THE GENEALOGICAL HISTORY OF THE CROKE FAMILY,

ORIGINALLY NAMED

LE BLOUNT

THE

GENEALOGICAL HISTORY

OF

THE CROKE FAMILY,

ORIGINALLY NAMED

LE BLOUNT.

BY

SIR ALEXANDER CROKE, D C. L. AND F. A S
OF STUDLEY PRIORY, OXFORDSHIRE

ΟΙΚΟΘΕΝ ΜΑΤΕΥΕ.
PINDAR

VOL. I.

OXFORD,
PRINTED BY W BAXTER,
FOR JOHN MURRAY, ALBEMARLE STREET, LONDON,
AND JOSEPH PARKER, OXFORD.
1823.

TO MY CHILDREN.

IT is an interesting object of curiosity, I believe, to most men, to search into the origin of their own families, to trace their lineal descents, and to collect the history of the individuals who compose them. However remote in time, or consanguinity, it is natural to experience in favour of our forefathers the real or imaginary influence of blood, and relationship. we enter affectionately into their concerns, we participate of their honours and prosperity, and are personally hurt at their misconduct, or misfortunes:

The connection between the ancestor and his posterity not only affects themselves, but is acknowledged by mankind in general. In every country, an ancient descent, and from persons of eminence, reflects honour upon those who can claim it the greatest nations have been ambitious of deducing their history from the earliest times, and where their real sources were lost in obscurity, they have adorned them with imaginary gods and heroes. These sentiments are undoubtedly founded in the innate and best feelings of the human mind, which delights in multiplying and extending the ties that bind us to our fellow-creatures. The love of our kindred is the first degree in the expansion of the heart, in its progress towards universal benevolence

> Self-love but serves the virtuous mind to wake,
> As the small pebble stirs the peaceful lake
> The centre moved, a circle strait succeeds,
> Another still, and still another spreads;
> Friend, parent, neighbour, first it will embrace,
> His country next, and next all human race[a].

I trust therefore that I have not been actuated by a silly vanity, or pride, by indulging a propensity so natural, and upon my return to my native country, after many years of absence occupied in the duties of an honourable station, if I have amused some of my vacant hours in collecting and digesting all the particulars I can discover relating to our own family. Its antiquity, and noble origin, the number of illustrious persons it has produced, and a variety of circumstances connected with it, seem to be not altogether unworthy of research, and relation.

Every day the task of inquiring into former ages becomes more difficult The knowledge of events gradually fades away, every generation, every year, annihilates the remembrance of persons, and facts,

> E di cento migliaja, che l'arena
> Sul fondo involve, un se ne serva appena[b].

My father, my grandfather, and my ancestors still more remote, were in possession of circumstances now totally forgotten, and, in the next generation, much of what is known to me will be no longer in memory. I have endeavoured therefore to preserve, before it be too late, whatever information still subsists, either in my own knowledge, or in the traditions of those who have

[a] Essay on Man, ep. iv. l. 363 [b] Ariosto, canto xxxv stanza 12.

gone before me. The pursuit has been to myself an innocent, and not unpleasant employment: the display of the rank and merits of your ancestors to you, my children, may prove an incitement to virtue and good conduct, and may "kindle in you a generous emulation, and a noble ambition to perform actions worthy of them[c]."

But another still more beneficial use may be made of this history. The review of so many persons and generations, passing rapidly over the theatre of life, may impress upon your minds a great truth, which I have lived long enough *to feel* in my own experience, but which, in the ardour of youth, you may probably have hitherto overlooked, That this world is nothing more than a succession of mere *phantoms*, which appear upon the stage for a short time, and then vanish for ever: and that to ourselves even, in what we seem to be, and to enjoy, it is equally unsubstantial. To the past we are dead, the present transitory moment can scarcely be said to exist, and the contingencies of to-morrow are still more visionary. You will then be satisfied that nothing can be considered as real but our future state, and that no object is worth the pursuit of a rational being but a happiness which is of a very different character from any thing to be seen in this life, unchangeable, indestructible, and eternal. If this lesson, one of the most valuable which the whole compass of science can teach you, from the moving pictures here represented, should strike you with such luminous evidence as it ought to do, and become the leading principle of your lives, I shall think my trouble amply rewarded.

In a few more revolutions of this planet, I shall myself be numbered with the ancestors of the family. In my person, in my character, and in the simple history of my life, I shall be as little known or remembered as they are now. Nothing of me

[c] Sir Harbottle Grimston's Preface to Croke James.

will remain to be discovered, by any idle person who may have the curiosity to enquire after me, beyond a register, a monument, and some slight scattered notices, which may have found their way into print, or may have been accidentally committed to writing. In future times, when this body shall be reduced to the dust from whence it came, may this little memorial be preserved, as a testimony of my respect for my predecessors, and of my love for my children, and even of those who shall be born after them; who "will never have known, or seen me, and whom I shall neither know, or see."

Believe me,

my dear children,

to be ever your affectionate father,

ALEXANDER CROKE.

Studley Priory,
January 1, 1823

CONTENTS.

BOOK THE FIRST.

FROM THE EARLIEST PERIODS TILL THE SETTLEMENT OF THE TWO BROTHERS, ROBERT AND WILLIAM LE BLOUNT, IN ENGLAND, IN THE YEAR 1066: OR THE HISTORY OF THE COUNTS OF GUISNES, AND THEIR ANCESTORS OF THE ROYAL FAMILY OF DENMARK.

BOOK THE SECOND.

THE SETTLEMENT OF THE LE BLOUNTS IN ENGLAND, AND THE HISTORY OF THE ELDEST BRANCHES, THE BARONS OF IXWORTH, THE BARONS OF BELTON, AND THE CROKE FAMILY.

PART I.

THE BARONS OF IXWORTH, AND BELTON.

BOOK II. PART II.

CHAP. I.

The conclusion of the Lords of Belton, and the origin of the Croke family.

CHAP. II.

CHAP. III

CHAP. IV.

The eldest son of Sir John Croke and Elizabeth Unton, Sir John Croke the Judge, and his descendants.

CHAP. VIII.

The three daughters of Sir John Croke and Elizabeth Unton

CHAP IX.

CHAP. X.

CHAP. XI.

END OF VOL. I.

VOL. II.

BOOK THE THIRD

THE HISTORY OF THE YOUNGEST BRANCHES, THE DESCENDANTS OF SIR WILLIAM LE BLOUNT, THE SECOND SON OF SIR ROBERT LE BLOUNT, AND ISABEL ODINSELS. 119

CHAP I

CHAP. II.

CHAP. III.

CHAP. IV.

CHAP. V.

CHAP. VI.

CHAP. VII.

In the Genealogies, No. 4. is cancelled, being comprehended in No 44. No. 44. is to be placed after the Introduction.

In the Copper Plates, there are four of Seals and Fragments at page 437.

APPENDIX.

AUTHORITIES REFERRED TO IN BOOK I.

I *The history of William, Count of Ponthieu. From Lambert.*

II. *The arrival of Sigefred. From the same.—His fortifying Guisnes.*

III. *The anger of Arnold, and the reconciliation. Ibid*

IV. *Sigefred's connexion with Elstrude. Ibid —Account of Sigefred's invasion, and the corruption of Elstrude, written by the Monks of St. Bertin's.*

V *The magnificence of Rodolphus. From Lambert*

VI. *Account of Rosella, and their children. Ibid.*

VII *The education of the children of Eustace. Ibid.*

VIII. *The invention of Saint Rotrude. From the Chronicle of Andres.*

IX. *A charter of Manasses, Count of Guisnes, and Emma, his Countess, to the Monastery of St. Leonard, with their seals.*

X *Contract of the Sale of Guisnes to the King of France —History of the Counts of Guisnes in Latin verse.*

XI. *Delivery of Guisnes by John, King of France, to Edward the Third.*

XII. *Extracts from records relating to Guisnes. From the Catalogue des Rolles Gascon, Normans, et François, in the Tower, Harleian Manuscripts, French Rolls, &c.—A catalogue of the Governors and Officers of Guisnes from Edward the Third, to Edward the Fourth*

IN BOOK II.

XIII *The estates of Robert, and William le Blount, in Domesday Book.*

XVI. *Account of the Knights and Monks of Ely. List of them from the* Tabula Eliensis.

IN BOOK III.

IN BOOK IV.

XXXV. *Proposals for drying malt with hot air. By John Busby, Esquire, F. R. S.*

XXXVI. *Some occasional verses*

XXXVII. a *A letter to Mr Bromley, respecting the Lancastrian schools.*

———— b. *Latin verses on winter and skating.*

XXXVIII. *A catalogue of the books and documents principally used in the Genealogical History.*

GENEALOGIES.

COPPER PLATES.

IN THE LETTER PRESS.

SEPARATE PLATES

As all these plates, except the map of Guisnes, and the head of Sir George Croke, were etched by myself, I have to apologize for their rudeness.

INTRODUCTION.

SIR HARBOTTLE GRIMSTON, in his preface to the Reports of his father-in-law, Sir George Croke, has correctly stated, that "he was descended of an ancient and illustrious "family called *Le Blount*," and that "his ancestor, in the time "of the civil dissention betwixt York and Lancaster, being a "fautor and assistant unto the house of York[a], was inforced to "subduct and conceal himself under the name of Croke, till "such time as King Henry the Seventh most happily reconcil-"ing those different titles, this our ancestor in his *postliminium* "assuming his ancient name, wrote himself Croke, alias Blount; "that of Blount being altogether omitted by the Judge's father "upon the marriage of his son and heir, Sir John Croke, with "the daughter of Sir Michael Blount, of Maple Durham, in the "county of Oxford." Which was about the end of the sixteenth century[b].

All authorities agree that the family of Le Blount is descended from two brothers, the sons of the Lord of Guisnes in France, who came over with William the Conqueror, and were then established in this country[c]. And the French historians have

[a] It is printed "Lancaster," but this is evidently a mistake

[b] Preface to Croke Charles, or Part the First.

[c] Collins's Baronetage, vol. ii. p. 367. iii. 665. Bigland, Garter King at Arms, in Nash's History of Worcestershire, vol. ii. p. 163. Dugdale's Baronage, Fuller, &c. &c. which will be more particularly stated hereafter.

traced the descent of the house of Guisnes from the royal family of Denmark.

The history of this family will therefore be divided into three Books.

The First Book will contain the account of the family from the earliest periods till the settlement of the two brothers Robert and William le Blount in England, in the year 1066. or the History of the House of Guisnes in Picardy, and, antecedently, in Denmark.

The Second Book will relate the settlement of the le Blounts in England, and the history of the eldest branches, the Barons of Ixworth, the Lords of Belton, and the Croke family.

The Third Book will comprehend the youngest branches, the Blounts of Sodington and Mawley; of Kinlet, Eye, and Kidderminster; the Lords Mountjoy; the Blounts of Iver and Maple-Durham; of Grendon, Bromyard, Orleton, and Eldersfield; of Burton-upon-Trent, Osbaston, and Tittenhanger; and others of the name.

Sir Robe[illegible]
d 1288.

= Isabel, da. an

Sir Robert le Blount, =
d. 1288 17 Edw I

BOOK THE FIRST.

FROM THE EARLIEST PERIODS TILL THE SETTLEMENT OF THE TWO BROTHERS, ROBERT AND WILLIAM LE BLOUNT, IN ENGLAND, IN THE YEAR 1066; OR THE HISTORY OF THE COUNTS OF GUISNES, AND THEIR ANCESTORS OF THE ROYAL FAMILY OF DENMARK.

Le Comte de Guisnes

ly of
vhose
avii[a].
id no
It is
ining
id of
The

of the
0 and

Rome,
ifying

more

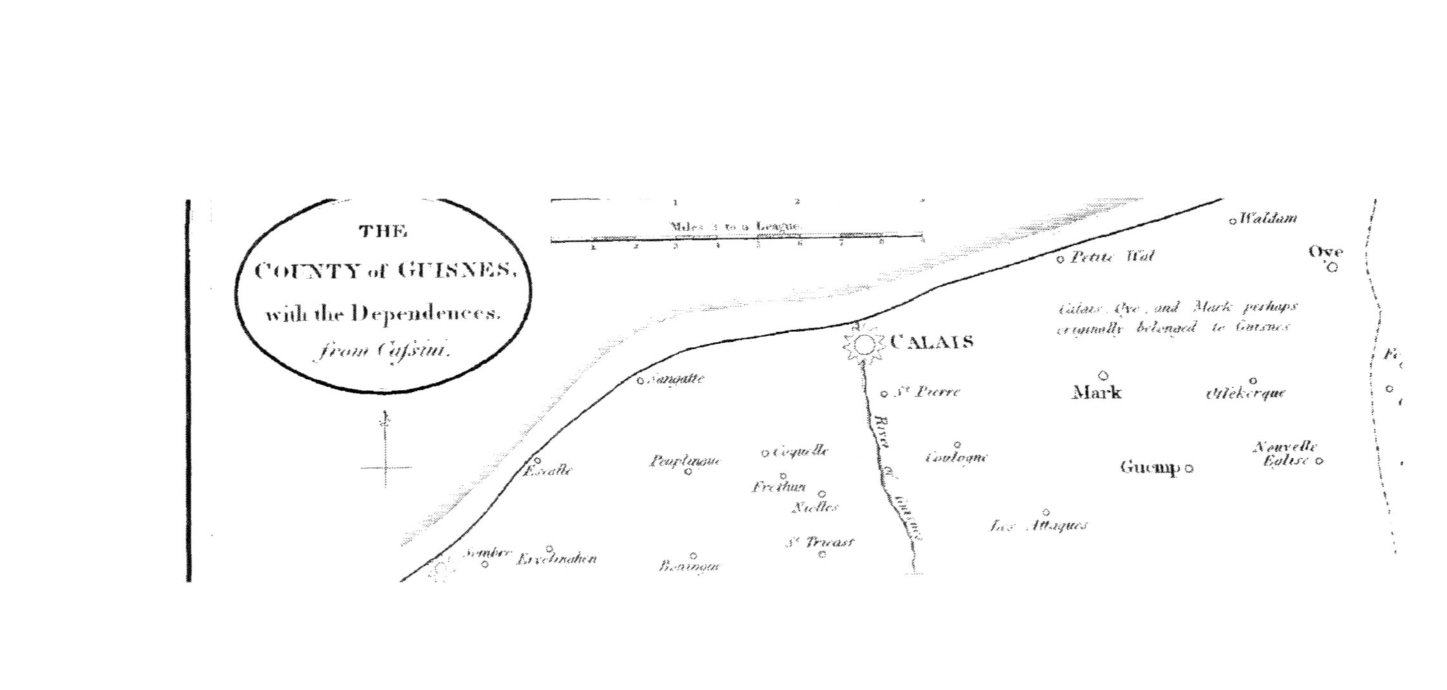
THE
COUNTY of GUISNES,
with the Dependences.
from Cassini.
Miles 3 to a League
CALAIS
Waldam
Petite Wal
Oye
Calais, Oye, and Mark perhaps originally belonged to Guisnes
Sangatte
S.t Pierre
Mark
Offekerque
Escalle
Peuplingue
Coquelle
Fréthun
Nielles
S.t Tricast
Coulogne
Guemp
Nouvelle Eglise
Les Attaques
Sombre
Ervelinghen
Bonningue
River of Guisnes

THE

GENEALOGICAL HISTORY

OF

THE CROKE FAMILY.

CHAPTER I.

The History of Guisnes, to the death of the first Count.

IT has been stated in some old authorities, that this ancient family of Le Blount took its rise from the Blondi, or Biondi, in Italy, whose historians derive them from the Roman Imperial family of the Flavii[a]. But a candid examination compels me to acknowledge, that I can find no evidence, or even probability, for this Italian and Roman descent. It is founded apparently upon no better ground than the similarity of meaning between the names of Flavius, or Flavus, of Blondi, or Biondi, and of Le Blount; all derived from the flaxen, or light colour of the hair[b]. The

[a] Collins's Baronetage, vol i. page 367. From the information of the family of the Blounts of Sodington, 1727 Rawlinson's MSS. B. vol lxxiii Art *Blount*, fol 110 and Habington's MSS. Descents of Worcestershire Families, in Bib Soc Antiq. &c &c.

[b] Thus the royal family of the Guelphs has been deduced from the Catuli of Rome, because the names in the Latin and German language are synonymous, both signifying little dogs, or *whelps* So the poetical historian, Gunther, says of Guelph the Sixth,

> Hunc ex Romano Catulorum sanguine clarum,
> Et genus et nomen, (nisi fallit fama) trahentem,
> Theutonicus verso Welphonem nomine sermo
> Dixerat, ambiguæ deceptus imagine vocis.

Gunther in Ligurin. lib. ix In Muratori, Antichità Estensi, vol. i. p 2. Some more

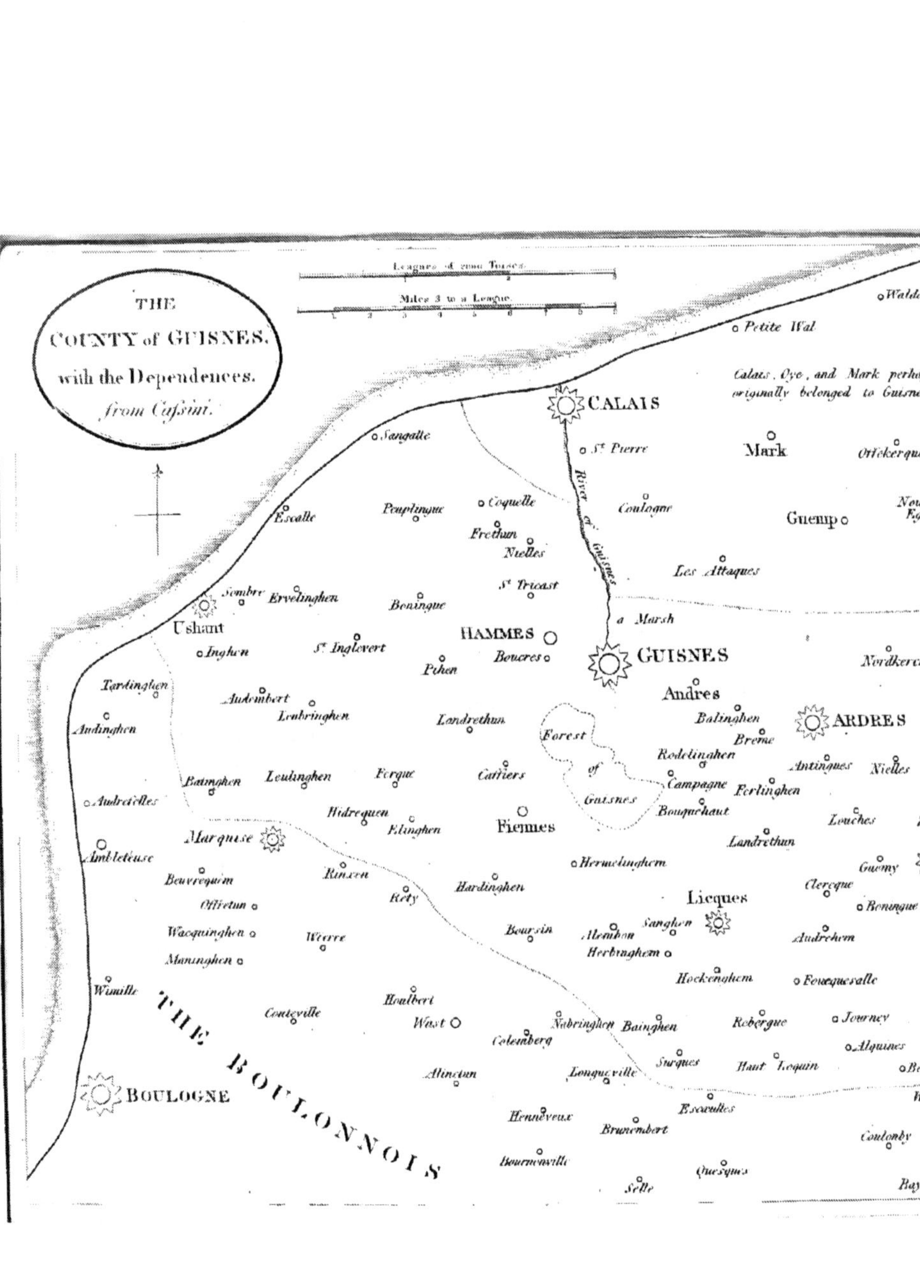
THE
COUNTY of GUISNES,
with the Dependences.
from Cassini.
Calais, Oye, and Mark perha
originally belonged to Guisne.
CALAIS
GUISNES
ARDRES
HAMMES
Ushant
Marquise
Fiennes
Licques
Andres
Mark
Guemp
BOULOGNE
THE BOULONNOIS
River of Guisnes
Forest of Guisnes
a Marsh

THE

GENEALOGICAL HISTORY

OF

THE CROKE FAMILY.

CHAPTER I.

The History of Guisnes, to the death of the first Count.

IT has been stated in some old authorities, that this ancient family of Le Blount took its rise from the Blondi, or Biondi, in Italy, whose historians derive them from the Roman Imperial family of the Flavii[a]. But a candid examination compels me to acknowledge, that I can find no evidence, or even probability, for this Italian and Roman descent It is founded apparently upon no better ground than the similarity of meaning between the names of Flavius, or Flavus, of Blondi, or Biondi, and of Le Blount; all derived from the flaxen, or light colour of the hair[b]. The

[a] Collins's Baronetage, vol. i page 367 From the information of the family of the Blounts of Sodington, 1727 Rawlinson's MSS B vol lxxiii Art *Blount*, fol 110 and Habington's MSS. Descents of Worcestershire Families, in Bib. Soc. Antiq. &c. &c.

[b] Thus the royal family of the Guelphs has been deduced from the Catuli of Rome, because the names in the Latin and German language are synonymous, both signifying little dogs, or *whelps*. So the poetical historian, Gunther, says of Guelph the Sixth;

Hunc ex Romano Catulorum sanguine clarum,
Et genus et nomen, (nisi fallit fama) trahentem,
Theutonicus verso Welphonem nomine sermo
Dixerat, ambiguæ deceptus imagine vocis.

Gunther in Ligurin lib. ix In Muratori, Antichità Estensi, vol. i. p 2 Some more

family of Le Blount is sufficiently noble and ancient not to stand in need of fictitious embellishments: and the real and well-proved deduction of the family from a Danish origin completely destroys the other supposition.

The county of Guisnes, the seat and patrimony of this family, before its arrival in England, is a part of the modern province of Picardy, which was never united under one government, like Normandy and Flanders, but was divided into many seigneuries, some of them held as fiefs of neighbouring lords; and the name of Picardy itself is of recent origin[c]. It is a very fertile country, and though a northern situation is unfavourable for vineyards, it abounds with corn and pasturage in an eminent degree It is bounded on the north-east by the districts of Calais, Marque, and Oye, and the province of Flanders, on the east by Artois, on the south by the county of Boulogne; and on the north-west by the sea. By a terrier made after it was reduced under the dominion of France, in 1558, it contained twelve *baronies*, Andres, Fiennes, Licques, Basinghem, Hames, Alembon en Surques, Courtebourne, Lamotte d'Andres, Laval, Cresseques, Zelthum, and Hermelinghem. As many *pairies*[d], Perrier, Losteborne, Nielles, Campagne, Autingues, Surgues, Bouvelinghem, Asquingoul, Reques, Fouquesolles, Ecclemy, and La Haye. Twenty-six *lordships*, Doncres, Nenviras, Berne, Wolfus, Leulingue, La Cressonniere, Steimbeque, Courteheuse, Saint Martin-en-Louches, Hondreconte-en-Breme, Le Fief du Briart-en-Frelinghem, d'Ophauve, Du Hied,

modern writers have derived it from a German root, from whence our word *help* is formed—Helfen *Leibnitz, Orig Guelf.*

So the real name of the Burleigh family was Sitsilt, an ancient Welsh name, which, after several variations, was at length changed to Cecil, upon the suggestion of Mr Verstegan, the celebrated antiquary, that they were descended from the Cecilii of Rome Aubrey's Lives, vol ii p. 28.

[c] Valesii Notitia Galliarum, p 447. Gibbon, vol xi. p. 1 For an account of the principal authorities, as well printed, as manuscript, which are referred to in this work, see the Appendix, No. XXXVIII.

[d] Pairies were fiefs, of which the possessors were bound to attend the court of their lord, where they were styled *peers, pares curtis,* or *curiæ.* They are so styled in the English, as well as the French law. Blackstone, vol ii p 54 In France, tout fief avait ses *pairies,* c'est à dire, d'autres fiefs mouvant de lui, et les possesseurs de ces *fiefs servans,* qui etoient censés *egaux* entr' eux, composoit la cour du seigneur *dominant* *Encyclopedie, voce Pairie.*

Landrethum, Croisilles, La Grange, Le Court, Bercq-en-Campagne, Dispendas, Sanghem, Marcamp, the abbey of Licque, and that of La Capelle, the priory of Ardres, the hospitals of Lostbourne, and of Saint Merlat, in Ardres. It contained thirty-three *parishes;* Ardres, Nielles, Louches, Breme, Rodelinghem, Bouquehault, Leulingue, Bonningues, Licques, Surques, Alembon, Sanghem, and Homelinghem, l'Hopital or l'Hotel Dieu de Saint Inglevert, Escales, Sangate, Wale, which does not now exist, Hervelinghem, Peuplingue, Pihen, Coquelle, Fretun, Nielles-en-Cauchie, Saint Tricat, Saint Martin in the Castle of Hames, Boucres, Saint Blaise, Guisnes, Eperleques, Andres, Balenghem, Campagne, and Capelle, now the Great and Little Cappe. Auderwic, Bredenarde, Tournehem, Ushant[e], and some lands besides, within the county of Artois, were amongst its *dependencies*[f]. Of these subordinate lordships, the barons

[e] Terrier de Guînes, Hist de Calais, vol. ii. p. 352 Amongst the Harleian Manuscripts, No. 3880, is a rental of the crown lands, and the King's revenues in Calais and Guisnes, taken by commissioners, who were Sir Richard Cotton, Comptroller of the Household, Sir Anthony St. Leger, Knight of the Garter, and Thomas Mildmay, Esquire, in the sixth year of Edward the Sixth It is entitled *Lands' Rental* The sums total are as follows:

	£	s.	d
The County of Guines	851	7	11
Lordship of Marc and Oye .	1447	18	4
Lordship and Castle of Hames .	383	15	3
Skimage de Calais . . .	620	13	0

Besides the town and marches of Calais.

[f] Whatever they might have been originally, Calais, Oye, and Marque, seem not to have been comprehended within the county of Guisnes very early. The foundation and the origin of the name of *Calais* are lost in obscurity. It was derived from the Caletes, if they ever visited that country, and may be corrupted from Scala, a port in Cæsar's time, if that were not Scales, or Escalle. The name Calais appears only after the twelfth century In 860, the Calaisis was part of Flanders, and a lordship distinct from the counties of Guisnes and Oye *Hist de Calais*, vol. i p. 446, where the boundaries are described From 864, it probably made part of the county of Guisnes, and was possessed by Baldwin Count of Flanders *Ibid.* 454. In 955, Arnold, the second, Count of Flanders and Boulogne, had a contest with the Abbey of St Bertin for Calais, which they pretended had been given them by Walbert, or Arnold le Vieux; but Arnold retained it against them He was still in possession of it after William of Ponthieu had taken Guisnes, &c and after Sifred's invasion, when he fortified it against his attempts. *Ibid* 496, 498 In 996, Baldwin IV. Count of Flanders, improved the port. *Ibid.* 502. In 1137, it was ceded by Charles le Bon, Count of Flanders, to the Count of Boulogne, p. 571. And in 1216, the

of Ardres became very powerful. Hames was erected into a Marquisate in 1658, as was Courtebonne in 1671, in favour of Charles de Calonne[g]. The twelve baronies and twelve pairies of Guisnes, were established as early as the year 1065[h].

The town of Guisnes is situated between Calais and Boulogne. It stands by the side of a marsh to the north-east, and a river rises near it, formerly called the Leda, which flows down to Calais It is surrounded on the other three sides by hills, and to the south is an extensive wood. At the time of the surrender to the French it was nearly square, encompassed on all sides by a large ditch filled with water, and defended by a rampart of earth, strengthened by freestone parapets The castle, which stood south of the town, was separated from it by a ditch, which was a continuation of that of the town, and surrounded likewise the castle It was built in the form of a pentagon, with five round bastions, and very high curtains In the middle stood a tower, called *La Cuve*, which was a square building, fortified without by a strong bulwark, and a second wall, defended by a wet ditch, and four towers at the angles[i].

Count of Boulogne gave Calais, Marque, and Oye, to Philip Augustus, King of France, as a portion with his daughter Matilda, p 630 And it continued in the Royal Family till it was taken by the English

Yet the Count of Guisnes had a judge in Calais in 1218 To a charter of Arnold of that date, among the witnesses is Wilhelmus de Undescote, Clerico Nostro, et Justiciario de Calais *Duchesne Pr* p 273 Justice was administered in Calais in the name of the Count of Boulogne, the lord, but the Counts of Guisnes had *allodial* lands there, which were not subjected to the ordinary jurisdiction of the lord, but to their own tribunal *Hist de Calais*, vol i p 637

The Counts, or Viscounts, of *Oye* were in the number of the twelve Peers of Flanders, and therefore it was not part of Guisnes, yet it was seized by Sifred *Hist de Cal* i 622 It afterwards was probably ceded with Calais, in 1137, by Charles le Bon, to the Count of Boulogne for in 1216 it was given by the Count of Boulogne to Philip Augustus, as before stated

As to *Marque*, the Abbey of St Bertin claimed it in 938, as having been given to it by the Count of Flanders The gift was controverted, and the Count kept possession *Hist de Cal* i 492 In 1147, it was held of the Count of Boulogne, and had for pairies under it and Oye, Coulogne, Walle, or Waldam, Offekirk, Hennin, and Ecluse. (*Ibid.* p 582,) and was at last ceded to Philip Augustus *Ante*

[g] Hist de Calais, vol i. p. 524

[h] Nobiliaire de Picardie Hist Cal ii 530, and 568

[i] From a plan of Guisnes, taken after the siege in 1588, printed at Rome, by Duchetti,

In an ancient picture in Windsor Castle, representing the interview between Henry the Eighth and Francis the First, in the year 1520, which took place between Guisnes and Ardres, there is a bird's-eye view of the market-place, church, and castle of Guisnes, with part of the town walls, and the surrounding ditch, of the morass, which lies on the north side of the town, and of the river, with a view of the adjacent country, as they were at that time[k].

After the capture by the Duke of Guise in 1558, the fortifications were entirely demolished by the French government, as useless; that frontier being sufficiently covered by the towns of Ardres and Calais.

The County of Guisnes was anciently comprehended within the Roman province of Belgica Secunda, and was inhabited by the Morini, a German race who had passed the Rhine, and expelled the original Celtic inhabitants. They were some of the most warlike people of Gaul, and for some time defeated the attempts which were made upon their liberty by Julius Cæsar. After they were subdued, it was from the *Portus Itius*, probably Ushant, in that territory, that he sailed upon his expedition to Britain[l]. The boundaries of the districts occupied by barbarous nations were fluctuating, and expanded, and contracted, with the weakness, or strength, of the neighbouring tribes. Much of what is now land was then occupied by the sea, or by morasses. Morinia is laid down by D'Anville, as extending along the sea-coast for about seventy-five miles, from Calais to Montreuil, on the river Canche, and of about half that breadth. Taruenna, now Terouenne, was the principal town[m]. It experienced the

Histoire de Calais, vol. ii. p. 310, referred to by Sir Joseph Ayloffe, in his Description of the Picture at Windsor Castle, page 19, note. There is also a rude plan of it in the British Museum, Cotton MSS.

[k] This picture has been engraved by the Society of Antiquaries, and a description was given of it by Sir Joseph Ayloffe, which was published in the Archæologia, vol. iii. p. 185, and separately, to accompany the print.

[l] The name of Morini was derived from the Celtic *Mor*, mare, the sea, as Armorica was. Valesii Notitia Galliarum. Cæsar, Bell. Gall. ii. 4. iii. 9, 28. iv. 20, 22, 37. vii. 76. Ushant was originally called Wit-sand, White sand, ab albedine arenæ.

[m] It continued to be the ecclesiastical capital of this country till 1553, when it was destroyed, and the bishopric divided into three bishoprics. Guisnes was then annexed to that of Boulogne. Hist. de Cal. Pref. 7. The Bishop of Terouenne was styled Episcopus Morinorum.

general calamities which afflicted every part of the Roman empire in its latter period. It was ravaged by the Huns, occasionally visited by the Northern pirates, and invaded by the Franks. Upon the death of Valentinian the Third, in the year 454, it ceased to be a part of the Roman empire.

Upon the dissolution of the Roman government, Morinia fell under the dominion of the Franks, who had then fully established themselves in Gaul, and it acknowledged the sovereignty of Childeric[n]. In the division of that country, upon the death of Clovis, it formed a part of the kingdom of Soissons. During this period it was governed, according to the political system of the feodal nations, by officers appointed by the King of France, under the name of Counts, whose principal residence was at Boulogne, and whose office was temporary, and various in extent. In process of time the Counts established their independence, and became the hereditary proprietors, or sovereigns, of the respective districts into which the country was apportioned.

In the subsequent dark periods, it is difficult to ascertain exactly who were the owners of the county of Guisnes, till it had its own and distinct Counts, about the middle of the tenth century. In the disputes which have arisen upon this subject, it has been severally given to the Abbey of Saint Bertin at Saint Omer's, the Counts of Ponthieu, of Boulogne, and of Flanders. But it is scarcely possible to reconcile, and to weave into one connected narrative, the insulated facts, and the confusion of names, which occur in the rude annals, and the documents which remain of those times, frequently of suspicious authenticity

Without entering into these uninteresting discussions, I shall shortly state what appears to be the most probable account, and descend to clearer times, and better established events.

In a dreadful eruption of the Huns and Vandals into Morinia, Leger the Second, the third Count of Boulogne, and his two sons, were slain, in the year 524. He was succeeded by his grandson Rodolphus in the county of Boulogne; but the county of Arques, which comprehended Sangate, Montour, Watte, Guisnes, and some other places, was detached from the county of Boulogne, and given to Matilda, the daughter of

[n] Mezerai, tom I p 236.

Leger, and who brought it in marriage to a prince of the house of Brandenbourg[o]. From her it descended at length to Agneric, the principal counsellor of Theodoric, King of Burgundy and Austrasia He was succeeded by his son Walbert, who was living in 660, was Count of Saint Pol, Ponthieu, and Arques, and with his son Bertin, so christened by St. Bertin, became a monk in the monastery of that name; and, dying without issue, his brother Saint Pharon, bishop of Meaux, and, next, his sister, Saint Phara, were his successors[p].

After the death of Saint Phara, this county remained for several years without a lawful owner, till Lideric, the first Forester of Flanders, created Count of Harlebec by Charlemagne, annexed it to his dominions, and it continued to be enjoyed by his successors[q].

One of these Foresters, Baldwin, surnamed Bras-de-Fer, the great-grandson of Lideric, married Judith the daughter of Charles le Chauve, King of France, and the grandson of Charlemagne. She was then a second time a widow Her first husband was Ethelwolf, King of England, who, after a year's residence at Rome, had married her upon his return through France. She was then only ten years of age; and as her husband lived only two years afterwards, she is said to have continued a virgin. After his death she incurred great censure by marrying Ethelbald, his son by a former wife; but, at the repeated exhortations of the clergy, he was induced at length to divorce her, and he lived not long afterwards. She returned to France, and was living at Senlis, where Baldwin saw her, fell in love with her, and, with the connivance of her brother, carried her off into Flanders, in the year 862. The King of France was offended, and assembled a council; the lovers were excommunicated, and a war was the consequence. By the interference of the Pope, a reconciliation was effected, and the marriage was solemnized with great magnificence at Auxerre[r].

[o] Malbr. lib ii p. 226 Hist de Calais, i. p 333, 334, 335

[p] Lambert, chap. 3, 4, 5, 6 Hist de Calais, p. 374

[q] Lambert, chap. 2, 6 Hist de Cal i 375. The claim of the Abbey of St. Bertin to the county of Guisnes was founded upon a supposed grant from Walbert It was proved not to have been comprehended in that grant, and the abbey was never in possession of it Ibid p. 416 Duchesne, p. 6

[r] Hist. de Cal i p. 449

Upon this event King Charles created his son-in-law Count of Flanders, and that county then extended from the Scheld to the Somme, and comprehended those of Boulogne, Saint Pol, Artois, and Guisnes. The King reserved to himself the paramount sovereignty, and the Count had under him the subordinate lords in the different districts[s].

Such was the origin of the Counts of Flanders, who afterwards extended their dominions, and acquired such power, that the first monarchs of Europe sought their aid, or alliance. From this time they were the immediate vassals of the crown of France, and the counties of Boulogne, Saint Pol, Artois, Ponthieu, Guisnes, and other counties within their territories, were held immediately of the county of Flanders, and as *arriere-fiefs* of the crown of France, having other lordships under them[t].

Baldwin the First died in 879[u]. His son and successor, Baldwin the Second, surnamed Le Chauve, died in the year 918[x]. By his wife Elstrude, the daughter of King Alfred, he left two sons. The eldest, Arnold, surnamed the Great, succeeded him as Count of Flanders. The youngest, Adalolphus, Adolphus, or Ardolphus, had for his inheritance the counties of Boulogne and Terouenne, Saint Pol and Guisnes, and was lord of the Abbey of Saint Bertin[y]. After the death of Adolphus, in 934, without children, his territories, including Guisnes, came to his elder brother, Arnold the Great. This Count,

[s] Hist de Cal i p. 452, 478

[t] Du Tillet, p 103 Uredius. Hist de Cal. i p 452, 479

[u] Though Lideric is stated by the Flemish historians as the first Forester of Flanders, doubts have been entertained by some other historians as to his very existence, and, at least, to his having had the government of Flanders L Art de Verifier les Dates, vol iii p 1 But Baldwin Bras-de-Fer is acknowledged, by the consent of all the historians, to have been the first Count, and that he was the son of Odoacer, the grandson of Enguerrand, and the great grandson of Lideric. It has been a question much agitated amongst the French lawyers and antiquaries, at what time fiefs became hereditary Montesquieu gives it as his opinion, that many fiefs were already hereditary by the end of the first race, and that Charles le Chauve established the succession to them by a general regulation Lib xxxi chap 28 Before that period perhaps no general rule can be laid down, each county must stand upon its own evidence

[x] Hist de Cal i. 479, 480 Duchesne, p 8 Lambert, chap 1

[y] Ibid

with the assistance of Louis D'Outremer, King of France, made war against the Count of Ponthieu, and took from him Montrieul, and other places. By his wife Alice, or Athele, daughter of Herbert the Second, Count of Vermandois, he had five children, who all died before him except his daughter Elstrude[z].

Arnold the Great was succeeded in 965 by his grandson, Arnold the Second, surnamed Le Jeune, the son of his eldest son Baldwin, by his wife Matilda, the daughter of Conrad the Pacific, King of Arles, or of Herman Billing, Duke of Saxony. Soon after his accession, Lothaire, King of France, and William the Second, Count of Ponthieu, took advantage of his minority, and attacked his dominions. This Count was descended from Engilbert, Silentiary, or Secretary, to Charlemagne, whose daughter, Bertha, he married, and who created him Count, or Governor, of Ponthieu. He was a man of learning, and at last retired from the world, and was Abbot of Saint Riquier William succeeded his father, Roger, in 957 at soonest Having been informed by tradition, that the territories of his predecessor, Walbert, had reached to the sea, he claimed the same extent of dominion, raised an army to support his pretensions, and, with the assistance of the King of France, he conquered the Boulonnois, the counties of Saint Pol, and Guisnes, in 965[a].

The ancient annals relate, that Count William divided his territories amongst his children, according to their different dispositions and pursuits To the eldest, whose whole delight was in arms and horses, he assigned his principal lordship of Ponthieu. The second son, who was a great hunter, had the woods and lawns of Boulogne. To the third son, who employed himself in the tranquil pursuits of agriculture, he gave the fruitful lands of the lordship of Saint Pol. To the fourth, whose principal occupation was the pasturage of his flocks and herds, he was preparing to allot the appropriate territory of Guisnes, when one of those sudden events, which were not uncommon in those unsettled times, defeated his intention , and his son was otherwise provided for, by a marriage with the daughter and heiress of Reinald, lord of Saint Valori[b].

[z] Hist de Cal. i p 487

[a] Ibid p. 409, 411, 422, 487, &c.

[b] Duchesne, p 5 Lambert, chap 15 Appendix, No. 1

This occurrence was the arrival of a Danish prince[c], named SIGEFREDE, cousin to the King of Denmark, who, with a numerous band of adventurers, drawn from the northern countries of Denmark, Sweden, and Norway, under the general names of Danes, or Normans, landed upon that coast, and took possession of the territory of Guisnes. The predatory habits of the Scandinavian nations, the recent success of Rollo, and others of their countrymen, and their beneficial establishments in France and England, were no doubt the principal incitements to this expedition, which had been preceded by several others on different parts of the same coast, but the immediate occasion of this attempt, and the reasons assigned for it, have been differently stated by the original writers Duchesne thinks it most probable, that, after Count William had subdued the Boulonnois, Saint Pol, and Guisnes, Count Arnold called in the assistance of the Danes, under Sigefrede and Cnute, to enable him to recover his dominions But he admits that this is mere conjecture, unsupported by any of the original historians and it seems inconsistent with the anger said to have been expressed by Arnold upon this invasion. There seems upon the whole no reason to disbelieve the circumstantial account given by Lambert, that Sigefrede was not only related to the King of Denmark, but that he was likewise a descendant of the blood of Walbert, Count of Ponthieu, Guisnes, and Saint Pol, and that he therefore claimed Guisnes as his lawful inheritance, and as having been unjustly detained from him by the Counts of Flanders, and Ponthieu. Upon whatever pretences he founded his claim, it is certain that he took possession of the country, with no opposition, probably about the year 965, being well received by the inhabitants as the descendant of their ancient sovereigns, and immediately built and fortified the castle, or, in the language of that age, the *donjon*, of Guisnes, and surrounded it with a double fossè[d].

[c] Un Prince Danois L'Art de Verifier les Dates

[d] Appendix, No III 1 Lambert assigns the year 928 to this invasion, as does Meier, in his Annals of Flanders, and Pontanus, Rerum Danicarum Historia, p 129 2. Duchesne supposes it not to have happened till 935 at the earliest For this event did not take place till after William of Ponthieu had conquered Boulogne, Saint Pol, and Guisnes, from Arnold But Arnold appears to have been in possession of Boulogne in 935, for, first, his brother Adolphus did not die till 933, or 934, when Arnold succeeded to the counties of Boulogne and St Pol, secondly, in the life of Saint Bertulph it is said, that Boulogne

Count Arnold, the lord paramount, was extremely angry at this violent intrusion into his fief, and summoned Sigefrede to appear before him to answer for his conduct. The high character and courage of this prince had procured him the friendship of many of the knights and nobles in the court of Flanders. Amongst these was Cnute, the brother of the King of Denmark, his own cousin, with whom he had lived upon terms of the closest intimacy, and who was in great estimation with Arnold. The occasion of his being in Flanders is not mentioned. Upon receiving the summons, Sigefrede called a council of his warriors, and, after hearing their different opinions, communicated to them his resolution of appearing before the Count of Flanders in person. Relying upon his interest in that court, and full of confidence in his own courage, he repaired to Sithieu, or Saint Omer's, where he found Count Arnold surrounded by his nobles and knights, amusing themselves with martial games[e]. When he arrived there, "recollecting," to use the words of Lambert, "that "fortune favours the bold," with an intrepid countenance he entered the assembly, and made his obeisance to the Count, and his nobles, with elegance and urbanity. He was received in a friendly and respectful manner by his cousin Cnute, and the rest of the court. Count Arnold at first shewed the haughty indignation of an offended sovereign; but the friends

having fallen to Arnold, he caused the body of that saint to be translated to Harlebecque, in Flanders, by the assistance of Wigfrid, Bishop of Boulogne and Terouenne, but the Chronicle of Flodoard relates, that he was not consecrated bishop of that place till 935. 3 The Art de Verifier les Dates assigns a still later period, 965, for which there seems to be good reason, assuming that the invasion did not take place till after the conquest of the Count of Ponthieu 1. Lothario, who assisted William, did not begin his reign till 954 2 Count William did not succeed till 957 at the earliest 3 Meier, lib. ii. Annal Fland and some other Flemish and French historians, relate, that the counties of Boulogne, &c. were not conquered by Count William till after the death of Arnold I which happened in 965 Without being perfectly satisfied, I have adopted the opinion of the Benedictine, as a submission to the authority of a learned chronologist It is often not easy to ascertain the exact date of events in those obscure periods, nor is it of much consequence.

[e] Sit-Diu, or Sithiu, originally called Hebbin-gahem, was at first only a small village Saint Omer, or Audemar, bishop of Terouenne and Boulogne, in 636, built an hospital and a church there, which afterwards became the cathedral of the bishoprick of St Omer He gave St. Bertin, a fellow-labourer, a place near St Omer's, where he built a monastery. Hence the names of St Omer's, and the Abbey of St. Bertin. The two institutions had a law-suit for the possession of the body of their founder Hist. de Cal i 365, 371

of Sigefrede interceded for him, and their repeated solicitations at length succeeded in mitigating the prince's anger. He held out to Sigefrede the right-hand of reconciliation, and friendship. The violence of the first occupation was overlooked, and Arnold deigned to bestow, and Sigefrede condescended to accept, the lordship of Guisnes, as a fief of the Counts of Flanders. The solemn ceremonies of investiture, fealty, and homage, were duly performed, and Sigefrede thus became the first Count of that territory, which he transmitted quietly to his posterity[f].

He is described as a man noble in mind, and illustrious in family, brave in all military affairs, of the highest rank, and greatly honoured in his own country of Denmark, as the cousin-german of the King, and second only to him in dignity[g].

Sigefrede married Elstrude, the daughter of Count Arnold the Great, and his wife Alice de Vermandois, and who was named after her grandmother, Elstrude, the daughter of King Alfred. He died soon after his marriage, leaving his wife pregnant with a son, who succeeded him in his titles and property.

It is related by some of the original historians, with many flowers of rhetoric, that the princess had been previously corrupted by Sigefrede, and that he died wretchedly in consequence of his crime, despised and forsaken by the world[h]. This story is not considered as entitled to credit by Duchesne and Du Tillet the celebrated French antiquaries, and is slightly alluded to by the learned Benedictine[i].

Nothing more is known of the history of the founder of the house of Guisnes. It must be supposed that he maintained his territories with the same valour and prudence by which he had acquired them, that, as was usual in those feudal ages, alternately a lord and a vassal, he supported

[f] See Appendix, No III

[g] Ibid The proper name of this Count was Sigefrede, from the Saxon ꞅiᵹe victory, and ꝼꞃeðe peace In German, *sieg* and *friede*, in Danish, *seier* and *fred* These are all different dialects of one and the same language Sifred is a contraction, and Sigefroy, and Sifroy, French corruptions of the name

[h] Elstrudem, cujus Sifridus nimio languebat amore Cui post multa amoris colloquia furtivaque ardoris oblectamenta, denium nolenti velle, immo nolle volenti, sine vi ludendo vim intulit, et eam clanculo impraegnavit Lambert d'Ardres, chap ii

[i] Appendix, No IV

his dignity and authority in his own court at his castle of Guisnes, and was a faithful counsellor, an upright judge, and a brave soldier, in the court of his sovereign of Flanders. The county of Guisnes was then in a wild and uncultivated state, and with few inhabitants Naturally a good soil, it improved by degrees in wealth and population, but at what æra the subordinate baronies and pairies were created perhaps is not easy to ascertain. It is certain that the full number existed in the reign of Baldwin the First, about a century afterwards[k].

But although the historians expressly state that Sigefrede was first cousin to the King of Denmark, they have not mentioned to which of them he was so nearly related, and have left it to be discovered from the chronology of that time. If his arrival in Picardy took place in the year 965, Harold the Sixth, who reigned from 930 to 980, must have been upon the throne: and Harold the Fifth was the grand-father of that sovereign, of Sigefrede, and his cousin Cnute, as he was the great great grand-father of Cnute, who swayed the sceptre of England with so much ability.

The families of Guisnes, Le Blount, and Croke, have therefore a right to enumerate the Danish kings in the catalogue of their ancestors. Denmark is one of the most ancient monarchies in Europe, and it has been observed, by no mean authority, that the regularity, and clearness, of their genealogies, and chronology, are a strong presumption in favour of the truth and accuracy of their historians[l]. They trace a succession of sixty-six kings. from Dan, the first founder of the monarchy, in the year before Christ 1038, to Harold the Sixth, who died in the year after Christ 980. It is not my intention to write a history of Denmark, nor do I mean to claim for an ancestor a sovereign who was a contemporary of King David. In the history of Denmark, during the great migrations of the northern hive, from the year of Christ 401, to 699, there is an unfortunate chasm, in which the name of King Biorno alone can be discovered to occupy an extensive space of two hundred and ninety-eight years. In the revolutions which may have happened in the intermediate time, it is impossible to connect the genealogy of the preceding, with that of the subsequent,

[k] Hist de Cal i 524

[l] Universal History, vol xxxii Modern Part

sovereigns. But from the election of Gormo the First, in the year of Christ 699, or 700, the descent of the royal family is regularly carried on from that monarch to Harold the Fifth, through a succession of thirteen monarchs of the same race, and chiefly in a descent of the title from father to son[m].

A strong and characteristic badge of the original Danish descent of this family was long preserved in the *cry of war* of the Counts of Guisnes, which was BERNE, BERNE, that is, *burn, burn*. A dreadful exhortation to slaughter and destruction, in the language of their northern ancestors whose expeditions were usually marked by sword and fire[n].

From the marriage of Sigefrede with Elstrude, daughter of the Count of Flanders, the subsequent Counts of Guisnes, and the families descended from them, are related to some of the most illustrious houses in Europe.

1. They are descended from Luderic, the first Count, or Forester, of Flanders, in the year 792. They were of course related to the subsequent Counts; to Matilda, the daughter of Baldwin the Fifth, who was the wife of William the Conqueror; to the five Latin Emperors of Constantinople, of the houses of Flanders and Courtenay; and to some of the principal heroes of the Crusades, Robert, Count of Flanders, Eustace, Count of Boulogne, and his two brothers, the celebrated Godfrey of Bouillon, and Count Baldwin. The Counts of Flanders intermarried likewise with many of the royal families of Europe, with daughters of the Kings of Burgundy, Italy, and France[o].

2. Elstrude was the grand-daughter and namesake of Elstrude, the daughter of Alfred the Great[p].

3. The Counts of Guisnes claim a direct descent from the Emperor Charlemagne, through Judith, the daughter of his grand-son, Charles le Chauve, and wife of Baldwin the First, Count of Flanders[q].

[m] See Genealogy, No. 1.

[n] Duchesne, p. 9.

[o] Oliver Uredius in Genealogia Comitum Flandriæ. Du Cange, Familiæ Byzantinæ, p. 217. See Genealogy, No. 2.

[p] The name of this princess is variously written in the English historians Aelstryth, Elftrita, Aelfryth, Aelfthrythe, Elstrude, Ethelswide, and Elfrida.

[q] Vix ulla est toto orbe Christiano præclara nobilitas, quin ex aliquo Comitum Flandriæ sit oriunda, atque ita genus suum ad Carolum Magnum referre possit. *Uredius* in Titulo.

No. 1.

KINGS OF DENMARK.

Gormo I.
elected A.D 699, or 700

Gotrick, his son

Olaus III. his son.

Hemming, his son.

Siward and Ringo, cousins to Hemming

Regner, son of Siward

Ivar, son

Siward, the Snake-eyed, brother to Ivar

Eric, the Bern, his son.

(Eric, the Usurper A.D 857.)

Cnute, the Little, son of Eric the Bern.

Frotho VI. son of Cnute, married Emma, daughter to the King of England

Gormo II surnamed Angle, being born in England, son of Frotho.

Harold V son

Gormo III = Daughter of Edward the elder king of England

Harold VI. First cousin to Sigefrede, reigned from A D 930, to A D 980

Cnute.

Swen A D 981

Harold.

Cnute the Great, A D 1015 King of England.

Hardiknute

Name unknown

Sigefrede, first Count of Guisnes, according to Lambert, &c &c A.D 965.

From the Universal History, Modern Part, vol 32

No. 2.

GENEALOGY OF ELSTRUDE, WIFE OF SIGEFREDE, THE FIRST COUNT OF GUISNES.

From Uredius, Muratori, Duchesne, Ducange, &c. &c.

Counts of Flanders.

Lideric, Forester of Flanders, A. D. 792.

Engelram, 802.

Odoacer, 832.

The Emperor Charlemagne.

Louis le Debonnaire, Emperor. = Judith.

Charles le Chauve. = Richild.

Guelph, Count of Weingarten, and Duke of Bavaria.

Henry the Black.
Henry the Proud.
Henry the Lion.
William of Winchester.
Otho the Boy.

14. William Cliton, Le Normand, elected Count of Flanders 1127.

15. Thierri D'Alsace, died 1168. = Sybilla D'Anjou.

16. Philip of Alsace, Count of Flanders.

Margaret D'Alsace. = 17. Baldwin V, as Count of Haynault, VIII, as Count of Flanders, d. 1195.

18. Baldwin IX. first Emperor of Constantinople, d. 1204. = Mary, da. of Henry the Liberal, Count of Champagne.

Henry, second Emperor of Constantinople, d. 1216.

Ioland. = Peter de Courtenay, third Emperor of Constantinople, d. 1218.

19. Jane, Countess of Flanders, 1206, married 1. Ferdinand, son of Sancho I. King of Portugal. 2. Thomas of Savoy. No issue.

20. Margaret II. succeeded her sister. From whom were descended the subsequent Counts of Flanders, till that country came to the house of Austria, by the marriage of the Emperor Maximilian with the daughter of Charles, Duke of Burgundy.

Robert, fourth Emperor of Constantinople, d. 1228.

Baldwin II. fifth Emperor, d. 1272. Constantinople recovered by the Greeks in 1261. = Maria, d. of John de Brienne, King of Jerusalem.

Their descendants retained the title of Emperor

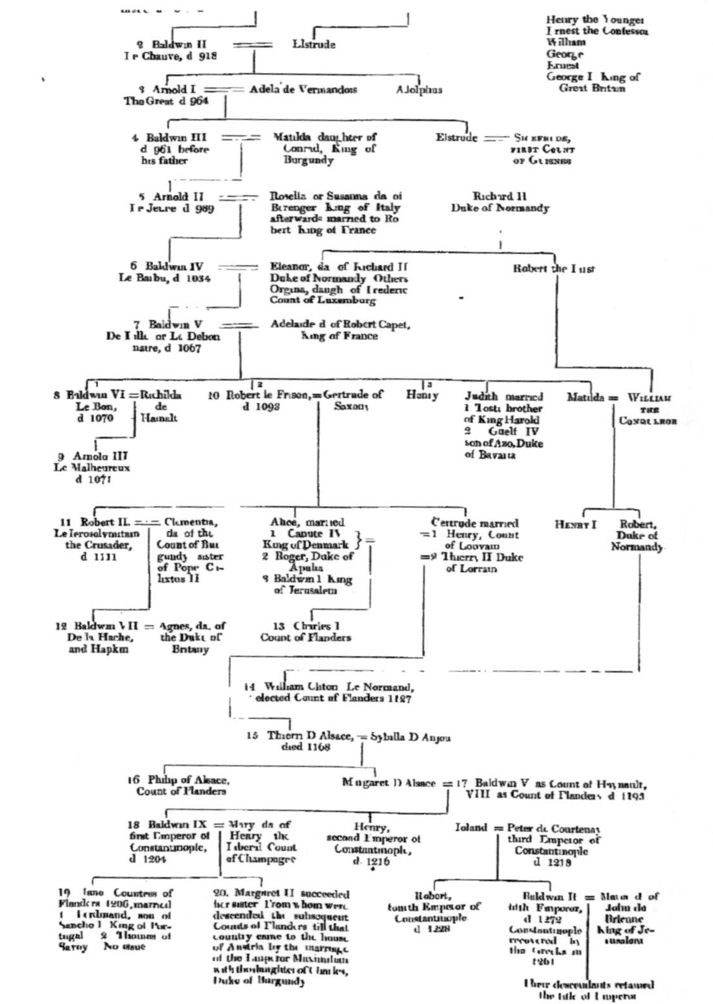

2 Baldwin II Le Chauve, d 918 = Elstrude
3 Arnold I The Great d 964 = Adela de Vermandois
Adolphus
Henry the Younger
Ernest the Confessor
William
George
Ernest
George I King of Great Britain
4 Baldwin III d 961 before his father = Matilda daughter of Conrad, King of Burgundy
Elstrude = Siceride, first Count of Guisnes
5 Arnold II Le Jeune d 989 = Rosella or Susanna da of Berenger King of Italy afterwards married to Robert King of France
Richard II Duke of Normandy
6 Baldwin IV Le Barbu, d 1034 = Eleanor, da of Richard II Duke of Normandy Others Orgina, daugh of Frederic Count of Luxemburg
Robert the First
7 Baldwin V De Lille or Le Debonnaire, d 1067 = Adelaide d of Robert Capet, King of France
8 Baldwin VI Le Bon, d 1070 = Richilda de Hainalt
10 Robert le Frison, d 1093 = Gertrude of Saxony
Henry
Judith married 1 Tosti brother of King Harold 2 Guelf IV son of Azo, Duke of Bavaria
Matilda = William the Conqueror
9 Arnold III Le Malheureux d 1071
11 Robert II Le Ierosolymitan the Crusader, d 1111 = Clementia, da of the Count of Burgundy sister of Pope Calixtus II
Alice, married 1 Canute IV King of Denmark 2 Roger, Duke of Apulia 3 Baldwin I King of Jerusalem
Gertrude married =1 Henry, Count of Louvain =2 Thierry II Duke of Lorrain
Henry I
Robert, Duke of Normandy
12 Baldwin VII De la Hache, and Hapkin = Agnes, da. of the Duke of Britany
13 Charles I Count of Flanders
14 William Cliton Le Normand, elected Count of Flanders 1127
15 Thierri D Alsace, died 1168 = Sybilla D Anjou
16 Philip of Alsace, Count of Flanders
Margaret D Alsace = 17 Baldwin V as Count of Haynault, VIII as Count of Flanders d 1195
18 Baldwin IX first Emperor of Constantinople, d 1204 = Mary da of Henry the Liberal Count of Champagne
Henry, second Emperor of Constantinople, d 1216
Ioland = Peter de Courtenay third Emperor of Constantinople d 1218
19 Jane Countess of Flanders 1206, married 1 Ferdinand, son of Sancho I King of Portugal 2 Thomas of Savoy No issue
20. Margaret II succeeded her sister From whom were descended the subsequent Counts of Flanders till that country came to the house of Austria by the marriage of the Emperor Maximilian with the daughter of Charles, Duke of Burgundy
Robert, fourth Emperor of Constantinople d 1228
Baldwin II fifth Emperor, d 1272 Constantinople recovered by the Greeks in 1261 = Mary d of John de Brienne King of Jerusalem
Their descendants retained the title of Emperor

4. Another Judith, grandmother to the former, and the wife of Louis le Debonnaire, was the daughter of Guelph, Count of Weingarten, and Duke of Bavaria. Through her they claim relationship to the Dukes of Brunswick, the ancestors of the present royal family of Great Britain, the Dukes of Bavaria, and Saxony, and the Italian branches of that family, the Marquisses of Este, of Liguria, and Tuscany, and the present Dukes of Ferrara, and Modena. A noble race, which has been immortalized by the splendid visions of Ariosto, and the more sober fictions of Tasso[r].

[r] Muratori, Antichità Estensi Leibnitz, Origines Guelficæ, and Gibbon's Antiquities of the House of Brunswick

CHAPTER II.

Of the subsequent Counts of Guisnes, to the end of the first male line.

THE posthumous son of Sigefrede was born about the year 966. He was under the tutelage of Arnold le Jeune, Count of Flanders, his first cousin and godfather, by whom he was named ARDOLPHUS, or ADOLPHUS, in memory of his great uncle, the Count of Boulogne and Saint Pol, and Abbot of Saint Bertin's. Count Arnold superintended his education, and when he arrived at an age capable of performing the duties of a knight and a sovereign, he conferred upon him the order of chivalry, and put him in possession of the county of Guisnes, to which he generously added the rich and extensive lands of Bredenard, which were situated between the river Vonne, and the bridge of Neullay[a]

Adolphus's affections were engaged by the charms of Mahaut, or Matildis, daughter of Ernicule, Count of Boulogne, and he obtained her in marriage. They had two sons; of whom Raoul, or Rodolphus, succeeded him, and Roger died in his youth[b].

RODOLPHUS, the third Count of Guisnes, married Rosella, the daughter of Hugh the Second, Count of Saint Pol She was so denominated, according to Lambert, from her roseate odours, or the roses in her complexion; but more probably after Rosella, the wife of Arnold le Jeune, surnamed Royne, or the Queen, from being the daughter of Berenger, King of Italy This marriage did not take place till after the year 1000, but how long after that time is uncertain[c].

It is related, that he distinguished himself by his military achievements, under kings and princes, in various and remote parts of the world, yet the particulars of his warfare have not been specified. The ecclesiastics, the only writers of this period, too often omit civil and military transactions[d].

[a] Lambert chap 12 13 [b] Ibid chap 14, 16 [c] Lambert, chap 16, 17 and Duchesne [d] Ibid

Proud of his martial renown, and his noble descent, his magnificence in his establishments at home, and upon his war expeditions, was greater than his revenues could support[e]. To supply his extravagance he oppressed his vassals, and all who were resident within his territories, with new exactions. He compelled them to pay annually a penny a head for all men, women, and children, who had lived there a year and a day, and fourpence upon every marriage and burial. A heavy tax when the precious metals were scarce! He introduced likewise a degrading species of servitude, by which all his subjects were prohibited from carrying any other arms than clubs, perhaps to prevent their revolt at his oppressions. It was called Colvekerlia, or Massuerie, and continued for many years This tax he transferred, by sale I suppose, to the lords of Hamme, as a perpetual feod[f].

To the great joy of the country, he was slain at a tournament at Paris, where he received two mortal wounds, and was thrown into the Seine This happened before the year 1036[g].

His eldest son and heir was named Eustace; and he had besides, as Lambert informs us, other sons, who did not degenerate from the virtues of their father in arms and martial deeds, and likewise daughters, whose lovely faces, and elegant forms, excited the admiration of the age[h].

EUSTACE, the fourth Count of Guisnes, was of a different moral cha-

[e] Appendix, No. V

[f] Lambert, chap. 36. In the Flemish language *colve* signified a *club*, *keule* in modern German, all derived from the Latin *clavus*, or an higher origin *Kerle*, as the Saxon *carl*, was a *countryman* Hence colvekerli, clavigeri rustici The poll-tax was likewise comprehended under the general term It was often exacted with insult, and particularly from new-married women, and was considered as of a very slavish nature Ignominiosum omnino, præsertim mulieribus recens nuptis, servitutis genus videtur indicari The editors of Du Cange in voce. I do not see what oppression it could have been to bear clubs. By the feodal law rustics were prohibited from carrying higher arms Si quis rusticus arma, vel lanceam, portaverit, vel gladium, judex, in cujus potestate repertus fuerit, vel arma tollat, vel viginti solidos pro ipsis recipiat a rustico Feod Lib II tit xxvii sect 5.

[g] Ad execrabiles nundinas quas torneamenta vocant, says Lambert, chap. 18 This shews how early they were in use They were condemned by the Council of Lateran, in 1164, under Alexander the Third, and persons slain in them were prohibited Christian burial Decret Greg. lib v tit 13

[h] Appendix, No. VI. Lambert, and the Chronicle of St Bertin.

racter from his father, and treated his subjects with justice and mildness[i]. Little is known of him: he appears to have been living in the year 1052, and to have died soon after. His wife was Susanna de Grammes, daughter of Siger de Grammes, *the most noble Chamberlain* of Flanders, by whom he had Baldwin, his eldest son, William, of whom nothing is said by Lambert; another son, named Remelin; and two daughters, Adela, and Beatrice. He provided that all his children, both sons and daughters, should be educated in the liberal studies of literature and his sons excelled in every military science, amongst the first young men of Flanders[k].

The fifth Count of Guisnes was BALDWIN THE FIRST, who succeeded his father before the year 1065, since he was at the Court of Philip the First, King of France, and attested a charter of that date[l].

The proper name of his Countess, Adela, was superseded by that of Christiana, which was universally bestowed upon her for her piety She is said to have been the daughter of Florent, or Florentin, a Duke of Lorrain, but as no duke of that name is known, Duchesne supposes that he was a powerful lord of that country, though not of ducal rank. According to other authors, she was the daughter of Bernard, Duke of Saxony, widow of Florent the First, Count of Holland, and was called Gertrude of Saxony[m].

In the war for the succession to the county of Flanders, in the year 1070, he embraced the party of Robert le Frison, against the heroine and tyrant Richilda; and in the year following displayed his valour in the battles of Montcassel and Broqueroies, in which she was defeated[n].

Baldwin was no less religious than his Countess. His pious intention of founding a monastery on his domains, was promoted and accomplished

[i] His subjects used to say of him,

Ex re nomen habes, vivas, Comes, hic, et in ævum!

A pun upon his name, Eustatius, eo quod semper et ubique *staret in bono* Lambert, chap 19, who adds himself, quod studuit,

Parcere subjectis et debellare superbos.

[k] Appendix, No VII Lambert, chap 23

[l] Duchesne and Preuv. p. 19

[m] Lambert, chap. 25. Hist. de Cal i p 517, who refers to Oudegherst and Scriverius

[n] L'Art de Verifier les Dates. Lambert, chap. 27.

by an accidental event. Upon a pilgrimage to Saint James in Galicia, in company with Enguerrand, lord of Lillers, and other noblemen, he fell sick, and was hospitably entertained at the Abbey of Charroux in Pictou[o]. In gratitude for this kindness, and edified by the exemplary regularity of that house, he agreed with the abbot that he should supply him with monks for his intended foundation, which he immediately proceeded to carry into effect. For his new establishment he chose the town of Andres, about two miles from Guisnes, where he built a magnificent church, on the site of the chapel of Saint Medard, and founded a monastery, which was dedicated to Saint Saviour, and Saint Rotrude, whose remains had been miraculously discovered[p] Monks from the Abbey of Charroux were transplanted thither. it was richly endowed by the Count, and numerous other benefactors, and in ten years' time was possessed of a fourth part of the county of Guisnes[q]. It became one of the most considerable abbeys in France, and was adorned with the stately monuments of the Counts of Guisnes. The charter of foundation bears date in 1084, and it was confirmed by the Bishop of Terouenne in the same year. It was made subject to the Abbey of Charroux, by which the abbot was elected, and to which it paid an annual rent of two marks of silver[r]. In 1211 the monks obtained from the Pope the privilege of electing their own abbot[s].

[o] Sancti Salvatoris Carofensis Monasterium Lambert, chap 26, 29, 30.

[p] For the history of the discovery of the body of Saint Rotrude, see Appendix, No. VIII

[q] This appears by an act of Manasses. Duchesne, Preuv p. 35. Hist de Cal vol i 567

[r] Gallia Christiana, vol x p 1602.

[s] Appendix, No VIII. Extract from the Chronicle of Andres. The charter of foundation, and the bishop's confirmation, are printed by Duchesne, Preuv p. 23, 25 The benefactions are all stated at length, and are very numerous They consist of land, houses, mills, gardens, farms, tithes, and other property Much of the land is described by days, terra quatuor dierum, prata triginta dierum; sometimes without mentioning the land, as quatuor dies, that is, as much land as a man can plough in a day with one plough, or a certain quantity of provisions for one day for the king's, or lord's, house It occurs in Domesday book in the latter sense, as nox does likewise Dimidia dies mellis Una dies de firma Firma trium noctium Spelman, Ducange Some of the benefactors give *themselves*, as well as their property Gotho dedit seipsum, dedit etiam totum prædium Eustachius, filius Hugonis fecit similiter Bernardus de Gisnes dedit hospitem, (a sort of Villains, Ducange,) unà cum comitatu, *et uxor ejus Gerberga attribuit seipsam cum pueris suis.* Rainerus del Bruc, et Segechins uxor ejus dederunt semetipsos, et totum prædium,

It may not be uninteresting to relate the future history of this abbey. When King Edward the Third took Calais, in 1347, the monks retired to Ardres, but afterwards returned, and reestablished the abbey. It was again destroyed by the troops of Henry the Eighth, when he took Boulogne in 1543, and was never rebuilt. No other monument of it afterwards remained than a house with a little chapel, at Ardres, which had been occupied by the monks in their secession, and retained the name of the Abbè Royal, and where the abbot of Ardres maintained a chaplain. To this small establishment were annexed the revenues of the ancient abbey, amounting to one thousand crowns, or three thousand livres a year. The body of Saint Rotrude was removed to the Abbey of Saint Bertin, where it continued to be one of its most valuable treasures[t].

The pious Adela died soon after this foundation, and was buried in the new monastery, where the solemn rites were performed by Gilbert, the first abbot. Her husband attended the funeral, and gave to the monks the use of the marshes of Ostinghehen, to celebrate an anniversary for the repose of her soul[u].

Baldwin had afterwards a contest, both in writing and by arms, with Arnold the First, Lord or Baron of Ardres, who refused to do homage to him for his territories, which were held as fiefs of the county of Guisnes. These barons were become rich and powerful; and Arnold was supported by a potent ally, Robert the Second, Count of Flanders, to whom he surrendered his allodial lands, and his castle, to hold of him as fiefs[x].

Count Baldwin died seven years after his Countess, and was buried near her at Andres, about the year 1091. He is said to have profited by his liberal education, and the study of the holy Scriptures. He was brave as a warrior, and correct in his morals. To his subjects and soldiers he conducted himself as a brother, rather than a superior, and exacted no

eorum Count Manasses, heir to Baldwin, agreed that each of his knights should give a carucate of land, or a rent of one hundred shillings. There are the names of Orbertus Wiscardus, and his brother Otgrinus. As most of the lands granted were in the county of Guisnes, all the gifts passed in the court of the Count. *Generalibus placitis* apud Gisnes, præsentibus militibus, et laicis, placitum observantibus, regionis Guinensis. Pr. p. 38.

[t] Hist. de Cal. i. p. 385, 583.

[u] Mentioned in the Charter, p. 25.

[x] L'Art de Verifier les Dates.

more than his just dues. He was a protector of widows and orphans, and a strenuous defender of the Church. Such is the excellent character given of him by Lambert, and which is not contradicted by any of his actions with which we are acquainted[y].

His children were six in number: Manasses, or Robert, the eldest. Fulk, who accompanied his cousin Robert, Count of Flanders, Eustace of Boulogne, Godfrey, and Baldwin, in the first crusade, and was made Count of Baruth, or Berytus, where he was buried Guy, Count of Forois, a place which the geographical knowledge of Duchesne has not enabled him to discover[z]: Hugh, first a priest, and archdeacon of the church of Terouenne, and who afterwards adopted the profession of a soldier, and received the order of knighthood. His eldest daughter, Adela, married Jeffrey, lord of Semur in the Brionnois, and "*resembling* "*her mother, shone like the sun for piety.*" Gisla, the youngest, married Wenemar, Chatelain of Ghent, of whom we shall have occasion to speak hereafter[a].

The sixth and last Count of Guisnes, in the male line, and who succeeded his father about the year 1091, was christened ROBERT, after his godfather, Robert le Frison, Count of Flanders, but he was usually called MANASSES, for it was customary in those times, as we are informed by Lambert, for persons to assume two names[b]. This nobleman frequented the court of William Rufus, and was in great favour with that king. He bestowed upon him in marriage an English lady of considerable possessions, Emma of Tancarville, daughter of Robert Lord of Tancarville, and Chamberlain of Normandy, and who was the widow of Odo of Folkestone[c].

The oppressive services of Colvekerlia, which had been imposed upon

[y] Lambert, chap 24.

[z] L'Art de Verifier les Dates says, (vol. ii. p. 785,) Gui, ch'un moderne, trompè par Lambert, fait Compte de Foris, en vertu d'un pretendu marriage avec la fille du Compte de Foris

[a] Lambert, chap 25

[b] Ex quo (Balduino, Christiana) suscepit famosissimæ nobilitatis sobolem, *Robertum* videlicet, qui ut tunc temporis erat consuetudo, et adhuc plerumque tenetur, *binomius* erat, sed suppressâ vocationis proprietate, inolescente usus assuetudine, dictus est Manasses. Lambert, chap. 25, 33.

[c] Lambert, chap 35.

the people of Guisnes by Rodolphus, still continued, and had been transferred by him to the lords of Hamme. A case, in which the fine upon marriage had been demanded with insolence, and indecency, from a bride, whose husband, William de Bocherdis, a *vavassor*, had resided in the country just long enough to bring him within the reach of the law, gave good reason for complaint. Havidis, the bride, applied to the Countess, who interceded in her favour with her husband. He abolished the grievance, and granted lands to the lord of Hamme, as a compensation for the perquisites which he lost by this emancipation[d].

Manasses was engaged in hostilities with Arnold the Second, Lord of Ardres, in 1093, because, after the example of his father, he had transferred to the Count of Flanders the feudal duties which he owed to the Count of Guisnes. In the course of this war, Arnold was besieged in Ardres. The city was taken, and he was compelled to retire into the castle, or donjon. This likewise being nearly forced, he collected his strength, and made a vigorous sortie with such effect, that he drove Manasses from his territories, and almost to Guisnes. A peace ensued, the Lord of Ardres at length acknowledged the sovereignty of the Count of Guisnes, and the princes were completely reconciled[e].

The remaining part of the history of this Count is confined to his benefactions to religious houses. By a charter, without date, but certainly executed before the year 1097[f], at the petition of Gilbert, abbot of Andres, he confirmed all former, and all *future*, grants to that monastery. It specifies minutely all preceding benefactions, which are very numerous. He likewise decreed that none of his successors, or vassals, or any lay persons whatever, should exercise any jurisdiction, or feudal rights, over the abbey, or any of its possessions, but that they should be subject only to the abbot and monks. Offenders against this privilege were to have their lands sequestered, and to pay a fine of one hundred pounds of

[d] Lambert, chap. 36. Lambert calls him, Veteranus sive Vavassorius, upon which Ducange in voce observes, Nondum mihi perspectum fateor cur Veteranorum nomenclaturâ vavassores donet Lambertus Ardensis.

[e] Duchesne, p. 94. Lambert, Preuv. p. 159, 163. L'Art de Verifier les Dates, tom. ii. p. 786.

[f] A charter of that date refers to it. Preuv. p. 37.

silver to the Count[g]. In 1102, he subscribed, as a witness, a donation to the abbey of Saint Bertin, and in 1119, some privileges were granted to the same through his hands[h].

In conjunction with his Countess Emma, he founded an abbey for nuns of the order of Saint Benedict, in the suburbs of Guisnes, in honour of the Holy Trinity, and Saint Leonard. The principal part of the endowment was from the Countess's possessions in England, and it was placed under the government of the Abbey of St. Bertin. Sybella, a lady from Lorrain, and related to Manasses's mother, was the first abbess[i]. Afterwards he bestowed upon it some churches and tithes in England, part of his lady's marriage-portion, and which, being of an ecclesiastical nature, he considered it as sinful for a layman to enjoy. These were the church of Niguenton, the churches or chapels of Alschot, and Celpham, and the tithes of Herst, and Bliseinghes, all in the diocese of Canterbury. The grants were confirmed by William, Archbishop of Canterbury, and possession was delivered by him, and Henry his Archdeacon. The original charter of foundation bears date in 1117; that of these farther gifts in 1120, and it is sealed with the seals of the Count and the Countess[k]. By other charters without date he gave to the same monastery the tithes of all cheese, cider[l], apples, wool, and sheep, which belonged to him in England, and woodbote, and right of common in Guisnes, with twenty-four measures of wheat from his mill[m]. This abbey continued till Guisnes was restored to France in the reign

[g] The charter itself from the Chronicle of Andres Duchesne, Preuv. p. 35. Firmiter etiam statuimus, ut nulli successorum meorum, vel hominum, ejusdem Cænobii homines liceat ad suam, vel cujuslibet laicalis personæ, justitiam cogere, nisi ante abbatem, vel coactivam *petitionem*, seu *incisuram* super ipsos instituere, vel animalia eorum suis servitus mancipare, vel quidlibet ex eorum substantiis auferre, sed omnia prænominata et omnia ad idem monasterium pertinentia, sub potestate et justitiâ abbatis et monachorum libera omnino in perpetuum permaneant Petitio, a tax Incisura, the same French, taille, tallia, talliage Ducange

[h] Archives of St Bertin, p. 38.

[i] Hist Cal i p 567 Chron of St Bertin. Duch. Pr p 41. 38. Gallia Christiana, vol x p 1606

[k] See the second charter in the Appendix. No IX

[l] Sicera.

[m] Archives of St Leonard's transferred to Bourbourg Duch. Pr 40

of Queen Mary, when the nuns were deprived of their English revenues and their French property was transferred to the Benedictine nuns of Ardres[n].

In 1124 he commuted some services of personal labour, which were performed by the inhabitants of Scales, now Escalle, for a pecuniary rent, and on condition that when a ship arrived from England, they should carry his goods from thence to his castle, three times a year, and should assist him in his wars[o]. In 1127, he made another grant to Saint Bertin's[p]. The church of Andres, and the spacious infirmary which was built by Rodolphus de Dovera, the friend and fellow-soldier of Manasses, having been burnt by lightning, he rebuilt them, with the assistance of other noblemen[q].

Soon after, oppressed by years and sickness, and full of trouble from the state of his family, he caused himself to be carried to the abbey of Andres, assumed the habit of a monk, and in a few days rendered up his spirit, in the arms of Peter, the abbot, in the year 1137. His widow retired to the abbey of Saint Leonard, and did not long survive her husband[r].

Count Manasses was of a robust make, and a gigantic size, but his countenance was beautiful, and his form elegant. He was dignified in his appearance, amiable for his virtues, and universally beloved. In his solemn acts he styled himself, Robert, *by the grace of God*, Count of Guisnes, which did not denote an independent sovereignty, but a greatness and power more than common. He maintained great state, and amongst the witnesses to his charters, we find the names of some of his officers, Elembert, Vice-count, Baldwin, Constable, William and Manasses, Sewers, and Eustace, Esquire to the Countess[s]. Whatever may be the opinion of modern times to the contrary, the noblemen who bestowed such large revenues upon the monasteries were real benefactors to society. The lands of the religious houses were better cultivated, and improved,

[n] Hist. de Cal i p 568 [o] Duch Pr p 40 [p] Ibid

[q] Chronicle of Andres, Duch p 41 [r] Lambert, c 49, 51.

[s] Duch. Pr p 40. Hist. de Cal i p 555. Comes Manasses elegantissimæ formæ specie laudabilis, essentiæ staturâ giganteus apparuit, et personali auctoritate grandævus, facie decorus, et aspectu, imò virtute, robustus, omnibus amabilis Lambert, chap 36 in fine. This appears in some measure from his seal

than those of the laity; and their tenants were used with more kindness, and exempted from the hardships of military service. The poor were relieved; learning was preserved, and communicated; means of education were supplied; and religion was maintained, and propagated.

Manasses, by his Countess Emma, had only one daughter, named Sibylla, or Rose, whom they married to Henry de Gand, Chatelain of Bourbourg. She died before her father and mother, in child-birth with Beatrice her sole offspring. After her death Henry married Beatrice de Gand, of the family of the lords of Alost. Manasses appears likewise to have had a daughter called Ade, but it is probable that she was not by Emma of Tancarville. He had likewise, before his marriage, a natural daughter named Adelaide, by a fair damsel of Guisnes. She was married to Eustace of Balinghen, and had five sons and a daughter. Her second husband was Daniel, brother to Siger, the second, Chatelain of Ghent[t].

The following are the seals of Manasses and Emma, annexed to their charter of 1120, which is in the Appendix[u].

[t] Lambert, chap. 34, 42. [u] Duchesne, Preuv. p. 39

BEATRICE, the only hope of the family, was of a weak and sickly constitution, and was afflicted with the stone and gravel[w]. At a proper age her grandfather procured a suitable match for her with a powerful English nobleman, Alberic de Vere, called by the French writers, Albertus Aper, or Sanglier, who was Lord Chamberlain, and Chief Justice of England, and the favourite of Henry the First, and King Stephen[x].

[w] Calculosa, et morbida Lambert

[x] Lambert, chap 43 The crest of the family of Vere is a boar, aper, sanglier—Edmondson's Baronage Dugdale in his Baronage, i p 188 is wrong in stating that it was the *first* Alberic de Vere, who married Beatrice de Guisnes For,

1 It is certain that the first Alberic had a wife named Beatrice, but it is equally certain that she had five sons and a daughter In the Monasticon, vol i p 436—438 is a charter by which Alberic, and his wife Beatrice, with their sons, Alberic, Roger, Robert, and William, grant the Church of Kensington and other gifts to the Abbey of Abingdon, for the soul of their son Geoffrey, deceased And there was a daughter named Rose, married to Geoffrey de Mandeville, Earl of Essex. Beatrice de Guisnes had no children, by the concurring testimony of the historians, (Lambert, Preuv p 32. Duchesne, p 30) it is fully confirmed likewise by the course of events, the fears of Manasses that he should leave no lineal descendants, and his divorcing, and marrying again, his granddaughter Beatrice, with the view of having an heir, (Preuv p 30, 32, &c) her bad health, for Lambert says, that she was matrimonii debitum solvere pertimescentem, (chap 50) Arnold's readiness to seize the country as next heir, De Vere's neglect, and no son's appearing to claim the county after her death The reason assigned for De Vere's not returning was, *quod de vitâ uxoris suæ non nimus quam de Guisnensis terræ comitatu desperaret*

2 The time does not agree The Charter to Abingdon Abbey was confirmed by King Henry the First in the year 1111, when seizin was delivered by Picot, Alberic's Dapifer, or Sewer, to Faritius the Abbot A few years afterwards (non multorum post decursum annorum) Alberic died, as is stated in the register of the Abbey. (Dugdale, eod loco.) But *our* Alberic was living at the death of Manasses in 1137

3 *Our* Alberic was a favourite with King Stephen, who did not begin to reign till 1137, when the first Alberic must have been dead

Alberic de Vere therefore, who married Beatrice de Guisnes, must have been the second Alberic, the son of the former, who was killed at London, in 1139, the fifth year of Stephen, and is related by the English historians to have been in the confidence of that monarch and to have been much employed by him in affairs of importance He was made Lord Great Chamberlain, and one of the King's Justices by Henry the First, was a man of talents and eloquence, and was sent by Stephen to appear for him at the ecclesiastical synod which was held in the fourth year of his reign. The turbulence of that reign, and the important situation which was held by De Vere, the sickly state of his wife, the want of children by her, the probability of her death, and the consequent loss of Guisnes, will

In case of her death without children, a very probable event, the next heir was Gisla the sister of Manasses, who was married to Wenemar, Chatelain of Ghent. Their son Arnold was an ambitious and enterprizing prince, who looked forward to the succession, and was prepared to seize upon Guisnes the first opportunity. With this view, even in the lifetime of Manasses, he had obtained from him the lordship of Tournehem, within the county of Guisnes, which afforded him a castle, and a station, within the territory[y].

Immediately upon the death of Manasses, in 1137, Henry of Bourbourg sent over to England to inform his son-in-law, of that event, and of the designs of Arnold Alberic came over, took possession of Guisnes, which was thus fallen to him in right of his wife, and did homage to Thierri D'Alsace, Count of Flanders. He returned immediately to England, to receive seizin from King Stephen of his wife's lands in that country, leaving her in Flanders with her father, and having appointed Arnold de Hammes, surnamed the Glutton, Bailiff, or Governor of Guisnes. Fully engaged by his honourable offices in England, having no prospect of children to continue the succession in his own family, and finding little attraction in his wife's infirmities, he never came back to Flanders[z].

In the mean time, Arnold, taking advantage of his absence, formed a powerful confederacy with William Castellan of St. Omer's, his father-in-law, and others, and seized upon the castle of Guisnes He was opposed by Henry of Bourbourg, and his allies; the war was carried on with

sufficiently account for his not going over to that country, and supporting a right which was so very precarious

Beatrice de Guisnes was his second wife His first wife by whom he had seven children, was Adeliza, the daughter of Roger de Iveri, and Adeline de Grentmaisnel, as is fully proved by Kennet, (Parochial Antiq p. 81 &c. ed 1695.) who states it as a palpable mistake in Dugdale, transcribed from Leland, that she was the daughter of Gilbert de Clare. (Baronage, vol. i p. 188)

It should seem that the title of Count of Guisnes was continued in the family of De Vere, for we find the arms of Aubrey de Vere, *Earl of Gyne*, and Oxeford, in the reign of Henry the Second, videlicet, quarterly, gules, and or In the first quarter a mullet of the second, (Ashmole s MSS vol 797.)

[y] Lambert, chap 44, 45, 50

[z] Ibid

various success, in which Guisnes was a scene of devastation, and at length Arnold obtained complete possession[a]. During this time, in vain did the partizans of Beatrice press De Vere to appear, and defend his wife's property. In this distressed state of her affairs, Baldwin, Lord of Ardres, made a proposal to Henry of Bourbourg, that if he would separate his daughter from De Vere, and give her to him in marriage, he would assist him in the recovery of Guisnes. The offer was accepted, and Beatrice was sent over to England under the care of a priest of Saint Omer's, and other attendants. Her ill-health, and other causes, were assigned as reasons for a separation; De Vere consented, and a legal sentence of divorce was pronounced by an ecclesiastical court. She returned to her father, and was married to Baldwin, with the consent of her liege Lord the Count of Flanders, but she died in a few days after the celebration of the nuptials, about the year 1142, and was buried in the monastery of Saint Mary de la Capelle. Her husband, Baldwin, soon after went to Palestine with Louis, King of France, and Thierri, Count of Flanders, and died there in 1146 On the death of Beatrice, Henry of Bourbourg quitted Guisnes, and left the undisturbed possession to Arnold, whose father, Wenemar, and his mother Gisla, being both dead, her rights now fully centered in him, and he thus became the first Count of Guisnes, of the second race, or of the house of Ghent. But Alberic, and Baldwin of Ardres, are enumerated as the seventh and eighth Counts[b]

[a] Lambert, chap 52—59 This war is described in verse by Lambert, who was a contemporary, in chap 55

[b] Lambert, chap 59, 60, 61, 62, 65

CHAPTER III.

Of the father of Robert and William le Blount.

HAVING thus given the history of this family till the extinction of the male line, and beyond the Norman invasion, it remains to ascertain which of these Counts was the father of Robert and William le Blount.

That they were the sons of a Count of Guisnes is sufficiently established by the records of the Herald's office, the tradition of the family, and the unanimous concurrence of every genealogical authority[a]. And since it is evident, from the high rank which they held in William the Conqueror's army, and the extensive lordships which he bestowed upon them, that they were of a noble and illustrious family, there is no reason to question these uniform accounts[b].

It may however be observed upon the history of the Counts of Guisnes, as related by the French historians,

First, That the surname of le Blount does not there appear.

Secondly, That there are no three brothers mentioned, of whom two were named Robert and William.

[a] This family of Blount, Blond, Blund, or le Blond, so named from fairness of complexion, is of noble extraction. The first mentioned in the records of the Herald's office are Robert le Blond, son of le Blond, Lord of Guisnes in Normandy and William le Blund, who is supposed by Sir William Dugdale and others to be the brother of Robert Genealogical Table by Ralph Bigland, Esq Garter King at Arms, in Nash's History of Worcestershire, vol. ii p. 163. Le Blound, Lord of Guisnes, in France, had three sons, who came into England with William the Conqueror. One returned into France, the other two, Sir Robert, and Sir William le Blound, remained in England, and gave a beginning to all the Blounts in the kingdom Collins, or rather Wootton, from the family Baronetage, vol ii p 367 and vol iii. p 665 The many genealogies in the Harleian collection, that of Rawlinson, and all the manuscripts, agree upon this point

[b] Camden styles Gilbert le Blount, son of Robert le Blount, *magnæ nobilitatis vir* Britannia, in Suffolk. Ixworth.

Thirdly, That no notice is taken that any of the family went over with Duke William

Fourthly, That the coat of arms of the Counts of Guisnes, being vairy, or, and azure, is different from that of the Le Blounts, whose most usual arms were lozengy, or, and sable or nebuly of six pieces, or, and sable.

1. To the first objection a decisive answer may be given Hereditary surnames were unknown both in France and England, till about the time of William the Conqueror, when they began to be introduced into both countries; and it was long after, not till about the reign of Edward the Second, before they came into general use *To search therefore for the ancient surnames of the royal and most ancient families of Europe is to seek after what did not exist*[c].

Surnames, indeed, given to individuals, were not uncommon, but they were arbitrary, and personal, and died with their possessors They were mostly in the nature of *sobriquets*, or nicknames, both good and bad, and were derived from their country, their possessions, place of birth, or habitation, from their occupations, professions, offices, and honours Others were given on account of the qualities, or habits, the perfections, or the defects of the mind, or the body, the colour of the complexion, or the hair, and even the most accidental occurrences, or associations They are to be met with in the history of all the nations of Europe Such were those of Edgar the Peaceable, Ethelred the Unready, Charles the Bald, Edmund Ironside, William Rufus, Geoffrey Grisogonel, or Grey-cloak, of Anjou, and in later times, Geoffrey Plantagenet, and the Duke of Guise, le Balafré.

At length these surnames began to be something more permanent, and to be continued from father to son; and thus gradually became family names. This took place in England, in a considerable degree, upon the Norman conquest, and many of the nobles and knights, who came over, retained and transmitted to their posterity, the appellations, some of them merely incidental, which they had brought over with them. To this new practice I apprehend the survey of Domesday Book very much contributed It bestowed upon the Norman adventurers "*a local habitation, and a name*" The authority of the great record of the nation gave stability to the names there entered, and their posterity, with the in-

[c] Camden's Remains

heritance of the fief, would naturally transmit the surname of the first possessor, in which it stood registered in the rolls of their sovereign lord.

But even long after that period, family names were subject to great fluctuations, and frequently underwent many changes. It was not uncommon for persons to take surnames different from their fathers. Of this many examples have occurred in our own country. For instance, Mortimer and Warenne, the founders of the noble families of those names, were brothers, and sons of Walter de Sancto Martino. The first Gifford was the son of Osbert de Bolebec. The first Lovels, Montacutes, Stanleys, and De Bergs, were respectively the sons of De Percival, Drogo Juvenis, de Aldeleigh, and Fitz-Adhelme. Besides these examples, Camden has given a remarkable instance of this practice, in a Cheshire family, not long after the Conquest, from authentic records. William Belward, lord of the Moiety of Malpasse, had two sons, Don David of Malpasse, surnamed le Clerk, and Richard. Don David had William his eldest son, surnamed de Malpasse. His second son Philip, was surnamed Gogh, one of the issue of whose eldest son took the name of Egerton. A third son, David, took the name of Golborne, and another that of Goodman Richard, the other son of William Belward, had three sons, who all took different surnames, Thomas de Cotgrave, William de Overton, and Richard Little; who had two sons, one named Ken-clarke, the other John Richardson. Here, as Camden observes, is the greatest variety of names, in one family, in only a few descents, and derived from most of the sources from whence they were usually deduced; from their place of habitation, in Egerton, Cotgrave, and Overton; from their complexion, in Gogh, that is red, from mental qualities, in Goodman, from stature, in Richard Little, from learning, in Ken-clarke; and from the father's name, in Richardson[d]. Even till the Reformation it was not unusual for ecclesiastics, upon taking orders, to exchange their family name for that of their town. The family name of William of Wykeham is unknown, and that of William of Waynflete was Paten, or Barbour[e].

[d] Camden s Remains

[e] Life of William of Wykeham, by Lowth, and of William of Waynflete by Dr. Chandler, who quotes Holinshead, p 232, for the frequency of the practice.

The family of Guisnes therefore, according to the usage of the times, having no surname, and the individuals of it being designated only by their Christian names, with the addition usually of their hereditary lordship, it is not at all extraordinary that the two brothers, Robert and William, should have acquired a name which did not belong to their ancestors Nor is it difficult to assign a reason for this peculiar addition. The Danes were a fair people; and whilst their countrymen in Normandy, who had migrated earlier, had been imbrowned by a longer residence in a more southern climate, the family of Sigefrede, who came over subsequently, might have still retained the national character of countenance, and the name of le Blount, in the Romance, or French dialect of the Latin tongue, would properly describe the light complexion and flaxen hair of the Scandinavian tribes[1]

It is not improbable that the Counts of Guisnes may have had the surname of le Blount, although it is not mentioned by the French historians The accounts of the family in England expressly state the father of these two brothers to have been Le Blount, Lord of Guisnes. The name itself is of foreign origin, and such attributes were very common at this time, and particularly amongst their kindred noblemen in the neighbouring provinces Amongst the old Counts of Boulogne we find a Guy à la Blanche Barbe, a surname not very unlike that of le Blount. Most of those names which were derived from personal qualities, of mind, or body, could scarcely have been assumed by the persons themselves, and must have been first given them by others, as a sort of nickname; most certainly in those which implied some defect. Many of the family of Guisnes might have been called *flaxen haired* for a long time before they adopted the epithet as their surname, or before a regular historian would apply it to them.

Secondly, and thirdly With respect to the second and third objections, namely, that the names of Robert and William do not occur, and that no notice is taken that any of the family went over with William the Conqueror, it may be observed, that all ancient pedigrees are imperfect, and many of the collateral branches, and the names of the younger chil-

[1] Blundus, blondus, color capillorum flavus, qui nostris Blond Du Cange in voce William Rufus is styled Blundus in some records

dren, are necessarily omitted. Most of the authentic accounts of the ancient families of Europe are taken from charters, grants to monasteries, and other conveyances, in which of course, the elder branches, who were possessed of the chief property, were the parties; the younger brothers had nothing to bestow It is to these benefactors likewise that the historians of those dark times have principally confined their narratives. The interests of their order, and the endowments of their churches, and monasteries, were the subjects most worthy of their attention. The adventures of the younger brothers of the family, and their embarking in an expedition which was so general, and extensive, were not objects of sufficient importance to find a place in those crude, and imperfect, annals.

The *fourth* objection, that the coat of arms of the Counts of Guisnes is different from that of le Blount, the history of armorial bearings will entirely dispel. With regard to the origin of coats of arms, which some heralds have carried up almost to Adam, an evident distinction must be made. The use of national, or personal, insignia, or symbols, taken from animals, and other objects, is very ancient. Such were the Roman eagles, and the peculiar standards of most nations. They were equally in use amongst the Northern barbarians, and were displayed by the feudal chieftains upon their banners, their shields, and helmets. In the Crusades, when the knights of so many different nations were assembled, completely covered with mailed armour, from the necessity of avoiding confusion, these appropriate marks became more general, and they assumed a more fixed and invariable character, as religious, as national, as family, and as individual distinctions; and the regulations which were unavoidably introduced, and observed, gradually formed the art, or science, of heraldry The subjects which formed these different ensigns were naturally taken from those pursuits which were most honourable, and most accordant to the manners and mode of life of those who bore them; from religion, war, and the chase. The cross of their Saviour, the arms and accoutrements of the knights, the war-horse and his trappings, the beasts of venery from the royal lion to the humble rabbit, the noble falcon, and his various prey, supplied an ample choice to gratify the fancy and taste of a gallant warrior.

Whatever capricious ornaments therefore the knights might occasionally display upon their banners, or armour, coats of arms, properly so called, were unknown in the time of William the Conqueror. It was not till the crusades that these marks of distinction began to assume a regular form It was not till a still later period, and by a gradual progress, that they became hereditary. This did not take place in France till the twelfth century[g], and, in England, till the time of Henry the Third, in the thirteenth[h]. The earliest known sculptured arms in this country are those on the shield of Geoffrey de Magnavilla, Earl of Essex, in the Temple Church, who died in 1144[i]. The oldest seal with a coat of arms is the great seal of Richard the First, in 1189, with two lions, or leopards, combattant; his next seal, made in 1195, bore three leopards passant[k]. In Montfaucon's Monuments of the French Monarchy, the first arms represented are those of Geoffrei le Bel, Comte of Main, who died in 1150 The most ancient French seal with arms is said to have been that of Louis le Jeune, who began to reign in 1137[l]. From the reign of Philip Augustus who began to reign in 1180, they are common. Amongst the seals of the Counts of Flanders, there is that of Robert le Frison, the tenth Count, affixed to a diploma of the year 1072, he is represented on horseback, and with a lion rampant on his shield. This may be thought an

In the ancient tapestry at Bayeux in Normandy, which represents the history of William the Conqueror, and Harold, and which was said to have been worked by Queen Matilda, but is certainly of contemporary date, and has been engraved by Montfaucon, in his Monuments de la Monarchie Francaise, vol i. though the shields in general have no ensigns on them, there are four, on which are pictured two monsters, a cross, and some leaves Upon these Montfaucon and there cannot be better authority, observes, Ces bouchiers sont chargez de quelques figures, deux de monstres, un d un croix, et l'autre de quelques feuilles, *ce ne sont point des armoiries* (*non tamen hæc gentilitia insignia erant*) Il est certain qu'il n'y en avoit point encore en ces temps-là qui passassent de pere en fils Les anciens mettoient souvent des marques à leur bouchiers Je ne doute point que depuis ces anciens Romains d autres nations n aient quelquefois mis des marques sur leur bouchiers, mais c etoit un pur caprice. Il n'y a eu de ces marques qui aient passé par succession aux familles qu' au *douzieme siecle* (Illa verò insignia queis familiæ distinguuntur, quæque ad filios et nepotes transierunt, *duodecimo sæculo cœperunt*) Montfaucon, I p 376 See Archæol vol xvii p 85. and vol xviii p. 359.

[h] Selden, Titles of Honour, Preface, p. 92

[i] Gough's Introduction to his Sepulchral Monuments, p 104

[k] Speed s History in Rich. I

[l] Edmondson, p 10

exception to the assertion, that arms were not in use so early. But in reality this must be referred to the arbitrary insignia occasionally adopted by knights. The lion does not appear again till it is introduced upon the shield of Philip of Alsace, to a diploma of 1163; after which it regularly becomes a coat of arms, and is on the seals of all the subsequent Counts[m] In Scotland there is no evidence of any coats armorial before William the Lion, who began to reign in 1165[n]. The oldest monument of any of the Roman Pontiffs with a coat of arms, is that of Clement the Fourth, at Viterbo. He died in 1268[o]. In short, no well authenticated examples of coats of arms are to be found which can prove that they were regularly established, or, indeed, were in use, as proper heraldic insignia, till after the first crusade. But for a long time, even after those periods, they were far from being fixed and permanent, and changes and variations frequently occurred. In the same family the son often adopted a different coat of arms from his father, and one brother was distinguished from another by a different coat of arms. Innumerable examples of such variations are to be met with in England, and even so late as in the instances of the last Earls of Chester, Winchester, and Lincoln[p].

Since then, at the time of William the Conqueror's expedition, heraldry had no existence, neither the Counts of Guisnes, or their sons, could have had any coats of arms When they were introduced into use, which was long after the Le Blounts had settled in England, it would have been no unusual occurrence that the two branches of the family, the one in Guisnes, and the other in England, should have adopted different bearings, from the want of mutual intercourse, or even for the very purpose of distinction.

It is even far from being impossible, or improbable, that the two coats of arms were originally the same, and that the subsequent difference was the effect of time, or accident. The two coats, the one, vairy, or, and azure, and the other lozengy, or, and sable, and barry, nebuly, or, and

[m] Ol Uredii, Sigilla Com Flandriæ.

[n] Lord Hale's Remarks on the History of Scotland.

[o] Edmondson's Heraldry, p 10

[p] The oldest grant of arms upon record is of Richard II. Richard the III first erected the Heralds into a college. Rowe Mores' Dedication. The banners of the twelve tribes of Israel are not mentioned in the Scriptures, but were the fancies of the Rabbies

sable, in their general appearance, both in the forms, and the colours, have a considerable degree of resemblance, and either of them may have been an accidental, and gradual, or an intentional, deviation from the other As the *leopards* of Normandy and Aquitain have imperceptibly become *lions* in the arms of England[q].

At what period the Le Blounts acquired their coat of arms cannot perhaps be easily ascertained. The first authentic emblazonment which I have met with, is in the reign of Edward the First, in the catalogue of the knights of that period, in an ancient manuscript in the British Museum[r].

It does not appear that, in fact, the Counts of Guisnes had adopted any coat of arms till the latter end of the twelfth century. Upon examining the ample collection of proofs and documents annexed by Du Chesne to his history, the earliest seal we find of any of the Counts of Guisnes is to a charter of Count Manasses, of the year 1120, already given. The impression is of a man on horseback, with a lance, or some other weapon, and a shield, without any coat of arms. The seal of his wife Emma, is a woman with a book in one hand, and a flower in the other[s]. So the seal of Count Arnold, in 1151, is a man on horseback. The oldest seals in that collection, which have coats of arms, are those of the three sons of Arnold, Baldwin the Second, in 1202, William, about 1177, and Siger, Chatelain of Ghent, in 1190, and 1198. Those of Baldwin have the usual arms of Guisnes; William has, in addition, a bend, and Siger, a chevron; to distinguish them being younger brothers[t].

There is no direct proof, therefore, that the Counts of Guisnes had any coat of arms before the year 1177, but there is presumptive evidence, from their seals, that they had none as late as the year 1151.

These objections are therefore of no weight, and the only point remain-

[q] As late as the reign of Edward I. the arms of England are thus blazoned Le Roy de Engleterre porte de goules, a iii Lupards passauns de or In an ancient manuscript containing nomina et arma nobilium qui cum Edwardo primo militabant. See more of this subsequently. Harleian MSS No 1068 p 71 and in the Catalogue published by Rowe Mores from another manuscript

[r] Ibid

[s] For the charter itself see the Appendix, No. IX.

[t] All these seals are engraved in the next chapter. They are taken from Duchesne

ing to be ascertained is which of the Counts of Guisnes was father to Robert Le Blount, and William Le Blount, the founders of the family in England, and to the other brother who returned to France.

The reigning Count of Guisnes, at the time of William's expedition, was Baldwin, who succeeded to the lordship before the year 1065, and died in 1191 Four sons only are mentioned by Lambert, Manasses, or Robert, the eldest, Fulk, Guy, and Hugh. This Robert could not have been the same with Robert Le Blount, because he succeeded to the lordship of Guisnes, and, though he frequented the court of King William, certainly did not settle in England. The name of William is not amongst them. Unless therefore there were other sons not stated by Lambert, the two Le Blounts were not the sons of Baldwin, at that time Count of Guisnes.

We must go back therefore to the late Count, Eustace, the father of Baldwin, and his children. Besides Baldwin, he is stated to have had a son, William, and another named Ramelin, but no other is mentioned. This might have been William Le Blount, for Lambert does not say what became of him. There might have been another brother named Robert, and Ramelin might have been the third who returned to France, and whose name is not known. These sons of Eustace were well qualified for the high prowess and the military rank of the Le Blounts, for it is said of them that they had been educated in the art of war amongst the first youths of Flanders[u].

But as there is no positive authority for these suppositions, let us ascend another step, to Rodolphus or Raoul, the father of Eustace. Besides Eustace, he is stated by Lambert to have had other sons, "who did not degenerate "from their father's merits in warlike exploits and accomplishments[x]." Amongst these were probably Robert and William Le Blount, and the other brother. The age of these sons agrees perfectly as to time. Rodolphus married after the year 1000, it is not known how long after. If we suppose that he married about the year 1010, his younger children would probably have been from forty to fifty years of age at the time of the Conquest Robert Le Blount must have been of that age, since his son Gilbert was capable of bearing arms, and accompanied William upon his

[u] Appendix, No VII. [x] Appendix, No. VI

expedition to England[y]. The high military command, bestowed upon the brothers, seems to imply a maturity of years and experience. In the painting at Ely, hereafter more particularly to be described, though a correct resemblance perhaps may not be found, yet even after repeated renovations, the general appearance was probably preserved, and in that of William Le Blount, we see the portrait of a warrior far advanced in life. Upon the whole therefore it seems best supported by facts, that the Le Blounts were the sons of Rodolphus, by his wife Rosella, daughter of the Count de Saint Pol.

[y] Dugdale, Monasticon, vol ii p. 184 Gilbertus veniens in conquestu cum Willielmo

CHAPTER IV.

Of the family of Guisnes, of the second race, or House of Ghent.

WE have now traced this family from its first origin to the end of the first race, to the time of the migration of the two brothers, and the detachment of the Le Blounts from the main stock. Before I proceed with their history, I shall relate the sequel of the fortunes of the house, and territory, of Guisnes.

The descendants of Manasses having become extinct by the death of his grand-daughter Beatrice without issue, his next heir was GISLA, his youngest sister. At the death of Beatrice, his brothers and his other sisters were dead, and none of them had left children, except Adela, who had been married to the Lord of Semur, and had a son She was older than Gisla, and had she been living would have had a claim prior to that of her sister But she had been dead some time, and, by the laws of that country, representation did not take place, and therefore a younger surviving sister was preferred before the son of an elder sister deceased, as being nearer of kin to the last possessor. The son of Adela, Jeffrey, Lord of Semur, appeared at first as a competitor, but he soon abandoned his claim[a].

GISLA was married to WENEMAR, Chatelain of Ghent, and Lord of Bornhem; one of the first noblemen in Flanders.

Ghent had formerly belonged to the Emperors, and was governed by Counts appointed by them. It was afterwards conquered by Arnold le Jeune, Count of Flanders, and, after being several times taken and retaken, was finally possessed by the Counts of Flanders, in the time of Baldwin le Barbu, about the year 1007 He appointed Lambert, a noble Lord, who was descended from the ancient Counts of Ghent, as the first hereditary Chatelain, Viscount, or Burg-grave of Ghent, and who was the

[a] Lambert, chap. 63.

ancestor of Wenemar. The ancient Counts, upon the first conquest, are supposed to have retired to Alost, and to have continued Lords of that place, retaining their original name of De Gand[h].

The Chatelaine after this was therefore an hereditary fief, held of the Counts of Flanders. It was the first in rank, and the Chatelains had the title of Illustrious. They had large domains, within which they had the right of taxation, of *haute justice*, and other feudal perquisites. It was their prerogative likewise to bear, in person, or by a proper knight of their blood, the standard, or banner, of the city of Ghent, whenever the citizens went to war under their Lord and Prince, the Count of Flanders. And the city was bound to give them a white horse, and a salary of one hundred livres Parisis a day, when upon that honourable service[c].

Wenemar, the son of Lambert the Second, who was grandson to the first Lambert, succeeded his father before 1088, in the Chatelaine of Ghent, and the Lordship of Bornhem. He was twice married. His first lady was named Lutgarde, and died without children. His second wife was Gisla de Guisnes. His name appears as a party, a guarantee, or a witness to various acts of that time, chiefly donations to monasteries, which, however important to those religious houses, are uninteresting to posterity. Having some contention with the people of Ghent, he retired to William of Normandy, Count of Flanders, who sent him as his ambassador to the Emperor Lotharius. He enjoyed his government for fifty years, and died in 1138, leaving his widow Gisla de Guisnes, who survived her husband, her brother Manasses, and her great niece Beatrice, and died about the year 1142.

The children of Wenemar and Gisla, were Arnold, Wenemar, Siger,

[h] Duchesne, p. 39, 299. Of the Lords of Alost, descended from the ancient Counts of Ghent, and named De Gand, was Gilbert de Gand, an ancestor of Beatrice, wife of Arnold II. Count of Guisnes, who came over with William the Conqueror, and received from him the Barony of Folkingham in Lincolnshire. His grandson, of the same name, was created Earl of Lincoln by King Stephen, and *his* brother, Robert De Gand, was Lord Chancellor. They were deprived of the Earldom of Lincoln, for supporting Louis of France, and Gilbert gave the Barony of Falkingham to Edward, eldest son of Henry the Third. *Camden, Britann in loco.* Of the family of Alost were likewise the Lords of Tenremonde.

[c] Duchesne, p. 299.

Baldwin, first a monk and afterwards a knight, and Margaret, married to Steppo, a knight of Ghent.

The seal of Wenemar affixed to a charter containing some grants to the Canons of Bornhem, without date, but perhaps about 1112[d].

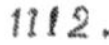

From Gisla the title to the county of Guisnes descended to her eldest son Arnold the First, who thus became the stock of the Counts of Guisnes of the *second race, or House of Ghent*, as before mentioned.

But Arnold did not succeed to the Chatelanie of Ghent, or the Lordship of Bornhem. After the death of Wenemar, Theodoric, Count of Flanders, displeased with Arnold for seizing upon Guisnes without his consent, took possession of Ghent, and appointed Roger, the Chatelain of Courtray, to be Chatelain. Arnold, to whom the office of right belonged, at length entered into a compromise, and agreed to surrender his claim, upon condition that Roger should marry his daughter, Margaret of Guisnes, as his second wife. Roger died in 1190, and leaving no children by Margaret, he was succeeded by Siger de Guisnes, her brother, and son to Arnold, who had married Peronella de Courtray, the daughter of Roger

[d] Duchesne, Pr. p. 67. from the archives of the Abbey of Afflegem. Of this and the other seals introduced, from the great accuracy of Duchesne, who copied them from the originals, and who has printed all the charters to which they are annexed, there can be no doubt of their authenticity. Yet he must have translated the *inscriptions* from their ancient form into a modern character.

de Courtray, by his first wife, Sarah de Lille. From him descended the subsequent Chatelains, who bore the arms of Guisnes, as well as those of Ghent, till the time of Hugh the Second, who succeeded in 1232 And from these descended the Barons of Saint John Steene, and Rassenghien, and the Counts of Isenghien, who will be hereafter mentioned[e]. The Lordship of Bornhem was likewise given to Siger[f].

We have before seen that Arnold, in the absence of Alberic de Vere, had taken possession of Guisnes. Upon the death of Beatrice, and his mother Gisla, he became the ninth Count of Guisnes. He is said to have been one of the bravest knights of his time, but the memory of his exploits has not survived. He was likewise a benefactor to several churches, and monasteries, and, amongst other benefits, he bestowed upon that of Saint Bertin the privilege of passing over his lands in their way to England, without paying any impost. His wife was Matilda the daughter of William, Chatelain of Saint Omer's. Upon a journey to England, to visit the property which had descended to him from Emma of Tancarville, the wife of his uncle Manasses, he was attacked in his own house, at a town called Newton[g], part of those possessions, by a disorder of which he died in 1169, and his body was removed to the hospital of Santingheveld, to be buried according to his own desire[h].

They had thirteen children, Baldwin, William, Manasses, Siger, Chatelain of Ghent, Arnold, Margaret, married first to Eustace de Fiennes, secondly, to Roger, Chatelain of Courtray, and Ghent, Beatrice, who married first, William Faramus, Lord of Tingry, and afterwards Hugh, Chatelain of Beaumez; Adelis, who had two husbands likewise, Hugh Chatelain of Lille, and Robert de Waurin, Lord of Senghin, Euphemia, Abbess of Saint Leonard's, Lutgarde, a nun who succeeded her sister; Matilda.

[e] Lambert, chap. 61 Duchesne, 300, 303

[f] The arms of the Chatelains of Ghent are sable, a chief, argent, with a coronet of a circle of gold, enriched with precious stones, bearing pearls, nine in sight

[g] Apud Niuentoniam Lambert, chap 73 Neuetona Chronicle of Ardres, p 100

[h] Lambert chap 73 As to the name of this Count, Lambert calls him Arnold, Duch Pr p. 89 In charters, his name is signed Arnulfus, Ernoldus, and Arnulphus, page 91 In one charter he styles himself Ernoldus, but the seal to the same instrument has Ernulfus, p 93, 94 Arnold the Second is called in a charter Arnoldus, his seal has Arnulfus In another, both charter and seal have Arnulphus

wife of Baldwin de Hondescote; Gisla, married to Walter de Pollar, Lord of Aa in Brabant, and Prince of Tyberios, or Tabarie, in the Holy Land; Agnes, who went to the Holy Land, married there, and was poisoned[i].

The seal of Count Arnold, from a charter without date, but probably about 1151, granting a free passage over his lands to the Abbey of St. Bertin[k].

He was succeeded by his eldest son, BALDWIN THE SECOND, the tenth Count of Guisnes, who was christened of that name by his godfather Manasses, in memory of his own father.

At a proper age, he received the honour of knighthood from the hands of Thomas à Becket, the Archbishop of Canterbury. The holy prelate in person girt on his sword, fixed his spurs, and conferred the stroke of chivalry; a ceremony which was attended with great splendour, and valuable gifts to the Archbishop; for whom he ever after retained the highest veneration[l].

[i] Lambert, chap. 48.

[k] From the Archives of that Abbey. Duch. Pr. p. 93.

[l] Archipræsul Thomas, qui eidem Comiti dudum in signum militiæ gladium lateri, et calcaria (o per omnia prædicandæ in eximio Christi sacerdote humilitatis virtutem) sui militis pedibus adoptavit, et alapam collo ejus infixit; quem tamen in ipso militatoriæ promotionis ejus die variis redemit munusculis, et lautioribus quam regalibus expensis.

It may perhaps, at first sight, be thought extraordinary that a military order should be conferred by an ecclesiastic, yet a little consideration of the nature of chivalry will shew that it was perfectly in character. Whatever might have been the origin of this institution, and however it might afterwards have degenerated, whilst it existed in its purity and perfection, it was entirely founded in religion. Besides the other duties, which were of a moral and Christian nature, to defend the catholic faith, holy church, and her ministers, were some of its first obligations. The previous preparations, the fasts, the night spent in prayer, the sermons, the sacrament, the baptisms, and the white habits, were the same ceremonies which accompanied the most solemn acts of religion The form of conferring knighthood itself was purely religious. It was regularly performed at the altar, mass was celebrated, and a peculiar form of prayer was used, to be still seen in ancient rituals. By whomsoever applied, the sword was always blessed by a priest, and the words of investiture invoked the name of God, Saint Michael, and Saint George. Some of the orders, as the Knights Templars, and of Saint John of Jerusalem, were decidedly monastic, and all of them partook of the monastic nature in their form, their vows, and their obligations. They were even sometimes considered as a species of priesthood, and the doubt whether all knights were not bound, like the clergy, to celibacy, was only dispelled by another indispensable part of their duty, love, and the service of the ladies[m].

It is no wonder, therefore, that an order so connected with religion, should be conferred by ecclesiastical, as well as lay, persons. Accordingly we find, that the right of making knights belonged to the pope, and other dignitaries of the church. In the Pontificale Romanum a form is prescribed for their creation by the pontiff in person[n] He claimed a right of authorizing others to make knights, even as late as the time of Julius the Third, in 1550. That pope, by his bull to the patriarchs of Constantinople, Alexandria, Jerusalem, and Aquileia, and other archbishops and bishops, being of his household chaplains, grants them the power of

Language scarcely affords Lambert sufficient expressions for his admiration of Saint Thomas à Becket, qui fecit magnalia in terra Ægypti, terribilia in mari, mirabilia in cœlo et in terra, super omnes, et in omnibus, magnitudinis virum, &c Lambert, chap 87

[m] De Sainte Palaye Mémoires sur l'ancienne Chevalerie.

[n] Selden, Titles of Honour, vol iii p 498

creating eight knights[o]. The Emperor of Germany was always knighted by a bishop[p]. In ancient times in England they were created both by ecclesiastical, and lay subjects The Abbot of Edmondsbury knighted many persons in the reign of William the Conqueror[q]. Lanfrank, Archbishop of Canterbury, bestowed that honour upon William Rufus, in his father's life time[r]. In a Synod, held at London, under Anselm, Archbishop of Canterbury, in 1102, in the reign of Henry the First, it was enacted, that abbots should not create knights[s]; though the practice seems still to have continued; for, amongst other authorities, in the statutes of the abbey of Reading, which were confirmed by Henry the First, and subsequent kings, the abbot is prohibited from making knights, unless when he is habited in his sacred vestments[t].

In the year 1170, when Thomas à Becket was returning to England, after his banishment, and passed through the county of Guisnes, he was met by Peter, Abbot of Saint Bertin's, by the command of Baldwin, and conducted from that monastery to the castle of Guisnes, where he was entertained with the greatest honour and magnificence. In the morning, before his departure, the Archbishop made a full confession of all his former life, to Geoffrey, Chaplain of the Count's chapel, humbly requesting his spiritual counsel, and commending himself to his prayers. He then took shipping for England, and his tragical end soon followed. Count Baldwin having afterwards obtained some relics of his body, placed them in the chapel of Saint Catherine, which he had built at de la Montoire[u].

His father Arnold, in his life time, had procured for Baldwin the Second, a match of great prudence, with Christiana, sole daughter of his vassal, Arnold, Lord of Ardres, Viscount of Marc, and Lord of Colewide, by his wife Adeline, sister and heiress to Baldwin, Lord of Ardres, father

[o] Milites et equites deauratas octo, ac eisdem militibus solita equitum deauratorum insignia concedere. Selden, Titles of Honour, p 506

[p] Ibid p. 495.

[q] Ingulphus, p. 901

[r] William of Malmsbury, lib iv cap 1

[s] Id de gest. Pontif ne abbates faciant milites.

[t] Nec faciat milites nisi in sacra veste Christi. *Seld.* ibid.

[u] Chronicle of Ardres, and Lambert, chap 75, 87.

of Lambert the historian[x]. Christiana was the heiress of those three lordships, which thus were united to Guisnes. Yet it was thought something of degradation for a lord to marry the daughter of his vassal Arnold's father, Elembert, Lord of Marc and Colewide, having been appointed by the Count of Guisnes his viscount, or lieutenant, he and his successors ever after retained the title of Viscount of Marc[y].

In Christiana's fortune was included some property in England, the manor of Tollesbury, or Tolleshunt, in the parish of Tollesbury in Essex. Arnold d'Ardres possessed here three knights' fees about the reign of King John. He had likewise lands in Kent, Essex, and Bedfordshire, which he lost by supporting the barons against the king. In after times Robert de Guisnes gave to Fulk Basset, Bishop of London, the homage of Henry de Mark in this place. In 1251 the Count of Guisnes held Tolleshunt for two knights' fees, and Fulk Basset, brother and heir of the bishop, at his death in 1271, held it of the king in capite, by one knight's fee, of his honour of Boulogne[z]

After the death of his wife in childbed, which happened upon the 2d of July 1177[a], to console his affliction, he gave himself up to study; and though his education, like that of most of the nobility of those times, had been illiterate, he made great progress in philosophy, and the knowledge of the holy Scriptures. He collected a considerable library, of which he appointed Hesard de Hesdin librarian, and built an organ for the nuns at Guisnes. The defects of his education were supplied by the lectures of learned men, whom he invited to his castle, and maintained. Some of their labours in his service have been specified. Landeric de Wallanio translated for his use the Song of Solomon from Latin into Romance[b], together with the Gospels for Sundays, and some Homilies. Alfrius

[x] Ad similitudinarium multorum exemplum nobilium, ducum, videlicet Regum et Imperatorum se humiliantium et propter similem causam sic uxoriantium, inclinavit se ad *hominis sui* filiam Lambert, chap 66, 67

[y] Duchesne, p 66 The arms of the Lords of Ardres were, argent, an eagle displayed, sable. For a coronet a wreath set with pearls Duchesne, Pr. p 86, 90

[z] Morant's Essex, vol i p 400 Dugd Bar.

[a] Lambert, chap 85, 86

[b] De Latino in Romanum. Lambert

interpreted the life of Anthony the monk. Another of the literati, named Master Godfrey, translated out of the same language a part of the Physics of Aristotle, as Simon de Bolonia did the work of Solinus de Naturâ Rerum. Walter, surnamed Silens, composed for him a book intitled Silentium, sive Romanum de Silentio, the Romance of Silence. Such was the Count's learning, that he was thought to equal Augustine in theology, Dionysius the Areopagite in philosophy, Thales the Milesian in mythology, and the most celebrated minstrels in lays of great exploits[c].

From his love of literature, Baldwin was naturally attached to the clergy, to whom it was almost exclusively confined. In 1178 we find him entertaining, in his castle at Ardres, William of Champagne, Archbishop of Rheims, who was returning from a pilgrimage to the tomb of Saint Thomas à Becket at Canterbury. In describing the feast given upon this occasion, Lambert relates a story strongly characteristic of the gross hospitality of the age. When the guests asked for water, to temper the strong wines which were set before them, the *Cyprus*, the *Hyppocras*, and the *Claret*[d], the attendants were directed, instead of water, to supply them with excellent wine of *Auxerre*[e]. The prelate perceiving the trick, "for there is "nothing hidden," says the historian, "which shall not be revealed[f]," asked his host for a cup of that water, without shewing his mistrust. The Count, arising from his seat, went to the side-board, and overturned and broke all the vessels of water, pretending drunkenness. "This piece of "politeness," says Lambert, "so much diverted the Archbishop, that he "promised to do whatever he should require, and at parting he presented "him with two vials of precious balsam[g]."

In 1179 he accompanied King Louis le Jeune to the tomb of Saint

[c] Lambert, chap 80, 81 In *cantilenis,* historiis, sive in eventuris nobilium, sive etiam in fabellis ignobilium, *joculatores* quosque nominatissimos æquiparare putaretur Lambert, chap 81

[d] Vino altero et altero Cyprico et Niseo, pigmentato, et clarificato. Lambert, chap 87

[e] Authisiodoricum vinum pretiosissimum.

[f] Nihil enim opertum quod non reveletur. Lambert, 87.

[g] Lambert, chap 87

Thomas à Becket. From Ushant they sailed to Dover, where his majesty was received with great honours by Henry the Second[h].

In the time of this Count an event happened of some importance to the county of Guisnes, the change of its sovereign lord. We have before seen, that it was a fief of the Counts of Flanders, as they were feudatories to the Emperor, and afterwards to the King of France. Philip of Alsace, Count of Flanders, married his niece Isabel, or Elizabeth, daughter of his sister Margaret, wife of the Count of Hainalt, to Philip Augustus, son of Lewis the Seventh, King of France, and gave as her portion a large part of the west of Flanders, and other territories. After the death of Philip of Alsace, at Acre, in 1190, there were many claims upon Flanders. His sister Margaret, as the next heir, took possession of it, and her husband Baldwin, Count of Hainalt, and Namur, assumed the title of Count Matilda of Portugal, the widow of Philip, was intitled to her dower; and Louis of France, the son of Philip Augustus, claimed what had been settled upon his mother at her marriage. After much discussion, a treaty, or a judicial decision, was made at Arras in 1191, by which the county of Flanders was divided, and Margaret had Bruges, Ghent, Ypres, Courtray, and Oudinard. Matilda, for her dower, Lisle, Douay, Orchies, l'Ecluse, Cassel, Furnes, Bailleul, Bourbourg, Berghes, Nieuport, and some other places To Louis were ceded, in perpetuity, Arras, Bapaume, Aire, St Omer's, Hedin, Lens, the homages of Boulogne, St. Pol, *Guisnes*, Lillers, Ardres, Richebourg, and all places to the south of Neuf-Fosse, comprising the Advowry of Bethune[i].

By this arrangement the Counts of Guisnes became at first the immediate vassals of the Crown of France. Afterwards Lewis the Eighth, the son of Philip Augustus, assigned these territories as the apannage of Robert of France, his youngest son. Saint Lewis erected them into a county, which was called Artois, in 1238, and Robert was created the first Count. The counties of Boulogne, Saint Pol, and Guisnes, were placed

[h] Hoveden in anno 1179

[i] Meyer Annal Flandriæ Anno 1191 Buzelini Ann Gall Flend p 248 Du Tillet, p. 105. Hist de Cal. i 610 Duchesne, Pr p 127

under the tenure of Artois, and thus became arriere-fiefs of the Crown of France[k].

Baldwin did not long observe the fidelity due to the French king. In 1192 he joined the Count of Flanders, at that time at war with King Philip Augustus. The French King marched a powerful army into Flanders, and reduced them to terms. A treaty of peace was signed soon after at Peronne, in which Guisnes, and the other places, which were the portion of Isabel, were finally ceded to Philip Augustus[l].

In 1196, Baldwin was again in arms, another treaty was made at Bailleul, and again broken. Philip invaded his territories a second time, and he was obliged to surrender himself a prisoner, with his two sons, Giles and Siger[m]. He was restored to his liberty after some years confinement, and, his health being injured by the imprisonment, he died on the 2d of January, in 1206.

His funeral was attended by thirty-three children, which he had by his wife, and other ladies who shared his affections after her death. For though a lover of learning, he was not indifferent to the charms of the fair sex[n].

Such was his prudence in the councils of princes, that he was said "to "shine as a precious gem in the crown of the kingdom of France, and a "valuable carbuncle in the diadem of the king of England[o]." So great was his wisdom and impartiality in the administration of the laws, that he was

[k] Le Roi Saint Louis ayant erigé, l'an 1238, l'Artois en Compté, mit dans sa mouvance ceux de Boulogne, de Guisnes, et de S Paul, qui devinrent par là des arriere-fiefs de la couronne *Du Tillet.* Arnold III in 1248, acknowledged, by an instrument under his seal, that he and his ancestors had done four liege homages to the Count of Artois; 1. for the Castle and County of Guisnes, 2 for the Barony of Ardres, 3. for the Chatelanie of Langle, 4. for the land which he had at Saint Omer's *Duchesne, Preuv* p. 287. quatre hommages liges

[l] Duchesne, p. 72. and Preuv p 127.

[m] Chronicle of St Bertin, Pr p 128.

[n] His enemies said of him, In tantum in teneras exardescit puellas, et maxime virgines, quod nec David, nec filius ejus Salomon in tot juvencularum corruptione similis ejus esse creditur Sed nec Jupiter quidem Lambert admits that he had so many children, quod nec pater eorum nomina novit omnium Lambert, chap 89

[o] In concilio principum adeo prudens dictus est idem Comes, quod in corona Regni Franciæ quasi gemma radiaret prætiosa, et in diademate Regis Angliæ quasi carbunculi petra corruscaret pretiosa. Lambert, chap 88

surnamed *the Just*. However irregular in his pleasures, his conduct as a prince and a man, in other respects, was correct, and virtuous. He was a protector of orphans and widows, hospitable to strangers, and a benefactor to churches and monasteries. He built chapels, repaired cities and castles, established markets, drained marshes, and was in every respect an active and public spirited sovereign. In his castle at Guisnes, he built a chapel, and, over the donjon, he erected a beautiful round house, covered with lead, and which contained so many chambers, and was so artfully contrived, that it was compared to the labyrinth of Dædalus[p].

The children of Baldwin the Second, and Christiana of Ardres, were ten. 1. Arnold, 2. William, 3. Manasses, Lord of Ronchoue, and Tiembronne, 4. Baldwin, Canon of the Church of Terouenne, and administrator of the Churches of Saint Peter near Montoir, of Stenentone, Stitede, Maling, and Baigtone, in England. He was killed in 1229, and his death was amply revenged by his nephew, Baldwin the Third, who compelled his murderers to go and bear arms in the Holy Land, for the good of his soul[q]. Though an ecclesiastic, he left children. 5. Giles Lord of Lotesse, 6. Siger, 7. Mabile, who married John de Chisom, 8. Adeline, married to Baldwin de Marquise, and Hugh de Malaunoy. 9. Margaret, wedded to Rabodon de Rumes, 10. Matilda to William de Tiembronne. The names of five of his natural children are mentioned.

The following Epitaph on the Countess Christiana, was written by Lambert[r].

HIC COMITISSA JACET, FLORENTI STIRPE CREATA,
PARQUE VIRO SOCIATA PARI, CHRISTIANA VOCATA.
JULIUS IN SEXTO NONARUM MENSE NOTETUR,
SICQUE DIES OBITUS IN SECULA LONGA CIETUR.
ANNUS MILLESIMUS, CENTENUS, SEPTUAGENUS,
SEPTIMUS, A CHRISTO STAT IN EJUS FUNERE PLENUS.

[p] Lambert, chap. 76. He repaired the fortifications of Tournehem, and Audrwick, and built Sangatte. Lambert, chap. 77, 86.

[q] Lambert, chap. 71, 72, 79.

[r] Lambert, chap. 71, 72.

The seal and counter-seal of Baldwin the Second, to a charter dated in 1202, confirming a grant of the tithes of Guisnes to the Abbey of St. Bertin[s].

The seal of his brother, William de Guisnes to a charter without date, but perhaps about 1177, by which he, his wife Flandrina, and his son William, grant to the Church of Saint Leonard the tithes of three parishes. St. Bertin, St. Peter, and St. Medard[t].

[s] Duchesne, Pr. p. 132. Archives of St. Bertin.

[t] Ibid. p. 100. From the Archives of that Abbey.

The seal of his brother Siger, Chatelain of Ghent, and that of his wife, Petronilla de Courtray. It is a grant of tithes to the Abbey of Afflegem, and bears date 1198[u].

The seal of his sister Margaret, wife first of Eustace de Fiennes, and afterwards of Roger Chatelain of Courtray, to a charter without date, granted to the Abbey of St. Bavon at Ghent[x].

[u] Duchesne, Pr. p. 464. Archives of the Abbey. [x] Ibid. p. 109.

He was succeeded by his son, ARNOLD THE SECOND, the eleventh Count of Guisnes, who likewise inherited from his mother the Lordships of Ardres, Marc, and Colewide. Upon her death, in the year 1177, he immediately claimed those lordships of his father, and, obtaining possession, assumed the title of Lord of Ardres. His education was completed in the Court of Philip, Count of Flanders. After receiving the order of knighthood from his father, in 1181, he employed the two next years in frequenting tournaments[y] in different countries, under the conduct of a brave and prudent knight named Arnold de Cayeu[z], and his nephew, who had been the companion of Prince Henry of England. In those early years, as we are informed by Lambert, he delighted to hear ancient men relate the edifying histories of the Roman Emperors, of Charlemagne, of Roland and Oliver, of King Arthur, the exploits of the English, of Gormund, Ysembarb, Tristan and Hisolda, Merlin and Merculf, the siege of Antioch, and the wars of Palestine[a].

His personal charms, and high reputation, inflamed the love of a noble widow, Ida, niece of the Count of Flanders, and, in her own right, Countess of Boulogne wife, first, of Matthew, whose surname is unknown; secondly, of Gerard, Count of Gueldres; and thirdly, of Bethold, Duke of Loringhen. After many clandestine meetings, the Countess paid him a visit at Ardres, where he entertained her splendidly, and only permitted her to depart upon her promise to return. Every thing was arranged, and the consent of Count Philip was obtained, yet Arnold was at last disappointed of the lady, and the county of Boulogne. Reginald, son of the Count of Dammartin, before this new connexion, had made proposals of marriage to Ida, to which she had been well-disposed, but her uncle, the Count of Flanders, unwilling to give up the profits of the wardship of the county of Boulogne, and disliking a French connexion, disapproved of the alliance. At this critical period, when the marriage with Arnold was entirely settled, Dammartin seized the Countess, not altogether without her acquiescence, and carried her off into Lorain. She contrived means to write to Arnold, to inform him of this pretended violence, and to request that he would deliver her from the hands of her oppressor. The too credulous lover, with some friends and followers, immediately engaged

[y] Et Behordicia. [z] Arnoldus de Chaiocho [a] Lambert, chap. 90, 91, 92.

in the enterprize, but no sooner were they arrived at Verdun, than Dammartin, informed of their coming by the Countess herself, took them all prisoners, and married the perfidious lady. After a captivity of some months, they obtained their liberty by the intercession of the Archbishop of Rheims. Lambert considers this unfortunate affair as a judgment upon him for having neglected to fulfil his vow of going to the Holy Land with Philip Augustus, and Philip Count of Flanders, and for having squandered the tithes, and the money, which had been exacted for that purpose, with thoughtless prodigality[b].

In his next matrimonial connection Arnold was the deserter. He was affianced to Eustachia, the youngest daughter of Hugh, Count of Saint Pol, but the celebration of the marriage was deferred on account of the tender age of the young lady. In the mean time, Henry, Chatelain of Bourbourg and Lord of Alost, died, in 1194, without issue, leaving Beatrice his sister sole heiress of his possessions. Arnold then abandoned Eustachia, paid his addresses to Beatrice, and was accepted. The marriage was celebrated with great magnificence at Ardres, and the new married couple received the nuptial benediction, were sprinkled with holy water, and fumigated with incense, as they lay in bed, by a procession of priests, led by Lambert the minister of the place, who relates the event. And the whole ceremony concluded with a long prayer by Count Baldwin, his father[c].

Arnold, being thus Chatelain of Bourbourg, and Lord of Alost and Waise, by this marriage, and Lord of Ardres, Marc, and Colewide, from his mother, in the lifetime of his father, assisted him in his war with the Count of Flanders against Philip Augustus, and was the principal means of taking the city of Saint Omer, in 1198, for which he received great rewards from the Count He surrounded Ardres with a large fossè, and gave protection to Matilda, the widow of Philip, Count of Flanders[d].

Upon the death of his father, Count Baldwin, he succeeded to the

[b] Lambert, chap 93, 94, 95

[c] Ibid chap. 149

[d] Ibid chap 151 Of this work Lambert gives a very rhetorical account, and describes the engineer, doctum geometricalis operis magistrum, Simonem fossarium, cum virgâ suâ, magistrali more, procedentem, et hîc illîc, jam in mente conceptum rei opus, non tam in virgâ, quam in oculorum perticâ, geometricantem. Ibid. c. 154.

county of Guisnes, in 1206. An enmity subsisted between him and Reginald, who was Count of Boulogne by his marriage with Ida, augmented, if not occasioned, by that marriage. Philip Augustus, as the ally of the Count of Boulogne, with a large army, entered the county of Guisnes in 1209, destroyed the castle of Bonham, and committed other devastations, till a peace was made in 1210[e], when Arnold did homage, and took the oath of fealty to King Philip Augustus and his son Louis But his adherence to the King of France proved extremely detrimental to his affairs. In the war which then raged between John, King of England, and Philip Augustus, the English army under the command of the Earl of Salisbury, together with the troops of Ferdinand, Count of Flanders, Reginald de Dammartin, and other noblemen, entered Guisnes in 1213, and laid waste a great part of the country A month after, in 1214, they returned again, and putting all to fire and sword, Arnold was obliged to retire to Saint Omer's. The city and castle of Guisnes were totally destroyed by the English, under the pretence that they had been compelled to pay a duty whenever they had passed through that country. Ardres was saved by the payment of a large ransom by the abbot. At length the hostile armies departed, and carried off Beatrice, and her children, into Flanders, where she was detained four years. Arnold was afterwards present with Philip Augustus at the battle of Bovines in 1214, where he had the satisfaction of seeing those enemies, who had so cruelly ravaged his territories, defeated, and many of them taken prisoners[f].

When John, King of England, had banished the prior and monks of Canterbury, in 1207, for electing Cardinal Langton Archbishop, at the nomination of the Pope, without his consent, the Count of Guisnes met them upon their entrance into his territories, to the number of eighty, and, after having regaled them at his castle of Tournehem, furnished them with horses for their journey to St. Omer's. Upon their arrival, they were met

[e] Lambert, chap 154

[f] Matthew Paris, An. 1216. Preuv 269 Chronicle of Flanders, Ibid. Chronicle of Ardres, Preuv 267 Matthew Paris, An 1214 Rex Anglorum Johannes misit principibus militiæ suæ, qui erant in Flandria, pecuniam magnam nimis, ut Regem Francorum inquietarent, et terras cum castris incursione bellica devastarent. At illi terram comitis de Gysnes ferè totam ferro flammisque discurrentibus contriverunt.

in the public place of that town by the monks of the Abbey of Saint Bertin in solemn procession. It was a moving scene, says the chronicle of Ardres, to see one convent thus embracing another, and shewing their love by mutual kisses of peace. They received a cordial invitation to reside with the monks of Saint Bertin, but Geoffrey, the prior, unwilling to render their generosity too burdensome, remained there himself with seven others, and the rest were distributed into different monasteries in France.

Arnold held lands in England, in Kent, Bedfordshire, and Essex, amounting to twelve knights' fees, part of the honour of Boulogne, which constitute him an English Baron[g]. And when Louis, the son of Philip Augustus, was invited into England by the barons, in their contests with John, Arnold accompanied him with fifteen knights in 1215, leaving his county to the ravages of the king of England[h].

In 1217, he obtained the release of his wife Beatrice, still a prisoner in the custody of the Countess of Flanders, who was intrusted with the government of that county, during the imprisonment of her husband Ferdinand, taken at the battle of Bovines. In 1215 and 1219 he served in the crusade against the Albigeois, with Prince Louis, and died in 1220. His Countess survived him four years, and built a monastery for nuns at Bonham, of which her daughter Beatrice was appointed the first abbess. It was destroyed by war, and by an inundation in 1395, and the nuns were transferred to Saint Colombe in Blendegne[i].

The children of Arnold the second, and Beatrice, Chatelaine of Bourbourg, were, Baldwin, Robert, Henry, Arnold, Beatrice, who took the veil in the Abbey of Bourbourg, and was the first abbess of the monastery of Bonham founded by her mother, Christiana, Matildis, who married Hugh de Chastillon, Count of Saint Pol; Adelis, and Beatrice. The second son Robert de Guisnes, and his brother and sisters are not mentioned by Lambert, and therefore were probably not born when his history concluded.

[g] Dugdale, Bar. i. 761

[h] Chronique ancienne de Flanders. Preuv 269 Matthew Paris

[i] Amongst her benefactions to the monastery at Ardres was a cask of excellent wine for the *pittance* of the monks Unum etiam peroptimum vini dolium adhuc vivens ad nos usque carricari fecit, et ad fratrum pitanciam assignavit. Preuv. 274

Robert's brother, Count Baldwin, by his will dated in 1244, left him a house in Baulinghem, and some land in Guisnes which had belonged to his sister M. perhaps Matilda[k]. He held the honour of Chokes in Northamptonshire, in the thirty-third of Henry III. 1248, and sold the manor of Gayton in the same county, with all his lands in England, to Ingelram Lord Fienles[l].

The seal and counter seal of Arnold the Second, on yellow wax, to a bond, by which he engages to pay a fine of fifty marks, if Walter de Formeselles should wage war against Philip, King of France, or his son Louis, as long as the King should exhibit justice in his court to the Count of Flanders, dated 1217[m].

Those of his Countess Beatrice, to an agreement between her, and her son Baldwin, to abide by the award of arbitrators in their disputes, dated

[k] Duchesne, p. 163. pr. 283.
[l] Banks, vol. i. p. 321.
[m] Duchesne, Pr. p. 271. from the king's Archives.

1222. It is on yellow wax, and was executed after her husband's death[a].

From this period we have no longer the assistance of the faithful historian of the family, Lambert of Ardres, and must be contented with such information as Duchesne has been able to collect from charters, and other ancient documents. He was the natural son of Baldwin, Lord of Ardres, the second husband of Beatrice de Bourbourg, by Adela, the daughter of Radulphus, a canon of that place; and was cousin to Arnold the Second, Count of Guisnes, to whom his book is dedicated. His ecclesiastical preferment was that of Priest, or Rector of the church at Ardres. His history of the Counts of Guisnes, and Ardres, begins with the earliest accounts of that country, from the year 800, and ends abruptly in the middle of the reign of Arnold the Second, before the year 1206, when it must be presumed that his death prevented the completion of his work. He professes to have taken the early parts of his history from authentic chronicles; he must have had access to the best materials, the documents of the family, and of the church at Ardres; and of the latter part he was a contemporary, and an eye-witness. He pursues the history of the Counts of Guisnes, in an uninterrupted series, till the

[a] Duchesne, p. 274. Archives of the Court of Isenghiem.

ninety-sixth chapter, when he breaks off suddenly, and begins the history of the Lords of Ardres, Bourbourg, and Marque, which is then introduced by something of a poetical fiction. During two rainy days and a night, when Arnold, and a company of knights, assembled at his castle at Ardres, were unable to pursue the amusements of the chase and the tournament, Walter de Clusa, an ancient sage, under which feigned name we must understand Lambert himself, related this history to the assembly to pass away the wearisome hours. "Applying his hand to his beard, and "combing it with his fingers, after the manner of old men[p]," he began his narrative, and continued it through more than fifty chapters, till the rain ceasing, the nobles returned to their manly occupations, and Lambert, in his own character, resumed his history of the Counts of Guisnes.

Lambert was learned in the literature of the age, and well acquainted with the ancient mythology, which he fails not to introduce upon all proper occasions. His heroes are compared to Hercules, Hector, and Achilles; his heroines to Cassandra, Helen, or Juno. He quotes Homer, but not in the Greek, Virgil, Ovid, Priscian, Eusebius, Jerom, Porphyry, Prosper, Sigebertus, and Bede When he is animated with his subject, he sometimes breaks out into a strain of poetry; but it must be admitted that his style is barbarous, like that of all the early writers of Europe, often too concise, at other times immoderately verbose, and full of antithesis, puns, and rhetorical amplifications. Every thing which concerns the interests of the church is stated with minute accuracy. He is affectionately attached to the family of Guisnes and Ardres, his relations, and patrons, but his partiality does not bias his judgment, or affect the truth of his narration, since he relates the faults of the individuals whose lives he writes, as well as their merits Upon the whole he may be considered as one of the most authentic historians of the middle ages, and as such is repeatedly quoted by Valesius, Ducange, and other antiquaries.

Baldwin, the second husband of Beatrice de Bourbourg and the father of Lambert, went to Jerusalem in 1146. He died at Sathania or Senchia, and at his own request was thrown into the sea. Thirty years afterwards, in 1176, an impostor appeared, who pretended to be Baldwin. Lambert

[p] Qui appositâ ad barbam dexterâ, et, ut senes plerumque facere solent, eâ digitis insertis appexâ, et appropexâ, apto in medium ore incipit, et dicit. Chap. 96. p. 499

was not at first certain of the falsehood of his pretences, and was accused wrongfully of favouring the deception for money, as he relates himself[p].

THE GENEALOGY OF LAMBERT D'ARDRES.

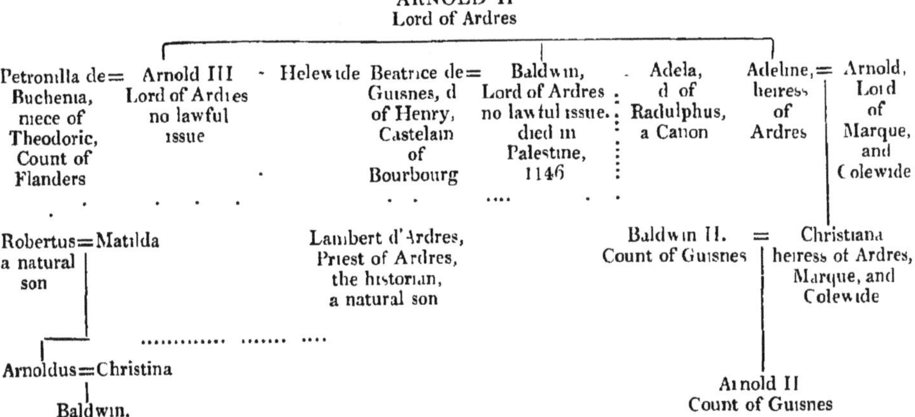

Baldwin the Third, the twelfth Count, succeeded his father in 1220, as Count of Guisnes, Chatelain of Bourbourg, and Lord of Ardres, and payed the relief which was due for his father's twelve knights' fees in Kent, Bedfordshire, and Essex[q]. He married Matilda de Fiennes, daughter of William, Lord of Fiennes and Tingry, and Agnes de Dammartin, sister of Reginald Count of Boulogne, and Simon de Dammartin, Count of Ponthieu. She was also cousin to Matilda, Countess of Boulogne, married to Monsieur Philip of France, uncle to Saint Lewis, and likewise cousin to Jane of Ponthieu, Queen of Castile and Leon

It would be tedious to relate this prince's temporary quarrels with some of the neighbouring nobles, his benefactions to monasteries, or his attendance at the translation of the body of Saint Bertin. In 1235 he was one of the noblemen who swore to endeavour to procure the marriage of

[p] Chap 141, 142, 144. [q] Dugdale, i p 761

Robert, brother of Saint Lewis, with the daughter of the Count of Flanders, and in the same year subscribed the complaint of the Barons of France to Pope Gregory the Ninth, against the prelates[r].

In 1233, Baldwin went to the assistance of Henry the Third, King of England, who was partial to foreigners, in his wars with the Barons Having been appointed to the command of Monmouth Castle, he was besieged in it by the Earl Mareschal of England. Baldwin made a vigorous sortie, in which after a bloody battle he took the Grand Mareschal prisoner. He was at the same time wounded by an arrow, but the wound was not mortal, and he afterwards greatly signalized himself by his gallant exploits in that country[s], where he had large possessions. A writ of right was brought against him by Robert de Davans, for a hide of land, and the twentieth part of a knight's fee in Telshant in Essex, in the twenty-first year of Henry III. 1236, when he appointed Peter de la Mote his attorney, in an imparlance[t].

He died in 1244, having made his will the same year, in which, amongst a great variety of bequests, he leaves two hundred livres to a knight to go to the Holy Land for the good of his soul[u].

By Matilda de Fiennes he had four children. Arnold, Baldwin, Lord of Sangate, Adelvie, married to William, Chattelaine of Saint Omer and Count of Fauquembergue, and Ida, the wife of Gerard de Prouny[x].

[r] Duchesne, Preuv p. 280

[s] Matthew Paris In anno 1233 Duchesne, Preuv. p 279, 280.

[t] R. Dod's MSS vol 103 fol 186 Essex Claus 21 Hen III Baldevinus comes de Gysnes, attornavit Petrum de la Mote in loquelâ que est in Com Essex inter ipsum et Robertum de Davans de una hida terre, et de vicessima parte unius feodi militis in Telshant

[u] Duchesne, Preuv p. 165.

[x] The will is a curious specimen of the old Flemish French A few extracts may be amusing Je Baudevvins Cuens de Ghisnes, e Castelains de Broborgh, fay à savoir à tos cheaus ki sunt e ki avenerunt, ke j'ai fait mon testament en teil maniere l'an del Incarnation nostre Seingeur M CC et XLIIII. le deluns apres le Tiphanie. (the Monday after the Epiphany) J'ay donei Robert mon frere me maison de Baulinghem ki fu M (de Mahaut de Guisnes) me sereur, e totte le tere ke le tenoit en la tere de Ghisnes, cho ai-je donei à luy e à son hoir s'il a hoir de son cors; e s'il n'avoit hoir de son cors, tot doit revenir au Comte de Ghisnes, ke kil soit, e cho luy ai-je donei por son homage e por son servige. J'ay donei à Adame de Tienbrone me nieche le bos de huonual tot ensi cumme je l'aquis à Monseingneur Manassie mon oncle.—J'ay donei à Clarenbaut mon clerc totte

The seal of Baldwin, with the counter seal, to a charter to the Monastery of Clairmaiest, relating to a rent in Rumingehem, dated 1240.

His son, Arnold the Third, the thirteenth Count of Guisnes, succeeded to that county, and to those of Ardres and Bourbourg in 1245 He was unfortunate during the whole course of his life.

me dime de Beauvoir, tot ensi cum je l' acatai à Monseigneur Avichart de Bochout, e mon palefroi ke je acatai à Monseigneur Philippe de Hondescote — A Robert d'Achiel mon grant palefroi, e mon haubergh, e mes cauches de toclenet, e unes convertures de fer A Borse mon garchon mon petit palefroi bai. A l'Abeie d'Andernes là je ai coisi me sepulture, et là je vuel gesir, X livreies de tere per faire mon aniversaire e che les aserra on à la tere ke je acatai à me Dame Alienor de Andernes, et mon cheval vairon e mon hauburgh e mes cauches à mon cors, e toutes les armures de mon cors A l'Abeie de Liskes X livreies de tere por faire mon anniversaire sollemnellement e con port la por en foir mon cuer e m'entraille A me filles tottes mes carettes, à tot les kevaux, e à tot le harnais, e tos mes pors, e totes mes vakes, e totte me bestaille e trestos mes bleis de mes granges, e mes hauberions, e mon autre meme harnais —A 'un chevalier por aleir outre meir por l'ame de mi C C lib. de parisis — E à cho à parfaire ai-je mis mes testamenteurs (executors) Duch Preuv p. 283

The wife of Arnold was Alice de Coucy, daughter of Enguerrand the Third, Lord of Concy, Marle, and la Fere, and, after the death of her brothers, heiress of those lordships. The ancient family of de Coucy, which thus centered in that of de Guisnes, was one of the most illustrious in France It derived its origin from the family of de Boves, so denominated from an old castle near Amiens[y]. Mary, the elder sister of Alice, was married first to Alexander the Second, King of Scotland, and was the mother of Alexander the Third, and afterwards was the wife of John de Brienne, surnamed of Acre, Grand Butler of France, youngest son of John de Brienne, King of Jerusalem[z]. The mother of Alice was Mary de Montmirel, the third wife of Enguerrand de Coucy, and heiress of the Lordships of Montmirel, of Oisy, of Crevecœur, Fertè Ancoul, Fertè Gaucher, Tresmes, and Belo, the Viscounty of Meux, and the Chattellainy of Cambray, all which lordships from this marriage subsequently came into the family of Guisnes[a].

Upon a journey to visit the court of Henry the Third, King of England, in 1249, Arnold was arrested by Roger Bigot, Earl of Norfolk, and Marshall of the kingdom, upon his own estate. He complained to the King, when the Earl pleaded a right of retaliation for a similar seizure upon the territories of Guisnes, where the Count had detained him as he was going ambassador to the council of Lyons, and had exacted a large fine. The affair was only ended, and the Count set at liberty, by the interference of Saint Lewis of France[b].

Afterwards, in the war, in which he supported the Countess of Flanders against the Count of Holland, the Flemings were defeated, and, with the young Count of Flanders and many other noblemen, Arnold was taken prisoner in a naval engagement near Walcheren, in 1253, and was compelled to pay a ransom amounting to near nineteen thousand pounds of our money, which he borrowed from his own subjects, the Echevins of the

[y] De Bova, or Castrum Bobarum, Preuv p. 343

[z] Anno 1239 Rex Scotiæ Alexander filiam cujusdam nobilis Baronis de Regno Francorum Engelrami de Cuscy, nomine Mariam, virginem elegantem, sibi matrimonialiter copulavit, et nuptias die pentecostes apud Rokesburc solemniter celebravit Mat. Par in anno Pr 383

[a] Duchesne, p 223, 230.

[b] Mat. Par An. 1249 Pr. 288

four bans of the county of Guisnes, that is, of Guisnes, Ardres, Audérwic, and Bredenard, and for which he gave them an hypothecation upon his lands in that county[c].

When Saint Lewis assumed the cross, he engaged himself as one of the knights who were to accompany him, but he did not go to the Holy Land, prevented probably by the embarassed state of his affairs[d].

To these misfortunes was superadded an inconsiderate, but what was then thought a meritorious, generosity, in numerous and large benefactions to churches and monasteries By these means, having contracted great debts, and reduced himself to the severest distress, he was obliged to sell the county of Guisnes, Montoire, and Tournehem, with other possessions, to Philip the Third, King of France. The contract of sale was executed at Paris in 1280 It begins by stating, that in consequence of his immense debts, and the mortgaging of all his property, moveable and immoveable, to his vassals, he was reduced to such extreme poverty, that he was unable to provide his wife and family with necessaries, and that, lest he should finally be obliged meanly to beg his bread, upon due deliberation he had resolved to sell his possessions in Guisnes The annual value was stated at one thousand, three hundred, livres Parisis. The price was three hundred thousand livres Parisis, and to be paid by installments He was likewise to receive an annuity of a thousand livres Tournois, for the lives of himself and his wife. The king was besides to pay all his debts which were charged upon the land of Guisnes, and was to assign him a competent *manor*, or castle, for his residence[e]. It appears that Ardres, Auderwic, and Bredenard, as dependences of the county of Guisnes, were comprehended in this sale, though not mentioned[f].

[c] The chronicle of St Bertin, and the bond to the Echevins Preuv p 288 The sum was 20,720 livres Parisis, which the Art de verifier les dates values at 25 875 livres Tournois, of the money of that time, or in the present money, 457,101 livres, 8 sols, 9 deniers At a rough calculation of 40 pounds sterling to 1000 livres, this will make something more than £18,280 Mezerai, t i p 608

[d] Extrait de l'Escrit des Chevaliers retenus pour aller avec le Roi S Louys outre mer, et des convenance qu'il fist avec eux —Ly Cuens de Guines soy dixiesme de Chevaliers, deux mille sis cens livres, et mangera à l'Hostel du Roy Pr 292

[e] See the contract, Appendix, No X

[f] The arrêt of Parliament in 1295, hereafter mentioned, states that what was claimed by

The time of his death is unknown. The poor and the unfortunate retire to their graves unobserved, and unnoticed!

The children of Arnold the Third and Alice de Coucy were six. Baldwin, the eldest, Enguerrand de Guisnes, the second son, who, upon the death of his maternal uncle, became Lord of Coucy, Oisy, and Montmirel, and was the ancestor of the second race of the family of De Coucy. John de Guisnes, the third son, obtained the Viscounty of Meaux, and the Lordships of Fertè Ancoul and Fertè Gaucher, upon a division between him and his brother Enguerrand. There was a daughter married to a nobleman in Ireland, whose names are unknown; another called Isabel, who married first Gaucher, Lord of Basoches, and afterwards the Lord of Faillovel; and a third, Alice, who was the wife of Walter Bertout, Lord of Malines[g].

The seal and counter seal of Arnold the Third, to a French charter, granted to the convent of Mount St. Eloy at Arras, exempting the monks from all duties on passing over his lands, dated in 1277[h].

his successor, were Fortalicium et villam Guinensem, Arde, Audrvic ac Bredenarde. Preuv. p. 301. And the son, facto patris sine terrà vixit. Poem. p. 285.

[g] This name is variously spelt, Aelide, Alips, and Adelize.

[h] Duchesne, Pr. p. 293.

His eldest son, BALDWIN THE FOURTH, inherited the Chattellanie of Bourbourg, and some other possessions. He married Jane de Montmorenci, sister of Matthew, Lord of Montmorenci, Great Chamberlain of France. He assumed the titles of Chattellain of Bourbourg, Count of Guisnes, Lord of Ardres, Auderwic, and Bredenard, and endeavoured to render his titles effectual by instituting a suit before the Parliament of Paris to recover the territories, which had been sold by his father, from King Philip the Third, under the *droit de retrait lignager*. The parliament decided, in 1283, that the suit could not be maintained, and that the Count could not claim the *retrait lignager*. This, in the French law, is a right in the descendants of the seller to redeem lands sold upon repayment of the purchase money. A law founded in the principles of the feudal times, to perpetuate the inheritances of great families[l].

He died in 1293, and left only two daughters, Jane and Blanch. Blanch was never married, and had for her portion the Lordship of Colewide, and the Chattellanie of Langle.

The seal and counter seal of Baldwin the Fourth, to a sale of lands to John le Vas, in French, and dated in 1284. It is broken in some places. In the dexter quarter of the shield are the arms of Ghent, sable, a chief argent, to mark his ancient extraction from that house[k].

[l] The arrêt of the parliament Pr. p. 300. Duchesne says, that the retrait lignager had no place in sales to the crown, but the arrêt does not state this reason, and this was a doubtful point in the French law. See Potier, Traitè des Retraits, Part I. ch. iv. sect. 194, page 164. This *droit* was not the general law of France till an edict of Henry the Third in 1581. Till then it prevailed only in particular provinces, and must have varied in different places. In 1293, he recovered, by an arrêt, ninety-five pounds for every year the king had held the mill of Bredenard. Some memoirs call his wife Catherine, others Beatrice.

[k] Duchesne, Pr. p. 301.

The seal and counter seal of his brother, John de Guisnes, Viscount of Meaux, Lord of Fertè-Ancoul, and Fertè-Gaucher, affixed to a remonstrance made by the nobles of Champagne to Philip, King of France, against certain grievances, sealed with their seals, in 1314[l].

Baldwin the Fourth having no son, his heir was his eldest daughter Jane, who was styled Countess of Guisnes, and was married, in 1293, to John de Brienne, the second Count of Eu, and Great Chamberlain of France. They finally succeeded in obtaining the restitution of the territories which had been alienated by Jane's grandfather. Upon a legal process, in the reign of Philip le Bel, an arrêt of the parliament, in 1295, restored to them the county of Guisnes, Ardres, Auderwic, and Bredenard, except such lands as were held of the Count of Boulogne. It was the ground of this decision, that Count Arnold the Third, previously to the sale, had settled those territories upon his son Baldwin in marriage, and therefore had no interest to alienate[m].

[l] Duchesne, p. 398.

[m] Terras in maritagium datas et assignatas. Arrêt. Pr. p. 301. et 304.

By this marriage of the heiress Jane, the county of Guisnes was transferred from the second race, the house of Ghent, to a third race, the Counts of Eu. John de Brienne was slain at the battle of Courtray in 1302, and left his son Rodolphus a child, under the guardianship of his mother. The marshes of Guisnes, which were said to have been held under the Counts of Boulogne, were restored in 1321, by King Philip the Fifth. The Countess Jane survived her husband near thirty years, and died in 1331. It does not appear that they had more than this one son[n].

The seal, and counter seal, of Jane, Countess of Eu, and Guisnes, to a charter respecting some dues from the Abbey of St. Bertin, dated 1324. The coats of arms are Guisnes and Eu. The latter is, azure, semé of billets, or, a lion rampant of the same[o].

[n] Pr. p. 305, 308.

[o] Duchesne, Preuv. p. 308. See the history of the Counts of Guisnes in Latin verse from Sigefrede to John de Brienne, Appendix, No. X

CHAPTER V.

Counts of Guisnes, of the third race, or the House of Eu.

JOHN DE BRIENNE, who died in 1302, and his wife Jane de Guisnes, were succeeded by their son RAOUL, or RODOLPHUS THE SECOND, in 1331, as Count d'Eu, and the sixteenth Count of Guisnes. He was Constable of France, and was slain by the stroke of a lance at a tournament at the marriage of Philip Duke of Orleans, on the seventh of October, 1345. His lady was Jane de Mello, Lady of Orme and Chateau-Chinon, daughter of Dreux de Mello, of an illustrious house in the diocese of Beauvais[a], and left a son and two daughters; Raoul, Jane, married, first to Walter de Brienne, Duke of Athens, secondly, to Lewis d'Eureux, Count d'Estampes, and Mary, who died young. His son RAOUL, or RODOLPHUS THE THIRD, inherited the counties of Eu and Guisnes, of which he was the seventeenth, and last Count; and he was likewise appointed to the honourable office of Constable of France.

Upon the invasion of France, by Edward the Third, in 1346, Philip the Sixth dispatched Rodolphus, and the Count de Tancarville, with a body of troops, to the defence of Caen, which was an extremely rich city, and was threatened by the English. The citizens were likewise in arms, and promised to make a brave defence. At their own request, and against his own opinion, Rodolphus arrayed them in battle beyond the bridge, and an attack was made upon the enemy, but upon the first discharge of the English, the citizens fled, and Rodolphus, and Tancarville, were obliged to surrender themselves prisoners to Thomas Lord Holland. The consequences of this victory, the taking of Caen, and the massacres and pillage of that city, have been fully related by the historians[b]. Rodolphus was carried into England, and remained there above three years, where he

[a] Hist. Cal i p. 697

[b] Hume, ii. p 450. ed. 4to. Froissart, liv. i chap. 122.

was treated by Edward with the greatest kindness. In 1350, he was permitted to return to France, to prepare the means of redeeming his liberty, and proposed to deliver up the town of Guisnes to Edward as his ransom. He went to Paris, and proceeded to the Hotel de Nesle, to pay his court to King John the Second, who had succeeded to the French throne. His reception was not such as he had expected, the monarch was displeased at his agreement to deliver up Guisnes, which would have opened the frontiers of his kingdom to the English, then in possession of Calais. He entertained likewise suspicions of his fidelity, and that he had formed dangerous connections with the King of England. These unfavourable impressions, however ill founded, had been inspired, or, at least, fomented, by Charles de la Cerda of Spain, who had executed the office of Constable of France during his captivity, and was desirous of obtaining that honour for himself. John, in consequence of these intrigues, caused him to be arrested by the Provost of Paris, and three days afterwards his head was cut off before the Hotel de Nesle, in the middle of the night[c], without any form of trial, in the presence of the Duke of Bourbon, the Count Armagnac, and other Lords. Charles de la Cerda, who was appointed Constable in his place, reaped little benefit from his treachery, having been soon after assassinated by the orders of the King of Navarre[d].

Rodolphus married Catherine, daughter of Lewis the Second, of Savoy, Lord of Bugei, and widow of Azzo Visconti, Duke of Milan

Not contented with having put Rodolphus to death, in this irregular manner, King John confiscated his possessions, gave the county of Eu to John D'Artois, son of Robert, Count of Beaumont, and reunited that of Guisnes to the domains of the Crown

The King of France did not long enjoy his new acquisition. Calais had been conquered by the victorious arms of Edward the Third, in the year 1347. It was not probable that the strong castle of Guisnes, in its immediate neighbourhood, would be left unattempted It was not however taken till five years afterwards, and by the stratagem of a private

[c] A l'heure de Matines, says a MS. Chronicle, that is, about the middle of the night

[d] L'Art de Verifier, ii p 789 Duchesne Hume, ii 474 Froissart liv i chap 144 Villani

individual, in a time of truce. An English archer named John Dancaster, having been taken prisoner by the French, was detained in Guisnes, and, not being closely confined, was permitted to work upon the repairs of the fortifications. Having discovered a concealed wall which went across the ditch just under the water, in the night he let himself down from the castle, passed the fossè upon it, and escaped to Calais, where he concerted the plan of his enterprize. With thirty men, habited in dark armour, he returned by the same way to Guisnes; they scaled the castle walls, slew the centinels, took the garrison by surprise, and made themselves masters of the place: and the next day they were reinforced by more troops from Calais. This happened in January, 1352. The governor, the Lord of Balinghem, was absent; and William de Beaucourray, his Lieutenant, was accused of treachery, and beheaded. The King of France complained to the Pope of this breach of the truce. The ambassadors of Edward pleaded, that the Count of Guisnes having been taken prisoner, had engaged to pay eighty thousand golden crowns for his ransom, or to surrender the county of Guisnes; that the ransom not having been paid, the county was forfeited to Edward, and that King John had cut off the head of the Count to deprive Edward of the ransom, or the county. The cause was heard in the Consistory Court at Rome, but the death of Pope Clement prevented sentence from being given[e].

[e] Thuanus, lib. xx cap 3 page 680 ed Buckley Stow's Chronicle, page 388 Edit 1592. Froissart differs as to the date Ce mois d Octobre, au jour que la confrairie Saint Oven fut celebree, prindrent les Anglois la ville de Gunes, durant les treves vol i. ch 153 page 160 Edit Denis Sauvage 1574

Essendo furata la contea Guinisi al Re di Francia, sotto la confidanza delle triegue, trasse in giudicio il Re d'Inghilterra a corte di Roma, suoi ambasciadori dicendo, che sotto la fede delle triegue prestata, il Re d'Inghilterra gli hauea tolto per furto la rocca, e la contea occupata per forza E per la parte del Re d'Inghilterra fu risposta, che havendo pei suo prigione il Conte di Guinisi, Conestabole di Francia, preso in battaglia, e dovendosi riscattare per lo patto del la sua taglia iscudi LXXX. mila doro, o in luogo di danari la detta contea di Guinisi E lasciato alla fede, acciò che procacciare potesse la moneta, il Re di Francia, appellandolo traditore, per non haverlo a ricomperare, o consentirgli la contea di Guinisi, il fece dicollare E cosi, contro a giustizia, privò il Re d'Inghilterra delle sue ragioni, lequali guistamente havea racquistate La quistione fu grande in concistoro, e pendeva la causa in favore del Re di Francia E però, innanzi che sentenzia se ne desse, il Re fece restituire la terra di Guinisi a quello Inghilese che dato glie l'havea E

After King John of France had been taken prisoner at the battle of Poitiers, by the treaty of Bretigny in 1360, Guisnes was formally ceded to the King of England, with Calais, Marq, Sangate, Couloigne, Hames, Wale, and Oye, as part of John's ransom. The letters of the King of France to the magistrates, noblemen, and subjects of that county, to deliver the possession to the King of England are quoted by Duchesne. And Edward appointed Matthew de Salperwic his Sovereign Bailly in that county, the fourth of December 1362[f]. The King of England, to secure the important post of Calais, removed all the former inhabitants, and peopled it with English, who were of course governed by the laws of their own country. Guisnes was permitted to enjoy its ancient laws and customs[g].

In the subsequent wars, various attempts were made by the French to recover their lost possessions in the county of Guisnes. In 1370, Ardres was attacked by an army of one thousand lances, under the command of the Constable of France, but they were repulsed with considerable loss[h]. The next attempt was more successful. In 1377, the first year of Richard the Second, the Duke of Burgundy with a powerful army invested it, and the garrison, commanded by John de Gumeny, being weakened by previous excursions, was obliged to surrender, and was permitted to retire, *vies et bagues sauvés*, to Calais. The castles of Ardwick, and Vauclingen submitted also[i].

King Richard the Second, in 1394, restored and confirmed to the nuns of the monastery at Guisnes, all their lands and revenues, both in Guisnes and England, of which they had been deprived in the wars[k]

seguendo la morte di Papa Clemente non ne seguì altra sentenzia. Istoria di Matteo Villani. Fir. Giunti, 1581. p. 118. He states the capture of Guisnes as above related.

[f] Duchesne, p. 182. Appendix, No. XI. In the act of cession, dated the twenty-sixth of October 1360, 35 Edw. III, Guysnes is surrendered to the King of England, a tenir en demesne et en fee, et en obeissance, ce que en fee, et en obeissance. The tenants are directed to render lige homage and obediences to the King of England.—Sauf notre droit en autres choses. Though not expressly stated, I suppose the King of England did, or ought to have done, homage for it to the King of France. MSS. Cotton.

[g] Hist. de Cal. ii. p. 351.

[h] Froissart, ch. 259.

[i] Ibid.

[k] Rhymer, iii. part iv. p. 94.

Upon the death of his first wife, a treaty was entered into for the marriage of Richard with Isabel, eldest daughter of Charles the Sixth, King of France, who was only seven years of age They were married by proxy, on the twelfth of March 1395, and it was one of the articles of the treaty that she should be conducted to Calais *vestue et enjoiallee*[l]. The King came over to receive her. He proceeded to Guisnes, and the French King came to Ardies. Between these two places there is a large plain, across which ran the line of boundary between the territories of the two sovereigns. Here was the place of interview, and it was covered with a great number of splendid tents. After several days spent in mutual festivities, accompanied as usual with magnificent presents, the young bride arrived with a numerous attendance of nobles and ladies, in superb habits, with garlands of gold and pearls. She made two obeisances upon her knees to her future husband, but he prevented the third by his kind embraces. Taking leave of her father and friends, she was conducted to Calais, where the marriage ceremony was performed by the Archbishop of Canterbury, on the third of November. After the death of Richard she returned to France, and in 1406 was married to Charles, Count d'Angouleme, afterwards Duke of Orleans[m].

The English took Balinghem, in 1412, and in return the Count de St. Pol plundered, and burnt the town of Guisnes, although he dared not attack the castle[n]. The next attempt against Guisnes was in 1436. Whilst the Duke of Burgundy was besieging Calais, as his army was exposed to frequent attacks from the garrison of that place, he sent the Lord of Croy to invest it After a vigorous resistance, the town was taken by assault. The castle proved impregnable, and the sieges of both places, after ineffectual efforts, were abandoned[o]. In 1454, Charles, Count d'Eu, conducted an enterprize against Guisnes. No sooner had he appeared before it than the garrison sallied out, defeated him, and hung sixty of the prisoners which they took[p]. Charles the Seventh, reconquered from the English all their possessions in France, except Calais and Guisnes.

[l] Rhymer, vol. vii p 811 [m] Froissart Hist de Cal ii p 81. [n] Monstrelet, ch 92 Hist. de Cal. ii 115 [o] Hist de Cal ii 150 [p] Ibid. p. 173

An attempt to take Guisnes was again made in the year 1514. After the capture of Terouenne, and the battle of Spurs, and Henry the Eighth had returned to England, the Count d'Angouleme, afterwards Francis the First, presented himself before it with eight thousand men, and a numerous artillery. The treaty for peace which immediately succeeded put an end to the siege[q].

Another interview between the kings of England and France, still more splendid than that between Richard and Charles, took place in the year 1520, between Henry the Eighth and Francis the First, in the plain between Guisnes and Ardres, which was called from this event the *Champ de Drap D'Or*. The magnificence of this meeting, in which the kings and the noblemen, of France and England exhausted their revenues in the rivalry of expense and splendor, has been related by all the historians, and has been celebrated in the lively description of Shakespeare[r]. The picture of this scene at Windsor castle is an elaborate performance, painted at the time, and contains a representation of every circumstance, from the beginning to the conclusion of the interview, with the strictest observance of historic and local truth, and it is embellished with the portraits of the principal personages[s].

After Henry the Eighth had taken Boulogne in 1544, the Dauphin undertook the siege of Guisnes, but after some severe losses, he contented himself with setting fire to some villages, and retreated[t].

In the twenty-fourth year of his reign, 1532, Henry the Eighth appointed commissioners to draw up ordinances and decrees for the government of the county of Guisnes, as he did likewise for Calais[u]. They regulated the succession to lands according to the law of inheritance in England, and the heriots to be paid upon deaths. At the expiration of seventy years, every tenant was bound to renew his title, and to pay a fine of a quarter of his rent. No English subject was permitted to marry a foreigner, without a licence. A widow's dower was to consist of half her husband's lands for life, and the fee simple of one tenth. All the inhabitants were compelled to learn the English language, and an English name was to be given to every child at its baptism. Sons were to be of age at sixteen,

[q] Hist de Cal vol. ii p. 215. [r] Hen VIII Sc 1 [s] See book i chap. 1. [t] Rhymer, tom vi p. 121 Hist de Cal ii 253 [u] In the Cotton MSS Faustina E vii 4, 5

and girls at fourteen years of age. No owners of castles were to suffer them to decay, and there were other less important regulations.

After the conquest of Calais and Guisnes, so mortifying to the French, they always looked forwards to their recovery The county of Guisnes, and the empty title of Count, were bestowed upon several families by the favour of the French King, though Ardres, and some small parts of it only, were in their possession.

The title was first claimed by the Viscount de Thouars. His claim was founded upon a descent from Margaret de Brienne, daughter of John de Brienne, the First, Count d'Eu, and who married Guy, the Second, Vicount of Thouars, and Lord of Talmond But his pretensions were without foundation, for Margaret was proved not to have been the daughter of Jane, Countess of Guisnes, as they alledged, but was the sister of John, the Second, Count d'Eu, the husband of Jane. The claim was therefore disallowed, yet the Lords of Tremouille, Dukes of Thouars, have always taken the title of Counts of Guisnes[x].

By the treaty of Arras in 1435, the nominal county was ceded by Charles the Seventh, to Philip le Bon, Duke of Burgundy. Louis the Eleventh, in 1461, gave it to Anthony de Croi, notwithstanding the opposition of Louis de la Trimouille, Vicount de Thouars. The King, in favour of De Croy, re-united the Barony of Ardres, and the Chatellany of Angle, to the county of Guisnes[y]. Afterwards Louis the Eleventh, by the treaty of Conflans, in 1465, gave the counties of Boulogne and Guisnes to Count Charolois, and made a compensation to the Lord De Croi But the Count becoming Duke of Burgundy, and being engaged in a rebellion against the King, Guisnes was taken from him, and given to Anthony De Croi, who was succeeded in it by his son Philip Philip revolted from the King, and attached himself to the Duke of Burgundy, upon which his lands were confiscated in January 1476, and the county of Guisnes, and Barony of Ardres, were bestowed upon Anthony, the natural son of Philip, Duke of Burgundy, surnamed *le Grand Bâtard*, upon whose death, in 1504, it reverted to the crown, from which it was never afterwards alienated[z].

[x] Hist. de Cal ii 17, 78. Duchesne, p 82

[y] Monstrelet, liv iii 97, 122

[z] Hist de Cal ii p 188 191 from the records Some of the French historians state,

But these shadowy honours were soon after converted into realities. At the treaty of peace concluded between Edward the Sixth, and Henry the Second, in 1550, the French King paid four hundred thousand crowns for the restitution of Boulogne. Calais was next recovered. The Duke of Guise made an unexpected march to this place, in the winter, a season when the greater part of the garrison was always withdrawn to England, and a fleet of ships blockaded it by sea. After a brave resistance, the governor, Lord Wentworth, was obliged to capitulate, and thus this important fortress, after being in the possession of the English for above two hundred years, was taken in eight days, in January in the year 1558.

The Duke next marched to Guisnes, of which Lord Gray was the governor, with a garrison of 1400 men The bulwarks of the city, after three days battering, were taken by assault. The Governor retreated to the castle, the tower de la Cuve, and whilst the French troops were engaged in plundering, they were attacked and driven out of the city, which the English then burnt The batteries were opened against the castle, and the bastion which defended the gate was shattered, and a breach opened. After some hard fighting the breach was abandoned by the besieged, who retired to the old castle The French having succeeded in taking possession of some other bastions, the governor capitulated, the twenty-first of January 1558[a]. Hammes, the county of Oye, Coulogne, Wales, Sangate, and all the other places, followed the example of Calais and Guisnes, and nothing now remained to the English of all their possessions in France.

that Guisnes was several times retaken by the King of France *L'Art de Verifier les Dates* says, that Charles the Sixth recovered it from the English by conquest, and was in possession of it in 1413, and that it was again reconquered by Charles the Seventh But nothing can be more certain than that the English were never dispossessed either of Calais or Guisnes till the final reconquest in the reign of Queen Mary The records in the tower and other evidences prove, that all the acts of ownership, in the nomination of the governor, and other officers, were performed by the Kings of England during the whole period, and at the very dates mentioned by the learned Benedictine See Appendix, No XII The donations by the Kings of France of this county were disposals of the lion's skin before the lion was taken, and have occasioned these mistakes

[a] Hist. de Cal ii. 308

This war was concluded by the treaty of Chateau Cambresis, in 1559, between Queen Elizabeth, and Henry the Second, when it was agreed that the French King should retain for eight years the possession of Calais, with the castle and town of Guisnes, and the rest of that country taken in the last war, and that after the term of eight years, he should restore those places to the Queen, or pay the sum of five hundred thousand gold crowns. For the performance of these conditions seven or eight merchants were security, and hostages were besides given[b] At the expiration of the time, in 1567, Elizabeth sent her ambassadors, Smith, William Winter, and Henry Norreys, to Charles the Ninth, to demand the restitution of these places, according to the treaty. The claim was resisted, and a long discussion ensued with the Chancellor de l'Hopital. This refusal was founded upon an article of the treaty by which it was agreed, that if the Queen should attempt any thing against the French King by arms, either directly or indirectly, he should be freed from the said agreement. And it was alleged that the English had sent auxiliary troops to Rouen, and had taken possession of Havre de Grace, which the King had been obliged to recover by force. It was answered by the ambassadors, that the French had first prepared for war, that they had supported Mary Queen of Scots, and sent troops to her assistance, and to invade England. Replies and rejoinders followed each other, the embassy was unsuccessful, and the French refused to surrender the town, or to pay the stipulated sum[c].

All the territories recovered from the English, including Guisnes, were united under one government, under the name of the *Pays Reconquis*, of which Calais was the capital, and it was divided into twenty-four cantons, or parishes. The ancient counties, baronies, pairies, and lordships, were united to the domains of the crown, and had no other lords, with some few exceptions[d].

[b] Treaties in 4 vols vol. ii. page 46 ed 1732.

[c] Thuanus, lib 41. Hist de Cal. ii. p 367. Hume says, that "all men of penetration "saw that the stipulations of the treaty of Chateau Cambresis were but a colourable pre-"text for abandoning Calais." vol v. p 19 But these discussions shew that the Queen was in earnest in endeavouring to recover those places.

[d] Hist de Cal ii. 313, 461, 352. Besides its connexion with this family, the account of

Guisnes appeared to me to be interesting, as it was one of the places possessed by this country in France; I had therefore a double motive to render it as complete as I could. A history of our ancient possessions upon the continent is a desideratum in English literature. That of Normandy would be particularly acceptable, especially since the local antiquities of that dukedom have been lately so much illustrated.

The Castle of Guisnes, in 1520.

CHAPTER VI.

Of other noble families of the House of Guisnes.

HAVING thus brought to a conclusion the history of the county of Guisnes, and the elder branch of the family, it may be necessary to say something of other noble families, descended from younger brothers of that house; which however I shall not pursue at any great length.

The Lords De Coucy[a].

We have before seen that, upon the death of his maternal uncle, named Enguerrand de Coucy the Fourth, Enguerrand de Guisnes, the second son of Arnold the Third, and Alice De Coucy, succeeded to the possessions of that family, by the name of Enguerrand the Fifth, and became the ancestor of the house of Coucy, of the second race. He was brought up at the court of his first cousin, Alexander the Third, King of Scotland, who married him to a noble lady named Christiana, daughter of Thomas Balliol[b], a relation of John Balliol, King of Scotland[c]. Upon his succession to the rich inheritances of De Coucy, he divided them with his brother, John de Guisnes, in 1311. By this partition, Enguerrand had the lordships of de Coucy, Marle, and la Fere, in Vermandois, Oisy and Hauraincourt, in Cambresis, Montmirail, Condè en Brie, and Chalon le Petit, with the Chattellanie of Chateau Thierry, and the Hotel de Coucy in Paris. John obtained the Chattellanies of la Fertè-Gaucher, and la Fertè-Ancoul, the Viscounty of Meaux, and the lands of Boissy, Tresmes.

[a] Duchesne, liv. vii.

[b] Camden, Lanc. Preuv. p. 415.

[c] Le Lignage de Couci, written in 1303, in Duchesne, Preuv. 390, 440, 441. Duchesne, p. 253.

Belo, and Romeny. The agreement was confirmed by Philip le Bel, and these large possessions were afterwards divided amongst their sons[d].

His grandson, Enguerrand the Sixth, in 1338, married Catherine of Austria, the eldest daughter of Leopold the First, Duke of Austria, and Catherine of Savoy, grand-daughter of Albert the First, Duke of Austria, and Emperor of the Romans, and great grand-daughter of Rodolph of Habsburg. The match was made by King Philip, who gave her a marriage portion of forty thousand livres tournois, for which was substituted a rent of two thousand livres, and he added twenty thousand livres more. In consideration of this fortune, Enguerrand settled upon her a dower of six thousand livres a year[e].

Their only son was Enguerrand the Seventh, who went to England, in 1360, as one of the hostages, by the treaty of Bretigni, for the restitution of John King of France. Here he was in such favour with Edward the Third, that he gave him in marriage his second daughter Isabel, and the title of Earl of Bedford, with lands in Morholm, Winsdale, Ashton, Ulverston, and Whittington, in Lancashire[f]. With part of his marriage portion he purchased the county of Soissons, which had been surrendered to King Edward by Guy de Blois, for his ransom, as one of the hostages for the King of France, with whom he was in great favour[g]. In right of his mother, Catherine of Austria, he claimed that Dutchy. The Emperor admitted his right, but was unable to assist him against the Austrians, who refused to receive him. He collected troops in France, and entered Austria, but the attempt was unsuccessful, and he was obliged to abandon his claim[h]. Afterwards he engaged in the expedition against the Turks in 1395, under the command of Sigismond, King of Hungary, and was taken prisoner by Bajazet, with the greater part of the French princes, at the siege of Nicopolis on the Danube. Upon setting out upon this ex-

[d] Preuv. p. 395. The agreement for the partition. There are some accounts of the possessions of the de Coucy family in England, in Banks's Dormant Baronages, vol. i. p. 321. Dugdale, Baron. vol. i. p. 761. but with many errors, which may be corrected from authentic documents in Duchesne, livres 6 and 7.

[e] The Settlement, Preuv. p. 407, 408.

[f] Camden, Bedf. Lanc. Ulverston. Duchesne, p. 266. Preuv. 415. Froissart.

[g] Preuv. p. 432.

[h] Pr. 420. Froissart.

pedition, a high compliment was paid him by Charles the Bold, Duke of Burgundy, who having appointed his son John, Count of Nevers, to command the French troops, put him under the care of the Lord De Coucy. He died in captivity, and his heart was buried in the monastery of the Celestins near Soissons, which he founded. After the death of Isabel of England, he married Isabel of Lorraine, daughter of the Duke of that province, who survived him, and, in 1399, married Stephen, Duke of Bavaria, father of Isabel, Queen of France. His children were only daughters, two by his first wife, and one by his second[i].

The eldest daughter, Mary, Countess of Soissons, lady of Coucy, and Oisy, married Henry de Bar, eldest son of the Duke of Bar, who was slain at the siege of Nicopolis She sold the lordship of de Coucy, in 1400, with the Chattellanies of Marle, and la Fere, to the Duke of Orleans, reserving the use during her life. The Duke used unwarrantable methods to compel her to this sale, and little of the purchase money was paid. She died soon after, having been poisoned at a wedding. The sale was held not to have been legal. The Chattellanies of Marle and la Fere returned to Robert de Bar[k].

The second daughter, Philippa, was educated in England, and married Robert de Vere, Duke of Ireland[l], Marquis of Dublin, Earl of Oxford, and Great Chamberlain of England. Her portion was Morholm, Wirisdale, Ulverston, and other places in Lancashire. Her husband proved unfaithful, he fell in love with a German girl, one of the Queen's maids of honour, whom he married, after he had been divorced from his wife[m].

[i] Duchesne, 270. Pr. 412 Froissart

[k] Duchesne, Pr 426. The Deed of Sale.

[l] He was created Duke of Ireland in the ninth of Richard II Dugd MSS. No. 34 f. 59

[m] Le Duc d'Irlande avoit à femme la fille au Seigneur de Coucy, laquelle estoit fille de Madame Ysabel, fille des defunts Roy et Royne d'Angleterre, qui estoit belle Dame et bonne, et de plus noble et haute attraction qu'il fut Et toutesfois il aima une des Damoiselles de la Royne regnante en Angleterre, une Alemande, et fist tant envers Urbain VI. qu'il se demaria de la fille au Seigneur de Coucy, sons nul tiltre de raison, fors par presomption et nonchalance, et epousa celle Demoiselle Et tout consentit le Roy Richard, car il estoit si aveuglè de ce Duc d'Irlande, que s'il eust dit, sire, cecy est blanc, et il fust noir, le Roy n'en eust dit du contraire Le mere de ce dit Duc fut moult grandement

Isabel, the only daughter of the second marriage, after the death of her father, and his widow, Isabel of Lorain, instituted a suit in law to recover her rights against her sister Mary de Bar, and the Duke of Orleans, and at length obtained the half of Coucy, Marle, and la Fere Philippa, being an English subject, and provided for in that country, had no claim to them[n]. Isabel married Philip of Burgundy, Count of Nevers and Rethel, youngest son of Monsieur Philip of France, called the Hardy, Duke of Burgundy, in 1409[o]

And thus this branch of the house of Guisnes, and the second race of the family of Coucy, ended in the royal family of Bourbon[p]

The Viscounts of Meaux[q]

Of the three sons of Arnold the Third, and Alice de Coucy, we have traced the descent of two, Baldwin de Guisnes, and Enguerrand de Guisnes, Lord of Coucy. We mentioned a third brother, John de Guisnes, who shared in the property of his maternal uncle, with his brother Enguerrand. By this partition he obtained the castles and Chattellanies of la Fertè-Gaucher, and la Fertè-Ancoul, the house of Tronoy or Dronay, the vineyards of Vaucelles, the land of Boissy, of Tresmes, Belo, and Rommeny. He had likewise the Viscounty of Meaux, from which he took his title His issue failing, were succeeded by Enguerrand De Coucy, youngest son of Enguerrand De Coucy the Fifth. After two descents, this branch ended in two daughters. Of these, the eldest, Alienor de Coucy, married Michael, Lord of Ligne in Hainault Jane, the youngest married John de Chastillon The youngest died, and Alienor succeeded to the whole property, and, dying without issue, was succeded by her aunt, Jane de Coucy, who was the wife of John de Bethune A daughter of this house, Jane de Bethune, Viscountess of Meaux, was married to Robert de Bar, whose daughter Jane de Bar, was wife of Lewis of Luxem-

courroucèe de son fil, et prit la fille au Seigneur de Coucy et la meit avecques elle, et en sa compaignie. Froissart, vol. iii. ch 77 He calls Oxford Acquessufford

[n] Pr p 427 The proceedings from the Register of the Parliament

[o] Monstrelet, ch 51 Preuv 436

[p] Duchesne, page 294

[q] Duchesne, liv 6, 7.

burg, Count of Saint Pol, by whom she had Peter of Luxemburg, Count of Saint Pol, and Viscount of Meaux, whose daughter, Mary of Luxemburg, married Francis de Bourbon, Count of Vendasme[r]

A second branch of the house of Guisnes, the Viscounts of Meaux, by this marriage centered in the royal family of Bourbon[s].

The Chattellains of Ghent.

We have likewise seen that the Chattellanie of Ghent came to Siger de Guisnes, a younger son of Arnold the First From him descended the subsequent Chatellains, the Barons of Saint John Steene, and of Rassenghien, and the Counts of Isenghien. Weary of the world, Siger quitted all earthly concerns, and entered into the order of Knights Templars The Chatellains of Ghent continued to be Lords of Bornhem, and Houdain Walter de Gand, surnamed Villain, second son of Hugh, the First, Chattellain of Ghent, and Lord of Saint John Steene, was the ancestor of the family of that latter title, and which retained likewise his surname of Villain[t]. The male line of the Chatellains of Ghent ended in Maria. She married Gerard, Lord of Sottenghien, a younger branch of the house of Enghien, in 1280. On the death of her son, and his issue, the Chatellanie fell to another female, Isabel, Viscountess of Melun, who had three husbands, first Henry of Louvain, secondly Alphonso of Spain, surnamed de la Cerda, son of Ferdinand, Prince of Castile, and Blanch, daughter of Saint Lewis, who after the death of Alphonso the Tenth, King of Castile, assumed that title, but was obliged to abandon it. By him Isabel was mother to Charles, Constable of France, and Count of Engoulesme. Thirdly, she married John, Viscount of Melun, Great Chamberlain of France, 1327. To him she brought the Chatellanie of Ghent, and other possessions, but from that time her descendants bore the title of Viscounts of Ghent[u].

[r] Duchesne, p 294.

[s] Ibid. Par ainsi les deux Branches des Seigneurs de Coucy, et des Vicomtes de Meaux, sorties de la maison de Guines, fondirent dans la Royale Famille de Bourbon, de laquelle est descendu le Roy Louys XIII. aujourd'huy regnant

[t] Duchesne, p. 337

[u] Ibid 359

The Lords of St. John Steene, surnamed Villain

After the Counts of Guisnes, the Chatellains of Ghent, and the Lords of Coucy, this branch was the most illustrious

The city and lordship of Steene, Saint John Steene, or de la Pierre, was transferred by one of the Counts of Flanders to a Chatellain of Ghent, in exchange for some rights in the town of Hulst it was enjoyed by the Chatellains till it was given as a portion to Walter de Gand, the second son of Hugh, before mentioned, who was surnamed Villain, or Villanus. This name was not uncommon, Duchesne mentions several who bore it, a cardinal priest, in a bull of Eugene the Third. Villain de Canny, Villain D'Arzillieres, Villain de Nuelly, in Villehardouin, and Villain D'Aunoy, appointed by that historian guardian of his lands in Champagne[x]. An uncle of Walter le Villain was surnamed Gerand le Diable. From a mere personal sobriquet this name become that of an illustrious family, whose cry of war was, *Gand à villain sans reproche.*

This family was divided into several branches, the Lords of Welle, Huysse, Morbeque, Lidekerque, and others[y].

The Lords of Rassenghiem, and Counts of Isenghiem.

From the marriage of John Villain the Third, Lord of Saint John Steene, and of Margaret de Gaure of Liedequerque, proceeded the two branches, the Barons of Rassenghiem, afterwards Counts of Isenghiem, and the Lords of Liedequerque, which barony and lordships with other possessions were acquired from her[z] I shall not relate all the particulars which may be collected of these noblemen; but it may be interesting to mention, that Martin Villain, in 1458, made a voyage to the Holy Land, and, upon his return, he passed by the kingdom of Cyprus, where Charlotte, Queen of Jerusalem, Cyprus, and Armenia, received him with great honours, and invested him with the Order of the Sword, with the privilege of conferring the same upon two other knights, or, at least esquires. Queen Charlotte's letter is dated at Nichosia, and was preserved amongst the muniments of the Counts of Isenghiem, and the coat

[x] P. 358 [y] Ibid 355 [z] Ibid 409

of arms of the Count received the addition of a sort of scroll round it, in which five swords were interwoven [a].

The territory and title of Isenghiem were acquired by the marriage of Adrian Villain the Third with Margaret, daughter of John de Staveles, Lord of Isenghiem, in 1525 From a barony it was erected into a county by Philip the Second of Spain, in 1582, as a reward for Maximilian Villain's services, particularly against the heretics in Flanders [b].

Many of the noblemen of these derivative families are occasionally celebrated in Froissart, Monstrelet, and other contemporary chronicles.

The county of Guisnes having been united to the possessions of the Crown of France, and all the foreign male lines of the family having become extinct, the blood of Sigefrede, the original founder, is no longer to be found, in a direct male descent, except in the families of Blount, and Croke.

[a] Duchesne, p 413. Preuv 621 [b] Ibid.

GENEALOGY OF THE COUNTS OF GUISNES.

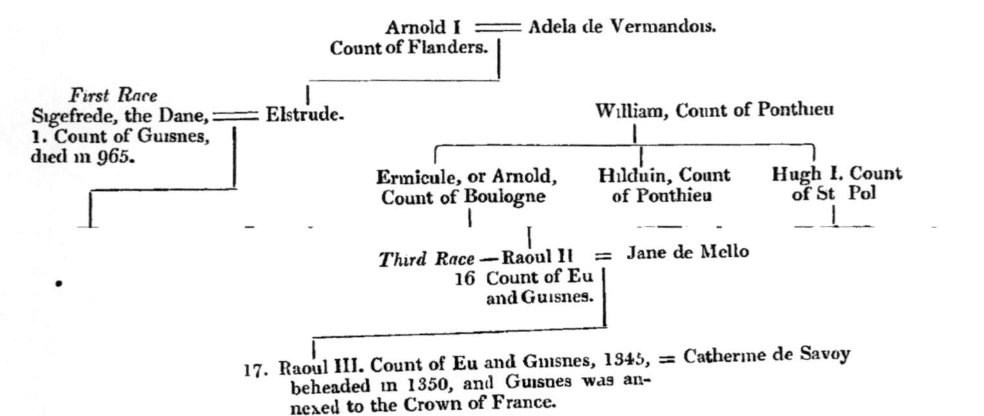

Arnold I = Adela de Vermandois.
Count of Flanders.
First Race
Sigefrede, the Dane, = Elstrude.
1. Count of Guisnes,
died in 965.
William, Count of Ponthieu
Ermicule, or Arnold,
Count of Boulogne
Hilduin, Count
of Ponthieu
Hugh I. Count
of St Pol
Third Race — Raoul II = Jane de Mello
16 Count of Eu
and Guisnes.
17. Raoul III. Count of Eu and Guisnes, 1345, = Catherine de Savoy
beheaded in 1350, and Guisnes was annexed to the Crown of France.

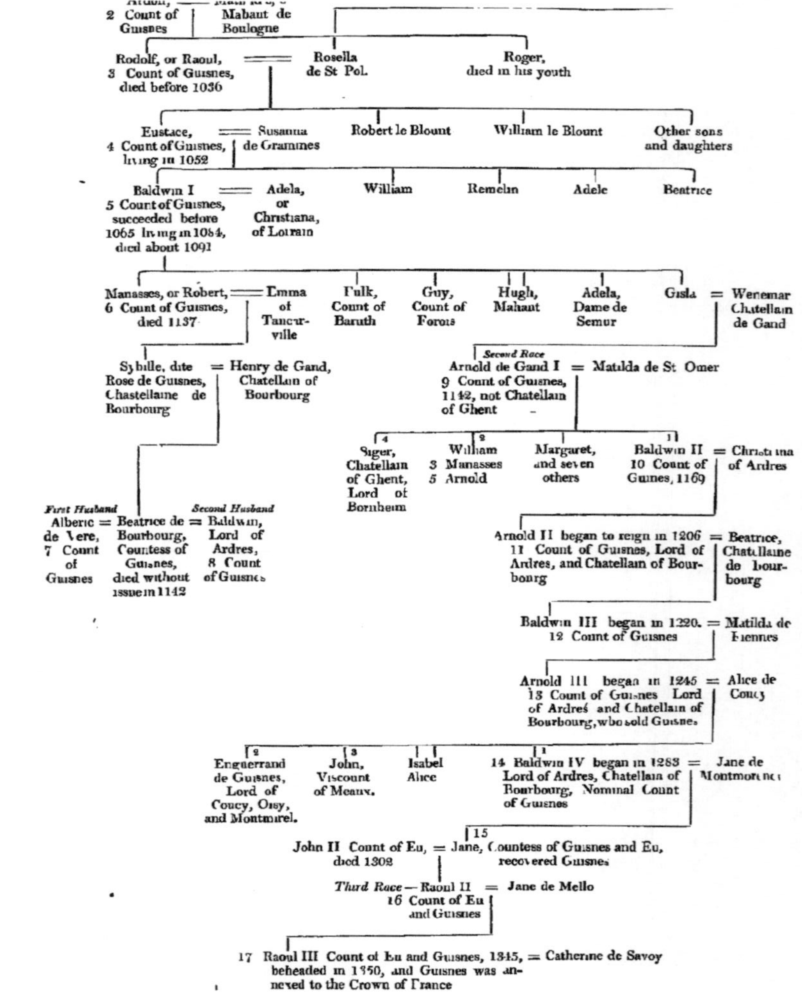

2 Count of Guisnes
Mahaut de Boulogne
Rodolf, or Raoul, 3 Count of Guisnes, died before 1036
Rosella de St Pol.
Roger, died in his youth
Eustace, 4 Count of Guisnes, living in 1052
Susanna de Grammes
Robert le Blount
William le Blount
Other sons and daughters
Baldwin I 5 Count of Guisnes, succeeded before 1065 living in 1084, died about 1091
Adela, or Christiana, of Lorrain
William
Remelin
Adele
Beatrice
Manasses, or Robert, 6 Count of Guisnes, died 1137
Emma of Tancurville
Fulk, Count of Baruth
Guy, Count of Forois
Hugh, Mahaut
Adela, Dame de Semur
Gisla
Wenemar Chatellain de Gand
Sybille, dite Rose de Guisnes, Chastellaine de Bourbourg
Henry de Gand, Chatellain of Bourbourg
Second Race
Arnold de Gand I 9 Count of Guisnes, 1142, not Chatellain of Ghent
Matilda de St Omer
4 Siger, Chatellain of Ghent, Lord of Bornheim
2 William
3 Manasses
5 Arnold
Margaret, and seven others
1 Baldwin II 10 Count of Guines, 1169
Christina of Ardres
First Husband
Alberic de Vere, 7 Count of Guisnes
Beatrice de Bourbourg, Countess of Guisnes, died without issue in 1142
Second Husband
Baldwin, Lord of Ardres, 8 Count of Guisnes
Arnold II began to reign in 1206 11 Count of Guisnes, Lord of Ardres, and Chatellain of Bourbourg
Beatrice, Chatellaine de Bourbourg
Baldwin III began in 1220. 12 Count of Guisnes
Matilda de Fiennes
Arnold III began in 1245 13 Count of Guisnes Lord of Ardres and Chatellain of Bourbourg, who sold Guisnes
Alice de Coucy
2 Enguerrand de Guisnes, Lord of Coucy, Oisy, and Montmirel.
3 John, Viscount of Meaux.
Isabel
Alice
1 14 Baldwin IV began in 1283 Lord of Ardres, Chatellain of Bourbourg, Nominal Count of Guisnes
Jane de Montmorenci
15
John II Count of Eu, died 1302
Jane, Countess of Guisnes and Eu, recovered Guisnes
Third Race—Raoul II 16 Count of Eu and Guisnes
Jane de Mello
17 Raoul III Count of Eu and Guisnes, 1345, beheaded in 1350, and Guisnes was annexed to the Crown of France
Catherine de Savoy

BOOK THE SECOND.

PART I.

THE SETTLEMENT OF THE LE BLOUNTS IN ENGLAND, AND THE HISTORY OF THE ELDEST BRANCH, THE BARONS OF IXWORTH, THE LORDS OF BELTON, AND THE CROKE FAMILY.

Le Blount.

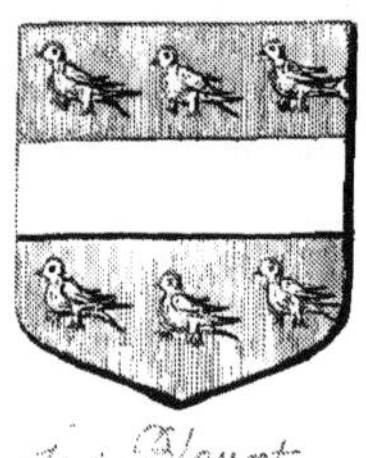

Le Blount

THE

GENEALOGICAL HISTORY

OF

THE CROKE FAMILY.

CHAPTER I.

The settlement of the Le Blounts in England.

WILLIAM of Normandy's preparations for the invasion of England animated the whole continent of Europe. Every motive which could influence the mind, in those days of chivalry, was in full action, the prospect of military fame, the hopes of extensive territories, the love of novelty and adventure, and the sanctity of an expedition which had been consecrated by the Pope [a]. From Normandy the warlike ardour principally extended to the nobles and knights of the neighbouring countries Amongst these, Baldwin the Fifth, Count of Flanders, was doubly related to Duke William. They were first cousins, Baldwin's mother, Eleanor, having been sister to Robert the First, William's father A still nearer connexion had taken place by the marriage of the Count's daughter Matilda with Duke William [b].

[a] In the Bayeux tapestry, the consecrated banner, sent by the Pope, is always introduced, and is argent, a cross or, in a bordure azure. Archæol xviii p 359. Walsingham says it represented a man fighting

[b] It is said by some authors that Baldwin IV had no child by Eleanor, and that Matilda was his grand-daughter by Orgina of Luxemburg. But it is certain that Matilda was nearly related to Duke William, he had a dispensation from the Pope to marry her; and Mauger, Archbishop of Rohan, the Duke's uncle, in a rebellion in Normandy, actually excommunicated him on pretence of the too near relationship between them If Eleanor had not been Matilda's grand-mother these facts cannot be accounted for Carte, vol. i p. 413 Rapin, i 165 has made a mistake in styling Matilda the daughter instead of the grand-daughter of Eleanor.

Tosti, brother to Harold, had married his other daughter, and, being at enmity with the King of England, had retired to the court of Flanders, full of complaints of the injustice which he had suffered, and he had engaged the protection of that Prince against his brother. The Emperor had given public permission to all his vassals to embark in the expedition. The Count of Flanders, therefore, had every inducement to employ all his influence to promote its success. Eustace, Count of Boulogne, was one of the principal noblemen who personally engaged in it. In concert with his relations the Counts of Flanders, and Boulogne, Baldwin the First, the Count of Guisnes, naturally supported the interests of the Duke of Normandy, with whom, and his wife Matilda, he was connected by the ties of consanguinity[c]. Three brothers of the house of Guisnes, who were probably uncles to Baldwin, and the sons of Rodolphus, a former Count, and his wife Rosella de Saint Pol, inlisted under the banners of the Duke. The name of one of them, who afterwards returned to France, has not been preserved, the other two were Sir Robert Le Blount, accompanied by his son Gilbert and Sir William Le Blount, who continued to reside in England, and were the ancestors of the family of that name.

The accounts of the Norman invasion are short and obscure. The list of the names of those who came over with William, in the Battel Abbey roll, varies much in the different copies which are now extant, and that document is not conclusive evidence, unless so far as it is confirmed by better authority. In four of those copies the name of Le Blount occurs, and it is omitted in the others[d]. As to their rank, and peculiar duties, Robert Le Blount was stiled Dux navium militarium, or Commander of the ships of war, and he was of the council of the Conqueror[e]. His

[c] See the Genealogies, Nos. 2, 3, 4 and book I chap 3

[d] The name of Le Blount is found in Duchesne in his Rerum Normanicarum Scriptores, page 9, in Fuller's Church History, page 151, in Holinshead, page 3; and in Stow, page 105. The name is omitted in the lists in Fox's Acts and Monuments, page 183; in two other lists in Holinshead, page 2, and in Stow, page 104, in Scriven's list, and in the rhyming catalogue in the Chronicle of John Brompton the Abbot, which begins

> Vous que desyrez assaver
> Les nons de grauntz de la la mer,
> Que vindrent od le conqueror
> William Bastard de graunt vigour &c &c.

[e] Sir Thomas Blount Chevalier fuit de concilio Ducis, (sc Willmi Conquestoris) Coles MSS. vol. xliii p 9 British Museum. *Thomas* is evidently an error for *Robert*.

brother William was General of the foot[f]. The exploits of the brothers upon this occasion, and the share which they had in the decisive battle of Hastings, have not been related; but the high station which they held, and the great rewards which they afterwards received from the Conqueror, are sufficient testimonies of their military merit.

Many circumstances have been related in local chronicles which are not of sufficient consequence to have found their way into the general histories. Of this kind are the events which took place in the Isle of Ely upon the conquest of England. Thurston, the abbot, and the monks of that rich monastery were the strenuous supporters of Edgar Atheling. After the unfortunate battle of Hastings, they afforded a safe retreat to many of the Saxon lords. The Earls of Chester and Northumberland, with other noblemen, and their followers, retired to that monastery with their treasures The natural difficulties of the country, which was inaccessible from its extensive marshes, seemed to promise them security, till some general efforts could be made to rescue the kingdom from a foreign yoke. Hereward, the son of Leofric, Lord of Brunne, a general of great renown, was elected to the chief command, and a plan of defence, and of hostilities against the Normans, was adopted in their councils of war. The strength of the place, the formidable force collected there, the length of time it continued, and the ineffectual attempts of his armies, had made the siege of Ely of sufficient importance to require the presence of William; and he marched thither in 1069, with a considerable force. A causeway was thrown up across the marshes, and several attempts were made to force a passage. But the works were imperfect, the resistance brave and well conducted, and, before any progress could be made, William was obliged to repair to his army at York, which had been taken by the combined armies of the English, Scots, and Danes The next year he returned to renew his attacks upon the island of Ely, and again failed in his attempts to pass the marshes. The preparations for another assault were defeated, and their forts were destroyed, in a sally made in boats, and commanded

[f] Collins's Baronetage, vol ii page 367 vol iii p 665 Nash's History of Worcestershire, vol ii. p 163 Dugdale's Baronage, vol i Blount Monasticon, vol ii. p. 184 Summons of the Nobility Fuller's Church History p 155. Speed's History of Great Britain, page 797 Dux *manuum* militarium in some of these is an error for *navium*

by Hereward in person, who, like Alfred, had got intelligence of their designs by visiting their camp in disguise. The king thus repeatedly baffled retreated to Cambridge, and, in his resentment for their protracted resistance, he confirmed his former seizure and alienation of the lands belonging to the monastery, in different parts of the kingdom. The monks repented of their resistance, and wished to surrender. The abbot, and some of the monks retired from the island, and waited upon the king at Warwick, with their humble submission. But their good will was all that was in their power. The lords refused to surrender, the monks who remained were kept under strict guard, and even in ignorance of what was going on, and the place was still vigorously defended. In the year 1071, though some reinforcements had been received, the skill of William's engineers, improved from experience, by a due combination of causeways and boats, forts and engines, formed a sufficient passage for the troops over the marshes and waters, and after several attempts, the defences were forced, and victory declared in William's favour. The garrison retreated, and great numbers were slain, or taken prisoners Amongst the latter were Earl Morchar, Siward, surnamed Bearn, and Egelwin, bishop of Durham Great cruelty was exercised upon some of the prisoners, and Hereward alone of all the leaders escaped. The king took possession of the monastery, accepted a fine of a thousand marks as an atonement, and, in the true spirit of the times, paid his devotions, with an offering of a mark of gold, to Saint Etheldreda, the founder and patroness of the Abbey[g]

Both as a punishment and a security, William sent forty of his principal knights, to be quartered upon the monastery. They had their banquets in the refectory, and each knight was allotted to a particular monk, as his host and companion. Amongst these knights was William Le Blount, who was assigned to the care and hospitality of Brother Wylnote. Great friendship and harmony subsisted between these martial and monastic pairs. There is reason to believe that the knights were not dissatisfied with their situation. " Of all the abbeys in England," says the witty Dr Fuller, " Ely bare away the bell, for bountiful feast-making, the vicinity

[g] Bentham's History of Ely.

"of the fens affording them plenty of flesh, fish, and fowl, at low "rates[h]."

When the king required the service of these knights in Normandy, upon the insurrection of his son Robert in 1077, their departure was a subject of mutual regret. But let the ancient historian of the Abbey relate "the "story," as it is translated by Dr. Fuller. "The soldiers with their "retinue are sent, they come, and here abide. Whereof each one is "delivered to some principal monk, as a captain to his lieutenant, or a "guest to his host. Now the king decreed that Bertwolde (MSS. Brith-"nodus) the butler should minister food to the soldiers and monks jointly "together, one with another, in the common hall of the monastery. What "need many words? these captains to their lieutenants, these guests to "their hosts, these soldiers to their monks, were most welcome for all of "them entertained each one, each one entertained all, and every one "mutually one another, with all duties of humanity. At length the fire "of the civil war being quenched, and the king established according to "his heart's desire, five years after, his severity in punishing being in "godly manner pacified, it pleased the king to withdraw this yoke, where-"with the pride of the monks was now sufficiently abated. And the "Conqueror reclaimed his soldiers to punish the ungodly insolence of his "son Robert, who at that time in outrageous manner kept riot in Nor-"mandy. But our monks (which is a wonder to report) did not only "with tears bewaile the departure of their dearest mates, the heroical "soldiers, and welcome guests, but howled out most fearfully, and beat "their breasts as destitute of hope, after the manner of a new married wife, "whose husband is violently taken away, at an unseasonable time, out of "her sweet arms unto the wars. For they doubted lest that, being for-"saken, they should be subject to the spoil, whereas they had lived "securely at ease, with their armed guests, to whose trust they had com-"mitted themselves and their goods. They being now all ready for their "journey, every one of our monks, many in number, investured in their "copes, in dutiful manner accompanied these gentlemen departing, unto

[h] Fuller's Church History, book 1 p. 299. In testimony of their merit in this respect he quotes an ancient couplet

Prævisis aliis, Eliensia festa videre,
Est, quasi prævisâ nocte, videre diem

"Hadenham, with songs, crosses, censers, processions, and all solemnity "that might be used.

"And returning home they took order that the arms (or rather, the por-"traits) of each soldier should be lively depainted upon the walls of the "common hall, where they took their repast together, to the perpetual "memory of the customed kindness of their soldier-like guests, the which "from time to time, from the predecessors to the successors, and from "obscure antiquity to our posterity at this day, are curiously set forth to "be viewed of all men, not without a pleasant delight, in such manner as "they glitter and shine honourable in the margent of this table[1]."

At the Reformation these pictures were destroyed, and the refectory of the monastery was converted into the present deanery of Ely. There is however an ancient painting, which was formerly in the possession of Doctor Knight, prebendary of that church, and now in the episcopal palace, which was probably copied from it. It consists of forty tablets, or pictures, each containing a knight, with the monk his companion, in their respective dresses as soldiers and Benedictines, with the coats of arms of each of the knights, as they are now borne by their families and descendants. Over it is the following inscription:

"Nomina et insignia militum singulatim cum singulis monachis "in ecclesia Eliensi collocatorum regnante Gulielmo Conquestore, "Anno Domini 1087."

The inscription over the picture of our ancestor is,

"Blundus Nabium Militarum Dux
"Cum Wlpnoto Monacho."

He is painted with a helmet and a red feather: his dress is scarlet, the helmet, and some pieces round his neck, are blue, to represent steel. Round his shoulders is a white scarf, and at the joints of his arms are large knobs with double bands, or bracelets, and he has a sword in his right hand. His appearance and beard denote the hardy veteran, but with an air of mildness and benevolence he stretches out his left hand, apparently in friendly converse with his companion, who is dressed in the

[1] See the original Latin, Appendix, No XIV, and the list of the knights.

Blundus nauium militarum
dux cum wylnsto Monacho

habit of his order. The meekness, resignation, and delicacy, of the holy father, form a striking contrast to the hardihood, and roughness, of the knight and soldier. Between them is the coat of arms still borne by the Blount family, barry, nebuly, or, and sable[k]

[k] As these pictures have been the subject of some controversy amongst the antiquaries, it may not be improper to give a short statement of their history

There appears to have been an original painting upon the walls of the refectory of the Convent, containing the portraits of the knights and monks, with their coats of arms, which was destroyed at the dissolution.

There are now remaining, 1st, the Ely Tablet, Tabula Eliensis, in the Episcopal Palace at Ely, which is on board, about three feet long, by two broad, and is said to have been copied from the original painting in the refectory. It consists of forty tablets, or pictures, each containing the portrait of a knight, with the monk his companion, with the coat of arms of each knight, as they were subsequently borne by their families The inscription at the top is, " Nomina et insignia Millitum singulatim cum singulis monachis in Ecclesia " Eliensi collocatorum regnante Gulielmo Conquestore, Anno Domini 1087 " Over each tablet is the name of the knight, and the monk This has been engraved in Bentham's History of Ely

2 A Parchment Roll, above a yard long, having a piece of green silk hanging before it In the middle is a Latin historical account of the transaction, and round it the arms of the forty knights. At the top are the arms of Saint Etheburg, (for Saint Etheldreda,) the foundress of the Convent, of Saint Ethelwald, Bishop of Winchester, of William the Conqueror, and of Robert de Orford, the fourteenth Bishop of Ely, who filled that see from 1301 to 1309, from 30th Edward I to 3d Edward II. which ascertains the period within which this document must have been made It was in the possession of Francis Blomefield, and was printed by him in a sheet of the Collectanea Cantabrigiensia, which he afterwards cancelled, and therefore is not now easily to be met with. What is become of the original does not appear. The Latin history in the middle was printed in the Gentleman's Magazine for 1779, page 585, and is in the Appendix, No XIV and there are many old copies of it, with variations

3 Fuller, in his Church History, book ii. page 168, has given a translation of the same history, with the coats of arms round it. Some mistakes he has made, as in calling Earl Morcar of Northumberland, Earl Margery.

4 There is a manuscript now in the British Museum, formerly in the King's Library, MSS 18 C 1 3 entitled, " Story found in the Isle of Ely ' This is a translation likewise of the same history, and has neither arms, or portraits

5. In Dugdale's Manuscripts, in the Ashmolean Museum, MSS No 6501 II. F. 2 is the same account, with the arms

Upon the whole the following observations may be made, respecting principally the authenticity of the Ely Tablet

1. If these traditions and written accounts may be credited, the monks, at the departure

The nobility, the high military rank, and the personal merit, of the two brothers, procured them the favour of the Conqueror, and were rewarded by extensive grants of land. Robert Le Blount appears in Domesday book as the possessor of thirteen lordships in Suffolk, namely, Gisswortha, afterwards called Ixworth, Walsam, Eascefelda, Wica, Sapestuna, Hepworda, Wica, Icswerda, Watefella, Gislincham, Westtorp, Wiverthestuna, Westledestuna. In Middlesex, he held Lekham, and part of Stanes. An ample inheritance was bestowed upon William Le Blount in Lincoln-

of the knights, caused pictures to be painted upon the walls of the refectory, as memorials

2 These pictures could not have been coats of arms, since they were not known in the time of William the Conqueror.

3. It follows therefore that they must have been *portraits*, which may well be signified by the word *insignia*, as they were put up in *honour* of the knights And it may be observed, that the Ely Tablet is intitled, Nomina et *insignia* Militum, though it contains their portraits

4 They were repaired from time to time, and it was perfectly natural that, when coats of arms were introduced, those of each knight should be added

5 After the pictures were so completed the Ely Tablet was copied from them The originals were perhaps separate pictures, not improbably as large as the life, though placed here in one piece The copier would in many respects adopt the practice and mode of his own time, as to the form of the letters in his inscriptions, his painting in oil, and other particulars

6 The Ely Tablet therefore probably gives a true representation of the original pictures, as they appeared at the time the copy was made that is the portraits, the first paintings, with the additional arms The objection made by Cole, that pointed, or rounded, helmets were not in use so early, or even before the fourteenth century, seems unfounded, as a helmet, nearly of the shape of that of William Le Blount, may be seen on the head of his cousin, Ernolphus, Count of Guisnes, in 1151 The coats of arms having been evidently introduced at a time long after that of William the Conqueror, no argument can be deduced from the shape of the escutcheons

These paintings are very rude The engravings of them in Bentham are very incorrect, and too much finished That of Earl Warren, in Watson's Memoirs of the Warren family, except something of the outline, is mere fancy The annexed etching was traced off the original painting, in which however one L has been by accident left out in the word *millitarum*.

See Book I chap 4 Bentham's Hist of Ely Fuller's Church History, book ii p 168 Stukely, in his second part of Origines Roystonianæ, who is very erroneous Cole's MSS in the British Museum, vol xxxi. page 100 to 107. Heylin, in his Examen Historicum, preface, p 4, written against Fuller, who answered it in his Appeal of Injured Innocence

shire, where seven lordships are recorded in his name. Faldingevide, Crocsbi, Torgiebi, Widcale, Catebi, Saltlatibi, and Schitebroc[l]

Sir Robert, from his principal lordships, was styled Baron of Icksworth, and Lord of Orford Castle. He married Gundred, the youngest daughter of Henry, Earl Ferrers, who was one of the commissioners for the survey of Domesday, and had two hundred and ten lordships given him by the Conqueror. His youngest son, Robert de Ferrers, was created Earl of Derby by King Stephen. It is not known who was the lady of William Le Blount. Time has obliterated all further memorials of the two brothers, nor is it known when they died, or where they were buried[m].

The heralds have given to Sir Robert Le Blount for a coat of arms, lozengy, or, and sable You have already seen that coats of arms were not in use so early. This coat was borne by his descendants, the Barons of Ixworth , and the heralds in this, as in many other cases, have worked upwards, and have attributed to the ancestor the bearings of his posterity. After the extinction of the Barons of Ixworth, it does not seem to have been borne by any others of the family[n].

To Sir William Le Blount have been attributed two coats of arms, to which the same observation applies. They are, first, barry, nebuly, of six pieces, or, and sable[o]. And, secondly, gules, a fesse between six martlets, argent · both of which have been borne by his descendants to the present time[p].

[l] See Domesday Book Appendix, No XIII and Dugdale, Baron.

[m] Dugdale, Baron. vol i. p 257

[n] Bigland &c. It appears however in a coat of arms of the Grendon family, on an old parchment in the possession of that family. See book iii. chap 5.

[o] Ibid.

[p] Rawlinson's MSS. B vol 73 f 110. 6

CHAPTER II.

The Le Blounts, Barons of Ixworth in Suffolk.

ROBERT LE BLOUNT, the first Baron of Ixworth, was succeeded in his possessions by his son GILBERT LE BLOUNT, the second Baron, who likewise came into England with William the Conqueror[a].

He founded a priory at Ixworth, for black canons, or canons of the order of Saint Augustine, and dedicated it to the Virgin Mary. Camden mentions it in these words. "Here is to be seen an ancient priory "founded by Gilbert Blount, a man of great nobility, and Lord of Ix-"worth[b]." At the dissolution, in the reign of Henry the Eighth, it was valued at £168. 19s. 7¼d. a year, according to Dugdale, and at £280 9s 5d. according to Speed; and it was then granted to Richard Codyngton[c].

His lady was Alicia de Colekirke, by whom he had William, his son and heir, and a daughter named Galina, or Galiena de Redel, who married Robert de Insula, or de l'Isle[d]. The arms of Colekirke were gules, a fesse, embattled, or, between two bells, argent[e].

It seems probable that Galiena derived her name of de Redel from her cousin Geoffrey de Redel, Archdeacon of Canterbury. Upon her marriage with Robert de Insula, that ecclesiastic gave her certain lands, which he afterwards exchanged for Rya, in the manor of Portar. The donation was confirmed by Henry the Second, and by Matthew Count of Boulogne[f].

[a] Dugdale, Monasticon, vol ii. p 184 [b] Britannia Ixworth, Suffolk [c] Monasticon Tanner's Notitia Monastica [d] Dugdale, ibid Genealogies, Collins [e] Bigland, Maple Durham Pedigree.

[f] Cartæ antiquæ Hen II confirmat donationem quam Galfridus Ridellus Archidiaconus Cantuariensis, fecit Roberto de Insula, et Galienæ, cognatæ suæ, filiæ Willmi Blundi, de Rya quæ fuit manerii Portar, in excange (something seems wanting here, perhaps pro terra) quam idem Gafridus dedit prefatæ Galienæ, ad maritandum honorato Roberto, et quam Mattheus Comes Bolon carta sua eis confirmavit R Dods MSS vol lxviii. f 59 William is a mistake for Gilbert, if Dugdale is right in making Galiena his daughter.

As Matthew was Count of Boulogne from 1160 to 1173, this gift must have been made between those years[g].

William Le Blount, the third Baron of Ixworth, lived in the reign of Henry the Second, and married Sarah de Monchampes, the daughter of Hubert De Monchampes, De Munchensi, or De Montecanisio, Lord of Edwardeston, or Elwaston in Derbyshire, son of Warine De Monchensi, a Baron in the time of Henry the First, who was son of Hubert De Monchensi, a baron, and Lord of Edwardeston in Suffolk, in the time of the Conqueror[h]. The priory at Ixworth having been destroyed in the wars, he rebuilt it, at some distance from the parish church, near which it had been originally erected[i]. The arms of De Monchensy were, or, three escutcheons, each, barry of six pieces, vairy, and gules[k].

His son Gilbert, or Hubert, was the fourth Baron, and married Agnes de Insula, or de l'Isle. The arms of de l'Isle were, or, a fesse between two chevrons, sable[l]

Hubert, son of William Blund is under the guardianship of the King. For eight years last past he was under the custody of the Bishop of Ely, and is of twenty years of age (thirty according to Dugdale.) He is the grandson of Hubert De Muntechenesy. He holds Ixworth, Effeld, Walesham, and Stratford, which were his father's[m].

In the Chartulary of the priory of Merton in Surrey is the following charter without date. "Brother Robert, Prior of Merton, and the Con-"vent there, to all the faithful in Christ, greeting. We make it known "to you that we have granted, and confirmed, to Alexander, Clerk, of

[g] William the fourth Count of Boulogne, who lived in the Court of Henry the Second, died in 1159 He left a sister Mary, who was Abbess of Romsey in England. Upon the death of William, Matthew d'Alsace, son of the Count of Flanders, carried her off in 1160, married her, and thus became in her right Count of Boulogne; and died in 1173 These lands were probably held of him under some manors granted to him, or his predecessors, by the King of England. Hist Calais, i 587, 599

[h] Bigland, Maple Durham Pedigree

[i] Tanner, and Dugdale Roger Dodsworth's MSS Rot Pip vol. xiii f 14

[k] Bigland, Maple Durham Pedigree

[l] Ibid

[m] R Dods. vol. xli. f 5 Rot. de dominabus puellis et pueris ex parte Rememoratoris R. in Scacco In anno 20 Hen II. 1173

"Fecham, the land which Gilbert Blount has given him, and his heirs, for "his service, to hold of us, rendering a rent of twelve pence[n]."

In the twelfth year of Henry the Second, 1165, upon the assessment of an aid for marrying the king's daughter, it was certified that Gilbert Blount, the father of William, in the time of King Henry, and at his death, held twelve knights' fees, but it was in the time of war, that he was disseized of five of them, of which three were in the king's lands[o].

Gilbert or Hubert had two sons, William and Stephen. Of Stephen I shall have occasion to speak hereafter.

WILLIAM was the fifth who inherited the Barony of Ixworth. At his father's death he was a minor, and was under the wardship of the Bishop of Ely. In the thirty-second year of Henry the Second, 1185, he was thirty-two years of age. He was possessed of the Lordship of Ixworth, Estelder, and Walcham in Suffolk, and Edulfesberg in Buckinghamshire[p].

In Norfolk, in Easter term in the seventh year of John, 1205, William Blund demanded of William Fitz Roscelin, the manor of Henford, as his right, and of which William Blund his grand-father had been seized in the time of Henry, the king's father, by taking the explees. To this record the following pedigree is annexed[q].

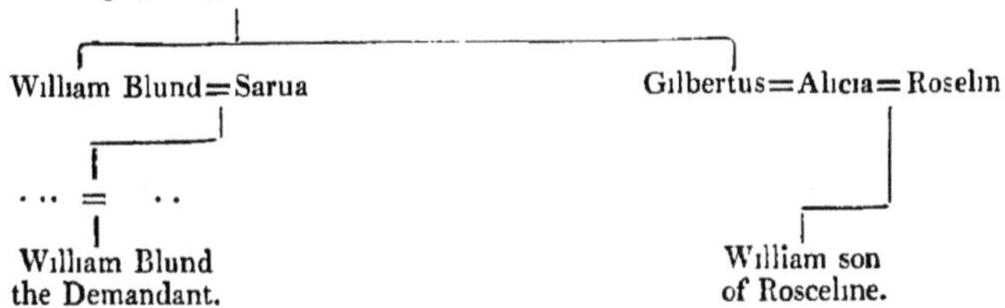

By this it seems that Sir William Le Blount, who married Sarah De Monchensi, besides his sister Galiena, had a brother named Gilbert, who had Henford for his portion, and which had been kept possession of, after his death, by William, son of Roseline, who had married Alicia, the widow of Gilbert.

In the pleas of the fifteenth of John, 1213, William Blund demanded against Warine Fitz Gerald, lands in Stivinton, of which his ancestor

[n] R Dods MSS vol. lv f 120. [o] Ibid vol. xlvii and vol lxxxix f 33. [p] Dugd Baron. [q] R. Dods. MSS vol. xcvii. f. 26.

Gilbert Blund was seized in the time of King Henry. His pedigree is annexed[r].

Gilbertus Blundus
|
Willelmus.
|
Hubertus.
|
Willelmus, the Demandant

His wife was Cecilia de Vere, who was the mother of a son named William, and two daughters, Agnes and Roisia[s]. The arms of de Vere were quarterly, gules, and or[t].

William le Blount, the sixth and last Baron, married Alicia de Capella[u].

In the fifth of Henry the Third, 1220, he paid scutage for the siege of the castle of Biham[x]. In the eighth year, 1223, William le Blund, and Alicia his wife, gave ten shillings to the church at Fairford in Gloucestershire[y]. In the twelfth year, 1227, there was a perambulation of the King's forest in Lancashire, by William Blount and others[z]. In the twenty-first year, 1236, William le Blount was sued by Walter de Fontibus, (Fountayn,) in a writ of right for the manor of Welldon Parva, in Northamptonshire, and had an imparlance[a]. In the twenty-ninth year of Henry the Third, 1244, when an aid for marrying the king's son was exacted, at the rate of twenty shillings for every knight's fee, Sir William le Blount paid seven pounds for seven knights' fees[b]. In the thirty-eighth year, 1253, when each fee was assessed forty shillings, towards making the King's eldest son a knight, he paid fourteen pounds[c].

In the disputes between King Henry the Third and the Barons, he supported Simon de Montfort, Earl of Leicester, against the King. A reference of their mutual claims having been made to the French King, in 1263, some of the English Barons went over to France to appear before him at Amiens. The Earl of Leicester set off, when his horse fell, and he broke his leg. Upon which accident, he and the other Barons sent a deputation of a few *wise men*, both of the clergy and the laity, to represent

[r] R. Dods. MSS vol 97 f 59. [s] Dugdale, Baron [t] Bigland [u] Dugd Baron. [x] R. Dods. vol. ciii. f 54. [y] Ibid. vol. cvii f. 128. [z] Ibid vol ciii f. 133 [a] Ibid. vol ciii. f 186 [b] Ibid. Rot Pip vol. xv. [c] Ibid

them; and of this number was the Lord William le Blount[d]. At the unfortunate battle of Lewis, he was standard bearer to the Earl of Leicester, and was slain, upon the 14th of May, 1264 He was attainted in Parliament, and dying without issue, his heirs were his two sisters. After the battle of Evesham, and the death of the Earl of Leicester, the next year, when Henry was established in full power, he made a merciful use of his victory. No attainders, except of the Montfort family, were carried into execution. And although the Parliament held at Winchester passed an Act to confiscate the property of all who had borne arms against the King, most of the forfeitures were remitted, easy compositions were made with others for their lands, and very small sums were levied even upon the most notorious offenders[e].

Such is the general account given of the consequences of the victory at Lewis, but it is difficult to ascertain precisely what forfeitures were exacted of Baron William. By the inquisition held upon his death, his property was found to consist of the manor of Wrabnasse in Essex, of Cley, Affield, Ixworth, and Walsham, and some lands in Level, all in Norfolk[f]. Matthew Paris says, that he was attainted, and all his lands in Ikesworth, Walsham, Hemestord, and other places, were given to Peter Camyneit, and Thomas de Grandisone, in the forty-ninth year of Henry the Third[g]. Some of his estates were certainly forfeited There is a record of the sixteenth year of Edward the Second, in which it is stated, that Edward the First had granted to William de Loghmaban lands in Blencogan, in Cumberland, which had belonged to Sir William le Blount, who had forfeited them as an enemy and rebel; and likewise the lands which Johanna, the widow of John le Blount, held in dower; that since the said lands were held of John de Weston, and Margaret his wife, in her right, they claimed the wardship of the lands, and the heir of William de Loghmaban, who was a minor, and likewise his marriage[h]. Yet his principal estates were not confiscated, his widow had her dower in the manor of Ixworth, which she held till her death in 1281, the tenth of

d Tyrrel, from Annals of St Augustine MS Mus Brit and Wykes

e Hume, ii p 228 ed 4to from Matthew Paris, p. 675

f Inquis Post Mortem, 48 Hen III The county is stated wrong in this record

g Hist in anno

h R. Dods MSS. vol xxxii. f. 95

Edward the First. and his two sisters succeeded to the inheritance of Ixworth, and his principal manors[i].

Agnes, his eldest sister, was married to Sir William de Creketot of Ovesdonne, who died in the 53d year of Henry the Third, 1268. Roisia, the youngest, was the wife of Robert de Valonys, Baron of Orford in Suffolk, fifth son, and heir, of Robert de Valonys and Isabella de Creke. William de Creketot and Robert de Valonys, their two sons, were coheirs of these lordships in right of their mothers.

By the death of Lord William, the last Baron of Ixworth, without male heirs, the title became extinct, and the property was thus transferred from the Le Blount family to those of De Creketot and Valonys[k] Creketot bore, azure, on a cross argent, five escalops, gules. De Valonys, argent, three pallets, wavy, gules[l].

In the seventh year of Edward the First, 1278, in the Pipe Roll, the estate of the late William le Blount paid to the scutage for Wales fourteen pounds, being for seven fees, at forty shillings each fee[m] In the hundred Rolls, about the same time, Alicia Blunda had wreck and other rights in Wrabenasse in Essex[n]. In Suffolk it was presented, that she had subtracted her suit to the hundred court of Risbrigg, for her tenement of Wratting[o]: that she held the manor of Ixworth of the King, of the Barony of le Blount[p]. that the Lords of Stoke, Domina Alicia le Blunde, Dominus Baldwin de Seyngeorge, Wilhelmus de Stok, Johannes de Tendring, Juliana Gifford, and Thomas Talbot, had from old times the assize of bread and ale in Stoke[q]. that Alicia la Blunt had lately claimed free warren in Haverille, and Withethersfeld, the jurors knew not by what warrant—that she claimed the same in Wrotting magna, and had subtracted her services in Wratting[r]. That in Kent she held one knight's fee in the town of Sneilwell[s]

[i] Inquis 10 Edw I Alicia uxor Willi Le Blount tenuit Icworthe manor, Suffolk

[k] Dugdale, Camden, &c The descent from Creketot and Valonys is continued in Dugdale's Monasticon. Ixworth, vol ii. p. 184. Sir William de Valonys had the ad vowson of the church of All Saints, with the chapel of St. Mary, of the gift of Sir William Blount, formerly Lord of the manor of Cley. Blomefield's Norfolk, vol. iii p 390.

[l] Bigland [m] Dods vol xvi f 41 [n] Page 163, 164 [o] Ibid p 172 [p] P 151 [q] P 143 [r] P 153, 195. [s] P 497, 500

CHAPTER III.

Le Blount, Baron of Belton, to Sir Thomas le Blount and Nicholas le Blount [a].

THE eldest male branch thus becoming extinct, we must ascend back to SIR STEPHEN LE BLOUNT, the second son of Gilbert le Blount the fourth Baron of Ixworth, and Agnes de L'Isle, as the root from whence the rest of the family proceeded He lived in the reign of Henry the Second, and married MARIA, the sole daughter and heir of Sir William le Blount of Saxlingham in Norfolk, the third in descent from Sir William le Blount, who came over with the Conqueror.

This original William le Blount had a son whose name is not known, and who was Lord of Saxlingham, in the time of Henry the First. His son Sir William le Blount lived in the reign of Stephen, and was father to

[a] This branch, the eldest after the extinction of the Barons of Ixworth, is entirely omitted by Bigland in his two pedigrees of the Sodington and Maple-Durham families, because they were not descended from it The principal authorities for it are, 1. A Pedigree drawn up about the reign of Charles the First, which belonged to Sir William Dugdale, and which was communicated by Dugdale Stratford Dugdale, Esquire, Member for the County of Warwick, his descendant It seems to be extremely accurate The Sodington branch is the only part which is continued to modern times, and it ends with the children of Sir George Blount, Baronet, who married Mary Kirkham 2 What Nash in his History of Worcestershire calls the Illuminated Pedigree It was drawn up at the College of Arms in 1642, is a vellum roll, ten feet and a half long, and about two feet eight inches broad, with the coats of arms drawn and emblazoned in their proper colours It was made for the Blounts of Grendon Court in Herefordshire, and therefore that branch is particularly described, and has been continued by Mr Roland Blount to the present times, in the possession of whose widow it now remains At the head are the effigies of Robert Lord Blount in a modern peer's robes, with a banner of the lozengy, Blount s arms, and of Sir William le Blount, in plate armour, with the nebuly arms of Blount on his surtout, and on his banner, argent a cross, gules 3 The Pedigree in Rawlinson's Manuscript, B vol 73 f. 110 4 The Manuscript printed in the Appendix, No. XX 5 Various records, deeds, and other documents, quoted in their proper places All this evidence places in a clear light many parts of the family which before laboured under great obscurity such as the marriages with Odinsels de Wiotham, Lovet, Stafford, Stury, &c &c Sir Thomas le Blount, Isabel and Eleanor Beauchamp, &c &c

Sir William le Blount, who lived in the times of Henry the Second, Richard the First, and John, and who had this only daughter Maria, married to Sir Stephen le Blount, who thus became Lord of Saxlingham. And thus the families of the two brothers who first settled in England became united, and they were both the ancestors of the subsequent families[b].

Sir Stephen le Blount in the first year of Richard the First, 1189, was on an assize[c]; and in the tenth year 1198, with Agnes his mother, held half a carucate of land in the manor of Thorphall, in the parish of Saxlingham in Norfolk[d].

Sir Stephen le Blount had two sons, ROBERT and JOHN[e]. His second son SIR JOHN BLOUNT married Constance one of the sisters and coheirs of RICHARD DE WROTHAM[f]. This family was descended from Geoffrey de Wrotham of Radeville near Wrotham in Kent, who was a domestic servant of several of the Archbishops of Canterbury; of whom Hubert Walter gave him certain lands at Wrotham. Geoffrey, by his wife Muriel de Lyd, had a son William, who was recommended by Archbishop Hubert to Richard the First, in the ninth year of whose reign he was appointed Warden of the Stanneries in Devonshire and Cornwall. His report of the execution of his office is still extant in the Exchequer[g],

[b] Rawlinson's MSS B vol. 73 f 119 b Pedigree by Vincent Eyre in Coll. Arm who has stated Stephen to have been the second son of William le Blount and Cecilia de Vere Bigland calls him a natural son His legitimate descent from Gilbert and Agnes is proved by the record next cited, by the Illuminated Pedigree, and Dugdale's Pedigree. The Sir Stephen le Blount, who was Chamberlain to Edward II in Scotland, and Warden of the Marches, must be a different person. Rot Scot 2 Edw II m. 16

[c] Placit Cap West

[d] Blomefield's Hist. of Norfolk, vol. iii p. 338, 340 In 1235, Ellen le Blund held the same of William Cardville, and the same year the heirs of Stephen le Blund held a quarter of a knight's fee of the Earl of Arundel. In 1306, William, son of Ralph le Blund, sold it to Peter de Norford In 1323, William le Blund possessed it In 1272, Ascelina, widow of William le Blund, sued out a writ against William, son of Warine de Munchensy, and Sapientia, widow of William de Cardville, for her dower in Saxlingham Ibid. That Saxlingham, the estate of Stephen le Blount, went in the line of Ralph le Blount, is a proof of the eldership of his branch.

[e] Dugdale's Pedigree The Illuminated Pedigree.

[f] Habington. Collins, Hutchins's Hist. of Dorsetshire, vol. i. p 284

[g] Lib Nig. Scacc. i. 102.

and his rules and ordinances still govern the affairs of the Stanneries. In the next year he had grants of the manor of Cathanger in Somersetshire, and the Bailiwick of North Petherton. In the first year of John he was Sheriff of Devonshire, still Warden of the Stanneries, and Forester of the King's forests in Somersetshire and Dorsetshire, which offices he held in the fifth year. His wife was Maud de Cornhall, who brought him two sons. William, the eldest, was Archdeacon of Taunton, in the reign of John, and succeeded to the property and honours. But being a clergyman, his brother Richard was substituted for him in his office of Forester. He died the third year of Henry the Third, 1218, when Richard de Wrotham, the second son, succeeded him. He was then a minor, and John de Mariscal and John de Erleigh were his securities for the performance of his office of Forester. In the twenty-sixth year of Henry the Third, 1241, he was a knight, and one of the justices of the Court of Common Pleas. He died in the thirty-fifth year of Henry the Third, 1250, without issue, when his heirs were William de Placetis, or Plessy, the son of his eldest sister Muriel; Constance, the wife of John le Blount; Emma, the wife of Geoffrey de Scoland, and Christiana, the wife of Thomas Picot. His property consisted of the manors of Mongton, Newton, Cathangre, and Ham, in Somersetshire; Crele and Heyghland in Kent; and other estates. William de Placetis had the office of Forester, the manor of Newton, and most of the property. His third son Richard took the name of De Wrotham[h].

An estate at Mosterton, or Mostern, in Dorsetshire, is the only part which I can trace in the Blount family. In the twentieth of Edward the Third, 1346, Thomas Blount held one sixth of a knight's fee there[i]. In the thirty-fourth year, 1340, John Blount held at his death two parts of a messuage and garden, and one carucate of land, at that place of the King in capite as of his manor of Marshwood, and Margaret his sister was his heir, aged thirteen years[k]. It should seem therefore that this branch of the family ended in that heiress. In the eleventh year of Henry the Sixth, Richard More held the manor, and the capital messuage called Blounts' Court[l].

[h] Inquis. P. M. Collinson's Hist. of Somersetshire, vol. i. p. 41. vol. ii. p. 63.
[i] Escaet. Hutchin. vol. i. p. 284. [k] Ibid. [l] Ibid. vol. i. 347.

Sir Robert le Blount, the eldest son, married Isabel, the daughter of the Lord Odinsels, who brought him as her portion the manor of Belton in Rutlandshire[m]. This was a family which had great possessions. The family of Limisie, in King John's reign, ended in two heiresses, of whom Basilia the eldest married Hugh de Odinsels, a Fleming, and Alianora the youngest David de Lindesey, a Scotsman. The partition of the estates between them was made in the fifteenth year of that King From Hugh de Odinsels proceeded two families The first was seated at Ichinton in Warwickshire, and continued till near the time of Sir William Dugdale. The second possessed Solihull and Maxtoke. Hugh lived in the fifth year of Henry the Third, 1220, and died in the twenty-third year, 1328. His son Gerard had livery of his lands, and paid a relief of fifty pounds: the relief for a knight's fee being only one hundred shillings, he must have held ten knights' fees. Gerard died the fiftieth of Henry the Third, 1265, and Hugh his heir being under age, the custody was granted by the King to his son Edmund Crouchback Hugh was of age the next year, and died the thirty-third of Edward the First, 1304. John, then twenty-eight years of age, was his successor, and died the tenth of Edward the Third, 1336, leaving his son John, twenty-four years of age, who in the twenty-fifth of Edward the Third, 1351, was outlawed, and the King seized his lands. They were restored to his son John, the thirty-first of Edward the Third, 1357. From him was a regular succession of heirs till the reign of Elizabeth, when John Odinsels was extravagant, became poor, sold the property, and ended the family.

The other family, at Solihull and Maxtoke, Sir William Dugdale observes, was soon, by heirs female, transferred to other stocks. Amongst these was Isabel The manor of Belton, her portion, was a large inheritance, and from this estate the le Blounts of this branch were called to Parliament, by the name and title of Lord Blount of Belton[n]. The arms of Odinsel were, argent, a fesse, and two mullets in chief, gules; with several variations[o].

In the eighth year of Henry the Third, 1223, Robert le Blund witnessed

[m] Rawlinson, Dugdale, and the Illuminated Pedigrees

[n] Rawlinson In Escaet 28 Edward I Belton was a knight's fee of Edmund Duke of Cornwall, p 160

[o] Dugdale's Warwickshire, p. 342.

the charter of foundation of Hilton Abbey, in Staffordshire, granted by Henry de Audethele[p]. In the fifteenth year, 1230, he held a burgage house in Salop[q]. In the thirty-seventh of Henry the Third, 1252, he sued for Robert Stater[r]. The thirty-eighth, 1253, Robert Blundus sued John Fitz-william for carrying away from his house his charters and his seal[s]. The fifty-second, he complained of trespass in his manor of Gayton in Lincolnshire[t]. He died in the seventeenth year of Edward the First, 1288, when Malculine the Escheater was commanded to seize into the King's hands all the land and tenements of which Robert le Blound, who held of the King in capite, died seised[u].

From Sir Robert le Blount the family divided into two great branches, descended from his two sons, Sir Ralph le Blount, and Sir William. Sir William le Blount, the youngest, was the ancestor of the Blounts of Sodington, Kinlet, Burton-upon-Trent, the Lords Mountjoy, those of Maple Durham, Grendon, and other families, which will be the subjects of the third book.

Sir Ralph le Blount, or Rodolphus, was probably so named from his ancestor Rodolphus, Count of Guisnes, the father of Robert and William le Blount As the eldest son he was of course the Lord of Belton. He married the daughter and heir of Sir —— Lovet, of Hampton Lovet in Worcestershire[x]. Her Christian name and that of her father are not mentioned, but she seems to have been either Cecilia, or Alicia, one of the daughters and heirs of Sir John Lovet, the son of Henry Lovet, who will be more particularly mentioned in the account of the Sodington family. She inherited Hampton Lovet from her father. It appears by the Testa de Nevil, about the first of Edward the First, 1272, that Henry Lovet held one knight's fee in Hampton Lovet of the Barony of William de Beauchamp[y]. In 1269 William Beauchamp presented to the church, I suppose on account of the minority of the heir[z]. This estate descended in this branch of the family, and not in that of Sodington. The arms of Lovet were, argent a fesse between six wolves' heads erased sable

In the fourteenth year of Edward the First, 1285, Sir Ralph le Blount recovered lands in Saxlingham which were his grandfather's, by the judg-

[p] Mon Ang 1 942 [q] Calend Rot Chart [r] Placit West [s] Ibid [t] Ibid
[u] Rot Orig Scacc [x] The Illuminated Pedigree [y] Testa de Nevil, p 40 [z] Nash

ment of Solomon de Ruffe[t]. The descent of this estate, some of the earliest property of the family, proves the seniority of this branch[u].

Besides Sir Thomas le Blount, it appears that Sir Ralph le Blount had an elder son, SIR WILLIAM LE BLOUNT, and that his wife was named Isabel. He was styled Lord of Belton. The estate there was settled upon him in tail, and to bar it, in the fifty-fifth year of Henry the Third, 1270, a fine was levied between William le Blount and Isabel his wife, querents, and Walter le Blount, deforcient, of one messuage, one mill, nineteen virgates of land, &c. in Belton, settled on William and Isabel in tail, who gave to Walter a virgate of land in Messeworth in Bucks[x] By a deed without date, Lord William le Blount gave to John Lovet lands in Brerhull in Bertone[y]. In 1306, William son of Ralph le Blount sold land at Thorphall in the parish of Saxlingham in Norfolk to Peter de Norford[z]. In 1315, in the ninth year of Edward the Second, William le Blount was Lord of Belton[a]. In 1323, William le Blount possessed land at Saxlingham[b]. In 1328, William le Blount presented to the Church of Hampton Lovet[c]. He must have died soon after that year, and without issue, since his brother Thomas, who died in 1330, was Lord of Belton. This Sir William le Blount could not have been the son of Sir

[t] Rawlinson and Dugdale's Pedigrees.

[u] Though contemporary, the following mercantile Sir Ralph le Blount I suppose was a different person He was Sheriff of London in the fourth year of Edward the First, 1276 Rawlinson In the Hundred Rolls, in the time of Henry the Third, and Edward the First, we find in London the ward of Ralph le Blount, and mention is made of Reginald le Blount, and William le Blount. Presentment is made of two walls erected in Kyron Lane by Ralph le Blount and the Abbot of Warden, to escape the attacks of thieves, the association of bad women, and filth in the night; another for exporting wool. Hund Roll, p 418 b 424, 480

[x] This is from a MS note of Le Neve, in the copy of Wright's History of Rutlandshire, in Gough's Collection, Bib. Bod. He adds, "See the Roll of Assarts of the Forest of Roteland to prove a William Le Blount possessed of Belton then Willm le Blount de Belton tenuit Belton Launde. Vide Rot Regard, 49 Edw III (1375) m 5 et ult" It is possible that this Sir William le Blount may have been the husband of Isabel Beauchamp, of the Sodington line, and his son Sir Walter of Rock, and that *a part* of the Belton estate had been settled upon him as the younger son

[y] Dugdale Appendix, No XVIII Art 5

[z] Blomefield, Hist Norf vol iii p 338, 340.

[a] Anecd. Coll Arm.

[b] Blomefield ibid

[c] Nash

Thomas, as he was in possession of Belton before Sir Thomas's death. Nor could he have been the person who married Isabel Beauchamp, because the estate at Saxlingham and the *Lordship* of Belton went in the elder branch, and not in the Sodington family.

The other son of Sir Ralph le Blount was SIR THOMAS LE BLOUNT. He is enumerated amongst the Knights who fought under that warlike monarch Edward the First That he was a brave, a faithful, and an accomplished soldier, may be inferred from the honourable trusts which were bestowed upon him by his sovereign. And though no memorials remain of his various campaigns, and military services, it may be presumed that he shared in the dangers and honours of the British conquests in Wales, Scotland, and France.

In the fourth year of his reign, 1310, King Edward the Second gave him the custody of his manor of Caldecote, near Kayrwent, in Gloucestershire, which had been held by John the son of Reginald, deceased[d]

In the fifth year, 1311, he was appointed Governor of Drosselan castle, in Wales, which he held till the twelfth year, 1318, when he was succeeded by Egidius de Beauchamp[e]. This castle is in the parish of Llangathen, not far from Grongar Hill, in the vale of Towy in Carmarthenshire. Some ruins of it still remain.

He married two wives the name of the first is not known His second was Juliana de Leyborne. This latter marriage took place in the nineteenth year of Edward the Second, 1325. Juliana was the daughter of Thomas de Leyborne, and the widow of John de Hastings, Lord Bergavenny[f]. She was a great heiress, and was usually styled the Infanta of Kent Her family was ancient, and had large possessions in that county. The greater part of their property had belonged to Odo, Bishop of Baieux, the half brother of William the Conqueror, whose estates had been confiscated by William Rufus. Sir Roger de Leyborne erected the

[d] Rot Orig in anno.

[e] Dugdale s Baron. vol. i p 519 and Rot. Orig in Cur Scacc 12 Edw II. Rex commisit Egidio de Bello campo custodiam castri Regis et ville de Droslan, cum pertinentiis, tenendum quamdiu Rex placuerit, eodem modo quo Thomas le Blound

[f] For Juliana de Leyborne, see Dugdale's Baron vol i p 531, 532 vol. ii. p 13, 14. The Inquis. post mortem at her death, and Hasted s History of Kent, vol ii p 206, &c &c

castle upon the manor from whence he derived his name, in the reign of Richard the First, whom he accompanied, with William de Leyborne, to the siege of Acre in 1191[x]. His son, Sir Roger de Leyborne, took an active part in the troublesome reigns which succeeded. Adhering to the Barons, he was taken prisoner by King John in the castle of Rochester, in 1215, but made his peace and was discharged. In 1251, he slew Ernulf de Mounterey at a meeting of the Round Table, at Waldon in Essex; the launce, which was unbated, entering through his armour, and it was supposed to have been done designedly, out of revenge for Ernulf's having broken his leg at a former tournament. In 1252 he attended King Henry the Third into Gascony. At first he adhered to the cause of the Barons against the King, but in 1263, he declared in favour of the royal cause, and was wounded in the King's service at Northampton. He was afterwards besieged in Rochester castle, and defended it successfully against the Earl of Leicester in person He was taken prisoner at the battle of Lewes in 1264, and was released upon an undertaking for his personal appearance before the parliament. He was again defeated by Leicester in Wales. In 1265 he was appointed by the King to treat with the city of London, which had incurred his severe displeasure by adhering to the rebellious Barons. After imprisoning some of their members, the King at last consented to restore the city to its liberties for a fine of 50,000 marks[y]. He was rewarded for his loyalty by valuable grants, and important offices, particularly after the battle of Evesham He was constable of Bristol in 1259, and was made Warden of the Forests beyond Trent, Steward of the King's Household, Warden of the Cinque Ports, Sheriff of Cumberland and Kent, and Governor of Carlisle, in 1267. In 1269 he assumed the cross to accompany Prince Edward to the Holy Land, but he died in the fifty-sixth year of Henry the Third, 1271. His two wives were, Idonea, the youngest daughter of Sir Robert de Vipont, Lord and Baron of Westmoreland; and his second, Eleanor, the daughter of

[x] List of the Knights at Acre. Ashmole MSS No. 1120 The arms of Leybourne were, Azure, six lions rampant, argent, 3 2 1 or 3. 3. Ashmole MSS No. 1120 Hasted, Hist Kent General History, page lxxvi

[y] Nichols s Leicestershire, vol i p 179 and 509

William de Feriers, and the widow of Roger de Quinci, Earl of Winchester, who survived him[z].

His son, William de Leyborne, received many marks of his sovereign's favour. In the fifty-sixth year of Henry the Third he had a grant in fee of the forest of Englewood. In the fourteenth year of Edward the First he entertained the King at his castle of Leyborne on the 25th of October. He was appointed the King's Admiral, Admiral of the southern seas, and Constable of Pevensey Castle, in 1295. The wardship, and marriage of Geoffry de Say was conferred upon him, and his ward married his daughter Idonea From the twenty-seventh year of Edward the First to the third of Edward the Second, he regularly received his summons to the Parliament as a Baron of the Realm. In the latter year, 1309, he died, leaving his widow Juliana surviving, and Juliana, his grand-daughter, then six years of age, his only heiress, his son Thomas de Leyborne having died before him.

But William de Leyborne had enfeoffed his son Thomas, and his wife Alice, before his death, with the manor of Leyborne, and other property. Thomas died in the thirty-fifth year of Edward the First, three years before his father, seised of the manor of Leyborne, which was held of the King as of the honor of Albermarle by half a knight's fee He left Alice his wife, who was the daughter of Ralph de Tony of Flamstead in Hertfordshire, and his daughter Juliana[a].

In the twenty-eighth year of Edward the First, Sir Simon and Sir Henry de Leyborne, two younger brothers, attended the King into Scotland and were knighted at Carlaverock[b]. In the list of persons summoned by that monarch, by his writs of the 8th of February, to attend his coronation, Henry de Leyborne and his consort were invited[c].

Juliana de Leyborne, the heiress of the family, was born in 1303, for she was six years old at her grand-father's death in 1309[d]. In her centered

[z] Dugdale's Baron vol ii p 13, 14 Selden, Titles of Honour, part ii. chap v. s 26 Upon the summons of the Barons, 5 Edw. I to assist upon the expedition against Wales, Roger de Clifford who married the eldest, and Roger de Leyburn, the youngest daughters of Robert de Veteri Ponte, acknowledged to owe the service of two knights' fees and an half each for their halves of the Barony of Westmoreland Seld from Rot Scut

[a] Ibid [b] Hasted, vol. i p. 489 [c] Ibid vol iii p 265 [d] Inquis. P M

the rewards of the merits of her ancestors, and the favour of so many sovereigns. Besides property in other places, the manor and castle of Leyborne, and the advowson of the church of Ridley, she inherited twenty-two manors in the county of Kent alone. Mere, in Reinham parish, was held by the service of walking as the Principal Lardner or Clerk of the Kitchen at the King's Coronation; and the privilege granted by Henry the Third to Roger de Leyborne was confirmed to his great-grand-daughter; that his *gavelkind* lands in Reinham, Upchurch, and Herclep should be held *in fee* by the fourth part of a knight's fee[e]. In addition to these, the manors of Langley, Colbridge, De la Gare, Wadeslade, Watringbury, Foukes, East Farbone, Bichnor, Swanton-Court, Goodneston, Easling, Queen-Court, Barton, Ashford, with Wall and Esture, Eleham, Packmanstone, Elmstone, Overland, Wadling, Ham, and Westgate, acknowledged her as their Lady[f].

These immense possessions Juliana de Leyborne transferred to three successive husbands: but she was so unfortunate as to have no children to inherit them.

Her first husband was John de Hastings, the eldest son of John de Hastings, Lord Bergavenny, by Isabel his wife; sister, and, at length, co-heir, to Aymer de Valence, Earl of Pembroke. At the death of his father in the sixth year of Edward the Second, 1312, he was of age. In 1323 he was made Governor of Kenilworth Castle, and died in the eighteenth year of Edward the Second, 1325, leaving his widow Juliana, and Lawrence, his son and heir, by a former wife, about five years of age[g]. The principal seat of the Hastings' family was on the Lordship of Bergavenny in Monmouthshire, and they likewise enjoyed great property at Fillongley, Allesley, Birdingbury, Aston Cantelupe, and other places in Warwickshire, which they acquired, by marriage, from the Cantelupe family[h].

[e] Thomas le Blount, and Juliana his wife, enfeoffed certain persons of the manors of De la Gare, Langell, and the third part of Herietsham, eighty acres of wood in Espling, Ospring, Hertelope, Ronham, Olivele, Aske, Sidingbourne, Tonge, Milstede, Merston, Rodemeresham, Kingestone, Upchurch, Dordan, and Middleton, in the county of Kent, as of the inheritance of Juliana R Dods. MSS. vol. 128 f 6.

[f] See each of these places respectively in Hasted's History of Kent

[g] Escaet R Dods vol 132 f 47

[h] Dugdale's Warwickshire in locis, and page 742 See Genealogy of Cantelupe, No. 19

In about a year after his death, in 1325, Juliana again married Sir Thomas le Blount. Besides what she inherited from her father and grandfather, she was now endowed with considerable property of her late husband Upon the death of John de Hastings, his estates were in the hands of the Crown, on account of the minority of the heir, and Edward the Third, in his first year, by John de Blomville, his Escheator, assigned to Sir Thomas le Blount and Juliana his wife, widow of John de Hastings, one of the heirs of Adomar de Valencia, late Earl of Pembroke, the following lands, as her dower.

The manors of	£.	s.	d
Sutton, in Norfolk, valued at	32	0	11¼
Winfaithing, in the same county	20	8	9¾
Invenesleshury, in Herts	8	19	11¼
Suthanyfeld, in Essex	10	9	10
Thurton, in the same	10	5	1
Reydon, in Suffolk	51	18	3¼
Towcester, in Northamptonshire	63	13	6
Some tenements in Fanges, in Essex	3	13	4
In Asshedon, in Bucks	1	10	0
In Southwark, Surrey	0	8	6

Making in all £203. 6*s*. 2*d* in annual value[i]

The manor of Birdingbury, in Warwickshire, had been granted to Sir John Paynel for his life; and upon his death, which happened before this marriage, it was assigned to Juliana, as part of her dower, the reversion and inheritance belonging to the son of her husband, Lawrence de Hastings. Accordingly we find that Sir Thomas le Blount, as patron, presented to the church at Birdingbury, Thomas le Blount, a subdeacon, in the year 1327. What relation this Thomas bore to him is not known[k].

Upon the death of Guy de Beauchamp, Earl of Warwick, in the ninth year of Edward the Second, 1315, as his son Thomas was a minor, various noblemen were entrusted with the care of his property. At first William de Sutton was appointed Constable of Warwick Castle, and in the twentieth year of Edward the Second, 1326, Thomas le Blount had the charge of that castle, as Constable or Governor. He did not however

[i] Rot. Orig in Cur Scacc 1 Edward III [k] Dugd War p 216.

long enjoy this honour, for in the first year of Edward the Third it was entrusted to Roger de Mortimer, during the remainder of the minority[l].

During the unhappy state of the kingdom in the last year of Edward the Second, though he held the office of Lord Steward of the King's household, he adhered to Queen Isabel, and after she had taken Bristol, and the King had fled into Wales, he gave her every assistance[m] Holinshead relates it in the following manner, which he has literally translated from the original historian, Walsingham. "After the Queen went to Bristol, the King in the mean time kept not in one place, but shifting hither and thither, remained in great care. Whereupon Sir Thomas Blount, an ancient Knight, and Lord Steward of the King's house, took his servants, with victuals, horses, and armour, in great plenty, and came to the Queen, of whom, and likewise of hir sonne, he was joifullie received, and divers of them which he brought with him were retained, and the others had letters of protection, and were sent away in loving manner[n]." Howe says, that by the breaking of his rod, he resigned his office, and shewed that the King's household had free liberty to depart[o].

Upon the accession of Edward the Third, he supplied the place of the Earl of Pembroke, who was still under age, at the Coronation[p]. He again served his country, and in 1327 was with the army which entered Scotland under Henry Duke of Lancaster[q]

After the death of Juliana de Leybourne, widow of Sir William de Leybourne and grandmother of the heiress, an Inquisition was held in the second year of Edward the Third, 1328, in Kent, when it was found that she held the manor of Eselyng, of the heir of Bartholomew de Badlesmere, who was under age, as of the barony of Chilham, by the service of one knight's fee; and a messuage, and eighty acres of ploughed land, and six of

[l] Dugd. War p 342 b. Rot. Orig Cur Scacc [m] Dugd Bar vol. i. p 519.

[n] Holinshead, page 339 Walsingham, 20th and 21st of Edward the Second Miles emeritus, Domini Regis Seneschallus se, cum totâ suâ familia, assumptis victualibus, armaturis, et dextrariis multis valdè, contulit ad Reginam Quem illa, cum filio suo, benigne suscepit, et quosdam de suis secum retinuit, quosdam datis literis protectoriis in pace dimisit. Walsingham, page 125. edit. Cambden. Dextrarii, Fr destriers, war horses. Du Cange

[o] History of England, page 225 [p] Rawlinson, vol. 73. f. 110, but with a mistake as to the reign. [q] Dugd Bar vol i p. 519

meadow, in Overland, of the Archbishopric of Canterbury, then vacant. And that Juliana, the daughter of Thomas de Leybourne, the wife of Thomas le Blount, was her next heir, and of full age. On the 13th of February, Thomas le Blount did homage for those lands[r].

In the twentieth year of Edward the Second, and the first and second years of Edward the Third, Sir Thomas le Blount was summoned to Parliament as a Baron[s]. He died in the fourth year of Edward the Third, 1330, leaving no issue by his second wife. There is no Inquisitio post Mortem amongst the records of the Tower.

In the same year, his widow Juliana married her third husband, Sir William de Clinton, younger brother of John de Clinton, of Maxtoke, ancestor of the Lords Clinton and Say, the Earl of Lincoln, and the Duke of Newcastle[t].

This marriage, and the great wealth he acquired by it, was the step to the future honours of William de Clinton. In the next year he was made Justice and Governor of Chester, Constable of Dover Castle, and Warden of the Cinque Ports. In 1351 he was summoned to Parliament as a Baron. Next year he was appointed Admiral of the Seas from the Thames westward. By patent of the 16th of March, in the eleventh year of Edward the Third, 1337, he was raised to the dignity of Earl of Huntingdon, with the creation fee of £20 per annum, payable out of the issues of that county, and a grant of a thousand marks per annum of land. In 1346 he paid an aid for knighting the Black Prince for the castle of Leybourne for one fourth of a knight's fee, which Thomas de Leybourne before held of Margaret de Rivers, and she of the King[u].

In the mean time, the son of her first husband, Lawrence de Hastings, was under the guardianship of his mother-in-law, Juliana. He was bred up in the court of Queen Philippa, the wife of Edward the Third, who seems to have interested herself in the young man's favour. When that Sovereign was at Newcastle, upon his Scotch expedition in 1333, having sent for the Queen to come to him, and considering that so long a journey might be dangerous to the child, he directed special letters to Juliana, desiring her to take him under her charge, as a person most proper to

[r] R Dods. MSS. vol. 84 fol. 8. Fines. [s] Dugdale, Baron. vol i p 519. and Summons of the Nobility, in annis. [t] Dugdale, i. 576, &c. &c. [u] Dugd Baron. Hasted, History of Kent.

undertake that trúst[x]. In the ninth year of that King, 1335, Sir John le Blount, and others, were assigned to enquire of all trespasses committed by Guy Bretons and others in the manor of Inteberwe, in Worcestershire, which belonged to Lawrence Earl of Pembroke[y]. In the eleventh year of Edward the Third, 1337, Lawrence de Hastings was committed to the tuition of Juliana's third husband, the Earl of Huntingdon, and he had an allowance of two hundred marks a year out of the Exchequer for his maintenance; and he held the manors of Winfarthing, and Heywood, in Norfolk, as his guardian. As soon as he came of age he was declared Earl of Pembroke, and he died in the twenty-second year of Edward the Third, 1348[z].

Sir William de Clinton, Earl of Huntingdon, died in the twenty-eighth year of Edward the Third, 1354, and was buried in the Priory at Maxtoke, which he had founded. Having no children, his heir was Sir John de Clinton, his elder brother's son[a]. Upon the Inquisition at his death it was found that he held, in conjunction with Richard Dallesle, yet living, the manor of Wybergh, and the manors of Thurton and Southingfeld, and the hamlet of Founge, and the advowson of the church of Thurton, in right of Juliana his wife, yet living, videlicet of her dower John, the son of John his brother, was his heir, of the age of twenty-four years[b].

Juliana, having survived her three husbands, became again possessed of the castle of Leybourne, and all the manors which she had inherited, in her own right. She made her will the 30th of October, 1363, died in the forty-third year of Edward the Third, 1369, and was buried according to her will in the new chapel, on the south side of the Church of St. Augustine's monastery, near Canterbury[c]. Upon the Inquisition which was held after her death, it was found that she had no heirs, either lineal or collateral, and all her immense possessions escheated to the Crown[d].

[x] Dugdale, Warwick p. 742. [y] Rot. Orig. in Scacc [z] Dugd Warw p 742.
[a] Dugd Bar [b] Escaet R Dods MSS. vol 51 f 61. [c] Dugd Baron Reg Cant Langham, f 115

[d] Inquis Post Mort 43 Edw III. See the Genealogy of Leyborne, No. 20 formed from Dugdale's Baronage, vol. i p. 531 vol ii. p 13. Ashmole's MSS No 825. part 5 fol. 10. No. 804 fol 34. R. Dods MSS. vol. 132 fol. 39 Hasted's History of Kent, vol. ii p. 206, &c.

By his first wife Sir Thomas le Blount had two sons, WILLIAM and NICHOLAS. SIR WILLIAM LE BLOUNT, the eldest, succeeded him as Lord of Belton[e]. NICHOLAS LE BLOUNT, the second son, was living in the 35th year of Edward the Third, 1361, and was the father of the second NICHOLAS LE BLOUNT, who lived in the reign of Richard the Second, and changed his name to Croke, an event which will be related in the next chapter[f].

SIR WILLIAM LE BLOUNT, the eldest son of Sir Thomas, was Lord of Belton, in the reign of Edward the Second[g]. He had a daughter Isabel, married to Alanus de Atkinson, and a son John. He was Knight of the Shire for Rutland in the twenty-eighth, twenty-ninth, and thirty-fifth years of Edward the First, and the seventh of Edward the Second, that is, in 1299, 1300, 1306, and 1313[h]. This was before his father's death, when he was summoned to the upper house. In the fourteenth year of Edward the Second, 1320, William le Blount, Lord of Belton, gave to Walter the son of Robert, the Bailiff of Belton, half a virgate of land, in Belton, for his life[i]. In the first year of Edward the Third, 1327, he had a charter of Free Warren for his manor of Hampton Lovett[k]; and in the fourth and sixth years, 1330 and 1332, grants of two yearly fairs at Belton, on the eve of St. Thomas, and on the eve, day, and morrow of St James[l]. In 1328, and 1332, he presented Thomas de Hugford to the Rectory of Hampton Lovet[m]. By a deed dated at Hampton Lovet, in the fortieth

[e] The Illuminated Pedigree makes the son of Sir Thomas le Blount, who married Leybourne, to have been Sir Thomas Blount, and says that he supplied the place of John Hastings at the coronation of Edward III And that *his* son Sir Thomas Blount was beheaded in 1400

[f] Manuscript, Appendix, No XX In the 28th year of Edward I 1299, Nicholas le Blount of Yorkshire released to Sir Roger Mynyot all his land in Eskelly, which had belonged to Richard de Stochilld R Dodsw vol. 91 f 181 Perhaps the first Nicholas A Nicholas le Blount was Rector of Weting in Suffolk, in 1315 Blomefield's Norfolk in loco

[g] Hist p. 109 n. [h] Wright's Rutland, p 14 [i] Dugdale's MSS. Ashmole MSS vol 39 fol. 47, et seq. Append No XVIII art 3 [k] Habington in Collins, vol iii. p 368 note Rot Chart p 159 [l] Dugdale, Baron. p 518 Rot Chart 6 Edw. III n 24 32 p 163

[m] Nash in loco In 1269 William de Beauchamp presented, perhaps as Lord on account of the minority of the heirs of Sir John Lovet In 1303 Peter le Blount, who in 1305 likewise, presented Radulphus le Blount, who was witness to a deed in 1322 See page 116. I know not in what right Peter presented

year of Edward the Third, 1366, he gave to his son Sir John le Blount, knight, and Elizabeth his wife, in franc marriage, certain lands in Hamslope, in Buckinghamshire. The seal is the nebuly arms of Blount[n]

The manor of Thichenapeltre, which is called in Domesday Book Tichenapletreu, was in Hampton Lovet, and was purchased, according to Nash, in the thirteenth year of Edward the Third, 1339, of Richard Bosler, or Bottiler; but by a deed preserved by Ashmole of John Alleyne, and Alice his wife, by William Blount, and John his son[o]. In the same year, Joan, late wife of Richard le Bosler, released to Sir John Blount, Lord of Hampton Lovet, the manor Thichenapeltre[p].

Sir John le Blount, his son, was Lord of Belton, Custos of the City of London, and Constable of the Tower in the reign of Edward the Third. In the first year of that King, 1327, he was summoned as a Baron to Parliament, by the name of the Lord Blount of Belton[q]. He had two wives · by the first, whose name is not known, he was the father of Sir Thomas le Blount, who succeeded to the Lordship of Belton, and whose history will be given in the second part of this book. His second wife was Elizabeth de Fourneaux, sole heir to her father Sir Simon de Fourneaux and Alice his wife, daughter of Sir Henry de Umfraville, and co-heir with Elizabeth Umfraville, who married Oliver St. John, ancestor of Lord Bolingbroke[r]. She inherited the great estates of Fourneaux, whose arms were, gules, a bend between six cross-crosslets, or[s].

In the nineteenth year of Edward the Third, 1345, Thomas de Hugford, Rector of Hampton Lovet, granted to Sir John Blount, and Elizabeth his wife, with remainder to William their son, the manor of Hampton Lovet, with the advowson, and the manor of Thichenapeltre[t].

Elizabeth survived her husband, and in her widowhood, in the eighth year of Richard the Second, 1385, founded a chauntry in the Abbey of Athelney in the county of Somerset. By the deed of foundation she agreed with Robert Hacche, the Abbot, that there should be found for ever two Chaplains, one of them to be a monk, the other a secular priest,

[n] Dugdale's MS Ibid App. No XVIII Art 2 [o] Ashmole, MS App No XVIII. Art. 27 [p] Habington. Ibid [q] Rawlinson's Pedigree, Dugdale's Pedigree. [r] Collinson's History of Somersetshire. Nash, vol. i p 536. [s] Habington They were quartered with Blount in St Augustine's Church, Dudurhull or Doderhill [t] Ashmole's MS App No XVIII Art 39

to say mass every day in the year, except Good-Friday, for the good estate of William Aungier, and Henry Roddam, and also for the said Elizabeth, the Lady Alice Stafford, the Lady Maud Stafford, and Robert Wrench, and all the other friends and benefactors of the said Elizabeth, And also for the souls of Sir John Blount, Sir Simon de Fourneaux, and Alice his wife, Sir Henry de Umfraville, and Isabel his wife, Sir William Blount, and Maud his wife, the Lady Julian Talbot, the Lady Elizabeth Cornwall, Sir Brian Cornwall, her son, Sir Richard Stafford, and Sir Richard Stafford the younger, Robert Flete, and Robert Stockton, and for the souls of all her friends and benefactors deceased. And it was farther agreed, that on the decease of the said Elizabeth Blount, or any other of the persons above mentioned respectively, annual obits should be kept on the days of their deaths, as also for the other persons who were dead at the time of executing the indenture. These services were to be performed at the Altar of the Holy Trinity in the Abbey Church of Athelney. And it was agreed that in case of the neglect thereof, the said Elizabeth and her heirs should have power to distrain upon the lands of the Abbot and Convent on their lands at Clavelshay in the parish of North Peverton[u].

Their son, Sir William le Blount, whose wife was named Maud, was therefore dead, and without issue in 1385. Alice, their only daughter and heir, married first Sir Richard Stafford, who was likewise dead in 1385, and had had a son Sir Richard Stafford, then dead also. Secondly, she married Sir Richard Stury, who died without issue in 1403 This Knight served Edward the Third and Richard the Second, in their wars, with Sir John Montacute, afterwards Earl of Salisbury. They both favoured the doctrines of Wycliffe, whose disciples attended their assemblies in armour, on account of the interruptions they were exposed to. When their attempts at a reformation recalled Richard the Second from Ireland, in 1394, he sharply rebuked Montague, and threatened to put to death Sir Richard Stury, if they did not renounce their opinions[x]. In the east window of Hampton Lovet in painted glass was the effigy of a knight in armour kneeling, with his name Sir Richard Stury under it, and two coats of arms: on the right, party per fesse, gules and or, six roses counter-changed, the buds

[u] Collinson's History of Somersetshire. [x] Ypod Neust. p 540 Walsingham, p. 351

counter-coloured, on the left, gules, a bend between six cross-crosslets, or, for Fourneaux[y], which proves Alice's descent from that family.

In 1396, by the name of Alice Stury Lady of Hampton Lovet, she presented to the church, and, in 1412, as the widow of Richard Stury[z]. By a petition, without date, addressed to the Earl of Warwick, describing herself as his tenant, and the late wife of Sir Richard Stury, she claimed two messuages, two plough lands, five acres of meadow, and other lands in Thichenapeltre, in the county of Worcester, as her rightful inheritance after the death of William le Blount her brother[a].

Afterwards, styling herself Lady of Hampton Lovet, she erected a chapel in the chauntry of St. John the Baptist in the church there, dedicated to Saint Anne, and endowed it with the manor of Bishampton, lands in Hampton Lovet, and in Otterton, formerly Cotterugge, to support two chaplains, to pray for the souls of Sir John Blount and Elizabeth his wife, her father and mother, Sir Richard Stafford, and Sir Richard Stury, her two husbands. The licence for this endowment from the Bishop of Worcester is dated the twenty-eighth of October, 1414, and in that year she presented a clerk to it[b].

She died in the fourth year of Henry the Fifth, 1415, and Sir John Blount of Sodington was found to be her heir[c], in the estates which came from her father Sir John Blount. The Fourneaux estates went to her mother's heirs, the descendants of John Bitton who married Hawise Fourneaux[d]. This was Sir John Blount, who married Juliana Foulhurst, and Isabella Cornwall, and died in 1424. The situation of the Belton branch of the family rendered it necessary to have recourse for an heir to so distant a relation. She had no children, her own brother was dead, her half brother or nephew, Sir Thomas Blount, had been beheaded in 1400, and her cousin Nicholas le Blount, had been attainted, went abroad, changed his name, and had lived in concealment in a distant country; and it must be concluded from this inquisition that no other relations remained of the descendants of Sir Ralph le Blount. Thus were the manors of Hampton Lovet, and Thichenapeltre, transferred to the Sodington branch. In the same year 1415, Sir John Blount presented to the church of Hampton

[y] Nash, ii p 538 [z] Nash [a] Ashmole, App. No XVIII Art. 40 and Habington, ibid [b] Dodsw vol 90. f 111 Nash, vol 1 p 543 [c] Escaet Dods vol 42. f. 47. [d] Collinson's History of Somersetshire.

Lovet, and the chapel of St. Anne[f]. Hampton Lovet descended to his son Sir John Blount of Sodington, by whom it appears to have been transferred to the Mountjoy family; for Sir Thomas Blount the Treasurer, presented to the church in 1419, 1421, 1422, 1432, 1445, and to the chapel in 1427, 1435, 1444, 1447, 1448, and 1453 And next, William Lord Mountjoy presented to the church in 1493, and to the chapel in 1512[g]; and in that family it continued till it was sold to the Packington family.

[f] Nash [g] Ibid

BOOK THE SECOND.

PART II

THE LORDS OF BELTON CONCLUDED, AND THE HISTORY OF THE CROKE FAMILY.

THE

GENEALOGICAL HISTORY

OF

THE CROKE FAMILY.

CHAPTER I.

The conclusion of the Lords of Belton, and the origin of the Croke family.

HAVING thus given the history of the children of Sir John Blount by his second wife Elizabeth Fourneaux, I proceed to Sir Thomas Blount, his only son by his first wife[a]. He succeeded as Lord of Belton. In the thirty-second year of Edward the Third, 1358, it was found by an inquisition not to be to the King's detriment to grant a licence to Sir Robert West, to give the manor and advowson of Compton Valence in Dorsetshire to Sir Thomas Blount for life[b]. At the coronation of Richard the Second, in 1377, he was deputy for John Hastings, Earl of Pembroke, a minor, in the office of Naperer, or Superintendent of the King's linen, in right of his manor of Ashele in Norfolk[c].

This knight, with his cousin Nicholas le Blount, whose descent I have already given, engaged deeply in the conspiracy which was formed, in the

[a] Dugdale's, Rawlinson's, and the Illuminated Pedigrees. [b] Inquis ad quod damnum in anno.

[c] Ibid. Baker's Chronicle. In these Pedigrees an intermediate Sir Thomas Blount is interposed between Sir John Blount and this Sir Thomas, but as the time scarcely admits of it, and as no particulars are mentioned of him, except that he lived in the reign of Richard the Second, I think it extremely probable that one Sir Thomas has been multiplied into two, as has sometimes been done by Dugdale, and other genealogists

year 1400, to restore Richard the Second to his throne after his deposition by Henry the Fourth. Since this transaction materially affected the family, by occasioning the extinction of the eldest line of the Belton branch, and the change of name, from le Blount to Croke, in the second line, it may not be improper to give some account of it, and of the causes which occasioned it

A long minority, a turbulent aristocracy, the ambition of the princes of the blood, and the King's imprudence, rendered the reign of Richard the Second one of the most unfortunate in the English annals. In the fluctuations of power between the parties of the King and his opponents, as each gained the ascendancy, their adversaries bled upon the scaffold, in their turn, the King's adherents, his enemies, and finally Richard himself, were sacrificed in the contest; and a foundation was laid for the civil wars which desolated the country for near a century. Expensive wars, the want of economy, in a tutelary and rapacious government, had early exhausted the treasury, and new and extraordinary taxes excited a general discontent in the kingdom, and dangerous insurrections of the people. When the King became capable of acting for himself, his thoughtless extravagance, his unbounded attachment to his favourites, and the oppression of his subjects to extort the means of supplying his necessities, gave general disgust, and excited the jealousy and resentment of a haughty nobility. The necessary defence of the kingdom against a projected invasion of the French, in 1386, required the aid of Parliament, and the party in opposition to the court, with the Duke of Gloucester at their head, seized this opportunity to compel the removal of the King's ministers, and to take the government into their own hands. A commission issued, to which the King was obliged to consent, to invest fourteen persons with powers totally subversive of the King's authority, his favourites and ministers were impeached, and most of them beheaded, or banished[d]

For some time the Duke and his party were completely masters of the kingdom, and Richard was obliged to acquiesce, but those measures were displeasing to the people; and as soon as circumstances were favourable, Richard emancipated himself from this restraint, asserted his royal authority in a council held for that purpose on the third of May 1389, and appointed

[d] Stat 10 Rich II 1387.

his own ministers. By these vigorous proceedings, and his subsequent judicious conduct, the King and his Parliament were cordially reconciled, he acquired the confidence of his people, and the kingdom for some years enjoyed an uninterrupted tranquillity.

But Richard unfortunately was not satisfied with the possession of a moderate and constitutional authority: he still feared the machinations of his enemies, he had experienced their oppressive insolence, he wished to protect himself against their power, and to raise himself above their control. It was declared by Parliament, that the King was as free in his royal prerogative as any of his predecessors, notwithstanding any statute in derogation thereof, particularly in the time of Edward the Second; and that if any statute had been made in prejudice of the liberty of the Crown, it was repealed and annulled[e].

In 1396 he strengthened his authority by an alliance with the French King, and a marriage with his daughter; and partly by force, and partly by an artful management, he had procured a parliament entirely at his devotion[f]. The Duke of Gloucester, and his party, alarmed at the King's proceedings, were entering into new cabals, when he was suddenly arrested and put to death, and many of his faction were seized, impeached, and beheaded. The Parliament proceeded to pass laws for the farther maintenance and extension of the royal authority. By one Act the whole power of the Parliament, after it was dissolved, was vested in eighteen commissioners, or any six of the lords, or three of the commoners, who composed it[g]. And though it was expressed to be merely for answering the petitions depending in Parliament then undetermined and undispatched, yet it was charged against him, that by colour of this grant they proceeded to other general matters according to the King's will[h]. This was a strong measure, and the whole power of the kingdom was thus devolved upon the King and a council entirely at his command. To render himself still more secure, it was made high treason to endeavour to procure the repeal of those statutes, solemn oaths for their observance were administered to all his subjects, and the sanction of religion was super-

[e] Rot Parl 15 Rich II 1391 [f] Articles against King Richard, Art 18, 19, 20

[g] 21 Rich II. ch 16 1397 [h] Articles against King Richard, Art 8.

added by a bull obtained from Pope Boniface to confirm them under the penalty of excommunication, denounced against all who should infringe them.

Though the King appeared now to be completely triumphant, and fully established in an independent and arbitrary power, under this seeming prosperity a general discontent prevailed through the kingdom, the oppressive exactions still continued, and the connection with France, the natural enemy of the country, was offensive to the prejudices of the English At this critical period, the King, by his unjust and injudicious conduct to the Duke of Lancaster, again roused the spirit of hostility, and occasioned his own ruin. After having banished that nobleman, without sufficient reason, upon the death of his father, Richard seized upon his opulent dutchy, and refused to admit him to the possession of it. Henry landed in England, and having taken a solemn oath that he had no other design than to recover his hereditary property, was supported by the greater part of the nation, Richard was deserted, and betrayed, and Henry of Lancaster mounted the throne doubly an usurper, by deposing his lawful sovereign, and by excluding the lawful heir of the house of Mortimer[1].

Yet although they had been overpowered for a time by the Lancastrians, the King had still many friends. The English people, always high spirited but generous and humane, though they could oppose the tyranny of a prince upon the throne, were filled with compassion towards their fallen monarch, who, after all, was rather inconsiderate than criminal. They were attached to the hereditary succession, and shocked at the perjuries and fraud by which Henry had obtained the crown. Some powerful noblemen, and a great number of Richard's adherents, determined therefore to take advantage of the spirit which was now rising in his favour, and to replace him on the throne The conjuncture seemed not unfavourable. The Welsh and the men of Cheshire were invariably in his interest. and assistance might be expected from France. The principal leaders in this conspiracy were John Holand Earl of Huntingdon, uterine brother to Richard, and a great warrior; his nephew Thomas Holand Earl of Kent: Edmund Earl of Rutland, and Thomas Lord Despenser, who had

[1] Richard was taken at Flint Castle, Aug. 19, 1399. Henry was crowned, October 13.

married Richard's cousin. These noblemen had all been the appellants against the Duke of Gloucester, and for their services in those impeachments had been promoted by Richard to the respective titles of Dukes of Exeter, Surrey, Albemarle, and Earl of Gloucester, of which honours they had been deprived in the first parliament of Henry. With these were John Montacute, Earl of Salisbury, an accomplished nobleman, who had been much in Richard's confidence, and had been sent by him from Ireland to take the command of the forces till his arrival · Ralph Lord Lumley, the Bishop of Carlisle, the Abbot of Westminster, Richard's two chaplains William Ferriby and Richard Maudelain, Sir Benedict Sealy, Sir Thomas le Blount, his cousin Nicholas le Blount, and many others.

The great power and vigilance of Henry, and the numerous armies which he could command, rendered any direct and open attack upon him altogether hopeless, and it was necessary to resort to some bold but secret attempt. The plan of the conspiracy was concerted at a dinner given by the Abbot of Westminster, on the 18th of December, 1399, at which were present the two Holands, Rutland, Despenser, Walsh, Roger Walden Archbishop of Canterbury[k], the Bishop of Carlisle, Maudelain, Pol King Richard's physician, and Sir Thomas Blount, who is styled "a wise knight[l]." It was here agreed to surprise Henry at a tournament to be held at Windsor on Twelfth-day, and a written agreement with their seals was entered into. The tournament was proclaimed, and Henry accepted of the invitation, every preparation was completed, the day arrived, and Henry was already at Windsor; when unfortunately the plot was discovered, either by accident, the treachery of Rutland, or some means not perfectly known, within a few hours of its being carried into execution. The King, upon receiving this information, instantly fled to London, and the Lords who came to Windsor soon after with a body of five hundred

[k] With the Duke of Gloucester the Earl of Arundel was impeached, and his brother, Thomas Arundel, Archbishop of Canterbury, was banished Roger Walden was thereupon consecrated Archbishop, and continued to the end of Richard's reign, when he was removed, and Arundel restored Walden was afterwards made Bishop of London Godwin De Præsulibus

[l] MS in the French king's library, called Ambassades, in Webbe's translation of the Metrical History of Richard, by Creton Archæol vol. xx p 217

lances, and six thousand archers[m], were disappointed of their object. Henry speedily collected an army of twenty thousand men, and appeared with them the next day at Kingston upon Thames. The conspirators, unable to oppose such a force, retreated in military array, with banners displayed, and every where proclaiming King Richard. The Earls of Kent and Salisbury, with two hundred horse, marched through Colnbrook, to Sunning near Reading, where Queen Isabel resided, who, though only eleven years of age was the object of Richard's tenderest affection.

Here the Earl of Kent, to raise the Queen's spirits, and to animate his adherents, declared that Henry of Lancaster had run away from them, and had been chased into the tower of London, and that Richard had escaped from prison, and was at Pomfret with an hundred thousand men: and he tore off the collars and other badges of the house of Lancaster from the Queen's attendants, who had been placed about her by Henry. Maudelain, the King's chaplain, who resembled that prince most remarkably in person and voice, clothed in royal habiliments, with a rich crown upon his head, marched with them, and personated the King; and having been much with his Sovereign, and employed in many confidential services, he was admirably qualified to favour the deception. From Sunning they proceeded to Cirencester, where a thousand men, chiefly archers, were collected on the evening of the sixth of January The Earl of Gloucester and Lord Lumley, with three hundred horse, proceeded towards South Wales, in hopes of being joined by Lord Berkeley in Gloucestershire[n].

In the town of Cirencester they were opposed by the inhabitants, and in the market place three hundred of them fought against two thousand[o], many women distinguishing themselves in the combat. Being defeated, the Earls of Kent and Salisbury were made prisoners, but one of their chaplains having set fire to some houses, with a view to rescue them, the

m Carte

n In the pardon of the Bishop of Carlisle, they were said to have appeared in arms at Bampton, in Oxon. Wantage, Faringdon, and Cirencester Carte, Hist of Eng'and ii 615. Rhymer. viii p 165

o Froissart

townsmen dragged them out of the Abbey, and beheaded them[p]. More than twenty of the principal conspirators fled to Oxford, where they were seized and beheaded in the Green Ditch. Amongst these were Lord Lumley, Sir Thomas le Blount, Sir Benedict Sealy, John Walsh, and Baldwin of Kent. Sir Bernard Brocas, Sir John Shelly, Maudelain and Ferriby, were put to death in London. The executions were performed with every circumstance of the most horrid barbarity.

Sir Thomas Blount was hanged, but the halter was soon cut, and he was made to sit on a bench before a great fire, and the executioner came with a razor in his hand, and knelt before Sir Thomas, whose hands were tied, begging him to pardon his death, as he must do his office. Sir Thomas asked, "Are you the person appointed to deliver me from this world?" The executioner answered, "Yes, Sir, I pray you pardon me." And Sir Thomas kissed him, and pardoned him his death. The executioner knelt down, and opened his belly, and cut out his bowels straight from below the stomach, and tied them with a string that the wind of the heart should not escape, and threw the bowels into the fire. Then Sir Thomas was sitting before the fire, his belly open, and his bowels burning before him, Sir Thomas Erpyngham the King's chamberlain, insulting Blount, said to him in derision, "Go seek a master that can cure you." Blount only answered, "Te Deum laudamus, Blessed be the day on which I was born, and blessed be this day, for I shall die in the service of my Sovereign Lord, the noble King Richard." The executioner knelt before him, kissed him in an humble manner, and soon after his head was cut off, and he was quartered[n].

[p] The king found it necessary to restrain the zeal of his partizans, by issuing a writ on the 8th of February, commanding that none in future should be beheaded or executed without form of law. Rhym. vol vii. p. 124. As a reward for this service, on the 28th of February, 1400, the king granted to the men of Cirencester the goods of Thomas, Earl of Kent, and John, Earl of Salisbury, and other traitors there taken, Rhymer, viii p. 130 and to the men four bucks from Braden Forest, and a cask of wine annually from the port of Bristol, and to the women six bucks and a cask of wine Ibid. p. 150.

[n] From la Relation de la Prise de Richard II. par Berry Roi d'Armes, a Manuscript in the French king's library, of which an account has been published by Gaillard, in his

The Earl of Huntingdon remained in London till after the battle of Cirencester, then went on board a vessel, and being hindered by contrary winds, was seized, committed to the Tower, and beheaded. Lord Despenser escaped from Cirencester, and embarked in a vessel of Bristol, but the Captain brought him back to that place, where the people decapitated him. Eight of the heads, and the mangled quarters of the Lords and principal persons, were brought to London in panniers, and carried in triumphal procession, on the 16th of January, with trumpets sounding, and the people shouting, and they were accompanied by eighteen Bishops, and thirty-two royal Abbots, and other prelates, and were then fixed upon London bridge. The Earl of Rutland, who seems to have made his peace by betraying his fellow conspirators, paraded through the streets with the head of Lord Spencer, his brother-in-law, carried upon a pole before him, and presented it to the King: and was followed by twelve waggons loaded with prisoners in chains. The Bishop of Carlisle, and the Abbot of Westminster were pardoned[o]. These cruelties were the prelude to the death of the unfortunate Richard, probably by starvation, and he was buried on the twelfth of March following[p].

By the attainder and death of Sir Thomas Blount, his estates were of course forfeited to the Crown. Upon the inquisitions which were taken, he was found to possess, in Hampshire, rents in Barramshe, the manor of Lyndhurst, rents in Pillee, a messuage and lands in Broklegh, the manor of Ryngewode, a messuage and lands at Wallop: in Wiltshire, at Larkestoke, the manor and a mill, a messuage and lands at Wodefold; at Bathampton, Rolveston, and Wyly, ten pounds of rent· and four pounds of rent at New Sarum· and that he died without issue[q]. It must be observed, that Belton is not mentioned in these inquisitions, probably because

account, &c of the MSS in the library of the King of France London, 1789 vol ii. p 197 It is referred to by Carte, vol ii p 642. from whom this extract is taken

[o] The Bishop of Carlisle was removed from the Tower to the Abbey of Westminster. Rhymer. vol viii p 150

[p] His scull has been examined, and no marks of any wound were perceived. Gough's Sepulcral Monuments, vol i p 163 King on Ancient Castles Archæol vol vi p. 313

[q] Escaet vol iii p 265 Rot Pat

it was in Rutlandshire, of which the inquisition is not remaining; unless it had been before alienated, which does not however appear. It was most likely now forfeited into the hands of the Crown, and was granted to Sir Walter Blount, since it is afterwards found in his possession, and was settled upon his wife Sancha. And thus the eldest line of the Lords of Belton became extinct.

In the mean time, Nicholas le Blount, and William Fitzwilliams, who with others upon the first failure of the conspiracy had been sent to different parts of the kingdom to excite a farther insurrection, raised each of them a good party of horse, with which they made an excursion as far as Brentford, where meeting with a body of one hundred and sixty of Henry's men, they defeated them, and took many prisoners. But all hopes of success being now at an end, and Henry's vigour and cruelty precluding all chance of safety, the chiefs engaged in this service held a council at midnight, and having ordered the common soldiers to betake themselves to their own homes, the principal officers, endeavoured to make their escape and to go abroad. Calais was as unsafe as England, for immediately upon the discovery of the conspiracy, on the 5th and 6th of January, writs were sent not only to all the counties in England, but to Peter Courtenay the captain of Calais, to arrest the Earls of Kent and Huntingdon, and all other traitors, and to seize their lands; and all liege subjects were commanded, under penalty of forfeiture of life and limb, not to conceal the said Earls, their officers, ministers, or servants, or any of their followers, adherents, or favourers[r]. They went therefore on board a small vessel at Pool, and arrived in safety at St. Maloes[s]. These were John Carrington, second son of Sir Thomas Carrington, who had received his military education under Sir John Neville in Gascony, where he served Richard the Second till he was twenty-five years of age[t]. His elder

[r] Rhymer, vol. vii p 120 [s] Croke MS

[t] This was John de Nevill, son and heir of Ralph, Lord Nevill, who served in the armies of Edward III. and Richard II and was much in France. In the 34th of Edward III he was there with the king and Sir Walter Manny, when he was knighted. In the 41st he succeeded his father as Lord Nevill Three years after he was retained to serve the king with forty men at arms, one hundred archers, and an hundred mariners After-wards with a larger number, and he was constituted admiral of the fleet In the 45th, 46th, and 47th years he served in France In the 1st and 2d years of Richard II. he was

brother being dead, he came into England, and continued with Richard till his capture in Wales[u]. With them were likewise Richard Atwick, Robert Newborough, William Lindsey, William Fitzwilliams, a younger son of John Fitzwilliams of Emley in Yorkshire[x], and Nicholas le Blount[y].

It is probable that Nicholas le Blount, having taken so active a part in the insurrection, and being so nearly related to Sir Thomas le Blount, was outlawed with the rest of those who had escaped, by which they became dead in law, and their estates were forfeited And although by a statute made in the 5th year of Henry the Fourth, in the year 1404, all treasons, insurrections, and rebellions, were pardoned, yet outlawries for such offences, declared by a court of justice, were excepted[z].

Having secured their retreat to the continent, they went to Paris, and brought to King Charles the first information of the murder of his son-in-law. These soldiers were too active to continue long in idleness, and the war in Italy, between the Emperor and the Duke of Milan, presented a fair field for their ambition[a]. A great connection and intercourse at this time subsisted between England and Milan. For some years a great number of English soldiers had served in Italy. The accomplished John Galeazzo Visconti, the reigning Duke, had received his education under the instructions of Britons, and Sir John Hawkwood, the great English warrior, had married Donnina, the natural daughter of Bernabo his uncle[b]. An event had taken place not

lieutenant of Aquitaine, and seneschal of Bourdeaux He died the 17th of October, in the 12th year of Richard II Dugdale's Baron vol i p. 296.

[u] Croke MS Appendix, No XX

[x] Amongst forty English who were killed by the Irish lords lez Tothils, on Ascension-day, in 1498, was John Fitzwilliams, perhaps the father of William Fitzwilliams Camden in anno. (MS p 19)   [y] MS

[z] Stat 5 Hen IV chap 15 Le Roi ad pardonez toutz maners de tresons &c et auxint les utlegaries, si nulles en eux ou aucun de eux soient pronunciez par celles enchaisons

[a] The battle of Brescia, mentioned in page 389, was fought on the 21st of October, 1401. Muratori, Annales d'Italia, vol ix p. 4.

[b] Sandford's Gen Hist p 360 Sir John Hawkwood was born at Sible-Henningham in Essex, the son of a tanner, and bred a tailor. Having being pressed into the king's service, he served in the wars in France with so much merit, that he was promoted, and knighted.

No 19.

THE BARONY OF BERGAVENNY IN WALES,

IN THE DAYS OF KING EDWARD THE FIRST

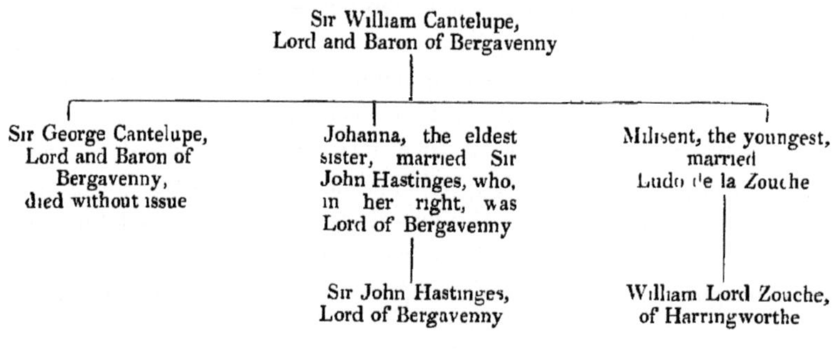

Ashmole MSS vol 825. part 4 f. 14

Cantelupe bore, Azure, three leopards' heads, jessant de lis, or
Ibid vol 797.

As a Sir Thomas de Blount bore these arms, with a bend ermine, (Ashm MSS vol 825 part 4 in fine,) perhaps it was Sir Thomas le Blount, who married Juliana de Leybourne, the widow of John de Hastings, and who might have borne them from being possessed of some of the Hastings, or Cantelupe, property, which his wife held in dower

No. 20

GENEALOGY OF LEYBORNE.

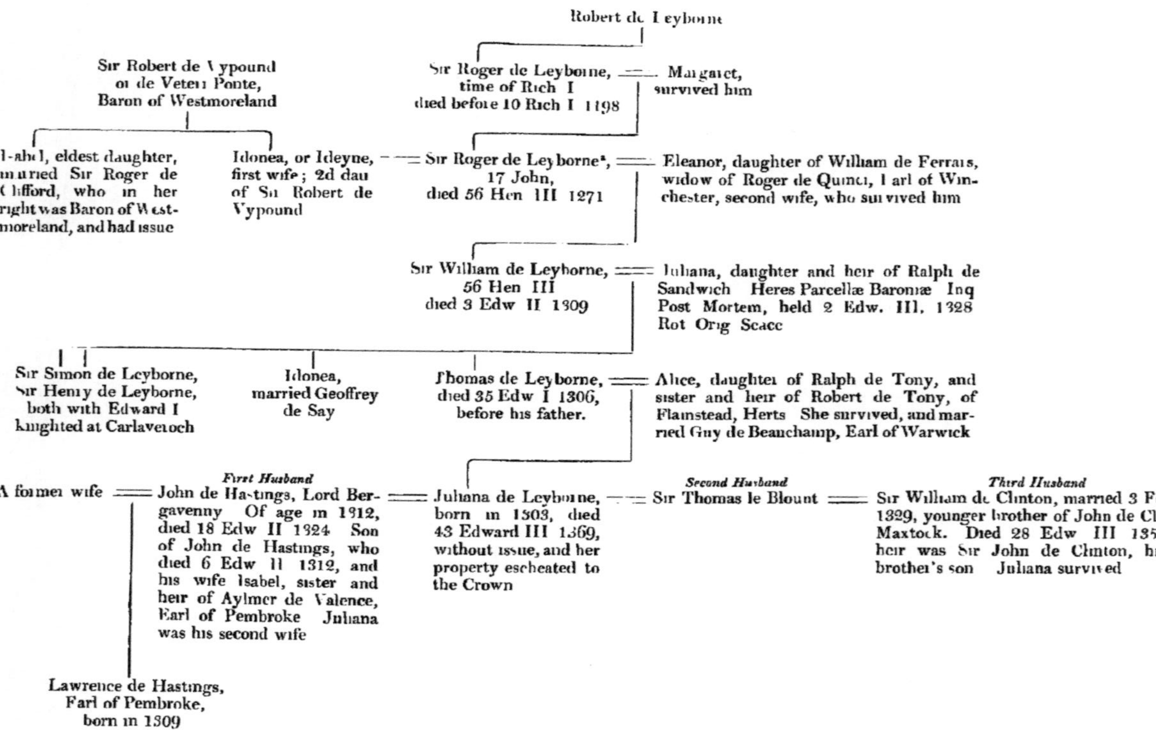

Robert de Leyborne
Sir Roger de Leyborne, time of Rich I died before 10 Rich I 1198
Margaret, survived him
Sir Robert de Vypound or de Veteri Ponte, Baron of Westmoreland
Isabel, eldest daughter, married Sir Roger de Clifford, who in her right was Baron of Westmoreland, and had issue
Idonea, or Ideyne, first wife; 2d dau of Sir Robert de Vypound
Sir Roger de Leyborne[a], 17 John, died 56 Hen III 1271
Eleanor, daughter of William de Ferrars, widow of Roger de Quinci, Earl of Winchester, second wife, who survived him
Sir William de Leyborne, 56 Hen III died 3 Edw II 1309
Juliana, daughter and heir of Ralph de Sandwich Heres Parcellæ Baroniæ Inq Post Mortem, held 2 Edw. III. 1328 Rot Orig Scacc
Sir Simon de Leyborne, Sir Henry de Leyborne, both with Edward I knighted at Carlaverock
Idonea, married Geoffrey de Say
Thomas de Leyborne, died 35 Edw I 1306, before his father.
Alice, daughter of Ralph de Tony, and sister and heir of Robert de Tony, of Flamstead, Herts She survived, and married Guy de Beauchamp, Earl of Warwick
A former wife
First Husband
John de Hastings, Lord Bergavenny Of age in 1312, died 18 Edw II 1324 Son of John de Hastings, who died 6 Edw II 1312, and his wife Isabel, sister and heir of Aylmer de Valence, Earl of Pembroke Juliana was his second wife
Juliana de Leyborne, born in 1303, died 43 Edward III 1369, without issue, and her property escheated to the Crown
Second Husband
Sir Thomas le Blount
Third Husband
Sir William de Clinton, married 3 Edw III 1329, younger brother of John de Clinton of Maxtock. Died 28 Edw III 1354 His heir was Sir John de Clinton, his elder brother's son Juliana survived
Lawrence de Hastings, Earl of Pembroke, born in 1309

[a] Dugdale names his wives differently 1 Eleanor Turnham. 2. Eleanor Vaux. Vol. ii p. 13, 14

many years before, which had still more contributed to promote the connexion between the two countries. This was the marriage of Lionel, Duke of Clarence, second son of King Edward the Third, with Violante, the sister of John Galeazzo.

These events had established a frequent communication between the English and the Milanese, and le Blount, with the other refugees, very naturally repaired thither, and entered into the military service of the Duke, who was at war with the Emperor, upon the following account. The predecessors of John Galeazzo Visconti had enjoyed only the title of Imperial Vicar, or Governor of Lombardy. He was created the first Duke of Milan, and his dominions were rendered nearly independent of the Empire, by the Emperor Wenceslaus, in consideration of one hundred thousand florins of gold, in 1395. The Germans were discontented with Wenceslaus, and a powerful party was formed against him. The Electors convoked a national assembly, and pronounced the solemn sentence of his deposition, in 1400. Amongst the charges against him, it was one that he had alienated the imperial domain of Milan, and raised a simple officer of the kingdom of Lombardy to the rank of Duke. The Count Palatine,

After the peace of Bretigni, with many other English adventurers, he went into Italy, and became the most celebrated commander of his age Bernabò, brother to Galeazzo the Second, and father of Giovanni Galeazzo, gave him his daughter Donnia in marriage He afterwards served the Pope, and at last established himself with the Florentines. He died at Florence, at a very advanced age, the 16th of March, 1393, the seventeenth of Richard II where a superb monument, with his picture or statue, was erected to his memory Sismondi's Histoire des Republics d'Itali, and all the Italian writers of that period Fuller's Worthies, Essex. Stow's Annals. Morant's Essex, ii 289, 290, who endeavours to prove him to have been lord of a manor, and not a tailor, but upon insufficient reasons. Hearne, in his preface to Leland's Itin vol iii p 5, refers to a Life of Hawkwood by Valens Villani, lib ix c 37. and for the companies, lib ix. c 109. x 27, 34. Froissart, b i c 214, 215. Montfaucon, ii 318, 322 Walsingham, Ypod Neust p 522 Muratori, An vol xii. Poggio, Hist Florent Buoninsegni See Memoirs of Sir John Hawkwood, read at the Society of Antiquaries, 25 Jan 1776, printed in the Bibliotheca Topographica Britannica of Nichols, vol vi art. 1. A portrait of him was given to the Society by Lord Hailes in 1775 His name is variously corrupted by the Italian writers Paulus Jovius calls him Aucuthus, others Giovanni della Guglia, or Agughia, John of the Needle; Aucud, Agudo, Kauchovod, and more correctly Falcone di Bosco. See a description and etching of the monument of Bernabò Visconti at Milan, 24 March, 1814, by T. Kerrich, Archæologia The Lords of Milan were the first Princes of Europe who maintained a standing army. Ibid. from Villani, in 1346.

Robert, was elected Emperor, the 21st of August, 1400, and was crowned at Cologne, the 6th of January, 1401, upon a capitulation of certain articles: and, amongst others, that he should re-establish the imperial domain in Italy.

In consequence of this engagement, and of the invitation of the Florentines, and some other Italian states, who were alarmed at the power and conquests of Galeazzo, the new Emperor, after having settled his affairs in Germany, assembled an army of fifteen thousand horse, and with the Duke of Austria, passed the Alps, in October, 1401, and approached the frontiers of Lombardy where he received an hundred thousand florins from the Florentines, with the promise of farther assistance[m].

From Trent, he summoned the Duke of Milan to surrender all the countries of which he had usurped the sovereignty, and threatened him, in case of disobedience, with his vengeance, and the ban of the empire. Giovanni Galeazzo returned a haughty reply, "That he possessed his dutchy in "virtue of a solemn concession by the legitimate sovereign, that he had "been invested conformably to the laws and ancient customs, that it did "not belong to Robert, a base usurper of the throne, the declared enemy "of their common sovereign, to trouble him in the possession of property, "so justly acquired and that he would repel force by force if he attempted "to make an hostile attack[n]."

Galeazzo was prepared to resist this formidable confederacy. He had already reduced to his dominion most of the northern part of Italy His army was commanded by the great constable Count Alberico Balbiano, who had been Grand Seneschal of the kingdom of Apulia, and some years before, in 1394, had entered into his service with an hundred lances. Under him the principal commanders were Facino Cane, and Otto Terzo. All the troops from every quarter which could be procured were engaged in his pay, and they amounted to four thousand lances, most of them select and experienced warriors[o] The arrival of the English was very seasonable, they readily engaged in the Duke's service, and amongst others, Carrington, Atwick, Newborough, Fitzwilliams, and le Blount, are particularly specified[p].

The first object of the Emperor was to endeavour to seize Brescia, as

[m] Corio, page 661 edition of 1565 [n] Corio—Pfeffel, Abrege [o] Corio

[p] MS ut supra

the possession of that place would facilitate the entrance of his armies from Germany. But that city being well provided with the means of defence, he could make no impression upon it Whilst he was engaged in this attempt, the principal part of his army, upon its march towards the city, was met by a select body of troops, including le Blount and his companions, which had been sent out of Brescia to attack them[q]. A desperate battle ensued. The post of greatest danger and honour was assigned to the English, they shewed themselves not unworthy of the military fame of their country; and by a furious onset on the Imperialists, broke their line, put them to flight, and contributed principally to the decisive victory which was obtained[r] The Emperor lost six hundred horse, the Grand Marshal of the Imperial army, and many other noble persons, were taken prisoners, and the remainder of the army escaped with difficulty from total destruction. The Emperor fled to Trent, his army was dispersed, and after some ineffectual attempts to retrieve his affairs, he was compelled to renounce all his designs upon Italy, and to return to Germany[s].

In this battle, Carrington and Newborough were however taken prisoners, and a large sum was paid for their ransom to a relation of the Bishop of Cologne. Galeazzo acknowledged with gratitude the merits and services of the English, and the splendid rewards which he bestowed upon them were worthy of the magnificent house of Visconti[t].

The Duke of Milan, by this important victory, being now secure in his dominions, and freed from all apprehensions from the Emperor, and the Italian states, proceeded to extend his conquests on every side. He had made himself master of many of the neighbouring states, had taken Bologna, and almost reduced Florence; and he had even prepared the ornaments of royalty for the purpose of being immediately crowned King of Italy, when he was seized with a violent fever, which put an end to his life and his projects, on the 3d of September, in the year 1402[u].

Galeazzo was a Prince of a superior understanding, great prudence, and humanity, and had received an extraordinary education under the most learned men of the age, in every department of science, and particularly in all the arts which are useful to a sovereign. But his ambition was equal to his talents, his magnificence and liberality were unbounded, and he wished

[q] Corio [r] MS [s] Corio Pfeffel [t] MS. [u] Corio. Pfeffel

to extend his fame throughout the universe[x] By his will, his dominions, which comprehended the finest parts of Italy, were divided amongst his three sons, who were all minors, and he left besides immense treasures, out of which he directed a monastery, several churches, and chapels to be erected, with suitable endowments[y]. To his eldest son, Giovanni Maria Inglese Visconti, who was only fourteen years old, he bequeathed the Dutchy of Milan, and some other places; to his second son, Philip Maria Anglo, Pavia; and to his legitimated son, Gabriel Anglo, Pisa, but the power of the Visconti family was much diminished by this partition of his dominions. The care of his children, and the administration of affairs, was intrusted to a council of seventeen persons The government was distracted by intrigues, and by factions struggling for power. The country became one promiscuous scene of murders, robberies, and violence: and the subject states asserted their independence[z]. The services of the English were no longer required, and they were ill treated by the Great Constable Alberico Balbiano[a], who, ungrateful for the benefits conferred upon him by the deceased Duke, basely deserted to the party of the Pope and the Florentines[b].

In this unhappy situation of affairs, the English, who had continued in Milan in the enjoyment of their wealth, and well-earned reputation, in 1404 resolved to leave Italy, and to return to England. They proceeded through France and Flanders. At Besançon Robert Newborough died, in consequence of a fall from his horse, and was buried in the Grey Friers' Church in that city, having bequeathed the greatest part of his riches, obtained in Italy, to his friend Carrington The others passed through Burgundy, traversed France, and arrived in Hainault, where they were entertained with great hospitality in the monasteries Here they met with two friers, lately arrived from England, from whom they obtained information of many particulars relating to Carrington's family, and of the state of matters in that country From Hainault they travelled through Brabant to Amsterdam. Being informed of the cruelty

[x] He began the celebrated cathedral at Milan in 1386, the finest Gothic building in Europe.

[y] Corio, pages 666, 667 [z] Ibid p 636 [a] MS [b] Corio, p 636 See a head of Giovanni Galeazzo, from a print by Agostino Caracci

which was exercised by King Henry the Fourth towards those who had taken part against him, they thought it prudent to change their names before they ventured to revisit their native land. John Carrington assumed the name of Smith, Fitzwilliams of English, and LE BLOUNT changed his name to CROKE. From Amsterdam they sailed for England, in a ship of Ipswich, near which place they landed in 1404.

During the life of King Henry the Fourth, they kept themselves in concealment, but after his death, in 1413, and they could appear in public with safety, they purchased lands, with the riches which they had acquired in Italy. Carrington, or Smith, settled in Essex, and dying in the year 1446, at the mature age of seventy-two, was buried in the church-yard of Reinshall Church, which was erected by himself.

Le Blount, or Croke, lived mostly in Buckinghamshire, at a place called Essendon. His friends, Carrington, Fitzwilliam, and the rest of his former companions in arms, frequently visited him, and they talked over their old exploits with mirth and pleasure.

The history of these transactions is contained in a curious original document, still preserved in the Croke family, and which is entitled, "*An* "*account how the Blounts in Warwickshire changed their name to* "*Croke*," and which is printed in the Appendix[c]. It is confirmed by contemporary and authentic historians.

Nicholas le Blount, or Croke, married Agnes Heynes, the daughter of John Heynes and Alicia at Hall. By the death of her brother, John Heynes, without issue, she inherited her father's property, and from this intermarriage the Crokes have ever since quartered the coat of arms of Heynes; argent, a fesse nebulè, azure, interspersed with besants, between three annulets, gules.

Alicia was the daughter of Walter at Hall, by Johanna, the daughter of Fulk Rycot. Alicia had a sister Johanna who married Henry Bruer. In the Rycot, and Bruer families, we meet with intermarriages with Senton, Frenshe, and Langfled. What the estates were which were thus acquired from the Heynes, or the at Hall families, or both, I have not been able clearly to discover, but in the manuscript from whence this account is

[c] No XX There was a Henry Croke with Henry the Fifth at the battle of Agincourt, in 1415. List of the Knights at that battle in Ashmole's MSS. No. 825, part 5.

taken, upon the pedigree, the names of Appulton, Kemington, Northempsey, Lyford, and Botely, all in the county of Berks, are written. From hence it must be inferred, that the property of the family was situated in those places[d].

The son of Nicholas le Blount, and Agnes Heynes, was JAMES CROKE, OR LE BLOUNT. His name is omitted in the "Dessenz," but it appears in the vellum pedigree, and in another pedigree in the Manuscript of Rawlinson

The son and heir of James was RICHARD CROKE, who married a lady named Alicia, but of what family is not related, by whom he had a son named JOHN CROKE, OTHERWISE LE BLOUNT, who will be the subject of the next chapter[e].

[d] Dessenz of Noble Noblemen Harl MSS No 1074 Art 39 f 55 printed in Genealogy, No 21.

[e] There was a Richard Croke, who was Nottyngham Pursuivant at Arms, and died in the twenty-second year of Henry the Seventh or Eighth, 1506, or 1530 Rex omnibus &c concessimus dilecto subdito nostro Thomæ Trcheron officium Persevanti, vulgariter Notyngham appellati—per mortem Richardi Croke, 30 Ap An Reg XXII Kennet in Bliss's Wood's Ath. Ox vol. i. p 259, note Weever mentions a Richard Crooke who was Windsor Herald in the reign of Henry the Eighth. Fun Mon p 676.

For this first part of the Croke family there are four documents 1 The account of the change of name, a manuscript printed in the Appendix No XX 2 A pedigree on vellum, beautifully illuminated, which begins with James Croke alias le Blountz, and ends with the children of William Croke, perhaps about the year 1670, penes me. 3 A pedigree in the Harleian Manuscript, No 1074, drawn up apparently in the reign of Henry the Eighth, which is here printed, Genealogy No. 21. 4 A pedigree in Rawlinson's Manuscript in the Bodleian Library, No B 74 p 131 There are some variations, and differences between them, which will appear in the following comparative view From the whole I have extracted what appeared the most probable account, upon comparing dates, times, and circumstances

1 *Account of change of name*	2 *Vellum Pedigree.*	3 *Dessenz Pedigree*	4 *Rawlinson's Pedigree.*
Thomas le Blount, Knight, of Warwickshire, temp Ed I	Jacobus Croke, alias les Blounts	Nicholas le Blount, alias Croke, married Agnes Heynes	Nicholas le Blount, Knight of Warwickshire, 35 Edw III
Nicholas le Blount, 35 Edw. III	Richardus Croke, married Alicia	Richardus Croke	James Blount
Nicholas le Blount, temp. Rich II	John Croke, married Prudentia Cave	John Croke, married Cave	Richard Blount
			John Croke, md Prudentia Cave.

No. 21.

THE GENEALOGY IN THE OLD MANUSCRIPT, INTITLED, "DESSENZ OF NOBLE NOBLEMEN."

Harl No. 1074. *Art.* 39. *fol.* 55, 56

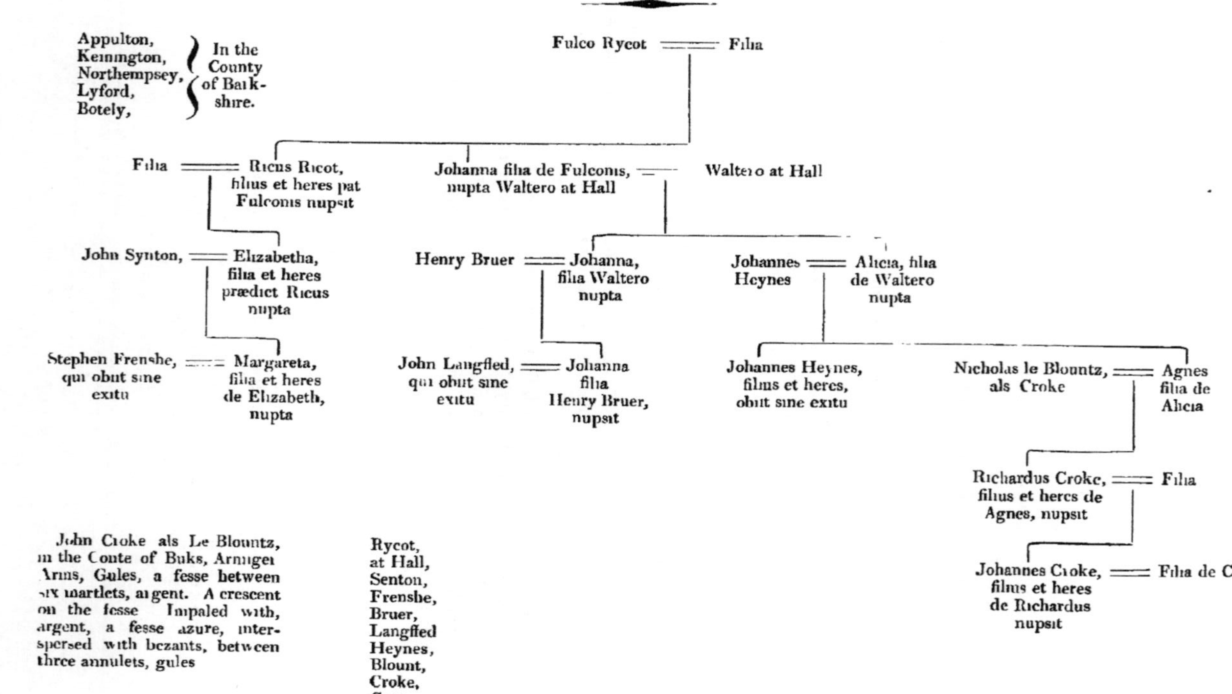

As there is a very ancient document of about this period, which contains the coats of arms of some of the le Blount family, this may be a proper time for considering their different bearings more particularly.

We have seen that three different coats of arms were borne by le Blount in the earliest times Lozengy, or and sable, by the Barons of Ixworth Barry nebuly, or and sable, and gules, a fesse between six martlets, argent, by the descendants of the first Sir William le Blount And there can be no doubt but that all the branches of the le Blount family are equally entitled to each of those arms, being lineally descended from those who bore them. Yet the lozengy arms have been laid aside since the extinction of the Barons of Ixworth[f]. And though at this day the Blounts generally use the nebuly arms only, and the Croke family the martlets; they were formerly borne promiscuously by all branches of the family. Thus in the Sodington branch, Peter le Blount used both coats, his brother Sir Walter le Blount of Rock had for his seal the nebuly arms, Sir William le Blount, son of Sir Walter, sealed first with the martlet arms, and afterwards with the nebuly arms[g]. They both were found in painted glass in the window of the chapel of the Blount family, in Mamble church[h]. And the martlets are introduced as the second quarter in the coat of Blount of Sodington in the Heralds' Visitation in 1634[i].

In a Manuscript in the Harleian Collection are the arms emblazoned of the knights of the several counties of England, in the time of Edward the First. Under the head of Warwickshire we find enrolled, "Sir William le Blountz," with his arms described, "unde of 6, or and sable." Sir Thomas le Blount with, "gules a fes entre 6 martlets argent[k]." The same Catalogue was published from other manuscripts by Rowe Mores, at Oxford, in 1749, under the title of Nomina et Historia Gentilitia Nobilium Equitumque sub Edwardo primo Rege militantium, in a small quarto in black letter[l]. He supposes the catalogue was written between

[f] They are introduced in the arms of Mountjoy Blount, Earl of Newport, in Mr Wm Blount's old parchment, but as they are the fifteenth quarter, and not stated to be Blount, I imagine they must be the arms of some other family

[g] See their seals post, p 125, 127, 130

[h] Nash's Worcestershire, vol. ii p. 157. Habington's MSS in Bib Societ Antiq

[i] In Coll. Arm c 30. [k] Harl. MSS. No. 1068 fol. 71.

[l] It was printed from R Dodsworth's MSS vol. 21 and Robert Glover's "Copies of Olde Rolls of Arms," in Queen's College library Mores printed only a few copies.

the fifteenth and nineteenth years of Edward the Second, 1321, and 1325, because Edmund of Woodstock, as Earl of Kent, and Hugh le Despenser, are mentioned; of whom the first was created Earl of Kent in 1321, the latter beheaded in 1325. Mores speaks in warm terms of this book, and says that it is, without a rival, the most ancient heraldic document existing. In this copy the names and arms are thus recited; Warwickshire, "Sir William le Blount, oundee de or et de sable. Sir Thomas le Blount de goules, a une fesse e vi merclos de argent." In the arms of the tilters at the tournament at Dunstable, in the second year of Edward the Second, 1308, in "le comte de Warwick" are Sir William le Blond, with the nebuly arms, and Sir Thomas le Blond, with the martlets[m]. These were probably Sir William, the son of Sir Walter le Blount, of Rock, who married Margaret de Verdun, and Sir Thomas le Blount who was the husband of Juliana de Leybourne. They are styled knights of Warwickshire, though the principal seat of one was at Rock or Sodington, in Worcestershire, and of the other at Belton, in Rutlandshire, because they were tenants of the Earl of Warwick, and therefore fought under his banner[n].

Yet this Sir William le Blount used seals both of the nebuly and martlet arms, as is already mentioned. Sir Thomas le Blount to the deed before recited has affixed a seal with the nebuly arms: and his eldest son used the nebuly arms likewise. It should seem therefore, that though, in their seals and private legal transactions, they used either coat, in war and tournaments, when from their being clothed in armour distinctions were necessary and usual, Sir William confined himself to the nebuly coat, and Sir Thomas to the martlets. Hence in the Croke Manuscript it is said, that Sir Thomas le Blount bore for his arms gules, a fesse between six martlets, argent, and that from him they have been derived to the Croke family, who are descended from his second son Nicholas, and have always borne those arms. And being so descended from a second son, in early times they bore a crescent

[m] Harl MSS. No 1068. So in Edward the Fourth's time. Ibid fol 115b. Dodsw vol 35 f 78. Ces sont les noms et les arms bannerets de Engleterre, arms as before Edw II.

[n] Hampton Lovet, Timberlake, and other manors belonging to the family, were held of the Earl of Warwick.

upon the martlet arms. The oldest emblazonment which I have met with is in the "Dessenz of Noble Noblemen," which was written early in the reign of Henry the Eighth. It commences with the second Nicholas le Blount, alias Croke, the grandson of Sir Thomas le Blount, and has the martlet arms with a crescent on the fesse[o]. The crescent is found likewise in the arms of John Croke, who married Prudentia Cave, the great grandson of Nicholas, and died in 1554, in brass upon his monument at Chilton, and in stone over the porch at Studley Priory In that of his eldest son Sir John Croke, in the same places, in a painted glass window at Studley Priory, and on a seal ring on his finger in his portrait[p]. The crescent was borne likewise by his eldest son Sir John Croke the Judge, and after this it was discontinued. The nebuly arms seem to have been continued in the elder branch of the Belton family.

[o] Harl MS. No 1074 Art 39. fol 55, 56 In this book in the genealogy of the King's of England, fol 172 6 Henry VIII. is the last, and Henry Prince of Wales is there. As he was born Jan. 1, 1509, and died Feb 22, old style, the book must have been written in 1510. The Lady Mary is in another hand and ink. It has the name of Henry Lilly, Rouge Dragon, written in it. Genealogy, No. 21.

[p] Penes me

CHAPTER II.

JOHN CROKE, ALIAS LE BLOUNT, ESQUIRE.—DIGRESSION, THE HISTORY OF THE PRIORY OF STUDLEY, ITS POSSESSORS, FOUNDERS, AND BENEFACTORS.—RICHARD CROKE, DOCTOR IN DIVINITY.

John Croke, or le Blount, Esquire, and Prudentia Cave.

THE year of the birth of JOHN CROKE, ALIAS LE BLOUNT, Esquire, the son of Richard and Alicia Croke, alias le Blount, does not appear. From his subsequent promotion it is evident that he must have been educated in the profession of the law. Of his early life, and the gradual steps of his advancement, no memorials have been preserved. We first find him, in the year 1522, one of the Six Clerks in the High Court of Chancery.

As the Chancellor had been almost always an ecclesiastic, these officers were anciently actual *cleri*, or in holy orders, and were regularly promoted to livings under the Chancellor's patronage. They were originally six in number: in the early part of the reign of Richard the Second, they were reduced to three; and by an ordinance in Chancery, of the twelfth year of that king, they were again restored to their first number. As clergymen they were incapable of marrying, and even when they ceased to be in orders, the ancient custom of their celibacy still continued; a restraint which was confirmed by the same ordinance, and was observed till the reign of Henry the Eighth[a]. In the fourteenth year of that monarch, 1522, a petition was presented to Parliament by John Trevethen, Richard

[a] Ordinatum est quod idem Custos Rotulorum jam habeat sex clericos, et non plures, scribentes in rotulis prædictis, ex causa supradicta, proviso quod nullus eorundem clericorum sic scribentium sit uxoratus Hargrave's Manuscripts, in the British Museum, No 221. page 22, entitled, " The Antiquitie of the Six Clerks."

Welles, Oliver Leader, John Croke, William Jesson, and John Lemsey, who then filled the office, and which was to this effect

"In most humble wise beseechen your highness, your true and faithful "subjects, and daily servants, the six clerks of your high court of Chan- "cery, that whereas of old time accustomed hath been used in the said "court, that all manner of clerks and ministers writing to the Great Seal, "should be unmarried, (except only the Clerk of the Crown,) so that as "well the Cursitors, and other Clerks, as the Six Clerks of the said Chan- "cery, were by the same custom restrained from marriage, whereby all "those that contrary to the same did marry, were no longer suffered to "write in the said Chancery, not only to their great hindrance, losing "thereby the benefit of their long study, and tedious labours and pains in "youth taken in the said court, but also to the great decay of the true "course of the said court. And forasmuch as now the said custom taketh "no place nor usage, but only in the office of the said six clerks, but that "it is permitted and suffered for maintenance of the said course, that as "well the said Cursitors, as the other clerks aforesaid, may and do take "wives, and marry at their liberty, after the laws of holy Church, and of "long time have so done without interruption or let of any person It "may therefore please your highness of your most abundant grace, with "the assent of the Lords Spiritual and Temporal, and the Commons in "this present parliament assembled, to ordain, enact, and establish, that "the said six clerks, and all others which in time to come shall be in the "same office, may and do take wives and marry at their liberty, after the "law of holy Church, and so married may hold their said office as they "should do before the said espousals" The petition was favourably received, and passed into a statute[b].

In the year 1529, when Sir Thomas More was appointed Lord Chancellor, he was at the head of the department[c]. That good and able man, upon coming into his office, found the Court of Chancery filled with many tedious causes, some of which had hung there for almost twenty years. To prevent the recurrence of these proceedings, which were so oppressive to parties, he endeavoured to apply a remedy, which was conformable to the manners of the times, and the character

[b] Stat. 14 and 15 Hen. VIII cap 8. 1522 3   [c] Spelman, Series Cancell. Gloss. in voce

of the Chancellor. He first caused Mr. Croke, the chief of the Six Clerks, to make a Docket, containing the whole number of all injunctions, which in his time had already past, or were depending, in any of the King's Courts at Westminster Then having invited all the Judges to dinner, in the presence of them all, he shewed sufficient reason why he had made so many injunctions. And they all confessed that they themselves in the like case would have done no less. He then assured them, "that if they themselves, to whom the reformation of the rigour of the law "appertained, would upon reasonable considerations in their own discre- "tion, as he thought in conscience they were bound, mitigate and reform "the rigour of the law, there should then from him no injunctions be "granted." To this offer they refused to condescend. "Then," said he, "for as much as yourselves, my Lords, drive me to this necessity, you "cannot hereafter blame me, if I seek to relieve the poor people's injuries." After this he said to his son Roper secretly, "I perceive, son, why they "like not this, for they think that they may by a verdict of a jury cast "off all scruple from themselves upon the poor jury, which they account "the chief defence. Wherefore I am constrained to abide the adventure "of this blame[d]."

Mr. Croke availed himself of the privilege of marrying granted to the Six Clerks. As his eldest son was born in 1530, his marriage must have taken place at least the year before. His lady was Prudentia, the third daughter of Richard Cave, Esquire, of Stanford-upon-Avon, in Northamptonshire, by his second wife Margaret, daughter of John Saxby, of Northamptonshire. This was an ancient family, descended from two brothers, Wyamarus and Jordayne, who were living at the time of the Conquest, and enjoyed several lordships in Yorkshire; from one of which, North and South Cave, they derived their surname, de Cave. She was sister to Sir Thomas Cave; and to Sir Ambrose Cave, who was Chancellor of the Dutchy of Lancaster, one of the Privy Council to Queen Elizabeth, and a most intimate friend of the Lord Treasurer Burleigh. It is related, that at a public ball at court her Majesty's garter slipped off as she was dancing. Sir Ambrose, taking it up, offered it to her, but, upon her refusing it, he tied it on his left arm, and declared that he would wear it for his mistress's

[d] Thomas More's Life of Sir Thomas More, page 218

sake as long as he lived. In the possession of the family is an original picture of him with the garter round his arm. Her nephew, Roger Cave, married Margaret daughter of Richard Cecil, and sister to William Cecil Lord Burleigh, the Lord High Treasurer to Queen Elizabeth[e]. One of their posterity, Sir Thomas Cave, was advanced to the dignity of a baronet in the year 1641: an honour which is still enjoyed by his descendants. The sufferings for the royal cause, in the reign of Charles the First, of the Reverend John Cave, Rector of Pickwell, are minutely related by Walker, in his history of the sufferings of the clergy, and afford a striking but not uncommon example of petty democratic tyranny[f]. His son was the learned Doctor William Cave, Canon of Windsor, and Chaplain to King Charles the Second, who wrote the *Scriptorum Ecclesiasticorum Historia Literaria*, the Lives of the Fathers, Primitive Christianity, and other works which still maintain their rank amongst the ecclesiastical historians of Great Britain[g].

On the 19th of September, 1529, the twentieth year of Henry the Eighth, he was appointed by patent Comptroller, and Supervisor of the Hanaper in Chancery, for his life[h]. On the 11th of June, 1534, the twenty-sixth of Henry VIII. the King granted to him the office of Clerk of the Inrollments in the Chancery for his life[i]. And in 1545, the thirty-seventh of that King, on the 6th of March, with Sir Anthony Lee, he had a grant of the manor of Senclers, and the Rectory of Stone, in Buckinghamshire[k]. In the first year of Edward the Sixth, 1546, six Serjeants at Law were made, and amongst them appears the name of "*Mr. Croke of the Inner Temple*." A full account of

[e] In Ashmole's MSS vol 836 fol iii is an original letter from Roger Cave's executors to the Lord Treasurer Burleigh, dated 2d of August, 1586, about his will and funeral.

[f] Page 220.

[g] Collins's Baronetage, vol. ii p. 164 and a Pedigree, Harl MSS No 1233 fol. 114 from Wymer and Jordanus Cave, to Sir Thomas Cave, the first baronet, in 1627. Printed in Genealogy, No. 22. but I have omitted the coats of arms.

[h] Warton in his Life of Pope, page 6, is mistaken in attributing this and other grants in the same reign to *Richard* Croke. I have examined the records, Rex Johanni Croke uni sex cler cancell concessit Officium Contrarotulatoris et Supervisoris Hanaperii ad vitam.

[i] Patent Rolls, 26 Hen. VIII 11th Jan Rex Johanni Croke concessit officium Clerici Irrotulamentorum omnium et singularum evidentiarum indenturarum, &c inter recorda Cancellariæ irrotulandarum, ad vitam.

[k] Patent Rolls, in anno

No. 22

NEALOGY OF CAVE

Maud, daughter to Peter de Mawle
Lord of Lockington

Anne, daughter to Sir Symon Ward

Alice, dau to Sir Geffrey Hotham

Mary, daughter and heir to Sir
Genill, of South Cliffe

Catherine, daughter to Roger Some
of Grindall

Anne, married to
Gilbert Stapleton,
of Bayton

Wimarus de Cave,
who gave all his lands in North Cave and South Cave to his brother Jordan Sans issue Temp Will Conq and Will Rufus

Jordan de Cave,
younger brother of Wimarus de Cave.

Brian de Cave, son and heir of Jordan Cave

Robert de Cave, married the da of Thos de Metham

Thomas Cave, son and heir of Brian, mar[d]. Joyce, da. of Sir William St Quintin.

Geffry Cave, son and heir of Thomas, married Mable Saltmarsh

Thomas, second son
John, third son
Piers, fourth son.

ne, married to
n Markenfield.

Alexander Cave,
Dean of Durham, and Prebendary of Holden, where he lyeth buried,

Peter Cave,
son and heir of Geffry,
Lord of South Cave,

the feast given upon the occasion is preserved by Dugdale. This perhaps was John Croke[l]. In the year 1547, the second of Edward the Sixth, he was elected Member of Parliament for Chippenham[m].

Afterwards being in much favour with King Edward the Sixth, in Michaelmas Term 1549, the third year of his reign, he was by him made one of the Masters of the Chancery[n].

There is still extant in manuscript a paper, in the nature of a report, upon the constitution of the Court of Chancery, drawn up by Master Croke, in 1554, the second year of Queen Mary, when Stephen Gardiner, Bishop of Winchester, was Lord Chancellor[o]. It is intitled, "Ordinances "explained by Master Croke, upon the estate of the Chancerye Courte in "Anno 1554" With the knowledge and accuracy of an ancient practitioner, he has stated minutely the different officers who compose the court, with an enumeration of their respective duties and privileges. The greater part of these regulations, I apprehend, are still the law of the court, but he mentions several customs, which savour of the simplicity of the good old times, and have been long abolished in modern practice. The Lord Chancellor, he states, had his diet out of the Hanaper, towards such charges as he was wont to be at. Of which some were then out of use, as to have, in the term time, such Masters of the Chancery as would come to his house to be at his table, and a Chancery table in his hall for the Clerks. Many of his officers always travelled with the Chancellor, and were allowed for horse-keepers and horse-meat: and there were three or four Clerks of the Almoner at meat and drink in the Chancellor's house, who, for their diet, served the poor suitors with their pens, without fees.

This Report will enable us to clear up a point of ecclesiastical history

[l] Dugd Or. Jur page 117 [m] Willis, Notitia Parliamentaria

[n] Croke Car Preface The time of his appointment appears by the following notes In a list of the Six Clerks in the first of Edward the Sixth, 1547, Croke appears at the head; Croke, Carter, Snow, Leder, Judd, Walrond In that for the third of Edward the Sixth, 1549, his name is omitted, and they stand thus, Carter, Snowe, Leder, Judd, Walrond, Powle (Lansdown MSS vol 163 fol 151) And in another manuscript, (Lansdown, vol 163, fol 84) there is "a noat of the Six Clarks, and when they succeeded.' Amongst these is, "Crooke departed Michaelmas 3d Edw. VI succeeded by Powle."

[o] Hargrave's MSS. British Museum, No. 249, f. 80 Lansdown MSS No 163 f 141 There is said to be another copy amongst the manuscripts of Lord Somers. It is printed in the Appendix, No. XXII

Alexander C[illegible] = Alice [illegible] to Sir Geffrey Hotha
1 [illegible]

Sir John Cave = Mary [illegible] heir to Sir Peter [illegible] of South Cliffe

Mary [illegible] — Sir Alexander = Catherine daughter to Roger Somervill of Crondall — Thomas second son; John third son; Piers fourth son

Sir Alexander = Constance daugh. to Roger Leeds, of Wintringham

Piers 2d son — Anne, daugh. to Ralf Engleby

John 3d son

Grace

Anne married to Gilbert Stapleton of Rayto

Catherine married to Sir John Markenfeld

Sir Alexander Lound Lord of Loundhall and Cave — Maud da. and heir

Robert Sheffield, of Butterwick of whom descended the Lord Sheffield and the Duke of Buckingham — Jennet da. and heir of Lound

[illegible] Cave eldest son of Pier = Mary daugh. to Burdett of Rodwell

John 3d son Abbot of Selby

Alexander 3d son of Piers

Thomas Cave [illegible] 1495 — The daughter of Passemer als. Cassemer of the county of Essex

the [illegible] of Harrington

Henry Cave 2d son — The daugh. of Belgrave of Bisby Com Leicest.

Elizabeth daugh. of Marrow of Church Lawford Com Warwick, first wife = Richard Cave ob. Aug. 2d, 1538. = Margaret daugh. of John Saxby Com Northampton 2 wife

John

Thomas — William mar^d a P[illegible]

1 William [illegible]
2 Christopher mar^d a C[illegible] at Stamford
3 Bartholomew mar^d a Wakley
4 Edward mar^d a knight live at Welford

Christopher — A dau. mar^d to Noble of Stamford — William Noble, Richard Noble, Justinian Noble

William — 1 John, 2 Peter

Marshall of Car[illegible] Com Nott.

Anne da. [illegible]

Margaret mar. Thomas Saunders of Harrington

Edward = Dorothy da. and coh. of Nichola Mallory Com Warwick

Sir Edward [illegible] Lord Chief Baron of the Exchequer mar^d the daughter of [illegible]

2 Lawrence Saunders, burnt at Coventry for the Gospel
3 [illegible] Saunders, [illegible] at Newbury
4 Robert Saunders married Margery Stanton Com. Leicest.
5 Blase Saunders married daughter of [illegible] Com Bucks
1 Daughter to [illegible] of Heathorp
2 Daughter to Smith of Com Warwick
3 Daughter to [illegible]

A daughter mar^d to Morgan of Com Northampton

[illegible] married Sir Thos. Andrew

1 Thomas that mar^d a Cotton of Cambridgeshire
2 Anthony Andrews
3 Son
4 Son

Margaret married to Thos. Boughton Com Warwick

Edward Boughton father to the Countess of Devonshire

1 [illegible] to William Wolley Com Staff
2 Dorothy to Smith als Harris Vide A
3 Prudence to Jo. Crook als Blunt Vide B
4 Bridget to Francis Tanfield Vide C

Sir Thomas Cave first son died 1534 = Elizabeth da. and coh. of Sir John Danvers of Waterstock

Anthony 2d son = Elizabeth [illegible] to Lovett

Clement 3d son mar^d a da. of Mallory ob. s.p.

Francis [illegible] son of Baggrave Doct. Juris Civilis — Margaret da. of Thos. [illegible] Com Sur LL.D.

Sir Ambrose Chancellor of the Dutchy of Lancaster and of the Privy Council to Qu. Elizabeth d. 1568 = Margaret eldest da. and coh. of William Willington

Margaret da. and heir mar^d to Henry eldest son of Sir Francis Knowles

Richard of Pickwell. = Barbary da. of Sir William Fielding

Brian. =

Edward, first son = Barbara d. and coh. of Sir W. Devereux

Richard [illegible] = [illegible] of Sir [illegible] Montague

Anne ob. infans

Roger 2d son d. 1586 — Margaret da. of Richard and sister to William Cecil Lord Burleigh Lord Treasurer [illegible] [illegible] husband [illegible] of [illegible]

Judith to Wm. Chester of London

Anne to [illegible] Hampden

Mary to John Nalgate

Mary to Sir Jerome Weston

Edward eldest son of Sir Thos. Cave of Waterstock

Elizabeth da. to Sir J. Conway

1 Anne to John Hunt.
2 Margaret [illegible] secondly to Dancet
3 Elizabeth to Sir [illegible] Stafford
4 Margaret to Sir Wm. Mexting
5 Mary to William [illegible]
Susan to John Bowes

Da. of Lolt, first wife = Sir Thomas — Da. of Lacy 2d wife

Anthony [illegible] mar^d Frances Dupont

3 Brian
4 Henry
5 ——
6 William

1 Margaret to [illegible] Babington
2 Dorothy to John Bernard

Sir Alexander = Daugh. of Sir John Brockett.

Sir Thomas first son ob. s.p.

Two younger children

Frances [illegible] mar^d [illegible]

Thomas

3 [illegible] mar. Thos. [illegible] of Walpole
5 Dorothy ob. 1603 married Arthur Evans
6 Isabel 1 to Chappendale of Humberstone 2 to John [illegible] and to Cleyney of [illegible]

John = Eleanor d. to Thomas [illegible] Com Staff

William mar^d da. of [illegible] of Osgodby

John third son Rector of Pickwell

William Cave D.D.

Alexander 2d son [illegible]

William first son of [illegible]

Sir W[illegible] Cave

1 Elizabeth mar. Walter Bagot
2 Margaret mar. Sir W. Skipwith
3 [illegible]
4 Dorothy to W. Hart

Sir Thomas Cave [illegible] = Eleanor sister to Sir [illegible] St. John [illegible] Markham of Cotham

[illegible] Cave = D[illegible] heir of Anthony Bennett

John [illegible] Dupont

Richard died in Italy sans 1606

Abigail 1 to Hen. Tresham 2 to the Lord Sherrard, of Stapleford

Anne to William Tufton of Essex

1 Bennet Lord Sherrard
2 Philip
3 George
4 Francis
5 William
6 Henry
John

Abigail
Anne
Emelin
Elizabeth

Penelope da. of Lord Wenman

Lucy died young

Dorothy married Sir Rowland Berkley

Ambrose [illegible]

[illegible] married

Mary married Sir Orland Bridgeman

A
Smith, als Harris of Leicestershire = Dorothy Cave
Robert — Francis — George. — Clement — William, drowned — Anthony — Ers[illegible]

B
John Crook als Blunt = Prudence Cave
John = The da. of Sir Ale[illegible]
John and other children

C
Francis Tanfield = Bridgett Cave
A daugh. to [illegible]
A daugh. to [illegible]
A daugh. to Barthol. Tate
Clement 2d son = Daughter of the Lord Mordant

[illegible] Jordan. [illegible] W. the Conq. and W. Rufus

Brian de Cave son and heir of Jordan Cave.

Robert de Cave married the da. of Thos. de Met[illegible]

Thomas Cave son and heir of Brian mar^d Joyce [illegible] of Sir William St. Quentin

[illegible] Cave son and heir of Thomas married M[illegible] Saltmarsh

Alexander Cave Dean of Durham and Prebendary of Holden where he lies buried [illegible] his nephew his heir

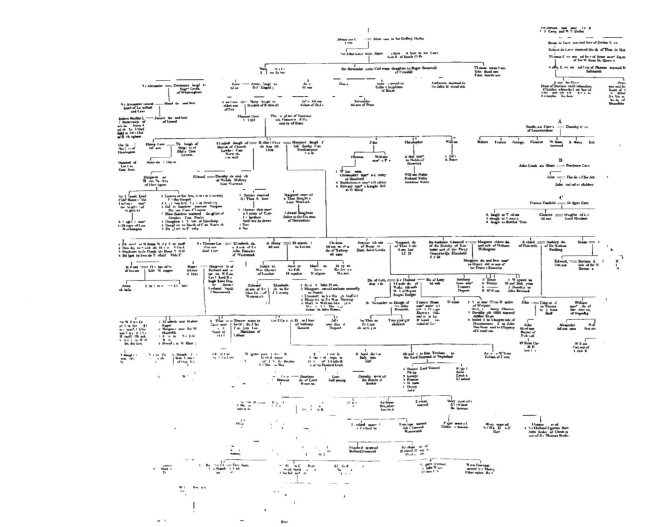

Peter [illegible] son and heir Lord of [illegible] Sir Alex[illegible] the da. of Bramflete

the feast given upon the occasion is preserved by Dugdale. This perhaps was John Croke[l]. In the year 1547, the second of Edward the Sixth, he was elected Member of Parliament for Chippenham[m].

Afterwards being in much favour with King Edward the Sixth, in Michaelmas Term 1549, the third year of his reign, he was by him made one of the Masters of the Chancery[n].

There is still extant in manuscript a paper, in the nature of a report, upon the constitution of the Court of Chancery, drawn up by Master Croke, in 1554, the second year of Queen Mary, when Stephen Gardiner, Bishop of Winchester, was Lord Chancellor[o]. It is intitled, "Ordinances "explained by Master Croke, upon the estate of the Chanceryе Courte in "Anno 1554." With the knowledge and accuracy of an ancient practitioner, he has stated minutely the different officers who compose the court, with an enumeration of their respective duties and privileges. The greater part of these regulations, I apprehend, are still the law of the court, but he mentions several customs, which savour of the simplicity of the good old times, and have been long abolished in modern practice. The Lord Chancellor, he states, had his diet out of the Hanaper, towards such charges as he was wont to be at. Of which some were then out of use, as to have, in the term time, such Masters of the Chancery as would come to his house to be at his table, and a Chancery table in his hall for the Clerks. Many of his officers always travelled with the Chancellor, and were allowed for horse-keepers and horse-meat: and there were three or four Clerks of the Almoner at meat and drink in the Chancellor's house, who, for their diet, served the poor suitors with their pens, without fees.

This Report will enable us to clear up a point of ecclesiastical history

[l] Dugd. Or. Jur. page 117. [m] Willis, Notitia Parliamentaria

[n] Croke Car Preface The time of his appointment appears by the following notes In a list of the Six Clerks in the first of Edward the Sixth, 1547, Croke appears at the head; Croke, Carter, Snow, Leder, Judd, Walrond In that for the third of Edward the Sixth, 1549, his name is omitted, and they stand thus; Carter, Snowe, Leder, Judd, Walrond, Powle. (Lansdown MSS vol. 163. fol 151) And in another manuscript, (Lansdown, vol. 163, fol 84) there is "a noat of the Six Clarks, and when they succeeded" Amongst these is, "Crooke departed Michaelmas 3d Edw. VI succeeded by Powle."

[o] Hargrave's MSS British Museum, No. 249, f 80 Lansdown MSS No 163. f. 141. There is said to be another copy amongst the manuscripts of Lord Somers. It is printed in the Appendix, No. XXII

hitherto left in uncertainty. The Lord Chancellor, as is well known, has a right to present to all benefices appertaining to the King, under a certain value. The reason and origin of this privilege appear upon the rolls of Parliament, in the reign of Edward the Third; that it had been immemorially granted by former Kings, to enable the Chancellors to provide for the Clerks of the Chancery, who were always in orders[p]. But then, and long subsequently, this patronage comprehended only benefices of *twenty marks* or under. The limitation has long since been extended to *twenty pounds*, for which no law or original authority is to be found, nor is the exact time known. Bishop Gibson, upon the authority of Hobart[q], supposes that the enlargement was *probably* made about the time of the new valuation taken in the reign of Henry the Eighth. So Professor Christian, in his notes upon Blackstone's Commentaries[r], says, "It does not appear "how this enlarged patronage has been obtained, but it is probable by a "private grant of the crown, from a consideration that the twenty marks "at the time of Edward the Third, was equivalent to twenty pounds in "the time of Henry the Eighth. It cannot be doubted that *since* the "new valor beneficiorum, pounds were intended to be substituted for "marks."

By "the ordinances explained" this point is determined. The presentation to all benefices of twenty *pounds*, or under, was first usurped by Cardinal Wolsey, probably with the King's consent. As the Cardinal was disgraced in 1529, the practice must have commenced long before the new valor beneficiorum was made, which was not till the year 1534. The words of the Report are these: "The guift of benefices of the King's "patronage of the value of twentie pounds, and under, be in the distribu"tion of the Lord Chancellor. The ould rent was twentie marks, but "because the Cardinal, when he was Lord Chancellor, did present, in the "King's name, his clearkes to benefices of twentie pounds by yeare, all "Lord Chancellors have since done the like." Master Croke must have stated this from his own knowledge, as he was one of the Six Clerks during the Chancellorship of Wolsey.

Sir Thomas Pope, the founder of Trinity College in Oxford, was originally destined to the profession of the law, and his earliest preferments

[p] Rot Parl 4 Edw III. [q] Hobart 214. Gibson's Codex, p. 763. [r] Edition of Blackstone, vol iii p 48 note.

were in that department; as Clerk of the Briefs in the Star Chamber, and Clerk of the Crown in Chancery. He received his instructions in the law of that court under the tuition of Maister Croke, and he always retained a grateful affection for the instructor of his youth; which he testified by his will, dated in 1556, in which is a bequest "of his black satin gown, "faced with Luserne spots, to *his old Master's son, Master Croke*[s]."

Nicholas le Blount, we have seen, was the first who bore the name of Croke, and, by his purchase of Easington, first introduced the family into Buckinghamshire. As all his original property, which descended to him from his ancestors, must have been confiscated by Henry the Fourth, he was indebted for whatever wealth he possessed to his own merit: and the foundation of the future fortunes of the Croke family was laid in Italy, by the munificence of the Duke of Milan. By his marriage with the heiress, Agnes Heynes, he obtained the inheritance of that family, which appears to have been situated in Berkshire Maister John Croke, by his purchases in Buckinghamshire and Oxfordshire, finally established the family in those counties. He was enabled to make these acquisitions by the very lucrative situations which he held. That of one of the Six Clerks was extremely profitable, for we find that, in the reign of Charles the First, six thousand pounds were paid to the Earl of Portland for procuring a man that appointment[t].

The office of Master of the Chancery was formerly of great rank and emolument. They were appointed by patent, and created by the solemn form of putting on a cap of dignity. They were styled the companions and co-judges, and were the real and effective assessors of the Chancellor; and the King's counsel in his Chancery. In the House of Lords they attended for the purpose of advising the Lords in those branches of learning which belonged to their occupation, in the common, the civil, and the canon law. They were allowed to wear their caps there, in the presence of their sovereign, and their present seats on the woolsacks in that august assembly are the remains of their ancient dignity. Besides their fees, they had other large perquisites and privileges. They were maintained in great luxury in the Hospitium, or Hostell of the Chancery, where the principal

[s] Warton's Life of Sir Thomas Pope, pages 6 and 164.

[t] Clarendon, vol i p 101. ed 1819

officers of that court lived in a collegiate manner. The King's Purveyors supplied them with provisions, and the Butler of England with wine; of which twelve tons were allowed yearly. A stately barge was kept upon the river for their voyages from the Hostell to Westminster-hall, and corn was allowed for their horses. They were found in lodging, food, fire, and apparel. Two robes, or liveries, were annually given them by the King, and delivered by the Chancellor. The winter robes were adorned with rich furs, those intended for the warmer season were lined only with taffety[u]. In the reign of Richard the Second a complaint was exhibited against them in Parliament, "that they were over fatte, both in boddie "and purse, and over well furred in their benefices, and put the King to "verry great cost more than needed[x]."

Many of these privileges and customs indeed were abolished before the time of Master Croke, as appears by his "ordinances," and some of them were compensated in money. Their principal emoluments were still undiminished. The ordinary and stated fees were not large, but a practice prevailed of receiving voluntary douceurs, the *honoraria*, from their clients, to a great amount. This practice, which was common to most of the public officers concerned in the administration of justice, even to those who were in judicial situations, was the occasion of Lord Bacon's disgrace, who had only followed the example of his predecessors. As late as the beginning of the reign of James the First, these fees, taken by the Masters of the Chancery, were a subject of complaint in the House of Commons, and an attempt was made to regulate them by an Act of Parliament. But as they were not exacted as strict dues, but freely and voluntarily offered by clients, as a debt of gratitude for beneficial services performed, prohibitory laws were of little efficacy, and the practice continued[y].

From the fair emoluments of his profession, Maister Croke might have been enabled to become the purchaser of a considerable estate. But the dissolution of the monasteries opened a new scene of wealth to those who

[u] Pannus et furfura, and pannus et sandallus, are the words of the Rolls, for all such allowances were made by warrant on record

[x] A treatise of the Maisters of the Chauncerie, written probably between 1596 and 1603 Published by Hargrave Tracts, p 314 vol 1

[y] Stat 1 Jac I cap 10 Abuses and Remedies of Chancery, by Norbury, in Hargrave's Tracts, vol. i. p 428.

had interest enough to obtain the gift, or the purchase, of the religious houses. The necessities of the King induced him to sell, by one extensive commission, a considerable part of their possessions for his immediate relief. The great quantity of land which came to market, the few persons who could command sufficient sums of ready money to become purchasers, and the pressure of the King's wants, which required an expeditious supply, occasioned them to be sold at a rate very inferior to their real value, and great numbers of persons raised large fortunes from this fruitful source.

In the year 1529, Master Croke purchased the estate and manor of Chilton, with lands in Wootton, and Hamme, in the county of Buckingham, of Lord Zouch. Easington, where his ancestor had settled in the reign of Henry the Fourth, was in that parish, which probably lead to the purchase. In the time of Edward the Confessor, Afric Fitz Goding held Chilton, and Easington[z]. At the Conquest it was taken from him, and given to Walter Gifford, and Ciltone and Hesington were two distinct manors. Walter Gifford was cousin to William the Conqueror, Earl of Longeville in Normandy, and Earl of Buckinghamshire. He had vast possessions, and his son founded Nutley Abbey, in the parish of Long Crendon. Chilton descended to that branch of the Giffords, who had the name of Bulbec, or Bolebec, and lived at their castle at Whitchurch in Buckinghamshire. Other families had possessions at Chilton, as Paganus de Dourton, Geoffrey de Sancto Martino, Hampden, and Grenville; holding I suppose of the chief Lord of the fee. In 1468, William Lord Zouch, of Haringworth in Northamptonshire, was seized of this manor: and it continued in his family till it was purchased by Master Croke[a].

The conveyance is dated on the 10th day of May, in the twenty-first year of the reign of Henry the Eighth, 1529. The consideration paid was five hundred marks: a yearly rent is excepted of £6. 13*s*. 4*d*. payable to the wife of Sir Christopher Garnyes, Knight, and before wife of Sir John Risley, for her life It is covenanted that the premises are of the yearly

[z] Brown Willis

[a] Delafield's History of Chilton, a manuscript in the Bodleian Library, printed in Dr. Bliss's edition of Kennet's Parochial Antiquities.

value of £19. 13s 4d. above all charges, and a fine was levied to complete the title[b].

And after the suppression of the monasteries, Henry the Eighth, in the thirty-third year of his reign, 1541, for the sum of two hundred and twenty-five pounds and five shillings, sold to John Croke and Prudence his wife, the manor of Canon Court, in Chilton, lately parcel of the monastery of Nokley, lately dissolved, as amply as it was enjoyed by Richard Rigge the last Abbot. By the same letters patent, were granted an estate at Merlake, which will be hereafter mentioned, and a house, with a garden on the west side of it, in Chancellor Lane, in London, which had both belonged to the Knights of St. John of Jerusalem[c].

Upon the acquisition of this estate, Mr. Croke erected the mansion-house of Chilton, which became the principal seat of the family. It was built in the form of an H. In the middle of the front, facing the great entrance, was a porch, embattled, and covered with lead, which advanced some feet from the house, and was ascended by steps On its face, just over the outward door, this inscription in capital letters was cut into the stone, alluding to the turret, IEHOVA TURRIS MEA, "The Lord is my tower." In the windows were many coats of arms of the family, and their connexions, in painted glass. There was likewise a gallery. The old house was altered, modernized, and new fronted by Richard Carter, Esquire, the subsequent owner of the estate, in 1740[d]. But the area, and the spacious dimensions of the old house, may even now be ascertained from the two extremities of the original building, which are still subsisting, and are distinctly marked on the *north* side, by two chimneys, and a good part of the wall, which are in an ancient style, the brick work being in diamonds of two colours; and, at the *south* end, by a Gothic door-way and window. All the bedrooms are still covered with old wainscot in small pannels, some of them of an ancient pattern, like scrolls of paper. I remember a fine stone gate-way, which formed the entrance from the street, consisting of a large arch for carriages, and a smaller by the side of it. Over it were carved these sentences in capital letters. DA GLORIAM DEO. DEUS NON DESERET. "Give the glory to God. God will not forsake us." And above, in carved work, pierced through the stone, OMNIA DESUPER,

[b] Studley Chartulary, fol 22 and f. 24.

[c] The Grant in Studley Chart. fol. 17.

[d] Delafield's History of Chilton.

"All things from above." Which last sentence, probably suggested by this inscription, is written on the picture of Sir John Croke, the Judge. This gateway was pulled down by Sir John Aubrey.

Ten years after his first purchase of Chilton, in the year 1539, he bought of Henry the Eighth the Priory of Studley, with all the possessions which belonged to it, for the sum of one thousand, one hundred, and eighty-seven pounds, seven shillings, and eleven pence[e]. It appears that he sold off all the distant estates of the Priory, and retained only the house, and manors, and other rights in the parish of Beckley.

The Knights of Saint John of Jerusalem were suppressed by the Act of Parliament passed in the thirty-second year of Henry VIII 1541. In the same year, together with the manor of Canon Court, and the house in Chancery Lane before mentioned, the King sold to John Croke, and Prudence his wife, a messuage called Merlake, in the parish of Beckley, in Buckinghamshire, parcel of the late Preceptory of Sandford, in Oxfordshire, lately belonging to the Hospital of Saint John of Jerusalem, with all their other possessions, and manorial rights there: to hold *in capite* by the service of the thirtieth part of a knight's fee, rendering three shillings yearly[f]

Master Croke in London lived at a house in Fleet Street, called the Charyate, or Chariate, and which had a garden to it He purchased this house, which was already in his possession, with two others adjoining it, in the year 1541. The sellers were Richard Holte, Citizen and Merchant-Taylor, and Thomasine his wife. The premises are described as all that messuage, called the Charyate, with two messuages and a garden adjoining, in which said messuage called the Chariate he now dwelleth. The consideration was £140, of which £60 was paid at the time of purchase, and the remainder by half yearly installments. Reciprocal bonds of two hundred marks each were given for the performance of the covenants, and the next year a recovery of the estate, which was freehold, was suffered in the Court of Hustings[g].

[e] See the History of the Priory of Studley, inserted after the account of Master John Croke

[f] The Grant, penes me. Studley Chartulary, fol 17

[g] Copies of the Deeds, in the Studley Chartulary, fol. 34 to 40.

Master John Croke, or le Blount, died upon the 2d of September, in the year 1554, and is buried at Chilton, in a chapel adjoining the chancel, and which is still the burying place of the family. His monument is a flat stone in the pavement, with the following inscription in the old black letter, written on brass plates, and on a fillet round the stone. It does not mention his age, which leaves the time of his birth uncertain

(At the head,)

Sit gravis hic somnus tamen ipse resurgere sperat
Marmoreo clausus Crocus in hoc tumulo.

(At the feet,)

Qui timent Dominum speraverunt in Domino.
Adjutor eorum et protector eorum est.

(Round the sides of the stone, on the fillet,)

Here lyeth buried John Croke the Calder, sumtyme one of the six Clerkys of the Kyngys Courte of the Chauncery, and afterward (one of) the Maisters of the said Chauncery, (which John) departed the second day of September, in the yere of oure Lorde God, MCCCCCLIIII. b.

The coat of arms on a brass plate is, a fesse between six martlets, with a crescent on the fesse, without any quartering, or impalement.

It is not known whether he left any children besides his son and heir, Sir John Croke I have a picture of an old man with a sensible look, which may probably be intended for him.

Over the porch of the house at Studley are his arms, in stone, Croke, as before, with the crescent; quartered with Heynes, and impaled with Cave, fretty, the colour of course not designated. The present family of Cave still bears azure, fretty, argent and for a crest, on a wreathe, a greyhound currant sable. On an escroll, proceeding from his mouth, for a motto, GARDEZ, alluding to the name, *Cave*, Beware.

His will is as follows, which was proved the 18th of October, 1555, on the oath of William Walker, Proctor of the Executor.

Chapel or Isle.

IN THE NAME OF GOD, AMEN, the xi day of June, in the yere of our Lorde God a thousand, fyve hundredth, fiftie and fower, and in the firste yere of the reigne of our sovereign Lady Quene Mary: I JOHN CROKE, of Chilton, th' Elder, make my Testament and last Will in this wise followinge. First, I bequeath my soule unto Almightie Godd, and my bodye to the erthe to be buried in Christian buriall. I bequeath to every of my servants, men and women, a blacke lyvery, at seven shillinges or eight shillinges the yarde; the men to have coates, and the women gownes, as speedily after my decease as may be provided. And I bequeath to Thomas Springe fortie shillinges. to Oswald thre poundes: to Sinewyn fortie shillings. to Stephen fortie shillings: to Meade fortie shillings: to Arthure fortie shillings· to Henry Chilton fortie shillings: to Henry the Bruer fortie shillings: and to Frances fortie shillings. I bequeath to Byrdesey twentie shillings: to the Miller twentie shillings: to Hawkyns twentie shillings· to Thomas the Carter twentie shillings· to John Chapman twentie shillings: to Alyanor Adys fortie shillinges to Sibill fortie shillings: to Amye twentie shillinges: to Johan Lovell twentie shillings: to Allice twentie shillinges: to Johan Maygott tenne shillinges I bequeath to John Coventree thre pounde six shillinges eight pence, and a black gown at tene shillinges the yarde: and to Sir Rauffe fortie shillings, and a blacke gowne of tenne shillinges the yarde: and to Mighell twentie shillinges. I bequeath to Jack twentie shepe: and to Robyn twentie shepe, and kepinge for them in Adingrove, or ellswhere sufficienthe, so longe as they shall contynue in service with my sonne, and my daughter, or at their bestowinge. I bequeath to Roger, the boye in my kitchin, twentie shillinges and to Alexander xx*s* : and to Norrice xx*s*. I bequeath to Anne Hunt tenne powndes: and to my cosin Anne Mason thre pownde, six shillings, eight pence: and to her sister Wise fortie shillinges: and to Prudence Mason that fyve pownde which my wife willed unto her, and XXXIII*s*. IIII*d* of my bequest besides: and to Mystris Conysby twentie shillinges· and to Prudence Edwardes £III. VI*s*. VIII*d* to her marriage. I bequeath to Anne Lee a tablett of golde, with a pommaunder in it. I will and bequeath to Anne Hunt, besides her annuity of twentie-six shillings eight pence by the yere, thirtene shillinges fower pence by the yere; to be taken and received of the rentes of my howses in Flete Strete at London, during her liffe. Also I will and bequeathe to Oswalde, my Butler, twentie shillings by yere during his lyfe, to be taken of the same rentes: also to Smewyn twentie shillinges by yere, to be taken of the same rentes, during his lyfe: and also to my cozin Thomas Ashwell fortie shillings by yere, during his lyfe, to be taken of the same rentes. Also I geve unto the same Thomas Asshwell the best of my geldinges that he will chose, after my Executour hath first chosen out twain for himself. I give to Sir George Giflorde a signet of golde, with a blue stone, and the best of my gownes that he will chose. Also I bequeath to John Croke, my sonne, and to Elizabeth his wiffe, my ferme of Adingrove: to have to them, and to theire assignes, for so many yeres as they and eyther of them shall lyve, enduring the term and lease of the said ferme: and, after their deceases, I give and bequeath the residue of yeres of the said ferme then to come, and of the lease of the same, to the heirs of the bodie of the saide John my soonne, lawfullie begotten, and, for lack of such issue, to the right heirs of me John Croke, th' elder. Also I geve and bequeath to every of my godchildren, in Chilton, and Esendon, fyve shillings a pece: and to Thomas Golde, the Attorney of the Common Place, eight powndes, in satisfaction for the cropp at Hayes that was in variance between him and me, and never yet dyscussed: yt contayned by estimation xii acres of wheate and rye newly sowen. Also I bequeath to the poore people of Beckeley, Studley, and Horton, fortie shillinges; and to the pore people of thes Townes following, (that is to say,) to Borstall twentie shillings: to Ockeley twentie shillings: to Brill fortie shillings: to Ludgarsall twentie shillings: to Dorton twentie shillings: to Wotton twentie shillings: to Asshendon and Pollicott twentie shillings: to Neather Wynchindon twentie shillings: to Cherdesley twentie shillings: to Crendon twentie shillings: to Shobyndon twentie shillings: to Ikford twentie shillings: to Wornall twentie shillings: to Chilton and Esindon twentie shillings. Also I give and bequeath to yonge Ciceley Croke my chain of golde, conteynyng in lyncks the nomber of a 148, and also my late wiffe's wedding ring. Also I give and bequeath to my olde companyons, the Feloweshipp of the Six Clerks, tenne powndes; to be bestowed by them in manner and forme followinge, that is to say, tenne marks thereof uppon such thinges as they shall thynke moste necessary for theire house, and fyve marks residue uppon a convenyent dynner whereunto I will require them to call Sir Richard Reade, the Clerks of the Petie Bagge, th' Examynours, and the Regester. I give unto Maister Leder my hope of golde. And of this my last Will and Testament, I ordeyn and make John Croke, my son, my Executour, to whom I will and geve all the residue of my goodes not before bequeathed. In witness whereof I have subscribed this my last Will and Testament, and sett to my seale, the day and year above written. Per me Johannem Croke—Robert Keylway—Edward Unton—Ciceley Unton—J. Coventre.

DIGRESSION

The History of the Priory of Studley, its possessors, founders, and benefactors.

THE materials for the earlier part of the history of the Priory at Studley, have been extracted from the ruins of antiquity by the industry of Bishop Kennet; the parish of Beckley, in which it is situated, having originally formed a part of the extensive honor, barony, or lordship, in which the parishes of Ambroseden and Bicester, the more peculiar subjects of his valuable work, were likewise comprehended.

Nothing more is known of this place before the Norman conquest, than that the village of Beccaule, which was bequeathed by King Alfred, in the year 901, to his relation Osferth, is supposed to have been Beckley[a], and that in 1005, Ailmer, Earl of Cornwall, founded an Abbey of Benedictine Monks, to whom he gave certain lands, which he exchanged with his kinsman Godwin for five mansions at Stodelege, now perhaps Studley[b].

Whoever was the possessor at the time of the Conquest, it was one of the estates which were seized by William, and bestowed upon his followers. Amongst these, Robert de Oyley enjoyed a considerable share of his sovereign's favour. Wigod de Walengeford, a powerful Saxon nobleman, had supported William's claim to the throne of England, and had hospitably entertained him in his castle at Wallingford. To gratify one of his adherents, and at the same time to ingratiate himself with his new subjects, in the year 1066, he bestowed in marriage to Robert de Oyley, Aldith, the only daughter and heiress of Wigod, who, after her father's death, which happened soon after, succeeded to his great estates. Upon this marriage, King William gave likewise to De Oyley two other lordships, the barony of Oxford, or De Oyley, and what was afterwards called the honor of Saint Valori, of which the head, or capital

[a] Kennet's Parochial Antiquities, page 39, from Ælfredi Vita MSS p. 194 This Beckley, Beccaulea, in a note to the will of King Alfred, Oxford, 1788, is said to have been in Sussex. [b] Ibid. p 46 Mon Ang. tom 1 p 254, 259

seat was at Beckley, and which contained a large extent of country, including Studley, Ambroseden, Mixbury, Northbrook, Arncott, and other manors.

The institutions of chivalry were the foundation of all the virtues of those rude times. The minds of the knights were elevated and refined by the love of God, and of the ladies, and by the sentiments of honor and courage required by their profession. The rivalship, incident to those engaged in the same noble pursuits, might have promoted divisions injurious to the public interests. But the children of chivalry were all considered as brethren, and a more intimate connexion subsisted between many of them in the voluntary association of *brothers, or companions in arms* Mutual esteem, and a similarity of ideas and pursuits, were the foundation of an exalted friendship, which received a peculiar form in these associations. They were entered into either for some particular enterprize, or generally, and for life. *The Brothers* took a solemn oath to share equally the labours, and dangers, the glory, and the profit of their adventures, and never to abandon each other in their perils, or misfortunes. Besides the oath, other fanciful ceremonies were sometimes employed: the knights mingled their blood, hearts of gold were given, or an exchange of armour was made; they received the sacrament, or jointly kissed the sacred vessel in which it was contained. Like members of the same family, they adopted the same dress and armour, and they had the same friends and enemies. The engagement was considered as of the most sacred and indissoluble nature. The obligation to assist *a brother in arms* was held to be paramount to every other duty, except that to the Sovereign alone, and even a distressed damsel might in vain implore the succour of the Knight, when necessity compelled him to fly to the relief of his companion. Knights of different nations frequently took upon them these mutual engagements, but the connexion was at once dissolved in case a war arose between their respective sovereigns[c].

This practice prevailed as early as the time of William, and such a connection subsisted between many of the knights who came over from Normandy: of these Eudo and Pinco are particularly mentioned[d]. Robert

[c] De Sainte Palaye, Mémoire sur l'ancienne Chevalerie, vol. 1. p. 224 Du Cange, Dissertation 21, sur Joinville, and Gloss voce Arma Mutare. [d] Dugd. Baron vol 1 p 439.

de Oyley had a fellow adventurer, and sworn brother, in Roger de Ivery[e]. In virtue of this engagement, when William the Conqueror bestowed two lordships upon De Oyley, upon his marriage, he honourably gave one of them to ROGER DE IVERY, about the year 1077. This was the lordship of which Beckley was the head. Before this gift Robert de Oyley had endowed his chapel of St George within his castle at Oxford with two parts of the tithe of Beckley, the tithes of Horton, and half a hide of land in Stodele. they were afterwards transferred to the Abbey of Oseney, in 1149[f]. This family of De Ivery was descended from Rodolph, maternal half-brother to Richard the First, Duke of Normandy · who having distinguished himself by killing a monstrous boar, in a hunting party with his royal brother, was rewarded for that service with the castle and lands of Ivery, on the river l'Evre, in Normandy, which gave him the title of Count[g]. Roger de Ivery was the son of Waleran de Ivery, who held a knight's fee in the bailywick of Tenechebrai in Normandy by the service of being Pincerna, or Cup-bearer, to the Duke[h] His son Roger enjoyed the same honour of being Cup-bearer to William, after his accession to the throne of England, and married Adeline, eldest daughter of Hugh de Grentmaisnel, and Adelidis his wife. Hugh came over with the Conqueror, and having distinguished himself in the battle of Hastings, was afterwards joined with Odo, Bishop of Baieux, and William Fitzosborn, in the administration of justice throughout the kingdom.

This lordship was then styled the Barony of Ivery, and constituted its owner an English Peer. Roger de Ivery likewise gave his name to the town of Iver, in Buckinghamshire, which belonged to him. He died about the year 1079, leaving three sons · Roger; Hugo, who had the manor of Ambrosden; and Geoffrey[i]. The eldest, ROGER DE IVERY, succeeded to the Baronies, and to the office of Cup-bearer. About the year 1086, he attended the King in Normandy, and was appointed

[e] Memorandum quod Robertus de Oleio, et Rogerus de Iverio, fratres jurati, et per fidem et sacramentum confederati, venerunt ad conquestum Angliæ, cum Rege Willielmo Bastard Iste Rex dedit dicto Roberto duas Baronias, quæ modo vocantur Doylivorum, et S Waleria Register of Oseney Abbey, MSS penes Decan et Capit. Æd. Christi. Kennet, 1066.

[f] Kennet, 1083 [g] Gul Gemet p. 288. [h] Norman Script p. 1048. [i] Kennet, p 62, 63, from Domesday Book and Oseney Register

Governor of the castle of Rohan, where he gave a proof of his courage and fidelity in defending it against one of the rebellious attempts of Robert, the King's son[k]. Upon the death of King William, in the disputes for the succession, with his relation Hugh de Grentmaisnel, he supported the title of Robert to the crown of England; for which he was banished by William Rufus in 1087, forfeited all his estates in England, and died in sorrow and disgrace. His misfortunes were considered by the monks of Worcester as a judgment for his having robbed them of the manor of Hampton[l].

Geoffrey de Ivery, the youngest son, was restored to his brother's possessions, and, dying without issue, the barony de Ivery fell to the Crown. But though the direct line was now extinct, yet some collateral branches long continued in the country[m].

About the year 1155, King Henry the Second bestowed this barony upon Reginald de Saint Valori, or, as it was called in England, Saint Walery[n].

This noble and ancient family were Lords of St. Valori in Normandy, a town so named from St. Valorie, a disciple of Columban, who was made Abbot of a Monastery in the territory of Amiens by Clothaire, in 589. The first person who is known of this family was Gilbert, who was styled the Duke of Normandy's Advocate de Sancto Gualerico. He married Papia, the daughter of Richard the Second, Duke of Normandy. His son was Bernard de St. Walery, father of Walter de St. Walery, who flourished under Duke Robert the Second, and with his son Bernard was present at the siege of Nice in 1096. Ranulph de St. Walery, who is recorded in Domesday Book, attended Duke William upon his expedition to England. Guy de St. Walery seems to have been his son, or younger brother, and died about the year 1141; leaving, by his wife Albreda, Reginald his son and heir[o].

[k] Kennet, p. 70, from Ordericus Vitalis, b iv p 546. [l] Ibid. p. 70 Mon. Ang tom i p 134. b. [m] Ibid. p. 83. Regist. de Oseney See the History of the House of Yvery, written by John, Earl of Egmont; printed, but not published, in 1764.

[n] Kennet first states, that this honor was given soon after the death of Geoffrey de Ivery to Guy de St. Valori, p. 83, but afterwards, p. 104, he says this is a mistake, and that it was first given to his son Reginald by Henry II. about 1155, and that Jeffrey was living in 1149

[o] Kennet, p. 83.

Reginald de Saint Valori having assisted the Empress Matilda, King Stephen seized his lordship of Haseldone in Gloucestershire, which he gave to John Saint John of Stanton. Henry the Second, upon his accession to the throne, restored it to Reginald, but as in the mean time it had been given to the Abbey of Kingswood, the monks were unwilling to relinquish their claim to it. At length Reginald having been enjoined as a penance by the Pope to found an Abbey of the Cistertian order, they surrendered it upon condition of his performing this injunction The abbey was erected at Haseldon, and the Abbot of Kingswood, with many of his monks, were translated thither. From hence, from a deficiency of water, they removed to Tettebiri, and afterwards, being ill supplied with wood, his son, Bernard de Saint Valori, procured from Roger de Berkley forty acres of land in Miretord near Kingswood, and transferred the Cistertian Abbey to that place. For which Bernard granted to Roger de Berkley freedom from toll in his port of Saint Valori[p]. Reginald soon after confirmed to the nuns of Godstow, Hermgesham, and Boreham, and whatever John Saint John had given them[q].

Reginald de St Valori was in great favour with Henry In 1155, soon after the death of Geoffrey de Ivery, the King conferred upon him the honor of Ivery, which from this time was called the honor of Saint Valori, or Walery[r]. Bishop Kennet has no where defined the exact extent of this honour. The lands of Roger de Iveri are thus stated in Domesday-book. In Peritune Hundred, Mixbury, Astall, Fulbrook, Etone, Northbrook, Horspath, Hensington, Heathrop, Clanfield, Barton, Beckley, Cheping Norton, Sherborn, Holton, North Leigh, Hampton-Gay, Wistelle, Cutslowe, Rousham In the first Gadre Hundred, Norbrook, Stoke Lyne In the second Gadre Hundred, Walcot, Woolvercot[s]. I think it extremely probable that the whole of these lands con-

[p] Mon. Ang vol i p 811 b 812. b Kennet, p 97, 113, 126 [q] Monasticon, vol. i. p 525 b. [r] Kennet, p 113

[s] I state the modern names as they are given by Kennet, Par. Ant p 67. In Domesday they are, Missebene, Estalle, Fulebroc, Etone, Nordbroc, Horspadan, Hansitone, Trop Chenefelde, Berton, Bechelie, Nortone, Scirburne, Eltone, Lege, Hantone, Wistelle, Codslaue, Rovesham, Norbroc, Stoches, Waltone, Ulfgarcote The wife of Roger de Iveri in Besentone Hundred held Letelape, (Islip) and Oxendone, (Oddington.) In Edward the Confessor's time, the manors of Burcester, (Bicester,) Ambroseden, Stratton, Weston, &c. belonged to Wigod de Walingford Domesday Book

stituted the honour of Iveri, and afterwards of Saint Valori. Some manors might in process of time have been detached from it by sale or gift, but it must be observed that it was held of the Crown by the same service of ten knights' fees, as long as it continued in the hands of a subject. At the death of Richard, King of the Romans, in 1272, the manors of Beckley, Ambrosedon, Blackthorn, Henley, and Willarstone only are mentioned[t]. The capital seat of the honour was at Beckley, where was a castle, in which Richard, King of the Romans, his son Edmund, Earl of Cornwall, and the other Lords resided. Upon the site where it stood, are still to be seen an ancient pigeon-house, and evident remains of foundations. Here of course the Lords of the dependent manors performed their suit and services[u].

Reginald was appointed a Commissioner to enquire what rents were due to the King in Normandy in 1161, and to collect a scutage, which was assessed in the same year upon the county of Oxford. He confirmed likewise to the monks of St. Frideswide at Oxford the manors of Knittinton in Berkshire, which had been given by his father. In 1164, he was one of the Barons in the Council of Clarendon, and was deputed with other Lords to wait upon Lewis, the King of France. He died about 1166, and left a son named Bernard, and a daughter called Matilda[x].

Matilda married William de Braose, a powerful Baron, and for her bold and resolute behaviour to King John, was miserably famished, with her eldest son, in Windsor Castle in 1210[y].

His son, Bernard de Saint Valory, the founder of the monastery at Studley, being abroad at his father's death, the King issued a precept to the Sheriffs of the counties in which his lands were situated, to secure his rights and property till his return[z]. For the livery of his lands he paid to the King five marks and a half, in which were included, half a mark for Beckley, and one mark for Horton. It appears by a charter of the year 1169, that he was still in possession of the original hereditary lordship of St. Valori in Normandy.

In 1171 he fell under the King's displeasure, his lands were seized, and the rents paid into the Exchequer. But his peace was soon made, and it

[t] Kennet, p. 276. [u] Ibid p. 295 [x] Kennet, in annis. [y] Mat. West. sub anno [z] Kennet, p. 123.

seems to have been a condition that he should give to the King his manor of Wolvercott, and the advowson of the nunnery of Godstow, near Oxford, both which estates he had acquired in frank marriage with his second wife Avoris, the daughter of John de St. John, Lord of Stanton[a].

He was a considerable benefactor to the monks. In 1172 he gave to the Abbey of Oseney a pool near the Thames, with a watercourse running to the mill, and the moiety of seventeen acres and a half of his demesne lands in the isle of Oseney. To the Hospital of St Giles in London he gave rents and privileges at Isleworth, and confirmed and enlarged his father's gifts to the nuns at Ambesbury[b]. He granted likewise a charter to the nuns of Godstow near Oxford, about 1172, with lands and fisheries[c]. King Henry the Second bestowed upon him the manor of Ardington, now Yarnton, in Berks, in 1180[d].

In the year 1184 according to Kennet, but Bishop Tanner supposes in 1176, or 1179, he founded the PRIORY OF STUDLEY, for nuns of the Benedictine order, dedicated to the Virgin Mary, and endowed it with half a hide of land in Horton. This is the earliest charter which is known, but it seems rather to imply that the convent was already in existence[e].

He was attending Richard the First in Normandy, when his father, Henry the Second, died in 1189. Soon after the coronation he again accompanied the King into Normandy, where he went to prepare for his expedition to Palestine. Bernard assumed the Cross with his sovereign, and, for his better success, in his passage through France, he founded an Abbey, which he called *Locus Dei*, *Lieu Dieu*, or *Godestow*, in 1191, in the county of Eu, upon the river Breston, which divides Normandy from Picardy[f]. To the convention which was made at Messina between Philip Augustus, King of France, and Richard, amongst the *fidejussores*, or securities, was Bernardus de St. Walery, or such of his heirs as should inherit St. Valori[g].

The events of this memorable crusade are well known, and the immortal honour acquired by Richard Cœur de Lion, and his brave associates.

[a] Kennet, p 127. [b] Ibid. [c] Kennet, p 128 [d] Ibid in anno
[e] Studley Chartulary. Bryan Twyne's MSS Kennet, in anno. Tanner's Notitia Monastica Dugdale's Monasticon. [f] Kennet, p 149 Gallia Christiana, vol x. p. 328
[g] The new edition of Kennet, in anno, from Rymer

The siege of Acre was then the principal scene of action It was here that the romantic bravery of Richard, and the Franks, met with a worthy adversary in the courage and virtues of Saladine. After two years the city was compelled to surrender; but this siege and victory were purchased at an immense expence of money, troops, and heroes. More than one hundred thousand Christians were slain, and every country in Europe had to lament the loss of its princes, nobles, and knights. Amongst these is enumerated Bernard de Saint Valori, who was shot through the head by an arrow from an arbalet, or cross-bow[h].

He was succeeded in his baronies by THOMAS DE ST. WALERY, who paid one hundred and seventy marks for the relief of his barony[i], and was likewise a considerable benefactor to the service of religion, and the second founder of the Priory of Studley. He married Adela, or Edela, heiress to the lordship of Saint Albine, near Dieppe in Normandy, and daughter of the Count of Ponthieu[k], of whom the following extraordinary story is related in the History of Picardy.

"Thomas de Saint Valery was travelling with his wife Adela, daughter of a Count de Ponthieu. They were attacked near a forest by eight armed men. St. Valery, after a severe struggle, was seized, bound, and thrown into a thicket. His wife was carried off, exposed to the brutality of the banditti, and afterwards dismissed in a state of nudity. She, however, sought for and found her husband, and they returned together. They were soon after met by their servants, whom they had left at an inn, and returned to their father's castle at Abbeville. The barbarous Count, full of false ideas of honour, proposed, some days after, to his daughter, a ride to his town of Rue, on the sea shore. There they entered a bark, as if to sail about for pleasure; and they had stood out three leagues from the shore, when the Count de Ponthieu starting up, said, with a terrible voice, "Lady, death must now efface the shame which "your misfortune has brought on all your family!" The sailors, previously instructed, instantly seized her, shut her up in a hogshead, and threw her into the sea, while the bark regained the coast. Happily a Flemish vessel passing near the coast, the crew observed the floating hogshead, and expecting a prize of good wine, took it up, opened it, and with

[h] Roger de Hovedon, p 685 [i] Kennet, p. 159 [k] Ibid p 156.

great surprise found a beautiful woman. She was, however, almost dead, from terror and want of air, and at her earnest entreaty the honest Flemings sent a boat ashore with her. She gained her husband's house, who was in tears for her supposed death. The scene was extremely affecting—but Adela survived it only a few hours. John, Count of Ponthieu, repenting of his crime, gave to the Monks of St. Valery the right of fishing three days in the year in and about the spot where his daughter had been thrown overboard[l]."

In 1193, Thomas de St. Valori gave his manor of Mixbury to the Abbey of Oseney. In 1202, he confirmed to the Abbot of Thame some land in Stoke, and in 1203 he confirmed his father's foundation of the Priory of Studley, with some new gifts[m].

In 1205, he confirmed to the monks of Bittledon lands in Dodford[n]. In 1206, he owed the King ten marks and nine shillings for arrears of scutage[o]. In 1207, he confirmed his father's foundation of Godstow in France. He afterwards incurred the King's displeasure, and his lands were seized by the Crown; for in 1209 he paid a composition of one thousand marks to recover them. The custody of his barony having been in the mean time committed to Robert de Braibroc[p].

In 1212, an Inquisition was taken of the honor of Saint Valori[q]. In 1213, Thomas de St. Valori, by adhering to the Pope and the French interests, again offended the King, who sent a precept to the Sheriff of Oxfordshire, with orders for putting in some discreet steward to take care of his lands and chattels, commanding him to be summoned to appear on a certain day. And another precept was sent to Ralph Hareng, Seneschal of the honor of St. Valori, requiring him to assign to Gerard de Rodes land to the value of twenty pounds out of the said estate[r].

In 1216, the King committed his estate to Ralph Harengod, to keep for the use of Thomas de Saint Valori[s], who confirmed the grants to Godstow Nunnery in Oxfordshire. In 1217, a precept was issued to the Sheriff of Oxfordshire to give Thomas de St. Valori possession of the lands

[l] The History of Picardy, quoted by Horace Walpole, from whom the above is taken. Walpoliana, vol. ii. page 128

[m] Kennet, in anno. Mon Ang tom i p 147 Studley Chart and Brian Twyne

[n] Kennet, p. 167 [o] Ibid p 168 [p] Ibid. in anno. [q] Ibid p 175

[r] Ibid in anno [s] Ibid p. 183

of his brother Henry, of which he had been disseized in the Barons' war, and Henry had seizen of his lands in Fulbroc in Oxfordshire, Northon and Sutton in Huntingdonshire, and Henton in Berks, where he had obtained a market[t].

Henry de St. Valori, brother of Thomas, late lord of the manor of Ambrosden, at a trial before the itinerant Judges in the county of Buckinghamshire, lost his lands in the said county by default to the King, because his attorney had not personally appeared in the court, after four days admonition, but would have pleaded for an *Essonium de malo lecti*, that is, that upon sickness of the party summoned, attested in the open court for four days successively, the Judges shall then appoint four knights to attend the sick person, and see him depute an attorney to appear for him. Which plea was now overruled by the Judges, because no attorney could have an attorney, as no proctor could have a proctor. Upon which Henry de St. Valori was judged in default, and his lands taken into the King's hands[u].

Thomas de St. Valori died in 1219, 4 Henry III. and left only one daughter, ALLANORA, who was married to ROBERT, surnamed Gastabled, EARL OF DREUX, a French peer, who was of the royal blood of France, being descended from Louis le Gros. He had livery of all the lands in England of her inheritance, including the honor of St. Valori, and in 1220 confirmed the gifts of Thomas de St. Valori to the Abbey of Oseney[x].

About 1227, all the lands of the Earl of Dreux were seized by the King, during some contests in France. He died in 1228, and was succeeded in his possessions in France, by his eldest son John, as Earl of Dreux and Brenne, and Lord of St. Valori, in Normandy. But the honor of St. Valori in England remained in the hands of the Crown. The arms of St. Valori were, two lions passant, which appears by a seal of Thomas de Saint Valori[y]. Allanora then married Henry, Earl of Sully[z].

Upon the disseizure and death of Earl Robert, the custody of his lands in England, which he held in right of his wife, was committed to RICHARD, EARL OF CORNWALL, the King's brother, in 1229, of which, in 1231, he had a full grant from his royal brother. But some part was

[t] Kennet, p 184 [u] Bracton, Hingham magna, cap. 4. Kennet, p. 198.
[x] Dugd Baron vol 1 p. 455 Du Tillet, Recueil, p 27, 38, 45 [y] R. Dods MSS. vol 20 fol. 58. [z] Du Tillet, p 27

allotted to Allanora, the widow of Robert. Richard, Earl of Cornwall, who had been elected King of the Romans, in 1256, died in 1272, and was succeeded by his son EDMUND, EARL OF CORNWALL, who dying without issue, in 1300, the honor of St. Walery descended to the King, EDWARD THE FIRST, as next heir[a]. This Barony was valued at ten knights' fees[b]. By King Edward the Second it was granted to his favourite PIERS DE GAVESTON[c], upon whose death in 1312 it again reverted to the King who immediately gave it to his new creature, HUGH LE DESPENSER[d]. Hugh granted it to his relation Sir John de Handlo[e] After this it appears to have been in various hands. In 1317, the King gave it to Isabel his Queen for life[f]. In 1332, John de Eltham, Earl of Cornwall. was possessed of it[g]. In 1337, Sir John de Handlo held the manor of Beckley for life, and William de Montacute, Earl of Salisbury, obtained a grant in fee in reversion after the death of Handlo In 1351, Edward the Black Prince held it by grant of the King as Duke of Cornwall[h] In 1357, Almaric de S. Amand was lord of the manor of Beckley[i]. From the want of sufficient documents, these intermediate possessions are not clearly understood, but in 1376, after the death of the Black Prince, the honor of St. Walery was ultimately vested in the Crown, with whom it has ever since continued parcels, or particular manors only, having been granted out[k]

In the fifth year of Edward the Sixth, 1551, the King, by his letters patent, dated the 24th of April, amongst other things, granted to Sir Walter Mildmaye the manor of Beckley, with all messuages, lands, tenements, woods, &c. in Beckley and Horton in the county of Oxford, to hold in capite by the service of the hundredth part of a knight's fee, as parcel of the honor of Ewelme. From him it was transferred to Sir Henry Norris, and thus came into the family of the Earl of Abingdon[l]

[a] Studley Chart f 42 In 1244, Philippa Basset, Countess of Warwick, gave to the Canons of Bicester seven shillings rent, which Roger de Stodley paid for a tenement in Stodley. Kennet, p. 232 R Dods MSS Pipe vol 15 f 120 vol 20 f 30 vol 42 f 127 vol 61. f. 38

[b] Studley Chart f 46 R. Dods MSS vol 14. f 246 vol. 15 f. 58, 285, 325. [c] Dugd Baron vol ii. p 42 Dugd MSS B i. 142 R Dods MSS vol. 35. f. 25. [d] Dugd Baron vol i. p 390 [e] R. Dods. vol 107 f 201 [f] Dugd. MSS C 138 [g] Year Book, Ed iii p 223 [h] Decree of Appropriation Studley Chartulary. [i] Dugd Bar vol ii p 20 [k] Kennet. [l] Studley Chartulary, fol 42

The extent of the manor of Beckley, and of what it consisted, is clearly ascertained by an inquisition taken on the death of Edmund, Earl of Cornwall, before the Escheator, on the 16th of November, in the twenty-eighth year of Edward the First, 1300. It is a very particular and minute account of the manor of Beckley, and Hamlet of Horton, and of all the messuages, the number of acres of plowed land, meadow, and wood, the names, rents, and services of every freeholder, bondman, cottager, and every other possession, right, and franchise belonging to the manor. The value of the whole is estimated at £44. 3*s*. 7¼*d*. a year; of which 6*s*. 8*d*. was held by the Prioress of Studley in free alms. It was held of the King, in capite, as of the honor of St. Valori, and King Edward was found to be the next heir[m].

Upon this inquisition, in the old chartulary, amongst other remarks, it is observed,

First, That neither the Prioress of Studley, nor the Lord of the manor of Ashe, nor any other person inhabiting, or having any lands, within the towns of Studley, Ashe, or Merlacke, is said or declared to be a freeholder of the manor of Beckley, or suitor to the court there, or to owe any manner of suit or service to the Lord of that manor.

Secondly, That no part of the manor of Beckley extendeth into any other county than Oxfordshire.

Thirdly, That no mention is made of the great parcel of ground called Otmoor, " which Moor at this day some would fain find to be parcel of " the manor of Beckley, but if it had been so in deed, and so known, " taken, and esteemed, in those days, it could not, nor should not, have " been so utterly forgotten, and so clearly left altogether out, and unmen- " tioned in the said presentment. And specially for that it is so great and " notable a quantity of ground, so beneficial a common, and so profitable " for fowling and fishing to all the inhabitants of six or seven townships " bordering round about it, who always together, videlicet, every of the " said townships, as well one as another, have ever used, and enjoyed the " said common, for all their flocks of sheep, herds of beasts, and all " manner of cattle, at all times, and have taken and enjoyed the profits of " the fowling and fishing at their pleasure, at all times. No one of the

[m] Studley Chartulary, fol. 46. b.

"said townships claiming any preheminence, or greater right, or interest "than the rest[n]."

It appears then, that when these observations were made, above two hundred years ago, the claim of the lord of the manor of Beckley to the lordship of Otmoor was considered as a new claim. Otmoor was not originally comprehended within the manor of Beckley, as is clearly proved by this inquisition. It was probably part of the wastes of the honor of Saint Valori, and that honor not having been granted out, the Moor remained the property of the Crown. The tenants of all the manors within that honor had of course right of common upon it: and the other neighbouring towns by usage: but being inconvenient for the occupation of those at a distance, the use and the right gradually became confined to the townships immediately surrounding it[o]. It would necessarily be under the jurisdiction of the court of the honor of Saint Valori, which was held at Beckley. After those courts were disused, the court of the lord of the manor of Beckley, which was held at the same place, naturally enough assumed some parts of their jurisdiction, gradually extended its authority over the neighbouring waste of Otmoor, exercised manorial rights over it, and made regulations, which being for the general good were acquiesced in. And this usurpation upon the Crown has been matured by time and possession into a perfect right

In the mean time, the Priory at Studley was augmented by various *donations*, as well by the *Founder*, *his heirs and successors*, as *by strangers*. The original foundation consisted of the house, and site, and half a hide of land in Horton, given by Bernard de Saint Valori. This gift was confirmed by his son Thomas de Saint Valori in 1203, who prescribed the mode of electing the Prioress. She was to be chosen with his consent, or that of his Seneschal, if he was absent abroad. Upon this nomination she was to be presented to the Bishop of Lincoln, and to appear at Saint Valori's court at Oxford to perform fealty. That is, a free election was left to the Religious, yet a congè d'eslire was first to be obtained from the Patron. He granted likewise pannage for feeding the Prioress's pigs[p].

[n] Studley Chartulary, fol. 49 b.

[o] The towns of Charlton, Fencot, Moorcot, Noke, and Oddington, were not part of the honor of St. Valori Kennet, p 61. et passim.

[p] Charter in Dugdale's Monasticon, vol ii p 486. Kennet, p 165, and Glossary, voce Advowson of Religious Houses

No. 23.

GENEALOGY OF THE LORDS OF SAINT VALORI

1 *Of De Iveri*

Rodolph
half brother to Richard the First, Duke of Normandy,
from whom descended

Waleran de Iveri,
Cup-bearer to
the Duke.

Hugh de Grentmaisnel, gave Charlton to St. Elrulfs in Normandy = Adelidis

Roger de Iveri, sworn brother to Robert de Oyley, acquired the lordship about 1077, died 1079. = Adeline, from her father held lands in Charlton. and the manors of Islip and Oddington She had a seat at Fencott Died 1111

Adeliz, married Alberic de Ver, junior, Lord Chamberlain of England

Roger, eldest son, forfeited his estates, 1087. Cup-bearer, and Baron

Hugh, Lord of Ambrosden, which he left to his brother

Geoffrey, restored to the Baronies. About 1112 died, without issue, and his estates escheated to the Crown, by whom they were granted to Hugh de Saint Valori, soon after

" said townships claiming any preheminence, or greater right, or interest " than the rest[n]."

It appears then, that when these observations were made, above two hundred years ago, the claim of the lord of the manor of Beckley to the lordship of Otmoor was considered as a new claim. Otmoor was not originally comprehended within the manor of Beckley, as is clearly proved by this inquisition. It was probably part of the wastes of the honor of Saint Valori, and that honor not having been granted out, the Moor remained the property of the Crown. The tenants of all the manors within that honor had of course right of common upon it: and the other neighbouring towns by usage: but being inconvenient for the occupation of those at a distance, the use and the right gradually became confined to the townships immediately surrounding it[o]. It would necessarily be under the jurisdiction of the court of the honor of Saint Valori, which was held at Beckley. After those courts were disused, the court of the lord of the manor of Beckley, which was held at the same place, naturally enough assumed some parts of their jurisdiction, gradually extended its authority over the neighbouring waste of Otmoor, exercised manorial rights over it, and made regulations, which being for the general good were acquiesced in. And this usurpation upon the Crown has been matured by time and possession into a perfect right.

In the mean time, the Priory at Studley was augmented by various *donations*, as well by the *Founder, his heirs and successors*, as *by strangers*. The original foundation consisted of the house, and site, and half a hide of land in Horton, given by Bernard de Saint Valori. This gift was confirmed by his son Thomas de Saint Valori in 1203, who prescribed the mode of electing the Prioress. She was to be chosen with his consent, or that of his Seneschal, if he was absent abroad Upon this nomination she was to be presented to the Bishop of Lincoln, and to appear at Saint Valori's court at Oxford to perform fealty. That is, a free election was left to the Religious, yet a congè d'eslire was first to be obtained from the Patron. He granted likewise pannage for feeding the Prioress's pigs[p].

[n] Studley Chartulary, fol 49 b.

[o] The towns of Charlton, Fencot, Moorcot, Noke, and Oddington, were not part of the honor of St. Valori Kennet, p 61 et passim.

[p] Charter in Dugdale's Monasticon, vol. ii p 486. Kennet, p 165, and Glossary, voce Advowson of Religious Houses

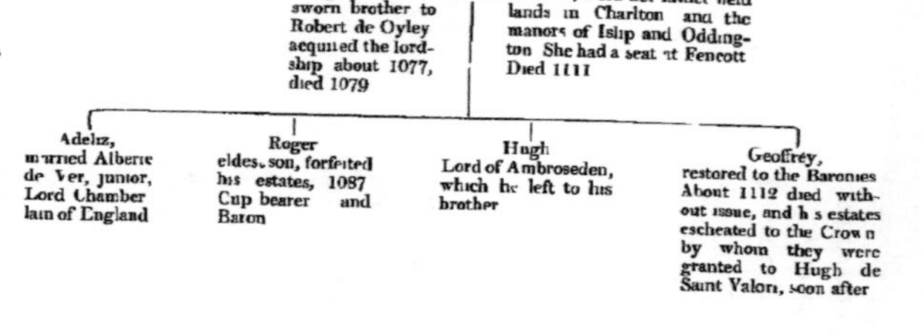
Roger de Ivery, sworn brother to Robert de Oyley acquired the lordship about 1077, died 1079
Adeline, from her father held lands in Charlton and the manors of Islip and Oddington She had a seat at Fencott Died 1111
Adeliz, married Alberic de Ver, junior, Lord Chamberlain of England
Roger eldest son, forfeited his estates, 1087 Cup bearer and Baron
Hugh Lord of Ambroseden, which he left to his brother
Geoffrey, restored to the Baronies About 1112 died without issue, and his estates escheated to the Crown by whom they were granted to Hugh de Saint Valori, soon after

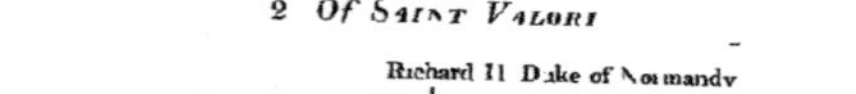

2 Of Saint Valori

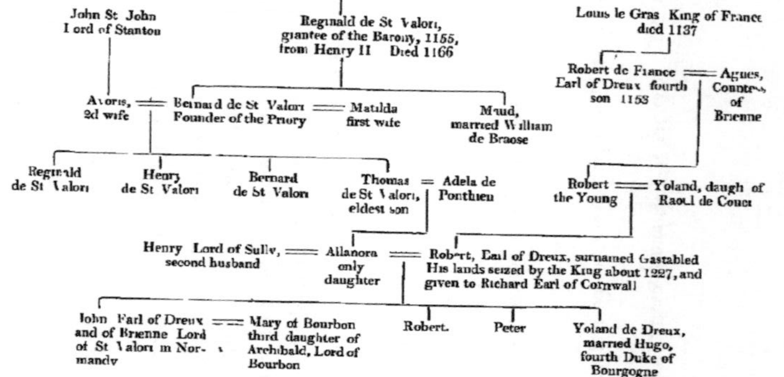
Richard II Duke of Normandy
Gilbertus Advocatus de S Gualerico
Papia
Bernard de Saint Valori
Walter de Saint Valori
Bernard de Saint Valori, living in 1096
Guy de Saint Valori Uncertain how related, son or younger brother to Ranulph de Saint Valori, who came over with the Conqueror He died about 1141 His wife Albreda survived him and married Walter de Wahull
John St John Lord of Stanton
Reginald de St Valori, grantee of the Barony, 1155, from Henry II Died 1166
Louis le Gras King of France died 1137
Robert de France Earl of Dreux fourth son 1153
Agnes, Countess of Brienne
Avoris, 2d wife
Bernard de St Valori Founder of the Priory
Matilda first wife
Maud, married William de Braose
Reginald de St Valori
Henry de St Valori
Bernard de St Valori
Thomas de St Valori, eldest son
Adela de Ponthieu
Robert the Young
Yoland, daugh of Raoul de Couci
Henry Lord of Sully, second husband
Allanora only daughter
Robert, Earl of Dreux, surnamed Gastabled His lands seized by the King about 1227, and given to Richard Earl of Cornwall
John Earl of Dreux and of Brienne Lord of St Valori in Normandy
Mary of Bourbon third daughter of Archibald, Lord of Bourbon
Robert.
Peter
Yoland de Dreux, married Hugo, fourth Duke of Bourgogne

Richard Earl of Cornwall and King of the Romans, brother to King John, had a grant of this Lordship in 1231 He died in 1272, succeeded by

Edmund his son, who dying without issue in 1300, the Honor of Saint Valori fell to King Edward the First, as next heir

By Edward II granted first to Peirs de Caveston, next to Hugh le Despenser Afterwards there were various possessors, if not of the Honor of St Valori, at least of the Manor of Beckley

From 1376 after the death of the Black Prince, ultimately vested in the Crown

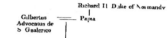

In August, in the ninth year of John, 1207, Thomas de Saint Valori granted a rent of three shillings in Beckley[q].

By another charter without date, he granted a carriage load of dead wood for firing weekly, to be taken out of Horton wood, by view of his Forester; and a piece of land to enlarge their garden[r].

Richard, King of the Romans, by his charter, granted to the Nuns twelve feet of land in breadth all round the priory in his demesne wood of Horton[s].

His son, Edmund, Earl of Cornwall, granted them one acre and half of his waste of Horton to enlarge their enclosure, by a charter dated the first of October, in the twenty-seventh year of Edward the First, 1298[t].

In 1226, Robert Earl of Dreux, Lord of Saint Valori, and Alanor his wife, daughter and heir of Thomas de Saint Valori, granted the advowson of the Church of Beckley to the Nuns of Studley. The grant was confirmed by Alanor after the death of her husband in 1234[u]. Hugh, Bishop of Lincoln, assigned certain tithes to the Nuns, in 1230[x].

The Nuns having recovered seizin of the presentation of the Church of Beckley against the King, and the Master of the Temple, Hugh Bishop of Lincoln, at the petitions of the King, and of Richard Earl of Pictou and Cornwall, and at the instance of the Nuns, with the consent of the Dean and Chapter, confirmed the right of advowson to them, and assigned to them a pension of ten marks from the said Church in certain portions after specified, together with the small tithes. These portions were, the tithes of corn of five hides of plowed land of the fee of the Lord of Saint Valori in Horton, with the tithe of hay thereunto belonging. The third part of the tithes of corn of two hides of the demesnes of Robert de Bosco, and John, the son of Alexander, in the town of Esses, with the tithes of hay. The tithes of corn of one carrucate of land cleared and cultivated by the Nuns in the town of Esses, provided that if they should clear any more land they should pay tithes for the same to the Church of Beckley, and they presented Nicholas de Anna, Clerk, to the Rectory, who was instituted by the Bishop, and took an oath not to molest the Nuns in the

[q] Dugdale. Kennet, p 169. [r] Dugdale, and Br. Twyne, No 4. [s] Dugdale. B Twyne, No. 13. [t] Dugdale. Br. Twyne, No. 14 [u] Dugdale. Studley Chartulary, f. 26. Br. Twyne, No 5, 6, 7, 8. [x] Br Twyne, No. 6, 7

said assignments of tithes[y]. This transaction took place in 1234[z]. In 1248, the Prioress again presented to the Church of Beckley[a]

Yet afterwards, for some reason which does not appear, the advowson was in the Lords of Saint Valori. For in 1283, Edmund Earl of Cornwall presented to the Church[b] In 1290 he presented Philip de Heddeshonere, in place of Richard de Sottewell, instituted to the Church of Frothingham[c]. On the death of Philip de Heddeshonere he presented Henry de Exon[d] In 1301, the King presented, as having the honor of Saint Valori descended to him[e]. In 1316, Sir John de Handlo presented Robert de Hanlo, Clerk, on the vacancy by the resignation of James de Berkhamstede[f]. Upon the institution of Robert de Hanlo to the Church of Haseley in 1318, Sir John Hanlo presented Edmund de Lodelawe[g].

During this period several controversies took place. In the year 1292 there was a suit between Philip de Heddeshonere, the Rector of Beckley, and Clementia the Prioress and convent of Studley, respecting the tithes of corn and hay which were claimed by the Prioress. By the consent of parties it was referred to the arbitration of Oliver, Bishop of Lincoln; who having made all due enquiries, in the presence of Edmund Earl of Cornwall, as patron of the living, decided in favour of the Prioress's claims, and a deed was drawn up and executed by the parties[h].

There was also a controversy between Sir Edmund de Lodelow, Rector of Beckley, and the Prior and convent of Saint Frideswide, the appropriators of Oakley, concerning the tithes of a wood called Godstowe-wood, which each of the parties asserted to be within their respective parishes. It was decided by the Bishop of Lincoln in 1328 in favour of the Priory, it being found that the wood was within the forest of Bernwood, and therefore within the parish of Oakley[i].

In 1345, in Michaelmas term, there was a trial between the King and the Prioress of Studley, for the taxation of three hides of land annexed to the Nunnery, in which the Prioress pleaded, that at the foundation three hides of land in the parish of Beckley were annexed to it, and that she was

[y] Studley Chartulary, fol 25 [z] Regis, Linc [a] Regis, Lincoln. [b] R Dods. MSS vol. 44 f 131. [c] Reg Lincoln. Ol Sutton [d] Kennet, new Edition [e] R Dods MSS. vol 107 f. 166. [f] Reg. Linc. Dalderby. [g] Ibid. [h] The Agreement. Studley Chartulary, fol. 7. [i] Chartular S. Frideswidæ. Kennett in anno.

taxed for them amongst the spirituals, or tenths. But the jury returned that she ought to pay for the same in taxation of the temporals[k].

At length the Nuns not only recovered the advowson of Beckley, but obtained the appropriation of the living. Margery, Prioress of Studley, by her petition to Edward, the Black Prince, to whom the advowson had been granted by his father, King Edward the Third, having shewn that her predecessors were seized of the advowson, and had presented their Clerks, who had been instituted by the Bishop of Lincoln, Prince Edward, adverting to the poor state of the Priory which was in his patronage, granted and quit-claimed to the said Prioress and convent the advowson of Beckley, to hold of himself and his heirs as Dukes of Cornwall. As the church was then void, he granted to them the presentation, and his licence to appropriate. These letters patent were dated the 9th of November, in the 25th year of his father's reign, 1351, and are recited in the letters patent of Edward the Third, dated on the 11th of November following, by which he confirms his son's grant, and gives his licence to appropriate[l]

The consent of the King and the Lord having been thus obtained, the appropriation was made by John Bishop of Lincoln, by his decree bearing date the 18th of the calends of May, in the year 1352. He states, as an inducement, that the possessions belonging to the Priory, since the last pestilence, had become so barren and slender, that they could not commodiously be maintained, or keep hospitality, or perform their other duties. Wherefore, that divine worship may be more perfectly increased in the said Priory, the said Religious being patrons of the Church, in the presence of the Chapter of Lincoln, and the Archdeacon of Oxford, the Bishop united, annexed, and incorporated the said Church to the Prioress and convent. Reserving a fit portion of the profits for the maintenance of a perpetual Vicar, to be instituted upon the presentation of the said Religious. And saving to the Church of Lincoln an annual pension of 6*s*. 8*d*. and for the Chapter 40*d*. Then follows the confirmation by the Dean and Chapter, in which the pension reserved to the Church of Lincoln is stated to be 10*s*.[m]

In the year 1524, a suit was instituted in the Archdeacon of Oxford's

[k] Dugd MSS A 2 f 323 [l] Studley Chartulary, fol 26 [m] Studley Chartulary, fol 27, 28.

court by the Prioress and Convent, against Ralph Cradoc and Robert Guillim, for subtraction of tithes arising in Beckley Park. The Prioress obtained a definitive sentence in her favour, which established her right, title, and possession, of perceiving all and all kind of tithes, as well great and small, as mixed and minute, and of what kind soever, in, of, and out of, all lands, fields, meadows, feedings, pastures, parks, and all other titheable places within the parish of Beckley[n].

Such were the benefactions by the Founder, and his successors, I proceed to state others which were made by *strangers*.

Soon after the foundation, Matilda, the daughter of Alan, the Hunter, (Venatoris) upon taking the veil, gave to the Convent twelve acres of plowed land upon Shulfhull, in Horton, with its appurtenances in meadow and pasture. Which gift was confirmed by Thomas de Saint Waleiys, discharging it from all secular services due to him[o].

Henry the Third, between the years 1229 and 1237, granted the Nuns to have one horse of burden travelling every day, once in the day, to bring them dead wood for firing from his wood of Panshale[p].

There are many documents relating to the donation of the church or chapel of Senekeworth, or Seckworth, with lands in that parish, in the beginning of the thirteenth century. This was a village, now no longer in existence, situated between Botley and Whitham in Berkshire, which chiefly belonged to the Abbey of Abingdon, and is now in Cumnor parish[q].

1. The charter of Robert de Senekeworthe, granting to the Priory of Studley the Church, with all lands, tithes, and dues; and one acre of land called Northsuture, and pasture for three beasts in his demesne. It has no date, but the time may be ascertained from the witnesses, who were H, and K, the abbots of Oseney, and Nutley, and P, the Prior of St. Frideswide's[r].

2. In 1218, a composition was made by Richard, Bishop of Sarum, that the Nuns should have a third of the tithes of corn of Seckworth; all

[n] Studley Chartulary, fol 29

[o] Ibid. fol. 15 a, and b Dedi Deo, et Ecclesiæ Sanctæ Mariæ de Stodleia, et monialibus ibidem Deo servientibus, cum corpore meo in religione. The name of Shulfhull is still retained.

[p] Br Twyne, No 9. [q] Ibid 55 [r] Ibid. No. 15.

other benefits belonging to that chapel in lands, tithes, and dues, with the tithes of Mercham, Cheleworth, and Boteley, to belong to the Vicar of the Chapel[s].

3. By his charter, Sir William de Senekeworth, granted to Dionysia his daughter, half a virgate of land, with a messuage, croft, and meadow; and two acres of arable land lying on one side at Schoolles, against Packstok, and on the other side adjoining the road called Eynshamwaye, and a marsh called Davidsmore[t]. It seems that Dionysia gave this land to the Priory.

4. Sir William, Lord of Senekeworth, her father, son and heir of Robert de Senekeworth, by his charter, without date, gave to the Nuns pasturage for four cows, and one bull, in all his lands, except the islands; and he discharged the virgate of land, which they held in Senekeworth, from all claim of hidage, scutage, *chirichseth*, and the custody of Windsor, and all other demands, except a rent of six pence to Robert de Boteley[u].

5. Sir William de Senekeworth, son of William, confirmed all the gifts of his father, and the half virgate of land which the nuns had of the gift of his sister Dionysia, and he discharged it of the custody of Windsor, suit of court, and all other demands[x].

6. William, Lord of Senekeworth, granted to the church of the Blessed Mary at *Senekworth*, in lieu of the tithes of his demesne meadow, the meadow called Welistdesham, containing five acres, and another between the Church-mead and the Thames. If any meadow now in Villenage should fall into his hands, it should be tithed; and least any instigated by an evil spirit should presume to disturb this Act, he confirmed it by the seal of R. Bishop of Sarum[y].

7. By a charter, William, the son of Henry, grants a virgate of land in Senekeworthe, with Crodyne-croft[z].

8. About 1181, a composition was made between the Abbot of Abendon and William, the Vicar of Seckworth, respecting oblations, and other obventions belonging to the Mother Church of Cumnor, by A and E. Abbots of Missendon and Dorkecestr, Philip and A. Priors of St. Frides-

[s] Br Twyne, No 16 [t] Ibid No 20

[u] Ibid. No 17. *Chirichseth*, that is, a certain quantity of corn which was paid to the church on St. Martin's day, Church-scot. Ducange, and Kennet, Par. Antiq p. 603

[x] Br Twyne, No. 22. [y] Ibid No 19 [z] Ibid. No 18.

wide and Esseby, by the command of Pope Lucius the Third. It mentions the church of Mercham, and Bayworthe[a].

The church of *Ilmere*, in Buckinghamshire, was given to the Nuns of Studley by Albritha, daughter of David de Romenel, and Thomas, the son of Bernard, in the reign of King John, which gift was confirmed by Peter of Blois, Bishop of Lincoln; and afterwards Hugh, his successor, appropriated it, and instituted a Vicar[b].

Hugh, the son of William of *Elsefield*, gave a virgate of land there, and, besides a hundred white loaves of that kind of bread which is called at Oxford *Blanpeyn*, which Ralph his Steward, and his heirs, were to deliver annually at Studley, upon the feast of the Assumption of Saint Mary[c].

A house at *Stratford* was given by William de Stratford, by a charter without date[d].

By a charter, Elias, the son of *William de Tetyndon*, gave the tithes of his demesnes in that parish, and if he should erect a chapel there, he should maintain the Chaplain. The gift was confirmed by Robert, Bishop of Lincoln, who held that see from 1235 to 1253[e].

Hugh, the son of *Henry of Abingdon*, confirmed the gift which Master Gilbert Mertel had made of premises in Ocks Street, which were of his fee[f].

The charter of Walkeline, the son of Roger, grants to Philip, the Miller of Oxford, a virgate of land in *Wendlebury*, rendering yearly six pence for some gilt spurs. And he warrants these tenements to whomsoever he shall assign them, whether a religious house, or otherwise[g].

About 1221, Ralph Harang granted a rent of ten shillings to be paid by Richard le Wose of *Forest-hill* for a pittance for the Nuns[h].

About 1221, Matthew, the son of Alan, gave a virgate of land at *Steeple-Aston*, in Oxfordshire[i].

But the principal donation was of the manor and advowson of *Craucumbe* in Somersetshire, and a manor in *Long Compton* in Warwickshire, by Godfrey de Craucumbe; perhaps about the year 1245.

[a] Br Twyne, No 23. [b] Ibid No. 24. Hugh Wallis, Bp. of Lincoln from 1209 to 1234 [c] Ibid. No 25 [d] Ibid No. 26 [e] Ibid. No. 27 [f] Ibid. No. 28. [g] Ibid No 29 [h] Ibid No. 35 [i] Ibid No 36

The town of Craucombe is about ten miles north from Taunton. Before the Norman invasion, Gueda wife of Godwin, Earl of Kent, in expiation of her husband's injuries to several monasteries, bestowed this manor on the church of Saint Swithun, at Winchester. At the Conquest it was seized by William, and given to the Earl of Morton, of whom Robert held it in Domesday Book. This Robert was surnamed de Constabulo from his office in Normandy. His son Robert possessed it in the beginning of the reign of Henry the First, and was succeeded by Simon, who called himself Fitz-Robert, and in the fifth year of King Stephen paid a fine to the King to have livery of the lands of Wimond de Craucombe, whose daughter he had married[k]. In the fourth of Henry the Second he paid a fine to have justice against Reginald Heirun, his wife's sister's husband[l]. And in the twelfth year of Henry the Second he was certified to hold one knight's fee of Robert de Beauchamp[m].

Simon Fitz-Robert having no issue, his lands were divided between his two brothers, Ralph and Godfrey. *Godfrey*, who inherited one half of the manor of Craucombe, assumed the name of *de Craucombe*, and was one of the most considerable men of his time. In the sixth of John he had a grant of the manor of Edston in Warwickshire. In the ninth year, a grant of the right of hunting, as well in, as out of forests, in all counties where he had lands[n]. In the sixteenth year of that King he was at Runnimede, and was sworn to the observance of the peace agreed to, and to support the authority of the twenty-five persons appointed to have the management of the kingdom. In that reign and that of Henry the Third, he was sent on several important embassies to the court of Rome. Henry the Third, in his seventeenth year, intrusted him to apprehend Hubert de Burgh, Earl of Kent, which he did at the head of three hundred men, and dragged him to the Tower out of a chapel near Merton, where he had taken sanctuary[o]. In the eighteenth year, the King granted to him the wood of Corseley, containing five acres, ten of moor, and thirty of heath, in the forest of Selwood; and in his nineteenth, the rights of free warren, a market, and a fair[p]. Afterwards, by the artifices of some sycophants, he was dismissed from the King's court, but in 1245 was retaken into favour

[k] Rot. Pip 5 Steph [l] Rot. Pip. [m] Lib. Nig. Scacc. 1 100 [n] Br Twyne, No 12. [o] Dugd Baron. vol 1 p 697 [p] Brian Twyne, No 10, 11

How much he was about the court appears by the great number of royal charters to which he was a witness.

By a charter without date, for the salvation of his own soul, and those of Alice and Johanna, his wives, he gave to the convent at Studley his manor of Craucombe, with the advowson of the church, *to clothe the Nuns:* except a messuage which William the shoemaker held of him in Craucombe, with half a virgate of land which he had given to Aufred Byssop: to hold of Robert de Beauchamp, with the borough, market, and all other rights, free from all suit to the county, the sheriff, and the hundred; by the service of one knight's fee, of the fee of Mortuyl[q]. The manor from this time obtained the name of Craucombe Studley. In the sixth of Henry the Eighth the Prioress made a grant of her moiety of the Church House towards the repairs of the parish church of Craucombe. The advowson was valued in 1290 at six marks[r]. On the 7th of June, 1459, the Prioress presented William Tybarde, the first President of Magdalen College, to the church of Craucombe[s].

As to *Long Compton*, the manor being vested in Edward the First, it was found, upon an inquisition held in the seventh year of his reign, that the Nuns of Studley in Oxfordshire had a carucate of land, which was granted to them by Geoffrey de Craucombe in pure alms, who had obtained it of Henry de Bohun, Earl of Hereford. That they had nine tenants holding several proportions of land, by the performance of certain servile works, and three acres of land in demesne, bestowed on them by Hubert de Burgh for the enlarging their court, and likewise a court leet and free warren. That John de Compton had two yard lands of the Hospital of Saint John in Oxford, for which he paid 6*s.* 8*d* to the Nuns of Studley per annum. In the thirteenth of Edward the First, Hugh de Plessetis and Ralph Pipard, who held the other half manor of Long Compton, claimed to have in common with the Prioress of Studley, a court leet, assize of bread and beer, gallows, weyfs, and to be exempted from suit to the hundred or county court, but it was found that the Prioress exercised these liberties in severalty[t].

[q] Dugdale s Monasticon, ad prædictas Sanctimoniales vestiendas.

[r] Taxat Spiritual Collinson's History of Somersetshire, 3 vols 4to 1791. vol. iii p. 515

[s] Chandler's Life of Will Waynflete from Reg Bath and Wells, p 93 note

[t] Dugdale's Warwickshire, Ed 2 1730 by W Thomas, D D. page 578. land in Halton, p 651. note to page 382 and lands in Shotswell, p 533.

A great number of houses, pieces of land, and rents, in the city of Oxford, were granted by different persons, at various times; chiefly in the thirteenth century; which are all described in the charters, with their situations and boundaries; but although these particulars might be interesting to an Oxford antiquary, they are too long to insert here. They may be classed according to their parishes.

In St. Mary's parish.

Clementia, the daughter of Robert Oweyn of Oxford, *in her virginity, and own liege power*, about 1261, granted a messuage near the house of the University; a mark of rent from the school of John Walens: four acres of meadow behind Oseney; all her right in the lands held by Roger de Orliens, tailor, in right of his wife Catherine, her sister, and all the rest of the lands and tenements of her father[u].

In 1276, William Pylle, of Oxford, granted a house called the School, between the *gable* of his own house, and Lawrence Kepeharm's; excepting the room abutting upon it, and the window looking into his own premises. If his wife Chrestina should survive him, and demand her dower in it, he binds his other lands, and discharges this tenement. It was afterwards called the Studley Schools, and brought half a mark of rent[x].

About 1214, Andrew Helegod gave part of his land in St. Mary's parish[y].

About the year 1241, Ralph Halegod, for his own soul, and those of his wives, Matilda, and Agnes, his father and mother, and his heirs, gave all his land in St. Mary's parish, which was held of the Church of the Holy Cross in Holiwell, for *the clothing of the Nuns of Studley;* which was agreed to by Juliana, the Prioress, with the assent of the whole convent. If any shall convert the land to other purposes, he is excommunicated. A rent of thirty-two pence to be paid[z].

In that year, an agreement was entered into, between John, Abbot of

[u] B Twyne, No 31. In meâ propriâ puellitate, et ligeâ potestate.

[x] Ibid No 32 Wood's Hist Oxon. vol. ii. p. 13. and Kennet, Par Antiq. *Camera forera* Forera is a head-land. *Visus extra dictam domum in tenementum meum.* I suppose, a window.

[y] Ibid. No 33

[z] Ibid. No. 34 ad vestitum Monialium de Stodleye.

Oseney, and Juliana, the Prioress of Studley, concerning an earthen wall, and the gutter of a sollar, in St. Mary's parish[a].

In the parish of Saint Mildred.

Philip, the miller, of Oxford, gave twenty-one pence of rent, paid by Peter, the son of Thorald, for the house which belonged to Humedon, the taylor, about 1221[b].

About 1260, an agreement was made between Walter the goldsmith, and Elizabeth, Prioress of Studley, respecting a rent of ten shillings from the house of Henry Gaieford.

Henry de Anna, formerly Rector of St. Mildred's[c], gave two houses, a sollar with cellars under it, in that parish, and another house in St Peter's. He granted likewise a rent, that twelve pence each might be paid annually to the *fifty Nuns of Studley* upon the day of his anniversary[d]. And Robert, son of Oein, gave four shops in Cobler's Street[e].

In St. Peter's in the East.

Lawrence, son of Harding, with the consent of his wife Agatha, gave all his land in Cattestrete, before Smithgate[f].

The nuns had a house called Sheld Hall, near New College, which was purchased of them by William of Wyckham, for an annual rent[g].

Edmund Turand gave a rent of four shillings, Henry the son of John Pille, the rent of a tenement; and Thomas de Blekkeley, the shop of Lawrence Leg[h].

In All Saints' parish.

Thomas, son of Henry, of Oxford, gave a rent of eight shillings from two shops, Celeyna, daughter of William Wakeman, a rent of twenty shillings, with power *of distress;* Adam, the son of Golde, of Oxford, four shillings of rent; Henry Punchard remitted his right in a house in the *Goldsmiths'* Street: and Lawrence Leg granted one mark of rent

[a] B Twyne, No 34, note [b] Ibid No 37. [c] Ibid. No. 43. [d] Ibid. No 42

[e] Ibid No 44 *Quatuor seldas,* shops, or stalls; *in cornesaria,* the coblery.

[f] Ibid No. 38 [g] Ibid. note. [h] Ibid. Nos. 39, 40, 41.

from his house in the Great Street. There is no date to any of these charters[i].

In St. Martin's parish.

Peter, the son of John, gave some land, Galfredus de Hengtestry (Hinxey) Burgess of Oxford, a *stall* in the *Butcher-row*; and Thomas de Henxtesey, Burgess of Oxford, remitted all his right in five shillings rent from a house in the Butcher-row[k].

In the seventeenth of Edward the Second, 1323, Roger, son of Nicholas at Nash, enfeoffed John Frelond of one messuage, one virgate of land, in *Horton*, formerly belonging to Walter at Hall. And in the fifteenth of Edward the Third, 1341, John Frelond enfeoffed Margery de Berchesdone, Prioress of Studley, with two tofts, twenty acres of plowed land, and three of meadow in *Becklegh* and *Horton*, formerly belonging to Walter at Hall, to find a chaplain to pray for his soul[l].

In the eighteenth of Edward the Third, 1344, John Frelonde, and William Attewode, of Studley, gave one messuage, nine oxgangs of plowed land, ten acres of meadow, six acres of wood, and sixteen shillings of rent in *East-Claydon*, and *Botel-Claydon*, to maintain a chaplain to celebrate a mass of the Virgin Mary every day in the conventual church of Studley[m].

Another capital donation was made to the priory, in the thirteenth of Richard the Second, 1389. This was the manor of *Esses*, *Ashe*, *or Nashe*, in the parish of *Beckley*, and in the counties of Oxford and Buckingham It was formerly the property of John de Esses, or at Ashe, and Eleanor his wife, son of Roger at Nashe, by whom it was granted to John de Appulby, and Margaret his wife, the thirty-fifth of Edward the Third, 1361. John de Appulbye, who was lord of Boarstall, granted it to Ralph Major, Vicar of the church of Beckley, and Roger Palte, of Newanton Purcel, Clerk of Studley, in the thirty-ninth of Edward the Third, 1365.

[i] Ibid No 45, 46, 47, 48, 49 *Distress*, Libero introitu ad *nanniandum* From *nam*, distraining, whence *withernam*, a distress by reprisal Saxon, niman, to take, and þẏþeꝛ contra. German, nehmen, and wieder. *Goldsmiths' Street*, Orfeveria. French, Orfevre, Auri Faber.

[k] Ibid. No. 50, 51, 52. A *stall*, stallum *Butcher-row*, Bocheria.

[l] Studley Chartulary, fol 15, 16. [m] R. Dods. MSS vol 56. f 134.

And in the thirteenth of Richard the Second, 1389, John Redhod, William Beknesfelde, and William Cok de Whateleye, enfeoffed Agnes at Halle, Prioress of Studley, with all their land in Ashe, which had belonged to John at Nashe, and which they had by the feoffment of Ralph Major, parson of the church of Waterstoke, and Roger Palte. In the next year Margaret, wife of Sir Gilbert Chastelyn, and afterwards of John Appulby, released all her right in Ashe, by a deed dated at Godstowe[n].

There are no remains of the town of Ashe, which stood upon the spot called Pinfold Green, where was the pound of the manor[o]. Traces of the name still continue in Nash Field, Asham Marsh, Asham Mead, and Asham Field

It appears, by depositions taken in the nineteenth year of Queen Elizabeth, that the Prioress of Studley had common without stint, for all manner of cattle in the very extensive track of country called the Quarters. Some tradition of this right still continues in two proverbial sayings, remembered by old people, that "if the grass grew upon Stanton church, "Studley might come and eat it off;" and another, that "Studley could "reach and fetch from Stanton church to Picket of Hay," which was said to have been near Winslow, ten miles off. It is extremely probable, that when this track of country was inclosed, the piece of ground called Menmarsh was allotted to Studley, in compensation for these extensive common rights. It appears by those depositions, that Menmarsh was part of the Quarters, and in an ancient terrier of the bounds of the parish of Beckley, it is stated, that the rivulet upon the common, there styled Denebrocke[p], divided the parish of Beckley from Brill or Boarstall; so that Menmarsh was in Brill or Boarstall parish, and the county of Buckingham[q]. So in the perambulation of the forest of Bernwood for the purpose of dis-

[n] Studley Chartulary, fol 9 a and b 10 a and b 11, 12, 15, 16

[o] It is so laid down in an ancient map, penes me

[p] Probably so called from the Danes, who fought many battles in Bernwood Forest See Kennet, p 35

[q] Fines et limites parochiæ Ecclesiæ parochialis de Becklеye Sepe vocatum Arngravehegh quod est inter quondam campum vocatum Borstallfelde dividit parochiam de Beckleye, à parochiâ de Brehull Et per illud sepe extendit se parochia de Beckleye, et ducit idem sepe rectè ad quendam rivulum Denebrooke nuncupatum, qui quidem rivulus pertendit usque ad clausum Domini Richardi Damori Qui quidem clausus dividit parochiam de Beckley à parochiâ de Woodperrye Studley Chart f. 3

afforesting so much of it as was in Oxfordshire, in the twenty-eighth year of Edward the First, in stating the boundaries between the Buckinghamshire, and the Oxfordshire parts, Denebrock is described as the division on that side[r].

There were besides a great number of other donations, of which the donors and the time are unknown, and which are specified in the subsequent grant of the priory. The original register of the monastery, which existed in the time of Bishop Tanner, is no longer to be found.

Of the Prioresses, I have been able to discover only the names of Juliana, in 1241[s]; of Alice de Craucombe, who was elected in 1250[t]; Elizabeth, Prioress in 1260[u]; Clementia, who was Prioress in 1292[x], Margery de Berchesdone, who died in 1377, and was succeeded by Elizabeth Freemantle, the Sub-prioress[y]; Agnes at Hall, in 1389[z], Catherine Copcot, who died in 1529, and was succeeded by Alice Whygill[a]. About the year 1266, there were fifty nuns[b].

The following is the seal of one of the Prioresses, perhaps Elizabeth, who held that office in 1260, or Elizabeth Freemantle. It represents the Virgin Mary and Child, under a tabernacle. Below, under an arch, is the

[r] Et sic per le Holewey usque Menmarshe, et sic usque le Hoke de Okewood apud Shortrudinsend, et sic usque le Denebroke ad caput occidentale de Orcherd de Oclewood, et sic ascendendo per le Denebroke usque Suthwellerne Studley Chartulary, fol 51 b. 54 and Kennet, page 323. 1294 and page 369. 1315.

Yet by permitting me to continue without dispute in the possession of Menmarsh for twenty-three years, till all the old witnesses were dead, who could have proved the full exercise of manorial rights over it by the lord of the manor of Studley, and by the perjury of a discarded tenant, who had vowed revenge, I was cruelly robbed of this piece of land, by two verdicts at Oxford Assizes, during my absence abroad If this judgment was correct, the Prioress of Studley had received no compensation for her common rights in the Quarters, and the manor of Studley in Oxfordshire, in the midst of forests and wastes, had little or no waste belonging to it The decision was as much against natural equity, as law

[s] Brian Twyne, MSS No 34 [t] Regist Lincoln in Kennet [u] B Twyne, MSS No. 34 note. [x] Studley Chartulary [y] Monasticon, vol iii. p. 13 [z] Coles's MSS. [a] Ibid. vol. 27 fol 85. Mus Brit. [b] B. Twyne, MSS. No 42 Henry de Anna gave annually quinquaginta monialibus xii denarios.

Prioress praying, and the inscription is Sigillum Elizabethe Priorisse de Stodle. The Seal of Elizabeth, Prioress of Stodley[e].

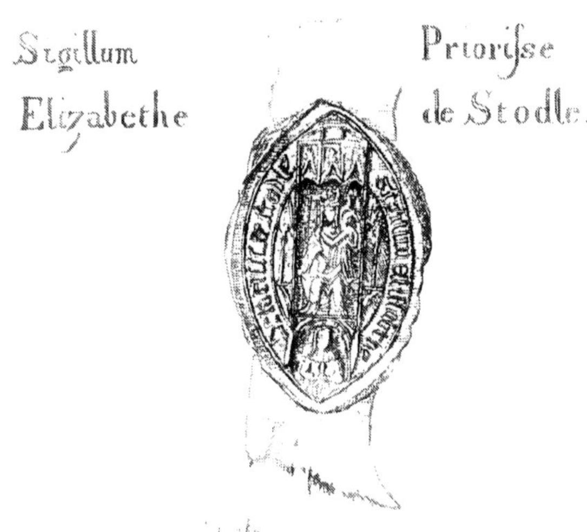

The habit of the Benedictine Nuns was a black robe, with a scapulary of the same, and, under that robe, a tunic of white, or undyed wool. When they went to the choir, they had over all a black cowl, like that of the monks.

The Priory was dissolved amongst the lesser monasteries, which had not above two hundred pounds a year, by the Act of the twenty-seventh of Henry the Eighth, 1536. At the dissolution, Johanna Williams was the Prioress, and there were fifteen nuns, whose revenue amounted in the gross, according to Speed, to £102. 6*s*. 7¼*d*. or in the clear, according to Dugdale, to £84. 4*s*. 4*d*.[d] Johanna Williams surrendered the Convent, and had a pension of £16. 6*s*. 8*d*. assigned to her, which she enjoyed in

[e] For this seal I am indebted to Henry Ellis, Esq. of the British Museum, whose attention and politeness render all researches in that extraordinary collection easy and pleasant.

[d] Dugdale's Monasticon. Tanner's Notitia Monastica.

1553, in which year there remained in charge, I suppose upon the Court of Augmentations, £3. 6*s*. 8*d*. in annuities, and in pensions to the nuns, to Katherine Copcote, £3. 6*s*. 8*d*. to Alice Yemans, £1. 13*s*. 4*d*. to Elizabeth Boulde, £1. 13*s*. 4*d*. to Susan Denton, and Margaret Wigball, £1. 6*s*. 8*d*. each[e].

It has been justly observed, that the dissolution of the monasteries was an act not of the Church, but of the State; prior to the Reformation, and effected by a King and Parliament of the Roman Catholic communion. The strictest members of that persuasion, and the most respectable characters of the times, among whom the Duke of Norfolk may be mentioned, accepted grants of the Conventual estates. Even the clergy thought it no sacrilege to share in these acquisitions. Bishop Gardiner commended the King for suppressing them, and Queen Mary made large grants of Abbey lands. Undoubtedly the suppression of the Convents facilitated the admission of Protestantism; but it was evidently undertaken on other principles[f].

In the thirty-first year of Henry the Eighth, 1539, the Priory, with all the possessions belonging to it, were purchased by John Croke, for the sum of one thousand, one hundred, and eighty-seven pounds, seven shillings, and eleven pence, and a grant was made of it by letters patent from the King, on the 26th day of February in that year[g]. The premises are described as the house and site of the Monastery, with the Church, the manor of Studley in the counties of Oxford and Buckingham, the manor of Crawcombe Studley, in the county of Somerset, the manor of Long Compton in Warwickshire, six pounds of rent in Crawcombe Beie in Somersetshire, the Rectory and Church of Beckley, the Rectory and Church of Hilmere, otherwise Ilmere, in Buckinghamshire, the Chapel of Senekeworth, or Sakeworth, in Berkshire, the advowson of the Church of Crawcombe Studley, the advowson of the Vicarage of Beckley, the advowson of the Vicarage of Hilmere, or Ilmere; all their possessions in Steple Barton, Steple Aston, Astwykes, Worton, Wighthill, Wightley, Benbroke, Bekbroke, Takeley, Weveley, Forstyll, Ellesford, Ellesfeld,

[e] Willis's Mitred Abbeys, vol ii. p 186 Warton's Life of Sir T. Pope, page 39

[f] Burn's Eccles Law, vol ii p 545

[g] Sept pars Patent. de anno R Hen Octavi tricesimo primo In the Rolls' Chapel.

Overhayford, Tetyndon, Tyvyton, Bekeley Parke, and Staunton, in Oxfordshire, and in Horton, Marlake, Okeley, Wornehall, Thomley, Wynchyndon, Kymbell, Hilmere, Ilmere, Est Claydon, Botel Claydon, Wighthill, and Wightley, in Buckinghamshire; and in Belgrave in Leicestershire, in Westcot Fairford in Gloucestershire, in Senekeworth, and Sakworth, in Berkshire, in Langeporte or Lamport in Northamptonshire, in Long Compton in Warwickshire, and in Crawcombe Studley, and Crawcombe Bere, in Somersetshire, and elsewhere: excepting the Prioress's wood, and all lands in Wroxton, Ardeley, Chesterton, and Wendlebury, in Oxfordshire. The whole was to be held of the King, in capite, by the service of the twentieth part of a knight's fee, and rendering six pounds fourteen shillings and two pence annually.

Of the reservations, Prioresses wood was granted by Queen Elizabeth, in her fourteenth year, to Christopher Hatton, Esquire, of whom it was purchased in the same year by Sir John Croke of Chilton[h]. And the fee farm rent of £6. 14*s.* 2*d.* and of three shillings for Marlake, were sold under the statute of the twenty-second of Charles the Second, chapter the sixth, to William Gape, and were by him conveyed to William Croke, Esquire, of Chilton, in the twenty-fifth of Charles the Second, 1672, for the sum of £123 9*s*.[i] The adjoining manor of Marlake, we have before seen, was purchased by Maister John Croke in 1541.

Of the very extensive possessions belonging to the Priory of Studley, thus purchased by Master John Croke, it appears that he sold off all the distant property, and retained only the house, the manor of Studley, the appropriation of Beckley, and other rights in that parish. The manor of Crawcombe Studley was transferred to the Kingsmill family, in which it still continues[k]. To whom the other estates were conveyed has not been traced. Out of the appropriation of Beckley, his son, Sir John Croke, conveyed to William Shillingford, otherwise Izod, by a deed dated the tenth of Elizabeth, 1568, the Rectory of Beckley, and some messuages and lands in the town of Beckley, reserving all rights and tithes in Studley, Horton, Ashe, Merlake, and Otmoor, except the tithes of beasts upon Otmoor belonging to the towns of Beckley, Noke, and Oddington[l].

[h] Grant, and Bargain and Sale. In Studley Chartulary, fol. 12, 13 [i] Deeds, penes me
[k] Collinson's Somersetshire [l] Deed

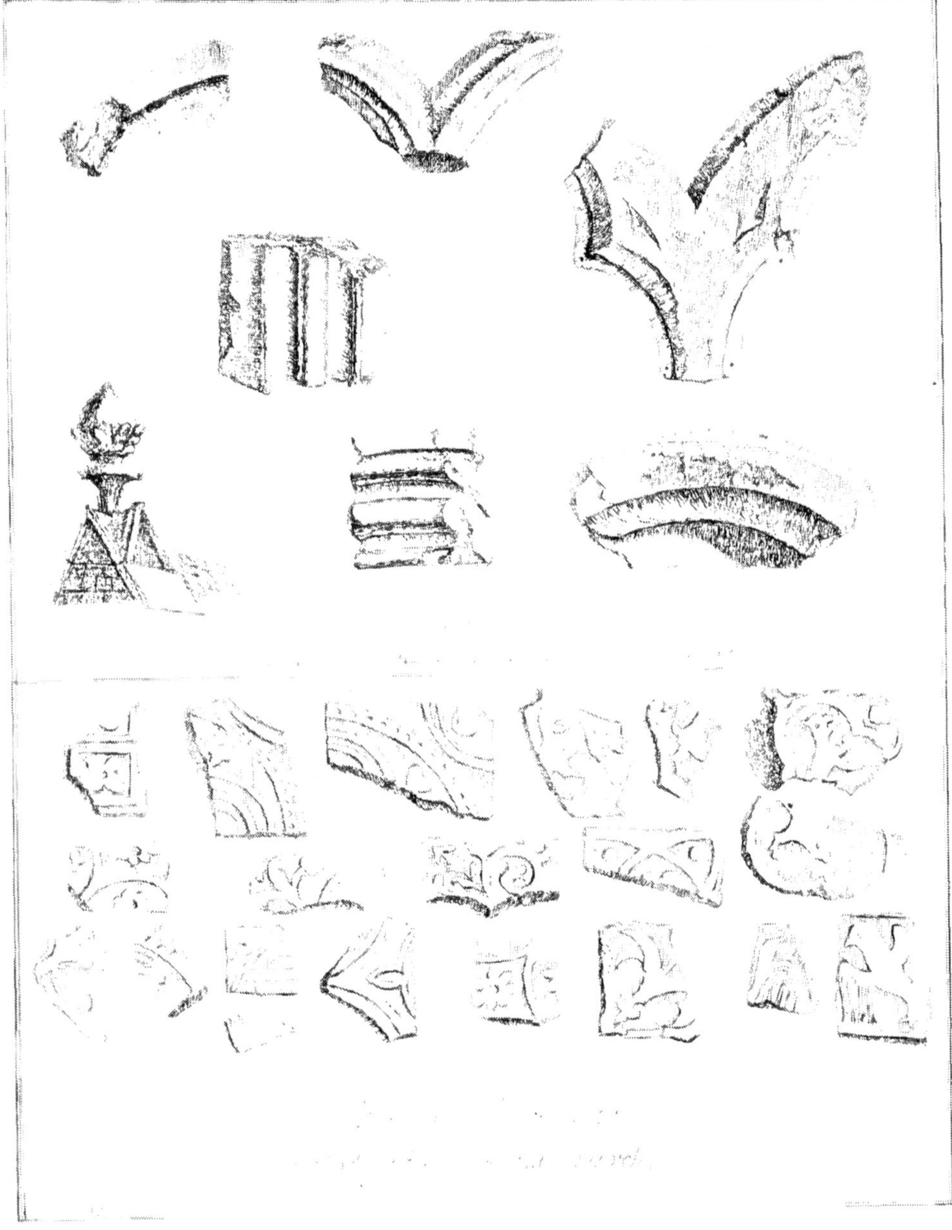

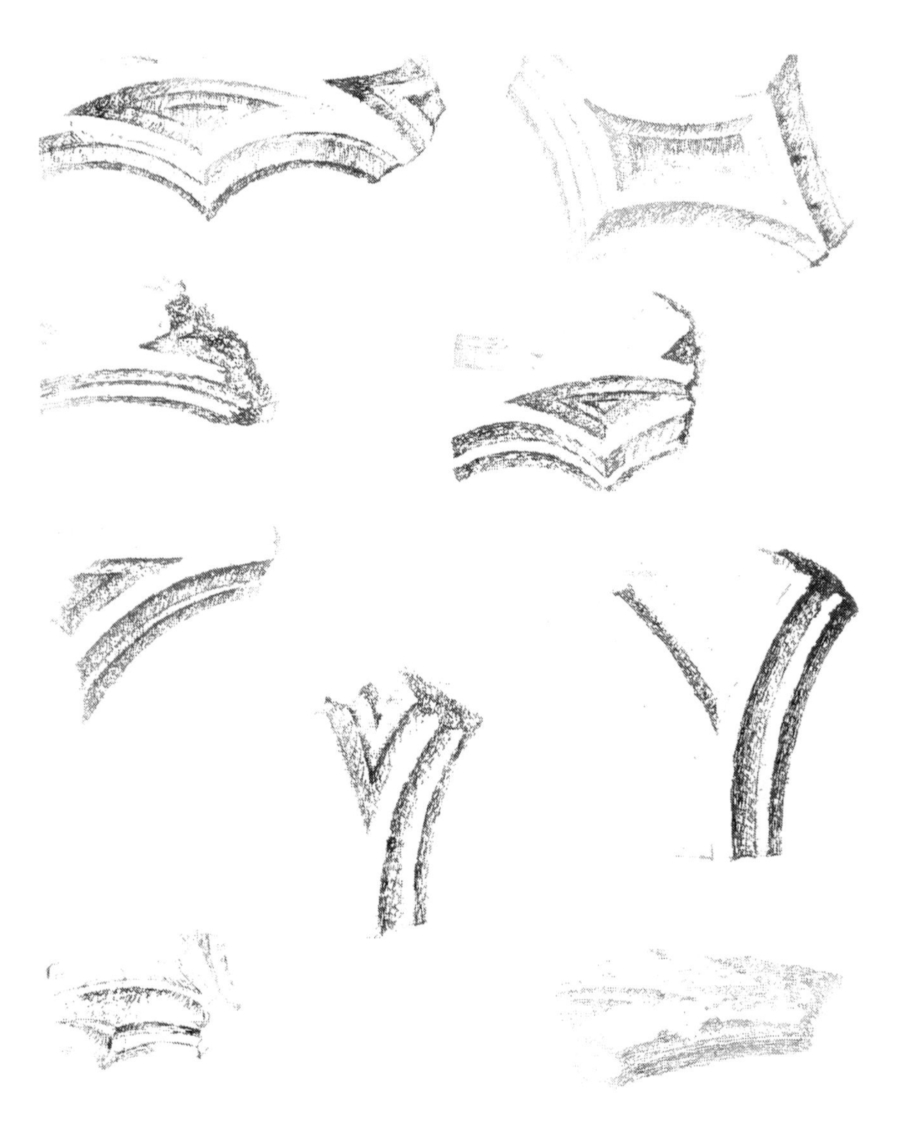

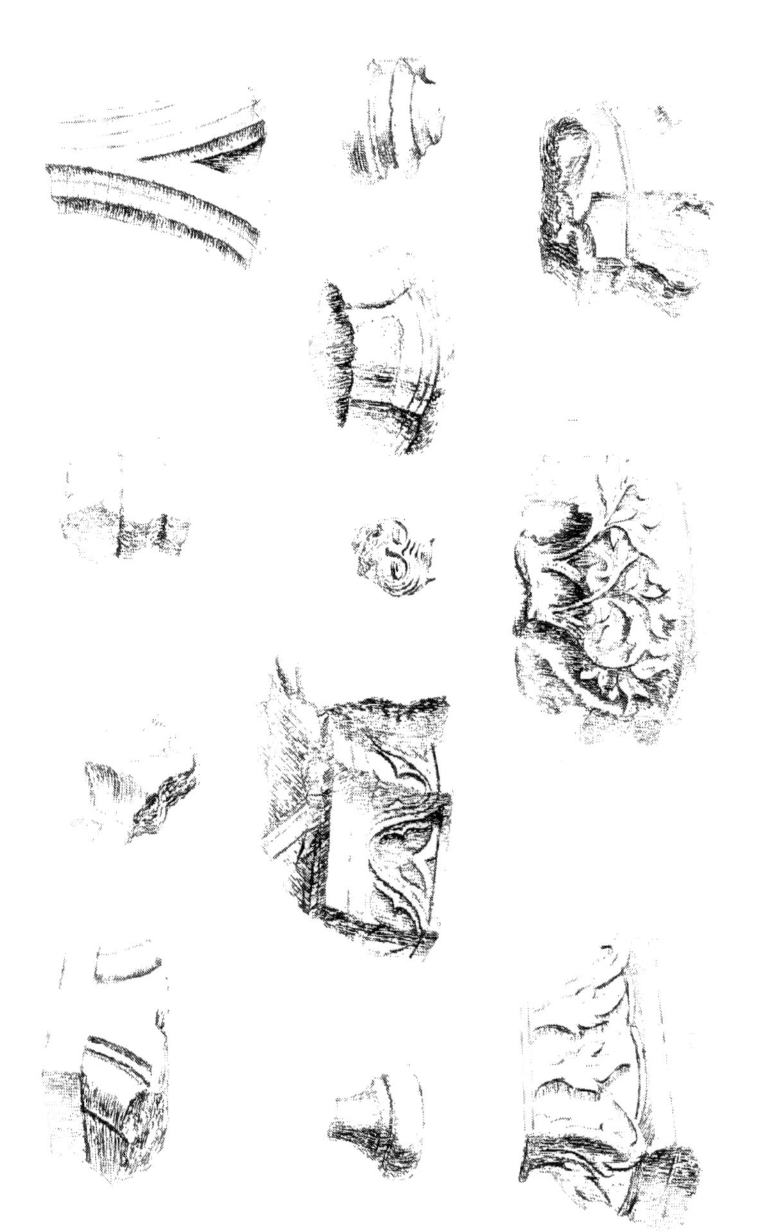

…e Seal of Elizabeth
…of Studley.

The … of the …nvent of St Mary,
of Studley.

… the Surrender in the Augmentation Office, 19 Novr 31 Hen VIII.

From many fragments which have been found of pillars, friezes, and capitals, of the Saxon and Gothic styles of architecture, admirably executed; and of very large windows, with a great quantity of flowered paving bricks, of what are usually called Norman tiles, the Priory must have been a handsome building; and there was a large Conventual Church[m]. How soon after the grant it was adapted to the purposes of domestic convenience, is not related I apprehend that the principal part of the walls of the present house were those of the Priory, and, in particular, the kitchen, the offices adjoining, and the eastern wing; but it must have been much altered, and the windows all made new[n]. As Master Croke, the purchaser, had built his principal seat at Chilton, it is probable that he did little to Studley, or even his son Sir John Croke, who resided at Chilton. I imagine that it was fitted up as a dwelling-house by Sir John Croke the Judge, the grandson of Master Croke. The old withdrawing room, the present dining room, had his arms inlaid over the chimney, being Croke with a label, impaled with Blount[o]. This proves that that room, at least, was finished by him, after his marriage, and in the life-time of his father. As his father did not die till Judge Croke was fifty-five years of age, he must have lived at Studley from his marriage till that event took place. The Chapel was built long after, by Sir George Croke, and the stables have the date of 1666, and the initials of Alexander Croke[p].

[m] See the etching of them I use the terms Saxon and Norman according to their usual acceptation, but the question of the origin of Gothic architecture has been very satisfactorily cleared up by late surveys of Normandy It is certain, 1. that what we improperly style Saxon architecture, was a clumsy imitation of the Roman orders, common all through Europe, and by the Normans introduced here 2 that the intersection of the arches, and the erection of groined ceilings, gradually suggested the pointed arch. 3 that the pointed arch naturally lead to all the other peculiarities of the Gothic style

[n] The present appearance agrees in this with the information received by Hearne in his Walk to Studley. See Appendix, No XXXIII

[o] I have preserved it

[p] Studley, or as it was formerly written, Estodeley, was probably derived from Eꞅꞇ East, Ƿoꝺe a wood, and Ley, uncultivated land, or Leʒe, a place. It would therefore signify, *a woody place to the east*, which is a proper description, being in the midst of woods, and to the east of the parish church, and the castle of Saint Valori

RICHARD CROKE, DOCTOR IN DIVINITY.

THERE was a person who lived about this time, whom we may with considerable probability include within the pale of our family, although there are not sufficient data fully to establish the relationship. This was Doctor Richard Croke, or Crocus, as he called himself in Latin, one of the first restorers, and most successful cultivators, of the Greek language in Europe.

The name of his father and mother are not known, but he is stated by Mosellanus, in a letter to Erasmus, to have been of an ancient and honourable family[a]. He was born in London[b], perhaps about the year 1492[c]. In his will, he mentions a brother, Robert Croke, of Water Horton in Warwickshire. This is all the knowledge we have of his connexions, but it is not improbable that he was the brother of John Croke, the Master in Chancery. They were contemporaries, and died within four years of each other[d]. He bore the name of Richard, which was that of Master Croke's father, and they both enjoyed the friendship of Sir Thomas More. The name of Croke is of rare occurrence out of this family.

From whatever family he was descended, he was under no great obligations to it. In his oration to the Cantabrigians, he complains that in his younger years, he was deprived of his paternal inheritance, by the iniquity of his relations. It is a proof of early merit, that he found in Archbishop Warham, a kind benefactor, who was at the expence of his maintenance and education[e].

[a] Juvenis cum imaginibus. Erasm. Op. Le Clerc, Epist. page 1596. D.

[b] Wood's Ath Oxon i col 85

[c] He was admitted Scholar at Cambridge in 1506, and as students then entered young, we may suppose that he was about fourteen years old

[d] John Croke in 1554, Richard in 1558

[e] Oratio de Græc. Disc. laudibus

Under such eminent patronage, he was elected Scholar of King's College at Cambridge, on the 4th of April 1506[f]. Soon after, lead by the celebrity of the Oxford professors, he removed to that University, and studied the Greek language under the famous William Groyn, and other learned men[g].

Having made great proficiency in Grecian literature, he went for farther improvement to Paris, where he was living in 1513. Whilst he resided there he seems not to have been well supplied with the means of pursuing his studies. Erasmus wrote to his friend Colet to send a few nobles to him, as a young man of good hopes, and who had been left destitute by some who had promised him their assistance[h].

His reputation for learning being now established, he went into Germany, and was the first public professor of the Greek language at Cologne, Louvain, Leipsic, and Dresden[i]. The exact time of his residence in these Universities is not ascertained; that he was at Leipsic in 1514, appears by a letter from Erasmus to Linacer[k]. He continued there for three years, and, amongst other eminent pupils, he taught the celebrated Camerarius[l]. With what honours he was received, and the success he met with there, the great number of his pupils, and the animated spirit and love for learning which he inspired, have been described

[f] Wood, ibid Regium Collegium cui meæ eloquentiæ rudimenta debeo Croc Oratio de Græc. Disc. laud

[g] Wood, ibid. Richardo Croco quondam ministro ac discipulo Grocini. Erasmus Epist. Coleto, page 131. C. Grocini doctissimi discipulus. Cai Hist. Cantab p 127

[h] Si quas pecunias habes in manibus, in hoc commissas, ut dentur in subsidium, rogo mittas aliquot nobiles Richardo Croco, quondam ministro ac discipulo Grocini, qui nunc Parisus dat operam bonis literis. Juvenis est bonæ spei, et in quem rectè beneficium collocaveris, nisi me planè fallit animus. Erasm. Epist. Coleto, 1513. page 131. C. In another, dated 29 Oct 1513, destituitur ille à nonnullis qui promiserant subsidium, page 131 F.

[i] Epistola Croci dedic. Martino Lenbelio Civi Lypsensi, præmissa operibus Ausonii, impressa 1515. Vale et Crocum tuum, primum literarum Græcarum, Coloniæ, Lovanii, Lypsiæque tuæ, publicum professorem. Ama, Vale

[k] Erasm. Linacro, 5 June, 1514. Crocus regnat in Academiâ Lipsiensi, publicitus Græcas docens literas Page 136 C. dated St. Omer's

[l] Joac Camerarii Vita P. Melancth. Usus ego sum Croco præceptore Lypsiæ puer penè triennio. In Grammaticâ sane doctrinâ Crocus excellebat, profitendo plurimorum studia excitaverat, reversus in patriam hoc opus doctrinæ reliqueiat inchoatum. Page 26.

in glowing language by Camerarius, who made such progress under his instructions, that, when the Professor was occasionally absent, the scholar supplied his place, though only sixteen years of age[m]. He was succeeded by Peter Mosellanus[n], upon his removal to Dresden, the last place of his residence upon the continent, and where he gave lectures for two years[o].

From hence he was invited to return to his native country, in 1517, and having been recommended for his great learning and eloquence, he became preceptor to the King in the Greek language, and was in great favour with him, and the English noblemen who were the patrons of literature[p]. In 1519, he was still attendant upon the court, and wrote to his friend Mosellanus to come to England, who however declined the invitation. Mosellanus, in a letter written at that time, says, that he wished to send some books of Croke to Hesse, but that they were not to be procured[q].

Upon the entreaties of Fisher, Bishop of Rochester, he returned to Cambridge, where he was appointed Greek Professor to succeed Erasmus[r]. This appears to have been in the year 1518, for there is a letter of the 23d of April from Erasmus, to congratulate him upon his ap-

[m] Joach Camerarii Epist Nuncupat, ad librum de Eruditione Comparanda Lugd. Bat. 1699 page 17 Giving an account of his early studies, he says, Advenit tum ad nos Richardus Crocus e Britanniâ, cum uberiore copiâ quasi mercis musicæ Cœpit profiteri interpretationem Græcæ linguæ Quis ad illum concursus factus? Quis honor externo habitus, vel qui potius non habitus? Quis tum vel labori, vel operæ, vel impensis pepercit? Fervebat opus, florebat ipse, nos incensi eramus discendi cupiditate

[n] Melch Adam. Vitæ Philosoph Germ. fol 1705 p 119, 120

[o] Dominus Richardus Crocus Anglus, qui hic biennio Græcæ literaturæ rudimenta cum summâ laude, et morum honestate, seminavit, et nunc patriam repetiturus, has tibi literas porrecturum se recepit H. Emsor Erasmo. Ex Dresdâ, Misniæ, 15 March, 1517. page 1592 D

[p] Crocus qui et Lypsiæ Græcas literas primus docuit, et ipsi Regi Henrico elementa Græca tradidit Stapleton de tribus Thomis, cap 5 Croke was King Henry's Greek master after his return from Leipsic. More's Life of Sir Thomas More, p 95.

[q] Mosellani Epist ad Jul. Pflugium Hessum nostrum rectissimè valere cupio, cui libellos Croci, quos cupit, jamdiu misissem, si haberi possent Nusquam, quod sciam, prostant Is noster Crocus in Aulâ Regis sui agit, et me jam literis in Angliam vocat Sed an fidendum sit nescio Misnæ, 1519 Jortin Erasm vol iii page 60.

[r] Wood. Knight's Life of Erasmus in Jortin, vol i page 22. Erasmo in *professione* linguæ Græcæ successit R. Crocus, vir disertus atque eloquens. Cai Hist. Univ. Cantab. page 127.

pointment to the professorship; which he styles, a splendid and honourable situation[s]. In his oration in commendation of Greek learning, which is dated on the calends of July the year following, he praises Erasmus highly, and speaks modestly of himself, as unworthy to succeed so great a man. In performing the duties of this office, so great were his labours, and so persevering his assiduity, that he had reason to complain, "that "his health was injured, and his countenance was become pale and "sickly[t]."

Afterwards, in 1522, he was appointed the first Public Orator at Cambridge, an officer who was before called Magister Glomeriæ: and he received a salary of forty shillings; which office he held till he was succeeded by Doctor Day in 1528[u]. By the University of Oxford he was offered a great stipend to reside there, and he was solicited to accept it by the Archbishop of Canterbury, Sir Thomas More, Linacer, and Grocyn On the other hand he was pressed by the Bishop of Rochester to continue at Cambridge; with whose request he complied[x]. In 1523, he was admitted to the degree of Bachelor in Divinity[y], and was elected Fellow of Saint John's College in Cambridge[z]. The next year, 1524, he was made Doctor in Divinity[a]. Then, or about that time, Wood says he was tutor to the King's natural son, the Duke of Richmond: but as that nobleman was then only five years of age, it was certainly later. The Duke went to Paris in 1532, and died in 1536, being only seventeen years

[s] Erasmus R. Croco suo S. D. Gratulor tibi, mi Croce, *professionem* istam tam splendidam, nec minus hororificam tibi quam frugiferam Academiæ Cantabrigensi, cujus commodis equidem pro veteris hospitii consuetudine peculiari quodam studio faveo Mihi nihil tuorum libellorum redditum esse scito Tantum Franciscus ostendit epistolas quasdam Græcas abs te recognitas, quas probavi; verum aiebat eas alteri missas. D Thomæ Grajo reddidi tuum Theocritum Bene vale, mi Croce charissime. Lovanio, 23 Aprilis, anno 1518 Col. 1678 F Dr Francis, Physician to Cardinal Wolsey.

[t] Croci Oratio ad Cantabrigienses.

[u] Wood, ibid. *Glomeria* is a barbarous word formed from *glomerare*, to collect together I suppose from collecting together the members of the University. Dominus Crocus qui primò advexit Græcas literas, erat *primus Orator*, et habuit, sicut Magister Glomeriæ stipendium xl[s] Ex libro D Matthei Cant. Dr Day succeeded about 1528. Ex libro Oratoris Publici Baker, in Coles's MSS vol 49 p 333.

[x] Croci Oratio ad Cantabrigienses

[y] Regist. Acad. Cant. Baker. [z] Ibid. [a] Ibid.

of age It was probably about the year 1529, or 1530, that Doctor Croke was his instructor, before he went to Italy, and when the Duke was at King's College[b].

Dr. Croke was intimately acquainted with all the learned men of his time, particularly those of his own country. His friendship with Erasmus appears strongly in a letter written by Mosellanus, of which Croke was to be the bearer, in 1517[c].

There is a letter from Sir Thomas More to him, preserved by his grandson, and which, allowing for the times and the man, must be allowed to be an elegant compliment.

"Whatsoever he was, my Crocus, that hath signified unto you that my love is lessened, because you have omitted to write unto me this great while, either he is deceaved, or else he seeketh cunningly to deceave you, and although I take great comfort in reading your letters, yet am I not so proude, that I should challenge so much interest in you, as though you ought of dutie to salute me everie day in that manner, nor so wayward, nor full of complaints, to be offended with you, for neglecting a little this your custom of writing For I were unjust if I should exact from other men letters, whereas I know myself to be a great sluggard in that kinde. Wherefore be secure as concerning this, for never hath my love waxed so cold towards you, that it need still to be kindled and heated, with the continual blowing of missive epistles. Yet shall you do me a great pleasure if you write unto me as often as you have leasure, but I will never

[b] Wood, ibid

[c] Petrus Mosellanus Domino Erasmo Lipsiæ, 24 Mar 1517. Deinde velut sponte currenti calcaria subdidit (ut literas scilicet Erasmo scriberet) Richardus Crocus, Britannus, juvenis cum imprimibus, tum utriusque linguæ litteraturæ cognitione non solum in Britanniâ, verum etiam Germaniâ nostrâ maximè clarus, qui in litterariis nostris confabulationibus, quoties tui nominis mentio esset facta (fiebat autem sæpè) non destitit suadere, hortari, ut me tibi insinuarem, neque enim hoc vel tibi fore ingratum, vel mihi pœnitendum, nempe quod te sit humanior nemo, neque quisquam και των πολλων magis omnibus sit expositus Aiebat præterea noster Crocus, se ita Erasmo conjunctum, ut epistolæ nostræ, vel hoc nomine, locus esset futurus istic honoratior, quod a se apportaretur · jam tum enim hinc in patriam solvere parabat His quasi stimulis excitatus calamum arripui, hæc utcunque scripsi, Croco perferenda dedi; quâ re si quid est peccatum, tuo Croco in nostrâ culpâ ignosces; is enim hujus audaciæ mihi auctor fuit (quod Græci dicunt) κορυφαιος Erasm Epist p 1596 D

persuade you to spend that time in saluting your friends which you have allotted for your owne studie, or the profitting of your scholars. As touching the other part of your excuse, I utterly refuse it, as there is no cause why you should fear my nose as the trunk of an elephant, seeing that your letters may without fear approche in the sight of any man; neither am I so long snowted that I would have any man fear my censuring. As for the place which you require that I should procure you, both Mr. Pace and I, who love you dearly, have put the King in mind thereof[d]."

When King Henry's divorce was in agitation, and, in consequence of Cranmer's suggestion, it was thought expedient to take the opinions of the foreign Universities; in the year 1530, Doctor Croke was sent into Italy upon that business: and he performed his commission with zeal, and fidelity. At the commencement of his progress, he was not invested with any public character, and had only a letter of recommendation to John Cassali, the English Ambassador. He went first to Venice, where he conferred with the divines and canonists, and even the Jewish Rabbis; and consulted the works of the Greek and Latin Fathers; which lay hid in manuscript, in the library of Saint Mark. Here he was intimate with Francesco Giorgi, the most learned man in the Republic, and who was called by the Pope, "*the Hammer of Heretics*[e]."

After continuing some time, he went to Padua, Bononia, and other cities. The question of the lawfulness of the King's marriage was at first proposed in general terms, without any direct reference to the case of Henry. When Doctor Croke found that the men of learning were mostly inclined to his opinion, he became more explicit, and at length ventured to go to Rome; where he endeavoured to procure himself to be made a Penitentiary Priest, that he might have the better access to the libraries. At this time, the Earl of Wiltshire, and Stokesley, Bishop of London, were sent as Ambassadors to the Pope, and the Emperor, and Cranmer accompanied them. In the disputes which took place between the families of Cassali, and Ghinucci, the King's ministers in Italy, he adhered to the Ghinucci; and the Cassali became of course his inveterate enemies. By Stokesley he sent over an hundred books, papers, and subscriptions[f].

[d] More's Life of Sir Thomas More, page 95. [e] Burnet's History of the Reformation, vol i p. 87. fol. edit [f] Ibid.

Though it was well known that bribes were given both by the Emperor. and Henry, yet an appearance of obtaining the disinterested opinions of the Universities was endeavoured to be preserved. Doctor Croke, in one of his letters of the 5th of August, 1530, to the King, protested that " he never gave, or promised any divine any thing till he had first freely " written his mind, and that what he then gave was rather an honourable " present than a reward." In another of the 7th of September, he writes, " Upon pain of my head, if the contrary be proved, I never gave any man " one half-penny, before I had his conclusion to your Highness, without " former prayer, or promise of reward, for the same." In his accounts still extant, the sums given appear to have been generally small, from one to thirty crowns, and the utmost was seventy-eight crowns. The Emperor's presents, and provisions, were more magnificent. Doctor Croke found the divines completely mercenary, and says, that " if he had money " enough he could get the hands of all of them in Italy[f] "

Many of his letters written during his stay in Italy are still extant[g]. In all of them he complained of the deficiency of his remittances, and that he had not money enough to support himself, and to pay his transcribers, and other necessary expences.

Having thus acquitted himself so much to the satisfaction of his employer, he was soon rewarded. On the 12th of January in 1531, he was presented by the King to the Rectory of Long Buckby in Northamptonshire[h]. A few years after, in 1535, this Rectory, including eight shillings payable yearly to the Prioress of Markeyate for a portion of the tithes, was valued at thirty-one pounds, eleven shillings, and three pence, out of which ten shillings and seven pence were deducted for synodals and procurations[i]. He does not seem to have resided upon his living, but to have kept a curate one of whom was called Sir William Castell.

[f] Burnet, ibid

[g] In the Cotton MSS Vitell. B 13 They are much burnt round the edges, but the principal part may be made out One of them, giving an account of the decision of the University of Padua, is printed by Burnet, vol i Appendix, page 88. Another by Strype, vol i Appendix, No 40 from Fox's collection There is another original letter in the Harleian MSS No. 416 folio 21 from Dr Croke to Henry VIII dated from Venice in 1530, 22 Oct concerning the prevarication of some Friars at Padua

[h] Reg Joh Longland Episc Linc Bridges's History of Northamptonshire, p 548.

[i] Rot in Offic Primit. No. 28. Ibid. p 547

Graduates having then the title of Sir, as Sir Hugh Evans in Shakespeare.

In 1532, he came to Oxford, and was incorporated Doctor of Divinity in that University. In that year, King Henry the Eighth converted Cardinal Wolsey's College into his own foundation, by his charter of the 18th of July, and Croke was appointed the third of the twelve canons. In the latter end of the same year, the new Dean, Doctor John Hygden, died, upon which the Canons wrote to Cromwell, the Secretary of State, requesting that he would intercede with the King that Doctor Croke might succeed him; but he was not appointed to the Deanery. In 1545, Henry dissolved his College, and established it as a Cathedral On this new foundation he was not made a Canon, but he received, as a compensation, a yearly stipend of £26 13*s*. 4*d* · when he retired to Exeter College, and lived there as a sojourner[k].

During his continuance at Oxford, he wrote some verses upon Leland, to reproach him with changing his religion, for Croke continued firm till his death in the Catholic faith Leland replied in the following witless epigram.

In Richardum Crokum Calumniatorem.

Me fatuum Crokus, fatuorum maximus ille,
 Imperio quodam prædicat esse suo.
Ut sim, me furiæ non torquent, illius urgent
 Clade Mathematicum nocte dieque caput[l].

It should seem that he afterwards went to reside at Cambridge, for Doctor Caius, or Keys, mentions that in 1551, a Doctor Richard Croke, being Deputy Vice-Chancellor of that University, together with Doctor Hall, discharged Christopher Frank, the Mayor of Cambridge, from his interdict, to which he had rendered himself subject, by refusing to take the usual oath to the Vice-Chancellor, but not till he had made submission, and done penance at the Augustine Church, on his knees, with a lighted taper before the blessed Virgin[m].

He died in London in 1558, having made his nuncupative will on the 22d day of August, being I suppose too ill to write. It was proved in

[k] Wood, by Gutch, vol iii p. 428. [l] Leland, Encomia Celeb. Virorum Collectanea, vol v p. 161 Wood, ibid [m] Caii Hist Cantab lb i page 107

the Prerogative Court of Canterbury on the 29th of August in the same year, in the following words.

In the Name of God, Amen, the 22d day of August, in the year of our Lord God a thousand five hundred fifty-eight. Richard Croke, Doctor of Divinity, Parson of Long-Buckby, in the county of Northampton, being then sick in his body, but of his perfect mind and memory, made and declared his last will and testament nuncupative in manner and form following. First he commended his soul to Almighty God, and all the holy company of Heaven, and his body to be buried in Christian burial. Then he made, named, and constituted Robert Croke, of Water Horton, in the county of Warwick, his brother, and Richard Carpenell, his servant, his Executors of his said testament, and last will; to whom he gave all his goods, chattels, and debts whatsoever. Witnesses hereof Will. Gent, and John Knight, Gent. Sir Will. Castell, Curate of Long Buckby, aforesaid, Will. Frend, and others. The will was proved by the oath of Christopher Robynson, Proctor of the Executors.

His known printed works, which are all extremely scarce, are these.

Oratio de Græcarum disciplinarum laudibus. Dedicated to Nicholas, Bishop of Ely, by an epistle dated cal. Jul. 1519. In quarto[n].

Oratio qua Cantabrigienses est hortatus ne Græcarum literarum desertores essent. Printed with the former. Before and at the end of these two Orations, Gilbert Duchet has a laudatory Epistle[o].

Richardi Croci Britanni Introductiones in rudimenta Græca. Dedicated to Archbishop Warham. Expensis providi viri Domini Johannis Lair de Sibeich[p].

Tabula Græcæ Linguæ, published in Germany: mentioned in the dedication of his Rudimenta Græca.

Elementa Grammaticæ Græcæ[q].

De Verborum Constructione. I suppose this is his translation of Theodore Gaza's fourth book De constructione, which he dedicated to the Elector of Mentz Printed at Lypsick, 1516, in quarto[r].

[n] Wood's Ath Ox col 86 [o] Ibid [p] Wood, and Ames's Typographical Antiquities, page 456 [q] Wood.

[r] Ibid. Grammatica Theodori Gazæ Latinè verterunt partim Erasmus, anno 1518, partim verò Richardus Crocus nostras, linguæ Græcæ apud Lipsienses professor omnium primus Hodius de Græcis illustribus, p 72

He translated into Latin, Chrysostom in Vetus Testamentum, and Elysius Calentius. This writer was a Latin poet, who was born at Naples, and died before 1503. He was preceptor to Frederic, the son of Ferdinand the First, King of Naples. His works were published in folio, the first edition it is not known when, the second at Rome in 1503, the third at Basil in 1554[s].

Opera Ausonii impressa per Valentinum Schumen, 4to. 1515, cum epistolâ præmissà dedicata Martino Lenbelio, Civi Lypsiensi, et annotaonibus[t].

[s] Tanner's Bibliotheca Britannica Hibernica, p 209. Moreri. [t] See ante.

CHAPTER III.

Sir John Croke, or le Blount, and Elizabeth Unton

THE family was now permanently established at Chilton, and Sir John Croke, the son of John Croke, Esquire, and Prudentia Cave, succeeded to the ample inheritance of his father. The tranquil life of a man of fortune affords few incidents for the pen of a biographer, and little which can interest posterity. But Sir John Croke was the patriarch from whose loins several distinct families proceeded, the descendants of his numerous children.

He was born in 1530[a]. The place of his education is not known, except that at seventeen years of age he was admitted of the Inner Temple, rather for acquiring the theory, than with a view to the practice of the profession of the law[b]. By Sir Harbottle Grimston, who married his grand-daughter, he is described as a man of great modesty, charity, and piety[c]. He resided in London at the house in Fleet Street, which had been purchased by his father, and which was a fashionable part of the town before elegance had migrated westward At his house in Chilton he seems to have maintained with dignity the highly respectable character of a country gentleman; filling, when his duty required it, the public offices which belonged to that station and occasionally taking his seat in Parliament

Early in life, when he was twenty-three years of age, in 1553, he married a lady of family, and high connexions, and who had likewise the youthful charms of fifteen. This was Elizabeth, the daughter of Sir Alexander Unton. Her family was seated at Chequers in Buckinghamshire, at Faringdon, and Wadley, in Berkshire In Faringdon church is

[a] From his monument

[b] "John Crooke of London was admitted of the Inner Temple, 10 June, 1 Edward VI '1547" Register of the Inner Temple

[c] Preface to Croke Charles.

a chapel called Unton's Isle, where are some of their monuments, of which the inscriptions are nearly obliterated, but which have been preserved by Ashmole[d]. Sir Hugh Unton, the great-grandfather of Lady Elizabeth Croke, married Sybell the daughter and heiress of William Fettiplace, the son of Thomas Fettiplace of Shifford in Buckinghamshire, Esquire, in the time of Henry the Sixth, whose wife was Beatrice, the natural daughter of John the First, King of Portugal. This sovereign married Philippa, the daughter of John of Gaunt, and had by her legitimate children, who succeeded him in the kingdom. By his favourite mistress Ines, or Agnes Perez, he had Beatrice, and a son named Alphonso, who was created Duke of Braganza, and was the ancestor of the present royal family of Portugal Beatrice had four husbands. The first was Thomas, Earl of Arundel. After his death she became the second wife of the great Gilbert Talbot, first Earl of Shrewsbury, the victorious general of the English forces in France, by whom she had a daughter named Ankaret, who died a child. Thirdly, she married John Holland, Earl of Huntingdon, and lastly, Thomas Fettiplace, Esquire. Her first and third marriages were unfruitful, and she left only one son, William Fettiplace, by her last husband. She was much beloved by her royal father, who upon the death of her first husband, in the fourth year of Henry the Fifth, wrote to Sir John Pelham, a favourite of that monarch, desiring him "to shew the Lady "Beatrice, his daughter, being deprived of her husband, the same favour "he had before shewn her." From this marriage the Untons quartered the arms of Fettiplace; which are gules, two chevrons, argent: and the Croke family, from this, and another marriage, which will be hereafter mentioned, claims a descent from the royal house of Braganza[e].

[d] History of Berkshire Faringdon came to the Crown by the dissolution of Beaulieu Abbey It was granted by Queen Mary to Sir Francis Englefield, after whose attainder Queen Elizabeth gave it to Sir Henry Unton In 1622 it was purchased of Sir John Wentworth, and other representatives of the Unton family, by Sir Robert Pye Wadley, in 1531, was the seat of the Untons from them it passed by a female to the Purefoys Henry Purefoy of Wadley was created a baronet in 1662, and the title is now extinct

[e] D Antonio Caetano de Sousa, Historia Genealogica da casa real Portuguesa, 6 vols 4to Lisbon, 1739 to 1748 Collins, Baronetage, vol. iii p 266 Ashmole's History of Berkshire, vol. ii p 213, &c Monuments at Childrey in Berkshire, Swinbrook in Oxford-

Sir Thomas Unton the son of Hugh, in the reign of Henry the Eighth, held lands in Fingest in Buckinghamshire, and was created Knight of the Bath, at the Coronation of Edward the Sixth.

His son, Sir Alexander Unton, had two wives, Mary Bourchier, by whom he had no children, and Cecill, the daughter of Peter Bulstrode, Esquire, of Bradborough in Buckinghamshire, by whom he was the father of Sir Edward Unton, Knight of the Bath, Henry Unton, and Lady Croke. Sir Alexander died in 1547[f] After his death, his widow Cecill married Sir Robert Kellaway, of Minster Lovell, in Oxfordshire, by whom she had an only daughter Anne, married to Sir John Harrington Lord Harrington of Exton in Rutlandshire. This nobleman was the eldest son of Sir James Harrington. In the reign of Elizabeth he was Lord Lieutenant of Rutlandshire, and Recorder of Coventry. King James in the first year of his reign created him Baron of Exton He and his lady were appointed to the care and tuition of the princess Elizabeth, who was born in 1596, and afterwards married Frederic the Fifth, Count Palatine of the Rhine, Duke of Bavaria, and King of Bohemia Lord Exton accompanied her into Germany upon her marriage, where he was taken ill, and died at Worms on the 24th of August, 1613. His widow was living in 1617. His only son survived him only a few months, and died young and unmarried. He left two daughters, who inherited the property. Of whom Lucy married Henry, Earl of Bedford, to whom she brought an estate at Minster Lovell, and ten thousand pounds in money. Frances, the other sister, and co-heiress, was the first wife of Sir Robert Chichester of Raleigh in Devonshire, Knight of the Bath, by whom she had a daughter, Anne, married to Thomas Lord Bruce, ancestor of the Earl of Aylesbury[g].

Sir Edward Unton, Knight of the Bath, brother to Lady Elizabeth Croke, married Anne, Countess of Warwick, daughter to Edward Sey-

shire, of Anne Fettiplace, married to Edmund Dunch, in Little Wittenham Church in Berkshire Fuller's Worthies Vertot's Revolution de Portugal Anderson's Genealogical Tables, pages 717, 718, 719 Noble's Memoirs of Cromwell, vol ii p 158

[f] Monument in Faringdon Church.

[g] Wills of Sir John and Lady Elizabeth Croke, and of their son, Sir John Croke Collins, Baronetage, vol ii p 227 Holland's Herwologia Anglica, 1620

THE GENEALOGY OF UNTON AND FETTIPLACE.

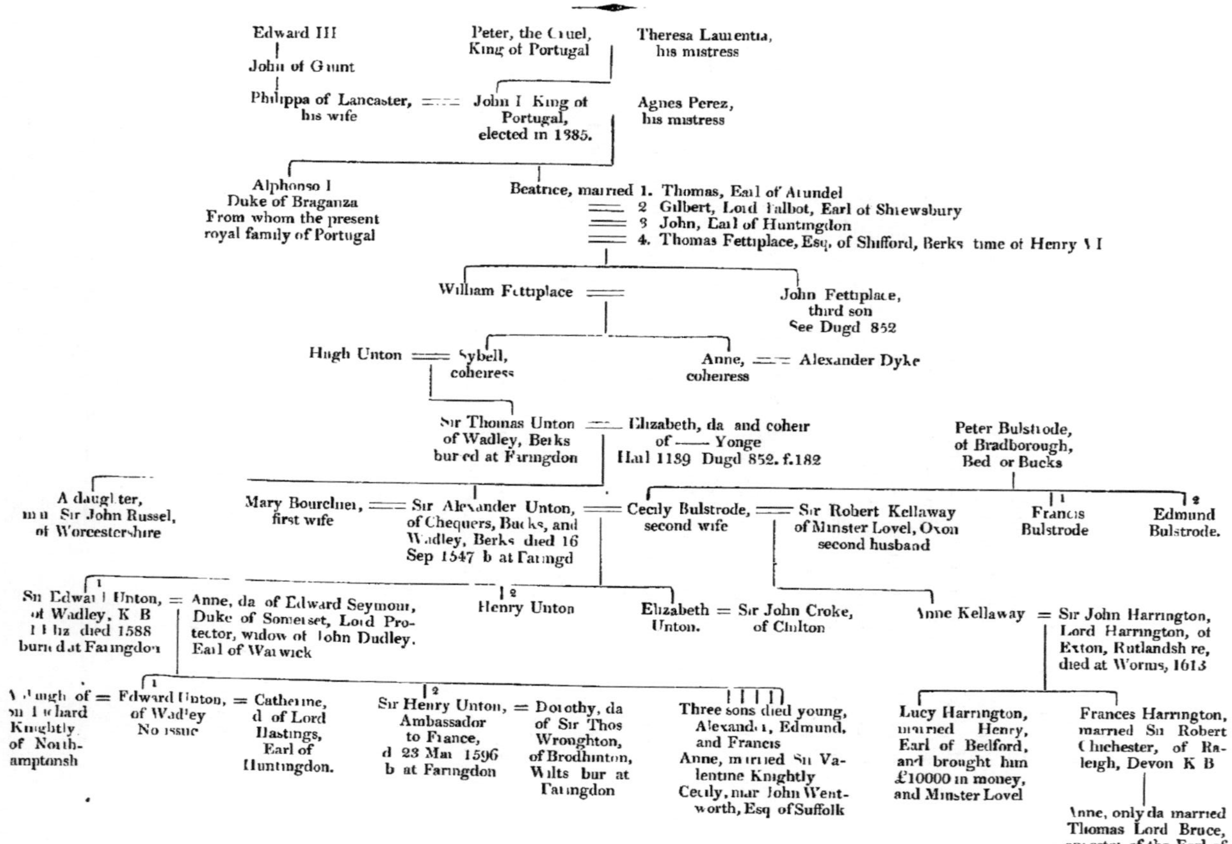

mour, Duke of Somerset, and Protector of England, widow of John Dudley, Earl of Warwick, and son of the Duke of Northumberland, by whom she had five sons, of whom three died young; Edward and Henry only survived, and succeeded one after the other, in their father's inheritance. Of the two daughters, Anne, married Sir Valentine Knightley, and Cecill to John Wentworth, Esquire[h].

Of the two sons, the nephews of Lady Elizabeth Croke, Edward Unton married two wives; first, a daughter of Sir Richard Knightley of Northamptonshire; and secondly, Catharine, daughter of the Lord Hastings, afterwards Earl of Huntingdon, but left no issue by either.

The other son, Sir Henry Unton, was educated at Oxford, and travelled over great part of the world. For his bravery he was created a Knight Banneret, by the Earl of Leicester, at the siege of Lutphen in 1586. He was twice ambassador in France. During his residence there, in the true spirit of the reign of Elizabeth, he challenged a French nobleman, in defence of the beauty, or honour, of his royal mistress. In the Bodleian Library is a manuscript which contains copies of his dispatches, and other papers, during his first embassy: the passport is dated 22 July, 1591[i]. His wife was Dorothy, the daughter of Sir Thomas Wroughton. He died upon his second embassy in France, the 23d of March, 1596, and was brought over and buried at Faringdon[k]. After his death, a collection of poems, written at Oxford in memory of him, was published by Doctor Robert Wright, Fellow of Trinity College, and afterwards Bishop of Litchfield and Coventry, who prefixed a good Latin preface[l]. Wright accompanied Sir Henry in his last embassy to the French King's camp at Lafere, in which he died[m].

Such was the noble family into which Sir John Croke married, and which soon after became extinct. To return to the account of himself[n].

[h] Monument in Faringdon Church [i] Bod. MSS. No. 3498 [k] Monument at Faringdon

[l] It is entitled, Funebria nobilissimi et præstantissimi equitis D. Henrici Untoni ad Gallas bis legati regii, &c a Musis Oxoniensibus apparata 1596 4to.

[m] Warton's Life of Sir Thomas Pope, Appendix, page 392. He inserts part of one of the poems

[n] See the Genealogy of Unton and Fettiplace, No. 24. From Harl MSS No 1139, a Visitation of Bucks in 1574 No. 1102 Visitation of Bucks in 1634, page 122, No. 3968. Ashmole's Berkshire Monuments in Faringdon Church Brown Willis's MSS. vol. 21. f. 19.

Sir Thomas Pope, the founder of Trinity College in Oxford, by his will dated in 1556, and which took effect by his death in 1559, in the fiftieth year of his age, bequeathed to him, under the affectionate name of "his old master's son, Master Croke," his gown of black satin, faced with lucern spots. This was the spotted fur of a Russian animal called a lucern, anciently much esteemed. It was usual in those times, when fashions were less changeable, and valuable articles of dress were considered as a substantial part of wealth, to leave them to particular friends, as a token of affection. This satin gown seems to have been his habit of ceremony, since he is represented in it by Hans Holbein in a fine picture, in the possession of the Earl of Guildford at Wroxton, and it appears in all his other portraits: Sir John Croke himself is painted in a similar gown[o].

In the year 1571, the thirteenth of Queen Elizabeth, he was elected Member of Parliament for Southampton, and he represented his own county as Knight of the Shire for Buckinghamshire, in the Parliament which met in 1572, having for his colleague Sir Henry Lee[p]. In 1575 he was appointed the first High Sheriff for the county of Buckingham, divided from Bedfordshire: till that year there having been only one High Sheriff for the two counties[q], and he then received the honour of Knighthood from the Queen Elizabeth[r].

Sir John Croke and Lady Elizabeth lived together above fifty-five years. He died on the 10th day of February, in the year 1608, in the seventy-eighth year of his age, and his lady followed him on the 24th of June 1611, in the seventy-third year of her age.

They had five sons, and three daughters, who lived to grow up: John, Henry, George, Paulus Ambrosius, and William: Cicely, Prudentia, and Elizabeth: and three children, who died young. He was buried in a very splendid manner: the expenees of his funeral amounted to £215 14*s.*[s], and his widow erected a fine monument in the chapel in Chilton church, which is appropriated as the burial place of the Croke family. Their effigies are lying under an arch supported by two black marble

[o] Thomas Warton's Life of Sir Thomas Pope, pages 6 and 164. [p] Willis, Notitia Parl. [q] Fuller's Worthies, Bucks, p. 140. [r] Ward, p. 303. [s] Account in the hand-writing of Sir George Croke, penes me.

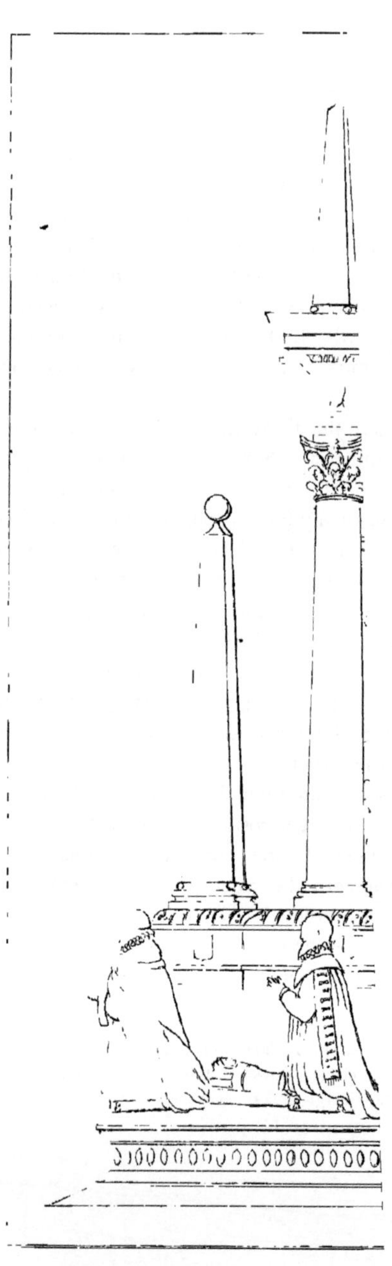

Sir Thomas Pope, the founder of Trinity College in Oxford, by his will dated in 1556, and which took effect by his death in 1559, in the fiftieth year of his age, bequeathed to him, under the affectionate name of "his old master's son, Master Croke," his gown of black satin, faced with lucern spots. This was the spotted fur of a Russian animal called a lucern, anciently much esteemed. It was usual in those times, when fashions were less changeable, and valuable articles of dress were considered as a substantial part of wealth, to leave them to particular friends, as a token of affection. This satin gown seems to have been his habit of ceremony, since he is represented in it by Hans Holbein in a fine picture, in the possession of the Earl of Guildford at Wroxton, and it appears in all his other portraits: Sir John Croke himself is painted in a similar gown[o].

In the year 1571, the thirteenth of Queen Elizabeth, he was elected Member of Parliament for Southampton, and he represented his own county as Knight of the Shire for Buckinghamshire, in the Parliament which met in 1572, having for his colleague Sir Henry Lee[p]. In 1575 he was appointed the first High Sheriff for the county of Buckingham, divided from Bedfordshire: till that year there having been only one High Sheriff for the two counties[q]; and he then received the honour of Knighthood from the Queen Elizabeth[r].

Sir John Croke and Lady Elizabeth lived together above fifty-five years. He died on the 10th day of February, in the year 1608, in the seventy-eighth year of his age, and his lady followed him on the 24th of June 1611, in the seventy-third year of her age.

They had five sons, and three daughters, who lived to grow up: John, Henry, George, Paulus Ambrosius, and William: Cicely, Prudentia, and Elizabeth: and three children, who died young. He was buried in a very splendid manner: the expences of his funeral amounted to £215. 14*s*.[s], and his widow erected a fine monument in the chapel in Chilton church, which is appropriated as the burial place of the Croke family. Their effigies are lying under an arch supported by two black marble

[o] Thomas Warton's Life of Sir Thomas Pope, pages 6 and 164. [p] Willis, Notitia Parl. [q] Fuller's Worthies, Bucks, p. 140. [r] Ward, p. 303. [s] Account in the hand-writing of Sir George Croke, penes me.

Corinthian pillars. Sir John is in armour, and Lady Elizabeth in the dress of the times. Round the front of the monument their children are all represented kneeling in the habits of their respective situations in life the figures are well executed, and the whole is a fine specimen of the taste and statuary of that age.

Above the figures of Sir John and Dame Elizabeth, in the centre, is the coat of arms of Croke, quartering Heynes, with a crescent. The same on the right hand, and on the left, Unton, quarterly

In front of the monument are the following eleven figures of the children, with a coat of arms to each.

1. Sir John Croke, the eldest son, in his dress as a Judge, scarlet robes and black coif. The arms are Croke, impaled with nebulè, or and sable, Blount.

2. A babe in swaddling clothes. This must have been their second child, who died an infant. The arms are Croke, with a crescent, azure, for difference, denoting a second son[t].

3. Henry Croke, in a bar gown, welted down the sleeves, denoting an utter barrister. Arms, Croke with a mullet, impaled with argent, a chevron between three eagles' heads erased, azure, for Honeywood.

4. Sir George Croke, habited as a Judge. Arms, Croke, with a martlet, impaled with gules, a bezant between three demi-lions' heads couped, argent, for Bennet In his own coat of arms he bore a mullet, as third son, not reckoning the infant.

5. Paulus Ambrosius Croke. In a plain bar gown, as having been a reader[u]. Two coats of arms · first, Croke, with an annulet, impaled with gules, a lion or griffin rampant, or, debruized of a bend, ermine, a chief, checky, or and gules, for Wellesborne. Second coat of arms, Croke, impaled with argent, two piles in chief, wavy gules, for Choe.

6. A little boy. Arms, Croke, with a fleur-de-lis.

7. A young man. Croke, with a rose.

8. William Croke, as a gentleman, in armour. Croke, with a quater-

[t] Ward supposes the three young figures to be grand-children, but the *differences* on the arms prove them to be children of Sir J Croke

[u] Chauncy's Hertfordshire, p. 303.

toil, impaled with azure, a chevron between three eagles' heads erased, argent, for Honeywood[x].

Then come the three daughters.

1. Cecil. Two coats of arms. First, sable, a stag's head caboched, argent, pierced through the mouth with an arrow, or; attired, and between them a cross patee, fitchee, or, for Bulstrode, impaled with Croke. Second, gules, within a bordure a chevron between three lions' paws, erased and erect, argent, armed azure. On a chief argent, an eagle displayed, sable. Impaled with Croke, for Brown.

2 Prudentia. Arms: a bend, gules, cottised, sable, charged with three pair of wings, argent, for Wingfield, impaled with Croke.

3. Elizabeth. Arms argent, within a bordure engrailed, gules, two chevrons, azure, for Tyrrel, impaled with Croke.

It appears that some part of this monument was not put up during the life time of Lady Elizabeth, for though two of her sons were judges, the youngest did not arrive at that dignity till long after the death of his mother.

The inscription on the monument is this

JOHANNES CROCUS, EQUES CLARISSIMUS, UNA CUM UXORE, ELIZABETHA, EX ILLUSTRI UNTONORUM FAMILIA. QUI PARITER SUAVE JUGUM CHRISTI, UNANIMI IN VERA PIETATE CONSENSU, SUSTULERUNT, VITAM DEO CONSECRARUNT, OPERA INDIGENTIBUS EXHIBUERUNT, EXEMPLUM POSTERIS RELIQUERUNT, IN HOC MONUMENTO CONDITI, RESURRECTIONEM JUSTORUM EXPECTANT.

JOHANNES OBDORMIVIT IN DOMINO X DIE FEBRUARII ANNO CHRISTI MDCVIII, ÆTATIS SUÆ LXXVIII. ELIZABETHA OBDORMIVIT IN DOMINO XXIV DIE JUNII, ANNO CHRISTI MDCXI, ÆTATIS SUÆ LXXIII.

PRÆVIUS AD CHRISTUM PROPERO, MEA LUX, MEA VITA.
CORDA DATE CHRISTO. METAM PROPEREMUS AD ISTAM.
VERE IGITUR FŒLIX, ET VITA, ET FUNERE, CROCUS.
EST BONA VITA BONIS, MORS BONA GRATA DEO.

[x] See as to Honeywood, in the Vellum Pedigree, it is argent, and the bearings azure

On the pavement below is a large flat stone, I suppose over the bodies, with this inscription, on a fillet of brass round it.

HERE LYETH BURIED SIR JOHN CROKE, KNIGHT, AND LADY ELIZABETH HIS WIFE, DAUGHTER OF SIR ALEXANDER UNTON, KNIGHT, WHO LYVED MARRIED TOGETHER 55 YEARES, 9 MONETHES, AND (obliterated) DAYS, FOR WHOME THIS TOMBE IS MADE, AT THE CHARGES AND DIRECTION OF THE SAID LADY ELIZABETH. THE SAID SIR JOHN CROKE DIED THE 10 DAY OF FEBRUARY, IN THE YEARE OF OUR LORD, 1608, AND THE SAID LADY ELIZABETH DYED THE 24 DAY OF JUNE, IN THE YEARE OF OUR LORD, 1611

Sir John Croke's coat of arms is thus blazoned, in painted glass, and in stone over the porch, at Studley. Croke, quartered with Heynes, a crescent for difference. Impaled with Unton, quarterly, the first and fourth quarters, azure, on a fesse, ingrailed, or, between three spear heads, argent, a greyhound, current, sable, armed, gules, for Unton. Secondly, gules, two chevrons, argent, for Fettiplace. Thirdly, azure, three griffons, segreant, argent, armed and langued, gules.

I have the portraits of Sir John and Lady Elizabeth. His is painted on pannel, and bears the date of 1596, ætatis 65. It is a three-quarters length. He is represented as a comely man in a green old age, with a grey beard; the hair which grows on his upper lip appearing almost to cover his mouth. He is dressed in a black silk doublet, worked and cut in small rows, with a gown of the same colour, flowered, lined and collared with fur; perhaps the same which was bequeathed to him by Sir Thomas Pope. He has a high crowned hat, with a band and rose. His sleeves have small ruffles, worked with an open edge. On his left hand, which bears a fringed glove, on the fore-finger he has a gold ring, with the single coat of arms of Croke, with a crescent on the fesse. On the fourth finger he has three rings, two broad plain gold rings, and between them a seal ring, with a death's head, and round it, DISCE MORI VT VIVAS. This ring is in my possession. It is gold, very heavy, and has the initials I. C. cut at the back of it. It belonged to his youngest son, William, who mentioned it in his will as an intended bequest to his grandson, Samuel

Davis, but he had afterwards erased it[y]. I have likewise what appears to be a copy of this picture, not so well painted.

Her picture is on canvas, a three-quarters length, larger than the other. She is a handsome woman, dressed in a large loose black gown, slashed in the sleeves, and shewing the white lining. She has a very large ruff round her neck, and ruffs round the wrists. Over her breast is a sort of broad band of white cambric, with lace down the middle, on which hangs a cameo of a head set in gold. Below this is a festoon of strings of pearls, and there are strings of dark beads round her wrists. Her head is dressed with a comb, set with pearls. On her left hand there is a ring with a square stone on her thumb, and another set with stones in the shape of a heart, on her fourth finger. In her right hand is a pinch of snuff. By her right side hangs a fan, and on her left a watch. The exact time when pocket-watches were invented does not appear to be known. The watch said to have belonged to Robert Bruce, King of Scotland, in the beginning of the fourteenth century, was a jocose imposition upon an antiquary. Henry the Eighth, and Charles the Fifth, had watches. There was one in Sir Ashton Lever's Museum, dated in 1541. In Queen Elizabeth's time they appear to have been a common article of magnificence. Malvolio, assuming the great man, talks of "winding up his watch." Hook, in 1656, by some said to have been the inventor, only improved the construction[z].

These two pictures were given to my father by Richard Ingoldsby, Esquire, of Dinton, the last male descendant of Sir Richard Ingoldsby, who married their grand-daughter.

[y] Will, penes me.

[z] Shakespeare's Twelfth Night, Act ii. sc. 8. Barrington, Archæol vol. v. p. 416. Ward's Lives, Hook, pages 169, 171, 179. Dr. Derham's Artificial Watchmaker. Beckman's History of Inventions, &c Waller's Life of Hook.

I have the wills of Sir John, and Lady Elizabeth, Croke, which give a curious picture of their affairs, and the manners of the times. His was made the 2d day of July, 1607. her's on the 1st of February, 1609[a]

It appears by these wills that they sometimes resided at their house in Fleet Street; of course during Sir John's attendance upon the Parliament, and in the country, at the Manor-house of Chilton, or the Lodge in the park there. They had a house for the purpose of husbandry, which was carried on extensively according to the usual custom of gentlemen in those days, almost every article of consumption being supplied from their own lands. No notice is taken of the house at Studley, which he had given up to his son John. Their coaches, the number of their horses, and servants, the gilded chambers, and the great quantity of gilt plate, in cups and covers, salt sellers and other articles, the chains of gold and pearls, the rings and jewels, the Turkey carpets, the great quantity of silk and linen, exhibit a picture of the simple splendor which reigned in the family of a rich country gentleman. The sums incidentally mentioned, and the appraisement at the end, afford a measure of the value of many commodities at that period Three steers, or dry kine, fat I suppose, are valued at £13. 6*s*. 8*d*. or £4. 8*s*. 10*d*. each. These modern times may perhaps smile at the minuteness, and simplicity, with which the different articles are enumerated, the knowledge displayed by a lady of family and fortune of the detail of her domestic establishment, and the particular care with which she disposes of her various pieces of apparel. The reader will not be displeased with the occurrence of antiquated names for various implements of ancient use; the mazlin cup, the suckling pot, the great livery pots, the kettle for driving of bucks, the basons and ewers, the armour and weapons for furnishing men for the wars, the lances, the morinspikes, the calivers, my lady's gowns and kirtles, of silk, velvet, taffety, and tufftaffety, not forgetting her holiday cloak of the latter material. The bowl of silver gilt with a cover, which Sir John bought of his eldest son, Sir John Croke, and which had been given him as a fee for his counsel in law by Sir Christopher Hatton, shews the estimation in which his legal opinions were early held. We may profit by the examples of the unfeigned sense of religion expressed

[a] The will of Sir John Croke is in the Appendix, No XXIV.

at the beginning of the wills, and reduced into practice at the end of them, in large bequests to the poor; by the love shewn to all their children and relations, in the great number of specific legacies, and by their considerate kindness to all their servants. All these and other circumstances will afford a fair specimen of the mode of living, the ideas, the plenty, the benevolence, and hospitality of those good old days, and will make these testaments interesting to all readers of taste and feeling.

The will of Lady Croke, being extremely long, is not printed. It may therefore not be improper to mention the various persons to whom she bequeaths legacies. These are, her daughter Brown, and her children. Henry Bulstrode, and his daughter Elizabeth Her daughter Whitlock, and her daughter Elizabeth Anne Searle, another of her daughter Brown's daughters, and her sister Dorothy Bulstrode that was. Edward Bulstrode Her daughter Winkefield, and her children, Robert, Richard, and Roger Winkefield. Her daughter Tyrrell. Her daughter Bennet Croke, and her children, Nathaniel, Henry, and Elizabeth. Her son Paulus Ambrosius Croke. Her son William Croke, his wife, and his children, Elizabeth, Catherine, Alexander, Edward, and Francis. Her sister Harrington Lady Umpton. Her nieces Wentworth, Chilwood, and Purefoy. Her cousin Francis Brown. Mrs. Denham of Oakley. Mary Hart. Mrs. Gurgeney. Sir Alexander Hampden. Her cousin Scudamore. With other legacies to servants and the poor. The residue was to be divided into three parts. The first, for the two daughters of her son Henry. The second, for the two daughters of her son William. And the third, for her executors, George Croke, Paulus Ambrosius Croke, William Croke, and Henry Wilkinson, Minister of Waddesdon.

Thus far we have only had to follow a single stem; but since the numerous children of Sir John Croke, and Elizabeth Unton, became each the founder of a separate family, I shall take them all in order, according to their seniority, allotting a chapter to each child, and the descendants. I shall follow the elder branch first to its extinction, then the next son, and so on to the last. Adopting in this respect the order which would be employed to hunt out the heirs to a paternal estate.

CHAPTER IV.

The eldest son of Sir John Croke, and Lady Elizabeth Unton, Sir John Croke, the Judge, and his descendants

AS Sir John Croke the Judge had five sons, who each became the head of a separate family, this chapter is subdivided into six sections, of which the first will be occupied by the Judge, and the other five by his sons, and their descendants.

SECTION THE FIRST.

Sir John Croke, the Judge, and Katherine Blount, his wife

OF the five sons of Sir John Croke, and Elizabeth Unton, four were educated for the bar, and two of them became illustrious ornaments to their profession.

The eldest son of Sir John Croke, and Elizabeth Unton, was named after his father. He was born in 1553, and was brought up to the law. He was admitted a Student of the Inner Temple the 13th of April, 1570, the twelfth year of Queen Elizabeth, and in due time was called to the bar.

Our ancient sovereigns interfered much in the private and domestic affairs of their subjects; and the influence, or direct power, of the King, or his ministers, was often exerted to promote the interests of favoured individuals. The lawyers of modern days would repel with indignation the interference of a prime minister in the government of their societies At this time an application to a Lord High Treasurer for his letter to the Benchers of one of the Inns of Court, to admit a young man to the bar, was not extraordinary. Amongst the manuscripts in the British Museum, is the following petition to the Lord Burleigh.

It is indorsed, "The humble petition of John Croke, gentleman, of the "Middle Temple, for your Lordship's letter to the Reader of the Middle "Temple, in his behalf, to be called to the bar[a]."

"To the Right Honourable the Lord High Treasurer of England.

"It may please your Lordship, I am an humble suitor unto you, for your Lordship's letter unto Mr Henry Hall, Reader of the Middle Temple, and the rest of the Worshipful of the Bench, in behalf of your suppliant, John Croke, gentleman, of the same house, that it would please him to accept of your suppliant in his call to the bar, (whereof they have a good opinion of him.) I therefore most humbly desire your Lordship to afford your honourable letter unto that end. For the which he shall be most bound to pray for your Lordship."

The relationship between the petitioner, and the Lord High Treasurer, was the ground of this application. Mr. Croke's cousin, Roger Cave, was married to Margaret, Lord Burleigh's sister, and his sister Prudentia married Sir Robert Wingfield, the son of Elizabeth, another sister of Lord Burleigh; but whether before, or after, this time does not appear.

He was made a Bencher of the Inner Temple, the 30th of January, 1591, Lent Reader of that Society, in 1596; and two years afterwards Treasurer, in which office he succeeded Sir Edward Coke[b]. In the latter end of the reign of Elizabeth he was appointed Recorder of the City of London[c]

In 1594, the thirty-seventh of Elizabeth, under the name of John Croke of Studley, he was jointly bound with Sir Michael Blount to Charles Blount, the last Lord Mountjoy, to pay a yearly quit-rent of twenty pounds, in consideration of his Lordship's surrendering the moiety of a certain number of acres of arable land, meadow, pasture, and wood, in the parishes of Benham, Winterburn, Stapleton, and Boswell, for the term of ninety-nine years[d].

Sir John Croke, besides his professional pursuits, served his country in

[a] This petition states him to have been of the Middle Temple, but in the Register of the Inner Temple is an entry, "John Croke of Chilton, admitted 13 April, 12 Elizabeth, 1570" Perhaps he was of both societies Lansdown MSS No. 107 fol 74 Burleigh Papers.

[b] Arms in the Inner Temple Hall Window. Register of the Inner Temple. Dugdale's Orig Jurid pages 166, 170 [c] Preface to Cro Car [d] Note to the Maple-Durham pedigree

a parliamentary capacity. In the year 1585, he was elected Member for Windsor, with Henry Neville, Esquire. In 1597, and again in 1601, he was chosen one of the representatives for the city of London[e].

In the year 1601, he gave to the newly established Library of Sir Thomas Bodley, "twenty-seven good volumes, of which twenty-five were "in folio[f]." The catalogue of them is printed in the Appendix, from the large vellum book of benefactions made by order of Sir Thomas Bodley, and preserved in the library[g]. He was likewise Sub-Steward of the University of Oxford[h].

In the last memorable parliament which was called by Queen Elizabeth, and which assembled on the 27th day of October, 1601, he had the honour of being chosen Speaker of the House of Commons. The manner and the ceremonies observed upon his appointment have been related by a contemporary writer[i].

Upon the meeting of the House, Sir William Knolles, the Comptroller of her Majesty's Household, proposed that they should proceed to make choice of a Speaker; and signified his opinion that Mr. John Croke, Recorder of London, and one of the Knights for the City of London, was "a very fit, able, and sufficient man to supply the whole charge of the "said office, being a gentleman very religious, very judicious, of a good "conscience, and well furnished with all other good parts." No contrary voice being delivered, Mr. Croke, after some large pause, stood up, and very learnedly and eloquently endeavoured to disable himself for the burthen of that charge; alledging his great defects both of nature and of art fit to supply that place, and shewing all full compliments for the same to abound in many other learned and grave members of the House. In the end, he prayed most humbly that they would accept of his due excuse, and be pleased to proceed to a new election. Upon which the Comptroller stood up, and said, That hearing no negative voice, he took it for a due election, which the House confirmed. Whereupon the Comptroller, and the Right Honourable Sir John Stanhope, her Majesty's Vice-Chamberlain,

[e] Willis's Notitia Parliamentaria [f] Wood's Annals Univ Oxon. by Gutch vol ii p. 922 [g] Appendix, No XXVI [h] Sir Leoline Jenkins, vol ii p 652. [i] Sir Simonds D'Ewes's Journals of the Parliaments, during the reign of Queen Elizabeth, 1682 fol

immediately set Mr. Croke in the chair. After some little pause, he returned thanks to the House for their great good opinion of him, and loving favour towards him, and prayed them to accept of his willing mind and readiness, to bear with his unableness and wants, in the service of the House, and referred himself to their good favour[k].

On the 30th of October, about one o'clock, her Majesty came by water to the Parliament chamber, where being placed in her chair of state, the members of the House of Commons, who had attended at the door of the said house, with their new Speaker elect, the full space of half an hour, were at last let in, and the Speaker was led up to the bar, by the hands of Sir William Knollys, and Sir John Fortescue, the Chancellor of the Exchequer, and presented to her Majesty, to whom after he had made three low reverences, he spoke in effect as follows.

"Most sacred and mighty Sovereign, upon your Majesty's commandment, your most dutiful and loving Commons, the Knights, Citizens, and Burgesses of the Lower House, have chosen me, your Majesty's most humble servant, being a member of the same House, to be their Speaker; but finding the weakness of myself, and my ability too weak to undergo so great a burthen, I do most humbly beseech your sacred Majesty to continue your most gracious favour towards me, and not to lay this charge so unsupportable upon my unworthy and unable self; and that it would please you to command your Commons to make a new election of another, more able, and more sufficient, to discharge the great service, to be appointed by your Majesty, and your subjects. And I beseech your most excellent Majesty, not to interpret my denial herein to proceed from any unwillingness to perform all devoted dutiful service, but rather out of your Majesty's clemency, and goodness, to interpret the same to proceed from that inward fear, and trembling, which hath ever possessed me, when heretofore, with most gracious audience, it hath pleased your Majesty to licence me to speak before you For I know, and must acknowledge, that, under God, even through your Majesty's great bounty and favour, I am that I am. And therefore none of your Majesty's most dutiful subjects more bound to be ready, and being ready, to perform, even the least of your Majesty's commandments I do therefore most humbly beseech

[k] D'Ewes, page 621

your Majesty, that, in regard the service of so great a prince, and flourishing kingdom, may the better, and more successfully, be effected, to command your dutiful and loving Commons, the Knights, Citizens, and Burgesses, of the Lower House, to proceed to a new election."

Then after he had made three reverences, the Queen called the Lord Keeper, to whom she spake something in secret, and after the Lord Keeper spoke in effect thus much.

"Mr. Speaker,—Her Majesty with gracious attention having heard your wise and grave excuse for your discharge, commanded me to say unto you, that even your eloquent speech of defence for yourself is a great motive, and a reason very persuasive, both to ratify and approve the choice of the loving Commons, the Knights, Citizens, and Burgesses, as also to commend their wise and discreet choice of yourself, in her gracious censure, both for sufficiency well able, and for your former fidelity and services well approved, and accepted of. And therefore her Majesty taketh this choice of you for *bonum omen*, a sign of good and happy success, when the beginning is taken in hand with so good wisdom and discretion. Her Majesty therefore commanded me to say unto you, that she well liketh of your election, and therefore she ratifieth it with her royal assent."

Then Mr. Croke, making three low reverences, answered in this manner.

"Most sacred, and most puissant Queen, Seeing it hath pleased you to command my service, by consenting to the free election of your dutiful and loyal subjects, the Knights, Citizens, and Burgesses, of me to be their Speaker, I most humbly beseech your Majesty to give me leave to shew unto you the dutiful thoughts, and earnest affections, of your loyal subjects, to do your Majesty all services, and to defend your royal and sacred person, both with their lives and goods. He then proceeded to make a vehement invective against the tyranny of the King of Spain, the Pope's ambition, and the rebels of Ireland; which he said were like a snake cut in pieces, which did crawl and creep to join themselves together again. He then offered his solemn prayers to heaven, to continue the prosperous estate and peace of the kingdom, which, he said, had been defended by the mighty arm of our dread and sacred Queen."

At this the Queen interrupted him, and cried out, "No, but by the mighty hand of God, Mr. Speaker."

He then proceeded to beseech her Majesty for freedom of speech, to every particular member of the House, and their servants. And lastly, that if any mistaking of any message, delivered unto him from the Commons, should happen, that her Majesty would attribute them to his weakness, in delivery or understanding, and not to the House, as also any forgetfulness, through want of memory, or that things were not so judiciously handled, or expressed by him, as they were delivered by the House

To which, after the Queen had spoken to the Lord Keeper as aforesaid, (after three reverences by the Speaker,) the Lord Keeper said in effect as followeth.

"Mr. Speaker,—Her Majesty doth greatly commend and like of your grave speech, well divided, well contrived; the first proceeding from a sound invention, and the other from a settled judgment and experience. You have well, and well indeed, weighed the estate of this kingdom, well observed the greatness of our puissant and grand enemy the King of Spain, the continual and excessive charges of the wars of Ireland, which if they be well weighed, do not only shew the puissance of our gracious Sovereign in defending us, but also the greatness of the charge continually bestowed by her Majesty, even out of her own revenues, to protect us, and the exposing of her Majesty to continual trouble, and toilsome cares, for the benefit and safety of her subjects. Wherefore, Mr. Speaker, it behoveth us to think and say, as was well delivered by a grave man lately, in a *Concio ad Clerum, Opus est subsidio nè fiat excidium.* Touching your other requests, for freedom of speech, her Majesty willingly consenteth thereto, but with this caution, that the time be not spent in idle and vain matter, painting the same out with froth, and volubility of words, whereby the speakers may seem to gain some reputed credit, by emboldening themselves to contradiction, and by troubling the House, of purpose, with long and vain orations, to hinder the proceeding in matters of greater and more weighty importance. Touching access to her person, she most willingly granteth the same, desiring she may not be troubled unless urgent matter and affairs of great consequence compel you thereunto: for this hath been held a wise maxim, " In troubling great estates, you must trouble seldom." For liberties unto yourselves, and persons, her Majesty hath commanded me to say unto you all, that she ever intendeth to preserve the liberties of the House, and granteth freedom even unto the meanest member of this

House: but her Majesty's pleasure is, you should not maintain and keep with you notorious persons, either for life, or behaviour, and desperate debtors, who never come abroad, fearing laws, but at these times; pettifoggers and vipers of the commonwealth, prolling and common solicitors, that set dissention between man and man, and men of the like condition to these. These her Majesty earnestly wisheth a law may be made against, as also that no Member of this Parliament would entertain, or bolster up, any man of the like humour, or quality, on pain of her Highness displeasure. For your excuse of the House and of yourself, her Majesty commanded me to say, that your sufficiency hath so oftentimes been approved before her, that she doubteth not of your sufficient discharge of the place you shall serve in. Wherein she willeth you to have a special eye, and regard, not to make new, and idle, laws, and trouble the House with them, but rather look to the abridging, and repealing, of divers obsolete and superfluous statutes; as also first to take in hand matters of greatest moment and consequence. In doing thus, Mr. Speaker, you shall fulfill her Majesty's commandment, do your country good, and satisfy her Highness's expectation Which being said, the Speaker made three reverences to the Queen, and the Members of the House of Commons returned to their own House, where the Speaker repeated the substance of what had been delivered by the Lord Keeper[1].

In this Parliament many matters of considerable importance were transacted. Amongst others, the redress of the great grievance of monopolies From the scantiness of the Queen's revenues, and the great expences of her government, she had adopted an expedient, which had not been unusual, to reward her servants by granting them monopolies by patent, which they either exercised themselves, or sold for large sums. They were lucrative to the holders, but oppressive to the country, by raising the price of commodities, and by restraining the freedom of commerce. A petition against them had been presented by the House to her Majesty in the last Parliament, but with little effect. A bill was now brought in, entitled, "An Act for the explanation of the common law in certain cases "of letters patent." It appeared that these monopolies comprehended a large proportion of the most useful articles of life, glass, pots, bottles, iron,

[1] D'Ewes, p. 600

steel, tin, oil, vinegar, salt, currants, salt petre, lead, brandy, beer for exportation, paper, cards, starch, sulphur, ashes, anniseed, tanning, and other particulars: and one proof of the abuse of them was produced by the instance of salt, which had been raised from sixteen pence, to fifteen shillings a bushel. Long debates ensued upon it. It was said by Mr. Francis Bacon, that the royal prerogative was too high to be debated; that her Majesty had both an enlarging and a restraining power; and that by her prerogative she might set at liberty things restrained by statute law or otherwise, and might also restrain things which were at liberty. Whatever might be the private sentiments of individuals, these high notions of the royal power seemed to be generally entertained by the House, at least they were openly asserted by many, and passed without contradiction. But although they might receive some countenance from the arbitrary proceedings of the House of Tudor, in the two following reigns they were fully discussed, and were proved to be contrary to the laws and constitution of England.

Whilst the bill was depending, the Queen, sensible of the general odium which these unpopular privileges had excited, and foreseeing from the spirited manner in which they were taken up by the House, that she should be compelled to abolish the monopolies, was desirous that it should appear as a gracious measure originating from herself. She sent therefore for Mr. Croke, and informed him of her intention of recalling the obnoxious patents. On his return to the House he stood up in his place, and gave the following account of the interview.

"It pleased her Majesty to command me to attend upon her yesterday in the afternoon, from whom I am to deliver unto you all, her Majesty's most gracious message, sent by my unworthy self. She yields you all hearty thanks, for your care and special regard of those things that concern her state, kingdom, and consequently our selves, whose good she had always tendered as her own; for our speedy resolution in making of so hasty, and free, a subsidy, which commonly succeeded, and never went before our councils, and for our loyalty. I do assure you with such and so great zeal and affection she uttered and shewed the same, that to express it our tongues are not able, neither our hearts to conceive it. It pleased her Majesty to say unto me, that if she had an hundred tongues she could not express our hearty good wills.

And further she said, that as she had ever held our good most dear, so the last day of our (or her) life should witness it; and that the least of her subjects was not grieved, and she not touched. She appealed to the throne of Almighty God, how careful she hath been, and will be, to defend her people from all oppressions. She said that partly by intimation of her council, and partly by divers petitions that have been delivered unto her both going to the chapel and also to walk abroad, she understood that divers patents, which she had granted, were grievous to her subjects; and that the substitutes of the patentees had used great oppressions. But she said, she never assented to grant any thing which was *malum in se*. And if in the abuse of her grant there be any thing evil, (which she took knowledge there was,) she herself would take present order of reformation. I cannot express unto you the apparent indignation of her Majesty towards these abuses. She said that her kingly prerogative (for so she termed it) was tender; and therefore desireth us not to fear or doubt of her careful reformation; for she said, that her commandment was given a little before the late troubles, (meaning the Earl of Essex's matters,) but had an unfortunate event, but that in the middest of her most great and weighty occasions, she thought upon them. And that this should not suffice, but that further order should be taken presently, and not *in futuro*, (for that also was another word which I take it her Majesty used,) and that some should be presently repealed, some suspended, and none put in execution, but such as should first have a tryal according to the law, for the good of the people. Against the abuses her wrath was so incensed, that she said, that she neither could, nor would, suffer such to escape with impunity. So to my unspeakable comfort she hath made me the messenger of this her gracious thankfulness and care. Now we see that the axe of her princely justice is laid to the root of the tree; and so we see her gracious goodness hath prevented our counsels, and consultations. God make us thankful, and send her long to reign amongst us. If through weakness of memory, want of utterance, or frailty of my self, I have omitted any thing of her Majesty's commands, I do most humbly crave pardon for the same; and do beseech the honourable persons which assist this chair, and were present before her Majesty at the delivery hereof, to supply and help my imperfections; which, joined with my fear, have caused me (no doubt) to forget something which I should have delivered unto you."

Nothing could exceed the astonishment, the admiration, and gratitude of the House, at this extraordinary mark of the Queen's goodness and condescension. Mr Wingfield, with tears in his eyes, said, that if a sentence of everlasting happiness had been pronounced unto him, it could not have made him shew more inward joy than he now did. Another compared it to the glad tidings of the Gospel; and said, that it ought to be written in the tablet of their hearts. Croke said, that his heart was not able to conceive, nor his tongue to utter, the joy he conceived of her Majesty's gracious and especial care for our good. Wherefore as God himself said, *Gloriam meam alteri non dabo*, so may her Majesty say, in that she herself will be the only and speedy agent for performance of our most humble and most wished desires. Wherefore let us not doubt but as she hath been, so she still will be, our most gracious Sovereign, and natural nursing mother unto us. Whose days the Almighty God prolong to all our comforts. Upon which the whole House answered, Amen[m]

It was unanimously voted, that the Speaker, with a committee, should wait upon her Majesty with the thanks of the House. When the time was fixed, Mr. Croke asked the House, "What it was "their pleasure he should deliver unto her Majesty?" Upon which Sir Edward Hobbie stood up, and said, "It was best he should devise "that himself, and that the whole House would refer it to him." Which reference was confirmed by the general acclamation of I, I, I[n].

In the afternoon, about three o'clock, about one hundred and forty members met in the great chamber before the Council chamber in Whitehall. When the Queen came into the Council chamber, and, being seated in her royal seat, attended with most of the Privy Council, and nobles about her, the Speaker and the Members were introduced, and after three low reverences made, Mr. Croke addressed the Queen as follows

[m] D'Ewes, p 657 [n] Ibid p 658

"May it please your excellent Majesty, I am, in the name of your most loyal subjects of the Lower House of Parliament, (whereof part are here prostrate at your sacred feet,) to present all humble, and dutiful, thanks for your most gracious message, sent of late by me unto them. For which they confess they are not able to yield your Majesty eyther answerable guifts, or comparable treasure, but true hearts they bringe, with promise of respect and duty, befitting true, and dutiful, subjects, even to the spending of the uttermost droppe of bloud in their bodyes, for the preservation of religion, your sacred person, and the realme. They cannot express the joy of their hearts by any sound of wordes, that it pleaseth your Majesty soe freely, and willingly, to grant them this access unto your sacred person. They come not, as one of tenn, to give thanks, and the rest to depart unthankful, but they come, all in all, and these for all, to be thankfull, not for benefitts received, which were sued for, and so obtained, but for gracious favours bestowed of your gracious mere motion, and of late published by your Majesty's most royal proclamation. They confess, that your sacred ears are always bowed down and open to all their suites and complaints, yet now your Majesty hath overcome them, by your most royal bounty, and as it were prevented them by your magnificent and princely liberality, for which, as for all other your gracious favours and royal and kingly benefits bestowed upon them, they give glory first unto God, that hath in mercy towards them placed so gracious and benigne a prince over them, praying to the same God to graunt them continuance of your so blessed, and happy, government over them, even to the end of the world. And, most gracious Sovereign, I confess I was not able in my heart to conceyve, much less with my tongue to utter, your princely and royal message, sent by me, your unworthy servant, to the Commons, soe in like manner I must acknowledge I am as unable to declare their humble, and dutiful, thankes for the same, for which my want and disability I crave pardon, first of your sacred Majesty, and of them all desire to be excused[o]."

The Speaker having ended his speech, with three low reverences, the Noblemen and Counsellors present, with the Speaker and Members of the House of Commons, all kneeled down, when her Majesty uttered these

[o] Harl. MSS.

gracious words following, directing them to Mr Speaker, with commandment to relate them from her to the Lower House of Parliament.

"Mr. Speaker,—I well understand, by that you have delivered, that you, with these gentlemen of the Lower House, come to give us thanks for benefits received. I pray you, let them know, that I return them all the thanks that can possibly be conceived in a kingly heart, for accepting my message in so kind a manner, and thanke you for delivering of it. But I must tell you, I doubt, and cannot be resolved, whether I have more cause to thank them, or they me. Howsoever I am more than glad to see sympathy between them and me, and I must tell you, that I joy not so much that I am a Queen, as that I am a Queen over so faithful and loving a people, as also that God hath set me over you, and preserved me so miraculously from dishonour, shame, oppression, violence, and infinite dangers, and practices, attempted by the enemies of God, and religion, against me. For which so mighty deliverance I yield all humble and hearty thanks to Almighty God. For the money you have so freely and willingly bestowed upon me, I will be no waster. You all know that I am neyther fast holder, nor greedy griper, nor hoarder of money; noe nor spender much upon myselfe. It shall all be bestowed for the defence of the kingdom, and theyr owne eyes shall see it, and a just account shall be made of all. Tell them, Mr. Speaker, that they may have a prince more wise, but never shall they have a prince more loving unto them, or more carefull of them for their wellfare, than myself will be. For I desire nothing more in this world, than to preserve them in peace, and to keep them from oppression and wrong. It was such a grief unto me when I heard that my people and loving subjects were by errors abused, that I could not be at rest, untill I had given them a remedy."

Here she paused; and bidding Mr. Speaker and the Commons to stand up and come nearer her, said, "that, as you have spoken unto me, soe I must speak to you, and trouble you with a longe speech The remedy of the grievances, and heavy wrongs, Mr. Speaker, for which they are so exceedingly thankful, I must say thus much in excuse of myself, That I never granted any of these Pattents, by my prerogative royal, to any of my servants by way of recompence for their good services done, but my intention was for a common good to the subject, as well as private benefit to them. Neyther did I ever sett my hand to any grant since I came to this place, but in my heart I thought no danger, but good should come to my subjects thereby. And, for my own part, I wish I may no longer live, than I shall endeavour to advance the Gospell, and the peace of my kingdom. But I must tell you, that those that sued to me for these, and such like pattents, dealt with me as physitions do with their patyents, who use to put into the pills they minister, either much aromatical powder, or guild them over to hide their bitterness and sourness. For they pretended to me, that all my subjects should have a public benefit and profit, as well as they should have private gain. This they pretended, and this I intended, but the executioners of them (like varletts) turn all to a contrary end. God knoweth against my heart; for God let me no longer live, than I shall endeavour, to my uttermost power, to doe all the good that may be for all my loving subjects, without any intention of preferring my private, much less any of my servants', good before them. Truly, Mr. Speaker, when this grievance came unto my ears, as I had great cause to be moved at their misdemeanors, so my heart was surprised with an extraordinary joy, when I understood that those gentlemen of the Lower House, that spake against the abuse of those monopolies, spake not against me that granted them, nor in malice to my servants, and others that had them, neyther for their private respect as being oppressed and wronged by the lewd executioners of them, but for their love to me, as well as for the public good in general. For they no doubt did perceive, that the gain of the pattents tolerated this long time, was a hazard of the losing of the love of my subjects, than which what can be more precious unto me!

"For this, Mr. Speaker, their loving and kind dealing with me, I can but thank them, and think of them as the best subjects I have. And for this their loving regard and care of me, this I will promise, that none that ever was before me in this realm, nor none that shall come after me, shall be more regardful of them than I will be, even to the hazard of my own life for their sakes. Alas, Mr. Speaker, what am I as of myself? without the watchful providence of Almighty God? other than a poor silly woman, weake, and subject to many imperfections, expecting as you do a future judgement; yet I hope assuredly this much, in the mercy of Almighty

God, that so long as I endeavour to my uttermost power to defend my people from private and open wrongs, shun oppression, and tyranny, that God will accept my willing heart for good, and not impute unto me the errors and culpes of my subjects For if that were not, intolerable and miserable were the state of a king. But howsoever I thanke Almighty God, that sendeth me such loving subjects, who are willing, as much as in them lyeth, to keep me from errors, which I might ignorantly have fallen into. Amongst these, and many other blessings which Almighty God hath vouchsafed to bestow on me, I thank God, notwithstanding all the attempts at danger, infamy, shame, oppression, and wronge exercised against me, by the enemies of the kingdom, this heart of mine was never possessed, or surprised, with any fear, or dread. This I speak not by way of bragging, or boasting, of my own strength, or power, but for it, and all his mercies bestowed upon me, I give all thanks possible, and so long I hope I dishonoured him not, nor speake flatteringly of myself. Many think it to be a great preheminence to be a King or a Queen. It is truth, the throne of a kinge is glorious without, but, Mr Speaker, I am not so blind, or simple, as to be ignorant, that with the glory there are many dangers, greifes, troubles, and vexations, and many other calamities and crosses, so that for my part, were it not more for conscience, than for any content I have, (except the love of my subjects, which is as dear to me as my life,) I could well be content that another had my charge. Well, Mr. Speaker, commend us heartily to all the Lower House, and soe I leave you to God, and your godly consultations."

She turned herself to Mr. Comptroller, and Mr. Secretary, willing them that they should bring the Gentlemen of the House to kiss her hand, before they went into their countries.

"Many things," the writer says, "through want of memory I have omitted, without setting down many her Majesty's gestures of honourable and princely demeanor, used by her. As when the Speaker spake any effectual or moving speech, from the Commons to her Majesty, she rose up and bowed herself As also in her own speech, when the Commons, apprehending any extraordinary words of favour from her, did any reverence to her Majesty, she likewise rose up and bowed herself[p]."

[p] I have given the last speech of the Speaker to the Queen, and her answer, from a

This account affords a fine specimen of the ceremonious and courtly style of the reign of Elizabeth.

In this Parliament many statutes were passed for the good of the country. Amongst these was the celebrated Act for the relief of the poor, the foundation of the present poor laws[q]. At the time this statute passed, it was thought not unwise, and to have been founded upon the humane principle of charity, and an useful plan of police. Either from a radical defect in the system itself, from the changes in the state of society, or from the mismanagement of those who were intrusted with the execution of it, by extending relief indiscriminately to those who are able to work, as well as to the sick and impotent, or perhaps from all these causes together, it has proved the scourge of the country, the basis of a system which has deranged the natural relations of society, of rich and poor, labourers and their employers, parents and children, husbands and wives; has relaxed industry and virtuous exertion, annihilated modest dependence, and destroyed charity. The ruinous consequences which have ensued from it, have compelled us to perceive at length a self-evident truth, that to support one part of the community, and that the most worthless, at the expence of the other part, which is the most useful and industrious, is an arrangement founded in palpable injustice, and in a false policy, totally subversive of the first principles of civil society: which was established to secure to every man the fruits of his own labour. There were other acts passed of less equivocal utility: for the relief of soldiers and mariners, for the redress of the misemployment of charities; for preventing perjury, and unnecessary expences in law, and for avoiding trifling and frivolous suits, for preventing idle misdemeanors, against fraudulent administrations; for the true making of woollen cloths; the recovery of marsh lands; the encouragement of the insurance of ships, and the assizing of fuel[r].

The business of this Parliament being ended, the Queen appointed a day to dissolve it, the 19th of December, 1601 For this purpose her Majesty being in the Upper House, the Members of the House of Commons were introduced, with Mr. Croke their Speaker, who addressed her Majesty to this effect.

manuscript in the British Museum, which is different from that published by D'Ewes, page 658, and is much fuller. Harleian MSS No 787. folio 127. the last in the book.

[q] 43 Eliz chap ii

[r] Statutes at Large

"That laws were not at first made with human pen, but by Divine ordinance, that politick laws were made according to the evil conditions of men, and that all laws serve not for all times, no more than one medicine for all diseases If he were asked, what were the first and chiefest thing to be considered, he would say, Religion. So religion is all in all, for religion breeds devotion, devotion breeds zeal and piety to God, which breedeth obedience and duty to the Prince, and obedience of the laws, which breedeth faithfulness and honesty and love, three necessary and only things to be wished and observed in a well-governed Common-wealth. And that her Majesty by planting true religion had laid such a foundation upon which all those virtues were so planted and builded, that they could not easily be rooted up and extirpated. And therefore he did acknowledge, that we ought and do acknowledge that we will praise God and her Majesty for it. And then he descended to speak of governments and laws of nations, among and above all which he principally preferred the laws of this land, which he said were so many and so wise, that there was almost no offence but was met with in a law. Notwithstanding her Majesty being desirous for the good of her land to call a Parliament for redress of some old laws, and making some new, her dutiful and loving subjects having considered of them, have made some new, and amended some old, which they humbly desire may be made laws by her most Royal Assent, which giveth life unto them. And so after thanks given for the pardon by which we dread your justice and admire your mercy, and a prayer unto her Majesty that she would accept as the testimonies of our love and duty offered unto her, with a free heart and willing spirit, four entire subsidies and eight fifteenths and tenths, to be collected of our lands and livelihoods" In speaking whereof, he mistook and said, four entire fifteenths and eight subsidies, but he was remembered by some of the council that stood near him, and so spake right as aforesaid; and having craved pardon for his offence, if either he had forgotten himself in word or action, he ended.

The which the Lord Keeper answered thus in effect. "First as touching her Majestie's proceedings in the laws for her Royal Assent, that should be as God should direct her sacred spirit; secondly, for your presentation of four subsidies and eight fifteenths and tenths, thirdly, your humble thankfulness for the pardon, for them and yourself; I will deliver her Majestie's commandment with what brevity I may, that I be not tedious to my most gracious Sovereign. First she saith, touching your proceeding in the matter of her prerogative, that she is persuaded subjects did never more dutifully; and that she understood you did but obiter touch her prerogative, and no otherwise but by humble petition; and therefore, that thanks that a Prince may give to her subjects, she willingly yieldeth. But she now well perceiveth, that private respects are privately masqued under publick presence. Secondly, touching the presentation of your subsidy, she specially regardeth two things, both the persons and the manner. For the first, he fell into commendations of the commonalty; for the second, the manner, which was speedy, not by persuasion, or persuasive inducements, but freely out of duty with great contentment. In the thing which ye have granted, her Majesty greatly commendeth your confidence and judgment; and though it be not proportionable to her occasions, yet she most thankfully receiveth the same as a loving and thankful prince, and that no prince was ever more unwilling to exact or receive any thing from the subject than she our most gracious Sovereign; for we all know she never was a greedy grasper nor strait-handed keeper, and therefore she commanded me to say, that you have done (and so she taketh it) dutifully, plentifully, and thankfully.

For yourself, Mr. Speaker, her Majesty commanded me to say, that you have proceeded with such wisdom and discretion, that it is much to your commendations; and that none before you hath deserved more. And so he ended after an admonition given to the Justices of the Peace, that they would not deserve the epithets of prolling Justices, Justices of quarrels, who counted champetrie good chevesance, sinning Justices who do suck and consume the wealth and good of the Common-wealth: and also against those who lie (if not all the year, yet) at least three quarters of the year in this city of London[r]."

Afterwards the House was dissolved by the Lord Keeper. Before the dissolution, Mr. Herbert Croft, one of the Members, addressed the Speaker in these words.

Mr. Speaker,—"Though perhaps my motion may seem unseasonable at this present, yet I beseech the House consider with me a speech made yesterday, that consisted of four parts, the scope whereof (it being Mr. Hackwell's speech) lays open the dangerous mischiefs that come by trans-

[r] D'Ewes, p. 618.

portation of ordnance, and that due reformation thereof may be had for restraint of private transporting; I would only put the House in mind, and you also, Mr. Speaker, that the gentleman which yesterday moved it, desired that Mr. Speaker might say something thereof to her Majesty, in his speech to be inserted. Which I do again desire, the more earnestly, because our bill is fallen (as he said) into an everlasting sleep, and we have now no remedy but by her Majesty."

Mr. Croke answered him.—"If it please you, upon the motion of the gentleman made yesterday, I mean to say something therein, both for your satisfaction, and performance of my duty, and therefore this matter shall need no further to be moved."

With which the House rested well satisfied, and so arose. But it is to be noted, that the Speaker said not one word in his speech to her Majesty touching that matter, which was greatly murmured at, and spoken against, amongst the burgesses, that the House should be so abused, and that nothing was done therein[s].

It was when the business of the monopolies was before the House, that certain witty verses, burlesquing some of the wise Members of the Parliament, and which began,

> Down came Sir John Croke,
> And said his message on his book,

were written by the polite and agreeable Sir Michael Hicks, a great wit of the times, and the intimate friend of Sir Fulk Greville, Sir Francis Bacon, Sir Walter Raleigh, Mr. Cambden, and other learned and eminent persons. But notwithstanding the testimony of the Secretary of State, Sir Robert Cecil, confirmed too by an oath, that "they were in his fancy as "pretty and pithy as ever he saw," and "the great entertainment they "found with her Majesty," and "the good sport she intended to have with "the author, when she saw him next," I fear I cannot, consistently with the delicacy and cleanliness of these fastidious days, mention even the subject of them, much less introduce the verses themselves[t].

In the first year of James the First, 1603, he was knighted, and made Serjeant at Law, with thirteen others. Upon their appearance in the

[s] D'Ewes, 689. [t] Collins's Baronetage, vol. i. page 343. De Crepitu in Parliamento.

Court of Chancery, to take the oaths, Sir John Croke, on account of his having been Speaker of the House of Commons, and having thereby gained a precedency before all other barristers, who were not Serjeants, by the direction of the Lord Keeper, appeared as Ancient, or first of the new Serjeants, although he was Puisnè, in admittance, to five of them. And he made a speech in that capacity, in all their names, and delivered unto the Lord Keeper a ring for the King. But when the solemnity of taking their degree was performed, in the Court of Common Pleas, Philips, because he had received the King's patent to be one of his Serjeants, came first, as Ancient Serjeant, by the appointment of Popham, the Chief Justice, with the assent of the greater part of the Justices and Barons. And Sir John Croke was brought to the bar, after the said five new Serjeants, who were his ancients in admittance and this was the rank assigned him. This was against the opinion of the Lord Keeper, and twelve of the Privy Council, who wrote letters, that as he had been Speaker of the Parliament, and had been knighted the Sunday before, he ought to have the precedence before the other Serjeants, notwithstanding their antiquity of admittance; and four of the Judges, Anderson, Gawdy, Fenner, and Yelverton, concurred in this opinion[u].

He was afterwards made a King's Serjeant, and Judge of the counties of Brecknock, Radnor, and Glamorgan[x].

In the fifth year of King James, 1608, on the 25th of June, upon the death of Sir John Popham, the promotion of Sir Thomas Flemming to be Chief Justice, and of Sir Lawrence Tanfield to be Chief Baron, Sir John Croke was made a Justice of the King's Bench: in which office he continued till his death. Upon receiving this preferment, his coat of arms was set up in the north window of the hall of the Inner Temple, and in the hall of Serjeant's-Inn in Fleet Street[y].

King James, in the thirteenth year of his reign, 1615, granted to him diverse coppices, woods, underwoods, and other land, in the forest of Bernwood, to hold for twenty-one years, rendering £51[z].

The arguments of Sir John Croke, as counsel, and his decisions as a judge, recorded in the contemporary reports, shew his eminence in his

[u] Cro Jac page 1 [x] Ibid. Table of the Judges, 5 Jac. [y] Cro. Jac page 181. Dugdale s Orig. Jurid p 166, 170 [z] Pat Rot 13 Jac. I part 2.

profession, and he is said to have been "famous for his wisdom, eloquence, "and knowledge in the laws[a]." He received a bowl of silver gilt, with a cover, as a present from Sir Christopher Halton, "for his council in "law[b]." Sir Christopher, though originally a member of one of the Inns of Court, had never followed the profession of the law. When he was appointed Chancellor, in 1587, in cases of difficulty he consulted his learned friends, and it may be presumed from this valuable present, that Sir John Croke was one of those of whose opinions he availed himself.

In 1609, Sir Thomas Bodley was guided by his advice, with respect to the best mode of endowing his celebrated library at Oxford[c].

There are in the British Museum, a short minute of a charge to the Grand Jury of Middlesex in 1604, of another at the Somersetshire Assizes at Monmouth in 1618, and a very long and able charge in the Court of King's Bench in 1613[d]. These minutes are written, according to the practice of the old lawyers in a motley dialect of law French, Latin, and English, though no doubt they were delivered, bating a few quotations, in the English language only. The charge delivered in the King's Bench contains a full and able specification of all offences which can come within the cognizance of the grand inquest, but expressed in the quaint language of that reign. Some of them would now appear curious. They are directed to inquire "de ceux que voile purtraiture le picture del Dieu semble al un homme oue grey beard. Car ceo est un damnable offence, il "n'est d'etre measured. Heaven is his throne, and the earth is his footstool, et pur ceo ils que voile undertake de measure Dieu doyent vuer "higher than the heavens cujus mensura (comme un dit) est altior celo, "latior terra, et profundior mare" In the reign of James, Recusants and Papists, and the Gunpowder treason, would not be forgotten, the learned Judge informed the Jury, "Ceo jeo dye pur leur amendment, ils seant "semblable al vipers labouring pur eat out the bowells del terre which "brings them forth. De Jesuits leur positions sont damnable, La Pape a "deposer Royes, ceo est le badge et token del Antichrist. Doyes etre

[a] Preface Cro. Car. [b] Will of Sir John Croke, his father. [c] Life of Sir Thomas Bodley, prefixed to the printed catalogue of manuscripts [d] Bibl Harl. No 583 fol 24 b. No 585. fol. 30

"carefull a discover eux. Receivers of stolen goods are semblable a les "horse leaches, which still cry, Bring, bring."

Amongst my own papers I have four annual speeches of ceremony made by Mr. Justice Croke when he was Recorder of London, upon presenting the Lord Mayor in the Exchequer in the years 1596, 1597, 1600, and another without date; one of these speeches is given in the Appendix[e].

The two following trials which were held before him may be mentioned as remarkable.

Dr. Dun, afterwards the celebrated civilian, when he was a student of Christ Church, had the misfortune to kill a boy. He brought down a special commission to Oxford, and was tried by Serjeant Croke, the Sub-steward of the University, and was acquitted[f].

In the year 1608, Sir John Croke, with Sir Thomas Fleming, Chief Justice, and Sir David Williams, gave sentence against the townsmen of Oxford, in the Court of King's Bench, in a dispute between the University and City for privilege of watch and ward. In which cause, besides sitting as Judge, he gave testimony, that the privilege in dispute had been asserted and used by the University above thirty years before, to his remembrance, without the claim of the town[g].

For the benefit of the students of the law, and of posterity, he published in 1602 a folio volume of select cases, which had been collected by the industry of Robert Keilway, who was Supervisor Liberationum Regis, or Surveyor of the King's Liveries, and which were decided in the reigns of Henry the VII. and VIII. others of which the time was unknown: cases in Eyre in the time of Edward the Third: a few in that of Edward the First: others reported by Judge Dalison in Philip and Mary, and Elizabeth: and some by Serjeant Bendloes, in Henry, and Mary. In a Latin preface, written not without some degree of classical elegance, and dedicated to the candid students of the law of England, he balances the motives for and against the publication of the work, and decides at length in favour of it by the advice of his friends, and the utility of cases, *in quibus multa acutè, multa subtilitèr disputata, (quæ tum inventionem, tum*

[e] Appendix, No XXV [f] Sir Leoline Jenkins, vol. ii p 652. [g] Wood's Hist Univ. Oxon. lib. i p. 386.

Judicium multum juvere possunt,) summo cum ingenio et Judicio determinata, quæ alibi non leguntur. The alterations, or improvements, which have been wrought in the law of England, by the ever-changeful course of time, the abolition of the feodal tenures, the extension of commerce, and other causes, have rendered those ancient cases of less use than formerly, but it is upon these old and solid foundations that the present admirable legal fabric has been erected, and, as Sir John Croke expresses it, *ex antiquis fontibus hodiernæ saluberrimæ aquæ hauriuntur*. He concludes his preface with four admonitory lines to the student.

Sit tibi cura magis multum, quam multa, legendi,
Immemor anne legit? Negliget ipse legens.
Quæ meminere sciunt, quod labitur utile non est,
Nosce quod oblitis tempus inane fuit [h].

Amongst the manuscripts of the Glynne family, at Ambroseden, were seven Arguments concerning the power and privileges of Parliament, by Mr. Mason, Mr. Calthrope, Mr. Attorney General, Justice Hyde, Justice Jones, Justice Whitlock, and Justice Croke [i].

In those times, the servants of the public were not so well rewarded for their services as at present, and Queen Elizabeth in particular was sparing of her remunerations. I have a letter from Sir John Croke to his brother George, in which he complains that he was much impoverished by his high situations, which led him into expences beyond what his fortune would support; and requesting the loan of five hundred pounds [k]. It appears too by his will, that, in his necessities, to provide for his children, and to sustain his public offices, he had sold to Sir George Croke the manor of Easington for seven hundred and fifty pounds [l]. Sir George had likewise a mortgage upon part of his property for five hundred and fifty pounds, and purchased of him his estate at Studley.

Sir John Croke married Catherine the daughter of Sir Michael Blount, of Maple-Durham in Oxfordshire, Lieutenant of the Tower, of whom I

[h] The Reports are intitled, Relationes quorundam casuum selectorum ex libris Roberti Keilway, Armigeri, qui temporibus fœlicissimæ memoriæ, Regis Henrici Septimi, &c &c [i] Vol. ii of the Catalogue of Oxford Manuscripts, page 51 No. 1992, 68. [k] This letter has been lost during my absence abroad [l] Ad publica onera evocatus sustinenda Will penes me.

have already spoken in the chapter upon that family. She was born the 11th of April, 1663[m]. Upon this marriage, the name of Blount was altogether omitted by his father, and the rest of the family, who had till that time styled themselves Croke, alias Blount[n].

In London, Sir John Croke resided at his house in Holbourne As his father did not die till he was fifty-five years of age, in 1608, and his mother, who had the use of the principal mansion at Chilton, lived three years afterwards, till 1611, I apprehend that he resided, when in the country, at Studley, till his mother's death This supposition is confirmed, by the admission of his third son Charles at Christ Church, as a Knight's son of *Oxfordshire*, in 1603[o]. How long the Priory continued in its original state, or whether any alterations were made in it by his father or grandfather, does not appear. It is extremely probable, that it was first converted into a commodious dwelling house by Sir John Croke the Judge. He certainly fitted up the old withdrawing room in the life-time of his father, and after his marriage, it was in small pannels, in divisions, with Doric pilasters between; and his coat of arms, inlayed in wood, was over the chimney, namely, Croke, with a label, denoting the eldest son, impaled with Blount When the wainscot was taken down to make the present dining room, at the back of the coat of arms was found written in ink, "*Mr. John Croke ye yonger att Studley, theis be &c.*" The same coat of arms, with those of his father, are in painted glass in the window of the same room, and those of Sir George Croke which are in a different style of ornaments, from having probably been put up at a later time, after he had purchased the estate. Sir John Croke's arms are likewise in stone over the porch, with the date 1587, when I suppose the alterations were made. The arms of Sir George Croke were evidently a subsequent addition. This porch appears to have been built on to the walls previously erected.

After his mother's death he lived at Chilton, where his will is dated in 1617, and died at his house in Holbourne, the 23d day of January, in 1619, aged 66 years He was buried at Chilton, and his monument is a flat marble stone, on the pavement of the Croke Chapel, with the following inscription upon a brass plate, written by himself.

[m] Gough's MSS Shropshire, No 2.

[n] Preface to Croke Charles, by Sir Harebottle Grimston.

[o] Ward's Lives of the Gresham Professors, page 306.

EPITAPHIUM VENERABILIS VIRI JOHANNIS CROKE.
EQUITIS AURATI, ET UNIUS JUSTICIARIORUM
DE BANCO REGIS, AB IPSO DUM IN
VIVIS ESSET CONSCRIPTUM.

DISSOLVOR LÆTUS, CHRISTUM SITIBUNDUS ADIRE.
SALVATOR, PROPERA, CORPUS, ET, EUGE, CAPE.
NON FUIT HÆC TRISTIS MEA MORS, SED JANUA VITÆ.
NON LOCUS EST LACRYMIS, NON DOLOR ULLUS IBI.
VITA BEATORUM CUM SANCTIS UNDIQUE SUAVIS
NIL MAGIS HAC DULCE EST: NAMQUE SOPORE JACENS
CORPUS ADIT TERRAM PATIENTEM, QUOD PARIEBAT,
ASTRA TENENT ANIMAM, QUAM DEDIT ANTE DEUS,
USQUE DIEM QUO NOSTRA SALUS DOMINUSQUE REDEMPTOR
ALTISONANTE TUBA SURGERE NOS FACIAT,
ABSTERGENS OCULIS LACRYMAS, ET VINCULA SOLVENS
MORTIS, UT ÆTERNA CORPORA LUCE MICENT.
HÆC MEA SPES, REQUIES, HÆC FIRMA FIDUCIA CORDIS,
VIVERE CUM CHRISTO, QUI MEA SOLA SALUS.

LONDINI OBIIT, JANUARII 23. 1619.
ANNUM AGENS 66.

Round the sides of the stone is likewise a fillet of brass, on which is cut the following words.

HIC JACET JOHANNES CROKE MILES, ET UNUS JUSTICIARIORUM DOMINI REGIS AD PLACITA CORAM IPSO REGE *TENENDUM ASSIGNATA*, DUM *VIXIRIT*, QUI OBIIT VICESIMO *TERCIO* DIE JANUARII, ANNO DOMINI MDCXIX ÆTATIS *SUI* LXVI.[p]

There is likewise a plate with his arms. Croke, quarterly, impaled with Blount, quartering nine coats. 1. Barry, nebuly, Blount. 2 Within a bordure, charged with ten saltiers, two wolves statant, Ayala 3. Vairy, Beauchamp. 4 A tower, Ayala. 5. A pale, Delaford. 6. A

p This epitaph seems to have suffered much from the ignorant artist who engraved it. *Tenendum assignata*, are palpable blunders, for *tenenda assignatus*, *vixirit*, for *vixerit* *tercio* for *tertio*, *ætatis sui* for *suæ* Some other parts are doubtful

chevron between three pheons, Spicer. 7. A fesse, dancette, between three mullets pierced, More. 8. A fesse between three annulets. 9. Barry of six, vairy and ermine.

In the window of the withdrawing room only four of the quarters of Blount are introduced. First, Blount, nebuly of six pieces, or, and sable. Secondly, argent, within a bordure, or, charged with ten saltiers, gules, two wolves, statant, sable, armed and langued of the third, Ayala. Thirdly, Or, a tower with three battlements azure, Ayala Fourthly, Vairy, Beauchamp. Over all, a crescent or, for difference. It is the same in stone over the porch.

His will was made the 28th of October, 1617, and is written in Latin. He left one hundred pounds, and all his household goods in his mansion house at Chilton, and all his plate, to his wife. To his son Sir John Croke, all his books, and the furniture in his houses in Holbourne, and Serjeant's Inn, with his seal at arms. To his son Henry, and his wife Brigitta, and their children, one hundred pounds. To his son Charles, twenty pounds. To his sons Unton and Edward, each, forty pounds, and an annuity of twenty pounds, to be paid out of Chilton To his daughter Rachel, bed furniture of the value of forty pounds. To each of his brothers and sisters, a silver cup of ten pounds value, with this inscription, *Timete Dominum, Honorate Regem, Diligite invicem.* (Fear the Lord, honour the King, love one another.) To his brother George, a gold ring of an ounce weight, with this inscription, *Fides adhibita fidem obligat,* (Fidelity exhibited, secures fidelity,) requesting him, by the fraternal love he bore him, to permit his son and heir to repurchase the manor of Easingdon. To each of his servants, twenty shillings. Upon all his family, and upon all who confess and love Jesus Christ, he implores the blessing of God. To his dearest aunt, Lady Anne Harrington, Baroness of Exton, he bequeaths a golden heart, with diamonds, of the value of twenty pounds. His wife, and his son John, are his executors, and his brothers George, Paul, and William, and his sons Henry and Charles, are the supervisors of his will By subsequent codicils he gives a pair of gilt salts, which had been his father's and grandfather's, to his son Sir John Croke, and to the poor in Chilton and Easingdon three pounds: to those of Studley and Horton, forty shillings

He had five sons, John, Henry, Charles, Unton, and Edward; and a daughter named Rachel: of all of whom I shall treat in order, appropriating a separate section to each.

I have his picture, painted on pannel, a half length. He is in his judge's robes, with a square cap, under which is a white cap, worn perhaps on account of baldness, or some other infirmity In his right hand is a bundle of papers. On the back ground is written, *Omnia Desuper*. I have likewise the picture of his wife, the Lady Katherine Croke, a handsome woman in a large ruff The dress and general appearance correspond with her statue on the monument of her father, Sir Michael Blount, in Saint Peter's Church in the Tower

SECTION THE SECOND.

THE ELDEST SON OF SIR JOHN CROKE THE JUDGE, AND HIS DESCENDANTS.

THE eldest son of Sir John Croke, the Judge, was likewise SIR JOHN CROKE, the fourth of that name, and the third of that title, having been knighted, in the life-time of his father, by King James the First[a]. He inherited the estate at Chilton, where he lived as a country gentleman. In 1628, the third year of Charles the First, he was elected Member for Shaftesbury[b].

He married two wives, the first was Eleanor, the youngest daughter and one of the coheiresses of Jervas Gibon, Esquire, of Kent. She had a considerable fortune, was only fourteen years of age, of a sickly constitution, and died in two years, being five months under sixteen. Her eldest sister married Mr. Robert Pointz; the second, named Gresill, Sir John Lawrence. After the death of Eleanor, Sir John Lawrence instituted proceedings at law, and in Chancery, against Sir John Croke, in 1618, to compel him either to pay £300, which was due to Sir John Pointz for the wardship of Gresill, or to relinquish his claim to Eleanor's lands. In his answer, Sir John Croke declares that he is willing to pay his contribution towards the wardship of Gresill, but that the lands of Eleanor, being of the nature of gavelkind, he was intitled to hold them for his life, as tenant by the curtesy, if he did not marry again, whether he had issue or not, that the provision in the will of Jervas Gibon, that if any of his daughters died before sixteen, her portion should accrue to the other sisters, must be understood *if unmarried*. And that the *inheritance* of the land descended to the two surviving sisters, by which Sir John Lawrence was bettered more than £300. All this appears in the petitions and answers of the

[a] Ward's Lives of the Gresham Professors, page 305. [b] Willis, Notit Parl

parties in Chancery before Sir Francis Bacon: but how the law-suit ended is not stated[c].

His second lady was Rachel, the daughter and heiress of Sir William Webb, Knight, of Motcomb in Dorsetshire. He died the tenth day of April, 1640, in the fifty-fourth year of his age, leaving three sons, and one daughter. He was buried under a plain marble stone on the pavement of the Chapel at Chilton, with the following inscription, which bears testimony to his devotion, learning, honour, and probity, and the proper discharge of his filial, conjugal, paternal, and friendly duties

M. S.

CINERES JOHANNIS CROKE DE CHILTON, EJUS NOMINIS QUARTI, IN AGRO BUCKINGHAMIÆ, MILITIS AURATI, HAC IN URNA SUNT REPOSITI, QUI TUBÆ NOVISSIMÆ AD SPEM ADHELANT.

	NUMINI DEVOTUS		PARENTIBUS SACER
VIR	LITERIS ERUDITUS	IDEM	CONJUGI MARITUS REDAMATUS
	FIDE SPECTATUS		LIBERIS PATER OPTIMUS
	PROBITATE INSIGNIS		AMICIS PRÆSIDIUM.

QUI, PATRIÆ ET PRINCIPI NATUS ET LIBATUS,
HINC PROPERE, AT FELICITER, FATO SUCCUBUIT.

OBIIT 10mo. DIE APRILIS, ANNO DNI 1640, ET ÆTATIS SUÆ 54° RELICTIS TRIBUS FILIIS, ET UNICA FILIA, QUOS SUSCEPIT EX RACHELE, DULCI CONJUGE, FILIA ET HÆREDE GUILLIELMI WEBB. DE MOTCOMBBE IN AGRO DORCESTRIÆ, MILITIS AURATI.

NON TOTUS PEREO

The arms on the monument are, Croke, quarterly. In an escutcheon of pretence, gules, a cross between four faulcons, or, for Webb[d].

SIR JOHN CROKE, the fourth of that name and title, was his son and heir In the life-time of his father he married a young lady of an excellent and amiable disposition, Jane, the daughter of Moses Tryon, Esquire. of

[c] Lansdowne MSS vol. 165. No. 95. fol 332. The petition and answer of Sir John Croke.

[d] The colours are not expressed on the monument, but they are in Guillim

Harringworth in Northamptonshire, but he was so unfortunate as to lose her in child-birth, in the twentieth year of her age, in 1636, leaving only a little daughter to console his afflictions. Her monument is a black marble on the pavement of the chapel at Chilton. The inscription.

M S.
ET VIRTUTI CŒLO FELICITER RECEPTÆ
JANÆ:
MOSIS TRYON DE HARRINGWORTH IN AGRO NORTHAMPT. ARMIG FIL. JOHANNIS CROKE DE CHILTON IN AGRO BUCKINGH. ARMIG. UXORIS.

QUAM

PARENTES	PIAM	
MARITUS	FIDELEM	HABUERE.
CONSANGUINEI	CARAM	
OMNES	AMABILEM.	

HANC

FAMILIÆ	DECUS
CONJUGIS	DELICIAS
AMICORUM	DESIDERIUM

IN IPSO FLORE FŒCUNDITAS ABSTULIT;
IX°. MAII V^{to}. A PUERPERIO DIE. A. C. 1636, ÆTATIS XX.
FILIOLA, UNICO TOT LACRIMARUM SOLATIO, SUPERSTITE.

The coat of arms is Croke, quarterly, with a label for difference, impaled with azure a fesse, crenellè, between six etoiles, or[e].

He married a second wife, but it is not known who she was.

During the civil wars, Sir John raised a troop of horse for the service of the King, by which means he very much embarrassed his estate. Mr. Ward says, that he was afterwards created a Baronet, but he was not able to learn the time of his creation, or to find his name in the English Baronetage[f].

I would willingly draw a veil over the misfortunes and crimes of this last but one of the family in the elder branch, but the historian must prefer

[e] The colours from Guillim, p 402

[f] Ward's manuscript additions to his lives of the Gresham professors, in the British Museum, page 305

plain truth before the gratification of his private feelings. We have before seen that Sir John Croke, the Judge, had impaired his fortune by the necessary expences of supporting the dignity of the high offices which he filled. His grandson was completely ruined. Poverty, unless it is occasioned by vice, is not dishonourable, and a series of unavoidable or laudable expences, or even a thoughtless imprudence, might have dissipated the paternal property of Sir John Croke, without affecting his character. The affair which I am about to relate can receive no mitigation by being attributed to the virulence of party spirit, or the gratification of an unfounded revenge, festering in a mind rendered acrid by distressing circumstances.

This was his cruel persecution of Mr. Robert Hawkins, and his endeavours to take away his life, in conjunction with several other persons, by a false indictment for a robbery in 1667 An account of Hawkins's trial was published in 1685, and is attributed by Wood to Sir Matthew Hale, before whom he was tried[g]. It was republished in 1710, about the time of Sacheverell's trial, to support the high church, by casting an odium upon the sectaries, and it is likewise in the State Trials[h]. The second edition is intitled, "The Perjured Phanatick, or the malicious conspiracy "of Sir John Croke of Chilton, Baronet, Justice of peace in com. Bucks. "Henry Larimore, Anabaptist preacher, and other phanatics, against the "life of Robert Hawkins, M. A. now living, and late minister of Chilton, "occasioned by his suit for tithes. Discovered in a trial at Alisbury, "before the Right Honourable Sir Matthew Hale, then Lord Chief Baron "of the Exchequer, and after Lord Chief Justice of England. Published "by his Lordship's command."

In his preface to the reader, Mr Hawkins gives the following account of "the occasion of this great difference."

"I was entertained by Sir John Croke, of the parish of Chilton, in the county of Bucks, Baronet, to attend as Chaplain in his house, and also to serve the cure of the said parish of Chilton, for which he did, under his hand and seal, promise to pay me fifty pounds per annum, he being impropriator of the said parish, and to pay it by quarterly payments. When I had faithfully performed my duty in both these capacities above two years, and in all that time had received no money from him, but upon

[g] Ath Ox vol ii col 426. ed 1. [h] Vol ii page 42. Edit. 1719.

some occasions had lent him several sums out of my own pocket, at last I was somewhat urgent with him for money, and then he told me plainly, that I did not know him as yet, for, as he said, he had cheated all persons that he had ever dealt with, and therefore I must not expect to speed better than they had done I told him, that I hoped for better things from him. But he replied, that he never intended to pay me any money, and therefore I might take my course.

"When I saw that, I went to London, and upon enquiry, found that Sir John Croke was outlawed after judgment, at the suit of Mr. Thomas and Mr. William Hellows, the one of London, and the other of Windsor, for a sum of money due from the said Sir John Croke to the said gentlemen; and that his manor of Chilton, with several farms, and the Rectory of the said parish, were extended into the King's hands, and a lease was granted from the Crown, under the seal of the Court of Exchequer, to the same gentlemen, and their assigns. I applied myself therefore to them, in order to persuade them to pay me for serving the same cure, out of the profits arising from the said Rectory: and they, by the advice of their counsel, granted me a lease of the said Rectory, with all the glebes, tithes, and other profits belonging to it, under both their hands and seals, to enable me to demand the same. Upon which I returned to Chilton, and acquainted Sir John Croke with what I had done, humbly entreating him to pay me what was due, and, upon that condition, I promised to deliver up the same lease But Sir John, instead of complying, told me I was a treacherous villain, and had undermined him in his estate, and therefore was not fit to live, and that the lease should be of no use to me; for that he would find out a way to prevent all my designs, and put a stop to all my proceedings, for he knew how to do my business to all intents and purposes, and bid me get out of his sight, or else he would knock me down immediately so I left him in a great rage and passion. Soon after this, he advised one Mr. Good, a Minister in the next parish, with the said Larimore, and others, to make a forcible entry upon my church in Chilton, which according they did, by breaking it open; and I indicted them for a riot upon that account at the next sessions at Buckingham. And then I desired several of the farmers to give me a meeting, in order to prevent a suit in law, if possible. When they came to me, I told them, that Sir John Croke owed me a great sum of money, for serving the cure at Chilton, which they knew to be true; and that he refused to pay me; and therefore, unless they would find out some way for me to be paid, I must put my lease in suit, and force them to pay their tythes to me, or compound with me for them. They replyed, that it would be unjust in me to make them pay their tythes over again, which they had bought of Sir John Croke, and had taken their farms tythe free. I replied, if they would let me see their leases, I would not insert any of those persons' names in my bill, whose leases bore date before the outlawry and extent; but all those whose leases were made since that time, were liable to pay their tythes to me, or else compound with me for them. But they reply'd, they would consult with Sir John Croke about the matter, and let me know his answer in a short time.

"So when they had discoursed with Sir John, they told me that he said, they needed not to fear what I could do to them by vertue of the lease, or upon any other account, for, as soon as I should begin the suit, and demand the tythes, he was fully resolved to do my business so effectually, as should stop all my proceedings.

"So when I saw I could not prevail to get my money either from Sir John Croke or the tenants, I was forced to exhibit my bill in the Exchequer, for tithes against Larmore, Mayne the Constable, Thomas Beamsly, Nicholas Sanders, and others; which I did in Michaelmass term, 1667, as may appear by the records of the Exchequer; and when the said Larmore, Mayne, and the rest above named, were served with subpœnas to answer my said bill, Sir John Croke soon after, viz. Wednesday, September the 16th, 1668, entered upon this conspiracy, with Larmore, to take away my life, as will fully appear by Mr. Brown's evidence in the trial, which shews how they prosecuted their malice, how justice was done, and my reputation as well as life secured by my acquittal: I shall only mention farther, the incouragement I had from my Lord Chief Baron, to prosecute several of the conspirators. He himself was pleased to direct the process for special bail, to order the Under Sheriff to demand £500 security of each; and, upon a motion at the Exchequer by Sir Richard Croke, and other eminent council, that less might be accepted, positively insisted upon the said order. But all ended in their hearty submission to me, and a reasonable composition with them; Larmore paid me £30.

Thomas Croxton £44 Thomas Beamsly £20. Mayne £15. Nicholas Sanders £12. In all £121. The others were secured by their poverty, and Sir John Croke lost his commission."

Though Sir John Croke was sufficiently culpable, this account is evidently much exaggerated, and in some parts a misrepresentation. The barefaced avowal, and even boast, of dishonest principles, here attributed to him, would shew a degree of profligacy scarcely credible in any man. This preface was written under a strong sense of injuries, with something of triumph, for having succeeded in escaping them, and it was published at a time when the author might hope to gain favour by blackening the puritans. Hawkins himself appears not to have been of the most unblemished reputation, for it is said by Anthony Wood, that "he was afterwards Vicar, but a poor one, "if not *scandalous*, of Beckley[1]."

This trial took place at Aylesbury, on the 11th of March, 1668, before Sir Matthew Hale, and Hugh Windham, Serjeant at Law. Hawkins was indicted for stealing two gold rings, one white Holland apron, two pieces of gold of the value of ten shillings each, and nineteen shillings in silver, belonging to Henry Larimore, upon the 18th of September. Sir John Croke was present in court, but quitted it abruptly before the conclusion. The best short account of this trial will be the summing up of Sir Matthew Hale to the Jury.

At the end of the examinations, the Lord Chief Baron (Hale) asked if Sir John Croke was gone, and informed the Court "that he had sent him "that morning two sugar loaves for a present. I did not then know so "well as now, what he meant by them, but to save his credit, I sent his "sugar loaves back again. I cannot think that Sir John Croke believes "that the King's Justices came into the country to take bribes, I rather "think, that some other person (having a design to put a trick upon him) "sent them in his name." And so taking the letter out of his bosom, he asked the gentlemen if it was his hand, which appearing, the Lord Chief Baron said, "he intended to carry it to London, and would relate the "foulness of the business upon occasion."

His directions to the Jury were to this effect.

[1] Ath Ox. vol ii col 426. Ed. i.

"You that are of the Jury, the prisoner at the bar stands indicted for robbing this Larimore, and you have heard at large, both the prosecutor's evidence to prove him guilty, (which if you do believe,) I never heard a fuller. And, secondly, you have also heard the prisoner's defence, wherein (as I think) he hath as fully answered the same charge. I shall first repeat the evidence against him, which consists of two branches, the first is the prosecutor's proof of this indictment; and, secondly, his charging him with other crimes of the like nature, as the stealing of Chilton's boots, and the picking of Noble's pocket

1. For to prove him guilty of robbing him, he observes this method:

First, He himself swears that he saw the prisoner at the bar commit the robbery.

Secondly, His son and sister swear that they saw him run out of the house at the same time

Thirdly, He brings in four or five persons, that swear the gold ring, and the five shilling piece, were found in the house of him that is now the prisoner at the bar.

Fourthly and lastly, He proves by two witnesses, that the gold ring and five shilling piece were pawned to him.

And for the first of these, Larimore swears, that upon Friday, the 18th of September last past, he locked his doors, between twelve and one of the clock at noon, and went out (leaving nobody at home,) to pluck hemp, about two furlongs from his house, where he stayed with the rest of his family, till within an hour and an half of sunset; at which time, he coming home, found his door open, and ran up into his chamber, and there through the chinks of the loft boards, he swears that he saw the prisoner, now at the bar, ransacking and rifling of a box, in the which was at that time a Holland apron, and a purse, in which purse were two gold rings, two pieces of gold, and nineteen shillings in silver, all which said rings, gold, and silver, with the said apron, he swears that he did see the prisoner now at the bar turn out of the said purse, take and feloniously carry away, except one piece or two of the silver, and shew the very purse out of which he saw him take them. If you compare the evidence with the indictment, you may see the policy of the prosecutor For he would gladly seem a moderate prosecutor, by indicting him for felony only, as the stealing of rings, money, &c But by his evidence, he would as gladly charge him with burglary also, for he swears, he broke open, or picked the locks of his doors, and box, which by law is the same.

And secondly, To corroborate this his evidence, he brings in two witnesses more, viz. his son and sister Beamsley, and they swear that they did, at the same time, see the prisoner, that is now at the bar, run out of Larimore's house, with a great bunch of keys in his hand, and he hid himself amongst beans and weeds: and note the keys, to intimate that by the help of those, he picked Larimore's locks.

Thirdly, He brings in his son, Dodsworth Croke, the Constable, and Tythingman, which all swear, that they found this gold ring, and five shilling piece of silver, in a basket, hanging upon a pin, in the house of the prisoner at the bar, with a few eggs, which the prisoner at the bar the day before had stolen from him

And, fourthly and lastly, He brings in one of Sir John Croke's sons and Mr. Good, who swear that the one pawned the ring, the other the five shilling piece, to Larimore.

Thus Larimore swears, he saw the prisoner rob him, his son and sister swear they saw him run out of the house, the same time, four more swear, that they found the ring and five shilling piece in his house upon search, and, lastly, two swear that the ring and five shilling piece were pawned to him. If all this be true, he must needs be guilty, and if so, altho' I have a great respect for his calling, yet that shall no way excuse him, but rather aggravate his crime.

And thus much touching the indictment.

And secondly, He seems to charge him with other acts of the like nature, as,

1. He brings in one Chilton to swear that the prisoner at the bar did steal a pair of boots from him, and four or five persons swear, that they did hear Chilton say he did

2. He brings one Boyce, from London, a person, I think, of no great credit, he swears, that he saw the prisoner at the bar, about two years ago, have his hand in the pocket of one James Noble, and that Noble said, that he lost a gold ring, and a piece of gold at the same time. This (if true) would render the prisoner now at the bar obnoxious to any Jury. Thus far the evidence against the prisoner at the bar.

Now we come to the prisoner's defence, which, because it is so full I shall be the briefer in it.

The parts of his defence were two, as himself observed.

1 He shews how too improbable it is.

And 2. How impossible it is that he should be guilty of this charge

First, That it is not likely that Larimore was robbed at all, because he did not declare it to any of his neighbours, as soon as he saw the robbery committed. Again, he varies as to the time when it was done, for that he told his brother Beamsley, that he had lost the ring and five shilling piece, before there was any difference between him and the prisoner at the bar, as appears by Mrs. Willcox, and that difference began in Michaelmas term, 1667. and before Sir John Croke he confessed that he had lost this a month before the prisoner was committed, which must be about the 19th of August, 1668. And in court, he swears, that he saw the prisoner rob him of the same gold ring, and five shilling piece of silver, upon Friday the 18th of September, 1668, an hour and an half before sunset, all this cannot be true, and for the warrant, that bears date a day before the robbery was committed, whereupon the Judge said to Larimore, Come, thou art a cunning fellow, for thou wentst to Sir Richard Pigott for a warrant on the 17th day, and wast not robbed untill the 18th day Larimore, thou knewest, it seems, upon the 17th day, that thou shouldest be robbed on the 18th day. that the prisoner at the bar should rob thee, surely thou canst divine, if all this be true. Again, is it likely, that when the prisoner was charged with flat felony at his own doors, the constable likewise threatening to break open his house to search, if he had been guilty, his wife and himself, having the opportunity of going abroad after they had so charged him, while they were gone to consult with Sir John Croke, as the prisoner at the bar sufficiently proved they did, that in all that time he would not have made his escape, or at least found a more convenient place to convey a ring and five shilling piece, than to let it remain all that time in a little basket, with a few eggs, hanging on a pin? Again, who came first into the room, where this egg-basket hung? Why, Larimore; and who took down the basket? Larimore; who turned out the eggs? Larimore, and who had the dressing of the eggs? Larimore. He is a special cook, you Gentlemen of the Jury; it is an easy thing for Larimore to juggle a ring and five shilling piece into a basket, he being the first that came into the room, as he put up his hand to take down the basket, he might with ease enough convey such things as these were into it All this, and many more, are probable circumstances, to move you and me to believe, that it is not possible, that the prisoner at the bar is guilty of this robbery, but that I must leave to you to consider of.

Again, the prisoner at the bar proves the whole business to be but a meer contrivance of Sir John Croke's and this Larimore, on purpose to ruin him, as is fully made manifest by the testimony of Mr. Brown, who justifies, that upon Wednesday the 16th of September last past, and but two days before this pretended robbery, he heard Sir John Croke advise this Larimore to fetch a warrant to search the house of the prisoner at the bar, and then to convey gold and silver into it; which having done, charge him with flat felony, and bring him before the said Sir John Croke, and no other Justice, he then promising to the said Larimore to commit him to the jail without bail, and hang him at the next assizes, which is now, and, as I take it, they do aim at it. You of this jury, if you do believe what Mr. Brown saith, it is as foul a conspiracy as ever was heard of, and I am apt to think it may be probable, because that Sir John Croke and Larimore did threaten to cast this Mr. Brown into prison, and so ruin him, if he came down, and testified his knowledge about this business, which thing is of a very ill consequence. Again, it seems likely that Mr. Brown may be credited, if you compare their actions with the times; for upon Tuesday Sir John arrested the prisoner upon a feigned action of an £100. Upon Wednesday the plot was concluded upon by Sir John Croke and Larimore, as may appear by Mr. Brown's testimony. On Thursday they procured of Sir Richard Pigott the warrant to search. On Friday, Larimore pretends that he was robbed, (tho' in truth there appears no such thing.) Upon Saturday the prisoner's house was broken open and he apprehended; and upon Sunday he was carried to jail, it was a good week's work But there is an honest man, said my Lord Chief Baron, (pointing at Mr. Willcox,) he knocks down all, for he justifies that he came to Larimore's house upon Friday the 18th of September last past, (it being the same day that he swears he saw the prisoner at the bar robbing him, and an hour and a half before sun-set,) and there continued till it was near night, and he further saith, that Larimore was with him all that afternoon. And he said, that Larimore was not robbed that afternoon, nor was Mr.

Hawkins there at that time. If this that Mr. Willcox saith be true, then all that Larimore, his son, and sister hath sworn, must needs be false.

And as touching the boots, Chilton swears that he had legged a pair of boots for the prisoner, and laid them in his shop window, for him to take along with him as he went by, which he did, and paid him for his work; and yet this Larimore, Sir John Croke, Croxtone, and others, did use their utmost endeavours, to stir up this Chilton to indict the prisoner for stealing of them, (Croxtone promising him to bear him out in it.) This can argue nothing else but malice in those persons. And for that which Boyce swears, is a story which can argue nothing else, for neither is Noble here to prosecute, nor can Boyce swear that the prisoner at the bar did pick his pocket, or that Noble ever said he did.

Thus I have repeated the evidence to prove him guilty, and have not, I think, omitted any thing in it that is material. Which if you do believe, he must needs be guilty. And also the prisoner's defence, which I think is sufficient. It is a plain case, and I suppose you need not go from the box, but that I leave to you."

And so the Jury, not stirring from the box, found Mr. Hawkins, *Not Guilty*.

On account of his debts, Sir John Croke, at this time, and afterwards, was a prisoner in the King's Bench, but continued in his house at Chilton under the superintendance of a keeper[k]. He sold the family estate at Chilton to — Harvey, Esquire, a citizen of London, of whose son Edward it was purchased by Richard Carter, Esquire, a barrister, and one of the Welch Judges: whose son George Richard Carter, Esquire, having an only daughter, Martha Catherine Carter, by her marriage with Sir John Aubrey, Baronet, about the year 1784, it became his property[l] This sale does not appear to have relieved Sir John Croke from his embarrassments, for he was removed from Chilton to London in a state of confinement, and died there, the exact time is not known[m].

His son was Sir Dodsworth Croke, who was knighted by King Charles the Second[n], and to whom the title of Baronet descended[o] Having no children, he was the last of the male line of the eldest branch

[k] Delafield's History of Chilton [l] Monument in Boarstall Church [m] Delafield
[n] Ward, MS Addit p. 305 [o] Delafield

of the family. The estate at Chilton having been sold, he lived to a great age in poverty and distress, at that place, and died without issue in 1728, as appears by this inscription upon a square stone in the chapel. "*Here* "*lieth the body of Sir Dodsworth Crooke, Knight and Baronet, who* "*died January the* 16*th*, 1728, *aged* 84 *years.*"

SECTION THE THIRD.

THE SECOND SON OF SIR JOHN CROKE, THE JUDGE, AND HIS DESCENDANTS, OR THE CHEQUERS BRANCH.

SIR HENRY CROKE

WHILST the eldest branch of the descendants of Sir John Croke, the Judge, thus withered in poverty, and discredit, his second son, Henry, by his prudence, and good conduct, raised a fair establishment of fame and fortune.

He was born, as is stated on his monument, in the *memorable year* 1588, when the country obtained safety and glory by the destruction of the invincible armada The honour of knighthood was conferred upon him by his Sovereign, and he is said to have been a man of letters, and of polite manners About the year 1616, he obtained the office of Clerk of the Pipe in the Exchequer[a], which is a lucrative place, not over burdened with any great expenditure of time, or labour[b]. His education, profession, and the previous steps which lead to this appointment, have not been related. In 1628, the third of Charles the First, he was Member of Parliament for Christchurch, in Hampshire[c].

By a discreet marriage he acquired a very considerable estate in Buckinghamshire. His lady was Bridget, the daughter and co-heiress of Sir William Hawtrey, Knight, of Chequers, in the parish of Ellesborough.

This was an ancient family, which had been long settled there. From the name, Hawtrey, a corruption of *Haute rive*, in Latin *de Altâ Ripâ*, it may be presumed to have claimed a Norman origin, or from the town of Hauterive in Languedoc, on the river Auriege, thirteen miles south of Thoulouse The earliest of the family who remains upon record is Sir

[a] Styled in Latin, Ingrossator rotulæ magnæ in Curiâ Scaccarii

[b] In the Court Calendar it is valued now at £651 a year, and is at present held by Lord William Bentinck.

[c] Willis Notit Parl

William de Altâ Ripâ, of Algerkirk in the county of Lincoln; and who appears to have acquired this estate by his union with Catherine, the daughter and co-heiress of Sir Chequers of Chequers. From him, by a descent of ten steps, we arrive at Sir William Hawtrey, Knight, the father of Bridget[d].

There are two flat monuments of this family in Ellesborough church. One has the effigies of a gentleman and lady, engraved on a brass plate, with two groups of figures, the one of eleven men, and the other of seven women, representing their sons and daughters. The brass fillets, with the inscription, have been torn off, but there is the coat of arms of Hawtrey. The other has an inscription on a brass plate in the old black letter

Of your charitie pray for the soules of Thomas Hawtrey Esquyer, and Sybell his wyffe whych Thomas decessyd the xvth **day of November in the yere of our Lorde God a** MCCCCC°. XL. IIII°. **and the sayd Sybell decessyd the . . . day of . in the yere of our Lorde God a** MCCCCC. . . . . **on whose souls and all Christen soules Jesu have mercy.**

Here lyethe the body of Marye somtyme the wyfe of William Hawtrey of this parysshe Esquyer, who departed this lyfe in travell of her fyrst chyld the xth **day of December in the yere of our Lord God** M. VC. L. V. **whose soule God pardon.**

The wife of Sir William Hawtree, the father of Bridget, was Winifred, the daughter of Ambrose Dormer, Esquire, of Great Milton in Oxfordshire, and sister of Sir Michael Dormer, who married Dorothy Hawtrey, sister of Sir William Hawtrey[e]. Sir William Hawtrey had no male issue, but he had three other daughters, Mary, married to Sir Francis Wolley; Anne, to John Sanders of Dinton; and Elizabeth, to Walter

[d] Visitation of Bucks, in 1574 Harl MSS No 1139 Pedigree of Hawtrey in Brown Willis, supra In the twenty-sixth of Elizabeth, the Queen granted to Michael Hawtrey, Philippa his wife, and William Hawtrey, their son, the Rectory and Advowson of the Vicarage of Wendover, for their lives, rendering 49*l* 16*s* 8*d* a year. The fine paid was 50*l*. Rot. Pat in Brown Willis, MSS vol xl fol 106.

[e] Monument of the Dormers in Great Milton Church. Brown Willis's MSS vol XIX. in Bibl. Bodl

Pye, son and heir of Sir Walter Pye. The estate at Chequers went with Bridget, the second daughter, to Sir Henry Croke[f].

Sir Henry Croke died of the stone, the first of January, in 1659, in the seventy-second year of his age, and was buried at Ellesborough. In the inscription upon his monument, which is a flat marble on the pavement, there is a singular thought, conceived in the quaint beauties of the language of those times, that "he did not love the poor, and therefore that "none might continue in poverty, was the constant object of his exertions, "and of the employment of his wealth."

P. M. S.

REQUIESCIT SUB HOC MARMORE DOMINI HENRICI CROKE, EQUITIS AURATI, DEPOSITUM, ANNOS XLIII CLERICI PIPÆ OFFICIO GAUDENS, TAM LITERIS QUAM MORIBUS HUMANISSIMI AN°. DN[i]. MIRABILI MDLXXXVIII° NATI: ÆTATIS LXXII, DOMINIQUE MDCLIX, PRIMO MANE, MENSE JANUARII, LITHIASI MORBO, DENATI

EX DIUTURNITATE JUDICIUM COMPUTETIS,
EX EUPHEMIA FIDELITATEM,
SINGULIS CHARISSIMUS SOLAS PAUPERES NON REDAMAVIT,
IDLOQUE, NE TALES PERMANERENT,
TUM OPE, TUM OPIBUS SATAGEBAT
ALBO OMNIUM CALCULO VIVEBAT,
SUO MORIEBATUR.

A coat of arms, Croke quartered, with a crescent for difference.

His lady, who died before him, is buried under a superb marble monument in the same church. She is represented in a recumbent posture, under an arch, supported by four Corinthian columns, and her *manly* virtues are celebrated in the following, rather extraordinary, epitaph. She died in 1638, and was buried on the fifth of July[g].

ECCUM NOMEN QUAM EMPHATICE MARMOREUM.
DURIORI SCILICET SAXO ÆQUE PERENNE.

[f] See the Genealogy of Hawtrey, Croke, Thurban, Russel, and Greenhill, No. 25.

[g] Ellesborough Register of burials.

No. 25.

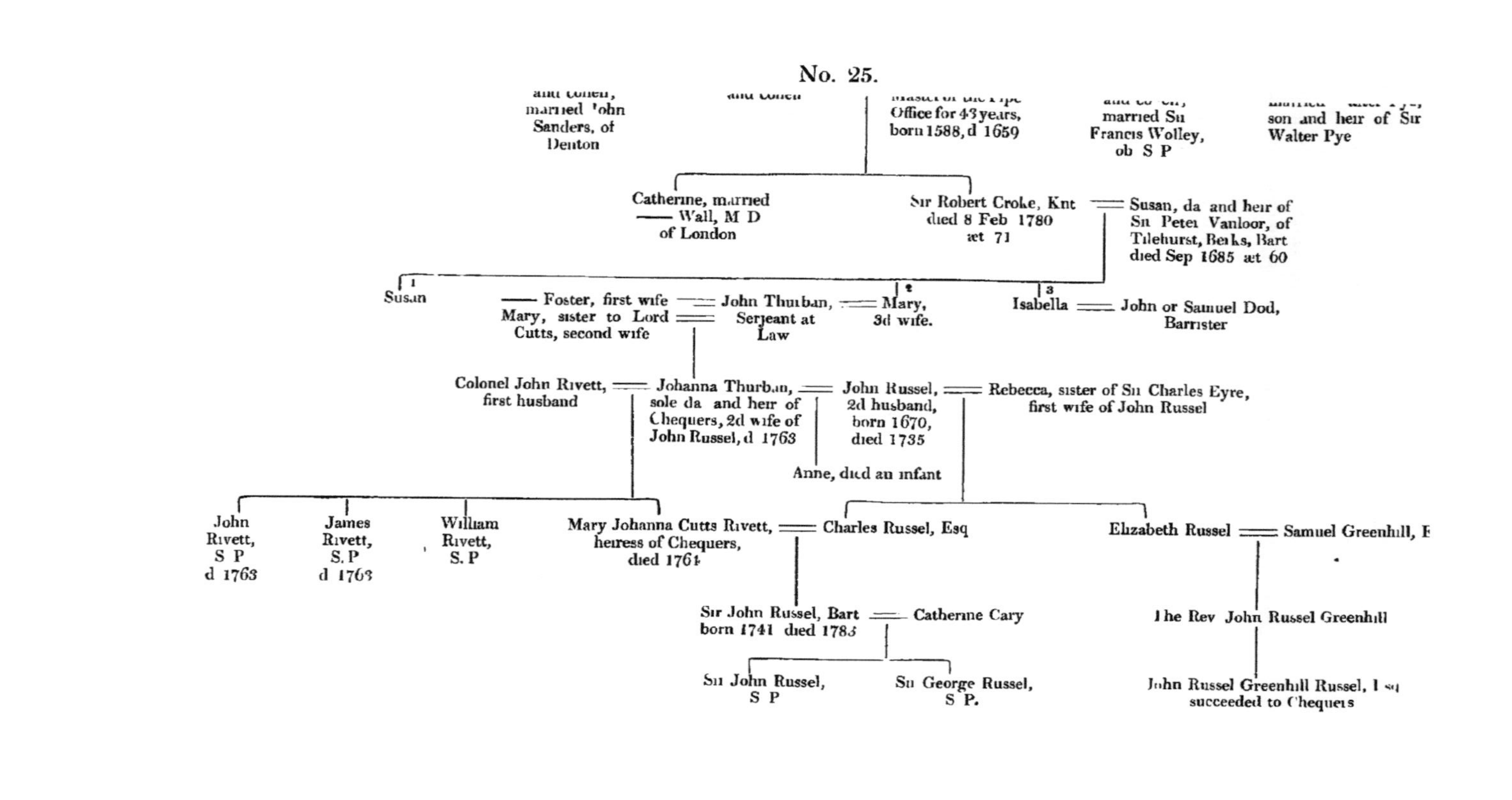
married John Sanders, of Denton
Office for 43 years, born 1588, d 1659
married Sir Francis Wolley, ob S P
son and heir of Sir Walter Pye
Catherine, married —— Wall, M D of London
Sir Robert Croke, Knt died 8 Feb 1780 æt 71
Susan, da and heir of Sir Peter Vanloor, of Tilehurst, Berks, Bart died Sep 1685 æt 60
1 Susan
—— Foster, first wife
Mary, sister to Lord Cutts, second wife
John Thurban, Serjeant at Law
2 Mary, 3d wife.
3 Isabella
John or Samuel Dod, Barrister
Colonel John Rivett, first husband
Johanna Thurban, sole da and heir of Chequers, 2d wife of John Russel, d 1763
John Russel, 2d husband, born 1670, died 1735
Rebecca, sister of Sir Charles Eyre, first wife of John Russel
Anne, died an infant
John Rivett, S P d 1763
James Rivett, S.P d 1763
William Rivett, S.P
Mary Johanna Cutts Rivett, heiress of Chequers, died 1764
Charles Russel, Esq
Elizabeth Russel
Samuel Greenhill, E
Sir John Russel, Bart born 1741 died 1783
Catherine Cary
The Rev John Russel Greenhill
Sir John Russel, S P
Sir George Russel, S P.
John Russel Greenhill Russel, Esq succeeded to Chequers

Pye, son and heir of Sir Walter Pye. The estate at Chequers went with Bridget, the second daughter, to Sir Henry Croke[f].

Sir Henry Croke died of the stone, the first of January, in 1659, in the seventy-second year of his age, and was buried at Ellesborough. In the inscription upon his monument, which is a flat marble on the pavement, there is a singular thought, conceived in the quaint beauties of the language of those times, that "he did not love the poor, and therefore that "none might continue in poverty, was the constant object of his exertions, "and of the employment of his wealth"

P M. S.

REQUIESCIT SUB HOC MARMORE DOMINI HENRICI CROKE, EQUITIS AURATI, DEPOSITUM, ANNOS XLIII CLERICI PIPÆ OFFICIO GAUDENS, TAM LITERIS QUAM MORIBUS HUMANISSIMI: AN^O. DN^I. MIRABILI MDLXXXVIII° NATI · ÆTATIS LXXII, DOMINIQUE MDCLIX, PRIMO MANE, MENSE JANUARII, LITHIASI MORBO, DENATI.

EX DIUTURNITATE JUDICIUM COMPUTETIS,
EX EUPHEMIA FIDELITATEM,
SINGULIS CHARISSIMUS SOLAS PAUPERES NON REDAMAVIT,
IDEOQUE, NE TALES PERMANERENT,
TUM OPE, TUM OPIBUS SATAGEBAT.
ALBO OMNIUM CALCULO VIVEBAT.
SUO MORIEBATUR.

A coat of arms, Croke quartered, with a crescent for difference.

His lady, who died before him, is buried under a superb marble monument in the same church. She is represented in a recumbent posture, under an arch, supported by four Corinthian columns, and her *manly* virtues are celebrated in the following, rather extraordinary, epitaph. She died in 1638, and was buried on the fifth of July[g].

ECCUM NOMEN QUAM EMPHATICE MARMOREUM:
DURIORI SCILICET SAXO ÆQUE PERENNE

[f] See the Genealogy of Hawtrey, Croke, Thurban, Russel, and Greenhill, No. 25.

[g] Ellesborough Register of burials

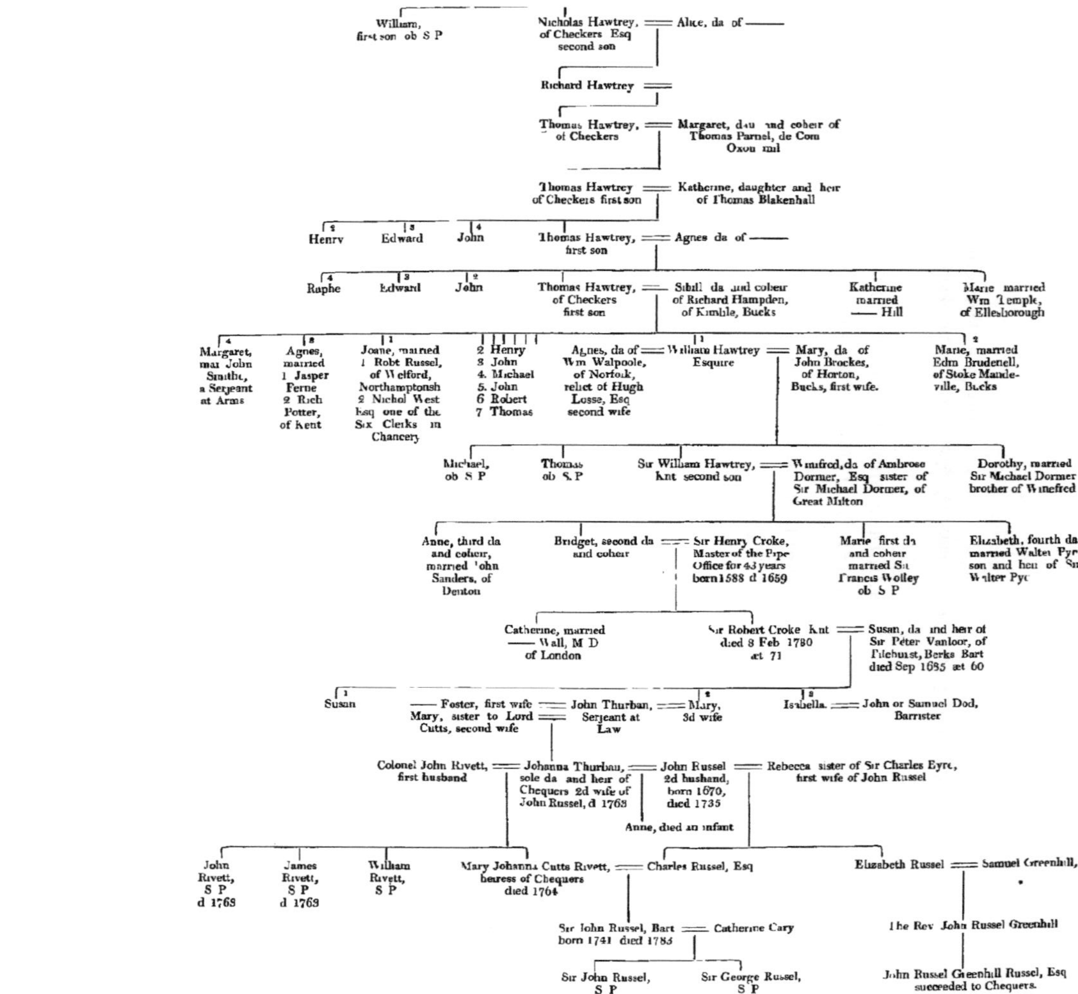

William, first son ob S P
Nicholas Hawtrey, of Checkers Esq second son ══ Alice, da of ——
Richard Hawtrey ══
Thomas Hawtrey, of Checkers ══ Margaret, dau and coheir of Thomas Parnel, de Com Oxon mil
Thomas Hawtrey of Checkers first son ══ Katherine, daughter and heir of Thomas Blakenhall
2 Henry
3 Edward
4 John
Thomas Hawtrey, first son ══ Agnes da of ——
4 Raphe
3 Edward
2 John
Thomas Hawtrey, of Checkers first son ══ Sibill da and coheir of Richard Hampden, of Kimble, Bucks
Katherine married —— Hill
Marie married Wm Temple, of Ellesborough
4 Margaret, mar John Smithe, a Sergeant at Arms
3 Agnes, married 1 Jasper Ferne 2 Rich Potter, of Kent
1 Joane, married 1 Robt Russel, of Welford, Northamptonsh 2 Nichol West Esq one of the Six Clerks in Chancery
2 Henry 3 John 4. Michael 5. John 6 Robert 7 Thomas
Agnes, da of Wm Walpoole, of Norfolk, relict of Hugh Losse, Esq second wife ══ 1 William Hawtrey Esquire ══ Mary, da of John Brockes, of Horton, Bucks, first wife.
2 Marie, married Edm Brudenell, of Stoke Mandeville, Bucks
Michael, ob S P
Thomas ob S P
Sir William Hawtrey, Knt second son ══ Winifred, da of Ambrose Dormer, Esq sister of Sir Michael Dormer, of Great Milton
Dorothy, married Sir Michael Dormer brother of Winefred
Anne, third da and coheir, married John Sanders, of Denton
Bridget, second da and coheir ══ Sir Henry Croke, Master of the Pipe Office for 43 years born 1588 d 1659
Marie first da and coheir married Sir Francis Wolley ob S P
Elizabeth, fourth da married Walter Pye son and heir of Sir Walter Pye
Catherine, married —— Wall, M D of London
Sir Robert Croke Knt died 8 Feb 1780 æt 71 ══ Susan, da and heir of Sir Peter Vanloor, of Tilehurst, Berks Bart died Sep 1685 æt 60
1 Susan
—— Foster, first wife ══ John Thurban, Serjeant at Law ══ 2 Mary, 3d wife
Mary, sister to Lord Cutts, second wife ══
3 Isabella ══ John or Samuel Dod, Barrister
Colonel John Rivett, first husband ══ Johanna Thurban, sole da and heir of Chequers 2d wife of John Russel, d 1768 ══ John Russel 2d husband, born 1670, died 1735 ══ Rebecca sister of Sir Charles Eyre, first wife of John Russel
Anne, died an infant
John Rivett, S P d 1768
James Rivett, S P d 1769
William Rivett, S P
Mary Johanna Cutts Rivett, heiress of Chequers died 1764 ══ Charles Russel, Esq
Elizabeth Russel ══ Samuel Greenhill, Esq
Sir John Russel, Bart born 1741 died 1783 ══ Catherine Cary
The Rev John Russel Greenhill
Sir John Russel, S P
Sir George Russel, S P
John Russel Greenhill Russel, Esq succeeded to Chequers.

ET VEL IPSI MONUMENTO MONUMENTUM;
NOMEN QUAERAS (LECTOR) SEU TITULUM POTIUS
VIRTUTUM, PIE VIXIT SPIRANS ETHICA
BRIGETTA CROKE:
MARITA PLUSQUAM AMICA
MULIER QUAM PENE NULLA,
FEMINÆ NIHIL HABENS NISI SEXUM,
CONSTANTIA FLORESCENS UXOR ADMODUM VIRILI,
MULTA PARTU MATER, ET AMORE MULTA,
CLARIS ORIUNDA PROAVIS, CLARIS ET DIGNA,
CUJUS VIGENTEM CINEREM RIGANS MARITUS,
OBRUTA DUM JACET HÆC TUMULO, JACET ILLE DOLORE.

The arms are, Croke, single, with a crescent, impaled with, argent, four lions rampant, between two cotises sable. For Hawtrey. Two crests, two swans' necks, Croke; and for Hawtrey, a bear's head, or, fretty, sable. There are likewise two single coats, one of Croke, and the other of Hawtrey, as in the impaled coat of arms.

His son and successor, not only in his estates, but likewise in the office of Clerk of the Pipe, was SIR ROBERT CROKE, Knight, who twice represented the borough of Wendover in Parliament, in the fifteenth and sixteenth years of Charles the First[i], and was knighted by that King at Whitehall, the ninth of August, 1641[k].

Like his father, he improved his patrimony by a prudent marriage. The object of his choice was Miss, or as young ladies were then called, Mrs. Susanna Vanloor, one of the three daughters and heiresses of Sir Peter Vanloor, Baronet, only son of Sir Peter Vanloor of Tylehurst in Berkshire. This last gentleman was born in Holland, in the province of Utrecht, was a wealthy merchant in London, and was naturalized by the authority of parliament. His mercantile and pecuniary services were often employed, and acknowledged, by his Sovereigns Queen Elizabeth, King James, and Charles the First, and he was rewarded by the title of a Baronet. He died September the sixth, in 1627, being above sixty years old, and was buried

[i] 15 and 16 Charles I Willis's Not Parl [k] Wood s Ath Oxon vol. ii. col 728.

at Tylehurst under a sumptuous monument[l]. By his wife Jacomina, the daughter of Henry Teighbott, he had only one son, of his own name, and six daughters of whom Anna married Charles Cæsar, son and heir of Sir Julius Cæsar, Privy Counsellor, and Master of the Rolls, and Mary, Sir Edward Powell, Baronet Sir Peter Vanloor, the son, married Susanna, the daughter of Lawrence Becke, of Antwerp, and had three daughters, Jacomina, Susanna and Maria. Susanna married Sir Robert Croke[m].

In 1661, Sir Robert Croke presented a petition to King Charles the Second, for restoring the ancient and established comptroll and legal course of the King's Exchequer. He states, that his Majesty's father, in the eighth year of his reign, by his letters patent, granted him the office of Clerk of the Pipe, or Ingrosser of the Great Roll of the Exchequer: that the ancient course of the Court had been observed from King Stephen, until of late, that the auditors obstructed the same by illegal and unsafe proceedings; and in particular that many rents had been omitted in the accounts and many sums lost to the Crown His Majesty, by an order of the seventh of June, 1661, referred the petition to the Chancellor, and others, who met at Serjeant's Inn, on the eighth of July, and made an order for the production and return of various documents, by the second of November, but what farther was done does not appear[n].

He died February the eighth, 1680, aged 71 years, and his lady in 1685, aged 60. They were both buried at Ellesborough, but their tomb-stones are now nearly covered by the pew of the Russel family[o]. They had six sons, and seven daughters[p].

The arms of Vanloor are, or, a garland, or orle of wood-bine, or honey-suckle, proper[q].

Robert Croke, Esquire, their eldest son, was Clerk of the Pipe, in his father's life-time who must therefore have resigned in his favour, after having enjoyed the office above twenty years. He died however without issue before his father, July the 30th, 1671, aged thirty-five years, and

[l] Ashmole's Berkshire, p 146 [m] Genealogy of the Vanloor family in Dugdale's MSS No 852 fol 324 It is signed by Pieter van Loor No 26 [n] Landowne MSS vol 259 fol 100 [o] Inscription [p] There was a Robert Croke, who took the degree of Doctor of Physic, 1 May, 1644, can it be the same person? Wood, Fasti, Oxon vol ii col. 728. [q] Blome's Catalogue of Baronets, at the end of Guillim

No. 26.

GENEALOGY OF VANLOOR.

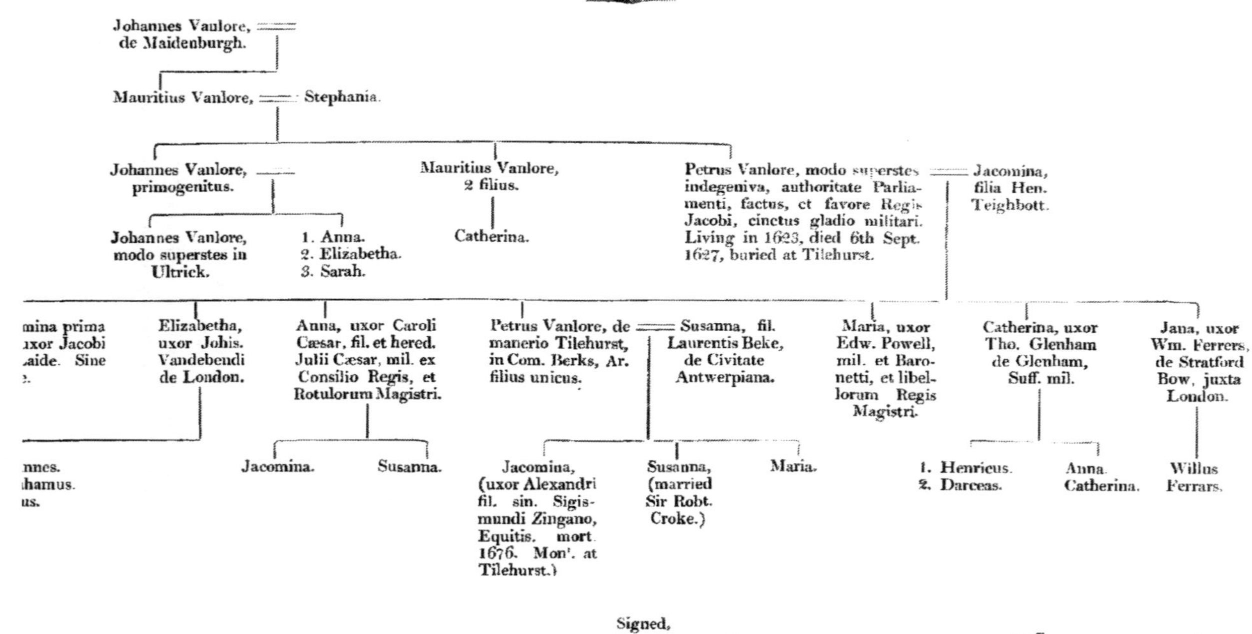

Johannes Vanlore, de Maidenburgh. =
Mauritius Vanlore, = Stephania.
Johannes Vanlore, primogenitus. =
Mauritius Vanlore, 2 filius.
Petrus Vanlore, modo superstes indegeniva, authoritate Parliamenti, factus, et favore Regis Jacobi, cinctus gladio militari. Living in 1623, died 6th Sept. 1627, buried at Tilehurst. = Jacomina, filia Hen. Teighbott.
Johannes Vanlore, modo superstes in Ultrick.
1. Anna.
2. Elizabetha.
3. Sarah.
Catherina.
mina prima
uxor Jacobi
aide. Sine
Elizabetha, uxor Johis. Vandebendi de London.
Anna, uxor Caroli Cæsar, fil. et hered. Julii Cæsar, mil. ex Consilio Regis, et Rotulorum Magistri.
Petrus Vanlore, de manerio Tilehurst, in Com. Berks, Ar. filius unicus. = Susanna, fil. Laurentis Beke, de Civitate Antwerpiana.
Maria, uxor Edw. Powell, mil. et Baronetti, et libellorum Regis Magistri.
Catherina, uxor Tho. Glenham de Glenham, Suff. mil.
Jana, uxor Wm. Ferrers, de Stratford Bow, juxta London.
nnes.
hamus.
us.
Jacomina.
Susanna.
Jacomina, (uxor Alexandri fil. sin. Sigismundi Zingano, Equitis. mort. 1676. Mon'. at Tilehurst.)
Susanna, (married Sir Robt. Croke.)
Maria.
1. Henricus.
2. Darceas.
Anna.
Catherina.
Willus Ferrars.

Signed,

Dugdale's MSS. No. 852. fol. 324.

was buried at Ellesborough, but his tomb-stone is likewise eclipsed by the Russel pew.

A second son, Henry Croke, died in 1662, only twenty-one years of age. His tomb-stone has a long laudatory inscription, nearly obliterated by the envious hand of time, and the footsteps of the profane. As far as it can be made out it is as follows.

HENRICI CROKE
QUOD MORI POTUIT HEIC CONDITUR
QUOD MORI NON DEBUIT HEIC PANDITUR.
QUI D^NI ROBERTI CROCI, EQUITIS AURATI,
NATU SECUNDUS, ANNUM AGENS XXI,
SUMMO MANE, CALENDIS JANUARIIS, AN. DM. M,DC,LXII,
VEL APOSTEMATE, VEL *ARTIUM* [r]
MORBO, SANE MEDICIS OCCULTO,
OXONII DELICIÆ, OCCUBUIT,
IISDEM HORA DIEQUE QUIBUS AVITUS
D^US HENRICUS CROCUS, EQUES AURATUS,
TRIBUS RETRO ANNIS OBDORMIVIT
NATALIUM SPLENDOREM VIRTUTUM PURPURA,
VIRTUTES OMNIGENÆ SCIENTIÆ IRIDE,
SCIENTIAS PURÆ RELIGIONIS CANDORE . . .
AUT SUI EXEMPLUM IMMORTALI . . .
TUM MORUM TEMPERIE TUM MORTIS TEMPORE .
EN CŒLESTEM AMBITIONEM . . . .
SIMULAC VIRILEM ATTIGISSET ÆTATEM
PERFECTIONE NON CONTENTUS HUMANA
AD HIERARCHIAM SANCTORUM . . .
Four lines obliterated.

A daughter Catherine was baptized the 23d of February, 1650, and died in 1657[s].

All the six sons and seven daughters of Sir Robert Croke, and Susanna Vanloor, died before their father, except three daughters. For Sir

[r] Artuum. [s] Ellesborough Register.

Robert, by his will, dated the 5th of May, 1679, gave all his manors and lands, in the parish of Ellesborough, to his wife Dame Susan Croke, for her life, and after her death to Susan, Mary, and Isabella, his three daughters, their heirs and assigns, for ever, in such shares as his wife should appoint[t]. Isabella the youngest daughter married John, or Samuel, Dod, a barrister Mary, the second, was the third wife of John Thurban, Serjeant at Law; by whom he had no children[u].

The whole of the estate at Chequers, I know not by what means, became the property of Serjeant Thurban; who left it to Johanna, his only daughter, by his second wife Mary, sister to Lord Cutts. She married, for her first husband, Colonel John Rivett, by whom she had three sons, John, James, and William, and a daughter, Johanna Cutts Rivett. Her second husband was John Russel, Esquire, by whom she had no children. The three sons dying without issue, the estate came to their sister Johanna Cutts Rivett This heiress married Charles Russel, Esquire, son of John Russel, who married Johanna Thurban, by his first wife Rebecca, sister of Sir Charles Eyre. They had an only son, Sir John Russel, Baronet, whose two sons by his wife Catherine Cary, Sir John Russel, and Sir George Russel, both dying without issue, the reverend Doctor John Russel Greenhill, as next heir, inherited Chequers He was the son of Samuel Greenhill, Esquire, by Elizabeth Russel, sister of Charles Russel before mentioned. The son of Doctor Greenhill, Robert Greenhill Russel, Esquire, Barrister at Law of Lincoln's Inn, and Member of Parliament for Thirsk in Yorkshire, is the present representative of the family, which is descended from Oliver Cromwell, the Protector's youngest daughter Frances, the relict of Robert Rich, having married their ancestor, Sir John Russel, Baronet[x].

The house at Chequers, in the parish of Ellesborough, is a fine old brick mansion, built by Sir Henry Croke, with a square court in the

[t] Sloan's MSS Mus Brit No 1691 fol 91 [u] Brown Willis, MSS vol iii. p. 36

[x] Genealogy, No 27 from the Visitation of Bucks, in 1574, by Richard Lee, Harl MSS No 1139 Brown Willis's MSS Noble's Memoirs of Cromwell, Gough's View of the family of Cromwell Nichols's Biblioth Topog vol vi. art 3 There was a Robert Thurborn, Student in Medicine, but in Orders, Warden of Winchester in the time of William of Waynflete, in 1429 Chandler's Life of Waynflete, p 15

No 27.

GENEALOGY OF RUSSEL.

Thomas Russel, Esq
of Yaverland, Isle of Wight,
died 18 Hen VI

Maurice Russel, Esq

William Russel, Esq of Surry

First Wife
Elizabeth, daughter of Sir Francis Cherry, Knt, buried at Chippenham, Oct 14, 1626
No children
= Sir William Russel, Baronet, of Chippenham in Cambridgeshire, Treasurer of the Navy Created January 19, 1629 30 buried at Chippenham, Feb 3, 1653-4
= *Second Wife*
Elizabeth, daughter of Thomas Gerard, of Burwell, Cambridgeshire
= *Third Wife*
Elizabeth, daughter and coheir of Michael Smallpage, of Chichester, Gent relict of John Wheatley, of Catesfield, Sussex

Children by the second wife:

1 Sir Francis Russel Bart died 1664, married Catherine Wheatley
- 14

2 Sir William Russel, Knt married Anne, daugh of —— Bendysh

3 Gerard Russel, of Fordham, two wives,
= Mary Cherry
= Mable Floyd
- by Mary Cherry: William = Elizabeth, da of Henry Cromwell, Ld Lieut Ireland; Gerard; John; Killephet
- by Mable Floyd: Mable = R Russel

4 Edward

5 Robert
6 John.
7 John
1 Elizabeth, mar 1. Edw Lewknor
- Mary

= 2 Dr. Gauden
2 Anne
3 Sarah

Children by the third wife:

William

Sir William Russel, Knt. created Baronet Nov 8, 1660.

Robert, by his will, dated the 5th of May, 1679, gave all his manors and lands, in the parish of Ellesborough, to his wife Dame Susan Croke, for her life, and after her death to Susan, Mary, and Isabella, his three daughters, their heirs and assigns, for ever, in such shares as his wife should appoint[t]. Isabella the youngest daughter married John, or Samuel, Dod, a barrister. Mary, the second, was the third wife of John Thurban, Serjeant at Law; by whom he had no children[u].

The whole of the estate at Chequers, I know not by what means, became the property of Serjeant Thurban; who left it to Johanna, his only daughter, by his second wife Mary, sister to Lord Cutts. She married, for her first husband, Colonel John Rivett, by whom she had three sons, John, James, and William, and a daughter, Johanna Cutts Rivett. Her second husband was John Russel, Esquire, by whom she had no children. The three sons dying without issue, the estate came to their sister Johanna Cutts Rivett. This heiress married Charles Russel, Esquire, son of John Russel, who married Johanna Thurban, by his first wife Rebecca, sister of Sir Charles Eyre. They had an only son, Sir John Russel, Baronet, whose two sons by his wife Catherine Cary, Sir John Russel, and Sir George Russel, both dying without issue, the reverend Doctor John Russel Greenhill, as next heir, inherited Chequers He was the son of Samuel Greenhill, Esquire, by Elizabeth Russel, sister of Charles Russel before mentioned. The son of Doctor Greenhill, Robert Greenhill Russel, Esquire, Barrister at Law of Lincoln's Inn, and Member of Parliament for Thirsk in Yorkshire, is the present representative of the family, which is descended from Oliver Cromwell, the Protector's youngest daughter Frances, the relict of Robert Rich, having married their ancestor, Sir John Russel, Baronet[x].

The house at Chequers, in the parish of Ellesborough, is a fine old brick mansion, built by Sir Henry Croke, with a square court in the

[t] Sloan's MSS Mus Brit No 1691 fol 91 [u] Brown Willis, MSS vol III. p 36

[x] Genealogy, No. 27. from the Visitation of Bucks, in 1574, by Richard Lee, Harl MSS No 1139 Brown Willis's MSS. Noble's Memoirs of Cromwell, Gough's View of the family of Cromwell Nichols's Biblioth Topog vol. II. art. 3. There was a Robert Thurborn, Student in Medicine, but in Orders, Warden of Winchester in the time of William of Waynflete, in 1429 Chandler's Life of Waynflete, p 15

No 27

GENEALOGY OF RUSSEL

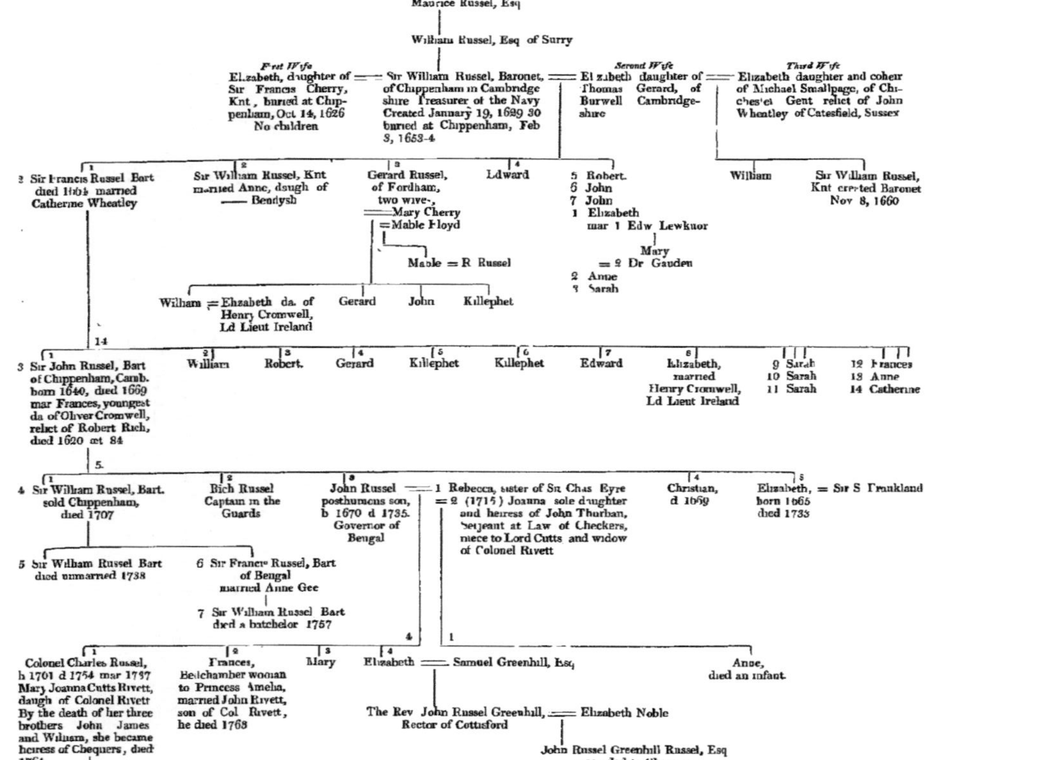

middle. It has lately been fitted up in the Gothic style, with great taste, and the rooms are large, and very beautiful. In the library is a valuable collection of original portraits of the Cromwell family, and some of the principal characters of that period. Amongst them are the pictures of Sir William and Lady Hawtree, Serjeant Thurban, and two full-lengths of Sir Robert, and Lady Croke[y].

[y] That of Sir Robert Croke is a fine portrait, and might have been painted by Cornelius Jansen, or Vandyck The other of Lady Croke is in a stiffer, more Gothic style, and being apparently older than the other, I am inclined to think is the portrait of Sir Robert s Mother, Bridget Hawtrey

SECTION THE FOURTH.

CHARLES CROKE, D.D.

CHARLES CROKE, the third son of Sir John Croke, the Judge, was a clergyman, and his success in his profession seems to have been the just reward of his merits. He was educated at Thame school, and was admitted a student of Christ Church in Oxford, on the 5th of January, 1603, as a Knight's son of Oxfordshire. He took the degree of Bachelor of Arts, April the 16th, 1608, that of Master in 1611, and became the principal Tutor and Lecturer in his college[a].

Upon the resignation of Mr. Richard Ball, the second Professor of Rhetoric in Gresham College, he was a competitor for that office with Mr. William Osbaldson On the 14th of January, 1613, he was elected, upon which occasion, the interest of his father, who had been Recorder of London, and was then one of the Judges of the King's Bench, was supposed to have given additional weight to the recommendation of his own acknowledged learning and abilities. The following letter, written by Dr King, formerly Dean of Christ Church, and then Bishop of London, is no mean testimonial in his favour.

"To the Right Worshipfull, my verie loving friends, Sir Thomas Ben-"net, and Sir Bapt. Hicks, Knights, with other the Committees for the "Rhetorique Lecture, in Gresham Colledge, these.

"Right Worshipfull,

"Understandinge that Mr. Charles Croke had a suite unto your "worthie company, in discharge of my love, which I beare to his name, "as also to his own good deservinge, I was bould to accompanie his "desires with some testimonie of my knowledge of him. Wee lived to-

[a] Ward's Lives of the Gresham Professors, page 306, with the manuscript additions

"gether in Christ Church, I his deane, he a member of that house, where "I observed and cherished his proceedinge from time to time, wherein he "prospered so well both for disputations and for other exercises of learn- "inge, that most of the place of lecturinge and government over others he "hath atteyned unto in that house. Which I speak not by report or "rumour, but am able truly to relate upon my perfect knowledge. His "religion is sounde and uncorrupt, according to the race from whence he "springeth. And for his honestie and virtuousness of lief, I could not "add more to men, that understand my speech, than that he is his father's "living image. Learning, religion, and virtue, I know, are what you "ayme at; which, when you shall find conjoyned in a person of birth and "blood, as well as of other qualities, you need not seek further to make "your election. And therefore, recommending you all to the integritie of "your good consciences, and the direction of the Spirit of God, I heartily "rest,

"Your worship's very assured friend,

"JO. LONDON."

London House,
Jan 14, 1613.

After his election, he was ordered to perform his first inaugural oration upon the first Friday in Hilary term following, which was upon the 28th of the same month[b].

This institution of Gresham College was established by the celebrated Sir Thomas Gresham, a noble merchant, in the reigns of Edward the Sixth, and Queen Elizabeth, who, like the Medici, was a great encourager of learning, and his benefaction took effect after the death of his lady in 1596. It was designed to be a third University of the kingdom, and, by its situation in London, to afford the means of obtaining knowledge to those, whose situation precluded them from a regular education in the more distant seminaries, particularly persons of the mercantile profession. Seven professorships, for divinity, law, physic, geometry, astronomy, rhetoric, and music, were appointed. The mansion-house of Sir Thomas was assigned for the residence of the Professors, who read their lectures

[b] Ward

twice in every week during the law terms, and received a salary of fifty pounds a year. This college was the cradle of the Royal Society. Many of the learned men, whose voluntary meetings were the origin of that useful establishment, were Professors here. The first members usually assembled in it, and had their public room, and their repository for curiosities there, for above fifty years, till they finally removed to Crane Court, in 1710[c].

In 1616, Mr. Croke was Junior Proctor of the University of Oxford, with the learned Dr. Saunderson, afterwards Bishop of Lincoln[d]. Upon the 24th of June, in the same year, he was instituted to the rectory of Waterstock, upon the presentation of his uncle Sir George Croke but he resigned it in the October following[e]. On the 5th of September, 1617, he was elected Fellow of Eton College, in the room of Mr. William Charke[f]. In 1619, he resigned his Gresham professorship, in favour of his cousin Henry Croke, who succeeded him on the 25th of May in that year[g]

Doctor Charles Croke had two wives. The first was Anne, the daughter of Sir William Grene, to whom there is a marble monument in Beckley church, against the wall of the chancel, at the south end of the communion table. On a plate of brass, having a lady kneeling against a table with a book engraved upon it, is this inscription.

THIS MONUMENT WAS ERECTED IN MEMORY OF ANNE CROKE WIFE OF CHARLES CROKE, AND DAUGHTER OF SIR WILLIAM GRENE, KNIGHT, BY CHARLES CROKE, HER SURVIVING HUSBAND, NOT IN ANY OPINION BRASS, OR MARBLE, CANNE EXPRESS HER WORTH, OR HIS OWNE AFFECTION, BUT TO TELL THE READER THAT IN THIS CHANCEL LYES HER BODY, THAT IS NOT IN SURER POSSESSION OF DUST, THEN IS HER SOULE OF HEAVEN, EXPECTING CONSURRECTION WITH THE JUST, FOR THE MERITS OF CHRIST

And on a brass plate, on a flat stone below,

HEARE LYETH BURIED THE BODY OF ANNE CROKE, THE WIFE OF CHARLES CROKE, THIRD SON OF SIR JOHN CROKE, KNIGHT, ONE OF THE JUSTICES OF THE KING'S BENCH, WHICH ANNE WAS THE

[c] Ward. Sprat's History of the Royal Society [d] Wood's Fast Oxon [e] Ward
[f] Ibid [g] Ibid.

DAUGHTER OF SIR WILLIAM GRENE, KNIGHT, OF GREAT MILTON, IN THE COUNTY OF OXFORD. SHE DEPARTED THIS LIFE JULY 24, 1619.

TE SEQUIMUR, CONJUX, PASSU QUO POSSUMUS ÆQUO,
ATQUE JACERE TUO TENDIMUS USQUE SINU,
POSUIT CONJUX MŒSTISSIMUS CAROLUS CROKE.

On the monument against the wall is a coat of arms Croke, impaled with, Azure, three stags trippant, or.

For his second wife, he married Anne, daughter of John Rivett, of Brandston, in the county of Suffolk, Esquire. By her he had an only son, who died young, and named John Croke[k].

In the year 1621, he was presented, by the Earl of Bedford, to the rich living of Agmondesham in Buckinghamshire. This obliged him to quit his fellowship at Eton College, which, by the rules of that society, was not tenable with any living, rated at more than forty marks; and Agmondesham is stated at £48. 16*s.* 0¼*d.*[h] On the 20th of June, 1625, he accumulated the degrees of Bachelor and Doctor in Divinity, and went out Grand Compounder. He was afterwards appointed a chaplain to King Charles the First[i].

Since his rectory was so valuable, it cannot be supposed that it was from mere lucrative motives that he undertook the education of some young gentlemen of rank and fortune, who seem to have been principally the sons of his particular friends. In this number were included, Sir William Drake of Amersham, Sir Robert Croke[l], and, that "miracle of his age for "critical and curious learning," as he is called by Anthony Wood, John Gregory, who was selected by Dr. Croke to wait upon those two gentlemen, as their Servitor, when they went to Christ Church, in 1624[m].

[h] Ward, 307 [i] Wood, Fasti Oxon vol. i. col 851

[k] Visitation of Bucks, 1575, and another in 1634. "Charles Croke, D.D now Rector "of Aymersham, and Chaplain to the King's Majesty, married Anne, daughter of John "Rivett, Brandston, com Suffolk, Esquire." Harl MSS. No 1533 fol. 65 b. No 1482 fol. 19. A pedigree in Harl. MSS. No 1102. fol 7. Brown Willis's MSS vol iii fol 36 Bibl. Bodl Ward says he always lived single

[l] Fast. Oxon vol ii. col 728.

[m] John Gregory was born at Agmondesham in 1607, the son of poor but respectable parents, and was probably educated gratis by Dr. Croke, who thus provided for his farther

Another pupil was Henry Curwen, Esquire, only son of Sir Patrick Curwen, of Warkington, in Cumberland, Baronet, who died at the age of fourteen, on the 21st of August, 1638, whilst under his care, and was buried in Agmondesham church. Under the title of a "Sad Memorial," he published the sermon which he preached upon the melancholy occasion, upon the fourteenth chapter of Job, verse the second, in quarto, at Oxford, in 1638[n].

He continued always very zealous in the interest of King Charles the First, during the rebellion, for which reason he was obliged to leave his native country, and retire to Ireland, soon after the unhappy exit of that Prince. His chief residence there was at Feathard, in Tipperary, but he died at Carloe near Dublin, on the 10th of April 1657[o]. I believe he left some posterity in that country.

education by this appointment He made a great progress in his studies, was successively Chaplain of Christ Church, Chaplain to Brian Duppa, Dean, afterwards Bishop of Chichester, then of Salisbury, in each of which churches Gregory had a prebend In the Rebellion he lost his preferment and retired in great distress to Kidlington, where he died in 1646 He wrote several very learned books, and was honoured with the correspondence of the greatest men of the age Biog Brit 1766 Supplement Ath Oxon ii col 100, 50, 728 Fast Oxon i 240, 252 His life prefixed to his Opera Posthuma

[n] Fast Oxon vol i c 851 His monument in Agmondesham church

[o] Ward s Lives, p. 308 from the information of Mr Benjamin Robertshaw, Rector of Agmondesham

No. 28.

A GENEALOGY

SHEWING THE RELATIONSHIP OF THE CROKE FAMILY WITH MANY OF THE PRINCIPAL LEADERS OF THE PARLIAMENT PARTY, IN THE REIGN OF CHARLES THE FIRST

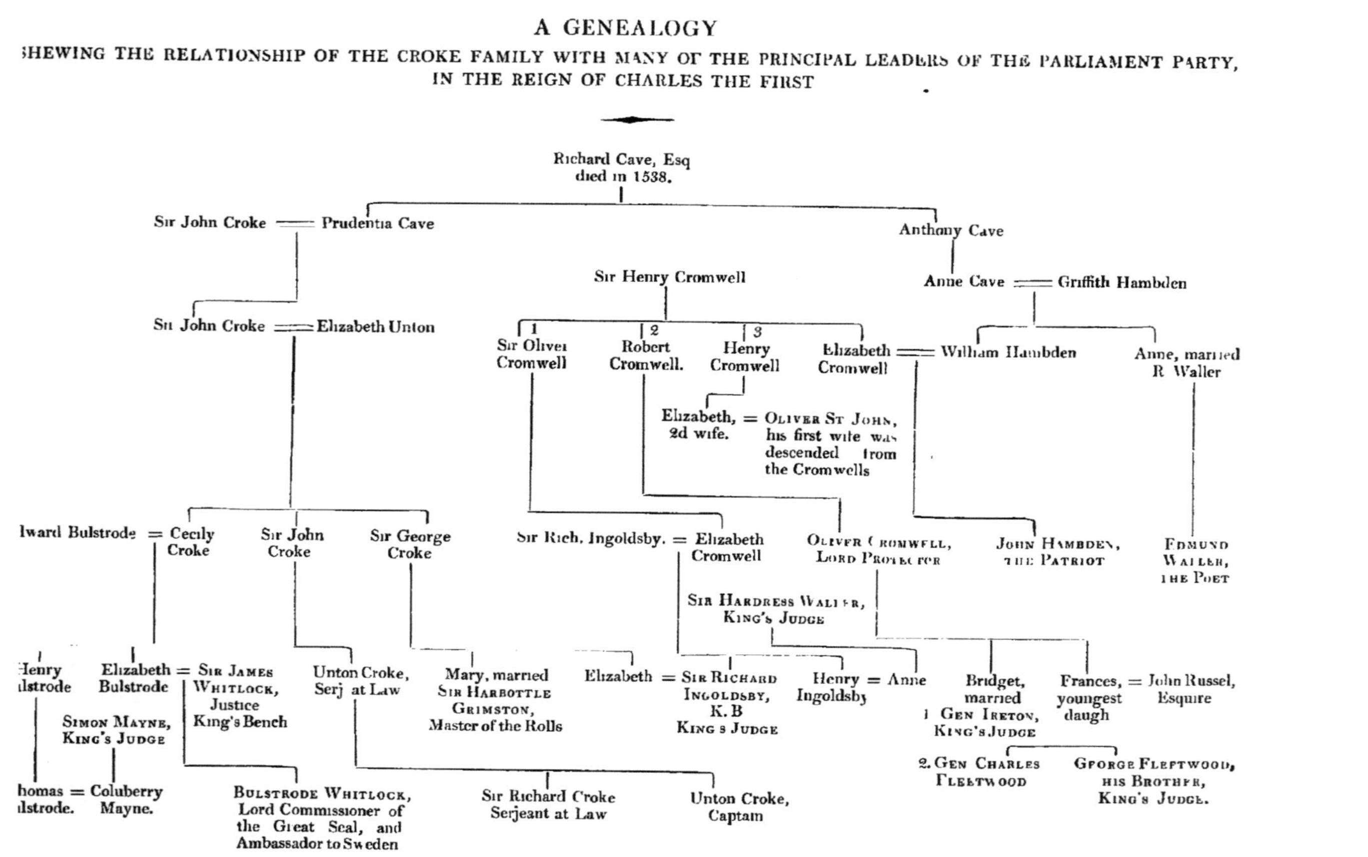

SECTION THE FIFTH.

SERJEANT UNTON CROKE, OF MARSTON.

THE influence of Hambden, and some other principal leaders in the opposition to King Charles the First, and who were persons of fortune and respectability in Buckinghamshire, extended in a considerable degree to their neighbours, and, accordingly, in the civil war which followed, we find the gentlemen of that county in general on the side of the Parliament. The Croke family was even more intimately connected with the heads of that party. To the Lord Commissioner Whitlock, Ingoldsby, Saint John, Hambden, Waller, the poet, Mayne, Grimstone, Sir Hardress Waller, and even to the Protector, they were nearly related by blood, or affinity[a]. We come now to a branch of the family, which was naturally swayed by the bias of its connections, and attached itself to Cromwell with zeal and fidelity.

The fourth son of Sir John Croke, the Judge, was born about the year 1594, and was named Unton after his grandmother He was admitted a student of the Inner Temple the 16th of November, 1609, called to the Bar the 26th of January, 1616, and to the Bench the 14th of June, 1635. He married his wife, whose name was Anne, the 8th of November, 1617, the daughter and heiress of Richard Hore, Esquire, of Marston In the first parliament of King Charles the First, in 1625, and in that which was summoned in 1640, he was elected Member for Wallingford, in Berkshire[b] In the latter year, he was Lent Reader to the society of the Inner Temple, when Sir Thomas Gardiner, Recorder of London, who lived some time at Cuddesdon, near Oxford, read the autumnal lecture[c]

He resided at Marston, a small village near Oxford, in a house which he acquired by his wife, and which was made use of by the Commissioners for the King and the Parliament army in the treaty for the surrender of Oxford, in May, 1646[d]. He was also for some time Deputy Steward of

[a] See the Table, No 28 [b] Willis, Notit Parl [c] Dugd Or Jud 168 [d] Wood's Hist Univ Ox lib I p 365.

the University to Philip Herbert, Earl of Montgomery and Pembroke[e]. On the 21st of June, 1654, he was called to the degree of Serjeant at Law.

In Thurloe's State Papers there is a letter, of the 2d of October, 1655, from Doctor John Owen, the Dean of Christ Church, to the Protector, in which he strongly intercedes in Serjeant Croke's favour, that he might be made a Judge.

"May it please your Highnesse,

"Your Highnesse was pleased to favour me not long since in my "request on the behalf of Mr. Serjeant Croke, and to mention your good "intendments towards him Least in the multitude of your weighty "affairs he might be forgotten, during the present opportunity of making "him one of your Judges, I am bold to remind your Highnesse of your "thoughts towards him, being fully assured he will never really forfeit "them. I dare not with any confidence assume unto myself a judge-"ment of the fitness of any person for such an employment, yet I have "most good ground to continue in my former persuasion of his ability and "integrity, so that I am most confident your Highnesse will never have "cause to repent of your doing him this favour, and that he will, in his "place, perform that which is the true service unto you, in an upright ad-"ministration of justice. That you may have the presence of our good "God, in a living sense of his unchangeable love in Jesus Christ, to your "person, and a gracious assistance in all your affairs, is the daily prayer of "him who is to

"Your highnesse most humbly and most faithfully devoted,

"JOHN OWEN[f]."

Oxford,
October 2, 1655

Whether the place was already promised, or for whatever cause is not known, it seems that the recommendation was not attended to.

In the list of Commissioners appointed in 1656, under the authority of an Act of Parliament, for the security of the Lord Protector, with power to try offenders for high treason, without the intervention of a jury, after the Lord Chancellor, and the Judges, the third person named is Unton Croke, Serjeant at Law[g].

[e] Wood's Hist Univ Ox lib ii 142

[f] Thurloe's State Papers, vol iv 65

[g] The Act itself in the King's Collection of Pamphlets published during the time of Charles the First, and the Commonwealth. Folios, volume 15.

Unton Croke acted likewise as a Justice of the Peace, and the following entries in the register of the parish of Marston of marriages performed by him in that capacity, during the great rebellion, may amuse the reader.

3 July, 1654. Edward Lyde, als Joyner, of Horspath parish, and Dorothy, one of the daughters of John Robinson of Whately, yeoman, were married by and with the consent of the said Jo. Robinson in this parish before Unton Croke, Justice of the Peace, according to the statute.

(Signed) UNTON CROKE.

In some of these entries it is stated, that the "contract" had been published in the parish church, in others, that it had been proclaimed on three several market days in the market place at Oxford. A family marriage occurs Martin Piggot, gent. of the parish of St. Pancrass in London, and Anne Croke, one of the daughters of Mr. Unton Crooke, Esq. married the 26th of August, 1657, by Martin Wright, Esq. Justice of the Peace.

His wife died before him, on the tenth day of June, 1670, in the sixty-ninth year of her age, and left him with ten children. He followed her in a few months afterwards, on the 28th day of January, 1671, being seventy-seven years of age.

On one flat stone in the chancel of Marston church are both their epitaphs.

O VIR, QUICUNQUE ES, PUSILLUM HOC TERRÆ, QUO MEUM TEGITUR CORPUS, MIHI NE INVIDEAS.

EX LU. CAP. 6°. VERS. 26. VÆ VOBIS CUM LAUDAVERINT VOS OMNES HOMINES.

UNTON CROKE, SERVIENS AT LEGEM, OBIIT 28° DIE JANUARII, AN°. DNI 1670[h], ANNOQUE ÆTATIS SUÆ 77°.

(On a brass plate below.)

MY FLESH SHALL REST IN HOPE. PS. 16. V 10.

HERE UNDER RESTETH, IN HOPE OF RESURRECTION, THE BODY OF ANNE, THE WIFE OF UNTON CROKE, SERJEANT AT LAW, WHO WAS MARRIED TO HIM 8th NOV. 1617, AND LEFT HIM AND TEN

[h] According to the manner of dating then in use, this must have been $167\frac{0}{1}$, or what we should now write, 1671. The date of the preceding year continued till the 25th of March

CHILDREN THE 10th DAY OF JUNE, 1670, AND IN THE 69th YEAR OF HER AGE.

The arms on the monument are, Croke, impaled with, sable, a chevron, between three cinquefoils, for Hore.

Of these ten children, the names of some are not known. Sir Richard Croke, the eldest son, Captain Unton Croke, the second, and Charles, will furnish materials for our history. Anne, the eldest daughter, we have seen was married to Martin Pigott, the second was named Mary; there was a second Anne, a Catherine, and another daughter, Caroline, who died the 19th of July, in the year 1670, in the thirty-sixth year of her age[i].

Sir Richard Croke, the eldest surviving son, was born about the year 1623. He followed, what may now be almost considered as the family profession, that of the law, and he proceeded in it till he obtained the highest rank, that of a Serjeant. He was admitted of the Inner Temple, the 24th of January, 1635, called to the bar the 5th of November, 1646, to the bench the 23d of November 1662, and was Autumn Reader in 1670[k]. At his admission he is styled *second* son of Unton Croke. His lady was Elizabeth, the daughter of Martyn Wright, Esquire, Alderman of Oxford. He was Recorder of that city for thirty years, and represented it in Parliament for twenty years.

After the death of King Charles, the property belonging to the Crown was taken possession of by the Parliament. The old royal Manor, or Palace, at Woodstock, the favourite abode of our kings from Henry the First to Charles the First, and which is rendered interesting from the confinement of Queen Elizabeth, and the anecdotes which are related of her employments and sentiments during her imprisonment, did not escape their unhallowed hands In 1649, Sir Richard Croke, his brother Captain Unton Croke, with the Captains Cockayne, Hart, Careless and Roe, and Brown, the surveyor, were the Commissioners appointed to survey, estimate, and sell, the manors, and houses at Woodstock, belonging to his

[i] So inscribed on a small flat stone in Marston chancel Visitation of Oxon In Coll Gonville et Cai, apud Cantab

[k] Arms in the Inner Temple Hall. Register of ditto In the register occur likewise the names of Charles, Henry, Francis, Robert, &c

late Majesty[l]. By some zealous partizans of the cavalier party, it was thought that the interference of supernatural agents might not be unserviceable to the cause of the Royal Martyr. When the Commissioners had taken possession of the Palace, they were assailed by the powers of darkness The adventures they met with were certainly extraordinary, but as they are " proved by irrefragable testimony," and are considered both by Anthony Wood, and Doctor Plot, as " worth the reading by all, " especially the many Atheists of the age," I hope I may be excused for inserting them.

The original account of this affair was published in a small quarto of thirteen pages, printed in 1660, but with the date of 1649, intitled, " The " just Devil of Woodstock, or a true narrative of the several Apparitions, " the frights, and punishments, inflicted upon the Rumpish Commis- " sioners, sent thither to survey the manors and houses belonging to his " Majestie." In the preface, it is said, that " the penman of this narrative " was a divine, and minister, and schoolmaster of Woodstock, a person " learned and discreet, and not biassed with factious humours; his name " Widows, who each day put in writing what he heard from their mouths, " and had befallen them the night before, keeping to their own words, " never thinking it would be made publick." It was printed after his death[m].

I give this story as it has been written by Dr. Plot, in his History of Oxfordshire, which is much shorter than the other, and though it differs in some few respects, as the days of the month, it agrees in the main circumstances with Widows.

" Amongst such unaccountable things as these, we may reckon the strange passages that happened at Woodstock in anno 1649, in the manor house there, when the Commissioners for surveying the manor house, park, deer, woods, and other the demesnes belonging to that manor, sat and lodged there. Whereof having several relations put into my hands, and one of them written by a learned and faithful person then living upon the place, which being confirmed to me by several eye witnesses of many of

[l] Wood Ath Oxon ii. 119

[m] This is a very scarce book It is to be found amongst the King's Pamphlets, in the British Museum, volume 859, article 10.

the particulars, and all of them by one of the Commissioners themselves, who ingenuously confest to me, that he could not deny but what was written by that person above mentioned was all true, I was prevailed upon at last to make this relation publick, (though I must confess, I have no esteem for such kind of stories, many of them no question being performed by combination,) which I have taken care to do as fully, yet as briefly, as may be.

"October 13, 1649, the Commissioners with their servants being come to the manor house, they took up their lodging in the King's own rooms, the bed chamber and withdrawing room, the former whereof they made their kitchin, the councel hall, their brew-house, the chamber of presence, their place of sitting to dispatch business, and a wood-house of the dining room, where they laid the wood of that ancient standard in the high park, known of all by the name of the King's Oak, which (that nothing might remain that had the name of King affixed to it) they digged up by the roots. October 14 and 15, they had little disturbance, but on the 16th there came, as they thought, somewhat into the bed chamber, where two of the Commissioners and their servants lay, in the shape of a dog, which going under their beds, did as it were gnaw the bed cords; but on the morrow finding them whole, and a quarter of beef which lay on the ground untouched, they began to entertain other thoughts

"October 17, Something to their thinking removed all the wood of the King's Oak out of the dining-room into the presence chamber, and hurled the chairs and stools up and down the room from whence it came into the two chambers where the Commissioners and their servants lay, and hoisted up their beds' feet so much higher than their heads, that they thought they should have been turned over and over, and then let them fall down with such a force, that their bodies rebounded from the bed a good distance, and then shook the bedsteds so violently, that themselves confest, their bodies were sore with it. October 18, something came into the bed-chamber, and walkt up and down, and fetching the warming-pan out of the withdrawing room, made so much a noise, that they thought five bells could not have made more. And October 19, Trenchers were thrown up and down the dining-room, and at them that lodg'd there, whereof one of them being shaken by the shoulder and awakened, put forth his head to see what was the matter, but had trenchers thrown at it. October 20,

The curtains of the bed in the withdrawing room were drawn to and fro, and the bedsted much shaken, and eight great pewter dishes, and three dozen of trenchers, thrown about the bed chamber again, whereof some fell upon the beds: this night they also thought whole armfulls of the wood of the King's Oak had been thrown down in their chambers, but of that, in the morning, they found nothing had been moved.

"October 21, The Keeper of their ordinary and his bitch, lay in one of the rooms with them which night they were not disturbed at all. But October 22, though the bitch kennel'd there again, (to whom they ascribed their former night's rest,) both they and the bitch were in a pitiful taking, the bitch opening but once, and that with a whining fearful yelp October 23, they had all their cloathes pluct off them in the withdrawing room, and the bricks fell out of the chimney into the room; and the 24th they thought in the dining-room, that all the wood of the King's Oak had been brought thither, and thrown down close by their bed-side, which noise, being heard by those of the withdrawing room, one of them rose to see what was done, fearing indeed that his fellow commissioners had been killed, but found no such matter; whereupon, returning to his bed again, he found two dozen of trenchers thrown into it, and handsomely covered with the bed cloaths.

"October 25, The curtains of the bed in the withdrawing room were drawn to and fro, and the bedsted shaken as before: and in the bed chamber glass flew about so thick, (and yet not a pane of the chamber windows broken,) that they thought it had rained money, whereupon they lighted candles, but to their grief, they found nothing but glass, which they took up in the morning, and laid together. October 29, Something walked in the withdrawing room about an hour, and going to the window, opened and shut it; then going into the bed-chamber, it threw great stones for about half an hour's time, some whereof lighted on the high bed, and others on the truckle bed, to the number in all of about fourscore. This night there was also a very great noise, as though forty pieces of ordnance had been shot off together, at two several knocks it astonished all the neighbouring dwellers, which 'tis thought, might have been heard a great way off During these noises, which were heard in both rooms together, both commissioners and servants were struck with so great horror, that they cryed out to one another for help, whereof one of them recovered himself out of a strange agony he had been in, snatch'd up a sword, and had like to have killed one of his brethren coming out of his bed in his shirt, whom he took for the spirit that did the mischief. However, at length, they got all together, yet the noise continued so great and terrible, and shook the walls so much, that they thought the whole manor would have fell on their heads At its departure, it took all the glass away with it.

"November 1, Something as they thought walk'd up and down the withdrawing room, and then made a noise in the dining-room. the stones that were left before and laid up in the withdrawing room, were all fetch'd away this night, and a great dale of glass (not like the former) thrown about again. November 2, came something into the withdrawing room, treading (as they conceived) much like a bear, which first only walking about a quarter of an hour, at length it made a noise about the table, and threw the warming-pan so violently, that it quite spoiled it. It threw also glass and great stones at them again, and the bones of horses, and all so violently, that the bedsted and walls were bruised by them. This night they set candles all about the rooms, and made fires up to the mantle-trees of the chimneys: but all were put out, no body knew how, the fire, and billets that made it, being thrown up and down the rooms; the curtains torn with the rods from their beds, and the bed posts pull'd away, that the tester fell down upon them, and the feet of the bedsted cloven in two· and upon the servants in the truckle bed, who lay this time sweating for fear, there was first a little, which made them begin to stir; but before they could get out, there came a whole coule, as it were, of stinking ditch water down upon them, so green, that it made their shirts and sheets of that colour too. The same night the windows were all broke by throwing of stones, and there was most terrible noises in three several places together, to the extraordinary wonder of all that lodged near them. nay, the very cony stealers that were abroad that night, were so affrighted with the dismal thundering, that for haste they left their ferrets in the cony boroughs behind them, beyond Rosamond's well. Notwithstanding all this, one of them had the boldness to ask in the name of God, *What it was? What it would have?* and, *What they had done, that they should be disturbed in this manner?* To which no answer was given, but the noise ceased for a while. At length it came again, and (as all of them said) brought seven Devils, worse than itself. Whereupon one of them lighted a candle again, and set it between the two chambers, in the door-way, on which another of them fixed his eyes, saw the similitude of a hoof striking the candle and candlestick into the middle of the bed-chamber, and afterwards making three scrapes on the snuff to put it out. Upon this, the same person was so bold as to draw his sword, but he had scarce got it out, but there was another invisible hand had hold of it too, and tugg'd with him for it, and pervailing, struck him so violently with the pummel, that he was stun'd with the blow. Then began grievous noises again, insomuch that they called to one another, got together, and went into the presence chamber, where they said prayers and sang psalms; notwithstanding all which, the thundering noise still continued in other rooms. After this, November 3, they removed their lodgings over the gate; and next day, being Sunday, went to Ewelm, where, how they escaped, the authors of the relations knew not, but returning on Monday, the Devil (for that was the name they gave their nightly guest) left them not unvisited, nor on the Tuesday following, which was the last day they staid. Where ends the history (for so he was stiled by the people) of the just Devil of Woodstock: the Commissioners and all their dependants going quite away on Wednesday, since which time, says the author that lived on the place, there have honest persons of good quality lodged in the bed chamber and withdrawing room, that never were disturbed in the least like the Commissioners.

"Most part of these transactions, during the stay of these Commissioners, 'tis true, might be easily performed by combination, but some there are of them scarce reconcileable to juggling: such as, 1. The extraordinary noises, beyond the power of man to make, without such instruments as were not there. 2. The taring down and splitting the bed posts, and putting out so many candles and so great fires, no body knew how. 3. A visible shape seen of a horse's hoof treading out the candle. And, 4. A tugging with one of them for his sword by an invisible hand. All which being put together, perhaps may easily perswade some man otherwise inclined, to believe that imaterial beings might be concern'd in this business: which if it do, it abundantly will satisfy for the trouble of the relation, still provided the speculative Theist be not after all a practical Atheist[a]."

To this account of Dr. Plot, we may add a few circumstances which he

[a] Plot's History of Oxfordshire, chapter viii sect 37.

has omitted, from Widows, and which more particularly relate to Sir Richard and Unton Croke

"On the 25th of October in the afternoon, came to them Mr Richard Crook the Lawyer, brother to Captain Crook, and now Deputy Steward of the manor. Mr. Hyans his Majesty's officer being put out To entertain this new guest, the Commissioners caused a very great fire to be made of near the chimney full of wood of the King's Oak, and he was lodged in the withdrawing room, with his brother and servant in the same room About the middle of the night, a wonderful knocking was heard, and into the room something did rush, which coming to the chimney side dashed out the fire, as with a stamp of some prodigious foot, then threw down such weighty stuff, what ere it was, (they took it to be the residue of the clefts and roots of the King's Oak,) close by the bed side, that the house and bed shook with it. Captain Cockayne, and his fellow, arose and took their swords to go unto the Crooks. The noise ceased at their rising, so that they came to the door, and called. The two brothers, though they were fully awaked, and heard them call, were so amazed, that they made no answer, until Captain Cockayne had recovered the boldness to call very loud, and came unto their bed side. Then faintly first, after with some more assurance, they came to understand one another, and comforted the Lawyer. This entertainment so ill did like the Lawyer, and being not so well studied in the point, as to resolve this the Devil's law-case, that he the next day resolved to be gone, but having not dispatched all that he came for, profit and persuasions prevailed with him to stay the other hearing, so that he lodged as he did the night before.

"On the 26th, the glass was thrown about the room. In the morning Mr. Richard Crook would stay no longer, yet, as he stopped, going through Woodstock town, he was there heard to say, "that he would not "lodge amongst them another night for a fee of five hundred pounds."

"On the 28th in the night, a noise, both strange, and differing from the foregoing, first awakened Captain Hart, who lodged in the bed chamber, who hearing Roe and Brown to groan, called out to Cockayne and Crook to come and help them, for Hart could not now stir himself. Cockayne would fain have answered, but could not, or look about, something he thought stopped both his breath, and held down his eye-lids. Amazed thus, he struggled and kicked about, till he had awaked Captain Crook, who, half asleep, grew very angry at his kicks, and multiplying words, it grew to an appointment in the field. But this fully recovered Cockayne to remember that Captain Hart had called for help. Then they heard Captain Crook crying out as if something had been killing him. Cockayne snatched up the sword that lay by their bed, and ran into the room to save Crook, but was in much more likelihood to kill him, for at his coming the thing that pressed Crook went off him, at which Crook started out of his bed, whom Cockayne thought a spirit, and made at him, at which Crook cried out, "Lord help, Lord save me!" Cockayne let fall his hand, and Crook embracing Cockayne, desired his reconcilement, giving him many thanks for his deliverance. Then rose they all, and came together, discoursed sometimes godly, and sometimes prayed. One night their book of valuations was found laid upon the embers, and burning; which was snatched up and saved.

The Commissioners applied to Mr. Hoffman, the Presbyterian minister of Wootton, who after consulting with two Justices of the Peace, Jenkinson and Wheat, refused to go to pray with them To this there is a marginal observation. "By which it is to be noted, that a Presbyterian "minister dares not to incounter an independent devil." A humorous ballad was written upon this occasion, and was printed in 1649, in one sheet in quarto, and intitled, "The Woodstock Scuffle," and is in the Appendix[o]. It is said, that this tragi-comic piece was performed by Joe Collins, the late King's Gardener, who hired himself to the Commissioners, assisted by his splay-footed bitch, and other confederates[p].

Sir Richard Croke had a considerable interest in his own county, and in the general election in 1654, supported his cousin, Lord Commissioner Whitlocke, as a candidate for the City of Oxford, and his son James in representing the County. Immediately after his election, James Whitlock, who was afterwards knighted by Cromwell in 1656, wrote the following letter to his father.

[o] Appendix, No XXVII [p] See the British Magazine for April and August, in 1757. For an account of the Palace at Woodstock, and Rosamond's Bower, see Warton's Life of Sir Tho. Pope, page 71, note

"For the Right Honourable his deare Father, the Lord Commissioner "Whitelocke, att Chelsey These, hast, hast.

"Dear Sir,

"I held it my duety, uppon the instant of the con-"clusion of the elections att this place, to acquaint you, that I am chosen "one of the Knights for the countey in the next parliament. I am told, "that the number of voyces might justly have given the first place to me; "but I freely resigned it to Lieutenant Generall Fleetwood, not suffering "it to be brought to tryall by the polle, which many of the countrey de-"sired The persons elected are, Lieutenant General Fleetwood, Mr. "Robert Jenkinson, Collonell Nathaniel Fynes, Mr. Lenthall, Master of "the Rolles, and myself.

"Many of your friends appeared really for me, amongst which, I can "experimentally say, none acted more effectually then my cousen Cap-"tain Croke, his father, and brother. The Citty of Oxford was pre-"pared very seasonably for me, wherein my cousen Richard Croke's "affections did particularly appeare; and I conceive that, if you shall be "pleased to waive the election for the Citty of Oxford, no truer friend "could be commended by you for their choice then my cousen Richard "Croke, in regard of his interest there, if you think it fitt. I shall say no "more at present in this hast, butt expect your commands in all things "who am

"Your most obedient sonne,

"J. WHITELOCKE[q]."

Oxford,
July 12, 1654

In 1659, he was appointed one of the Commissioners for settling the militia for the County of Oxford, under the ordinance of Parliament for that purpose. He died on the 15th day of September, 1683, in the sixtieth year of his age, and is buried under a handsome marble monument, erected against the wall, in the chancel of Marston church, by his son Wright Croke. The epitaph speaks highly of his devotion to the true catholic religion, his fidelity to his clients, and his friendship for all mankind;

[q] Whitelocke's Journal of the Swedish Ambassy, vol ii p 419

and it states, that he was much beloved by both the King Charleses It is conceived in the following words

M. S.

RICHARDI CROKE EQUITIS, SERVIENTIS AD LEGEM, PER VIGINTI ANNOS OXONII BURGENSIS, PER TRIGINTA RECORDATORIS, UTRIQUE CAROLO DILECTISSIMI, DEO ET RELIGIONI VERE CATHOLICÆ SEMPER DEVOTISSIMI, CLIENTIBUS FIDELIS, ET TOTI HUMANO GENERI AMICABILIS. QUI VIXIT OMNIBUS AMANDUS, OBIITQUE 15° DIE SEPTEMBRIS AN. DNI 1683, ÆTATIS SUÆ 60, OMNIBUS FLENDUS, PRÆCIPUE FILIO SUO MŒSTISSIMO WRIGHT CROKE, QUI HOC, ERGA PATERNAM VIRTUTEM, ET EX AMORE SUO, OPTIMO PARENTI, MONUMENTUM POSUIT.

The coat of arms is, Croke, quarterly, on the fesse, a label, on a martlet, sable; denoting the eldest son of a fourth son[r].

Sir Richard Croke had three sons, Richard, Wright, and Charles[s].

[r] Rawlinson, MSS Pedigrees.

[s] The following is a specimen of the malice, and wit of the cavalier party against their adversaries, and of the Fescennine licentiousness of the Universities in those times. It is part of a Terræ-filius, spoken in the Theatre at Oxford, at the Public Act, in 1674, and preserved by Anthony à Wood, in his Diary, volume 52, page 25, under the year 1714

Oratio habita in Theatro Oxoniensi per Henricum Gerard, A. M è Collegio Wadhamensi, et Academiæ Terræ-filium —Cum hoc Doctore (Dr. Smith, Canon of Christ Church) jungamus illius coexecutorem Recorderum nostrum Oxoniensem, qui cum sit magister memoriæ oppidanis, (Mr Crook,) Terræ-filius ipsi paucis erit è memoria Noverint, igitur, universi per præsentes, prædictum dominum, Dominum Recorderum Oxoniensem, non haventem timorem Dei ante oculos, sed motum ab instigatione Diaboli, Oliveri, vendidisse, vel vendendos exposuisse, omnes et singulos boscos, subboscos, catellos, matellos, pascuas, pratas, et pasturas, Regii manerii Woodstockiani, die 25° Octobris, anno 1649 Noverint deinde universi, prædictum Dominum causam habuisse cum Diabolo, misere tamen jactatum fuisse, Barbarum enim illum Diabolum à summo gradu ad imum præcipitem dedisse. Noverint insuper universi per præsentes, eodem tempore, Diabolum contra illum *habeas corpus* issuasse, at secundum meritum debuisse *habeas animam* issuasse. Non mirum tamen est illum hunc Diabolum hostem habuisse, cum tot Diabolos hospites sibi ascivit? Diabolum scilicet Rebellionis, Diabolum Hypocrisis, Diabolum Fraudis, et Diabolum Fanaticismi et cæteros quoscunque oppidanos Diabolos

Richard died in the 16th year of his age, in January 1671, having been entered of the Inner Temple, and a monument was erected to his memory in Carfax Church at Oxford, with the following inscription, which attributes to him the appropriate virtues of his age; a good disposition, great hopes of his future proficiency, the fear of God, and an exemplary dutifulness towards his parents

MEMORIÆ SACRUM.

HIC JACET HUMATUS RICHARDUS CROKE, DE INTERIORI TEMPLO LOND. GENT. FILIUS ET HÆRES APPARENS RICHARDI CROKE AR APPRENTICII IN LEGE, ET RECORDATORIS CIVITATIS OXON, ET ELIZABETHÆ UXORIS EJUS, FILIÆ MARTINI WRIGHT GENT DEFUNCTI, UNIUS ALDERMANNORUM DICTÆ CIVITATIS OXON. VIXIT JUVENIS BONÆ INDOLIS, ET MAGNÆ SPEI, EXEMPLAR TIMORIS ERGA DEUM, ET OBSEQUII ERGA PARENTES OBIIT . . . DIE MENSIS JANUARII, ANNO SALUTIS NOSTRÆ 1671, ANNOQUE ÆTATIS SUÆ 16 CURRENTE

JEHOVA DEDIT, JEHOVAH RECEPIT. SIT NOMEN
JEHOVÆ BENEDICTUM.

His eldest son having thus died young, Sir Richard Croke was succeeded by his second son and heir, Wright Croke, who was born about 1658. This young man was entered at Lincoln College in Oxford the 6th of July, 1677, and gave early indications of talent and scholarship. There is a considerable Latin poem of his in the Musæ Anglicanæ, in praise of the Saxon language, written when he was at college It is a proof of some merit in a composition, that it is placed in a select collection with the works of Addison, Smith, and others of our best writers of Latin poetry, and that it does not suffer by the proximity[t]. But these seeds of genius do not seem to have been matured to any good purpose. It does not appear that he followed any profession, or engaged in any pursuits, which might have been useful to himself, or others. Nothing indeed farther is known of him than that he had a wife, whose name was Mary, that he died on the 7th day of June, 1705, in the forty-seventh year of his age,

[t] Musæ Anglicanæ, vol iii p 225

and his lady on the 29th of March, 1717, aged 61 years Of his family, it is recorded on the same monument which he erected to the memory of his father, that he lost three children in their tender years; and the parish register of Marston contains the names of two other sons, Richard, baptized 11th of October, 1687, Charles, baptized 7th of April, 1689, and a daughter, Caroline, baptized 31st of January, 1691. In the same register are entered the baptisms of Anne, daughter of Richard Croke, 16th of July, 1699, and of Thomas, son of Richard Croke, 30th of May, 1703 Whose children those were I am at a loss to know, as Sir Richard Croke died in 1683, and Richard, the son of Wright Croke, was only 12, and 16 years of age, at those two baptisms

The inscription, on the monument in Marston chancel, under that for Sir Richard Croke, is this.

PROPE ETIAM JACET WRIGHT CROKE, ARMIGER, PRÆDICTI RICHARDI CROKE, EQUITIS, FILIUS, HÆRESQUE, QUI EX HAC VITA DISCESSIT 47 AN. ÆTAT. JUNE 7th, 1705.

ITEM WRIGHT CROKE, ARMIGERI, FILII TRES, QUI TENERIS IN ANNIS DEFUNCTI SUNT.

PROPE ETIAM JACET MARIA, UXOR CHARISSIMA WRIGHT CROKE, QUÆ OBIIT 29° MARTII 1717, ÆTATIS 61.

Of Charles Croke, the other son of Sir Richard Croke, nothing is known.

We have seen Sir Richard Croke in favour with the leading powers in the great Rebellion: his brother Unton Croke entered early into the parliament army, in which he had the command of a troop of cavalry Though he was never promoted to the rank of a general, he was an active partizan, and an able officer in that species of desultory warfare, which was peculiarly calculated for the cause in which he was engaged.

Whilst the King was at Oxford, he was stationed in the garrison at Abingdon, with a large body of the parliament army, under Major General Browne. This was a scene of very active service, from being a situation so near the head quarters of the enemy, and Unton Croke distinguished himself upon every occasion where the cavalry were employed. Amongst other gallant actions, he went one night with his party, and seized and carried off a great number of horses belonging to the King's troops, whilst they were grazing in the meadows adjoining to Magdalen College. For this hazardous and useful piece of service he was promoted to a company[u].

In the year 1649, Lord Fairfax, Generalissimo of the parliamentary army, with his Lieutenant General Cromwell, and other officers, came to Oxford, at the time of the Commemoration, where they were splendidly entertained by the University, with feasts, and with learned and congratulatory speeches. Fairfax and Cromwell were created doctors of law[x]. Degrees were given to other officers, according to the recommendation of the generals. Sir Hardress Waller, Colonels Harrison, Ingoldsby, Hewson, Okey, and some more, were admitted to the degree of Master of Arts, and Unton Croke was created Bachelor of Law[y]. In the October following, with his brother Sir Richard, he was one of the Commissioners appointed by the Parliament to take possession of the King's Palace at Woodstock, for the valuation and sale of the royal property there, as before mentioned.

The Lord Commissioner Whitelocke was in several ways related to the Croke family, and was born in the house of Sir George Croke, his mother's uncle, in Fleet-street[z]. When he went upon his embassy to Sweden, with a magnificent train of attendants, he was accompanied by two of his cousins. In his own account he thus describes them. Amongst the gentlemen of the first degree, who were admitted to the Ambassador's table, and who had servants and lacquays in Whitelock's livery, was "*Captain* "*Unton Croke, of the army, kinsman to Whitelocke, son of Serjeant* "*Croke, of an ancient family in Oxfordshire, and of good parts and con-* "*dition*[a]." Unton had the particular permission of the Protector to go[b]. His brother Charles, mentioned hereafter, was the other. They sailed for Sweden in November, 1653, and returned in June, 1654. Of Captain Unton Croke's gallantry in this embassy, Whitelocke tells the following story. "The 22d of February, Captain Croke, Whitelocke's kins- "man, and one of his gentlemen, chose for his Valentine, Monsieur

[u] Wood's Athenæ Ox. part ii. coll. 755. [x] Whitelock, p. 389. [y] Wood, Ath. Ox. ii. p. 755. [z] Wood's Ath. Ox. art. Whitelock, part ii. coll. 399. [a] Whitelock's Ambassy to Sweden, vol. ii. Append. p. 463, and 465. [b] His Letter to Cromwell, Thurloe's State Papers, vol. iii.

"Woolfeldt's lady, and sent a present of English silke stockins and gloves, "which she took so well, that, he going to wait on her as his Valentine, "she treated him with great respect, and gave him a ringe sett with a "fayre ruby, and sixe little diamonds about it, of the value of eighty "pounds, a present fitt for a lady to give, who was the daughter and sister "of a king[c]." Monsieur Woolfeldt was a nobleman of family and fortune in Denmark, and had the place of Reichs Hoffmeister, or Great Chamberlain, in that country. His lady was the King of Denmark's daughter by a *left-handed wife*, that is, a second wife, whom the King, having issue by his first wife, takes in marriage by the left hand, and the issue cannot inherit the crown[d]: a kind of marriage well known amongst the German nations[e]. Woolfeldt was at that time in Sweden, having been banished by the King of Denmark for favouring the rights of the people.

In the beginning of the next year, 1655[f], Unton Croke was of material service to the Protector. The general discontent of the nation at the usurpation of Cromwell, and more particularly after the dissolution of the Parliament on the 22d of January, began at that time to shew itself in open mutinies, and still deeper conspiracies. All parties, the republicans, the army, and the royalists, were dissatisfied with an arbitrary power, erected upon the ruins of the monarchy and of liberty, and exercised with oppression and tyranny. A conspiracy, usually called the *Cavalier Plot*, was very generally entered into to restore the King. Cromwell, who had information of every thing which passed, was justly alarmed at these combinations, which he knew to be very extensive, and favoured by some of the principal persons in his government, and who had been his chief supporters. To counteract their designs, he employed confidential agents in all parts of the kingdom. In this service, Captain Unton Croke, with his troop, was stationed in the west, and had his emissaries in every quarter

[c] Ambassy, vol. i. p 454 [d] Ambassy, i. p. 280 [e] See the Introductory Essay to the case of Horner on Liddiard, page 115 It is fully treated of by Heineccius in his Elementa Juris Germanici, lib i tit 10 § 214 and the whole of title 13 [f] At that time the year began the 25th of March, till that day the date of the preceding year continued, either alone, or with the following year also, written like a fraction Wagstaffe's expedition was in what we should now call 1655, yet being before the 25th of March, Unton Croke's Letters are dated 1654, or $165\frac{4}{5}$

With, or without, specific directions, he apprehended all persons who were with reason suspected of being disaffected to the government. Of his seizure of Adjutant General Allen he has given an account to the Protector[g].

"Feb. 7, 1654.

"*Concerning Adjutant Allen.*

"Sir John Davis, Baronet, reports, that the said Adjutant said, at his last being in London, he was with the Protector, and had roundly told him his mind, and that he did nettle the Protector extremely; that he departed from him in a huffe, without any leave, and that immediately he took his horse and came out of London.

"About the end of November last he met in Exeter a kinsman of his wife's, one Mr. Reynell, who was chosen a member of the last Parliament, but had deserted. He told the said Mr. Reynell, they were quiet in Ireland, as to the common enemy, but there were many discontented there, as well as here. He said there was talking of disbanding some there, and that he was pitched upon to inform a Committee concerning it, and other the affaires of Ireland, but he was resolved to say nothing in it: he said there might be mischief, besides the danger of disbanding any there, that there could not be 5000 drawn into the field, and there was 40000 to be kept under. He did highly commend Lieutenant General Ludlowe, and said he was come already, or coming into England That he intended to be himself in Ireland in February, but would first go to London.

"The said Mr. Reynell telling him he was ready to act in the country as a Justice of the Peace, though he could not as a Parliament man. For that the best way (as he thought) to be secured against the common enemies was to acquiesce in and under the present government, he answered, that he happly might think so likewise, but there were many of another mind, and the Protector might have overruled all, according to the interest of honest men, without taking so much power to himselfe, which did displease many.

"All company, that have, since his last coming from London into these

[g] All the following letters, which are in Thurloe's State Papers, I have examined and corrected by the originals, which are in the Bodleian Library

parts, conversed with him, do report him to be a person highly dissatisfied with the present government.

There are divers strangers, particularly from Somerset, and about Bristol, that came to his meetings, which are often on week days. He rides commonly with a kind of vizard over his face, with glasses over his eyes, and this he did on the 5th of last month, being Friday, riding to a meeting at Luppitt, within this county, and that which did not a little cause suspicion of him, was the coming at that time of Hugh Courtnay (that had been, or is, an officer in Ireland) to Mr. Prowze's house, a Cavalier of good estate; where the said Courtnay scarce spoke any thing but treason, most bitterly reviling the present government and his Highness, said he was then going to London, where, and thereabouts, he was sure to meet hearts and hands enough to carry on the Anabaptistical interest, that his government should not stand many months, and that deliverance was at hand.

We have not picked out the venom of his discourses, but fairly represented the same.

JO. COPLESTON[h].
UNTON CROKE[i].

Captain Unton Croke to the Protector.

May it please your Highness,

If my letter of account concerning Adjutant General Allen (which I sent up with divers papers inclosed in it by same post that he wrote to your Highness) be not yet come unto your Highness's hands, I cannot but suspect there hath been some ugly practise used in diverting the intelligence, which at large I presented your Highness with, and also an endeavour to render me negligent and remiss in my duty towards your Highness. And least what I have reason to fear should prove true, that your Highness is yet in the dark concerning all passages of the seizing the Adjutant's person, and other things relating to him, I shall presume humbly to reiterate what I formerly hinted unto your Highness. So soon as I

[h] He was Sheriff of Devonshire, represented Barnstaple in the Parliament in 1656 and 165$\frac{7}{8}$, and was Knighted by Oliver, 1 June, 1655 Noble, i. 443

[i] Thurloe's State Papers, vol. iii p 140. Original, vol 23. f 43

received your commands for securing his person, which came to my hands this day eight days in the evening, within few hours afterwards I set forth of Exon, towards his father-in-law Mr. Huish his house, where I heard the Adjutant was. To which place I came about break of the next day, and having enquired of some servants of the house, whether the Adjutant were there, they told me he was, and in bed. So soon as I heard this, I resolved, according to what the High Sheriff and I agreed on the night before, imagining it might conduce much to the advantage of your Highness, to seize on his trunks, and them to search for papers, thereby to discover his designs, and to know who were his correspondents. But unhappily, he had sent them up to London some few days before so that I was deprived of my intention. And here, my Lord, if he could quarrel at any thing in his apprehension, it was at this action, where I was necessitated to send two or three soldiers to enter in his chamber, with the first that carried him news of my being come to the house least he having notice, if he had any papers there, might convey them away. Some few letters were found, which I inclosed in my last letter to your Highness. They were writ to him from some discontented spirits, and many dissatisfactory clauses contained in them. 'Tis true, my Lord, the soldiers wore their swords by their sides, and alighting from their horses, took their pistols in their hands, but that the least violence was used, or any ill words gave, or any thing that looked like an affront, I do deny, and well know, that he cannot lay any thing to the charge of myself or any man that was with me. I should now, my Lord, render your Highness an account of what words passed between us, but, hoping that my former letter is, ere this, in your Highness's hands, I shall forbear, only this I shall add, that, according to your Highness's instructions, I confined him to his father's house, he giving me a note under his hand, that he would there remain until your Highness's further pleasure were known. This day I sent him your Highness's letter, and I desired him to remember his promise unto me in continuing at the present where he was. All that possibly the High Sheriff and myself, with the greatest care and diligence we have used, can of a truth make out against him, is this, that to two persons of very good quality in this county, in his discourses, he vented these words. To the one he said, (and that in a high bravado) that he was not ashamed to say, that he was dissatisfied with the present government: and that he had declared so much (said he) to your Highness; and added, that, in discourse with your Highness, he very much nettled you, and having put your Highness into a chaffe, he left you, and then took his horse, and came into the country, without taking leave. To the other gentleman he said, they being entered into several discourses, and the gentleman asking him some question concerning Ireland, as to the peace thereof, &c to which the Adjutant replied, they were free from the common enemy, but there were those, that were discontented there as well as here. He added, that it was reported, that some in Ireland should be disbanded, which he thought could not be done, and then, entering into a high commendation of Lieutenant General Ludlow, he concluded the Irish discourse. After this, the gentleman took the occasion to express the great sense of happines that he, and the whole nation had, by your Highness's government. To which the Adjutant replied, that he perceived he thought so, and it may be, so might he; but he thought many others were of another mind. And then said, that your Highness might have overruled all, according to the interest of honest men, without taking so much of the government to youiself, which, he said, displeased many. My Lord, these words will be exactly proved. Many others I have heard, in many places spoken, but cannot prove them. All the country rings of his dissatisfaction, which he spares not to tell every where, especially at the meetings of such of the baptized church, where he resorts, but doth it so cunningly, that I cannot yet discover him further, though, without all question, his work hath been in those parts to dissatisfy the people. They have had divers meetings of late upon the week days, to which places he hath gone disguised with kind of vizard: and this also can be proved I sent over all Dorsetshire and Devon, enquiring after Colonel Sexby, and Courtney, but as yet cannot hear of them, and your Highness need not doubt in the least of my vigilancy and care in all respects over those that are your Highness' and nation's enemies. I have faithful scouts in all parts of this country, who do correspond with me, and if any thing be hatching, I hope the Lord will make me instrumental to discover and suppress it. I have, according to your Highness' commands, acquainted the baptized Church in Exon with your Highness's favour towards them, who have sent this inclosed letter of thanks to your Highness. I now take leave humbly to subscribe myselfe,

Your Highness's most humble
and devoted servant,
UNTON CROKE[k]

Exon,
February 7, 1654

In another letter from him, of the 21st of February, he relates his securing some other gentlemen, who might have been instrumental in any insurrection His own Lieutenant had been apprehended as a disaffected person, and some of his soldiers, who had been sent to take Colonel Sexby, had been imprisoned at Weymouth. These events he fully stated and explained in two other letters to the Protector, of the 5th of March.

Captain Unton Croke to the Protector.

May it please your Highness,

By the last post I acquainted your Highness of the peace and quiet that was in these parts, and what I had done in relation thereunto, by securing such gentlemen as (if any trouble should have arisen) might have been instrumental in acting much mischief. And I humbly desired your Highness's commands, whether I shall continue their restraint, or enlarge them I also acquainted your Highness, that I had not been careless in making the most curious search after Sexby, having had parties out after him both in Devonshire and Dorsetshire. Some of them are not yet returned. which makes me hope they have tract him, and that by the next your Highness may receive a further account from

(May it please your Highness)
Your most humble and obedient Servant,
UNTON CROKE[l]

Exon,
February 21, 1654

[k] Thurloe, iii p. 143 Original, vol 23 f 59 [l] Ibid vol iii p 165 Original vol 23. f 203

Captain Unton Croke to the Protector.

May it please your Highness,

Receiving your commands on Saturday night last by the post, I made all possible speed to repair to Weymouth, to receive an account of the late detention of my soldiers, and also to be informed of the particulars your Highness gave me in charge, and I have most faithfully and impartially (according to my best judgement, and as the brevity of time would also permit) couched every particular in this enclosed narrative Hitherto your Highness hath (I confess) received no satisfaction from me concerning my Lieutenant. Indeed, my Lord, I know not how he stood in your Highness's thoughts, nor what was the reason of his long absence from my troop. I only accidentally heard that he was detained upon suspicion that he did not well relish the present government. My Lord, I think he is more a stranger unto me than unto any officer in the regiment. He was placed in my troop (but not by my choice) immediately before the time your Highness gave me liberty to attend my Lord Whitelocke into Sweden. So that, before my going thither, I had not a week's acquaintance with him, and since my return I have had as little of his company: so that I am very incapable to know his principles. But, my Lord, I am informed by others that know him very well, that he is of a dangerous temper, and neither well inclined to the good old way of God, nor to the government of your Highness. My Lord, this I thought my duty to speak, not out of any prejudice I have to the person of the man, from whom I have received all respect that could have been expected, but that I could not be silent having so fair a call from your Highness to spend my opinion I profess, my Lord, I am so far from desiring his continuance, that I rejoice at your Highness's resolves in giving him his dismission. And since your Highness is pleased to think of such a course, I beseech you, my Lord, grant me the liberty of making an earnest request unto your Highness, which if you will be pleased to grant, I shall freely engage all that's dear to me in this world, that your Highness shall never have cause to think your favours . . . . It is, my Lord, that my Cornet (who is a plain downright honest man, one that is well principled, and that hath borne command in my troop now for more than five years, and an exceeding good and careful soldier) may be my Lieutenant, and that your Highness will confer my colours on a brother of mine who hath been some years in my troop, and is not unapt for the place. He is, my Lord, well disposed, and of a gracious spirit. The High Sheriff of Devonshire, Col. Copleston, hath lately honoured him with one of your Highness's commissions for a company (which he hath already raised) in his regiment: but, my Lord, I imagine that that is now near at an end; and therefore it is that I presume thus earnestly to importune your Highness in this manner, hoping I may live to express my gratitude, and to declare more amply than I hitherto have had opportunity to do, how much I am,

May it please your Highness,

Your most faithful and obedient Servant,

UNTON CROKE[m].

Weymouth,
March 5, 165$\frac{4}{5}$

A paper of Captain Unton Croke concerning Col. Sexby

The Mayor of the town, Captain Hurst, the Governor of Portland, Captain Green that commands a frigate, and Cornet Brockhurst that belongs to Jersey island, confessed to me, that the soldiers demeaned themselves very civilly without giving offence to any; and the reason why they were detained was purely upon this account, that they came to search for Colonel Sexby without an order in writing.

The soldiers came unto Weymouth on the 20th day of February last past about five a clock at night, made some enquiry at a distance, whether Colonel Sexby were in town or no. They were told that if he were in town, he was at Captain Arthur's house, (who is the Grand Customer of that place, but a man esteemed of no good principle,) for there he was servant to a lady, to whom for many years he had professed friendship, and many people thought that it still continued. One of the soldiers throwing aside his arms, addressed himself to the said Captain's house in quality of a countryman, and knocked at the door, whereupon a maid servant came unto him The soldier asked her whether Colonel Sexby were in the house or no, for he had a desire to speak with him She replied, she could not tell, but she would in an instant inform him, and so went in and called Mis Ford unto him, Sexby's supposed mistress. When she came, she demanded of the soldier his business. He told her, he had a message

[m] Thurloe, iii p 193 Original, vol. 24 f 91

and letter to deliver to Colonel Sexby. She desired to know from whom The soldier answered, from a very good friend of the Colonel, one Mr. Hugh Courtney. Mrs. Ford said, that the Colonel was not within, but if he would leave the message and letter with her, she would take order to have it delivered unto him, that so a time and place might be appointed for them to meet. The soldier told her that unless he could see him he would not deliver the letter, and so departed. Immediately after this. Mrs. Ford calls one Dudley unto her, (who is deputy to Captain Arthur, and acts all things under him,) and tells him that there were troopers in town, enquiring after Colonel Sexby She willed him to enquire, if he could, what was the business; and if he could learn it, she desired to be informed before any soldiers came down to the house to make search after him. He promised he would make enquiry, and then went up to the inn where the soldiers quartered, and entered into discourse with them. He told the soldiers, that he knew their business, and what it was they came about, and told them it was to apprehend Sexby. And for his part he loved the Protector so well, that he would assist them in the business. He said that Sexby was in town, and at the house of Captain Arthur: and if they should be wise, and keep his counsel, he would carry them to his very chamber door: but he told them, they must search very well, for the house was large, and many by places in it; that without a strict scrutiny, little good could be done. The soldiers were very joyful at this news, and did intend that night, though very late, to go and search the house. And when they were provided and ready to go, Dudley's mind changed, he denied all that was said before, and would not go forth with them, so that all the business for that night seemed to be quashed. E're this time, the news went for current about the town, that soldiers were come to apprehend Col. Sexby; whereupon, Coronet Brockhurst, Captain Lambert, one Major Hardinge, and Mr. Waltham, (the two last, I am credibly informed, are high flown men in their principles, and direct friends to Sexby and Joyce,) these four much questioned why it was the soldiers came to look after any man without a written order. Some of them examined the soldiers, who presently confessed the design; and notwithstanding that they made out what they could, to whom they belonged, from whence they came, and what was their business, yet they thought it convenient to secure the soldiers. And that night some of Captain Lambert's seamen were placed in the house, where the soldiers were, to take care none should come to them, nor they go to any. The next day the soldiers were had to the Mayor, and by the instigation of the aforesaid gentlemen, he thought them very fitting to be secured, until such time as he should send for Captain Hurst, Governor of Portland. He desired the soldiers to repair to their quarters, and entreated Coronet Brockhurst and Captaine Lambert to bear them company, which was to watch over them About noon Captain Hurst comes They incited the Captain to proceed against the soldiers, as they had done the Mayor before. He concurred with them, so the soldiers were then disarmed, and made prisoners indeed.

By this it appears, that if Sexby were in the town, he had liberty enough given him to make his escape.

I do find that the Mayor and Captain were very innocent from any design in the business; they did it merely at the request of others. Neither can I learn that either the Mayor or Captain have any relations or near acquaintance with Sexby; but some of the other gentlemen have

I cannot discover what the principles of the Captain are. They are not much taken notice of any way, but sure I think by his discourse, he desires to be quiet, and doth not appear to be of a turbulent spirit. I pressed him to discourse as to present affairs, but he was very wary. I asked him his thoughts of Major General Harrison, who was his prisoner. He was very affectionate towards him in his expressions, often saying, he was a good man. He told me that the Major General had desired liberty of him to speak upon some places of Scripture sometimes to his soldiers, which he had granted him: and he did usually preach to them. There is no commission officer but himself in the castle, otherwise I had discoursed with more. The Captain told me that he had little acquaintance with Sexby, but he knew Joyce very well, and hinted to me, as if he owned all his preferment from him He told me that he was at London, about three weeks since, and desired to speak to Sexby about some business, but could not. for he was then told that Sexby was with his Highness, and that he had much conference about the plot, but that he heard Sexby was very free, and gave satisfaction He told me that Colonel Harrison wondered to hear that Sexby should be suspected. He thought him only to be a decoy for his Highness, because he observed all those that Sexby had been with were secured; but he himself at liberty, though pretended to be searched for. Colonel Harrison also added, that Sexby was with him, but he knew him to be a treacherous fellow, and would have nothing to do with him. This imperfect unmodelled narration is all that at present can be made forth by

UNTON CROKE[n].

After the events here related, Colonel Sexby was suspected of having dispersed some papers directed against the government. Cromwell sent for him to secure him, but he fled. Upon which, Cromwell pretended, on account of ancient friendship, to employ him as his agent at Bourdeaux. He accepted of the employment, but being near seized by the magistrates there, he made his escape[o]. He was the writer of the celebrated pamphlet called, Killing no Murder, of which he acknowledged himself to be the author. He died in the Tower[p].

Notwithstanding the vigorous police of the Protector, the conspiracy still existed in full force, and a day for a general rising was even appointed. The design so far succeeded, that in several counties armed parties began to assemble, and, in the month of March, attempts were made to seize Shrewsbury castle, Chirke castle, and other strong places. In the west the conspiracy broke out most into action. On the 11th of March, a party of about two hundred horse, under the command of Sir Joseph Wagstaff, Penruddock, Jones, and Grove, some of the principal gentlemen in that part, with other persons of fortune and consequence, entered Salisbury at the time of the assizes, at midnight, proclaimed King Charles the Second, seized the Judges, and having taken away their commissions, set them at liberty; the Sheriff they carried away with them. Not finding themselves supported by the country, as they expected, they retired into Devonshire: of which Captain Croke having timely intelligence, pursued them with his troops, overtook them at South Molton, and defeated them most completely, after a sharp conflict[q]. Penruddock, Jones, and Grove, with many others, were taken prisoners, but Sir Joseph Wagstaff and

[n] Thurloe, iii p. 194 Original, vol. 24 f 87 [o] Ludlow, vol. ii p 82. [p] Noble's Memoirs of Cromwell, vol ii p 66. n [q] Whitelock's Memorials, page 601. Ludlow's Memoirs, vol ii page 69 Clarendon's Hist of the Rebellion.

Mr. Mompesson escaped. Captain Croke's two letters to the Protector upon this occasion, which were published in the Gazette, will give the most authentic account of this transaction[r].

" A Letter to his Highness the Lord Protector, from Captain Unton Crooke, signifying the total defeat of the cavaliers in the west, under the command of Sir Joseph Wagstaffe.

Published by his Highness's special commandment. London, printed by Henry Hills and John Field, printers to his Highness, 1654. [March 17.]

A Letter, &c. as in the title page.

May it please your Highness,

Yesterday morning, being Tuesday, I marched with my troop to Hunnton, being fifteen miles eastward from Exon, with intention to stop the enemy from coming further westward, but gaining intelligence that they were come that way, and that they would be too strong for me, I made my retreat to Exon, the next morning I understood they were in the march for Cornwall, and in order thereunto they were come to Collumpton, within ten miles of Exon, I heard they were much tired, and then number two hundred, and therefore imagined that if they should gain Cornwall, it might be much prejudicial, I was resolved to hazard all that was dear to me rather than let them have their end, and thereupon marched towards Collumpton with only my own troop, I had no more for this service, but when I came near that place, I understood they were marched to Tiverton, whither I pursued them with all speed, but there mist them also, but received information that from thence they were gone to South Molton, twelve miles further, still in order for Cornwall, thither I resolved to follow them, they took up their quarters about seven of the clock this night, and by the good providence of God, directing and assisting me, I beat up their quarters about ten of the clock, they disputed it very much with me in the houses for more than two hours, firing very hot out of the windows; they shot seven or eight of my men, but none I hope mortally wounded, they shot many of my horses also; but, my Lord, we broke open many houses, some of them yielded to mercy; I promised them, I would use my en-

[r] They are preserved in the British Museum. See catologue of printed books

deavours to intercede for their lives, I have taken most of their horses, about fifty prisoners, amongst whom are Penruddock, Jones, and Grove, who commanded those horse, each of them having a troop. Wagstaff I fear is escaped, he was with them, but at present I cannot find him, yet hope to catch him as soon as day-light appears. I will raise the country to apprehend such stragglers, which for want of having dragoons, narrowlie escaped me My Lord, they are all broken and routed, and I desire the Lord may have the glory. I beseech your Highness to pardon this unpolisht account, I can hardly indeed write, being so weary with extreme duty, but I hope by the next to send your Highness a more perfect one, and a list of the prisoners, many of them, I suppose, being very considerable. Colonel Shapcot of this county was pleased to march with me on this design, and was with me at the beating up of their quarters, and hath shewed himself wonderfully ready, in every respect, to preserve the peace of this county. My Lord, I remain,

May it please your Highness,

Your most obedient and most humble servant,

UNTON CROOK.

From South Moulton,
March 15, 1654, about two
or three o'clock in the morning.

" A second Letter to his Highness the Lord Protector, from Captain Unton Crooke, signifying the total defeat of the cavaliers in the west, under the command of Sir Joseph Wagstaffe.

Published by his Highness special commandment.

London, printed by Henry Hills and John Field, printers to his Highness, 1654. [March 20th.]

A second Letter, &c. as in the title page

May it please your Highness,

I gave your Highness last night an account how far I had pursued the enemy that came out of Wiltshire into Devon, I sent your Highness the numbers of them, which I conceived to be two hundred, it pleased my good God so to strengthen and direct me, that although I had none but my own troop which was not sixty, that about ten a clock at night, I fell into their quarters at a town called South Molton, in the county of Devon ; I took, after four hours dispute with them in the town, some sixty prisoners, near one hundred forty horses and arms. Wagstaffe himself escaped, and I cannot yet find him, although I am still sending after him, this party of them was divided into three troops, Colonel Penruddock commanded one of them, and was to make it a regiment, Colonel Groves commanded another, and was to compleat it to a regiment, Col. Jones the third, and was to do the like; these three gentlemen are of Wiltshire, and men of estates. One of Sir Edward Clark's sons was with them, he was to be Major to Penruddock, the prisoners tell me that we killed him.

I have brought all the prisoners to Exon, and have delivered them over to the High Sheriff, who has put them into the high gaol Your Highness may be confident this party is totally broken, there is not four men in a company got away, the country surprize some of them hourly, the Major of South Molton, being with me in the street, was shot in the body, but like to do well.

I have nine or ten of my troop wounded

I remain,

Your Highness most

obedient servant,

Exon, Mar 16, 1654 UNTON CROOK"

A commission of oyer and terminer was issued for the trial of the prisoners, but Chief Justice Rolls, the Judge, who had been seized at Salisbury, and was nominated upon the commission, refused to attend, as being too nearly implicated in the affair The Attorney General, Prideaux, was sent down to prosecute. Many were found guilty of treason. Penruddock and Grove were beheaded. Lucas, and many inferior criminals, were executed, Jones, being allied to Cromwell, was pardoned.

After this defeat, Unton Croke was still upon the alert, to extinguish all the remains of the conspiracy In June he was in Oxfordshire, and apprehended a great number of disaffected persons

Captain Unton Croke, and H Smith, to the Protector

May it please your Highness,

In pursuance of your instructions we have seized the persons of the Lord Lovelace, Sir John Burlacie, Sir Thomas Pope, John Osbaldiston, Esq. who were included in the list sent us from your Highness, Sir William Walter, and Col. Sands, are, as we hear at London, and so out of our reach. We have also secured the Lord of Falkland, George Nappier, Thomas Whorwood, Esq. who are dangerous and disaffected persons. We intend to-morrow morning to send them to Worcester, that being the nearest place where there is convenience for confinement. We also sent for my Lord of Lindsay, whose residence is in this county, a person sufficiently known to your Highness, as we suppose; but at his own importunity, and Colonel Coke's, we have adventured to leave him at his house, untill your Highness shall signify the contrary, but we thought it a duty to act what we did incumbent on,

May it please your Highness,

Your most faithfull humble servants,

H. SMITH.

Oxon June 6th, 1655 UNTON CROKE.

Here was in this town one Coll. Colt, who formerly served the king, and esteemed a very dangerous person, we made attempts to seize him, but he having notice, fled from us, as we hear, to London[s]."

In November, disturbances were still apprehended, and Unton was still active, as appears by a letter from Major General Berry, followed by a second, in which he requests the Protector to perform his promises to Captain Croke

Major General Berry, to Secretary Thurloe, dated Worcester, 17th of November, 1655.

Sir,

I came this last night to Worcester, where I met with your Letter, as also some intimations from his Highness, which I can find Captain Croke hath taken notice of, and given his Highness an account of his proceeds thereupon, &c[t].

Major General Berry, to the Protector.

May it please your Highness,

I have only one public business of great import-

[s] Thurloe's State Papers, iii. p. 521. Original, vol. 27. f. 101. [t] Thurloe, vol iv p 211 Original, vol 32. f 569

ance, that I make bold to trouble your Highness withal, having always found you ready to accept such motions, and that is, that your Highness would please to make good your word to Captain Croke; but it must be whilst you live, or otherwise we fear it will never be done. You know what plotting there is against your person, and if any of them should take, what will become of our preferments? Only for my own part, I may hope for something when you die, if any thing be left, because I am promised it in the word of a King, from whom I crave pardon, and a grant of this humble request of

Your Highness's most
devoted Servant,
JA. BERRY[u]

Salop,
Dec 1, 1655.

The failure of this attempt was fatal to the designs of the royalists; and the annihilation of their very sanguine hopes filled them with indignation against the principal instrument of their defeat. Unton Croke was accused of a breach of the terms upon which Penruddock, and the others, had surrendered. It was pretended that they had capitulated only upon the express condition that their lives should be spared. The charges of perfidiousness and falsehood were liberally bestowed upon him, and are conveyed to posterity in the sermons of Dr. South[x], and the Fasti of Anthony à Wood[y] But upon an accurate consideration of all the circumstances of the case, whatever may be the merits, or demerits, of the cause in which he was engaged, Unton Croke must stand acquitted of this crime.

With respect to the fact, whether any such direct and express terms had been granted them as the inducement to their surrender, Ludlow informs us, in his Memoirs, that "*Major Croke absolutely denied any such* "*thing*[z]." In his letter to the Protector, published in the Gazette, and written immediately upon the spot, no such capitulation is mentioned, nor do we find that his account was contradicted at the time. All that he states is, that they defended themselves, firing very hot out of the windows,

[u] Thurloe, vol iv p 274 Original, vol. 33 f 45

[x] South's Sermons, ed. 1715. vol i page 124 in a note, perhaps written by Dr King, the publisher of South's Sermons.

[y] Fasti Ox. part ii col 755

[z] Memoirs, vol ii p 71 ed Edinburgh, 17.

for two hours, that the troops broke open many houses, that "*some of* "*them yielded to mercy, and he promised them that he would use his* "*endeavours to intercede for their lives*" A very different thing from a surrender upon express terms. Penruddock, in the speech which he made at his execution, stated the articles to have been life, liberty, and estate, and said that *they were drawn by his hand*[a]. This implies that they were in writing, in which case they must have been deposited with the parties who were to have the benefit of them: many persons must have seen them, and they would have been capable of proof.

Indeed the promise of interceding in their favour, which Unton Croke admits that he made to some of them, was in reality the utmost engagement to which his power extended Without entering into the learning of the writers of the Law of Nations, relating to *sponsions*, or treaties entered into by subaltern officers, it must be remarked, that this was not a case of war, but a case of a rebellion against an established government; which would of course be subject not to the laws of war, as between two enemies, but, to the municipal laws of the country, as between the Sovereign and the subject. A commander sent to reduce rebels, could have no power, without an express authority to that effect, to stipulate with them for the preservation of their lives, and, in case of capture, they would still be amenable to the laws of treason. It is justly observed therefore by Lord Clarendon, though his account of this transaction in other respects is evidently stained with the colouring of party, that "*Major* "*Croke had no authority to enter into any such convention*[b]."

After all, if such conditions had in reality been made, with, or without, sufficient authority, the performance of them did not rest with Unton Croke, but with the Protector. It was not Unton Croke who put them to death: but, after they had been condemned upon a trial before a jury of their countrymen, it was the Protector who inforced the sentence, and suffered them to be executed: which it was not in Unton Croke's power to prevent

To *some*, who yielded to mercy, he fairly stated, that he promised to

[a] State Trials, vol ii p 259 ed 1730. 19 April, 1655 Trial of Penruddock

[b] Clarendon's Hist of the Rebellion, ed folio, vol iii p 435

intercede for their lives His conscientious performance of this promise affords a very strong presumption that he was not capable of acting perfidiously towards the others. By two letters in Thurloe's Collection, it appears that he addressed himself both to Cromwell, and his Secretary, in their favour, and that with warmth, and earnestness.

Captain Unton Croke to Secretary Thurloe.

To the Honourable John Thurloe, Esquire, Secretary of State at Whitehall. These, Hast, hast, hast.

Honourable Sir,

Upon my Lord Protector's letter, I immediately sent away Mr. John Penruddocke, and Francis Jones, within some few hours after I received an express from you, clearing any doubt I might make of the person, because there were two of the name in gaol, but the considerablenesse of the person guides me aright. Sir, I wrote to his Highness lately, concerning five men, (who are the most inconsiderable of the company, not one of them being of estate or quality as I can learn,) to whom I promised, who kept a house against me four hours, that I would intercede to his Highness for their lives. Sir, I shall press it to you *with importunity*, that you will move it to his Highness, that so, if any be thought worthy of pity, as to have their lives, that his favour may extend to those men, though not for their own sakes, yet in regard of my reputation, because I lye under a promise to them. Sir, hereby you will infinitely oblige,

Sir, your most humble servant,

UNTON CROKE[c].

Exon,
March 2, 1655

At the time of holding the commission for their trial at Salisbury, he wrote again.

Captain Unton Croke to Secretary Thurloe.

Honorable Sir,

I received yours at Exeter on Saturday last, and accordingly repaired to Sarum, to attend the Judges, where I at present am You were pleased to put me in hopes, that his Highness might be intreated for the sparing of

[c] Thurloe's State Papers, vol. iii p 281. Original, vol 36. f 23

those five persons I wrote about, and promised me your assistance, in the promoving my request. Sir, I do again intreat your intercession, and that, if it be possible, by the very next post, I may be ascertained whether there is a possibility of their reprieval. One of them is Wake, two brothers, whose names are Colliers. I profess I have forgot the others' names, but they are all five contemptible persons; yet, *by reason of my engagement, I cannot but continue my importunity, that they might be spared.* Sir, I am very tedious with you, but I hope you will pardon,

Honorable Sir,
Your very humble Servant,
UNTON CROKE[d].

Sarum,
April 12, 1655.

These letters evidently proceed from an honourable mind, extremely desirous, not of formally satisfying an engagement by a cold application, but of accomplishing the object of it effectually; and they shew that sensibility of reputation which always attends a man of honour. Upon the whole, it is impossible for every impartial person not to draw the conclusion, that the vehement abuse, which was heaped upon this officer, proceeded rather from the virulence of a disappointed party, than from any foundation in truth.

The suppression of this conspiracy, which threatened to shake the protectoral throne, and was chiefly effected by the vigorous measures of Unton Croke, gave great satisfaction to Cromwell. To provide for his future security he immediately established his projeet of dividing England into cantons, under the government of twelve Major Generals, and of levying a tenth part of the estates of all the royal party. Unton Croke was promoted to the rank of Major, and two hundred pounds a year. out of the forfeited estate of Mr. Mompesson, was settled upon him for his services[e].

In 1658, the zeal and insolence of the Anabaptists and other sectaries being very violent against the University of Oxford, the colleges, and students, they had laid a plan to destroy all "both root and branch" as they called it The Protector, having received information of their designs, sent orders to Major Unton Croke, at this time at Oxford, with some

[d] Thurloe, p 368 Original, vol 25 f 315

[e] Ludlow's Memoirs, vol ii. p. 72.

troops of cavalry, to have a vigilant eye towards their proceedings. Upon which he appointed parties of horse to patrole the streets, night and day; and particularly upon the 8th of May, the time fixed for the attempt. The scholars were armed for the protection of their own colleges. A general panic prevailed. Many of the members of the University quitted the place, some hid themselves, or left their colleges and took refuge in the town, and others of the more godly party prayed day and night to be freed from the danger. By the activity of Major Croke, and his troopers, the intended insurrection was prevented, tranquillity was completely restored, and the University saved from total destruction[f].

Upon the death of Oliver Cromwell, in 1658, he appeared in support of his son Richard, and at the head of his troop, with the Mayor, Recorder, and Town-Clerk of Oxford, proclaimed the new Protector before Saint Mary's church and at other places, where they were liberally pelted by the loyal young students of the University with carrot and turnip tops[g]. In that year, he was appointed High Sheriff for Oxfordshire, by Richard Cromwell, and his council; in which capacity he made a double return of members for that county[h], and, in the same year, with his brother, Sir Richard Croke, was returned as Member of Parliament for the city of Oxford[i]. This was afterwards quoted in the House of Commons, as a case in point, to prove that a person might be returned for a borough in a county for which he was High Sheriff[k]. In King Charles the First's time it was considered as a disqualification, and that monarch appointed four of the popular leaders Sheriffs, to incapacitate them from being elected members, which was submitted to[l]. In the writ indeed there was formerly a clause, *Nolumus autem quod tu nec aliquis alius Vicecomes dicti regni aliqualiter sit electus.* But as early as the reign of Queen Elizabeth the constant practice was otherwise, as is proved by Sir Simonds

[f] Wood's Hist. Univ. Oxford, ed. Gutch, p. 684. [g] Anthony Wood's Life, p. 115. [h] Journals, House of Commons. [i] Willis's Not. Parl. vol. i. p. 277, 291. [k] Douglas, Election Cases, vol. iv. p. 121. note p. 161.

[l] Sir Edward Coke, and other members, who had taken an active part against the Duke of Buckingham, were made Sheriffs in 1625, and so could not be chosen parliament men. Whitelocke's Mem. pages 2, 6. In 1629, Mr. Long was fined 2000 marks in the Star-Chamber, and imprisoned, for serving as a Member of Parliament, when he was Sheriff. Whitelocke, p. 14.

D'Ewes, and he adds a substantial reason for it, that "otherwise it had "lain in the power of any sovereign to have disabled as many persons as "he chose, and he might have dis-furnished the house of its ablest mem-"bers[m]."

After the removal of Richard Cromwell from the Protectorship, April 22, 1659, the governing powers began to look towards the revenues of the universities; and all human learning was despised by the saints. Some thought that the universities should be quite abolished, but the more moderate were of opinion, that they should be modelled after the form of Leyden, and other Dutch universities, and should have three colleges left for the study of the three great faculties, of divinity, law, and physic; each to have a professor. The most active person in promoting this plan was said to have been Major Croke. For this opinion respecting the university he was censured by Dr. South[n]. Soon after, he was appointed one of the Commissioners for Oxfordshire, by the act for settling the militia.

In the disputes which arose between the republican party and the army, when the principal point in debate was the re-establishment of the remains of the long parliament, or the calling of a new one, a party appeared for the old parliament in Wiltshire, under the command of Colonel Croke, "who having told divers of Ludlow's friends (as he relates "it himself) in that country, 'that the principal reasons of his dissatis-"faction with the proceedings of the army had been taken from what "Ludlow had said in the late council of officers,' he prevailed with divers "of them to side with him, and so marched towards Portsmouth, in order

[m] Journal, page 381

[n] Sermons, vol i page 124 ed. 1715 "Should God in his judgement suffer England "to be transformed into a Munster, should the faithful be every where massacred, should "the places of learning be demolished, and our colleges reduced not only as *one* in his "great zeal would have it, to three but to none, yet assuredly hell is worse than all this" To this is subjoined a note, I suppose by the Editor, Doctor William King, to explain to whom he alludes "Unton Croke, a colonel of the army, the perfidious cause of Penrud-"dock's death, and sometime after High Sheriff of Oxfordshire, openly and frequently "affirmed the uselessness of the Universities, and that three colleges were sufficient to an-"swer the occasions of the nation, for the breeding up of men to learning, so far as it was "either necessary or useful."

"to join Sir Arthur Haslerig, and Colonel Morley, who had already possessed themselves of that place, and declared for the restitution of the parliament[o]." On the 11th of January, 1660, he was made Colonel of Berry's regiment by the Parliament[p].

Weary at length of the endless confusion which prevailed in the kingdom, with the moderate men of all parties, together with his relation Ingoldsby, he cordially supported the re-establishment of a more stable government, in the restoration of the ancient race of monarchs. After General Monk had arrived in London, on the 29th of February, accordingly, Colonel Unton Croke, and his regiment, declared their concurrence with him[q]. After the Restoration, when his regiment was disbanded, he appears to have led a retired life: sometimes in Devonshire, from whence he married his wife, at Cheddington in Bucks, at Grandpoole in the south suburbs of Oxford, at Headington Wick, and other places. He was living in a gouty condition, at or near London, in 1690 but his affair with Penruddock was never forgotten by the loyalists[r]. He married, first, the daughter of Sir Charles Wise, and had by her one daughter at least. His second wife was the daughter of Mr. Mallet, a merchant of Exeter by whom he had a son of his own name. What became of his children is not known.

Charles Croke, a younger son of Serjeant Unton Croke, and brother to Colonel Unton Croke, was a Commoner of Christ Church College at Oxford[s]. He accompanied his cousin, Lord Whitelocke, upon his embassy to Sweden, in the years 1653, and 1654, as one of his Pages, of whom he had four, Henry Elsing, son of the Clerk of the Parliament, was another[t]. He served some years in his brother Unton Croke's troop of horse, and after his return from Sweden, Colonel Coplestone, the High Sheriff of Devonshire, honoured him with one of the Protector's commissions for a company, which he had already raised, in his regiment. But that being near an end, Unton Croke, in a letter to the Protector, dated 5 March, 1655, requests that he would confer the vacant colours in his troop upon

[o] Ludlow's Memoirs, vol ii p 283. [p] Whitelock, p 694. [q] Ibid p 699. [r] Wood's Ath Oxon col. 755. [s] Wood's Fast Oxon. ii c 755. [t] Whitelocke's Ambassy, vol ii. p 465 Appendix.

his brother, of whom he speaks as "not unapt for the place, well disposed, "and of a gracious spirit[u]" Wood informs us, that after he had taken many rambles, had been a soldier, and had seen the vanities of the world, he published at London in 1667, a book in octavo, intitled, *Youth's Unconstancy*.

[u] See the letter already printed, p. 533, 534, from Thurloe's State Papers, vol iii

SECTION THE SIXTH.

THE fifth and youngest son of Sir John Croke, the Judge, was EDWARD CROKE, of whom it is only known by his monument, that he died young on the 4th of February, 1626, and was buried at Chilton, where, on a flat stone, is the following inscription, upon a brass plate, of which the sentiments are superior to the poetry

A coat of arms above, Croke with an annulet

AVE, VIATOR.

STAY HERE, THOU GENTLE PASSENGER,
AND VIEW THIS YOUNG MAN'S CHARACTER.
HERE LYES THE BODY OF A SONNE,
NEXT TO HIS SIRE THAT TO GOD IS GONE.
THE NEXT STEP FORWARD, GRANDSIRE HOLDES,
AND GREAT GRANDSIRE THIRD PLACE ENFOLDES[1].
THEIR VIRTUES SPEAKE THEIR PRAYSES BEST.
AND HEERE THEIR BODYES QUIET REST

VALE, LECTOR.

READER, NOW PASSE, AND CREDIT THIS,
WHO LIVETH WELL SHALL GO TO BLISSE,
AND WHO SO RUNNES A HOLY COURSE,
AS THESE HAVE DONNE WHOM I REHEARSE,
WHEN AS HE VIEWS THIS CHARACTER,
WILL WISH HE WERE INHERITOR
UNTO SUCH WORTHYES MEN THAT WERE
RENOWNED WHILST THEY LIVED HERE

HIC JACET EDWARDUS CROKE, QUI OBIIT QUARTO DIE FEBRUARII, 1626.

[1] This alludes to the situation of their places of burial

Sir John Croke, in his will, mentions his daughter Rachel, but he probably speaks of his daughter-in-law, Rachel Webb, wife of his son, Sir John Croke.

This finishes all the descendants of Sir John Croke, the Judge.

CHAPTER V.

The Waterstock Branch

HAVING gone through all the descendants of Sir John Croke, the Judge, I return to his brother HENRY CROKE, the second son of Sir John Croke, and Elizabeth Unton He was a barrister, and was dead when his mother made her will in 1607. His wife was Bennet Honywood, the daughter of Robert Honywood, of Charing, in Kent, Esquire, and sister to his brother William's wife, and who was buried the 27th of October, 1638, at Waterstock. He is represented on the monument of his father and mother in a bar gown, with his coat of arms, Croke, with a mullet, impaled with argent, a chevron between three eagles' heads, erased, azure: for Honywood. His children were, Anne, Nathaniel, Henry, and Elizabeth Anne married William Walpole, Esquire, of Little Bursted, in Essex; and Elizabeth was the wife of —— Nicholas, a barrister. I believe Nathaniel died young[a].

HENRY CROKE, son to the last Henry, was born about 1596. He was entered at Christ Church College, in Oxford, on the 17th of January, 1610, being only fourteen years of age; where he continued till he had taken his degree of Master of Arts, and then removed to Braze-nose College[b].

A testimonial, addressed to Doctor George Abbot, Archbishop of Canterbury, was given him in 1618, from the principal members of both his colleges, certifying his abilities for any employment either in Church or State, suitable to his years, being then twenty-two years of age, but for what purpose it was obtained does not appear, unless for his ordination.

[a] Harl MSS No 1533 a visitation of Bucks, in 1675 Ward, Waterstock Register
[b] Ward, 305.

Reverendissimo in Christo patri, Georgio divina Providentia Archiepiscopo Cantuariensi, et totius Angliæ primati et metropolitano, nos, quorum nomina subscripta sunt, pro merito et dignitate tanti viri debitam cum honore reverentiam. Cum Henricus Croke, e collegio Ænei Nasi in Artibus Magister, certis de causis ipsum in hac parto moventibus, literas nostras testimoniales de vita sua, laudataque morum integritate, concedi petierit; nos tam honestæ petitioni ejus, quantum in nobis est, obsecundare volentes, testamur, et testatum facimus per præsentes, Henricum Croke ad secundam annuum suscepti gradus magisterii, quo in Æde Christi et Ænei Nasi collegio versatus est, sedulam studiis dedisse operam, vitamque suam sobrie ac pie per omnia instituisse; ad hæc, in iis rebus, quæ ad religiorem spectant, nihil unquam, quod scimus, eum aut credidisse aut tenuisse, nisi quod catholici patres veteresque episcopi ex doctrina Veteris Novique Testamenti collegerunt, quod ecclesia nostra Anglicana jam tenet, approbat, et tuetur; adeoque dignum fore, ut ad quodcunque munus in ecclesia, vel republica, ætati suæ competens promoveatur. In cujus rei testimonium nomina nostra hisce præsentibus apposuimus.

SAM. RADCLIFFE, Pr. coll. Æn. Nas.	GUIL. GOODWIN, Vicec. Ox.
JOANN. PICKERING.	EDM. GWINNE, Subdec.
EDW RITSTON.	JOHANN. WESTON, Præbend.
GABR. RICHARDSON.	GUIL. BALLOWE, Thesaur.
RADUL. RICHARDSON.	CHRIST. WHITE, Magist.
PHILIPP. CAPPAR.	JOHANN. MORRIS, Magist.

The names in the first column were of Brazen-nose, in the second, of Christ Church[c].

The next year, his cousin Charles Croke resigned his Professorship of Rhetoric, at Gresham College, and he was chosen to succeed him, upon Wednesday the 26th of May, 1619, being then but twenty-three years of age. Upon that occasion he obtained another testimonial from Christ Church college, where he had been longest resident.

Universis Christi fidelibus, ad quos hoc præsens scriptum pervenerit, nos, quorum nomina subscripta sunt, pro merito ac dignitate cujusque

[c] Ward, 309.

personæ debitam reverentiam. Cum pium sit et æquitatis officio consentaneum cognitæ veritati testimonium perhibere, et Henricus Croke, Artium Magister, ex Æde Christi Oxon. certis de causis ipsum hac in parte moventibus, literas nostras testimoniales de vita sua laudabili, merumque integritate, sibi concedi petierit, nos tam honestæ petitioni deesse non potuimus. Quare testamur, et testatum facimus per præsentes, dictum Henricum Croke per septem annos in Æde Christi Oxon vixisse, doctrinæ suæ atque eruditionis Christianæ non vulgare apud nos specimen edidisse, eundem fuisse et esse probis et honestis moribus, bona fama, religione sincera, et conversatione integra, adeoque dignum, qui ad qualecumque munus in ecclesia, vel republica, ætati et gradui conveniens promoveatur. In cujus rei testimonium nomina nostra his præsentibus apposuimus. Datum die decimo octavo Maii anno Dom. 1619.

EDM. GWINNE Subdec.	ROB. BURTON, Theol. Baccal.
JO. WESTON, Doct Jur. Civ.	JO WALL, Theol Baccal.
THO. MANNE, Theol Baccal.	ROB WHITEHALL, Theol Baccal.[d]

Trinity term beginning that year on the next Friday after his election, which was the day for reading the Rhetoric Lecture, he was ordered to perform his Latin oration that morning according to custom. It is probable that he had prepared his composition from an expectation that he should be chosen, as the time was short, and the electors would otherwise scarcely have required that duty from the youngest professor they had ever chosen He held the office with great credit for eight years, and resigned it April the 13th, 1627, having then taken his degree of Bachelor in Divinity[e].

He left Gresham College upon a design of marriage, which he accomplished soon after, for upon the 18th of July following, he married Sarah, the daughter of the Reverend Henry Wilkinson, Rector of Waddesdon, in Buckinghamshire. And the reason of his quitting his professorship some months before his marriage might probably be to favour the election of his wife's brother, Edward Wilkinson, who succeeded him in it[f]

[d] Ward, 309 [e] Ibid [f] Ibid

No 29.

THE WILKINSON FAMILY

Collected from Wood, Ath. Oxon

The Rev William Wilkinson, of Adwick, Yorkshire

Henry Wilkinson, born at Halifax in Yorkshire, 1566, Fellow of Merton, 1586, related to Sir H Saville, the Warden, B D; Rector of Waddesdon in 1601, one of the Assembly of Divines in 1643; died 1647, buried at Waddesdon. *Ath Ox* ii 59. = Sarah, only da of Arthur Wake, Canon of Ch Ch *Ath. Ox* i 491

Dr John Wilkinson, D D Wife, Catherine Tutor to Prince Henry, son of James I, Principal of Magd Hall, ejected in 1643, restored in 1646, Parliamentary Visitor On rejection of Dr Oliver, President of Magd Coll 1648; buried at Milton, 1649

Children of the Rev William Wilkinson:

John Wilkinson, of Magd Hall Visitor in 1648, M D 1649, died 1655, lived at Doncaster *Ath Ox.* ii 770

Henry Wilkinson, *junior*, or Dean Harry, born 1616 B D and Principal of Magd Hall in 1648, D D in 1652, ejected in 1662, died 1690; buried in Suffolk *Ath Ox* ii 645 = Elizabeth, died 1654, aged 41, buried at Milton

Children of Henry Wilkinson and Sarah: 6 sons, 3 daughters

John Wilkinson, born 1603, died 1664, æt 61, buried at Waddesdon

Edward, born 1607 Professor of Rhetoric at Gresham College

Henry Wilkinson, *senior*, or Long Harry, born 1609, one of the Assembly of Divines in 1643, Rector of St Dunstan's in 1645, Visitor Vice-President and senior Fellow of Magdalen College, Canon of Christ Church, D D 1649, succeeded Dr Cheynel as Margaret Professor in 1652; ejected in 1662, died 1675 Promoted taking the Spur Royals *Ath Ox* 748, 397

Sarah = Henry Croke 1627

The family into which he married produced several divines of considerable eminence in the Presbyterian party. His father-in-law, who was born in 1566, and died in 1649, had been elected Fellow of Merton, by the interest of Sir Henry Saville, to whom he was related, obtained the Rectory of Waddesden, and was one of the Assembly of Divines in 1643. His wife was Sarah, the only daughter of Dr. Arthur Wake, Canon of Christ Church, and father of the learned Sir Isaac Wake, Orator of the University of Oxford, author of Rex Platonisus, and afterwards Ambassador to Savoy[g].

The brother of Mr. Henry Wilkinson, was Doctor John Wilkinson, who was tutor to Prince Henry, son of James the First, Principal of Magdalen Hall, and, in 1646, one of the Parliamentary Visitors of the University. In 1648, he was appointed President of Magdalen College, and died in 1649. At this advanced period of his life, oppressed by years and weakness, he was persuaded by the avarice of his wife, and his nephew Henry, to take part in a very disgraceful transaction. The founder of Magdalen College had provided a sum of money for the expenses of law-suits, and other occasional demands, and which was deposited in old gold, or spur-royals, in the tower of the college. Dr. Wilkinson, with the college officers, broke open the door, discovered the treasure, and they divided it amongst them: the President had an hundred pieces, and the Fellows each thirty. All the college shared in the spoil, in the whole there were nine hundred pistolets, and each piece produced sixteen shillings and six-pence[h]. Wood states the whole amount at £1400.

Doctor Henry Wilkinson, usually styled *senior*, nephew to the President of Magdalen, son of the Rector of Waddesden, and brother to Sarah Wilkinson, was one of the Assembly of Divines likewise, Rector of Saint Dunstan's, one of the Parliamentary Visitors, Vice-President, and Senior Fellow of Magdalen College, Canon of Christ Church, and Margaret Professor of Divinity; and died in 1675[i].

There was another Doctor Henry Wilkinson, commonly called *junior*,

[g] Wood Ath. Oxon. ii 59. As there has been some confusion respecting these divines, from there being several of the same name, I have made out a correct pedigree of them. No. 29.

[h] Chandler's Life of William Waynflete, 1811, page 290. Wood, ii. 748

[i] Ath. Oxon c. 397.

who was cousin to the last, being the son of the Reverend William Wilkinson, of Adwick in Yorkshire; brother to the Rector of Waddesden, and the President of Magdalen. This Henry was made Principal of Magdalen Hall, in 1648, and had a brother John, who was a physician[k]

Soon after Henry Croke's marriage, his uncle, Sir George Croke, presented him to the Rectory of Waterstock, and, upon the 25th of June, 1640, he took the degree of Doctor in Divinity. Sir George Croke having by his will left him the house and estate at Waterstock, upon his death in 1641, he succeeded him as Lord of the Manor. He died in 1642, and was buried on the 20th of April[l], in the chancel of his own church, without any monument to his memory[m]

He had four sons, George, John, Henry, baptized 7th of May, 1640[n], and Samuel, baptized 1st of April, 1642[o], and one daughter, Mary, born in 1635, who died in her infancy[p].

Of the great number of persons, who compose the genealogy of a numerous family, few will be found whose lives can afford much entertainment, or instruction. Of many, no remembrance whatever is preserved; the men of fortune pursue their amusements, the men of business their occupations, without supplying any materials which can be interesting to futurity. When we meet with a man of science and philosophy, who has employed his mind in pursuits useful or ornamental to mankind, we may be allowed to dwell upon the subject with some degree of pleasure and satisfaction

Sir George Croke, the eldest son of Doctor Henry Croke, after his father's death, inherited the estate at Waterstock His uncle Sir George Croke, the Judge, left him one hundred pounds, to be laid out in the purchase of an annuity, towards his maintenance and education[q] He was appointed Fellow of All-Souls College in Oxford, by the Parliamentary Visitors, and on the 27th of February, 1651, was created Master of Arts, by virtue of a dispensation from Oliver Cromwell, the Chancellor of the University[r]

He married Jane, one of the fourteen children of Sir Richard Onslow, the ancestor of the celebrated Speaker of the House of Commons, and the

[k] Ath. Oxon. ii. c 646, 770. [l] Waterstock Register [m] Ward [n] Waterstock Register [o] Ibid [p] Ward [q] Will penes me [r] Wood Ath Oxon vol ii col 777

present Earl of Onslow. Sir Richard Onslow, in the time of Charles the First, espoused the side of the Parliament, in which he served in three sessions for the county of Surrey. He raised a regiment, and was one of the select committee who waited upon Oliver Cromwell to persuade him to assume the title of King; and was afterwards made one of his peers. He was a man of an elegant and polite mind, and a particular friend of Sir Anthony Ashly Cooper; with whom he concurred in bringing about the Restoration of Charles the Second[s]. Upon the return of the King, he received the honour of Knighthood, and was appointed High Sheriff for Oxfordshire in 1664[t]

Sir George Croke appears to have been actively engaged in the various pursuits which occupied men of science at that philosophical period, when the Royal Society was first instituted, and enrolled amongst its members so many persons of eminence, and he was elected a Fellow the 8th of February, 1676[u]. Dr. Plot, in his Natural History of Oxfordshire, has dedicated to him a plate of undescribed plants, natives of Oxfordshire, in which he styles him "a learned and curious botanist[x]." Of the different branches of that interesting science he attended more particularly to gardening, and was curious in exotic plants[y]. Lawrence, in his New System of Agriculture[z], says, that he was the first who brought the Plane Tree into England: which Miller supposes must have been the Occidental, or Virginian Plane. for the Oriental Plane was introduced by Lord Bacon[a]. Evelyn, in his Sylva, says, that "the introduction of the true Plane Tree amongst us is perhaps due to the great Chancellor Bacon, who planted those still flourishing at Verulam. As to mine, I owe it to that honourable gentleman, the late Sir George Croke of Oxfordshire, from whose bounty I received an hopeful plant, now growing in my villa[b]."

Anthony Wood gives an account, that he visited Sir George Croke at Waterstock, on the 30th of June, in 1668, and was much pleased by lodging in a room there, called the King's room, because Henry the Sixth had slept there. And that in December of that year, he spent his Christmas

[s] Collins's Peerage, vol v p 327, 330. [t] Wood, ubi supra. [u] Books of the Society [x] Page 149. [y] Ward, p 311 [z] Page 247 [a] Dictionary in voce [b] Voce Platanus, vol ii p 62. Edit. Hunter, 1812 The first edition was in 1664

at Sir George's, with Francis Dryer, a foreigner of Bremen, who had been residing at Oxford for the purpose of consulting the Bodleian Library[c].

In a correspondence with Mr. Oldenburg, the Secretary of the Royal Society, and which is preserved in their letter books, Sir George appears to have been an astronomer, an anatomist, an amateur in medicine, and to have been engaged in discovering a method to find the longitude at sea.

A vapouring French physician, a Monsieur Dennis, who was employed "par ordre du Roi à faire des experiences, dont tout le monde recevra de "grands avantages," transmitted to England in 1673, "un essence merveil-"leuse," which he pretended would staunch effusions of blood even from wounded arteries. It had been tried "aux yeux de toute la cour, et de "tout ce qu'il y a de scavans medicins et chirurgeons." The ingenious inventor had obtained the Royal Privilege for the exclusive sale of it in France, and he confesses that he expected to derive "bien de l'argent" from England, "car pour une pistole de dispense, on en tireroit plus de "mille." A pretty reasonable profit. Some of it was transmitted to Sir George Croke, who in a series of experiments fully proved the inefficacy of the medicine, and annihilated the golden mountains of the charlatan.

About the same time he brought forward a proposition for the finding of the longitude. Having stated the insufficiency of all former methods, by the eclipses of the moon, her place in the zodiac, distance from the fixed stars, or entrance into the ecliptic line, by the satellites of Jupiter, or any other celestial observations, or the variations of the magnetic needle; he assumes, that a correct measurer of time would be the only certain method, an opinion which succeeding experience has proved to be true. Since then to obtain an accurate time-keeper was the principal object, he examines and rejects the various kinds in use, dials, water, sand-glasses, and pendulums, and then proposes a new horologium, of his own invention, in which Mercury was made the measure of time *per descensum*, upon the principle of an hour-glass. In Latin, the language of science, he describes the invention, and explains its various advantages

Mr. Oldenburg, in his answer, after many compliments, informs him, that the invention of mercurial hour-glasses had occurred to Tycho Brahe,

[c] Life of Anthony Wood, p 217, 214

the Danish astronomer, many years before, who had failed in the experiment, and complained "that Mercury had played the knave with him," that another man, Smith, had attempted the same thing with no better success; and that it was his own opinion, and that of his philosophical friends, that the method would not answer.

Sir George, in his reply, assures the Secretary that he had never seen those authors; but with the true sanguine spirit of an inventor, so far from being disheartened by this information, he is glad that his opinion is confirmed by so good authority. He does not like it the worse because they failed in the experiment, which he supposes was owing to its being ill conducted. He obviates some farther objections, and wishes it to be tried with greater accuracy. He proposes that Mr. Hook, or some able mechanic, should make an instrument upon his plan. But I suppose it did not succeed ultimately, as nothing farther was heard of it[d].

Sir George Croke died the 17th of November, 1680, at the house of his brother Henry, in the Haymarket at London, from whence his body was conveyed to Waterstock, and was buried in the chancel, without any monument, near to his great uncle Sir George Croke, the Judge, and his wife, who died about four years before him, March the 11th, 1676[e].

He left only two daughters, Elizabeth, and Sarah, who was born the 19th of April, 1669[f]; one of them married Sir Thomas Wyndham, and Mr. Delafield was informed that Sir Richard Onslow courted the other, but whether he married her he could not be certified[g]. There being no son, the estate was sold to Sir Henry Ashhurst. This gentleman was one of the trustees appointed by Mr. Boyle for his lectures. He was a staunch puritan, and a particular friend of the celebrated Mr. Baxter. In 1688, he was created a Baronet. The estate still continues in this family, but in 1695, the ancient seat was pulled down, and a new one of brick was built in its place. This, in turn, was demolished, and an excellent new stone house was erected, by Sir William Henry Ashhurst, one of the Justices of the King's Bench: and father to William Henry Ash-

[d] See Monsr. Denys's letter, and the correspondence between Sir George Croke and Mr Oldenburg, respecting the Styptic, and the finding the longitude, from the Letter Books of the Royal Society, in Appendix, No XXVIII

[e] Wood, ibid [f] Waterstock Register [g] History of Chilton

hurst, Esquire, the present representative in Parliament for the county of Oxford[h].

Of the other three sons of Doctor Henry Croke, John was a courtier, and Gentleman of the Bedchamber to King Charles the Second. He died in November, 1670, and was buried at Waterstock. Henry was a linen draper in the Haymarket Of Samuel no account has been preserved[i].

[h] Ward, p. 312. and MSS notes. Wood, Fast. Oxon Life of A. Wood p 581

[i] Ward, p. 311 Waterstock Register

Sir George Crooke one of
the Iuſtices of the Kings Ben

CHAPTER VI.

Sir George Croke, the Judge, and his descendants.

SECTION THE FIRST.

SIR GEORGE CROKE, the third son of Sir John Croke and Elizabeth Unton, was born about the year 1560, in the beginning of the reign of Queen Elizabeth[a].

He passed his infancy and his tender years under the care of a discreet and affectionate mother, and exhibited, from his childhood, the same excellence of mind and disposition, which accompanied him through life He received the first part of his public education at the school at Thame, which had been founded by Lord Williams, and was formerly of much celebrity. At the age of fifteen, in 1575, he was entered of Christ Church College in Oxford, to improve his talents, by the cultivation of the sciences, and the study of philosophy. After some residence, he was removed to the Inner Temple, of which he had been admitted a Member. on the 7th of February, in the seventeenth year of Queen Elizabeth, 1574 and where he employed the remainder of his youth in the study of the common law[b]. At what time he was called to the bar does not appear In 1597, the 39th of Elizabeth, he was elected a Representative in Parliament for the borough of Berealston in Devonshire[c]. He was made a Bencher of the Inner Temple, the 5th of November, 1597, was Autumn Reader in 1599, Treasurer in 1609, and Double Reader in 1617[d]. The Inns of Court, at that time, constituted a Juridical University, where exercises

[a] From the dates, ætatis 66, 1626, on his picture, and his monument

[b] Sir Harbottle Grimston's Preface to his Reports. Wood s Hist. Univ Oxon Register of the Inner Temple, and his arms in the Hall window

[c] Willis s Not. Parl

[d] Pref Cro Car Ward, p 305 Temple Register

were performed, lectures read, and degrees conferred, in the common law as in other Universities in the canon and civil law[e]. From the Benchers, or Ancients, one was appointed to read lectures annually in the summer vacation to the students, and was called the Single, or Autumn Reader: and one of them, who had formerly read, gave his lectures in the Lent vacation, and was called a Double Reader[f].

Upon the 29th of June, 1623, the twenty-first year of King James, he received from Williams, the Lord Keeper, and Bishop of Lincoln, in the presence of the King at Greenwich, an order signed by the King for him to be made a Serjeant at Law, and at the same time was knighted, and appointed the King's Serjeant. On the 3d of July following, he received the King's writ to that effect, dated the 26th of June; and in Michaelmas term, he was accordingly called to the rank of a Serjeant, with fourteen others, amongst whom were, Bridgeman, Sir Heneage Finch, Davenport, Bramston, and others, who afterwards arrived at high dignities in the law[g].

A happy union of learning, judgment, memory, talents, industry, and integrity, could not fail to open the road to fame and wealth. Sir George Croke appears to have had great practice as advocate, and was particularly celebrated for his skill in pleading causes[h]. His name occurs continually, as counsel, in the cases of the contemporary reporters. Of his zeal, and honest prejudices, in favour of the parties in whose causes he was engaged, so natural to a warm and honourable mind, he has frankly made a confession in his argument in Selden's case. "The "counsel have, of either side, pressed such reasons and arguments as they "thought convenient for the maintaining their opinions, and perhaps "with a prejudicate opinion: as I myself, by mine own experience, when "I was at the bar, have argued confidently, and I then thought the law "to be of that side for whom I argued. But after being at the bench, "weighing indifferently all reasons, and authorities, I have been of a dif-

[e] Blackstone, vol. i. p. 23. [f] Coke, Preface to vol. iii. of his Reports.

[g] Cro. Jac. p. 668, 671. Pref. Cro. Car.

[h] Judicio acri, et memoria tenaci fruebatur, quibus additâ singulari industriâ, amplissimum juris cognitionem, maxime autem in iis quæ ad causas agendas spectant, adeptus est. Denique virtutibus intellectualibus morales adjecit, fidem utique integerrimam, et munificentiam egregiam. Wood, Hist. et Antiq. Univ. Oxon. vol. ii. p. 64.

"ferent opinion, and so the law hath been adjudged, contrary to that "opinion, which I first confidently conceived[i]."

In 1618, when the citizens of Oxford, endeavoured to procure a new charter, which would have been injurious to the University, the Earl of Pembroke, the Chancellor, having notice of it, obtained a copy, which was examined by the University, and many exceptions were taken to it. They were put into the hands of Mr. John Walter, and Mr. George Croke, the Barrister, who digested and drew them up in due form[k].

Though the exact amount of his profits cannot be ascertained, there is sufficient proof that he acquired considerable wealth by his profession. As a younger brother he could have inherited no great fortune from his father. I had a letter from his elder brother, Sir John Croke, the Speaker of the House of Commons, and afterwards Judge, to borrow five hundred pounds of him, as is before mentioned

Before the year 1615, he purchased of Sir William Cave, the estate at Waterstock, which is now the property of William Henry Ashhurst. Esquire. This estate had come into the Cave family, by the marriage of Sir Thomas Cave, brother to Sir George Croke's grandmother, Prudence Cave, with Elizabeth Danvers, daughter and heiress of Sir John Danvers of Waterstock. For many years it had been in the Danvers family, as appeared by the coats of arms formerly in painted glass in the church and mansion-house. There were the quarterings and impalements of many families, with which they intermarried· Bruly, Quatermain, Mansel, Fowler, Verney, and others. Amongst them were those of William Waynflete, Bishop of Winchester, George Neville, Archbishop of York, and James Fenys, the latter with the date of 1480. That the arms of William of Waynflete were there, may be easily accounted for. Joan Danvers, relict of William Danvers, Esquire, was a benefactress to Magdalen College, in the life-time of the founder. In 1453, she granted the manor of Wike, alias Staneswyke, at Ashbury in Berkshire, which had descended to her from Rafe Stanes, to Waynflete, and other trustees, for the new Hall, which was afterwards transferred to the college. In return, the President and Society entered into an obliga-

[i] State Trials, vol. vii. [k] Wood's Annals Univ Oxon by Gutch, vol ii p 331.

tion to celebrate exequies *cum notâ* for her soul, and the souls of her husband, and of Matilda de Vere, Countess of Oxford, for which they were allowed a pittance. These obits continued till the Reformation, when they were changed into commemorations[l]. The arms of Waynflete were probably put up in remembrance of the connexion which subsisted between him and Joan Danvers, or to record a visit which he made to Waterstock. It was a very usual mark of respect, paid to persons of rank, and was frequently given by the visitors themselves. George Neville was brother to the celebrated Earl of Warwick, who was surnamed the King-maker, and was Archbishop of York from 1464, to 1476. It does not appear why his coat of arms was put up at Waterstock[m]. James Fenys, I suppose, was Lord Say and Seal, to whom the Danverses were related. For William of Wykeham's daughter Margaret married Sir William Fenys, (or Fiennes,) Lord Say and Seal. Edward Fenys, Lord Say and Seal, married Margaret, daughter of Sir John Danvers, and and his sister Elizabeth Fenys, married William Danvers. In the house were likewise the arms of Knolles, Harrington, and others, I know not how connected[n].

In 1621, he purchased Studley of his nephew, Sir John Croke of Chilton, and, besides lands in Chilton, given in exchange, he paid the sum of £1800 in money for it. I find receipts, which have been preserved, for the sum of £2420, before paid in 1600, to his brother Sir John Croke, the

[l] Chandler's Life of William Waynflete, 1811, page 86, 252.

[m] Godwin de Præsulibus, vol ii p 275. who has recorded an account of the magnificent dinner given at his installation.

[n] See post, the Genealogy of Barker from William of Wykeham, No. 42. See the account of the coats of arms in the church and mansion house at Waterstock, as they were in the year 1660, from Hutton's Collections for Oxfordshire. Rawlinson's MSS. Bibl. Bod. No 397. fol 343. in the Appendix, No XXXI. and the arms in the church rudely tricked by Wood. Wood's MSS Ashm. Mus No 8548 f 52. As they had survived destruction in the Rebellion, what became of those in the church? Those in the house, I suppose, were destroyed when it was taken down. In an heraldic visitation I find, Edwardus Cave de Waterstoke, Ar. filius tertius Thomæ Cave, milit. Duxit in uxorem Elizabetham filiam Johannis Conway de Arrowe in com. Warw. mil. et habuit exitum Fulconem. Harl. MSS. No. 5868, and Lee's visitation of Oxfordshire, in 1574, page 33. Anthony Wood's MSS. No. 8474, 12.

NO. 30

GENEALOGY OF BENNET

Thomas Bennet, of Clopcot, Esq near Wallingford, in Berks = Anne, daughter of — Molines, of Mackney, Com Oxon

Elizabeth Tisdale = Richard Bennet, first son and heir.

Mary, da. of Robt Taylor, Sheriff of London, 34 Eliz = Sir Thomas Bennet, third son, Sheriff of London 1594, 36 Eliz Lord Mayor, 1 Jac I 1603, when he was knighted

Children of Richard Bennet:

2 John Bennet, LL D ...r to the Earl of ...ville, of Dawley, died 1627, ...ried Anne Weeks.

1 Ralph Bennet, from whom the Bennets of Morden

3 Thomas, Alderman, &c two sons

Children of John Bennet:

1 ... Bennet, ...Dawley, ...arried ...thy Crofts.

2 Sir Thomas Bennet, LL D Master in Chancery

6 sons:

1 ..., K B. ...ron ...lston, ...ar II

2 Heneage, Earl of Arlington, by Car II 1672

3 Robert, S P

4 Charles, 1 son, and 2 daughters.

5 | 6 Thomas Edward S P

Isabella, mother to the Duke of Grafton

...arles, created Earl of Tankerville, 1714

Children of Sir Thomas Bennet:

Anne, married to William Duncombe, of Brickhill, Bucks

Mary = Sir George Croke

1 Simon, of Beechhampton, in Bucks, married Elizabeth, da of Sir Arth Ingram, Baronet, 1627, obiit S. P. 1632.

2 Richard, a merchant, married Elizabeth Cradock, afterwards married to Sir Heneage Finch

John, or Thomas Bennet

Simon Bennet, of Beechhampton, heir to his uncle = Grace, da and coheir of Gilbert Morewood; murdered at Colverton, 19 Sep. 1694, ætat 63, buried at Beechhampton

Three daughters

Edward Osborne, Lord Latimer, eldest son to the Earl of Danby, Lord Treasurer, afterwards Duke of Leeds = 1 Elizabeth, born 1659, died 1680 S P

John Bennet of Habington, Com Cantab. = 2 Grace, born 1664, had issue.

James Cecil, Earl of Salisbury, obiit 1694 = 3 Frances, born 1670

Judge, said to have been for lands bought at Studley, and for a further sum of £1200 in 1621, to his nephew, "due as by agreement[o]."

The exact time of his marriage has not been stated. His lady was *Mary*, the second daughter of Sir Thomas Bennet, by his wife, who was named likewise Mary, and was the daughter of Robert Taylor, Esquire, Sheriff of London, in the thirty-fourth year of Queen Elizabeth. Sir Thomas Bennet was the third son of Thomas Bennet, Esquire, of Clopcot near Wallingford in Berkshire, was Sheriff of London in the year 1594, and Lord Mayor in the first year of King James the First; by whom he was knighted. And he was brother to Richard Bennet, the ancestor of the Earl of Arlington, in the reign of Charles the Second, and of the present Earl of Tankerville Lady Croke's elder sister Anne, married William Duncombe, of Brickhill in Buckinghamshire, Esquire. Simon, her eldest brother, was seated at Beechampton in Buckinghamshire, married Elizabeth, the daughter of Sir Arthur Ingram, and was created a Baronet in 1627 Richard, her second brother, was an eminent merchant in London, and the grandfather to three heiresses, who became the wives of Lord Latimer, John Bennet, Esquire, and James Cecil, Earl of Salisbury. His widow Elizabeth, daughter of William Cradock, Esquire, afterwards married Sir Heneage Finch[p].

Upon the 11th of February, 1624, the twenty-second year of James, he was created one of the Justices of the Common Pleas, then more usually called the Common Bench, in the place of Sir Humphrey Winch[q]. In Hilary term, 1627, with the rest of the Judges, he subscribed some orders to be observed in the houses of the Courts of Law· as he did afterwards, in 1630, for the government of the Inns of Court and Chancery[r].

After the death of Sir John Dodridge, in 1628, the fourth year of King Charles, there being then five Judges in the Common Pleas, the King, intending to reduce them to their usual number, upon the 23d of September, having had communication with the Lord Keeper Coventry, nominated Sir George Croke to be one of the Justices of the King's

[o] Penes me

[p] Collins's Peerage, vol iii page 364 edition 1756. By an error he calls her Margaret, instead of Mary See the Genealogy of Bennet, from Collins, and Brown Willis's MSS vol. 19. No. 30.

[q] Cro Jac. page 699 [r] Dugd. Orig. Jurid p. 321.

Bench, and signed a warrant the same day for his patent, and another warrant, reciting his first patent of Justice of the Common Pleas, and determining his pleasure concerning that place, saving all wages and sums due. The patent of Justice of the King's Bench was dated and sealed upon the 9th day of October, the patent of revocation of his former appointment upon the 10th, and both were delivered to him upon the 11th, when he was sworn in[s].

Upon this occasion a question was raised respecting his precedency. Previously to this removal, he had three puisnès, or juniors, upon the Bench; one in the Common Pleas, and two of the Barons in the Exchequer, and there was no clause in his patent, saving his superiority, precedency, and antiquity, as had been the case in the second patent of Justice Nichols. It was doubted therefore, whether his appointment to the King's Bench was not to be considered as a new appointment, which would bring him in as puisnè to all the Judges, whose rank is determined according to the date of their patents But all the Judges, assembled at the Lord Keeper's house, agreed, "That he needed not such a saving "For his patent continued untill the time he was Judge of the King's "Bench, and he never ceased to be a Judge, but was translated only" And they conceived that "the patent of revocation of his place as Justice "in the Common Pleas was needless, because, by making him Justice in "the King's Bench, his former patent was in law determined, according "to the case in Dyer, 5 Mar 159, yet for better security, there was one "made, according to the president of Justice Jones his patent, when he "was removed out of the Common Pleas to be Judge in the King's "Bench[t]."

Towards the conclusion of Sir George Croke's life, in the disputes between the King and the Parliament, the kingdom had arrived at one of the most important crisises in which any country was ever involved. Each party pretended to found its claims upon law and right, and it must be admitted, that, at the commencement of the contest, they were both on the side of the Parliament For it was indisputably the object of the King, however excellent his private character, to render his power despotic, and independent of his Parliament, whilst it was, at least, the ostensible

[s] Cro Car p 127 [t] Ibid

purpose of the Parliament, to maintain the ancient free constitution of the country.

But the state of the question was soon changed. Charles had complied with every reasonable demand, and had surrendered every offensive part of his prerogative. This period may be fixed, at the time when he gave his assent to the bills for the abolition of the High Commission Court, and the Star Chamber. The subject had then obtained the confirmation of every right, which was essential to his freedom. The Crown was left in possession of all the prerogatives, which were absolutely necessary to the executive power, and of no others. And the constitution was settled, nearly according to its present form, which is justly considered as a model of political wisdom.

From this time it became evident, that no concessions on the part of the Crown were sufficient to satisfy the Parliamentary leaders, and that they had a settled design to overturn the established laws and constitution, to abolish the monarchy, and to establish a republic in its place. They began by depriving the King of the command of the militia, and were proceeding to strip him of every part of his just authority. Farther submission would have been to betray the sacred trust, with which he was invested, and he was compelled to make a stand in his own defence, and that of the lawful constitution of his country. A civil war was the consequence, which ended in the King's defeat, the triumph of his adversaries, and the erection of a commonwealth. The struggles for power between different factions, the inevitable concomitant of that unstable form of policy, ended in a military government, and the tyranny of Cromwell. The people, at length, having experienced the inadequacy of all the projected schemes of government to promote their happiness, and sensible that they had only been the dupes of crafty and ambitious men, were glad to retrace their steps, and to return to the old legitimate limited monarchy.

Such is the short history of this contest. It was the fortune of Sir George Croke to live in the earliest part of it only, when the Crown was assuming very unjustifiable powers. To establish, and rivet them upon the people, the Courts of Justice were used as the principal instruments, and no means were left unattempted, by threats, persuasion, and promises, to render them subservient to the views of the court. The virtuous Sir Edward Coke, and several others, had been removed for want of sufficient servility. The place of Chief Justice was occupied by Finch, a man whose talents were employed only to gratify his ambition and most of the other Judges were awed, or cajoled into submission. Wherever the Crown was interested, the decisions were uniformly in its favour, and these partial judgments were amongst the principal causes of the subsequent calamities

In these unjustifiable proceedings Sir George Croke did not concur; and unterrified by the menaces, and uninfluenced by the fascinations of power, upon every occasion, followed the dictates of his own conscience, and gave his opinion in favour of the rights of the people. Although he was but little supported, and his opinions were generally overruled by the majority of the Judges, yet they had great influence upon the public mind, and contributed not a little to those measures by which the liberties of the country were finally established. To appreciate properly the merit and the utility of his conduct, it will be necessary to shew how much those liberties were indangered by the attempts of the Crown.

Of the three absolute rights of man, which civil society was instituted to protect, that of *personal security*, indeed, in the enjoyment of life and limb, could not well have been violated in a civilized country, or by any but a most lawless and savage despot; but powers which were totally subversive of the other two rights, *personal liberty*, and the *right of property*, were claimed and exercised by this unfortunate monarch. Nor was any thing further wanting to establish a perfect despotism, than his succeeding in these attempts, for a sovereign who can *imprison* or *tax* his subjects, without control, has the unlimited command over a nation Upon these two essential points the country found an able supporter in Sir George Croke

First. PERSONAL LIBERTY, by which no man can be imprisoned unless by due course of law, is essential to a free state. In every country where the magistrate or the sovereign is invested with the power of arbitrary imprisonment the subject is completely inslaved, and holds every other right by a precarious tenure.

I shall say nothing of the High Commission Court, or the Star Chamber, because, however inconsistent with liberty, they were certainly established by the law of the land, till they were abolished by Act of Parliament. But the most objectionable and illegal power assumed by the

King, was that of *imprisonment by a warrant from the Privy Council, without bail, and for a great length of time, without the parties being brought to trial.* Such imprisonments had frequently taken place in the last and former reigns. Charles continued to exercise a power which he believed to be lawful, and he exerted it, with little scruple, upon every occasion, where the public or even the private, conduct of individuals, had unfortunately incurred his displeasure. In 1626, *Sir Dudley Diggs*, and *Sir John Elliot*, were committed to the Tower, for exercising a truly legitimate right, in being managers for the Commons in the impeachment of the Duke of Buckingham. They were however soon released[u]. The Earl of Arundel was committed for having married his son to the Duke of Lenox's sister; but he was released upon the application of the House of Peers[x]. Of those who refused to lend the King the sums required by the Commissioners of loans, some were sent on board ships to serve as mariners, others were pressed as soldiers, *Sir Peter Hayman* was dispatched upon an errand to the Palatinate, and many others were imprisoned in close confinement, in common jails, and out of their own counties. Just before the meeting of the Parliament, in 1627, they were all discharged[y]. Many were imprisoned without any cause shewn, and when it was certified, upon their being brought up by *habeas corpus*, that they were committed by his Majesty's command, they were returned back to prison[z].

These harsh measures occasioned the interference of Parliament, and the celebrated Act, called the *Petition of Right*, was the consequence; by which it was enacted, that no freeman should be imprisoned, unless by the lawful judgment of his Peers, or the law of the land[a]. But this law, conclusive as it seemed, proved no security to the subject, and arbitrary imprisonments by the Privy Council again took place. Even the writ of *habeas corpus*, which the law had provided as a remedy in cases of false imprisonment, was evaded, by removing the persons committed from prison to prison, and other artful means[b].

These unjustifiable proceedings were opposed by Sir George Croke. Upon every motion for an *habeas corpus*, or for a discharge from custody, where the party was legally intitled to it, he always gave his decided opi-

[u] Whitelocke, p 6 [x] Ibid. [y] Ibid p 8 [z] Ibid [a] 3 Car. I. [b] Whitelocke, page 13

mon that it should be granted: though his vote was often rendered nugatory by the number of the other Judges.

Thus in the case of *Atkinson* in 1629, who had been committed by the Lord Chamberlain, for suing a servant of the King, without his leave, had been once delivered by an *habeas corpus*, and was again committed by the Lord Chamberlain; Sir George Croke, with Jones, and Whitelocke, in opposition to Hyde, the Chief Justice, granted a new *habeas corpus* [c].

But the principal case was that of the celebrated *Selden*, who, with *Hollis*, *Hobert*, *Elliot*, *Heyman*, *Coriton*, *Long*, *Stroud*, and *Valentine*, were committed for their language and proceedings in Parliament; which the King, in his speech upon the dissolution of it, was pleased to call "*the* "*seditious conduct of some vipers*" A particular statement of this case will shew the oppressive nature of this power which was assumed by the Crown, and the vexatious manner in which it was exercised.

The first warrant of the Privy Council, under which they were committed to prison, was dated the 2d day of April, 1629, and stated no cause, but only *His Majesty's pleasure and commandment.* A month afterwards, on the 7th of May, a second warrant issued for their detention, "*for notable contempts committed against the King and government, and* "*for stirring up sedition.*" They applied for writs of *habeas corpus*, but upon the day when they were to have been brought up to hear the opinion of the court upon them, the prisoners did not appear, and therefore could receive no benefit from the writs. This was a manœuvre on the part of the King, who had removed some of them from the prisons in which they were before, and to the keepers of which the writs had been directed, and had committed them to the Tower. A letter was sent from the King to the Judges, dated the 27th of July, 1629, to inform the court of the reason why he had not suffered them to appear, "*that they had carried them-* "*selves insolently and unmanneredly towards the King and the Judges,* "*and therefore he did not think their presence necessary, until their* "*temper and discretion should be such as to deserve it*" *Selden* and *Valentine* were however permitted to appear the next day. Three hours after, came another letter from the King, to inform the Judges, that "*upon*

[c] Whitelocke, page 13 b

"*more solemn deliberation, Selden and Valentine were not to be brought* "*up, but that all should receive the same treatment.*" He recommended likewise that the opinions of all the other Judges should be taken. From this intended delay, the court could give no opinion upon the writs of *habeas corpus*, and the parties continued in prison the whole of the long vacation. Towards the end of the vacation the King sent for the Chief Justice, and *Judge Whitlock*, and told them "*that he was* "*contented they should be bailed, if they would express their sor-* "*row for the King's being offended with them.*" In Michaelmas Term the prisoners were brought up, and informed that the court was willing to discharge them upon giving bail, and also finding sureties for their good behaviour. In prescribing these conditions, *Sir George Croke* did not concur with the other Judges, and was of opinion that they were intitled *to be bailed absolutely*, but his opinion was overruled by the rest. The prisoners considered these conditions as illegal, since sureties for good behaviour were never required but from persons held to have been guilty of some heinous, or at least infamous crime, and it was an implication that they were guilty of the matters objected Upon their refusal to find such sureties, they were therefore remanded to close custody in the Tower, and the Chief Justice informed them at the same time, that *perhaps the court would not afterwards grant an habeas corpus.* A denial of justice, which was considered, by all the eminent lawyers present, as a monstrous perversion of the law, but which was adhered to by the court: for upon a subsequent application of Mr. Littleton for another *habeas corpus*, for the question to be again argued, the Judges refused, and said, that *unless Selden would certify under his hand that he would enter into such a security, they would no more grant an habeas corpus*[d].

Proceedings were commenced against them in the Star Chamber, but they were dropped. Sir John Elliot, Hollis, and Valentine, were prosecuted in the Court of King's Bench, and were fined and imprisoned by the sentence of the court[e]. But Selden was not proceeded against, and was detained in prison upon the original grounds, of not putting in sureties for his good behaviour[f]. In the end of November, by a warrant from the Privy Council, his close confinement was relaxed, and he was permitted

[d] State Trials, vol vii p 29, &c. Rushworth, Whitelock. [e] Ibid. [f] Selden's Vindiciæ Maris Clausi, p 1433 a 1428 b

some liberty within the walls of the Tower, and to see his friends Soon after he procured himself by an *habeas corpus* to be removed to the Marshalsea prison, from thence, in May, 1630, to the Gate-House, in Westminster, from whence he was again remanded to the Marshalsea During this time, many applications were made, at different intervals, to procure his liberty by *habeas corpus*, but all in vain; till at length, in May, 1631, by the interest of the Earls of Arundel and Pembroke, he was discharged, upon giving *bail for his appearance only* After making his appearance in the Court of King's Bench from term to term, according to the tenor of his bailment, in January, 1634, upon his petition to the King, he was absolutely discharged[g].

Thus was a member of Parliament, one of the first characters in the kingdom for learning, talents, and respectability, by a mere mandate of the Privy Council, illegally kept in custody, without being convicted of any crime, or brought to trial, for the space of six years; of which, for near nine months, he was in close confinement, for above two years more, in prison, with more or less indulgence; and for the rest of the time in the legal custody of his bail. Nor was this a mere nominal imprisonment, within the rules of a court, but during part of the time close and severe During the nine months he was in the Tower, his friends were denied all access to him, and he was prohibited for three months from the use of books, paper, pens, and ink. At length leave was obtained from the Privy Council that he might have the use of certain books, of which he gave a catalogue[h]. Nineteen sheets of writing paper were allowed him, marked each by the Lieutenant of the Tower, of which, and of whatever he might write upon them, a regular account was required to be given[i].

These oppressions, in violation of the Petition of Right, engaged the attention of Parliament in the year 1640, and produced the celebrated *habeas corpus act*, a noble remedy, and which was finally completed by subsequent statutes. In the debates upon that Bill, the indignation of the House of Commons was justly excited by these cases It was resolved, that "*there was a delay of justice towards Mr. Selden, Hollis, and the* "*rest, in that they were not bailed upon the writs of habeas corpus.*"

[g] Vindiciæ That is 1635 [h] They were the Bible, both the Talmuds, some modern books of Talmudical learning, and Lucian [i] Selden's Vindiciæ

"*That Sir George Croke, then one of the Judges of the King's Bench,* "*was not guilty of this delay, and that Mr. Selden, Hollis, and the* "*others, should have reparation for their respective damages and suffer-* "*ings against the Lords of the Council, and the Judges of the King's* "*Bench,*" and the sums of £5000 each were awarded to most of them[k]. *Hyde*, *Jones*, and *Whitelocke*, were named as the guilty persons, but *Whitelocke's* son, afterwards Ambassador in Sweden, having assured the House, that his opinion and carriage in the case of *habeas corpus* were well known to have been the same with that of *Judge Croke*, which was confirmed by *Hambden* and others, he was considered by the House in the same degree with that Judge, as to their censure and proceedings[l].

2. The other most important right is that of PROPERTY; which was likewise invaded. If the King could take the money of his subjects without their consent in parliament, property was no longer secure; parliaments, being no longer necessary, would be laid aside, and the Sovereign would be despotic The various attempts to establish this power in the Crown which had been made in the early part of Charles's reign, had been strenuously resisted, and, as it was conceived, the claim itself had been finally annulled by the Petition of Right. But this statute was soon evaded, and still farther efforts were made to render the King independent of his parliaments This was done by the writs, which issued by the King's sole authority, to tax all the counties in England for the ostensible purpose of finding ships, and furnishing them with men and provisions

The general occasion of raising this tax was not fictitious. The other powers of Europe were in arms. The coasts were actually much infested by pirates, to the great prejudice of commerce That the narrow seas were not guarded was one of the grievances complained of by the House of Commons, in 1625. That pirates infested the coasts, that trade had

[k] Journals of the House of Commons, July 6 and 8, 1641. Selden's opposition was merely on account of what he considered as the illegality of the King's proceedings, not any enmity to the monarchy itself At a subsequent period, upon the intended removal of the Lord Keeper Littleton, the King proposed to deliver the seals to Selden, whose affection to him was not doubted. They were not however offered to him, because it was thought he would refuse them, on account of his age and dislike of business. Clarendon, vol i part ii page 770 ed 1819.

[l] Whitelocke's Memorials, page 37

decayed, and the national honour suffered, was a charge against the Duke of Buckingham. The Dutch had become masters of the sea; and the disputes relating to the fisheries had given occasion to the celebrated controversy between Grotius and Selden, respecting the freedom of the seas[m]. It had become necessary to support the honour of the kingdom by a more powerful fleet. Nor was there afterwards any suggestion that the money which was raised had been embezzled, or misapplied. In the summer of 1635, by the help of this tax, a powerful navy of sixty ships had protected the narrow seas, and the trade of the country; the Dutch fishing boats, which had encroached upon the British territories, were repressed, and they had been compelled to pay thirty thousand pounds for a licence to fish in those waters. But if the right of levying this tax had been once established, there was no security as to the future application of the money raised, and it would have afforded an unlimited fund for any purpose to which the King might think proper to apply it[n].

At first, in 1634, writs had been directed to the *Cinque Ports*, and other maritime places only, to prepare a certain number of ships· which was not much objected to, or opposed. But the next year, 1635, the King, intending to increase the navy still more, issued new writs, directed not only to the maritime places, but to every county in England. It was a favourite measure with the King, and to ensure its success, *the Lord Keeper Coventry*, by his Majesty's command, in his usual address to the Judges, before their departure to hold the Assizes, on June 17th, 1635, required them to take every occasion in their charges, and otherwise "*to let the people know how careful his Majesty was to preserve his* "*honour, and the honour of the kingdom, and the dominion of the sea,* "*and to secure both land and sea by a powerful fleet, that foreign nations* "*might see that England was both able and ready to keep itself, and all* "*its rights.*" And the Judges were to let them know, "*how just it was* "*that his Majesty should require this supply for the common defence.* "*and with what alacrity and chearfulness they ought, and were bound* "*in duty, to contribute to it.*" In December of the same year the King privately took the opinion of the Judges upon the general question.

For the most part, the tax was submitted to and paid, and, in parti-

[m] Whitelocke, p. 22, 3, and 6 [n] Clarendon, i. p 121

cular, the sum of twelve thousand pounds, which had been assessed upon the county of York. But many, as Whitelocke observes, were not convinced by the Judges of its legality, great discontent was expressed, and actions were brought against the officers employed in the execution of the writs[o]. Upon this opposition, the King required the more solemn opinion of the twelve Judges, upon a case stated in a letter addressed to them on the second of February, 1636. Every exertion was made by Lord Chief Justice Finch to obtain an answer favourable to the Crown. By great solicitation, promises of preferment, and even threats, he at length procured the following opinion[p]

May it please your most excellent Majesty,

We have according to your Majesty's command, every man by himself, and all of us together, taken into consideration the case and question, signed by your Majesty, and inclosed in your royal letter; And we are of opinion, that when the good and safety of the kingdom in general is concerned, and the whole kingdom in danger, your Majesty may by writ, under the great seal of England, command all the subjects of this your kingdom, at their charge, to provide and furnish such number of ships, with men, munition, and victuals, and for such time as your Majesty shall think fit, for the defence and safeguard of the kingdom from such danger and peril· And that by law your Majesty may compel the doing thereof, in case of refusal or refractoriness: And we are also of opinion, that in such case, your Majesty is the sole judge, both of the dangers, and when, and how the same is to be prevented and avoided

Jo. Brampston.	Rich. Hutton.	Geo. Vernon.
Jo. Finch.	W. Jones.	Fra Crawley.
Humph. Davenport.	Geo Croke	Robt. Berkley
Jo. Denham.	Tho. Trevor.	Fra. Weston.

This opinion was thus signed, the 7th of February, 1636, by all the twelve Judges; but, at the time, two of them, at least, Sir George Croke, and Mr. Justice Hutton, dissented from it, and subscribed for conformity only. It was published, and inrolled in all the courts of law.

[o] Whitelocke, p. 24 [p] Ibid. p 23

Amongst those who had opposed these writs was *John Hambden, Esquire*, a gentleman of family and fortune in Buckinghamshire. He was proceeded against in the Exchequer, and the cause was tried, upon a demurrer, before all the Judges, in the Exchequer Chamber.

By the writ it was commanded, that the county of Buckingham should provide a ship of war of 450 tons, with 180 men, and all things necessary, and should bring her to Portsmouth by the 1st of March, provided for six and twenty weeks, for the defence of the kingdom, the guarding of the sea, the security of the subjects, and the safe conduct of ships, the sea being infested with pirates. To effect this, power was given to the Sheriff to assess each person within the county according to his state and faculties, and to enforce compliance by distress and imprisonment. The sum assessed upon *Hambden* was twenty shillings, which he refused to pay, and the legality of the charge was the question to be decided.

The whole nation regarded with the utmost anxiety the event of this celebrated trial, one of the most important which ever came before a court of justice. On the one side, the power and prerogative of the Crown were at stake, and, on the part of the subjects, it involved their dearest interests, their liberty, persons, and estates It was argued, on the behalf of Mr Hambden, by St. John, and Holborne, and for the Crown, by Sir John Banks, the Attorney General, and Sir Edward Littleton, the Solicitor General; and afterwards by the twelve Judges. The cause was conducted with talents and exertions, equal to its importance. The arguments were elaborate, learned, and powerful. Reason, history, and authorities, were appealed to. Laws and statutes, from the remotest antiquity, to the present times, precedents, Parliament rolls, records, and decisions of courts, particularly of the Exchequer, to the number of upwards of three hundred, were produced, on one side, or the other, at the bar or on the bench.

After the counsel had concluded their arguments, which occupied twelve days, the Judges separately delivered their opinions at length; beginning with the junior, according to the usual practice of the court. After five of the Judges, Sir Francis Weston, Sir Francis Crawley, Sir Robert Berkley, Sir George Vernon, and Sir Thomas Trevor, had delivered their opinions in favour of the Crown, Sir George Croke, on the 14th of April, 1638, contrary to expectation, gave his judgment for Hambden. His non-concurrence in the opinion delivered to the King, to which his signature appeared, had not been generally known. From the persuasions of the King's friends, from his unwillingness to differ from his brethren upon the Bench; and perhaps from his benevolent wishes, not to give occasion to disturbances in the country, and to foment the divisions and the vehement party spirit, which now began to shew themselves, and of which he foresaw and feared the consequences, he had resolved to deliver his opinion for the King, and to that end had prepared his argument. Yet a few days before he was to argue, upon discourse with some of his nearest relations, and most serious thoughts of this business, he resolved not to give an opinion which in his real judgment he could not approve. He was particularly confirmed in this resolution by his lady, who was a very good and pious woman, and told her husband upon this occasion, "*that she hoped he* "*would do nothing against his conscience, for fear of any danger, or* "*prejudice to him or his family; and that she would be contented to* "*suffer want, or any misery with him, rather than be an occasion for* "*him to do or say any thing against his judgment, and conscience.*" A noble example of spirited and honourable conduct in a lady! Upon these and other encouragements, but chiefly upon his better thoughts, he suddenly altered his purpose and arguments, and when it came to his turn, he argued and declared his opinion against the King[q]

Before he proceeded to his argument, he obviated a difficulty, which had been much pressed by the Solicitor General, *That the case had been resolved by the opinions of all the Judges under their own hands* He admitted that he had set his hand to two opinions, of which the first in December, 1635, being more general, he still maintained, but with respect to the second opinion before stated, he confessed, " that he subscribed his " hand, but he then dissented to that opinion, and then signified his opi- " nion to be, that such a charge could not be laid by any such writ, but by " parliament. But the greater part seeming absolutely to be resolved " upon that opinion, some of them affirming that they had seen diverse " records and precedents of such writs, satisfying them to be of that " judgment, he was pressed to subscribe with them, for that the major " part must involve the rest, as it was said to be usual in cases of differ-

q Whitelocke's Memorials, page 24

" ence, and for that the lesser number must submit to the major, although " they varied in opinion, as it is in the courts, if three Judges agree in " opinion against one, or two, where there are five Judges, judgment is " to be entered *per curiam*. And in cases of conference and certificate of " their opinions, if the greater part did agree and subscribe, the rest were " to submit their opinions. And this by more ancient Judges than " myself was affirmed to be the continual practice. And that it was not " fit, especially in a case of this nature, so much concerning the service of " the King, for some to subscribe, and some to forbear their subscriptions. " And that although we did subscribe, it did not bind us, but that in point " of judgment, if the case came in question judicially before us, we " should give our judgments as we should see cause after the arguments " on both sides.

" Hereupon I consented to subscribe, with such protestations, only for " conformity. But this being before arguments heard on both sides, or " any precedents seen, I hold that none is bound by that opinion. And " if I had been of that opinion absolutely, now having heard all the argu- " ments of both sides, and the reasons of the King's counsel to maintain " this writ, and the arguments of the defendant's counsel against it, and " having duly considered the records and precedents, cited and shewed to " me, especially those of the King's side, I am now of an absolute opinion " that this writ is illegal, and declare my opinion to be contrary to that " which was subscribed by us all. And if I had been of that opinion, " yet, upon better advisement, being absolutely settled in my judgment, " and conscience, in a contrary opinion, I think it no shame to declare " that I do retract that opinion, for *humanum est errare*, rather than to " argue against my own conscience."

After this manly avowal of his conduct and sentiments, he proceeded with his argument. He stated six points. FIRST, that the command to make ships at the charge of the inhabitants of the country, not being by authority of Parliament, was illegal, and contrary to the *common law*. SECONDLY, that it was expressly contrary to diverse *statutes*. THIRDLY, that it was not to be maintained by any *prerogative royal*, nor allegation of *necessity* or *danger*. FOURTHLY, that, admitting it were legal to lay such charge upon *maritime* ports, yet to charge an *inland* county is illegal, and not warranted by any former precedent. FIFTHLY, I shall examine the *precedents and records*, cited to warrant the writ. And, SIXTHLY, I shall examine this particular *writ*, and do conceive it is illegal, and not sufficient to ground this charge.

The FIRST point he proved, by shewing, that this was the first writ since the Conquest, which went to any inland county to that effect, and therefore that it was against the common law. That the common law of England settleth a freedom in the subjects in respect of their persons, and giveth them a true property in their goods and estates, so that without their consent, either actual, or implicite, by a common ordinance which they consented unto by a common assent in Parliament, it cannot be taken from them, nor their estates charged; and for this purpose the law distinguisheth between bondmen, whose estates are at their Lord's freewill and disposition, and freemen, whose property none may invade, charge, or unjustly take away, but by their own free consent; and this constitutional doctrine he proved by numerous authorities. That if it were allowed, no man would know what his charge may be, for they may be charged as often as the King pleases, and with making as many ships as should be appointed And, besides, it is left in the power of the Sheriff, to charge any man's estate at his pleasure.

SECONDLY. If the common law were doubtful, it is made clear by diverse express statutes, which he stated; from that of the twenty-fifth year of Edward the First, by which it was enacted, that "no aids, taxes, "or prizes, should be taken, but by the common assent of the realm," to the Petition of Right passed in the third year of the King. Amongst which, the Act of the twenty-first of Henry the Fourth, was shewn to be directly to the very point, stating, that "of late commissions had been "made to cities and boroughs, to make barges and barringers, without "assent of Parliament, and therefore declaring them void."

THIRDLY. And whereas the arguments had been, that the kingdom being in danger, there could not so suddenly any Parliament be called, and the kingdom might be lost: the writ so mentioning, and that being *recordum superlativum*. To all these he answered, amongst other things, that the suggestions of danger in the writ were not absolute, or sufficient And if they were, that we are not always bound absolutely to believe them: because many times untrue suggestions are put into writs and patents, which may be traversed. Yet the law doth not impute any untruth to the King, but that he is abused therein, and attributeth the falsehood to those who misinformed him.

If the danger were real, yet a charge must not be laid upon the subjects without their consent in Parliament; for either it is near, and then present provision must be made by men's persons, and the present ships of the kingdom, which the King may command, but he cannot command money out of men's purses. But if the danger be further off, the King may call his sages together for such defence. And here, if there be time to make ships at the charge of the counties, there is time enough to call a Parliament. And seven months are allowed by the writ to prepare the ships.

Where it has been urged, that this writ is warranted by the King's prerogative, to this I answer, that I do not conceive there is any such prerogative, for if it were, I should not speak against it, for it is part of our oaths to maintain the prerogative. But if it is against the common law and the statutes, then there is no such prerogative, for the King can do nothing contrary to the law. *Nihil aliud potest Rex in terris quam de jure potest.* And whatever is done to the hurt or wrong of the subjects, and against the laws of the land, the law accounteth, that it is not done by the King, but by some untrue and unjust informations, and is therefore void. And if it be illegal to impose such a charge, it is not to be considered as a matter of royal power, but as a matter done upon a false suggestion, to be imputed not to the King, but to those who advised him.

The royal power, indeed, is to be used, in cases of necessity, and imminent danger, when ordinary courses will not avail, as in cases of rebellion, sudden invasion, and the like. But in a time of peace, and no extreme necessity, legal courses must be used, and not royal power. But there can be no such necessity or danger conceived, that may cause these writs to be awarded. For the laws have provided means for defence in times of danger, without taking this course, for the King hath power to command all persons to attend with arms, at the sea coast, to defend the kingdom, and also to make stay or arrest of the ships of merchants, to go with his navy, to any part of the kingdom for defence thereof. And this was always conceived to be sufficient. This course he shewed had been always taken, and no other was resorted to, even in the case of the threatened invasion by the Spanish Armada.

FOURTHLY. If it were legal to lay such charge upon maritime ports, yet, to charge an inland county with making ships, where there are no shipwrights, masters, or mariners, and is utterly unconversant with sea affairs, is not legal, for it commandeth an unreasonable and impossible thing to be done, which is contrary to law. For *lex non cogit ad impossibilia.*

But the FIFTH and great point, and indeed the chief argument in favour of the Crown, was a multitude of records and precedents, which had been cited to warrant the writ, and to shew, that the King had done nothing but what his progenitors have done.

I confess this allegation much troubled me, when I heard these records cited, and so learnedly and so earnestly pressed to be so clear, that they could not be gainsayed But having perused them, and satisfied my judgment therein, I now answer, that if there were any such precedent, (as I shall shew there was not one,) to prove this writ to be usual, yet it were not material, for now we are not to argue what has been done *de facto*, for many things have been done, which were never allowed, but our question is, what hath been done, and may be done, *de jure*, and then as it is said in Coke, *multitudo errantium non parit errori patrocinium.* Multitudes of precedents, unless they be confirmed by judicial proceedings in courts of record, are not to be regarded; and none of these were ever confirmed by judicial record, but complained of.

But to give a more clear answer unto them. Upon serious reading of all the records which have been sent me on the King's part, I conceive that there is not *any precedent or record of any such writ.*

It is true, that before the twenty-fifth year of Edward the First, there have been some writs to maritime towns, to provide and prepare ships upon just cause of fear of any danger, sometimes at the King's charge, but sometimes at the charge of the towns, which occasioned the complaint in Parliament, in the twenty-fifth of Edward, and the making of that statute, and there is no record of that reign since, to maritime towns, to prepare ships at their own charge.

In the time of Edward the Third, indeed, writs were again awarded to maritime towns, to send ships at their own charge, which were the principal cause of the statute 14 Ed. III. c. 1. After that statute, no such writs or commissions issued, but one, but that is fully satisfied, for it was grounded upon an ordinance of Parliament, in the first year of Richard the Second.

After this general answer, he took a view of all the records which had been cited, near ninety in number, and shewed that none of them proved these writs to be legal, that they were only for arrays of men with arms, and for collecting ships in the ports and maritime places; and none of these at their own expence, since the statute of the fourteenth year of Edward the Third, and none to make or prepare ships at the charges of the counties, upon any occasion whatever.

Having discussed the principal question, he proceeded in the SIXTH place to examine the writ itself, which he proved not to be legally issued, or warranted by any former precedent

That the motives mentioned in it were not alledged as certain, and were besides not sufficient. That all former precedents for providing ships had alledged, that great navies had been armed by foreign princes to invade the kingdom: but to make such preparations against pirates was never heard of, but the course had been, for the Admiral to secure the coast with a few ships. That the command of the writ to inland counties to find a ship, which is impossible, and to find provisions for the men out of their own county, is contrary to law. That the command to the Sheriff to assess men at his own discretion, is not legal That the power of imprisonment is illegal, being contrary to *Magna Charta*, and other statutes. That other parts of the writ could not be performed. That it was not certified, so long after the writ had issued, that a ship had been provided, and therefore that there is no cause to charge the defendant.

Lastly, he objected to the *mode of proceeding*, and that the writs of *Certiorari* and *Scire facias* were irregular, and not good.

He concluded therefore, upon the whole matter, that no judgment could be given to charge the defendant.

I have omitted many lesser arguments, particularly those of a mere legal nature, and I have only given the heads of the principal, as every position was proved at great length, by quotations and authorities To every impartial mind, it must have carried complete conviction, and I will venture to say, that a more learned, masterly, luminous, or dignified argument, was never delivered in a Court of Justice.

He was followed, in favour of Hambden, by Sir Richard Hutton, and Sir Humphrey Davenport, the Lord Chief Baron, and by Sir John Denham, without any argument, as he was not able to attend.

An elaborate answer to Sir George Croke, and the other arguments in favour of Hambden, was given by Sir John Finch, the Chief Justice of the Common Pleas, abounding with much ingenious sophistry, and which rather served to make more manifest the weakness of the King's cause. than to support it The principal foundation of his reasoning was the supposition of a case of danger to the kingdom, of the sufficiency of the King's writ to prove it, the necessity that he should provide against it, and the consequential power of calling for the assistance of all his subjects for defence. It was alledged, that the power of imposing this charge must be solely vested in the King. for since the laws had intrusted him with the power of defending the kingdom, it must necessarily have given him the means of executing his trust. With regard to the precedents produced, it was denied that they were irrelevant, and if they were *not directly in point as to the very mode*, they were in point as to the principle, namely, that the King had called upon his subjects for their services in time of danger That no distinction could be made between the sea and the land, for that the sea was the King's as well as the land, and he might command the services of his subjects on the one, as well as the other.

The statutes against the power of raising talliage, aids, and other taxes, were evaded by nice distinctions, and it was said that they must be understood only of *unjust* exactions, and such as were levied for the King's *own emolument*, and not of a revenue raised for the good of the country, and for necessary defence. And, still farther, this necessary power for the defence of the kingdom was said to be one of the *high prerogatives* of the King, and that though Acts of Parliament might "take away the flowers "and ornaments of the Crown, they could not take away the Crown it-"self, they could not bar a King of his regality, and therefore Acts to take "away his royal power in the defence of the kingdom, or to bind him not "to command his subjects, their persons, and goods, and, I say, said the "Chief Justice, their money too, are void."

It was said that the writ does not command an assessment, but ships to be provided; that the assessment was not absolutely necessary, and therefore that it was not a talliage, but a service. Yet, with the inconsistency natural to those who argue against the truth, when pressed with the reasoning of the impossibility of finding a ship in an inland county, he observed, that it was to be performed by the money raised. In answer to the objection, that by law no man could be compelled to go out of his county, it was stated, that the sea and land made but one entire kingdom, and therefore that going to sea was not going out of the realm, that the question before the court was not on an imprisonment, but on an assessment, and that if the writ was illegal in form and circumstances, yet that would not make the command illegal for substance

Notwithstanding the able arguments in his favour, judgment was given *against Hambden*, but a great part of the nation was satisfied that the decision was contrary to law, and the Judges were loaded with reproach and infamy, for prostituting the dignity of a court of law to the favour of a prince[r]. The argument of Sir George Croke, from his known learning, independence, and integrity, had great weight with the country, which was justly alarmed at this subversion of its best rights, and the proceedings in this case were one of the principal causes of the subsequent calamities.

In the Parliament of 1640, it was unanimously voted by the two Houses, that " *ship-money, the extra judicial opinion of the Judges, the writ it-*" *self, and the judgment against Mr Hambden, were against the laws*" *of the realm, the right of property, and the liberty of the subjects,*" *contrary to former resolutions in Parliament, and to the petition of*" *right. And were so declared by an Act of Parliament 16th Car*" *cap.* 14." The records of that judgment, and the opinion of the Judges, were ordered to be brought into the Upper House by the Chancellor, and chief Judges, to be vacated and cancelled.

The next day a committee was appointed to draw up a charge of treason against such as had been abetters therein, Finch, who was now the Lord Keeper, and the rest of the Judges[s] Finch appeared upon his impeachment, and made a very submissive speech in the House of Commons, yet he was voted a traitor, amongst other charges, for " soliciting, persuading, " and threatening the Judges to deliver their opinions for the levying of ship-" money," but he made his escape into Holland[t]. Sir Robert Berkley

[r] Clarendon i. page 122 See his strong censure of the Judges [s] Whitelocke, p 37 [t] Ibid p. 38

was afterwards impeached of high treason, and the Usher of the Black Rod was sent to the Court of King's Bench, when the Judges were sitting, and took Judge Berkley from off the Bench, and carried him away to prison. He redeemed himself, by supplying the Parliament with ten thousand pounds[u]. Subsequently another charge was brought in by the Commons against five of the other Judges, Brampton, Trevor, Weston, Davenport, and Crawley, for their opinions in favour of ship-money[x].

The situation of a Judge is an unthankful office. The party who gains his cause thinks that he has only obtained his own, and feels no gratitude for the justice of a decision in his favour, but the losing party usually considers himself as aggrieved, and too frequently harbours resentment against those who have decided against him. Even the high character of Sir George Croke was not sufficient to shield him from the malice of disappointed suitors. In the year 1640, an attack was made upon him by a Mr. John Cusacke, a man of good family in Ireland, and great nephew and heir to Sir Thomas Cusacke, sometime Lord Chancellor of that country[y]. He was an attorney, and had written some pieces in support of the royal prerogative. He came over to England for the recovery by law of some property belonging to his uncle, in which he seems not to have been successful. Whether in the prosecution of these claims Sir George Croke had given a decision against him in the court in which he presided[z], or for what other cause, does not appear, he certainly entertained much resentment against him, which he endeavoured to gratify in the form of law. As a Solicitor in the Star Chamber, he procured a subpœna to be sued forth in that court, at the suit of two persons named, Wingfield Honnings and Leonard Henricke, but without their authority or knowledge, against Sir George Croke, Knight, without giving him any other title, and caused it to be served upon him by a common porter. In further prosecution of his wicked design, he had prepared a bill to be preferred against him, charging him with giving an unjust judgment in the Court of Chancery. against Honnings and Henricke. Upon an informa-

[u] Whitelocke, p. 391. [x] Ibid. p. 45. [y] Sir Thomas Cusacke was made Chancellor of Ireland, 4th of August, 1550. He was of Cussington and Lismullen, in the county of Meath. Archdall's Irish Peerage, vol. v. p. 38. [z] See Cusacke's case, Car. 128. Qu. whether the same? 4 Car. I.

tion filed in the Star Chamber against him, by Sir Ralph Whitfield, the King's Serjeant, the Court decided, on the 10th of June, 1640, that Cusacke had been guilty of a great offence, which was much aggravated, in respect it was against a Judge of the realm, without giving him that addition which of right belonged to him, being a person in the opinion of the whole court of great learning and unspotted integrity, and one that in all his judgments had shewed himself a worthy and honest man. Wherefore they adjudged that Cusacke should be committed to the Fleet, till he had given security never to meddle with the sollicitation of causes, should pay a fine of £500, and be set in the pillory, and carried through Westminster Hall, and to all the courts there, with a paper on his head declaring his offence, and in every court was to acknowledge his offence, and ask Mr Justice Croke forgiveness There is a pedantic but humble letter from Cusacke to Sir George, dated from the Fleet, 18th of June, 1640, acknowledging his offence, and imploring forgiveness; but whether he succeeded in obtaining his pardon is not known, as Sir George had declared that "he did not seek a revenge for the abuse of his private person, but "of his public function, that the estimation thereof, which is holy, and a "general preservative of all public felicity, may be preserved[a]." This is the case alluded to in Viner's Abridgment, that a bill in the Star Chamber abated, because it was brought against Sir George Croke only, without the addition of his office and dignity of Judge, which is said to have been cited by Jones, in Trinity term, 16 Car I soon after it happened[b].

As Sir George Croke, in his public situation, ably supported the most valuable rights of his fellow subjects, in *his private capacity* he was equally their benefactor, in promoting religion, and by charitable institutions.

In the year 1629, he gave one hundred pounds to Sion College, the corporate association of the clergy of London, and which was employed in purchasing books for the library[c].

He erected a chapel in his mansion house at Studley, and in his life-time settled a stipend of twenty pounds a year for a clergyman, who should

[a] Viner's Abridgment, vol. ii p 94 Title Additions, G 25 [b] The sentence of the court, 10th of June, 16 Car. and Cusacke's Letter, MSS with me

[c] Ward, MS Additions to his Lives of the Gresham Professors British Museum, to p 305 from the History of Sion College, p 41

Studley Alms-House 1639.

preach once every Sunday, there, or in the chapel at Horton[d]. This was a great convenience to his own family, the poor people in the alms-house, his tenants, and neighbours; the parish church being at Beckley, at the distance of two miles. There was previously no place for divine service at Studley, since the suppression of the convent, and the chapel of the contiguous hamlet of Horton was unendowed, and supported only by the voluntary subscription of the inhabitants, who paid eight pounds a year to the vicar of Beckley, or his curate, for reading prayers there. But there were seldom, or never, any sermons, till Sir George Croke, before the erection of his own chapel, first allowed ten pounds a year to several clergymen for preaching upon Sundays, once a fortnight[e].

He likewise appointed an annuity of ten pounds a year "*to the minister* "*of Chilton, if he should be a preaching minister, and should preach once* "*at least every Sunday in the parish church*[f]."

At Studley he also erected an hospital or alms-house, for the relief, habitation, and maintenance, of four poor men, and four women. It is a substantial, but plain, brick building, and has the following inscription upon it.

DOMVS. PRO.
RELEVAMINE. PAV
PERVM. ERECTA.
ANO. DOMINI. 1639.
SOLI. DEO. GLORIA.
NIHIL. HOMINI.

By the same deed in which he had provided for the clergyman, and which is dated the 23d of May, in the 15th year of Charles I. 1639, he endowed it with a rent charge of sixty pounds a year, out of his estate at Easington. It was a comfortable retreat for age and want. They were supplied with the necessaries of life, a warm house, clothes, and fuel, and an allowance in money, which was sufficient at that time to afford a decent maintenance. The men were to be of the age of threescore

[d] Deed of the 23d of May, 15th Car. 1639

[e] The affidavit of J Coxhead, 7th of Feb. 1638 MS penes me

[f] Deed ut supra

years, and the women fifty, unless they were lame or blind: and were to be elected by such persons as should be owners of the mansion houses of Waterstock and Studley, and the persons elected were to be out of the parishes of Chilton, Waterstock, and Beckley. They had each a room in the building, and a separate garden behind it. Their allowances were, two shillings every week, once every two years a livery gown of broad cloth, of colour London russet, and the other years, two shirts and smocks, and half a chaldron of coals, or two loads of wood, yearly.

A set of excellent orders for their regulation was drawn up, and signed by him, the 21st of September, 1639, and which is still extant[g]. They bear the marks, not of a narrow superstition, but of an enlarged and liberal mind, and the object appears to have been, not merely the relief of indigence, but the encouragement of industry and good morals. No persons of indifferent character were to be admitted, or could be permitted to continue. Such only were eligible as were poor indeed, and well reputed of for religion, and good conversation, no cursers, or common swearers, no idle persons, or drunkards, none having committed fornication, or adultery, no hunters of ale-houses, no gadders, or wanderers abroad from house to house, no tale-bearers, no busybodies, but such as shall live without common scolding, or brawling, and quietly and peaceably with their neighbours. After their admission, they were not to live in idleness, but to dispose themselves to such work as they were able, that they might get somewhat towards their maintenance, that they might eat their own bread, and give unto others, and to keep themselves when they were sick. None were to wander, or beg alms; none was to lodge with them in their chambers, but one of them was to help another, as in charity they should. Cursing, or swearing, getting drunk, or sitting above half an hour at an ale-house, unless with some strange friend, were fined for the two first offences, and occasioned expulsion for the third. They were to attend divine service on Sundays, both morning and evening, and twice daily, in the chapel, or alms-house.

Such was the judicious, and well-arranged plan, upon which this good and wise man formed his charitable establishment. It is still kept up, and maintained, as much as possible, according to the disposition and intention

[g] See the Appendix, No XXX

of the founder. The specific allowances of clothing, and fuel, are, of course, of the same intrinsic value as formerly, but the pecuniary payments, from the depreciation in the value of money, are now become scarcely sufficient for their support. An evil which might have been prevented, by reserving the rent charge in corn, and apportioning the allowance according to the price of that standard article of life[h].

The general estimation in which Sir George Croke was held for integrity, a sense of duty, and a disposition to promote every useful institution, occasioned his being appointed a trustee for several benefactions for the advancement of learning, and the improvement of the condition of the poor.

Though the extraordinary talents of Lord Bacon had created a revolution in science, and had discovered the just method of studying nature in her own works, like all other novelties it made at first but a slow progress. The reign of James was abundant enough indeed in learning, but it was directed towards matters of religion, and unprofitable disputation, and the interest of Lord Bacon could never obtain the authority of the King to found a public establishment for the encouragement of natural knowledge which was afterwards in some measure effected by the institution of the Royal Society[i]. In the mean time it was left to the exertions of individuals, and amongst these, Sir William Sedley by his will, dated in 1618, bequeathed the sum of two thousand pounds, to be laid out in the purchase of lands, to found a professorship of Natural Philosophy in the University of Oxford Such however was still the prejudice in favour of Aristotle, that the new professor was directed to lecture in his books of *physics, de cœlo et mundo, de meteoris,* his *parva naturalia, de animâ, et de generatione, et corruptione*[k]. After his death, an estate at Waddesden, in Buckinghamshire, of the value of one hundred and twenty

[h] It appears by the old accounts of the Alms-house, that, during the Rebellion, such charitable institutions were made to contribute to the government, and that in the year 1651, out of the rent charge of sixty pounds, four pounds fourteen shillings and sixpence were paid *for ten months tax for the army;* which is more than ten per cent. In the first and subsequent Acts for imposing the land tax, charitable foundations were exempted 1st William and Mary

[i] Sprat's History of the Royal Society, p 151.

[k] Wood's Hist Oxon. by Gutch.

pounds a year, was purchased with this money, and conveyed to the University, by a deed of the 11th of December, 1622, in which Sir George Croke appears as a trustee[l].

He was likewise appointed a trustee, with the Earl of Essex, and other persons of rank and consequence, of the valuable estates given by Henry Smith, Esquire, to charitable uses, of which the benefits were "so widely "diffused, applied to so many purposes, and gladdened the hearts of so "many persons in very different stations of life." Every parish in the county of Surry partakes to this day of his benefactions, besides many other places They were directed to be applied to the relief of poor prisoners, and of hurt and maimed soldiers; for the portions of poor maids in marriage; apprenticing children, and setting up poor apprentices; amending the highways; for losses by fire, or shipwreck; for the relief of aged, poor, or infirm people, of married persons having more children than their labour could maintain, poor orphans, such poor as keep themselves and families to labour, and put forth their children to be apprentices at the age of fifteen; and to provide a stock always in readiness to set such persons to work as were able; for the ransom of poor captives, being slaves under Turkish pirates; for the use and relief of his poorest kindred; to buy impropriations for the maintenance of godly preachers, and the better furtherance of knowledge and religion; the teaching and educating poor children; and money to be lent in sums of twenty pounds, half a year at a time. A more extensive charity, or a more proper application of it, can scarcely perhaps be found[m].

In the year 1639, or 1640, this pious and learned Judge, finding his ageand infirmities to increase, and being desirous, before he put off his decaying and declining body, to have some leisure to examine his life, and to prepare for that great day, wherein all must render an account to the Supreme Judge of all their actions, was an humble suitor to King Charles for his writ of ease, which was denied, and yet in effect granted[n].

[l] Wood's History of the University of Oxford, lib. ii. p 42. [m] Collections relating to Henry Smith, Esq published by William Bray, Esq. in 1800 [n] Sir Harbottle Grimston, Pref. to Cro Car.

To the King's most excellent Majesty.

The humble petition of your Majesty's humble Servant, Sir George Croke, Knight, one of the Justices of your Bench,

Humbly sheweth,

That he having by the gracious favour of your Majesty's late Father, of famous memory, and of your Majesty, served your Majesty, and your said late Father, as a Judge of your Majesty's Court of Common Pleas, and of your Highness' Court, called the King's Bench, above this sixteen years, is now become very old, being above the age of eighty years. And by reason of his said age, and dullness of hearing, and other infirmities, whereby it hath pleased God to visit him, he findeth himself disabled any longer to do that service in your Courts, which the place requireth, and he desireth to perform, yet is desirous to live and die in your Majesty's favour.

His most humble suit is, that your Majesty will be pleased to dispense with his further attendance in any your Majesty's Courts; that so he may retire himself, and expect God's good pleasure: and during that little remainder of his life, pray for your Majesty's long life and happy reign.

GEORGE CROKE.

To which he received the following answer from the King.

Upon the humble address, by the humble petition of Sir George Croke, Knight, who, after many years service, done both to our deceased Father and Ourself, as our said Father's Serjeant at Law, and one of his and our Judges of our Benches, at Westminster, hath humbly besought Us, by reason of the infirmity of his old age, (which disableth him to continue to perform to Us that service, he much desireth to have according to his duty done,) his further attendance might be by Us, in our grace, dispensed with, to the end all our loving subjects, who have and shall faithfully serve Us, (as We declare this our servant hath done,) may know, that, as We shall never expect, much less require, or exact from them, performances beyond what their healths and years shall enable them, so We shall not dismiss them, without an approbation of their service, when we shall find they shall have deserved it, much less expose them in their old age to neglect. As our princely testimony therefore, that the said Sir George Croke, being dispensed withal, proceeds from Us, at the humble request of the said Sir

George Croke, (which We have cause and do take well, that he is rather willing to acknowledge his infirmity by his great age occasioned, than that by concealing of the same any want of justice should be to our people,) and not out of any our least displeasure conceived of him, do hereby declare our Royal pleasure, That We are graciously pleased, and do hereby dispense with, the said Sir George Croke's further attendance in our said Bench at Westminster, and any our circuits. And, as a token of our approbation, of the former good and acceptable service, by the said Sir George Croke, done to our deceased Father and Ourself, do yet continue him one of our Judges of our said Bench: and hereby declare our further will and pleasure to be, That, during his, the said Sir George Croke's life, there shall be continued and paid by Us unto him, the like fee and fees, as was to him, or is, or shall be by Us, paid to any other our Judges of our said Bench at Westminster, and all fees and duties, saving the allowance by Us to our Judges of our said Benches, for their circuits only.

After he had thus retired from the laborious duties of his judicial office, he spent the remainder of his life at Waterstock, in the enjoyment of his friends, and the appropriate exercises of holy meditation and devotion.

In public transactions, there is a certain degree of formality and stiffness; we see only the external man, it is always, therefore, particularly interesting to view a great character in his undress, in retirement, in the bosom of his own family, and even in trifling circumstances of his private and domestic manners and habits The little anecdotes of this nature, introduced with so much judgment by Plutarch, have made his lives the favourite of all ages and nations. In Montaigne, and the works of our relation Whitlock, we see the man himself, as well as the accurate chronicler of his times. Of Sir George Croke, in this respect, little can now be found, and none of his correspondence has been preserved. There is however a memorandum, written by his nephew Alexander Croke, in which he gives an account of a conversation, which passed between him and his uncle, after his retirement from business, about the disposal of his property, which, though in itself trifling, and of little consequence, may not be uninteresting from the description of the place and manner in which it took place, and the amiable kindness of Sir George to his relations.

"Memorandum, that upon the 21st day of June, 1641, I being then at Waterstock, and my uncle, the Judge, being then pleased to declare unto me his purpose of settling Studley and Easington upon me, in case his son should die without issue, and then using unto me many kind speeches, and amongst others, said unto me, that he did account of me as of one of his children. I then moving of him, (that if his purpose therein should continue,) and that what he intended that way, were to be to my eldest son only, that he would be pleased so to order it, that my said eldest son might in some kind be beneficial unto my son William He was then pleased to give me answer to this effect. "Nephew, I give the land unto "you, and you may dispose of any part of it, as you will, yourself." I then replied, "Sir, is it your pleasure, that I should do so?" He answered, "Yes, when I am dead, but whilst I live you cannot do it." And farther declared, that it was his intention and meaning, that provision should be made for my wife, and for my younger children, and said, "that "he intended to do it himself, and to have done it, although I had not "spoken." And upon my saying, that what I moved him in, proceeded from myself, out of my tender care of my children, and least peradventure I might die in his life-time, his answer unto me was, "that it was "well done, and if I died in his life-time, he would take order." And then, as he was walking on the mount, he was pleased to say unto me, that "my family consisted of two branches, and that Studley should be "for my eldest son, and Easington for my younger," and said, that "for "ought he knew, he would make it so before he slept," and then said, that "he would have me build an house at Easington, and that he would "allow timber, and be at the charge of building, as far as an hundred "pounds would go." All this passed in the parlour and garden, at Waterstock, and upon the mount, the day and year above written. And upon the Saturday following, I attending on my said uncle, between Thame and Cuddington, he was pleased then to say unto me, that "concerning "the matter I moved him in, his will was in his nephew Hampson's "keeping, but if it pleased God that he lived till Michaelmas, he said he "would do it." And afterwards, upon occasion of using my son Richard's name, with mine and others, in the purchase of the land, which he intended to have bought of Nicholas Lovell, in Easington, which he said he intended towards his alms-house, but was pleased to declare, that "although

" my son's name were therein used, yet his intention was, that my son " William should have Easington," and did likewise at one or two times more declare himself unto me to this purpose, " that it might be, Easing- ' ton one day might be my son William's.

ALEX. CROKE"

On the same paper is another memorandum.

" Memorandum, that in the year 1641, about Bartholomewtide, I being then at Waterstocke, and my uncle, the Judge, speaking of Easington, was pleased to say unto me to this effect, that " it might be, Easington " might come unto me and my son William sooner than I did imagine" And at another time, about Michaelmas, in the same year, my said uncle, having shewed me then the survey of Studley, was pleased, amongst other speeches, to speak unto me to this effect, that " it might be, that it might " one day come to me, and mine, but there would be a great many be- " tween me and home, his daughters and their children." And used some such like speech unto me at one other time before, and at one other time, in the same year, as he was riding on the way between Waterstock and Chilton, to the best of my remembrance, used words to this effect, that " he would purchase some other lands for his alms-house, and take off " the charge from Easington.

ALEX CROKE[a] "

Soon after these transactions, he departed this life upon the 16th of February, 1642, in the eighty-second year of his age, and was buried at Waterstock, on the 3d of March, where there is a monument to his memory erected against the wall of the chancel near the communion table. It is an arch, with Corinthian pillars, under which he is represented in his judicial dress, leaning upon a scull, and with a book in his hand Underneath is the following inscription.

GEORGIUS CROKE, EQUES
AURATUS, UNUS JUSTICIARIORUM
DE BANCO REGIS, JUDICIO LYNCEATO
ET ANIMO PRÆSENTI INSIGNIS, VERI-

[a] The original MS. in the hand-writing of Alexander Croke penes me

TATIS HÆRES, QUEM NEC MINÆ NEC
HONOS ALLEXIT, REGIS AUTHORITATEM
ET POPULI LIBERTATEM ÆQUA LANCE
LIBRAVIT. RELIGIONE CORDATUS, VITA
INNOCUUS, MANU EXPANSA, CORDE
HUMILI, PAUPERES IRROGAVIT,
MUNDUM ET VICIT, ET DESERUIT,
ANNO ÆTATIS LXXXII. ANNO
REGIS CAROLI XVII. ANNOQUE
DOMINI MDCXLI

Sir George Croke left behind him, amongst his contemporaries[p], the general character of abilities, and deep learning in his profession, unblemished integrity, sincere religion, and amiable manners and the justness of their opinion is sufficiently evinced by the history of his life. In a turbulent period, when faction ran high, he was not considered as a partizan, but he supported the steady and unbiassed dignity which became a judicial situation. He lived in habits of friendship with many of the popular leaders, without approving of their republican principles, or abetting their violent proceedings. As he maintained the royal prerogative, as far as it was conformable to the laws of the country, although he decided those great constitutional points in favour of the liberty of the subject, yet his not having been removed from his office, and the King's gracious answer to his petition for leave to retire, are proofs that he had not forfeited the favour of his Sovereign. He happily quitted the world before the scenes of confusion which followed; had he lived, it is probable that, like Sir Matthew Hale, he would have continued to hold his commission, without acknowledging the authority of the usurpers; since it was necessary that justice should be administered, whoever might be in possession of the government.

The following character of him was written by Sir Harbottle Grimstone, his son-in-law; whose personal acquaintance with him, and his own experience as a lawyer, enabled him to discriminate his various excellencies.

"He was of a most prompt invention and apprehension, which was

[p] Wood's Hist Univ Ox lib ii p 42 before quoted in a note; Whitelocke, and every author by whom he is mentioned. His monument states his death in 1641. As it was in February, this, according to the new-stile, was in 1642.

accompanied with a rare memory, by means whereof, and through his sedulous and indefatigable industry, he attained to a profound science and judgment in the laws of the land, and to a singular intelligence of the true reasons thereof, and principally in the forms of good pleading. He was of an universal and admirable experience in all other matters which concerned the Commonwealth. He heard patiently, and never spake but to purpose, and was always glad when matters were represented unto him truly and clearly, he had this discerning gift, to separate the truth of the matter, from the mixture and affection of the deliverer, without giving the least offence. He was resolute and stedfast for truth: and as he desired no employment for vain glory, so he refused none for fear, and by his wisdom and courage in conscionably performing his charge, and carefully discharging his conscience, and his modesty in sparingly speaking thereof, he was without envy, though not without true glory. To speak of his integrity and forbearing to take bribes, were a wrong to his virtue In sum, what Tacitus saith of Julius Agricola, his wife's father, who was a Governor in our Britain, I may truly say of this *Agricola*[q], our Reverend Judge, my wife's father, *tempora curarum, remissionumque divisa, ubi conventus ac Judicia poscerent, gravis, intentus, severus, et sæpius misericors: ubi officio satisfactum, nulla ultrà potestatis persona: tristitiam, et arrogantiam, et avaritiam exuerat, nec illi, quod est rarissimum, aut facilitas auctoritatem, aut severitas amorem, deminuit* "That he well and discreetly divided the seasons of his affairs and vacations In times of audience and judgment, he was grave, heedful, and austere, and yet merciful too. That duty performed, no face any more or shew of authority severe and stately looks were laid apart in such sort, that neither his gentle and courteous behaviour weakened the reverence, nor his severity the love due to his person." He was of a strict life to himself, yet in conversation full of sweet deportment and affable, tender and compassionate, seeing none in distress whom he was not ready to relieve, nor did I ever behold him do any thing more willingly than when he gave alms: he was every way liberal, and cared for money no further than to illustrate his virtues. he was a man of great modesty, and of a most plain and single heart, of an ancient freedom and integrity of mind, esteeming

[q] Γεωργος Taciti Agricola, sect ix

it more honest to offend, than to flatter, or hate. He was remarkable for hospitality, a great lover and much beloved of his country, wherein he was a blessed peace-maker, and in those times of conflagration was more for the bucket than bellows, often pouring out the waters of his tears to quench those beginning flames which others did ventilate. In religion, he was devout towards God, reverent in the church, attentive at sermons, and constant in family duties. Whilst he lived, he was the example of the life of faith, love, and good works, to so many as were acquainted with his equal and even walkings in the ways of God, through the several turnings and occasions of his life[r], and he died full of commendation for wisdom and piety; and left such a stock of reputation behind him, as might kindle a generous emulation in strangers, and preserve a noble ambition in those of his name and family to perform actions worthy of their ancestors[s].

Of the following poem, I know not the author. I found it in manuscript amongst my papers

An Elegy on Judge George Croke.

This was the Man, the Glory of the Gown,
Just to himself, his Country, and the Crown,
The Atlas of our Liberty, as high
In his own Fame, as others' Infamy.
Great by his Virtues, great by others' Crimes,
The best of Judges in the worst of Times.
He was the first who happily did sound
Unfreedomed Loyalty, and felt the Ground.
Yet happier to behold that dawning Ray,
Shot from himself, become a perfect Day,
To hear his Judgement so authentic grown,
The Kingdom's voice the Echo to his own.
Nor did he speak but live the Laws, although
From his sage Mouth grave Oracles did flow.
Who knew his Life, Maxims might thence derive,
Such as the Law to Law itself might give.
Who saw him on the Bench, would think the Name
Of Friendship, or Affection, never came

[r] Preface to Cro Car. [s] Preface to Cro Eliz

Within his Thoughts. Who saw him thence, might know
He never had, nor could deserve, a Foe.
Only assuming Rigour with his Gown,
And, with his Purple, laid his Rigour down
Him nor Respect, nor Disrespect, could move,
He knew no Anger, and his Place no Love.
So mixt the Strain of all his Actions ran,
So much a Judge, so much a Gentleman.
Who durst be just, when Justice was a Crime,
Yet durst no more, in so unjust a Time.
Nor hurried by the highest Mover's Force,
Against his proper, and resolved, Course;
But when our World did turn, so kept his Ground,
He seemed the axe on which the Wheel went round.
Whose Zeal was warm, when all to Ice did turn,
Yet was but warm, when all the Word did burn

The reports of cases, decided in the different tribunals, are the repositories of the common law, and of the interpretation of the statutes After the year books, no public officers were appointed to perform the duty of reporting, but it was left to the industry of individuals. From his earliest attendance in Westminster Hall, Sir George Croke had taken a regular series of notes of cases which were adjudged in the Courts of King's Bench, and Common Pleas, during the whole time that he frequented them as a student, or advocate, or presided in them as a Judge He began when he was about twenty-four years old, and continued them till within a year or two of his death They were bequeathed by him, with the principal part of his library, to his son-in-law, Sir Harbottle Grimston, who published them, having been brought up, as he says of himself, at the feet of this Gamaliel. They were written in a very small, close, and intricate hand, and in the old Norman, or French, language, which custom had rendered more familiar and expressive to the old lawyers than their native tongue; but they were published by Sir Harbottle in English, contrary to his own opinion, by the injunction of some persons of authority In regard they were too bulky to be comprised in one volume, he divided them into three parts, according to the reigns of the three princes, in which the decisions took place. And in consequence of the advice of Lord Coke to students, "*that they should read the later* "*reports first*," and that he might vouch the principal persons in the profession then living, for their correctness and candour, he began with the publication of *the last part*, those cases which occurred during the reign of *King Charles the First*, when he was Judge as well as Reporter. This first volume, or part, was printed, with the approbation of the Judges, in the year 1657; and, by the authority of the Parliament, a monopoly was granted to Sir Harbottle for the sole publishing of it[t]. There was a squabble between some printers respecting it, which was published and printed on one side of a sheet of paper[u]. A long preface is prefixed, giving an account of the work, and an history of the author and his family. *The second part*, of cases during the reign of *King James*, came out in 1659, and the *first part*, of the reign of *Queen Elizabeth*, in 1661, which is dedicated by Sir Harbottle Grimston to King Charles the Second, with all those expressions of an ardent affection, which subsisted between Charles and his subjects, in the early days of his restoration. The reports themselves begin about the time when those of Sir James Dyer end, and comprehend a series of cases adjudged during a period of near sixty years, from the twenty-fourth year of Queen Elizabeth, 1582, to the sixteenth of Charles the First, 1640, an extraordinary length of time for the exertions of one man. They contain an immense mass of law, of the highest authority, with a regular journal of all the changes which took place in the principal department of the profession, and an interesting account of the legal formalities and ceremonies used in the creation of Serjeants, Judges, and other high officers, and of many of the usages and rights of the common law. The method used is likewise excellent. They are not swelled out with the pleadings and arguments at large, but each case is shortly stated, according to the points discussed and adjudged, the reasons are plainly and succinctly stated; and a happy medium is observed between a wearisome diffuseness, and an imperfect brevity

I have a portrait of him, a three-quarters length, in his dress as a Judge, with the coif His left hand leans on a table covered with a green cloth,

[t] It is amongst the King's folio pamphlets in the British Museum, No 13. See the Appendix, No XXIX

[u] Journals, House of Com 9 June, 1657, page 551. order signed Hen Scobel, at the end of Cro Car

and there is a curtain behind him of the same colour. There is written on it, ætatis 66, anno domini 1626. I have likewise another picture, apparently a copy from the other. Mr. Pennant mentions that he saw at Gorhambury, the seat of Lord Grimston, near Saint Alban's, a portrait of Sir George Croke, a half length in his robes, and another of his lady in black, with a lawn ruff[t], but, on examination, I found it to be a copy of his mother's picture, Elizabeth Unton.

There is a small oval head of him, engraved by Hollar[u], another larger by Robert Vaughan, which is prefixed to his Reports, with this inscription *Vera effigies Georgii Croke Equitis aurati et utriusque Banci Justiciarius, temp. Car. Reg. Ut vultus hominum, ita simulacra vultûs, quæ marmore, aut ære finguntur, imbecilla, ac mortalia sunt. Forma mentis æterna, quam tenere et exprimere, non per alienam materiam, et artem, sed tuis ipse moribus possis*[x]. Granger[y] mentions two others, by Gaywood, and R. White, but I have never seen them

His buildings, the chapel and the alms-house, still remain at Studley. His coat of arms, dated 1622, is carved in stone, over the porch of the mansion, impaled with Bennet, that of his wife, viz. gules, a bezant between three demi lions rampant, argent, langued azure, with a mullet, to denote his being a third son. The same arms, in painted glass, are in the old withdrawing room, with the two crests, that of Bennet being out of a mural coronet, or, a lion's head gules, charged with a bezant on the neck. The same arms are in the chapel, and two of the bed rooms

Sir George Croke left two wills, the first, relating principally to his real, the second to his personal property. The first is dated the 25th of May, 1639, and is to the following effect[z] He desires to be buried after a Christian's manner of burial, without any unnecessary ceremonies, or charges, especially of hearse, heralds, or offerings. He left an annuity of £20 to his brother William Croke, to be paid by his wife, and others, out of Easingdon, and £80 a year, as before limited, to the alms-house, and chaplain. He bequeathed *Studley* to his conusees and grantees, under a

[t] Pennant's Journey from Chester, and he quotes Lloyd, ii 267? [u] The original plate of Hollar is in the Bodleian Library, and, by the favour of the Vice-Chancellor and the other Curators, I have been permitted to have some impressions taken off for this work [x] Tacit in vita Jul Agricolæ Socrei sui, sec 46 [y] Biographical Dictionary [z] The original is in the possession of William Henry Ashhurst, Esq of Waterstock

fine before levied, to the use of his son Thomas for life, then to the conusees for ninety-nine years, then to the heirs of the body of his son Thomas by any other wife that he might have other than Anne his now wife, with liberty to Thomas, with the assent of his mother, and of any two others of his executors, to limit all or any part of Studley to any his wife that he hath, or shall have, for term of her life for a jointure, then to his conusees during the ninety-nine years, and afterwards to the use of such children of Thomas, and the heirs of their bodies, as his son, by the assent of his mother, and two executors, shall appoint; and for default of such appointment, then after his decease, to such of the children of Thomas, and the heirs of their bodies, as the testator's wife and executors should think fit And for default of such issue, to his brother, William Croke, for life, remainder to the use of his nephew Alexander, and his heirs male; giving security for the payment of £2000 for the testator's daughters.

Easington he left to his wife for life, or widowhood, then to his son Thomas for life, with power to sell, with the consent of the executors: then to the conusees for ninety-nine years, as before limited as to Studley and, after that term ended, then to the heirs of the body of his son by any other wife than Anne; and, for default of such issue, to his nephew Alexander Croke, and the heirs male of his body, giving security for the payment of £1000 to his daughters.

Waterstock he bequeathed to his wife for life, or widowhood, then to his son for life, then to his executors for ninety-nine years, then to his son and the heirs of his body by any other wife than Anne, with liberty, with the consent of his mother and two executors, to appoint the same to any wife he now hath, or shall have, for life for a jointure, and, after such estates, then to the conusees, to dispose thereof to such of the children of Thomas, and the heirs of their bodies, as he, with the consent of his mother and two executors, should appoint; and, for default of such appointment, to such of his son's children as the executors should think fit. And for default of such issue, then to his nephew Henry Croke, son of his brother Henry, and then to his son George Croke, giving security for £3000 to his daughters.

We have before seen, that the estate at Waterstock went, according to this will, to his nephew Doctor Henry Croke, and afterwards to his son

Sir George Croke: that at Studley went to his brother William, as will hereafter appear.

The will of his personal property is dated, at the beginning, on the 20th of November, 1640, and, at the end, on the 3d of December, and was proved on the 3d of May, 1642. In this he bequeaths to the poor of Chilton, Waterstock, Studley, and Saint Dunstan's in the West, five pounds each, and three pounds to the parish where he shall die. To the minister of Chilton 40s., of Waterstock £5; but if his nephew Henry is parson there, £10. To his wife £300, and her jewels, &c. part of his plate, and the use of the remainder for life; afterwards to his son, or, if dead, to be sold and divided amongst his daughters. A part of the plate is excepted, and given to his son. To his wife, half his household stuff, and furniture, at Waterstock, and the use of the other half for life, or widowhood; then to his son Thomas. His household stuff at Studley to his son, and two hundred pounds for the better furnishing the house at Studley. To his wife, her wearing apparel, coach, coach-horses, and harness, one nag for her own use, except the bay nag given him by his son-in-law, Thomas Lee, which was to be returned to him, a double gelding, and two geldings for servants, and his carts and cart geldings, kyne, &c. &c. To his brother William Croke, a piece of plate of the value of £10, and the sum of £100, and his wearing apparel, except his robes used by him as a Judge, which were to be disposed of by his wife by gift or otherwise. To his son-in-law, Harbottle Grimston, Esquire, and his daughter Mary, £20 in plate, and to their children, George, Mary, Elizabeth, Sarah, and Thomas, £100 each. To Harbottle Grimston all his books concerning the common law, lying or being usually in his study, or closet, at Serjeant's Inn, both printed books, and written, except his books of Statutes, and the Abridgments of Statutes, and those which concern the office of a Justice of Peace, which books so excepted he devises to his son Thomas. And he desires his said son-in-law, that if he shall not proceed in the practice and profession of the law, as perhaps, after the death of his father, he may not think it convenient for him to do, that then he would dispose of them between his nephew Edward Bulstrode, Unton Croke, and George Walton. To his son-in-law, Thomas Lee, Esquire, and his daughter Elizabeth, his wife, £20 for plate; and to their sons, Thomas, and George, and their daughter

Mary, £100 each. To Richard Jervois, Esquire, and Frances his daughter, his wife, £20, and to their daughters, Lucy and Mary, £100 each. All his books concerning the common law, except the book commonly called the Commentary upon Littleton, and the Book of Statutes, and Abridgment of Statutes, and Dalton's book concerning a Justice of Peace, lying and being in his study at Waterstock, to his nephew Unton Croke, Esq. Also all his books concerning the common law at Studley, to his nephew Edward Bulstrode, Esq. to whom he forgives a debt of £50. The books excepted in his study at Waterstock, to his son Thomas. All his divinity books in English, except the three new books of Martyrs of the last edition, and the English Bible in folio at Waterstock, to his wife, the book of Martyrs and Bible to his son, his wife to have the use for life, or widowhood. To his son, all his Latin books, and books written in Latin, French, or any other language not before given. Legacies to his servants. To his nephew and godson, George Croke, son of his nephew Doctor Henry Croke, £100, for an annuity towards his maintenance and bringing up in learning. To his wife, one complete armour for a horseman, and two armours for two footmen. The residue of his armour to his son. Debts owing from his brother William to be released. His wife, his nephew Bulstrode Whitelocke, Thomas Hampsted, Alexander Croke, Esquires, and his good neighbour, William Tipping, to be his executors. His wife to have the sold administration, and the others to be coadjutors, and to have £20 each. And whereas Lord Bayning, Viscount Sudbury, had appointed him one of his executors, and he had not intermeddled in his affairs, though he had joined in the probate, and the other acting executor was dead, and the executorship was now come to him by survivorship, he appoints Lady Anne, widow of Lord Bayning the son, his executrix of the said estate. Signed George Croke. *Christus mihi vita, mors mihi lucrum* Witnesses, Har. Grimston, Tho. Hampson, L. Hurst, Fran. Croke, Robert Newburgh, John Cammocke, Robert Durham.

His lady, Dame Mary Croke, survived him fifteen years, and dying on the first of December, 1657, was buried at Waterstock, under a flat stone in the chancel near her husband. She appointed Colonel Ingoldsby, and Giles Hungerford, Esquire, her executors, and bequeathed five pounds to the alms-house, to which she had given many benefactions in money during her life, and settled upon it a small close in Easington[a].

The inscription upon her tomb-stone is as follows

HERE LYETH THAT HONOURABLE LADY, DAME MARY, RELICT OF SIR GEORGE CROKE, KNIGHT, LATE ONE OF THE JUDGES OF THE KING'S BENCH, WHO FOR HER PIETIE, CHARITIE, AND OTHER EMINENT VIRTUES, WAS THE HONOR OF HER SEX WHILST SHE LIVED, AND SCARCE LEFT HER EQUAL WHEN SHE DIED. SHE DEPARTED THIS LIFE, DECEMBER THE 1st, 1657.

They had only one son, named Thomas, and three daughters, Mary, Frances, baptized the 25th of September, 1618[b], and Elizabeth

Of the children of Sir George Croke, little is known of his only son Thomas, nor indeed of the exact time when he died. He appears to have been bred to the law, for he was a member of the Inner Temple, and was admitted on the 26th of April, 1619, into the chambers of his uncle, Paul Ambrose Croke, who was a Bencher of that society[c]. Mr. Wood says, that he was "a sot, or a fool, or both[d]" But he quotes no authority for this assertion, and the legacy of his father, in his will, in which he leaves him "all his Latin and French books, or books in any other language, "with his Statute books, Abridgments of Statutes, such as concern the "office of a Justice of the Peace, and any others undisposed of," are a bequest not very well adapted to such a character But as Sir George in his will left the bulk of his law library to Sir Harbottle Grimston, it should seem that at that time he had laid aside the study of the law, and had chosen the life of a country gentleman. This will was made Dec. 2d, 1640, and it there appears to have been settled, that after his decease, his son was to live at Studley, and his lady to continue at Waterstock, as he devises to him part of his plate, the household goods at Studley, and £200 for better furnishing that house. Thomas was living on the 21st of June, 1641, a few months only before his father's death. Whether he survived him or not is uncertain. At that time in the conversation with his nephew

[a] The old alms-house accounts, sub anno 1647, &c penes me [b] Waterstock Register [c] Ward's MS. Inner Temple Register, vol. ii. fol 125 [d] Life of A Wood, p 581

[illegible]

nearly as it was [illegible] about 1640.

Alexander, he spoke of his succeeding to the Studley estate, after the death of his son Thomas, as if it were a probable event, perhaps from the state of his son's health. There is no proof that his son ever inherited any part of his property, as Waterstock went to his daughters, and Studley to his nephew Alexander. Thomas was married, and his wife's name was Anne, as appears from Sir George's will in 1639.

Of Sir George Croke's daughters, *Mary*, the eldest, married *Sir Harbottle Grimston, Baronet*: *Elizabeth*, the second, had two husbands, the first was *Thomas Lee, Esquire*, of Hartwell, in Buckinghamshire, and her second husband was *Sir Richard Ingoldsby, Knight of the Bath*: *Frances*, the third, married *Richard Jervois, Esquire*.

After just premising, that Stephen Moore, ancestor of the Baron Kilworth, Viscount Mountcashell, of the kingdom of Ireland, married the granddaughter of Sir George Croke, I have not discovered by which of his children[e], I shall proceed to give some account of his sons-in-law.

[e] Debrett's Peerage, Ireland, p. 734.

SECTION THE SECOND.

SIR HARBOTTLE GRIMSTON, who married MARY, the eldest daughter of Sir George Croke, was one of the most respectable characters of that eventful æra. He was descended from an ancient family, and was born at Bradfield Hall, near Maningtree, in Essex, about the year 1594. He was the second son of Sir Harbottle Grimston, Baronet, who was the representative for that county, and was one of those who were imprisoned for a long time for refusing to pay the loan money. He was educated for the law, and was a member of Lincoln's Inn, but upon the death of his elder brother, he abandoned his profession. Falling in love with Sir George Croke's daughter, her father would not bestow her upon him unless he would return to his studies, which he did with great success, and became eminent as an advocate[a]. In 1638, he was appointed Recorder of Colchester; and at the meeting of the Long Parliament, in 1640, he was chosen one of the representatives for that place.

In his political conduct, though no enemy to the monarchy, he warmly opposed the illegal oppressions of the Crown, and was a zealous defender of liberty and the laws. His learning and talents were considerable, and his eloquence powerful. Upon every important question, his conduct was animated, his language vehement, and he inveighed against those, whom he considered as the enemies to his country, with unsparing severity[b]. Upon all measures in opposition to the King, and in the most important committees of that memorable parliament, for the redress of grievances, and for bringing obnoxious ministers to justice, he was always an active member. He was one of the first who proposed calling to account those who had been concerned in levying ship-money. In 1641, he was of the committee

[a] Burnet, Hist of his Own Times.

[b] Upon one occasion he called Secretary Windebanck, the very pander and broker to the Whore of Babylon. Rush v. 122 Hume, vi 411.

to prepare the charge against the Earl of Strafford; and, in 1642, upon that for vindicating the privileges of Parliament, upon the King's going down to the House to demand the five members. In the same year, when the Parliament had passed the ordinance of the Militia, he accepted a commission as one of the Deputy Lieutenants of the county of Essex[c]. Soon after the King had erected his standard at Nottingham, Sir Thomas Barrington and Grimston seized upon Sir John Lucas and his Lady in Essex, and committed them to prison, and Lucas was proclaimed a traitor for assisting the King[d]. He was one of the Commissioners named by the Commons, in 1647, to go down with a congratulatory declaration to the army, and of another for disbanding part of the army[e]. During the memorable siege of Colchester by the Parliament army, the King's troops took possession of Sir Harbottle's house at Bradfield Hall, where they placed two hundred musqueteers, and two troops of horse. This party plundered and ruined the house, took away and destroyed all the furniture, and turned out his lady[f]. In 1647, he was one of the Committee of Appeals from the Visitors appointed to reform the University of Oxford[g].

But during this time he was far from going all lengths with the Parliament. In 1643, he refused to subscribe the solemn League and Covenant, and discontinued sitting in the House till it was laid aside[h]. In September, 1648, he was appointed one of the Commissioners of the Parliament to treat with the King in the Isle of Wight, and was extremely desirous of a compromise between him and the Parliament. He, and Hollis, on their knees, begged the King to dispatch the business with all possible haste, before the army, then in the north, could interfere, and they assured his Majesty, that "*if he would frankly come forward, and send them back "with the concessions that were necessary, they did not doubt but that he "would in a very few days be brought up with honor, freedom, and "safety, to the Parliament, and matters brought to a present settlement.*" But the King unfortunately could come to no resolution, and the treaty failed. The King however was well pleased with Sir Harbottle's conduct, who, upon his return to Parliament, pressed the acceptance of the King's concessions[i]

When the King was brought to his trial, the persons in power had such

[c] Whitelock, p 56 [d] Ibid 59 [e] Ibid 252 [f] Ibid 308, 9, 10. [g] Wood's History, by Gutch [h] Burnet [i] Burnet's Hist of his Own Times, vol 1. p 44. Ed. folio.

apprehensions of Sir Harbottle's duty to his Majesty, and his interest with the army and people, that they put him under confinement, and did not release him till after the King's death. An order for his discharge was signed by Fairfax, on the 30th of January, which states that he had engaged himself not to act, or to do any thing to the disservice of the Parliament or army[k]. He afterwards resigned the Recordership of Colchester, on the 6th of July, 1649, and went abroad for some time with his son for his education[l].

A man of Grimston's sound principles was not likely to be a friend to Cromwell, and he joined in a strong opposition to him and the Independents. During the disputes which began to take place between the Parliament and the army, at a meeting of the officers, it was proposed, "*to* "*purge the army.*" Upon which Cromwell said, "*he was sure of the* "*army, but there was another body that had more need of purging,* "*namely, the House of Commons, and he thought the army only could do* "*that*" Grimston reported these speeches of Cromwell to the House of Commons, and introduced the business by a speech, in which he stated, that "he had a matter of privilege of the highest sort to lay before them, "which concerned the very being and freedom of the House." He then charged Cromwell with the design of putting force upon the House, and proved the words which he had used by witnesses. Cromwell fell down upon his knees, and made a solemn prayer to God, attesting his innocence, and his known zeal for the Parliament, and submitted himself to the providence of God for his protection. This prayer was uttered with great vehemence, and was accompanied with many tears; and he so confused and wearied out the members by a very long speech, in which he endeavoured to persuade them that the witnesses were not to be believed, that nothing farther was done in it[m]. But he soon afterwards proved the truth of the charge, by his forcible dissolution of the Parliament

When Cromwell summoned a Parliament in 1656, according to his new model of representation, Grimston was elected as one of the sixteen members for the county of Essex He was not however permitted to sit in the House, being in the number of those who were rejected by the council, for

[k] Archdall's Peerage of Ireland, in seven vols 8vo 1789. vol. v. p 193. [l] Biog. Brit. note F. [m] Burnet

refusing to recognize the Protector's government, or for being otherwise obnoxious to him. Upon which he joined in the strong and severe remonstrance which was published by the excluded members, against the oppression and tyranny of Cromwell, and by which they protested against the present assembly as not being the representative body of England But this remonstrance was not attended to by the Protector, his Council, or the Parliament[n]. After being thus excluded from the House of Commons, he was principally employed in following the practice of the law. As he was known to be a well wisher to the ancient government of England, he united himself with those who prepared the way for the King's restoration. In February 1660, he was appointed one of the Council of State, in which the principal power was vested by the old Parliament, before its dissolution. Upon the meeting of the new Parliament, he was chosen Speaker; an high honour, to be appointed to preside in an assembly, which was about to perform such signal services to the country, as the abolition of tyranny and anarchy, and the restitution of lawful government! Upon the 11th of May he sailed to Holland, to wait upon the King, at Breda, with Sir John Granville, who had been the chief organ of communication between the King, General Monk, the army, and the Parliament[o].

After the Restoration, he was much in favour with the King, and had the honour of entertaining him, on the 25th of June, in 1660, at his house in Lincoln's-Inn Fields. Upon presenting the money bill to his Majesty, on the 13th of September, he made an elegant and loyal speech[p]. He was in the commission of Oyer and Terminer for the trial of the Judges of Charles the First, who sat at Hicks's Hall, 9th of October, 1660. Upon the 3d of November the same year, without any solicitation, he was made Master of the Rolls, an office which he held above twenty-three years, till his death. The same year he was appointed Chief Steward of Saint Alban's, and Recorder of Harwich, and from the Restoration till his death, he continued to be one of the Representatives in Parliament for the borough of Colchester[q].

He published, as I have before mentioned, the Reports of his father-in-

[n] Whitelocke, p. 640 [o] Burnet. [p] Biograph. Britan sub nomine [q] Biog. Brit.

law, Sir George Croke, who had left them to him, with his study of books at Serjeant's Inn. He has prefixed long prefaces to each of the volumes, in which he has given an account of the Judge and his family. Several of his speeches have been preserved in Rushworth, and other contemporary collectors

Sir Harbottle's second wife was Anne, daughter of Sir Nathaniel Bacon, niece to the great Lord Bacon, and widow of Sir Thomas Meautys. Of Henry Meautys, elder brother of Sir Thomas, he purchased the house and manor of Gorhambury. It had belonged to the monastery of Saint Alban's, and, at the dissolution, was granted to Ralph Rowlatt, Esquire, whose son conveyed it to Sir Nicholas Bacon. His eldest son Anthony Bacon, left it to his brother, the great Lord Bacon, who gave it, after his death, to Sir Thomas Meautys, one of the Clerks of the Privy Council, and his private secretary, and confidential friend. Sir Thomas Meautys's only daughter Jane dying without issue, it became the property of her uncle Henry Meautys. There was another connexion between the families, for Sir Nathaniel Bacon married Jane, the daughter of Hercules Meautys, Sir Thomas's great uncle[r]. Lord Bacon had built a small house within the bounds of the old city of Verulam, and about a mile from Gorhambury, called Verulam House, at an expence of nine or ten thousand pounds: which was most ingeniously contrived, his Lordship being the chief architect. It was sold about 1665 or 1666, by Sir Harbottle Grimston, to two carpenters, for £400, of which they made £800 Gorhambury House was built by Sir Nicholas Bacon. There is extant a particular and very curious description of both these houses[s].

Sir Henry Chauncy gives this character of Sir Harbottle Grimston, "He had a nimble fancy, a quick apprehension, a rare memory, an eloquent tongue, and a sound judgment. He was a person of free access, sociable in company, sincere to his friends, hospitable in his house, charitable to the poor, and an excellent master to his servants[t]."

The celebrated Bishop Burnet lived many years under his protection, as

[r] From the deeds in the possession of Lord Verulam Clutterbuck's History of Hertfordshire, vol i Ed 1815

[s] Letters in the Bodleian Library, vol. ii. page 228 [t] Hist and Antiq of Hertfordshire, p 465.

Preacher at the Rolls Chapel He was a kind patron to him, and greatly assisted and encouraged him in writing the History of the Reformation[u]. When King Charles the Second was offended with Burnet, about his conduct in the affair of the Duke of Lauderdale, and sent Secretary Williamson to Sir Harbottle, to desire him to dismiss him, he excused himself, and said " that he was an old man, fitting himself for another world, " and he found his ministry useful to him." Burnet was grateful for these acts of kindness, and says in his History of his Own Times, " Since I was " so long happy in so quiet a retreat, it seems but a just piece of gratitude " that I should give some account of that venerable old man." After stating some particulars of his life, which we have already related, Burnet adds, " His principle was, that allegiance and protection were mutual obligations, and that the one went for the other. He thought the law was a measure of both; and that when a legal protection was denied to one that paid a legal allegiance, the subject had a right to defend himself. He was much troubled when preachers asserted a divine right of regal government. He thought it had no other effect but to give an ill impression of them as aspiring men; nobody was convinced by it; it inclined their hearers rather to suspect all they said besides; it looked like the sacrificing their country to their own preferment; and an encouragement of princes to turn tyrants. Yet he was always looked at, as one who wished well to the ancient government of England.

" He was a just Judge; very slow, and ready to hear every thing that was offered, without passion or partiality. I thought his only fault was, that he was too rich; and yet he gave yearly great sums in charity, discharging many prisoners by paying their debts. He was a very pious and devout man, and spent every day at least an hour in the morning, and as much at night, in prayer and meditation. And even in winter, when he was obliged to be very early on the bench, he took care to rise so soon, that he had always the command of that time, which he gave to those exercises. He was much sharpened against popery, but had always a tenderness to the dissenters, though he himself continued always in the Communion of the Church.

" His second wife, whom I knew, was niece to the great Sir Francis

[u] Preface to that History

Bacon She had all the high notions for the Church and the Crown, in which she had been bred; but was the humblest the devoutest, and best tempered person I ever knew of that sort It was really a pleasure to hear her talk of religion, she did it with so much elevation and force. She was always very plain in her clothes, and went often to jails to consider the wants of the prisoners, and relieve or discharge them, and, by the meanness of her dress, she passed but for a servant trusted with the charities of others When she was travelling in the country, as she drew near a village, she often ordered her coach to stay behind, till she had walked about it, giving orders for the instruction of the children, and leaving liberally for that end[x]

"In 1684, old Sir Harbottle Grimston lived still to the great indignation of the Court, on account of his known dislike to the Roman Catholic religion. When the 5th of November came, Burnet begged him to excuse his preaching at the Rolls, 'for that day led one to preach against popery, and it was indecent not to do it' Sir Harbottle said, 'he would end his life as he had led it all along, in an open detestation of popery.' Burnet, thus compelled to preach, did it effectually, and chose for his text 'Save me from the lion's mouth, thou hast heard me from the horns of the unicorn,' which was interpreted by the court, perhaps not unjustly, as levelled against the King's coat of arms and his conduct. This occasioned much anger, and the King wrote to Sir Harbottle to dismiss him from being Preacher at the Rolls, as a disaffected person. He was obliged to comply, and Burnet travelled abroad. Sir Harbottle died soon after, nature sank all at once, and he departed, as he had lived, with great piety and resignation to the will of God[y]."

He was well read in the ancient Fathers of the Church, and wrote in Latin, for the use of his son, a small manual, containing the duty of a Christian He also left in manuscript, a journal of the several debates in the treaty with Charles the First in the Isle of Wight[z].

He died on the 31st of December, 1683, being near ninety years of age, and was buried at Saint Michael's church, at Saint Alban's By his first

[x] Burnet's History of his Own Times, vol. 1 p 382 folio edition [y] Burnet, page 596

[z] Archdall's Irish Peerage, vol v page 194. note He seems to have varied in the spelling of his Christian name. In the two first volumes of Sir George Croke's reports, it is printed *Harebotle,* but in the last volume, *Harbottle,* as it is now written by the family

No 31

GENEALOGY OF GRIMSTON,

Descended from Silvester de Grimston, of Grimston, in Yorkshire, Standard-bearer to William the Conqueror

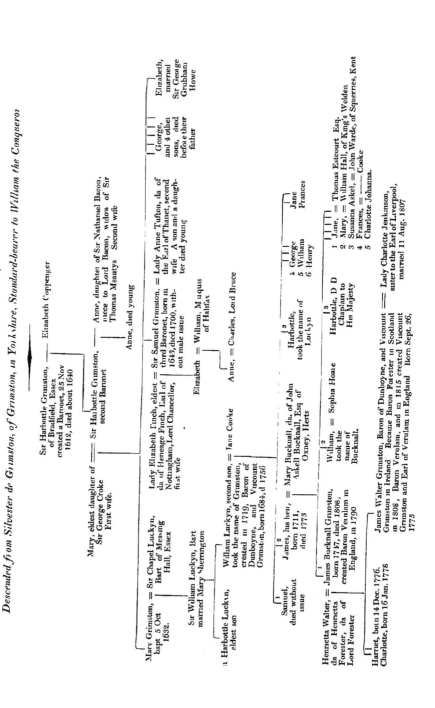

Sir Harbottle Grimston, of Bradfield, Essex created a Baronet, 25 Nov 1612, died about 1640 — Elizabeth Coppenger

Mary, eldest daughter of Sir George Croke First wife. = Sir Harbottle Grimston, second Baronet — Anne, daughter of Sir Nathaniel Bacon, niece to Lord Bacon, widow of Sir Thomas Meautys Second wife

Anne, died young

Mary Grimston, bapt 5 Oct 1632. = Sir Chapel Luckyn, Bart of Messing Hall, Essex

Lady Elizabeth Finch, eldest da of Heneage Finch, Earl of Nottingham, Lord Chancellor, first wife = Sir Samuel Grimston, third Baronet, born in 1643, died 1700, without male issue = Lady Anne Tufton, da of the Earl of Thanet, second wife A son and a daughter died young

George, and 4 other sons, died before their father

Elizabeth, married Sir George Grubham Howe

Sir William Luckyn, Bart married Mary Sherrington

Elizabeth = William, Marquis of Halifax

Anne, = Charles, Lord Bruce

1 Harbottle Luckyn, eldest son

William Luckyn, second son, took the name of Grimston, created in 1719, Baron of Dunboyne, and Viscount Grimston, born 1684, d 1756 = Jane Cooke

1 Samuel, died without issue

2 James, his heir, born 1711, died 1773 = Mary Bucknall, da. of John Askell Bucknall, Esq of Oxney, Herts

3 Harbottle, took the name of Luckyn

4 George
5 William
6 Henry

Jane
Frances

Henrietta Walter, da of Henrietta Forester, da of Lord Forester = 1 James Bucknall Grimston, born 1747, died 1808, created Baron Verulam in England, in 1790

2 William, took the name of Bucknall. = Sophia Hoare

3 Harbottle, D D Chaplain to His Majesty

1 Jane, = Thomas Estcourt Esq.
2 Mary, = William Hall, of King's Welden
3 Susanna Askel, = John Warde, of Squerries, Kent
4 Frances, = —— Cooke
5 Charlotte Johanna.

Harriet, born 14 Dec. 1776.
Charlotte, born 16 Jan. 1778

James Walter Grimston, Baron of Dunboyne, and Viscount Grimston in Ireland Became Baron Forester in Scotland in 1808, Baron Verulam, and in 1815 created Viscount Grimston and Earl of Verulam in England Born Sept. 26, 1775 = Lady Charlotte Jenkinson, sister to the Earl of Liverpool, married 11 Aug. 1807

lady, the daughter of Sir George Croke, he had six sons, five of whom died before him, and three daughters[a]. By his second wife Anne he had no children. He was succeeded in his title and estates by his son Samuel, who married, first, Lady Elizabeth Finch, daughter of Heneage Finch, Earl of Nottingham, and Lord Chancellor, by whom he had only one daughter named Elizabeth, and who married William, Marquis of Halifax. Sir Samuel Grimston's second wife was Lady Anne Tufton, daughter of the Earl of Thanet, by whom he left one daughter only

Of Sir Harbottle Grimston's daughters, Mary, who was christened at Waterstock, 5th of October, 1632, was married to Sir Chapel Luckyn, of Messing Hall in Essex, whose grandson William Luckyn, was the adopted heir of Sir Samuel Grimston, took the name of Grimston, and, in 1719, was created Baron of Dunboyne, and Viscount Grimston, of the kingdom of Ireland. His grandson, James Bucknell Grimston, was created Baron Verulam in England, in 1790. His son, the present peer, James Walter Grimston, succeeded to the title of Baron Forester, in Scotland. upon the death of Anna Maria, the last Baroness, in 1808, and in 1815, was created Viscount Grimston, and Earl of Verulam, in England. He was born the 26th of September, 1775, and married Lady Charlotte Jenkinson, daughter of Charles, the first Earl of Liverpool[b].

The arms of Grimston are, Argent, on a fesse, sable, three mullets of six points, pierced, or; and in the dexter chief, an ermine spot. Crest, on a wreath, a stag's head, couped, proper, attired, or.

At Gorhambury, are portraits of Sir Harbottle Grimston, one at full length, and another in his robes, as Master of the Rolls[c].

[a] Sir George Croke, in his will, dated 20th November, 1640, leaves one hundred pounds each to George, Mary, Elizabeth, Sarah, and Thomas, the children of his son-in-law Harbottle Grimston, Esquire, and his daughter Mary The other sons must have been born afterwards.

[b] Archdall's Peerage of Ireland, and all the peerages

[c] Many of his speeches and some letters are extant in the histories and collections of the times. Whitelocke's Memorials, Clarendon, Rushworth, Thurloe, Nelson, Kennet, &c &c. See the Genealogy of Grimston, No. 31.

SECTION THE THIRD.

ELIZABETH, the second daughter of Sir George Croke, had two husbands, THOMAS LEE, ESQUIRE, and SIR RICHARD INGOLDSBY.

To the first she was married at Waterstock, on the 30th of September, 1633[a]. This was THOMAS LEE, ESQUIRE, of Hartwell, in Buckinghamshire, the ancestor of the present Baronet of that name and place, and who was descended from an ancient family, which was supposed to be a younger branch of the Leghs, or Leighs, of Cheshire, derived from the Venables. They settled in Buckinghamshire about the beginning of the reign of Henry the Fourth. Their original seats appear to have been at East Claydon and Morton, in that county; where we find William Lee, Esquire, who died in 1486. By the marriage of his descendant, Sir Thomas Lee, Knight, with Eleanor, the daughter of Michael Hampden, Esquire, of Hartwell, they acquired that estate, and made it their principal residence. Sir Thomas and Eleanor had twenty-four children, and Thomas, their eldest son, married Jane, the daughter of Sir George Throckmorton, of Fulbrook, in Buckinghamshire, by whom he was the father of Thomas Lee, Esquire, the husband of Elizabeth Croke[b].

Thomas Lee and Elizabeth Croke had three sons and a daughter, Thomas, William, George, and Mary. William is not mentioned in Sir George Croke's will, and was perhaps then dead. Mary married Sir William Morly, of Barecourt, Knight. The name of their son Thomas occurs occasionally in the annals of the times. Though probably, from his Buckinghamshire connections, he took part with the Parliament, he was a promoter of the King's restoration. On the 23d of December, 1659, with his father-in-law Colonel Ingoldsby, and Colonel Howard, he waited upon Lord Chancellor Whitelocke, to persuade him to go over to the King with the Great Seal[c]. Upon the King's restoration he was created a

[a] Waterstock Register [b] Collins's Baronetage, vol iii p 149 ed 1741

[c] Whitelocke's Memor p 692 The name of Colonel Lee occurs several times in those memorials, I suppose the same person

GENEALOGY OF LEE OF HARTWELL.

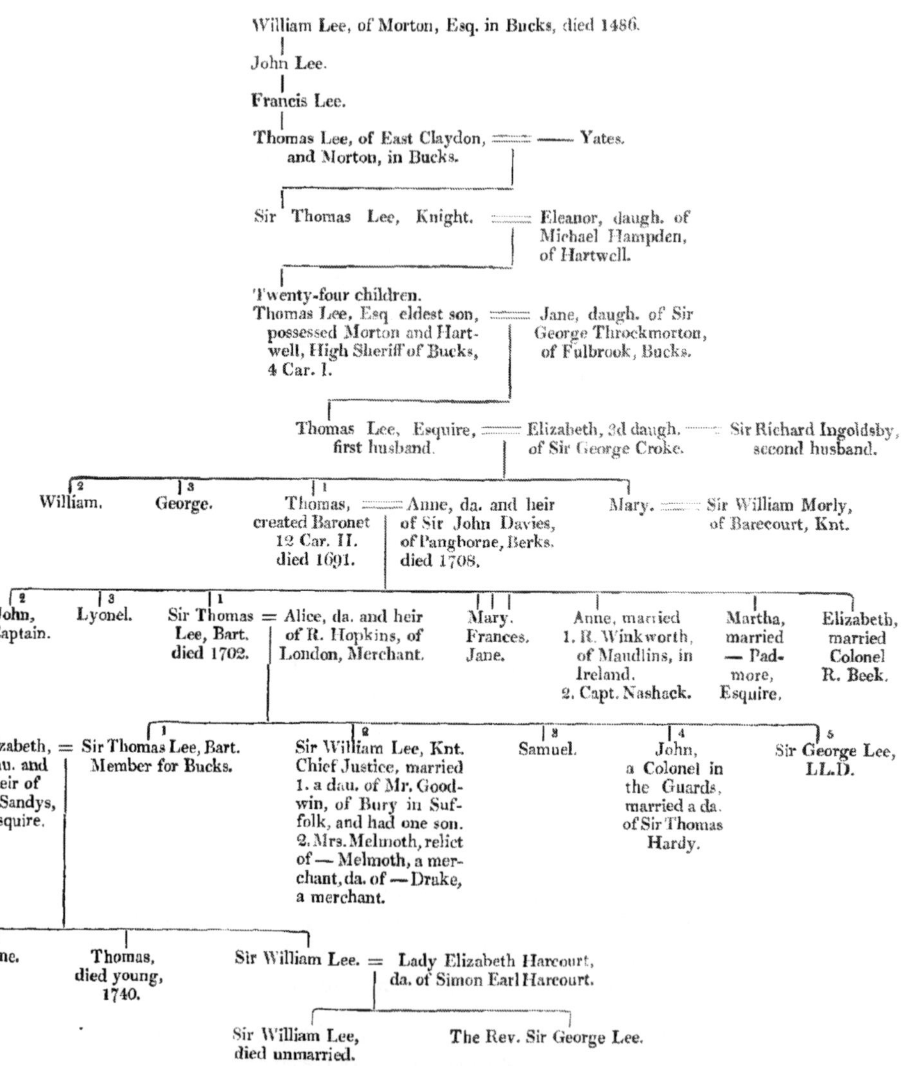

Baronet, and died in 1691. His lady was Anne, the daughter and heir of Sir John Davies, of Pangbourne in Berkshire, by whom he had a son of his own name, who was singularly fortunate in his children, whom he had by Alice, daughter of Richard Hopkins, Esquire, a merchant in London. Besides his eldest son, who was likewise another Sir Thomas, and represented his county in Parliament, two of his other sons had the merit and good fortune to arrive at the summit of their respective professions[d]

William, the second son, was bred to the common law, and became Lord Chief Justice of England. His younger brother, George, was an advocate in the Civil Law Courts, where his integrity and abilities promoted him to the situation of Dean of the Arches, and Judge of the Prerogative Court, when he was knighted, and made one of the Lords Commissioners of the Admiralty, and a Privy Counsellor. But his talents were not confined to his profession: he was an active Member of Parliament, and joined the party of the Prince of Wales in opposition to Sir Robert Walpole. He was much in the confidence of the Prince, and afterwards of the Princess Dowager, of Wales. His answer to the Prussian Memorial was considered as a master-piece in the science of the Law of Nations[e], and his decisions in Prize Causes in the Court of Appeals established his fame in every state in Europe[f].

The last Sir Thomas Lee, brother to the two Judges, having lost his eldest son, Thomas, at eighteen years of age, was succeeded by his youngest son, Sir William Lee. This gentleman married Lady Elizabeth Harcourt, daughter of Simon Earl Harcourt; one of the most accomplished noblemen of his time, Preceptor to the Prince of Wales, afterwards George the Third, and Ambassador to the Court of France. Lady Elizabeth survived her husband several years: and their eldest son, Sir William Lee, having died without issue, the present Baronet is the Reverend Sir George Lee.

The arms of Lee are, azure, two bars, or. Over all a bend, countercompony, of the second and gules. The crest, a bear, passant, sable, muzzled, collared, and chained argent[g].

[d] Collins's Baronet vol iii p. 149 Brown Willis's MSS vol 19

[e] Montesquieu, Lettre XLV. Nous lisons ici la réponse du roi d'Angleterre au roi de Prusse, et elle passe dans ce pays-ci pour une réponse sans réplique.

[f] Blackstone's Commentaries, vol iii. p 70 [g] See the Genealogy of Lee, No. 32.

SECTION THE FOURTH.

THE second husband of ELIZABETH CROKE was SIR RICHARD INGOLDSBY, Knight of the Bath. Amongst the sons-in-law of Sir George Croke, we have hitherto seen only lawyers or private gentlemen. We have now to present the reader with a soldier, of no small reputation in those military times.

Sir Richard Ingoldsby was the second son of Sir Richard Ingoldsby, of Lenthenborough in Buckinghamshire, Knight, by Elizabeth his wife, the daughter of Sir Oliver Cromwell, of Hinchinbrook in Huntingdonshire, and consequently, he was cousin to the Protector. The Ingoldsby family was originally of Lincolnshire. Sir Roger de Hyngoldyeby held in Foulbeck, Hetham, Westby, and Heryerby, three knights' fees, rendering yearly for Castle Ward thirty shillings, about 1230[a]. They removed to Lenthenborough in Buckinghamshire, in the reign of Henry VI. of which Ralph and John Ingoldsby were the joint purchasers. Ralph had a commission in 1448, to provide ships for the defence of Aquitaine, and John, in 1468, was appointed a Baron of the Exchequer[b]. Sir Richard Ingoldsby's eldest son, Francis Ingoldsby, by his extravagance, dissipated his fortune, sold Lenthenborough, and became a Pensioner in the Charter House. The second son was Sir Richard Ingoldsby, who married Elizabeth Croke.

He was educated in the public school at Thame, and by the persuasions of his parents, entered early into the Parliament army. He was soon made a Captain in Colonel John Hambden's regiment, in which he fought against the King, and, in a short time, by the interest of Cromwell, he was promoted to a regiment of horse. Colonel Ingoldsby was a man of great

[a] Dñs Rogerus de Hyngoldyeby tenet in Foulbeck, Hetham, Westby, et Henerby, tria feoda militis redd'. pro Ward Castri xxs' Blount's Fragmenta Antiquitatis, page 456 Beckwith's ed. 4to 1815

[b] Noble's Memoirs of Cromwell, vol ii p 181.

personal strength, and undaunted bravery. In an age of enthusiasm and hypocrisy, he escaped the general contagion; and without aspiring to the character of a saint, he retained the honest frankness of a soldier, and the pleasant and sociable manners of a gentleman. Although he was so unlike those with whom he associated, and was known to be no enemy to monarchy, he was highly esteemed by the republican party, and was much in the confidence of Cromwell[c].

A man of such a character, and so nearly related to Cromwell, was of course engaged in all the principal transactions of the time. He was elected a Member of the Long Parliament in 1640. In 1644, his name appears in the list of officers of Sir Thomas Fairfax's army, which was voted by the Lords and Commons, as Ingoldsby, Colonel of Foot[d]. In that year he was obliged to surrender himself to the King's officers, but regained his liberty[e]. In 1645, he attacked the King's troops near Taunton, with considerable slaughter[f], and was employed in the siege of Pendennis castle, where it was reported he was shot in reconnoitring[g]. After the surrender of Oxford to the Parliament, 24th June, 1646, Colonel Ingoldsby was appointed Governor of the garrison. Though no place had been more loyal before the surrender, afterwards it became of all others the most remarkable for sectarianism and sedition.

It was resolved by the Parliament to reform the University, and to bring the members to a conformity with the prevailing opinions. Six commissioners were sent down, to prepare the way for a general reformation. At the head of these was the celebrated Doctor Cheynell. They were of the Presbyterian faction, and preached, and disputed indefatigably, to remove the *scruples of weak-minded brethren*. They met with great opposition from the army there stationed, which consisted of Seekers, Anabaptists, Independents, and *gifted men* of every denomination; who maintained the perfect equality of all Christians, and abhorred the doctrines and the regular establishment of ministers, in the Presbyterian assemblies. Conferences and disputations were frequently held between the leaders of the different sects. Amongst these, one William Earby, a

[c] Wood's Ath. Ox. ii col 757 [d] Whitelocke, p 132. [e] Noble's Memoirs of Cromwell, vol. ii. p 186. [f] Whitelocke, p 144. [g] Ibid p 204

soldier and an eminent preacher, publicly maintained, that "the fulness "of the Godhead dwelt in the saints in the same manner, though not in "the same manifestation, as it doth in Christ, and that they would have "the same worship, honour, throne, and glory, that Christ hath, and a "more glorious power to do greater works than ever he did before his "ascension." He had many followers in this extraordinary doctrine, till Colonel Ingoldsby, his commander, cashiered and discharged him for his abominable blasphemy[h].

Upon the resolutions of the House of Commons, for disbanding the army, in 1647, and the discontents of the military upon it, after the result of Fairfax's Council of War was communicated to the House, the money sent for disbanding Colonel Ingoldsby's regiment was recalled Three thousand pounds of this money were stopped by some of Colonel Rainsborough's men[i]. After the King was taken prisoner, there was a petition to the General, in October, 1648, from Colonel Ingoldsby's regiment, "for justice to be done upon the principal invaders of their liberties, namely, "the King and his party." It does not appear that Ingoldsby himself concurred in it, as the soldiers at that time were deliberative bodies, independent of their officers[k].

Though he was appointed one of the King's Judges, he never sat in the court, always abhorring the action in his heart, and having no other interest in the national disputes than his personal affection for Cromwell. The day after the sentence was pronounced, he had occasion to speak with an officer, who, he was told, was in the Painted Chamber, when he came thither, he found Cromwell, and the rest of the Judges, who were assembled to sign the warrant for the King's death. As soon as Cromwell saw him, he ran up to him, and, taking him by the hand, drew him by force to the table, and said, "though he had escaped him all the while before, "he should now sign that paper as well as they." Which he, perceiving what it was, refused with great passion, saying, "he knew nothing of the "business," and offered to go away. But Cromwell and others held him by violence, and Cromwell, with a loud laughter, taking his hand in his, and putting the pen between his fingers, with his own hand writ.

[h] Wood's Hist [i] Whitelocke, p 253 [k] Ibid 341

Richard Ingoldsby, he making all the resistance he could; and he afterwards said, "if his name there were compared with what he had ever "writ himself, it could never be looked upon as his own hand[l]."

After the University had been reformed, and regenerated, by the Parliamentary Visitors, Fairfax, Cromwell, and a large party, were invited there to the Commemoration, in May 1649, and were received with great honours. Degrees were given to most of them, and that of Master of Arts was conferred upon Ingoldsby. Amongst the ejected members of the University, Whitehall who had been expelled from Christ Church, by cringing and flattery to Ingoldsby, was made Fellow of Merton[m].

In September of that year, a formidable mutiny broke out at Oxford, amongst the Levellers. They published a representation to the army and nation, declaring their intention of "freeing them from the excise, which "eats into the bones of poor people, from cut-throat tithes, lawyers, and "law Latin." They imprisoned their officers, set guards, fortified New College, and committed many acts of hostility. The mutineers expected to have been joined by great numbers, and even the whole army. Before they could increase to any very considerable party, by the care of Ingoldsby the governor, and the other officers, they were dispersed, some of them were tried by a court martial, and two were shot, others disbanded and otherwise punished Some of them, who belonged to Ingoldsby's regiment, were pardoned at his request. The University was greatly alarmed, and, after tranquillity was restored, it was voted, that "calling into consideration that special service which divers officers of war "had effected in quieting the tumultuous soldiers in the garrison, a civil "visit and thankfulness should be tendered to them by the Vice-Chan-"cellor, Proctors, and Heads of Houses, and that Major General Lam-"bert and Colonel Ingoldsby should be presented severally with gloves, "in the name of the University." And thanks were voted by the House of Commons to them for their services therein[n].

In 1650 he was sent by the Parliament into Ireland with General Ludlow. Here he was particularly distinguished. In the same year, with

[l] Nalson's Trial of King Charles Clarendon, Hist vol. iii. p 1011 Ed 1819 [m] Wood's Ath. Ox [n] Wood, by Gutch, p 626 Whitelocke, pages 408, 409, 410, 411

three troops of horse, he charged 3000 horse and foot of the Irish, near Limerick, under Colonel Grace, and totally routed them[o]. In 1651, finding about two hundred horse grazing near the city of Limerick, he followed them to the gates, where those that escaped the sword, the Shannon devoured. The enemy lost about an hundred men, a hundred and fifty arms, and a thousand cows, oxen, and sheep[p]. In July, 1651, Cromwell sent Ingoldsby's regiment to General Lambert, who were in Scotland[q]. In the year 1651, he purchased the estate at Waldridge, in the parish of Dinton in Buckinghamshire, which then became the seat of the family. In 1652, the Irish burnt Portumny town, and Colonel Ingoldsby relieved them, routed their horse, and surrounded their foot in a bog[r].

In the year 1653, when Cromwell was determined to humble the Parliament, he called a council of officers at Whitehall to determine respecting the settlement of the country, and putting a period to that assembly. Hopes were entertained that they would dissolve themselves, but Colonel Ingoldsby came back to Cromwell, and told him that the House was engaged in debate of an act which would occasion other meetings and prolong the session. Upon which Cromwell was so enraged, that with a party of soldiers he marched to the House, ordered the mace to be taken away, turned out the members, and locked the door. Thus, by one bold measure, he destroyed the celebrated Parliament which had murdered the King, and governed the nation for so many years, and put an end to the Republic[s]. He was now declared Protector, and a Council of State was appointed, by the fundamental instrument of government. Of this Council, Ingoldsby was nominated, and was afterwards summoned by writ to sit in the Upper House, or House of Peers. upon its erection in 1657.

Anthony Wood informs us, that about this time, Cromwell committed him to the Tower, for a short time, for beating at Whitehall a person, whom he calls "the honest innkeeper of Aylesbury." This I suppose was one of Ingoldsby's lively sallies, in which his zeal had the upper hand of his discretion[t]. In 1654, he was one of the Commissioners for "eject-

[o] Whitelocke, p 450 Ludlow, vol i p 359. [p] Whitelocke, June 20th, 1651
[q] Whitelocke, July 28th, 1651 [r] Whitelocke, p. 513 [s] Whitelocke, page 529
[t] Fast. Oxon. ii col 758.

"ing scandalous, ignorant, and insufficient schoolmasters" for the county of Buckingham[u].

After the death of Oliver Cromwell, he continued to be faithfully attached to his son Richard, when he was ungratefully betrayed, and deserted, by his own relations, and by those who owed their elevation to his family. Richard was not insensible of his merit. When an officer was brought before him for murmuring at the promotion of some persons who were known to have been cavaliers, he asked him, "Whether he would have "him prefer none but those that were godly? Here, continued he, is "Dick Ingoldsby, who can neither pray, nor preach, and yet I will trust "him before ye all." And Henry Cromwell, the Lord Lieutenant of Ireland, always spoke of him by the familiar, but affectionate appellation of "honest Ingoldsby[x]." In 1659, he was one of the Commissioners of the Militia for Bucks.

Yet however well disposed himself, he was not always properly seconded by the soldiers under his command. When Lieutenant General Fleetwood, in opposition to the new Protector, had assembled his officers at Saint James's, and had appointed a general meeting of the army there, Richard ordered a counter-rendezvous at the same time at Whitehall. Most of the officers and soldiers repaired to the General amongst others, three troops of Colonel Ingoldsby's horse marched also to Saint James's, with part of two more; so that he had only one entire troop of his regiment to stand by him Even many of Richard's own guards deserted him, and he was left almost unprotected[y]. In this distress of Richard, amongst contending and virulent parties, and whilst he was wavering between contradictory proposals, Ingoldsby was one of those real friends who suggested the most prudent line of conduct for him to adopt, if he had been of a capacity to embrace their counsels, and of sufficient courage to have executed them. They persuaded him "to adhere to the Parliament, to reject the demands of the army, and to "punish their presumption." Ingoldsby, Whaley, and Goffe, declared their resolution to stand by him, and one of them, probably Ingoldsby, offered to kill Lambert, whom they looked upon as the author of the con-

[u] The Commission [x] Ludlow's Memoirs, vol. ii. p 171. Ed. Edin 1751 [y] Ludlow, ii p 176

spiracy against him, if he would give him a warrant for that purpose. Richard rejected their advice, dissolved the Parliament, and was deposed[z].

When the Council of Officers had thus freed themselves from the superior authority of a Protector, they knew that they could not long hold the government in their own hands, if they did not immediately remove Ingoldsby, Whaley, Goffe, and the other officers who had dissuaded Richard from submitting to their advice, from their command in the army, as they had great interest there. They were accordingly removed, and were replaced by Lambert, and the other officers who had been cashiered by Oliver[a].

The Cromwell family having now totally fallen from all its power and honours, Colonel Ingoldsby, who had no republican principles, readily concurred with the party which accomplished the restoration of the monarchy. Before the arrival of Monk in London, on the 23d of December, 1659, with his son-in-law, Mr. Lee, and Colonel Howard, he waited upon Whitelocke, the Lord Commissioner of the Great Seal, and discoursing with him upon the probability of their success, proposed that he should go over to the King with the Great Seal. Whitelocke would not consent to their overtures[b].

After Monk was appointed General of the Forces, he gave Colonel Rich's regiment to Ingoldsby. Before the order could be put in execution, Rich, hoping to prevail with his men, as he had formerly done, to declare for the republicans, went down to their quarters. Upon his arrival most of them promised to remain faithful to him, but when Colonel Ingoldsby came down, as he had great personal interest amongst them from their having been under his command in the time of Cromwell, he prevailed with the greatest part of them to desert Rich, who, finding himself abandoned, yielded the rest of the men to him, and declared his resolution to acquiesce[c]. Rich was afterwards committed to prison by the Council of State, for persuading his soldiers to obey the Parliament, and to stand against Charles Stuart[d].

On the 25th of February, 1660, he was sent by Monk with forces to

[z] Clarendon, iii. p 876 [a] Clarendon, iii. p 877 [b] Whitelocke's Memorials, p 692 b [c] Ludlow, ii p 356 [d] Whitelocke, p 699 b

quiet the regiment at Bury[e], and he was appointed a member of the Council of State[f]. He surprised likewise the Castle of Windsor, where there was a great magazine of arms and ammunition, and displaced the Governor who had been appointed by the Rump Parliament[g].

At this critical time a most important service was performed by Ingoldsby. Whilst the great business of the Restoration was in a state of trembling uncertainty, an event happened which had nearly destroyed the King's hopes, defeated all the prudent designs of Monk, and was near again plunging the nation into all the miseries of civil war. The near prospect of the changes which were expected to take place had filled the republican party with the most gloomy apprehensions, and their ruin and destruction appeared to be inevitable. The greater part of the army, and even many of the soldiers who were under General Monk, had been inflamed, by artful agents, with a sense of their own desperate condition. Whilst they were in this state of mind, and wanted only a proper opportunity, and a leader of vigour and capacity, to break out in great strength, General Lambert, a man of the greatest enterprize, and military skill, and highly popular with the army, made his escape from the Tower, where he had been for some time confined by the Parliament. Monk, and the Council of State, were in the greatest agony. Officers were sent by Lambert to the soldiers who were dispersed in different parts of the kingdom, and were all expected to join him; on the other hand, no small danger was apprehended from assembling troops to oppose him in their present state of jealousy and dissatisfaction

With great expedition, Lambert drew together four troops, and appeared in arms near Daventry, waiting for the other parts of the army. General Monk, upon the first intimation of his proceedings, appointed Colonel Ingoldsby to attend and watch all his motions with his own regiment of horse: a service in which he very willingly engaged, from his enmity to Lambert, on account of his malice to Oliver and Richard, and an affront which he had himself received from him: and his own regiment was the more faithful to him, for having been before seduced by Lambert to desert from him. Ingoldsby, being joined with a good body of foot, under Colonel Streater, used so much diligence in waiting upon

[e] Whitelocke, p. 698 [f] Wood, Fast Ox. ubi supra [g] Clarendon, iii p. 1011.

Lambert's motions, before he was suspected to be so near, that Hasleing, son of Sir Arthur, one of his four captains, was taken prisoner. Hasleing told them that he was dissatisfied with Lambert's design, and had quitted him, and hoped to be set at liberty. But Ingoldsby informed him, that unless he would bring off his troop also from Lambert, his deserting them should be of no advantage to him. He promised to use his best endeavours, and was permitted to return, and soon afterwards he brought over his troop to Ingoldsby[h]. From the information thus obtained, Ingoldsby marched hastily, and came in sight, before it was known that he was in pursuit of his enemy. Lambert, surprised at this discovery, disheartened by the desertion of one of his troops, and the superiority of the enemy, and probably wishing to gain time, offered a parley, which was agreed to. Lambert proposed that Richard should be restored to the Protectorship, and promised to unite all his credit to the support of that interest. But Ingoldsby, sensible of the folly and impossibility of that undertaking, and having devoted himself to a better cause, rejected his overture, and told him, that he himself was one of those who pulled down Richard, and now would set him up again, and that they had no commission to dispute, but to reduce him and his party[i]. Both parties prepared for engaging, but another of Lambert's troops forsaking him, his courage failed him, and no fighting took place, except that one of the troopers fired a pistol at Ingoldsby. Lambert, concluding that his safety depended upon his flight, endeavoured to escape by the swiftness of his horse. Ingoldsby, keeping his eye still upon him, and being as well mounted, overtook him, and made him prisoner with his own hand, after he had in vain used great and much importunity to him. that he would permit him to escape. Some officers of the greatest interest with the fanatical part of the army, and whose designs were most apprehended by Monk, were taken with him. This capture took place on the 23d of April, 1660. Upon their return, they found the roads full of soldiers, marching to join Lambert, and, if their plans had not been crushed *at that very instant*, they would have become in a few days a very formidable power[k]. Ingoldsby first brought his prisoners to Northampton. It was

[h] Ludlow. [i] Whitelocke, 701. [k] Clarendon, iii p 962. Whitelocke, p 701. a Ludlow, ii 376.

here that Lambert, as Ingoldsby told Burnet, entertained him with a pleasant reflexion for all his misfortunes. The people were in great crowds applauding, and rejoicing for the success. Upon which Lambert put Ingoldsby in mind of what Cromwell had said to them both, near that very place, in 1650, when, with a body of officers, they were going down after their army that was marching into Scotland, the people all the while shouting, and wishing them success. Lambert upon that said to Cromwell, he was glad to see they had the nation on their side. Cromwell answered, " Do " not trust to that; for those very persons would shout as much if you " and I were going to be hanged." Lambert said, " he looked on him- " self as in a fair way to that, and began to think Cromwell prophe- " sied[l]."

Ingoldsby returned to London, and brought his prisoners to the Privy Council, who committed them to the Tower, and other prisons. By this seasonable victory, all apprehensions from the discontent of the army were removed, and the business of the Restoration proceeded, without further interruption. with moderation and firmness[m]. From this time the King's party, who had hitherto sheltered themselves in obscurity, appeared publicly, and avowed themselves. And, through Mr. Mordaunt, who was known to be entirely in the King's confidence, Ingoldsby, with many of the Council, and officers of the army, made direct tenders of their services to Charles[n]. On the 26th of April, 1660, the House of Commons ordered a day of Thanksgiving, " for raising up Monk, and other " instruments, in delivery of the nation from thraldom and misery." And thanks were voted to Monk, for his eminent and unparalleled services, and to Ingoldsby[o].

The King would admit of no applications from any of his father's Judges, or hearken to any propositions on their behalf. To this, Ingoldsby formed an exception. From the deposal of Richard, he had declared that he would serve the King, and told Mr. Mordaunt, " that he would per- " form all the services he could, without making any conditions, and " would be well content, that his Majesty, when he came home, should " take off his head, if he thought fit; only he desired that the King might

[l] Burnet's Hist of his Own Times, vol 1 p 85 Ed. folio, 1724 [m] Clarendon.
[n] Ibid [o] Whitelocke, p 701 b

4 L

"know the truth of his case" namely, that he had never once been present at the trial of the late King, and had been compelled by force to sign the warrant, as before related. But though his Majesty had within himself compassion for him, he never would send him any assurance of his pardon; presuming that, if these allegations were true, there would be a season when a distinction would be made, without his Majesty's declaring himself, between him and the others of that bloody list, which he resolved never to pardon, nor was Ingoldsby at all disheartened with this, but pursued his former resolutions, steady in the King's cause[p].

Upon the Restoration, in the Act of Indemnity which was passed, and did not extend to any of King Charles the First's Judges, Colonel Richard Ingoldsby was excepted by name, and he was declared capable of bearing any office, ecclesiastical, civil, or military, and of serving in Parliament[q]. At the King's Coronation he was created Knight of the Bath. He afterwards retired, and passed the remainder of his life in a quiet repose at Waldridge. Of his two younger brothers, Henry was a Colonel, and Thomas a Captain, in the Parliament army[r]. Henry was created a Baronet, by Cromwell, on the 31st of March, 1658, and was re-created by Charles the Second[s]. Sir Richard served in Parliament, after the Restoration, in the Parliaments which were summoned in the 13th, 31st, and 32d years of Charles the Second, for the borough of Aylesbury[t], died in 1685, and was buried in Hartwell church, on the 16th of September. His wife was buried at Dinton, May the 7th, 1675[u]. He left an only son, Richard, and a daughter Anne, who married Thomas Marriot, Esquire, of Ascot, in Warwickshire.

His son, Richard Ingoldsby, Esquire, of Waldridge, married Mary, the only daughter of William Colmore, Esquire, of the city of Warwick. They had seven sons, and as many daughters. He died the 14th of April, 1703, and his wife in 1726[x]. Their sons were, Richard, William, Thomas, a second Richard, Francis, Henry, and John. The daughters, Elizabeth, Mary, Anne, Letitia, Jane, Sarah, and Henrietta[y].

All the sons died children, except Thomas, the third. He was born in

p Clarendon, iii. p. 1011. q 12 Car. II. cap xi. sect. 45. r Wood's Fasti, vol ii. col. 757. s Noble's Memoirs of Cromwell, vol. i. p. 441. t Ibid. u Noble. x His monument in Dinton Church. Register there. y Dinton Register.

THE GENEALOGY OF INGOLDSBY OF LETHENBOROUGH, IN THE PARISH OF BUCKINGHAM

Sir Roger Ingoldsby = Lord of the Manor of Skymord and Ingoldsby Lane

John Ingoldsby ob S P

Roger Ingoldsby = son and heir

Roger Ingoldsby =

Roger Ingoldsby = —— daughter of Thomas Kelly

Thomas Ingoldsby = Mary daugh of Thomas Frene

Ralf Ingoldsby of Lethenborough = Agnes daughter and heir of William Bardwell

Richard Ingoldsby of Lethenborough — —— daughter of John Hines of Northamptonshire

Richard Ingoldsby of Lethenborough = —— daugh of John Greenway Justice of the Peace for the County of Bucks tem Hen VIII

—— daughter of William Sander of Welford Com Northampton first wife = Francis Ingoldsby — —— daugh of —— Crispe and relict of —— Dormer 2d wife

Sir Richard Ingoldsby = Elizabeth daughter of William Palmer of Waddesdon

Francis Ingoldsby, 2d son. Issue

= Francis Ingoldsby

John

Sir Richard Ingoldsby of Lethenborough Knt = Elizabeth daughter of Sir Oliver Cromwell of Hinchinbrook Hunt.

Dorothy married 1 Christopher Pigott of Doddershall, Esquire 2 to Simon Stuart 3 to Maximilian Petty

Agnes married to Richard Saunders, of Dynton Bucks Esq.

7 Thomas

8 William

1 Elizabeth

1 Francis Ingoldsby sold Lethenborough and became a Pensioner in the Charter house. = Lettice dau of Crawley Norton of Offley Herts

2 Sir Richard Ingoldsby of Waldridge in Dynton Knt of the Bath, died in 1685 = Elizabeth, third dau of Sir George Croke widow of Thos Lee of Hartwell Esq She died in 1675

3 Sir Henry Ingoldsby, of Lethenborough Bart = Anne dau. of Sir Hardress Waller

6 Sir George Ingoldsby a Loyalist served the King in the Civil wars, killed in the Dutch wars = Daughter of —— Child of Ireland

1. Francis
2. Richard
3. Elizabeth

2 Anne
3 Lucy
4 Lettice

Richard Ingoldsby of Waldridge Esq ob 14 April 1708 only son Seven sons and seven daughters = Mary daugh of Wm Colmore of Warwick died at Beaconsfield in 1726

Anne, married to Thos Marriot of Ascot, Warw

Anne married to Sir Francis Blundell of Ireland Bart, mother to Sir Mountague Blundell

Sir William Ingoldsby Bart = —— only daugh of Sir Kingsmill Lucy Bart.

Anne only child living in 1708

Charles Ingoldsby killed in a duel = —— daugh of — Gore Bart of Ireland

Ingoldsby, Lieut General

Richard b. 1680 d 1687

William b 1681 d 1682

Elizabeth b. 1683 d 1705

Mary b 1684

Anne b 1685

Letitia b 1686 d 1711

Jane b 1687 d 1691

Thomas Ingoldsby of Waldridge, Sheriff of Bucks, and in 1731 Member for Aylesbury born 1689 died 1768 = Anne, daugh of John Lambrey Esq of Tangier Park Hants d. May 21 1741 aged 40

Richard b 1690 d 1700

Sarah b 1691 d 1692

Frances b 1698

Henry d 1693

John d 1697

Henrietta

1689, and inherited the estate at Waldridge. He was High Sheriff for Buckinghamshire, and, in 1731, was Member of Parliament for Aylesbury. He died in 1768. His wife was Anne, daughter of John Limbrey, Esq of Tangier Park, in Hampshire, and she died the 21st of May, 1741, aged forty years[z].

They had an infant, who died in 1736[a]; but their only surviving child was Martha Ingoldsby, who, on the 7th of January, 1762, married George Powlet, Esq. who on the death of the Duke of Bolton, in 1794, became Marquis of Winchester, premier Marquis of England[b]. The Marchioness died the 14th of March, 1796, and the Marquis in 1800. Their son was Charles Ingoldsby Powlet, the present Marquis of Winchester, Earl of Wiltshire, and Baron Saint John[c].

The arms of Ingoldsby are, ermine, a saltier engrailed, sable. Crest, a griffon[d].

FRANCES, the third daughter of Sir George Croke, married JOHN JERVOIS, ESQUIRE, of whom I have not been able to learn any particulars.

[z] Her monument at Dinton [a] Dinton Register [b] Ibid [c] Peerage
[d] See the Genealogy of Ingoldsby, No. 33. from Brown Willis's MSS vol xix Harl MSS No 1102 corrected, and continued from Deeds, the Dinton Register, &c.

CHAPTER VII.

HAVING exhausted the family of Sir George Croke, the Judge, I proceed to his brother, PAULUS AMBROSIUS CROKE, the fourth son of Sir John Croke, and Elizabeth Unton.

He was a Barrister of the Inner Temple, of which he was admitted a student, and described as late of Clement's Inn, the 18th of February, 24 Elizabeth, 1582: was called to the Bar the 5th of July, 1590. made a Bencher the 10th of May, 1605: and was Lent Reader in 1608[a]. The manors of Cotsmore and Barrow, in Rutlandshire, were purchased by him[b].

His first wife was Frances Wellesborne, whose monument was in Saint Catherine Cree's Church in London, and the epitaph is preserved by Stowe[c]. *Frances Croke, the loving and beloved wife of Paulus Ambrosius Croke, of the Inner Temple, Esquire, was one of the daughters, and heirs, of Francis Wellesborne, Esquire, of Hanny, in the county of Berks. She deceased the* 10*th of July, in the year* 1605, *aged* 22 *years.*

Well borne she was,
but better borne again.
Her first birth
to the flesh did make her debtor,
The latter in the Spirit
by Christ hath set her
Freed from fleshes debts,
Death's first and latter gains.
Wives pay no debts
Whose husbands live and raigne.

Inner Temple Register. Arms in the Inner Temple Hall window. Ward, 306. Dugd. Or. Jud. p. 167.

[b] Wright's Rutlandshire, page 40.

[c] Survey, page 149. There was a grant of the manor of Esyndon in the county of Bucks for time of his life to Christopher Wellesborne, in the reign of Henry the Fifth, or Richard the Third. Harleian MSS. No. 433. Art. 465.

The first line alludes to the origin of this family. Eleanor, eldest daughter of King John, married Simon Mountford, Earl of Leicester, by whom she had six children. Richard, the fifth son, changed his name from Mountford to Wellesbourne, and was the ancestor of that family[d].

His second wife was Susanna, the daughter of Thomas Coe, or Choe, of Boxford in Suffolk, widow of Humphrey Milward, Esquire, of London, and before the wife of Thomas Carter, Esquire, of London and Walthamstow[e].

He died on the 25th of August, in 1631, and Mr. William Fletcher was admitted to his chambers in Hare Court, on the 3d of November, in the same year[f].

On Sir John Croke's monument he is represented in a barrister's gown, with two coats of arms for his two marriages. First, Croke, with an annulet, impaled with, gules, a lion rampant, or debruised of a bend, azure; a chief, checky, or and gules: for Wellesborne. The other coat is, Croke, as before, impaled with argent, two piles in chief, wavy, gules, for Coe.

By his first wife he left one daughter only to inherit his estates. She was married to Sir Robert Heath, Attorney General, and afterwards Lord Chief Justice of the King's Bench. Their only daughter, Margaret Heath, married Sir Thomas Fanshaw, Knight, of Jenkins, in the parish of Barking, in Essex. They had an only daughter likewise, Susanna Fanshaw, who became the wife of Baptist Noel, Esquire, second son of Baptist, Lord Viscount Camden, who was seated at Luffenham in the county of Rutland. They left one son, Baptist Noel, who became Earl of Gainsborough, upon the death of his cousin, Wriothesley-Baptist, Earl of Gainsborough, without male issue, in 1690[g]. This title became extinct in 1799, but the present family of Noel, Viscount and Baron Wentworth, is descended from the same ancestors[h].

[d] Baker's Chron. p 83. [e] Harleian MSS No 1533 page 65 b A visitation book of Buckinghamshire [f] Ward p 306 [g] Collins's Peerage, vol. ii. p. 522 Delafield [h] Peerage, i 272.

CHAPTER VIII

SECTION THE FIRST

CECILY CROKE

BEFORE I proceed with the history and descendants of William Croke, the fifth and youngest son of Sir John Croke and Elizabeth Unton, I shall dispatch their three daughters, CECILY, PRUDENTIA, and ELIZABETH.

CECILY, the eldest, had two husbands: the first was EDWARD BULSTRODE, Esquire, of Hedgerly Bulstrode, in Buckinghamshire, the second, SIR JOHN BROWN, Knight.

Her first husband was descended from an ancient family, and from Richard Bulstrode, who was Keeper of the Great Wardrobe to Margaret, the Queen of Henry the Sixth, and, afterwards, Comptroller of the Household to King Edward the Fourth. His great grandmother was Mary, the daughter of the celebrated Sir Richard Empson, one of the Barons of the Exchequer, who, with Dudley, was an able instrument in the hands of Henry the Seventh, to extort money from the subject under the forms of law; and who was attainted of high treason, arraigned, found guilty, in violation of justice, and beheaded on Tower Hill, to gratify the people.

Edward Bulstrode, and Cecily Croke, had two sons, Henry and Edward, and a daughter, Elizabeth. Their eldest son, Henry, was the father of Thomas Bulstrode, who married Coluberry Mayne, and thereby formed a connection with two families, of whom I shall have occasion to speak hereafter, the Maynes, and the Bekes. Their daughter, Elizabeth Bulstrode, married SIR JAMES WHITELOCKE, Knight, one of the Justices of the King's Bench, who was born in 1570. He was an able and an independent man, and disapproved of the method sometimes used by the King, of sending to the Judges for their opinions upon questions beforehand, and said that if Bishop Laud went on in his way, he would kindle a flame in the nation[a]. He concurred with Sir George Croke upon the point of granting writs of *Habeas Corpus*. When actions for false imprisonment were brought against some of the members of the High Commission Court, with a view of checking the oppressive measures of that tribunal, and the King personally interfered with his absolute command to stop the proceedings, Whitelocke insisted upon it, "that "it was against law to exempt, or privilege, any man from answering "the action of another man that would sue him." The Judges stood firm, refused to obey the command of the King, and he was at length obliged to abandon this unlawful exercise of authority[b]. After his death, when it was moved, as before related, that Selden and the other prisoners should have reparation out of the estates of the Judges who had refused to bail them, Whitelocke was excepted, and it was stated, that he had been a faithful, able, and stout assertor of the rights and liberties of the free-born subjects of this kingdom, for which he had been many ways a sufferer, and particularly by a strait and close imprisonment, for what he said and did as member of the House of Commons[c].

His son has given the following character of him. "In his death the "King lost as good a subject, his country as good a patriot, the people as "just a judge, as ever lived All honest men lamented the loss of him. "No man in his age left behind him a more honoured memory. His "reason was clear and strong, and his learning deep and general. He had "the Latin tongue so perfect, that sitting Judge of Assize at Oxford, "when some foreigners, persons of quality, being there, and coming to "the court, to see the manner of our proceedings in matters of justice, "this Judge caused them to sit down, and briefly repeated the heads of "his charge to the Grand Jury in good and elegant Latin. He under-"stood the Greek very well, and the Hebrew, and was versed in the "Jewish histories, and exactly knowing in the history of his own country, "and in the pedigrees of most persons of honour and quality in the "kingdom, and was much conversant in the studies of antiquity and

[a] Whitelocke's Memorials, page 13 [b] Ibid p. 15. [c] Ibid. p. 37.

"heraldry. He was not by any excelled in knowledge of his own pro-"fession of the Common Law of England, wherein his knowledge of the "Civil Law (whereof he was a graduate at Oxford) was a help to him, "as his learned arguments will confirm[d]."

Sir James Whitelocke was a member of the original Society of Antiquaries, in the reign of Queen Elizabeth, with Sir Robert Cotton, Camden, and other eminent men[e].

There are in manuscript, the Lectures of James Whitlock, Esquire, in the Middle Temple, read August the 2d, 1619, upon the Statute 21 Henry VIII. chapter 13; and, A Treatise upon Combats[f]. Several of his speeches are in The Sovereign's Prerogative, and the Subject's Privileges discussed. Printed at London, in 1657. There are also two short pieces written by him, published in Hearne's Curious Discourses[g]. 1. A Discourse of the antiquity and office of Heralds in England. It consists of three pages, and is dated 28 November, 1601 2. Of the antiquity, use, and privileges of places for Students, and Professors of the Common Law of England: in six pages. He left likewise an account of his own life, written by himself. And, notwithstanding his full practice in his profession, he neglected not his study of the Bible, but collected notes throughout both the Old and New Testaments. His lady likewise wrote a Collection of promises and precepts out of the Book of God[h]. He died in 1632.

The son of Sir James Whitelocke and Elizabeth Bulstrode, was BULSTRODE WHITELOCKE, who became eminent as a man of general learning, a lawyer, a politician, and a negociator.

He is included in that list of superior characters, with whom it was the pride and boast of Lord Clarendon to have associated in his youth. At first setting out in life, they both ran the same course, and opposed the illegal proceedings of Charles. Afterwards, whilst Clarendon followed the fortunes of his Sovereign, Whitelocke, as was natural from his connections with the principal leaders, was attached to the side of the Parliament; yet, as his former friend observed, "with less rancour and malice "than other men, and never led, but followed, and was rather carried

[d] Whitelocke's Memorials, page 17 [e] Life of Sir Robert Cotton, annexed to the catalogue of the Bodleian, and other Manuscripts, page 8 [f] Bodleian MSS No 7858 [g] Pages 90, 129 [h] Swedish Ambassy, vol ii Appendix, p 433, 436

"away with the torrent than swam with the stream[i]." He has been accused of a want of stability of principle, and of always adhering to those who were in power: but the review of his life will shew this charge to be unfounded. He was too good a moralist, and lawyer, not to distinguish what was right; he had too much sound sense for an enthusiast; and he was too honest to give his sanction to what he believed to be wrong. Accordingly we find him opposing many of the unlawful proceedings both of the King, and of the Parliament, and entirely adverse to the elevation of Cromwell. When he had freely delivered his opinion upon any point, and it was always in favour of peace and moderation, and his farther opposition could be no longer effectual, he acquiesced under measures which he could not control, and submitted to authorities which it was not in his power to resist. This conduct proceeded not from weakness, but, as he has explained it himself, from principle. "All casuists," he said, "agree, that if a government be altered, and another power in possession of it, all private men are bound to submit to the present powers, "because they are ordained of God[k]."

Bulstrode Whitelocke was born on the 6th of August, 1605, in the house of Sir George Croke, his mother's uncle, in Fleet Street[l]. He received the first part of his education at Merchant-Taylors' School, and was admitted, in Michaelmas term, 1620, a Gentleman Commoner of Saint John's College in Oxford, where he was recommended to the particular care of the President, afterwards Archbishop Laud, who was his father's contemporary and intimate friend[m]. For the fatherly kindness which he experienced he was ever grateful; and when that prelate was impeached, he refused to be upon the committee appointed to draw up the charges against him. Without having taken a degree, he removed from hence to the Middle Temple, where he was called to the Bar, and became a celebrated practitioner.

During his residence in that society, together with Hyde, Noy, Selden, and other great lawyers, he was one of the principal managers of the superb masque, which was exhibited by the Inns of Court in February, 1633, before King Charles and his Queen, at Whitehall, at an expence

[i] Life of Lord Clarendon, vol. i. p. 59. ed. 1761. [k] Swedish Ambassy, vol i. p. 335
[l] Wood's Ath. Ox part ii col 399 [m] Whitelocke's Memorials, p 33 ed 1682. Wood

of above twenty thousand pounds. In the arrangement of these festivities, the whole charge of the music was intrusted to him, and it was an accomplishment in which he excelled. He has given an entertaining account of the whole exhibition, apparently *con amore*[n].

But these delights were soon to be exchanged for less pleasing occupations. As a sound lawyer, he could not approve of the Ship-money, and he was much consulted by Hampden in his great cause Yet so little was he of a seditious disposition, that he refused to support the Covenanters of Scotland, and advised his friends not to foment those public differences, or to encourage that nation in their opposition to their natural Prince[o].

In the Long Parliament, which met on the 3d of November, 1640, he was elected Member for Marlow, and defended the memory of his father, who was wrongfully accused of having refused to bail Selden upon an *Habeas Corpus*[p].

When the Earl of Strafford was impeached, he was chosen Chairman of the Committee appointed to draw up the articles against him, and to speak to some of them. Of his manner of conducting that trial, Lord Strafford observed to a private friend, "that others had used him like advocates, but "that Palmer and Whitelocke had treated him like gentlemen, yet had "omitted nothing that was material to their cause[q]"

He was frequently employed by the House of Commons to draw up some of the most important bills, and other instruments; as the Act that the Parliament should not be prorogued, adjourned, or dissolved, without their consent, which finally established the supreme power of that assembly[r].

In the debates upon the militia, in 1641, he made an excellent speech, in which he declared it to be his opinion, that the power of the militia was neither in the King alone, nor in the Parliament, but jointly in both: in the King for *command*, in the Parliament for *pay*, which is the present true constitutional doctrine[s].

When matters were coming to an extremity with the King, and it was proposed in Parliament to raise an army in their defence, Whitelocke

[n] Memor p 18 [o] Biog Britan [p] Wood, ubi supra Memor. p 37.
[q] Memor p 37, 41. [r] Ibid. p. 43. [s] Ibid p 53.

highly disapproved of it, and with great eloquence deprecated the miseries of a civil war, which he painted in the most lively colours, and with a prophetic spirit foretold, that in the progress of it, they would be obliged to surrender their laws, liberties, properties, and lives, into the hands of an insolent soldiery. He then proposed, that all peaceable means should be resorted to, before they had recourse to such desperate measures[t].

His opposition was unavailing, and he therefore concurred in the future proceedings of the Parliament. He accepted the office of a Deputy Lieutenant of the counties of Oxford and Buckingham, in 1642, and with Mr. Hampden, and a body of troops, dispersed the King's Commissioners of Array, who met at Watlington to raise men for his service. Afterwards, with a gallant company of horse, raised chiefly amongst his neighbours, he marched to Oxford with Lord Say, and about three thousand troops, and took possession of it. It was proposed to fortify that city, and to seize the college plate, and Whitelocke, who was very much beloved there, was named as a fit person to be the Governor. This advice was not followed by Lord Say, and that important station was soon after occupied by the royal army. In October, his seat at Fawley Court was plundered by Prince Rupert's brigade, and in November, Whitelocke was with the forces which opposed the King at Brentford[u].

In January, 1643, the Parliament sent propositions for peace to the King at Oxford, when he was one of the six Commissioners, and principally drew up the papers during the treaty; which came to nothing[x].

As he opposed any undue extension of their authority both in the King and the Parliament, he was equally adverse to any extraordinary power in the sectarian clergy. In 1644, the Assembly of Divines, of which he was one of the lay members, presented their opinion to the House of Commons, "that the Presbyterian form of Church government should be "settled, and that it was *jure divino*." In the debates upon that subject, Whitelocke delivered his opinion in the House of Commons against the divine right of presbytery, and that point was in consequence negatived[y]. So afterwards, when the Presbyterians petitioned to have the power of excommunication, and suspension, he opposed it, and shewed the unreasonableness and ambitious nature of the demand[z].

[t] Memor. p 57. [u] Ibid p 59 [x] Ibid p. 63 [y] Ibid p. 106 Wood
[z] Memor p 163

After the battle of Newbury, which happened upon the 27th of October, 1644, he was one of the Commissioners named to carry to the King at Oxford the propositions of peace, which had been agreed to by both Houses. When employed upon this service, in an accidental interview with him and Hollis, his Majesty expressed his particular regard for them, and was satisfied of their wishes for peace. He requested their opinion, *as friends*, what they apprehended might be a proper answer to the message of the House, and was likely to facilitate a peace: and he desired them to set it down in writing: which they did, and the King adopted some parts of their paper[a]. This treaty, which, like the others, was only a solemn farce on the part of the Parliament to cajole the people, of course produced no good effect. The secret intercourse, which had taken place between Hollis and Whitelocke, and the King, was betrayed by the treachery of Lord Savile, and they were impeached of high treason, for advising with the King, contrary to their trust. It was only by the great exertions of their friends, that they escaped being sent to the Tower, and were at length cleared from the charge[b].

The Earl of Essex, who was jealous of the power of Cromwell, and the Scotch Commissioners, who were offended with him likewise, were carrying on their intrigues to get rid of him. One evening, Maynard and Whitelocke were sent for by Essex, to meet the Commissioners, and other friends. It was proposed by the Scotch Chancellor, to remove Cromwell, by proceeding against him as *an incendiary*, under the treaty between the two nations. Whitelocke spoke against it, and advised them not so to proceed, upon which the design was abandoned After this time, Cromwell, who was informed of every thing, shewed himself more kind to Whitelocke[c].

He voted against the Self-denying Ordinance, answered the arguments which were advanced in favour of it, and stated the injury which the State would suffer from laying aside the many brave men, who had rendered it such material services[d].

In 1645, he was one of the Commissioners at the treaty of Uxbridge, of which the proceedings are too much the subject of general history, to re-

[a] Memor p. 109 [b] Ibid p 148, 156 [c] Mem p 111 [d] Mem p 114 Clarendon is wrong in stating that Whitelocke appeared for passing the Ordinance Hist Reb vol ii p 795

quire being here related[e]. After the failure of that negociation, in the debate about sending farther proposals of peace to the King, he supported the motion to the utmost of his power. In the same year he was appointed one of the Commissioners of the Admiralty, and Steward of the revenues of Westminster College[f]. He was accused of holding intelligence with the King, but he justified himself against the charge, and had afterwards £2000 voted to him for his losses[g]. Although he was far from agreeing with them in their politics and conduct, yet he states himself to have lived much in 1645 with Sir Henry Vane, Mr. Solicitor, Mr. Brown, and other grandees of that party, and was kindly treated by them[h].

With Selden, Maynard, and St. John, he procured the abolition of the Court of Wards, and all the oppressive system of wardships: an improvement in the laws of the country, which was adopted after the Restoration[i].

Upon all occasions he shewed himself a friend to learning. He preserved the Lord Keeper Littleton's books and manuscripts from being sold by the Sequestrators[k]. He preserved the Herald's College, in opposition to the ruling powers, who were levellers of all ranks[l]. He caused also the King's manuscripts at Whitehall to be removed to Saint James's, and preserved. And again, in 1648, at the instance of Mr. Selden, he undertook the care of the royal library and medals, to prevent a design of their being sold and sent abroad[m]. At the siege of Oxford, he used all his interest to have honourable terms granted to the garrison, and that the colleges and libraries should not be plundered. With Selden he assisted Patrick Young, formerly his Majesty's Librarian, to print the Septuagint, from a valuable manuscript[n] and in 1656, there was a great meeting of learned men at his house, by an order of the House of Commons, to consider the translations of the Bible. It was agreed that the English translation was the best in the world, though some mistakes were pointed out. But the dissolution of the Parliament rendered their enquiries fruitless[o].

In December, 1646, he earnestly promoted the Ordinance for taking away

[e] Memor p 120 [f] Mem. p. 137 [g] Wood, and Memor. [h] Memor p 176 ed. 2. 1645. Oct. 14 [i] Memor p 199 [k] Ibid p 166. [l] Ibid p. 203 [m] Ibid p 289, 400. [n] Ibid p 259. [o] Ibid. p. 645

all coercive power of Committees, and all arbitrary power from both or either of the Houses of Parliament, and was usually on all Committees relating to foreign affairs[p] And he opposed the disbanding of the army, because he knew that the soldiers would not submit to it, and bad consequences would ensue. This ingratiated him still more with Cromwell and the officers. He kept a strong garrison in his house at Fyllis Court, near Henley[q].

During all this time, he applied himself closely to the practice of his profession, and attended the Assizes. In March, 1647, he was appointed one of the three Commissioners of the Great Seal, for one year, with a salary of one thousand pounds. By this appointment he acquired honours, and the style and title of Lord Commissioner Whitelocke, but he was no gainer in point of income. His practice in the law before brought him in near two thousand pounds a year, and the profits of his new office were not above fifteen hundred. He has related, as an instance of the industry of the Commissioners, that they determined in one day thirteen causes, and forty demurrers in the afternoon, and sometimes sat from five in the morning till five in the evening[r]

In May, in the same year, his friends, and some who wished for his absence, proposed that he should be appointed Lord Justice of Ireland, to exercise the civil government of that country, but he was unwilling to undertake it. Cromwell and his party were likewise against his going away, as they frequently consulted with him, and made much use of his advice[s]. He refused also the office of Recorder of the city of London[t].

The next year, 1648, in July, the Earl of Pembroke was made Constable of Windsor Castle, and Keeper of the Park and Forest, and he appointed Whitelocke his Lieutenant[u] In October he was called to the degree of Serjeant at Law, and was appointed by the House of Commons Attorney General of the Dutchy of Lancaster, and one of the King's Serjeants[x]. When those who obtained promotion in the law came before him to take the oaths, he usually addressed them in learned speeches, in which he treated of the antiquity and the nature of their offices. Several of them are preserved in his Memorials: such as his discourses upon the

[p] Memor. p 234 [q] Ibid p 217 ed 2. 28 July, 1646 [r] Mem p 294, 322, 359
[s] Ibid p 253 [t] Ibid p 271 [u] Ibid p 319 [x] Ibid p 337

Court of Exchequer, upon the rank of Serjeants, and of that of Judges[y].

When Colonel Pride stood at the door of the House of Commons, on the 6th of December, 1648, to exclude those members who were obnoxious to the party in power, he suffered Whitelocke to pass as a friend to Cromwell and the army[z]. Whilst things were in an unsettled state, on the 21st of that month, the Speaker, Lieutenant-General Cromwell, Sir Thomas Widdrington, another of the Lords Commissioners of the Great Seal, and Whitelocke, met by appointment to consult upon the state of affairs, the conduct of the army, and the settlement of the kingdom. Widdrington and Whitelocke were ordered to draw up the heads of their discourse for consideration; by what means they might endeavour to bring the army into a fitter temper, and procure the restitution of the secluded members, the answer to be given by the army to the message of the House; and a proposal of settlement between the army and the House. In this important duty they were intrusted with the confidence of both parties[a].

He was next named by the House, upon the Committee to consider of the charges to be brought against the King. But he never attended the Committee, and entirely disapproved of the King's trial and execution[b]. In February he was appointed to draw up the Act to take away the House of Lords, though he had declared his opinion against that measure[c].

After the King's death, and the new seal of the Commonwealth was made, on the 8th of February he was voted to be the first of the new Lords Commissioners. Sir Thomas Widdrington refused to accept of the office under the new government. Whitelocke modestly wished to be excused, but stated his reasons why he had no objection to it, "that the "business was the execution of law and justice, without which men "could not live together:" and, with respect to any objections which might be entertained against the legal authority of Parliament, "that a "strict formal performance of the ordinary rules of law had hardly been "discerned on either side, from unavoidable necessity:" that for himself "he thought his obedience due to the House of Commons, there "being no other visible authority in being but themselves[d]."

[y] Memor. p 344, 347, 392 [z] Ibid p. 355 [a] Ibid p 357. [b] Ibid p 359 [c] Ibid [d] Ibid p 372.

On the 14th of February, he was nominated one of the Council of State, whose powers were to command the militia and navy, and for one year. In the next year he was again appointed[e]. He refused to subscribe the test appointed by Parliament, approving the proceedings of the High Court of Justice which tried the King[f]. Whitelocke was still in high favour with Cromwell. On the 24th of February, in 1648, Cromwell and Ireton went home with him from the Council of State, and supped at his house. They were all cheerful, and well pleased, and discoursed of God's providence, and the miraculous events which had happened. In going home late, they were stopped by the guards, who pretended not to know them, but did it to shew their vigilance[g]. On the 14th of March he drew a declaration to satisfy the people respecting the proceedings of the Parliament[h]. On the 1st of June, he was chosen High Steward of the city of Oxford, and on the 6th of July resigned his office of Attorney General of the Dutchy[i]. In 1649, he was one of the Governors of the school and alms-houses at Westminster[k]; and in November, made a long speech in the debate for excluding lawyers from the House of Commons[l].

In 1650, when Fairfax had his scruples about the lawfulness of invading Scotland, Cromwell, Lambert, Harrison, Saint John, and Whitelocke, were appointed by the Council to confer with him, and to persuade him to undertake it. Notwithstanding their arguments, Fairfax declared he would rather lay down his commission than do it. The issue of the conference was reported to the House, upon which Fairfax was removed from his command, and Cromwell was appointed General and Commander in Chief[m], upon which occasion Whitelocke was one of the four Members appointed to meet and congratulate him. Cromwell presented each of the four Members with a horse, and two Scots prisoners. Whiteloocke gave his two prisoners their liberty[n].

After the defeat at Worcester, on the 10th of December, 1651, a meeting was held at Cromwell's request at the Speaker's house, consisting of some members of parliament, and officers of the army, for the settlement of the nation. The lawyers were generally for a mixed monarchical govern-

[e] Memor p. 376, 425 [f] Ibid p 377 [g] Ibid. p 378. [h] Ibid p 380 [i] Ibid p 397 [k] Ibid. p 411. [l] Ibid. p. 431. ed. 2 [m] Ibid p. 445 [n] Ibid p 509 ed 2 10 Sept 1651.

ment, and the soldiers for a commonwealth. Whitelocke spoke in favour of a monarchical government, and proposed that a time should be appointed for Charles Stuart, or the Duke of York, to come in to the Parliament, upon proper terms. Cromwell evaded, and put off that question, and they parted without coming to any resolution: but that artful politician by this conference discovered the inclinations of the persons present; a knowledge of which he afterwards availed himself[o].

Near a year afterwards, on the 7th of November, 1652, Cromwell had a private conference with Whitelocke upon the same subject, to sound him, and to endeavour to gain him over to support him in his design of assuming the supreme power. Cromwell urged the necessity of some high authority to restrain, and keep things in order, and asked him what he thought of *some person's* taking upon himself the office of *King*. Whitelocke highly disapproved of it, and told him that, as to his own person, the title of King would be of no advantage to him, because he had all the power already, and that it would be attended with great envy, and opposition. That the question, at present, was *national*, between a *monarchy* and a *free state*. If he assumed the title, it would be merely *personal* between *Cromwell* and *Stuart* The friends of a commonwealth would all desert him, and his cause would be ruined. He suggested therefore, that Cromwell should enter into a private treaty with Charles, to restore him upon certain limitations to secure their religious and civil liberties, and to protect himself, and his friends. If he did this, he might be as great as ever a subject was Cromwell thanked him for his advice, but from this time his carriage towards him was altered, and he did not consult with him so often, or so intimately, as before[p].

On the 20th of April following, in 1653, at the meeting at Cromwell's lodgings at Whitehall, when he proposed that the Parliament should be dissolved, which was supported by the Officers, as the best way to advance themselves to the civil government, Whitelocke spoke against it, as a dangerous thing, neither warranted in conscience, or wisdom. It was expected that the Parliament would dissolve itself; but when Ingoldsby came from the House of Commons, and informed Cromwell that the members

[o] Memor. p. 491 [p] Ibid. p 523.

were prolonging their sittings, he immediately marched down with a party of soldiers, and cleared the House[q]. Into Cromwell's Parliament, which was summoned by his writ dated the 8th of June, Whitelocke was not admitted[r]. His commission of the Great Seal was superseded by the vote for taking away the Court of Chancery[s].

When Cromwell found that Whitelocke was not to be moulded to his purpose, and that he was likely to oppose his design of assuming the sovereignty of England, which he was now about to carry into execution, fearing his talents and influence, he was determined to get rid of him in an honourable manner[t]. It was first proposed that he should be appointed one of the Commissioners for the civil government of Ireland, which he refused. Another favourable opportunity soon offered itself[u].

It was the policy of Cromwell, and the other leaders, to enter into treaties with foreign powers, in which the legitimacy of their government must necessarily be recognized. There was no power so friendly to them as the Queen of Sweden. Like her father, she was attached to the protestant cause, and was desirous of cultivating alliances against the popish interests. The protestant princes of Germany were weak and divided, the protestants of France were subdued, the Swiss were too distant, and the Dutch and the Netherlands were in league with the Danes, and at war with England No nation therefore was in a condition to be so serviceable to her as England. On the other hand, it was an important object to the Commonwealth, by a treaty with Sweden, to procure a powerful ally, to promote commerce, to open a free trade through the Sound, and to strengthen themselves against the Dutch and the Danes.

Christina had already made some overtures, and it was resolved to send an Ambassador Extraordinary to Sweden. Whitelocke was unanimously appointed by the Council of State to that office. When it was to be notified to him, Sir Gilbert Pickering, the Secretary of State, having written what Cromwell called "a very fine letter," he took the pen himself, and wrote as follows, with his own hand.

q Mem p 529 r Mem p 532 s Mem p 543 t Mem. p 526 u Mem p 536 Ed 1732. 16th of June, 1652

For the Right Honourable the Lord Whitelocke, one of the Commissioners of the Seal. These.

My Lord,

The Council of State, having thoughts of putting your Lordship to the trouble of being Extraordinary Ambassador to the Queen of Swizland, did think fit not to impose that service upon you, without first knowing your own freedom thereunto; wherefore they were pleased to command our services in making this address to your Lordship, and hereby we can assure you of a very large confidence in your honour, and abilities for this employment. To which we begging your answer, do rest,

My Lord,

Your humble servants,

September 2, 1653

O. CROMWELL.
GIL. PICKERING.

The coldness of the climate, the dangers of the northern seas in winter, the chance of capture, the detriment which his affairs, private and political, might suffer in his absence, and his suspicion, that it was not intended as a favour, were reasons which induced Whitelocke to decline the appointment. But although this civil letter seemed to leave it to his own free choice, he soon found that his refusal would not be admitted. In two private conversations with him, Cromwell urged his acceptance with extraordinary earnestness, and in the most friendly manner; assuring him that it would be a most important service to the Commonwealth, and the Protestant cause; with high compliments to his abilities, and promises of future kindness. When he had at length prevailed with Whitelocke to undertake the office, he thanked him in the most cordial terms, as for a favour done to himself, and sent him a present of a fine sword, and a pair of rich spurs. And indeed it would have been difficult to have found a person better fitted for the situation. His being of a good family, and of polished manners, his former travels, his acquaintance with languages, his knowledge of the various interests of Europe, his firmness and courage, his eloquence, judgment, and discretion, qualified him in a peculiar manner for that delicate employment. Of his skill in foreign politics they had

had sufficient experience: and he had been always consulted in all questions of that nature: as in the dispute with Holland, about the dominion of the British seas[x].

The embassy was set forth with great splendor. Whitelocke's retinue consisted of one hundred persons. In the first class, which comprehended the gentlemen who were admitted to his table, were two of his sons, and his cousin, Captain Unton Croke, whose brother Charles was one of the Pages. With two frigates, two store-ships, a ship of war, and a light catch, they sailed from Gravesend, on the sixth of November, 1653, and, after a most stormy passage, arrived at Gottenburgh on the fifteenth From hence, they went by land to Upsal, where the Queen was residing. They were received with the greatest honours, both by the Queen and the people, but of the foreign Ambassadors, Don Antonio Piementel de Parada, the minister from Spain, was the only one who paid his respects to him. He had many enemies, who were instigated by the Dutch and Danish Ambassadors, and he was in some danger of assassination from the royal party, as had happened to Dorilaus and Ayscham. By his noble and magnanimous conduct, he gained the esteem of those who were at first not inclined to befriend him, and he maintained punctiliously the dignity of the nation which he represented. To guard against the daggers of the cavaliers, he never went abroad without a large attendance well armed.

The Queen soon entertained a high opinion of him, from his honourable conduct, and his candour, particularly in presenting to her at first all his instructions without reserve, or distrust. She admitted him to frequent private audiences, and treated him with perfect confidence. With herself in person, in reality, the whole negociation was carried on, and Whitelocke found her easier to deal with than her prime minister, the Chancellor Oxenstiern, an old and wary politician.

The many conversations which Whitelocke has detailed, exhibit a curious picture of the character and manners of that extraordinary woman. With business she usually intermixed lively sallies, and pleasantry. Upon one occasion she asked him how many wives he had had, and upon his in-

[x] Mem. p. 556 Ed. 2. 23d of June, 1652

forming her that he had had three, and had children by all of them, she exclaimed, " *Par Dieu vous estes incorrigible*[y] !"

At a concert, she led him by the hand to a lady who was called *La Belle Comptesse*, the wife of Count De La Garde, and desired him to discourse with this lady, *her bed-fellow*, and tell her if her inside was not as beautiful as her outside. Whitelocke found her to correspond to this description, and to have great modesty, virtue, and sense. The Queen then pulled off the Countesses glove, and gave it to Whitelocke, for a favour The other she tore in four pieces, and gave to some great persons. In return, Whitelocke sent the Countess a dozen pair of English white gloves, which were much esteemed[z]

At a collation, to which he invited the Queen, upon May-day, " *by the* " *custom of England, as she was his mistress*," her Majesty expressed her contentment, with much drollery, and gaiety of spirit. Amongst other frolics, she commanded him " *to teach her ladies the English salutation*, " which, after some pretty defences, their lips obeyed, and Whitelocke " most readily[a]."

The nuptials of *Baron Horne* and the Lady *Sparre* were celebrated at Court with great magnificence. In the evening when they began dancing *the brawles*, the Queen came to Whitelocke to take him out to dance with her, which he did. After it was over, and he waited upon her to her chair of state, she exclaimed, " *Par Dieu, these Hollanders are* " *lying fellows* " Upon his requesting an explanation of her meaning, she said, " The Hollanders reported to me, that all the noblesse of Eng- " land were of the King's party, and none but mechanics of the Parlia- " ment party, and not a gentleman among them; now I thought to try " you, and to shame you if you could not dance: but I see that you are a " gentleman, and have been bred a gentleman[b]." She likewise bestowed upon him the Order of Amaranta, which she had instituted[c].

Whitelocke's visit to Sweden was just at the critical time when Christina was about to resign her crown. He had the honour of being waited upon by the Prince, who came to Upsal to succeed

[y] Journal of the Swedish Ambassy, vol. i p. 297 [z] P 420 [a] Vol ii p 126.
[b] P 154. [c] Wood

her; and was present at the Ricksdagh, or Swedish Parliament, summoned to give consent to the resignation; which took place whilst he was yet lying in the harbour of Stockholm.

Though there was little difficulty in arranging the terms of a treaty, to which both parties were so well disposed, a considerable delay took place before it was concluded. The Swedish court waited to know the event of a treaty which was negociating between England and Holland. As soon as intelligence arrived of the conclusion of that treaty, the other between England and Sweden was immediately signed, on the 11th of April, 1654.

This treaty comprehended the articles of mutual friendship, free trade, and reciprocal benefits, which are usually agreed upon between allied nations. Each country was to be permitted to trade with the enemies of the other, except in contraband. What was to be comprehended under that description was to be the subject of future discussion. The goods of an enemy might be seized on board the ships of either nation, but passports and certificates were to be conclusive evidence that none such were on board. It was agreed to maintain the freedom of navigation in the Baltic, the Sound, and other seas, and to give mutual assistance for promoting and establishing it.

This business being completed, after five months residence, Whitelocke sailed from Stockholm on the 31st of May, 1654, landed at Lubec, traversed part of Germany, sailed again from Gluckstadt, and after another dangerous voyage, in which his vessel struck on a sand bank, and was nearly lost, he arrived in safety on the shores of England, on the 30th of June.

The treaty, and Whitelocke's conduct in Sweden, were highly approved of by Cromwell and the Council; but empty compliments were all that he was likely to receive. Even the balance of his accounts, and the sums which he had advanced beyond his allowance, were left unpaid. Two years afterwards, by the very great exertions of his friends, the Parliament voted him £500, the sum he had expended beyond what he had received, and £2000 more for his services. But the Protector was not pleased with this favour of the Parliament to him[d]. Whitelocke observes, that *it*

[d] Memor. p. 645. 18 Jan. 1656.

was the practice of Cromwell, after his turn was served, to cast off his instruments!

When the new King of Sweden was seated on his throne, he sent an Ambassador to England, in 1655, to ratify the treaty, and to arrange such points as had been reserved for farther discussion. The Lord Fiennes, Whitelocke, and Mr. Strickland, were appointed Commissioners to treat with him. Many and warm discussions took place, especially as to whether pitch, tar, hemp, and flax, should be considered as *contraband*. At length it was agreed that they should be so considered, *only* during the war between England and Spain. The new treaty was signed on the 17th of July, 1656. After the Restoration, a new treaty was entered into, between Charles the Second and the King of Sweden, in which almost all the articles of these two treaties were introduced And this is the last permanent treaty now subsisting between the two countries, and which still continues to define their political and commercial relations.

During Whitelocke's absence in Sweden, Cromwell had taken upon him the sovereign power, under the name of *Protector*. Although this was contrary to Whitelocke's opinion and advice, yet he accepted from him the renewal of his commission as Ambassador: which was sent over to Upsal. After his return, he was continued as first Commissioner of the Great Seal, and was appointed one of the Commissioners of the Exchequer, on the 4th of August, 1654[e]. At the meeting of Oliver's second Parliament, on the 4th of September, Whitelocke, as first Commissioner, carried the purse with the seal before him[f]. In this Parliament he was chosen for the county of Buckingham, and the boroughs of Oxford and Bedford, and was Recorder of Bristol[g]

On the 23d of April, 1655, an ordinance was made by the Protector and his Council for the better regulating and limiting the jurisdiction of the High Court of Chancery: which Whitelocke and Widdrington refused to execute. Whitelocke's objections were "not only to the new regu-"lations themselves, as inconvenient, injurious, and prejudicial to parties in "the court, but to the authority by which they were enacted, which he "knew had no legal power to make a law; and he had taken an oath to "execute the place of Commissioner *legally and justly*. He did not, how-

[e] Memor. p. 580. [f] Ibid p 582. [g] Mem Sept. 1654

"ever, scruple the authority of his Highness, and the Council, as to the "command of matters concerning the government of the Commonwealth." Upon this refusal the Seal was taken from them[h]. But the Protector, as Whitelocke states, "being good-natured, and sensible of his harsh proceedings against him and Widdrington, for keeping to that liberty of "conscience which himself held to be every one's right, and that none "ought to suffer for it," intended to make them some recompence, by appointing them, in July, 1655, Commissioners of the Treasury, with the Colonels Mountague and Sydenham, with salaries of one thousand pounds a year each[i].

Though Cromwell found that Whitelocke could not be made a tool of to further his ambitious views, he still retained the outward appearance of friendship for him, and frequently consulted him, particularly about foreign affairs. He knew that his opinions, though sometimes not very flattering to his inclinations, were always sound and judicious; and that he could always depend upon his sincerity. In these conversations he often pressed Cromwell to have recourse to frequent Parliaments, advice with which he was not disposed to comply, though he was not offended by it[k].

He was appointed one of the Committee of Trade and Navigation, which was a favourite measure of Cromwell, and was established the 2d of November, 1655: and he made an able report upon the copper trade with Sweden[l]. He was nominated as an Ambassador Extraordinary to Sweden a second time, in January, 1656, but Whitelocke thought "that "he had had danger and trouble enough in his former Ambassy, without "the least reward; but instead of it, had met with neglects and slightings, "besides being money out of pocket." He therefore endeavoured to avoid this appointment, and the design was afterwards abandoned[m].

In Cromwell's third Parliament, which met the 17th of September, 1656, he was elected Knight for Buckinghamshire, and was not one of those members who were excluded from sitting in the House by Cromwell and his Council[m]: and he was appointed to fill the office of Speaker, during the indisposition of Sir Thomas Widdrington, for which he

[h] Memor. p. 602 [i] Ibid p 608 [k] Ibid p 647, 664 [l] Ibid p 617, 632 [m] Ibid p. 643

received the thanks of the House, and it was agreed, that in the short time of his being Speaker, by his holding them to the points in debate, they had dispatched more business than in all the time before of their sitting[n].

When the Parliament had framed their Petition and Advice to Cromwell, that *he should take the title of King*, Whitelocke was made Chairman of the Committee appointed to confer with him upon it. Though he disliked some things in the Petition, and therefore refused to present it, yet he spoke in favour of the principal point, and advised Cromwell to comply with it. Upon this, and other important affairs, Cromwell consulted with the Lord Broghill, Pierrepoint, Whitelocke, Wolsey, and Thurloe, in private meetings, when he used to lay aside his greatness, would be very familiar, and, by way of diversion, would make verses with them, and every one must try his skill in poetry. Tobacco and pipes were commonly introduced, and he would smoke himself. From this buffoonery he would again return to serious business, and he followed their counsel in most of his great affairs; but not in complying with the Petition and Advice[o] Nor was Whitelocke's conduct upon this occasion inconsistent with the principles which he had formerly avowed Though the illegal proceedings of Charles had originally occasioned his opposition to him, he had been led, through his particular connection with the parliamentary party, much farther than he intended to go, and was in reality a friend to monarchy. When the restoration of the exiled family seemed impossible, he thought the re-establishment of the monarchical form of government, even in the person of Cromwell, preferable to a republic. The existence of a King was necessary to give life to the laws and constitution of the country, to which Whitelocke was sincerely attached[p]. What perhaps had never happened before, Cromwell's fears overcame his inclinations and his ambition, and he refused the title. That of Protector was substituted in its place, with power not inferior. At his solemn inauguration, Whitelocke, with a drawn sword in his hand,

[n] Memor p 645 [o] Ibid p 647.

[p] See the account of this conference, published in 1660, under the title of Monarchy asserted to be the best, most ancient, and legal form of government

sat with his son, Richard Cromwell, in one of the boots of his state coach[q].

Whitelocke was far from supporting all the measures of Cromwell and the Parliament. He disapproved of the Committee for ejecting scandalous and insufficient ministers, which was an instrument of great oppression to the clergy[r]. About the same time he made application to Cromwell for the Provostship of Eton, "as a thing of good value, quiet, and honourable, "and fit for a scholar," but he met with a refusal: his service, as he observes, was past, and therefore there was no necessity of a recompence[s]. Cromwell, however, still continued upon apparently friendly terms with him, and summoned him as one of the sixty members of the *Other House* of Parliament, the new House of Peers, on the 11th of December, 1657[t]. Yet not being satisfied with the public transactions, he lived much in retirement[u]. In April, 1658, he was appointed of a Committee to hear appeals from Guernsey and Jersey[x]. He was nominated in the Commission of the High Court of Justice, for the trial of Doctor Hewet and the other conspirators against the Protector, but he never sat with them: the establishment of that court being against his judgment, which was, that they should be tried in the Upper Bench, according to law[y]. Upon the capture of Dunkirk, overtures were made to him to be Governor of it, which he refused to undertake[z]. On the 21st of August, a bill was signed by the Protector, about a fortnight before he died, for a patent to make Whitelocke a Viscount, an honour of which he refused to accept[a].

Upon the accession of Richard, he presented an address to him from Buckinghamshire[b]. During his Protectorship, he constantly attended the business of the Treasury, and was again made Commissioner of the Great Seal, with Fiennes and L'Isle. Richard had a particular respect for him, and consulted with him, the Lord Broghill, and others, about dissolving the Parliament. Most of them were for it. Whitelocke dissuaded him from it. and always declared his judgment honestly, and for the good of the Protector, when his advice was required[c].

[q] Memor. p 662 [r] Ibid p 664 [s] Ibid. [t] Ibid p 665 [u] Ibid p. 673 [x] Ibid p 674 [y] Ibid. [z] Ibid [a] Ibid p 675 [b] Ibid p 676 [c] Ibid p 678

After the deposition of Richard, and the army had assumed the government, he was removed from his office of Commissioner of the Great Seal. When part of the Long Parliament was restored, and appointed a Council of State, he was named one of the members of it. He was falsely accused of holding a communication with Charles and Hyde, from which he justified himself[d]. He was named as a Commissioner to mediate a peace between Sweden and Denmark, which he declined[e]. As President of the Council, he was most active in suppressing the insurrection of Sir George Booth.

Monk seems to have been desirous of availing himself of his services, and wished him to have been one of the Commissioners for Scotland; but Whitelocke refused[f]. He was one of the Committee of ten members of the Council of State, who were nominated by the army on the 17th of October, 1659, to consider of fit ways to carry on the government[g]: and of a new Council of twenty-three persons, named on the 22d, for the management of public affairs, under the name of the Committee of Safety. This office he was at first unwilling to undertake, and only consented to prevent, if possible, the army from governing by the sword. And he was of a special Committee of that Board, to consider of a form of government. The Great Seal was again delivered to him[h]. At first he took an active part against Monk, and with the Committee issued Commissioners to raise forces against him: and he even received from them a commission to raise a regiment of horse himself. He represented to the city that Monk designed to bring in the King by a new civil war, and Lambert was ordered to march against him.

Whilst affairs were in this perplexed state, Whitelocke proposed to Fleetwood, that, since it was evidently Monk's design to bring in the King, he should either assemble all their forces and see what stand they could make against it, or else send some trusty person to the King with a tender of their services to restore him; and he offered to go himself. Fleetwood at first seemed willing, and had even desired Whitelocke to prepare himself for the journey; but after meeting with Vane, and some officers, he declared he could not do it without Lambert's consent, who

[d] Memor. p 680 [e] Ibid p. 681 [f] Ibid p 685 [g] Ibid p 686. [h] Ibid. p 687

was at too great a distance. The next day, Colonel Ingoldsby told Whitelocke that his condition required that he should go to the King, with the Great Seal, which overture he did not comply with[i]. By the restored Members of the Long Parliament he was treated with much severity, and Scot said, that he should be hanged, with the Great Seal about his neck. Being informed of their intention to send him to the Tower, he retired into the country, and ordered his wife to carry the Great Seal to the Speaker[k].

In this seclusion he continued till the King's restoration was completed After that event, during the debates upon the Bill of Oblivion, he petitioned the House of Commons, and on the question being propounded, whether he should be one of the twenty persons excepted out of the general pardon, it was negatived by a considerable majority. He spent the remaining fifteen years of his life in retirement, mostly at Chilton Park in Wiltshire, where he died of the stone on the 28th of July, 1675; and was buried at Fawley near Marlow, in an isle which he had built for a burying place for himself and his family. It is said that he waited upon the King, after the Restoration, to beg his pardon for all that he had transacted against him, and that his Majesty bid him "*Go, live* "*quietly in the country, and take care of his wife and sixteen children*" Queen Christina, in an interview with Charles the Second, informed him, that, in his Embassy to Sweden, *she had never heard him speak a dishonourable word against his Majesty*[l].

Lord Commisssioner Whitelocke had three wives The first was *Rebecca*, the daughter of Thomas Bennet, Esquire, Alderman of London, by whom he had only one son, Sir James Whitelocke, who was settled at Trumpington, near Cambridge. He was first a Captain; afterwards Fellow of All Souls College; then a Colonel in the Parliament army, Knight for Oxfordshire, September 3, 1654, Knighted by Oliver, January 6, 1650, Burgess for Aylesbury, January 27, 1658[m]. He left two sons, both of whom died unmarried. His second wife was *Frances*, daughter of William, Lord Willoughby of Parham, and Frances, daughter of John, Earl of Rutland. He had nine children by her, and she died the 16th of May,

[i] Memor. p 692, 693. [k] Ibid. p. 693. [l] Memorials [m] Wood s Ath Ox part ii col 401.

1649 His third wife was the widow *Wilson*, whose maiden name was Carleton, who survived him, and by her he had several children. In the year 1664, he mentions that he had then fourteen children, and had lost three. The eldest of the last marriage inherited Chilton Park, and his son was living in 1772. At that time, of all Sir Bulstrode's numerous issue there were none left in the male line, except Mr. Whitelocke of Chilton Park, Mr. Carleton Whitelocke, and his son, a Student in the Middle Temple[n]

In his retirement, Lord Whitelocke wrote the Annals of his own Life, not with a view of being published, but for instruction to his children. They contained likewise the public transactions of the country, and various dissertations upon subjects of divinity, law, politics, history, and antiquity[o].

Of these a part was printed in folio, in the year 1682, under the name of Memorials of the English affairs from the beginning of the reign of King Charles the First, to the Restoration. Arthur, Earl of Anglesea, was the Editor. This is a most valuable account of that eventful period. The concern which the author had in the public affairs of the country, and his intimacy with the chief actors, enabled him to relate events with accuracy, and to ascribe them to their genuine motives. Upon every occasion he has shewn the greatest impartiality both as to the measures themselves, and the characters of those who were concerned in them. His style is easy, and without affectation, and though his work is not wrought up into a regular uninterrupted narrative, it derives some advantages from the form of a journal, in the correctness of dates, and the introduction of an infinite number of facts, which would not find their place in a regular history.

Another part was published by Doctor Morton, in the year 1772, in two volumes in 4to. intitled, A Journal of the Swedish Ambassy in the years 1653 and 1654, from the Commonwealth of England, Scotland, and Ireland, written by the Ambassador, the Lord Commissioner Whitelocke. It is a most interesting history of every thing relating to that ambassy, full of anecdotes of the celebrated Queen Christina, and her court, and related in so lively a manner, as to make us present, as it were, in every scene he describes, and to enter into his very inmost thoughts and feelings.

[n] Dr. Morton's Dedication to the Swedish Ambassy, &c. [o] See his preface to it in the Appendix, No I. of the Swedish Ambassy, vol ii page 429

"In those pages," says his learned Editor, "the political man will find no "contemptible model of doing business; the family man may extract that "which suits his laudable purposes, and the individual, the moral, and "the religious man will see his form delineated, and be instructed where to "seek his end." It is greatly to be wished that the remainder of his Journal was published.

His Essays ecclesiastical and civil were published in octavo, in 1706. His Notes upon the King's Writ for choosing Members of Parliament, issued in the thirteenth of Charles the Second, being Disquisitions on the Government of England by King, Lords, and Commons, were published in 2 vols. in 4to in 1766. A most learned and constitutional book.

Many of his speeches were published separately in his life-time, of which Wood has given a list. Others are in Rushworth's Collection; as those upon the trial of the Earl of Strafford. His speeches in the conference with Cromwell, to persuade him to take upon him the title of King, are to be found in the account of the conference printed in 1657, under the title of, Monarchy asserted to be the best form of Government[p].

The second husband of CECILY CROKE was SIR JOHN BROWN, KNIGHT. I have not discovered any particulars relating to this second marriage, which took place before the 1st of February, 1609; because her mother, in her will of that date, styles her "my daughter Brown."

[p] See the Genealogy of Whitelocke, Bulstrode, Mayne, Beke, &c. Whitelocke, from Brown Willis's MSS. vol. 19. Harl. MSS. 1102, a visitation of Bucks in 1634. Bulstrode from the same, Harl. 1102. p. 44. and Harl. No. 1193. p. 51. Mayne from Harl. No. 1102. Willis, ibid. Beke, ibid. and Brown Willis's MSS. vol. iii. page 46. Harl. 1102. p. 61. b. Harl. 1193. p. 68. No. 34.

Two sons, died unmarried

No 34

THE GENEALOGY OF WHITELOCKE, BULSTRODE, MAYNE, AND BEKE

See likewise the Genealogy of Upton, No 24

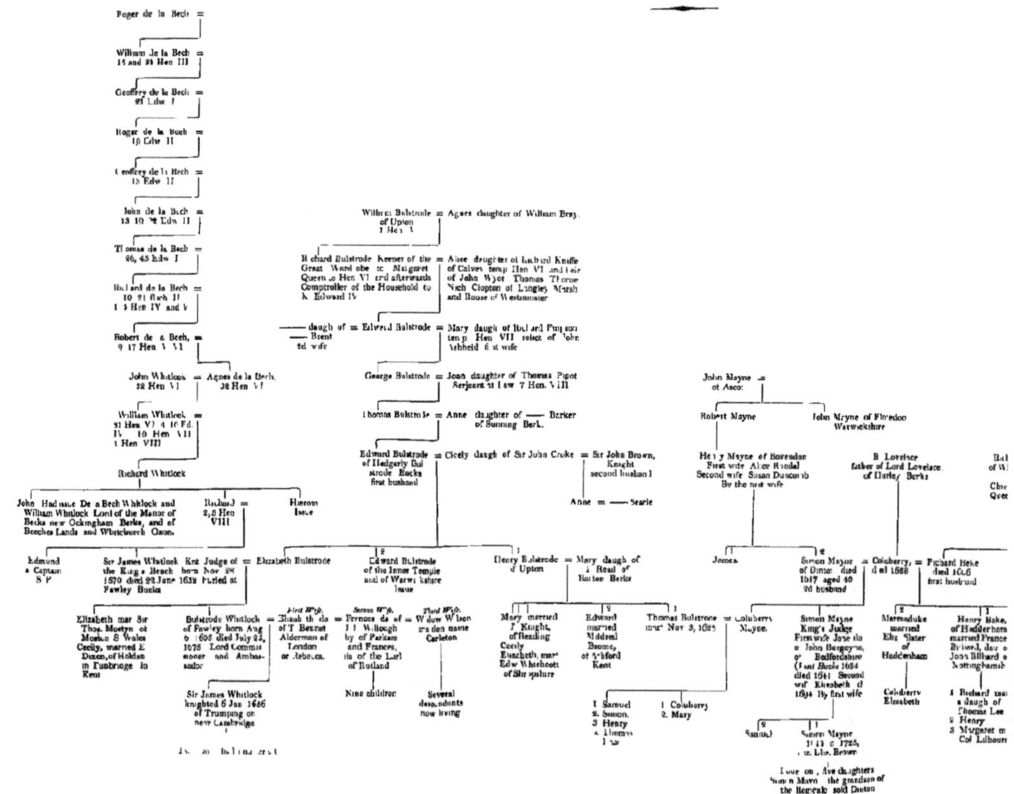

No. 35.

THE GENEALOGY OF WINGFIELD.

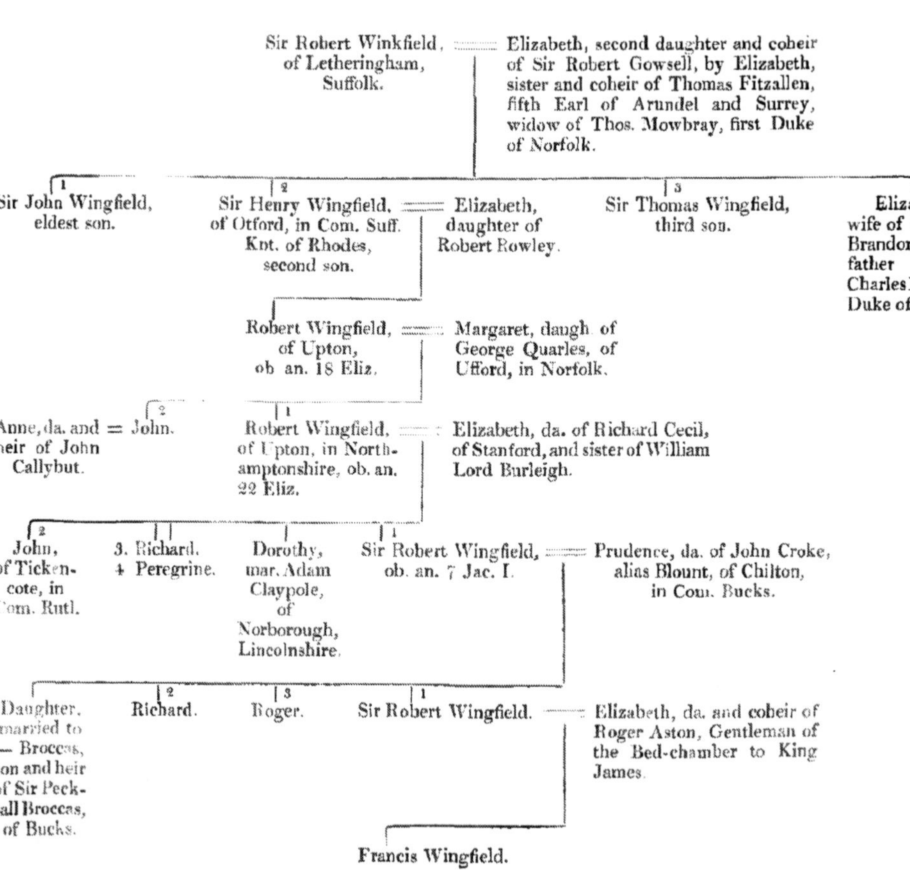
Sir Robert Winkfield, of Letheringham, Suffolk.
Elizabeth, second daughter and coheir of Sir Robert Gowsell, by Elizabeth, sister and coheir of Thomas Fitzallen, fifth Earl of Arundel and Surrey, widow of Thos. Mowbray, first Duke of Norfolk.
1 Sir John Wingfield, eldest son.
2 Sir Henry Wingfield, of Otford, in Com. Suff. Knt. of Rhodes, second son.
Elizabeth, daughter of Robert Rowley.
3 Sir Thomas Wingfield, third son.
Elizabeth, wife of Sir Wm. Brandon, grand-father to Sir Charles Brandon, Duke of Suffolk.
Robert Wingfield, of Upton, ob an. 18 Eliz.
Margaret, daugh. of George Quarles, of Ufford, in Norfolk.
Anne, da. and heir of John Callybut.
2 John.
1 Robert Wingfield, of Upton, in Northamptonshire, ob. an. 22 Eliz.
Elizabeth, da. of Richard Cecil, of Stanford, and sister of William Lord Burleigh.
2 John, of Tickencote, in Com. Rutl.
3. Richard.
4 Peregrine.
Dorothy, mar. Adam Claypole, of Norborough, Lincolnshire.
1 Sir Robert Wingfield, ob. an. 7 Jac. I.
Prudence, da. of John Croke, alias Blount, of Chilton, in Com. Bucks.
Daughter, married to — Broccas, son and heir of Sir Peck-sall Broccas, of Bucks.
2 Richard.
3 Roger.
1 Sir Robert Wingfield.
Elizabeth, da. and coheir of Roger Aston, Gentleman of the Bed-chamber to King James.
Francis Wingfield.

SECTION THE SECOND.

PRUDENTIA CROKE, the second daughter of Sir John Croke and Elizabeth Unton, married Sir Robert Wingfield, Knight, who died in the seventh year of James the First. He was the son of Sir Robert Wingfield, by his wife Elizabeth, the daughter of Richard Cecil of Burleigh, and sister of William Lord Burleigh, Lord High Treasurer, whose sister Margaret was married to her cousin Roger Cave[a]. His great grand-father was Sir Henry Wingfield, of Orford, in Suffolk, a Knight of Rhodes[b]. Sir Robert Wingfield and Prudence Croke had three sons, Robert, Richard, and Roger, and a daughter married to —— Broccas[c], son and heir of Sir Pecksell Brocas, of Buckinghamshire[d].

Some of this family were settled at Brantham, and Letheringham in Suffolk, Stones Castle in Kent, and Kimbolton Castle in Huntingdonshire; and were of great antiquity, and noble descents and alliances[e].

Their coat of arms is, argent, on a bend, gules, between two cotizes, sable, three pair of wings joined in lewer, as the first.

[a] Collins's Peerage, vol ii. p 190. [b] Pedigree in the History of Northamptonshire by Bridges and Whalley, vol. ii. page 508. Ed. 1791. [c] Dame Elizabeth Croke (Unton's) Will, penes me. [d] Harl. MSS No 1411 fol 27 where is a pedigree of the Wingfield family, printed in Genealogy, No. 35. [e] Guillim, page 384. Ed 1660.

SECTION THE THIRD.

ELIZABETH, the third daughter of Sir John Croke and Elizabeth Unton, married SIR JOHN TYRRELL, of Heron in Essex. Her epitaph at Chilton has recorded all we know of her

Here lyeth Elizabeth Tyrell, late wife of Sir John Tyrell, of Heron, Knight, and daughter of Sir John Croke of Chilton, Knight, who had one daughter named Dorothy, who died in her infancie And the said Elizabeth died the 16*th of February, Anno Domini* 1631, *being the* 57*th yeare of her age.*

Against the wall is the monument Within an arch, a lady kneeling at an altar, an infant before her. At the top, a coat of arms, in a lozenge, argent, two chevronels, azure, within a bordure, engrailed, gules, for Tyrrell, impaled with Croke. Below another coat of arms, Quarterly 1 Tyrrell. 2. Paly, argent and sable. 3. Gules, on a chevron argent, three dolphins of the field 4. Argent, a cross, between four escalops, sable.

This was an ancient family, descended from Sir Walter Tyrrel, who held the lordship of Langham in Essex, in the time of William the Conqueror, and shot William Rufus with an arrow in the New Forest, they were divided into several branches, which possessed large estates in Essex, Suffolk, Buckinghamshire, and Oxfordshire, and two of them were created Baronets. The titles and the name are now become extinct.

Of the elder branch little is recorded, except the names, the marriages, and the estates One Sir John Tirrel was appointed by Henry the Fifth Captain of the Carpenters for the new works at Calais, to be paid twelve pence a day The sufferings of another Sir John Tyrrel, in the royal cause of Charles the First, are commemorated in the following epitaph in East-Hornden church.

ΕΠ' ΑΥΤΟΝ,

SEMEL DECIMATUS,

BIS CARCERATUS,

TER SEQUESTRATUS,

TACET QUOTIES SPOLIATUS,

I. ELDEST BRANCH OF TYRRELL, OF HERON IN GREAT THORNDEN IN ESSEX, SPRINGFIELD BARNEY, ESSEX, OF GIPPING IN SUFFOLK, AND BEECHES IN ESSEX.

Sir Walter Tyrrell, of Langham, Essex, in time of William the Conq

Sir Henry Tyrrell.
Sir Richard Tyrrell
Sir Edward Tyrrell
Sir Geoffrey Tyrrell
Sir Lionel Tyrrell

Sir Edward Tyrrell = Maud, or Anne, da and heir of —— Burgate, in Suffolk

Sir Hugh Tyrrell, of Great Thornden in Essex, Edw III. Gov of Carisbrook Castle in 1378, 1 Rich II = Joan, daugh and coheir of James Flamberd

Sir James Tyrrell, of Heron, in Thornden = Margaret, dau and heir of Sir William Heron

Sir Walter Tyrrell, of Heron = Jane, da and coh of Sir Wm Swynford, of Essex, Knight

Elizabeth, or Elianora, da of John Flamberd, second wife = Sir Thomas Tyrrell = Alice, dau of —— d'Adeleigh First wife No issue

Sir John Hawkwood, of Essex

Sir William Coggeshall, of Little Samford Hall, Essex = Antiocha.

Children of Sir Thomas Tyrrell and Elizabeth:

- William Tyrrell, jun of Beeches, in Essex, third son
- William Tyrrell, of Gipping, in Suffolk, second son
  - James Tyrrell,
- Sir John Tyrrell, Capt of the Carpenters at Calais, Hen V Treasurer of the Household to Hen VI First husb = Alice, da and coheir of Sir Wm Coggeshall, of Little Samford Hall in Essex She died 1422 = John Langham, Esq of Pantfield, Essex, second husband

Mary. | Martha, married Sir Thos Drury, of Overstone, Northamptonshire | Anne | Elizabeth

1 Sir Charles Tyrrell, died 1735 æt 11 | 2 Sir John Tyrrell, Bart | 3 A son.

SECTION THE THIRD.

ELIZABETH, the third daughter of Sir John Croke and Elizabeth Unton, married Sir John Tyrrell, of Heron in Essex. Her epitaph at Chilton has recorded all we know of her

Here lyeth Elizabeth Tyrell, late wife of Sir John Tyrell, of Heron, Knight, and daughter of Sir John Croke of Chilton, Knight, who had one daughter named Dorothy, who died in her infancie And the said Elizabeth died the 16th of February, Anno Domini 1631, being the 57th yeare of her age.

Against the wall is the monument Within an arch, a lady kneeling at an altar, an infant before her. At the top, a coat of arms, in a lozenge, argent, two chevronels, azure, within a bordure, engrailed, gules, for Tyrrell, impaled with Croke. Below another coat of arms, Quarterly 1. Tyrrell. 2. Paly, argent and sable. 3. Gules, on a chevron argent, three dolphins of the field. 4 Argent, a cross, between four escalops, sable.

This was an ancient family, descended from Sir Walter Tyrrel, who held the lordship of Langham in Essex, in the time of William the Conqueror, and shot William Rufus with an arrow in the New Forest; they were divided into several branches, which possessed large estates in Essex, Suffolk, Buckinghamshire, and Oxfordshire; and two of them were created Baronets The titles and the name are now become extinct.

Of the elder branch little is recorded, except the names, the marriages, and the estates. One Sir John Tirrel was appointed by Henry the Fifth Captain of the Carpenters for the new works at Calais, to be paid twelve pence a day. The sufferings of another Sir John Tyrrel, in the royal cause of Charles the First, are commemorated in the following epitaph in East-Hornden church.

EII' AYTON,

SEMEL DECIMATUS,

BIS CARCERATUS,

TER SEQUESTRATUS,

TACET QUOTIES SPOLIATUS,

I. ELDEST BRANCH OF TYRRELL, OF HERON IN GREAT THORNDEN IN ESSEX, SPRINGFIELD BARNEY, ESSEX, OF GIPPING IN SUFFOLK, AND BEECHES IN ESSEX.

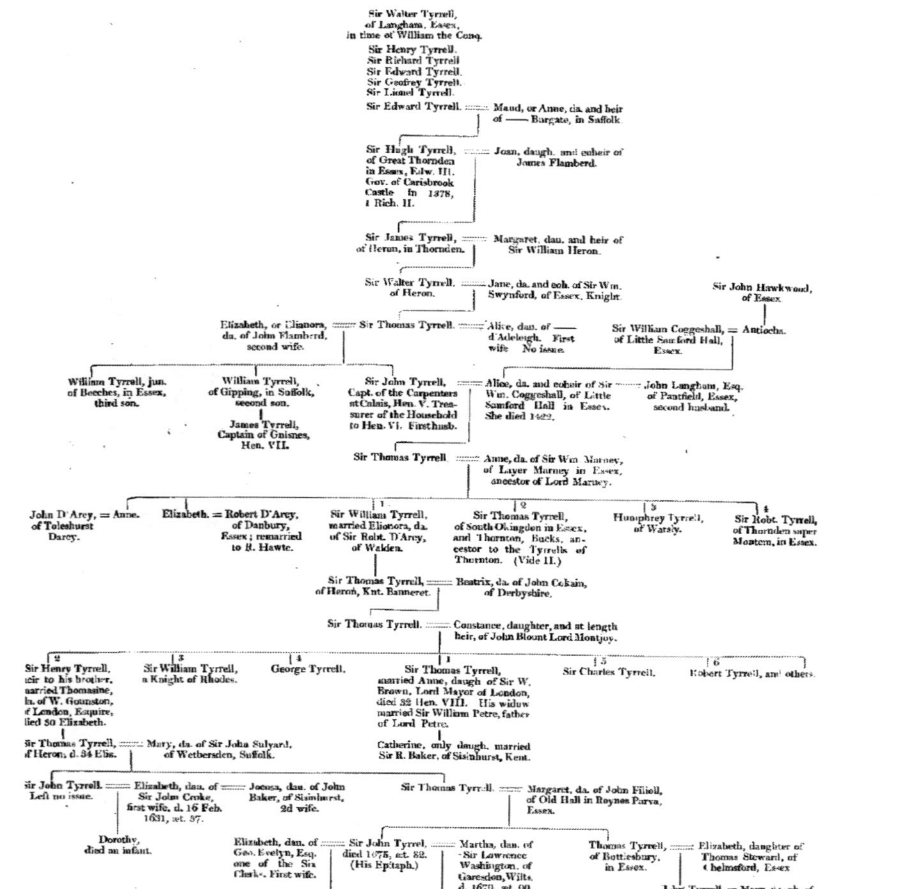

Sir Walter Tyrrell, of Langham, Essex, in time of William the Conq.
Sir Henry Tyrrell.
Sir Richard Tyrrell
Sir Edward Tyrrell.
Sir Geofrey Tyrrell.
Sir Lionel Tyrrell.
Sir Edward Tyrrell. = Maud, or Anne, da. and heir of —— Burgate, in Suffolk.
Sir Hugh Tyrrell, of Great Thornden in Essex, Edw. III. Gov. of Carisbrook Castle in 1378, 1 Rich. II. = Joan, daugh. and coheir of James Flamberd.
Sir James Tyrrell, of Heron, in Thornden. = Margaret, dau. and heir of Sir William Heron.
Sir Walter Tyrrell, of Heron. = Jane, da. and coh. of Sir Wm. Swynford, of Essex, Knight.
Sir John Hawkwood, of Essex.
Elizabeth, or Elianora, da. of John Flamberd, second wife. = Sir Thomas Tyrrell. = Alice, dau. of —— d'Adeleigh. First wife. No issue.
Sir William Coggeshall, of Little Samford Hall, Essex. = Antiocha.
William Tyrrell, jun. of Beeches, in Essex, third son.
William Tyrrell, of Gipping, in Suffolk, second son.
James Tyrrell, Captain of Gnisnes, Hen. VII.
Sir John Tyrrell, Capt. of the Carpenters at Calais, Hen. V. Treasurer of the Household to Hen. VI. First husb. = Alice, da. and coheir of Sir Wm. Coggeshall, of Little Samford Hall in Essex. She died 1422. = John Langham, Esq. of Pantfield, Essex, second husband.
Sir Thomas Tyrrell. = Anne, da. of Sir Wm. Marney, of Layer Marney in Essex, ancestor of Lord Marney.
John D'Arcy, = Anne. of Toleshurst Darcy.
Elizabeth. = Robert D'Arcy, of Danbury, Essex; remarried to R. Hawte.
1 Sir William Tyrrell, married Elionora, da. of Sir Robt. D'Arcy, of Walden.
2 Sir Thomas Tyrrell, of South Okingdon in Essex, and Thornton, Bucks, ancestor to the Tyrrells of Thornton. (Vide II.)
3 Humphrey Tyrrell, of Warsly.
4 Sir Robt. Tyrrell, of Thornden super Montem, in Essex.
Sir Thomas Tyrrell, of Heron, Knt. Banneret. = Beatrix, da. of John Cokain, of Derbyshire.
Sir Thomas Tyrrell. = Constance, daughter, and at length heir, of John Blount Lord Montjoy.
2 Sir Henry Tyrrell, heir to his brother, married Thomasine, da. of W. Gounston, of London, Esquire, died 30 Elizabeth.
3 Sir William Tyrrell, a Knight of Rhodes.
4 George Tyrrell.
1 Sir Thomas Tyrrell, married Anne, daugh. of Sir W. Brown, Lord Mayor of London, died 32 Hen. VIII. His widow married Sir William Petre, father of Lord Petre.
5 Sir Charles Tyrrell.
6 Robert Tyrrell, and others.
Sir Thomas Tyrrell, = Mary, da. of Sir John Sulyard, of Heron, d. 34 Eliz. of Wetbersden, Suffolk.
Catherine, only daugh. married Sir R. Baker, of Sisinhurst, Kent.
Sir John Tyrrell. Left no issue. = Elizabeth, dau. of Sir John Croke, first wife, d. 16 Feb. 1631, æt. 57. = Jocosa, dau. of John Baker, of Sisinhurst, 2d wife.
Sir Thomas Tyrrell. = Margaret, da. of John Filioll, of Old Hall in Raynes Parva, Essex.
Dorothy, died an infant.
Elizabeth, dau. of Geo. Evelyn, Esq. one of the Six Clerks. First wife. = Sir John Tyrrell, died 1675, æt. 82. (His Epitaph.) = Martha, dau. of Sir Lawrence Washington, of Garesdon, Wilts. d. 1670. æt. 90. Second wife.
Thomas Tyrrell, of Bottlesbury, in Essex. = Elizabeth, daughter of Thomas Steward, of Chelmsford, Essex.
John Tyrrell, = Mary, daugh. of of Billericay. Giles Allen, of

Charles,
died unmarried,

John Robert Spencer =
Philips, of Riffham

No 37

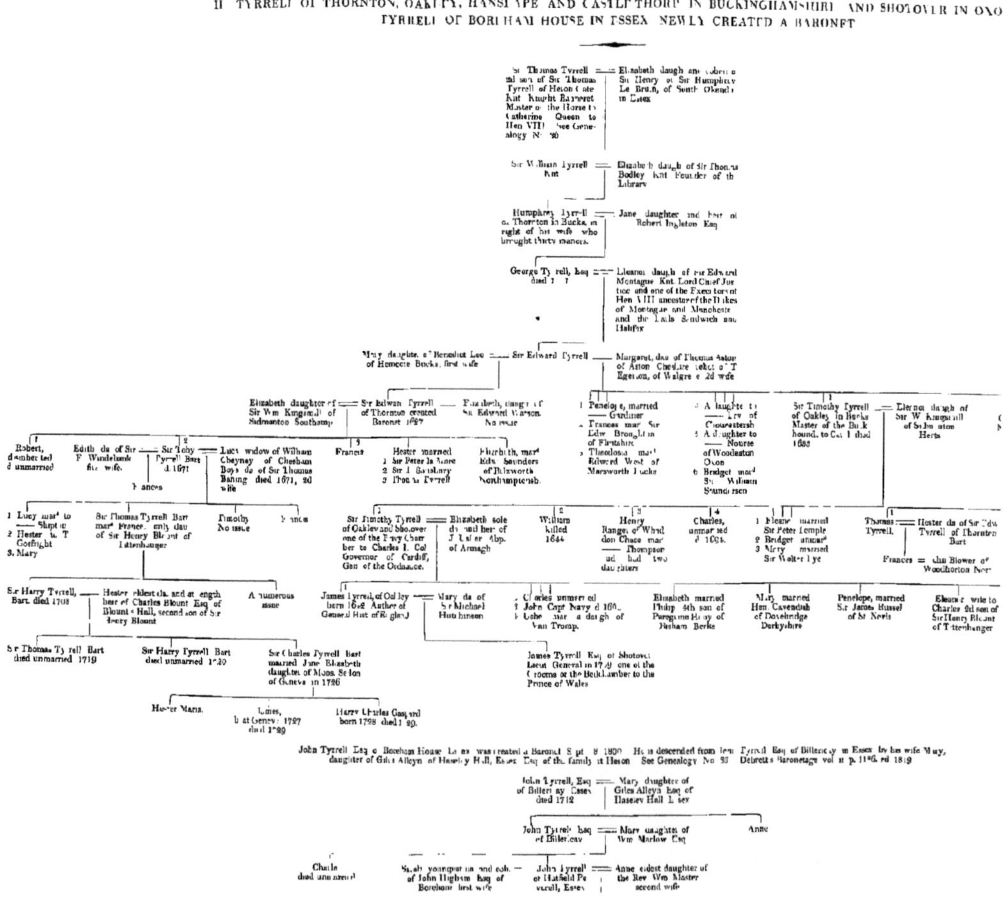

TYRRELL OF THORNTON, OAKLEY, HANSLAPE AND CASTLETHORP IN BUCKINGHAMSHIRE AND SHOTOVER IN OXO
TYRRELL OF BOREHAM HOUSE IN ESSEX NEWLY CREATED A BARONET
Sir Thomas Tyrrell
Sir William Tyrrell Knt
Humphrey Tyrrell of Thornton in Bucks
George Tyrrell, Esq
Sir Edward Tyrrell
Sir Edward Tyrrell of Thornton created Baronet 1627
Sir Timothy Tyrrell of Oakley and Shotover
Sir Harry Tyrrell, Bart. died 1708
Sir Thomas Tyrrell Bart died unmarried 1719
Sir Harry Tyrrell Bart died unmarried 1730
Sir Charles Tyrrell Bart
James Tyrrell of Oakley
James Tyrrell Esq of Shotover
John Tyrrell Esq of Boreham House

HIC JACET INHUMATUS,
JOHANNES TYRREL,
EQUES AURATUS,
OBIIT DIE MARTIS, APRILIS 3°. A.D. 1675. ÆTAT. 82.

The deeds of men of fortune, and soldiers, seldom survive them, the works of authors have something of a longer existence. The last but one of the Oakley and Shotover family, James Tyrrel, Esquire, who was born in 1642, was educated at Queen's College in Oxford, and afterwards studied, without practising, the common law, in the Inner Temple, where he was called to the bar. Upon his marriage, he retired to his patrimony at Oakley, and was one of the Deputy Lieutenants, and a Justice of the Peace, for Buckinghamshire, from which offices he was removed by King James the Second, for not complying with his designs for the restoration of popery. He became a voluminous author, and wrote an History of England to the reign of William the Third, in five volumes folio; and another work intitled *Bibliotheca Politica*, or an Enquiry into the Ancient Constitution of the English Government, in folio likewise, and other books.

His son, James Tyrrel, was the last of the Shotover family, served in the army, arrived at the rank of Lieutenant General in 1739, was one of the Grooms of the Bedchamber to the Prince of Wales, represented the corporation of Boroughbridge in Yorkshire in three Parliaments, was Governor of Gravesend, and Tilbury Fort, and Colonel of a regiment. He died without issue, and left the estate, and the house at Shotover, which was erected by himself, to Baron Schutz, by whose descendants it is now possessed[a].

[a] Collins's Baronetage, Ed 1741 vol ii. p. 76 vol iii p 510 See the Genealogies of Tyrrell, No. 36, and 37.

CHAPTER IX.

William Croke, and his descendants

WE have now traced, to the full extent, the descendants of the four eldest sons, and the three daughters, of Sir John Croke and Dame Elizabeth Unton, the patriarchal stock of the family. We have seen all the male lines of them gradually and in succession becoming entirely extinct, vanishing from sight, or transferring their blood and property through females to other families. The youngest branch, which lived at Studley, has been favoured with a longer duration.

This branch was descended from William Croke, Esquire, the fifth son of Sir John Croke and Elizabeth Unton. We have before related, that his brother, Sir George Croke, bequeathed to him the estate at Studley for his life, with remainder to his son Alexander in tail male, which thus became the seat of his family. He does not appear to have engaged in any profession or other active pursuit: an ample testimony is borne by Sir Harbottle Grimston to the amiableness of his character: "that *he* "*was a man of an humble spirit, and piously disposed, addicting himself* "*wholly to a country life.*"

If education and example can influence the mind, he was blessed with a wife who was probably of a disposition similar to his own. This was *Dorothy*, the daughter of Robert Honywood, Esquire, of Charing, in Kent. Her mother, Mary, was a lady who has been much celebrated for her piety, the multitude of her descendants, and the length of her life. Her father, Robert Atwaters, or Waters, Esquire, of Royton, in the parish of Lenham, in Essex, was a man of fortune, who left only two daughters, coheiresses, Joyce, the eldest, who married Humphrey Hales, Esquire, of the Dungeon, in Canterbury, and Mary, the youngest, who brought the estate at Royton, another at Charing, and some other property, to her husband, Robert Honywood; then of Henewood, in the parish of Postling, in

No. 38.

A GENEALOGY UPON VELLUM,

BEAUTIFULLY DRAWN, WITH THE COATS OF ARMS EMBLAZONED, IN THEIR PROPER COLOURS

Iacobus Croke alias Les Blounts — Gulielmus Huniwood

The aforenamed Mary, daughter and coheire of Robert At-waters, of Royton in the County of Kent, Esquire, wife of Robert Honnywood of Charinge in the same County, Esquire, her onely husband, had at the time of her decease lawfully descended from her, 367 children, (viz) 16 of her own body, 114 grand children, 228 in the third generation, and 9 in the fourth Almighty God having gratiously protected her, from many dangers and afflictions, both of body and minde, she in Christian and comfortable manner did depart this life, in her eldest sonnes house, at Markshall in the County of Essex, the xi[th] day of May, Anno Domini 1620 in the 93d year of her age, and 44th of her widowhood, and according to her desire lieth buried in Kent, wheare she was borne.

The coat of arms of Croke, quarterly, with a crescent, and a crest, two swans' necks, proper, beaked gules, conjoined with an annulet, azure, bearing in their beaks two annulets, or, issuing from a wreath, argent and gules, with helmet and mantlings, fully emblazoned.

The arms of Honywood, quarterly with Barnes, and At-waters. Crest, on a wreath, argent and azure, a wolf's head ermine, langued, gules, with helmet and mantlings, fully emblazoned.

CHAPTER IX.

William Croke, and his descendants.

WE have now traced, to the full extent, the descendants of the four eldest sons, and the three daughters, of Sir John Croke and Dame Elizabeth Unton the patriarchal stock of the family. We have seen all the male lines of them gradually and in succession becoming entirely extinct, vanishing from sight, or transferring their blood and property through females to other families. The youngest branch, which lived at Studley, has been favoured with a longer duration.

This branch was descended from WILLIAM CROKE, ESQUIRE, the fifth son of Sir John Croke and Elizabeth Unton. We have before related, that his brother, Sir George Croke, bequeathed to him the estate at Studley for his life, with remainder to his son Alexander in tail male, which thus became the seat of his family. He does not appear to have engaged in any profession or other active pursuit an ample testimony is borne by Sir Harbottle Grimston to the amiableness of his character "that *he "was a man of an humble spirit, and piously disposed, addicting himself "wholly to a country life.*"

If education and example can influence the mind, he was blessed with a wife who was probably of a disposition similar to his own This was *Dorothy*, the daughter of Robert Honywood, Esquire, of Charing, in Kent. Her mother, Mary, was a lady who has been much celebrated for her piety, the multitude of her descendants, and the length of her life Her father, Robert Atwaters, or Waters, Esquire, of Royton, in the parish of Lenham, in Essex, was a man of fortune, who left only two daughters, coheiresses, Joyce, the eldest, who married Humphrey Hales, Esquire, of the Dungeon, in Canterbury and Mary, the youngest, who brought the estate at Royton, another at Charing, and some other property, to her husband, Robert Honywood; then of Henewood, in the parish of Postling, in

No 38

A GENEALOGY UPON VELLUM,

BEAUTIFULLY DRAWN, WITH THE COATS OF ARMS EMBLAZONED, IN THEIR PROPER COLOURS

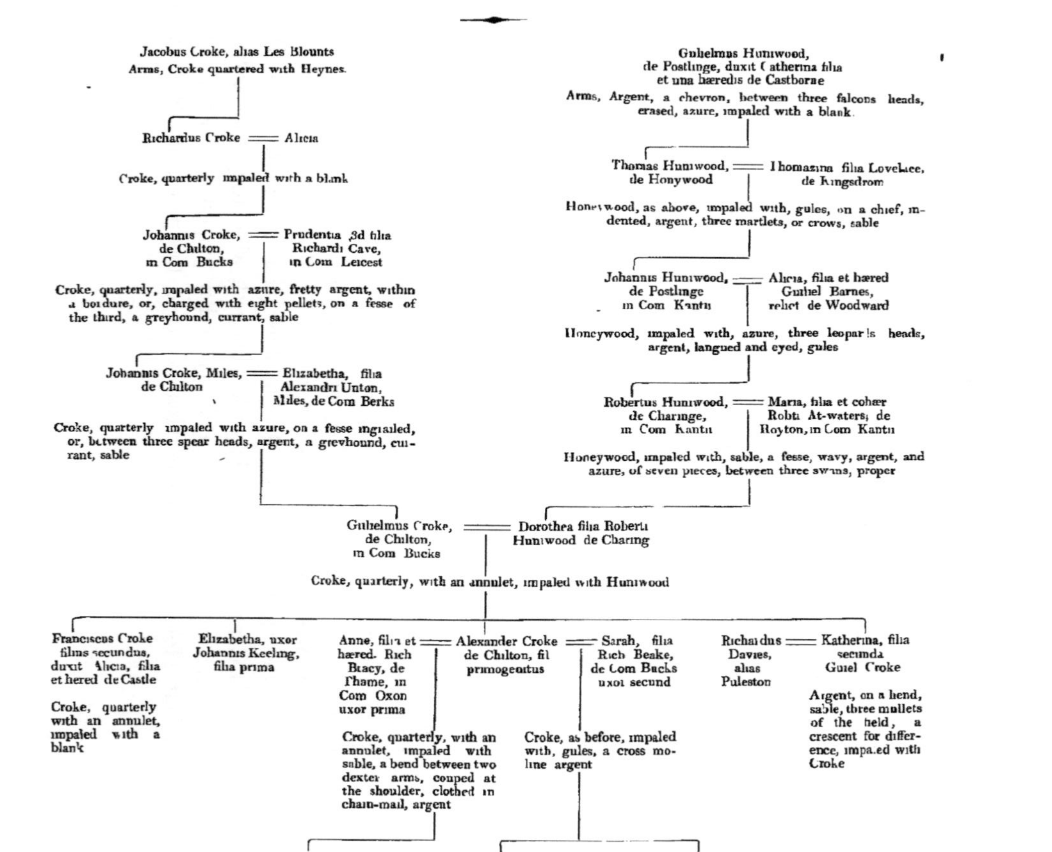

Kent. Mary was born in the year 1527, and married in February, 1543, at 16 years of age. Her husband died in the year 1576, and she lived to see three hundred and sixty-seven descendants of whom, sixteen were her own children, one hundred and fourteen grandchildren, two hundred and twenty-eight in the third generation, and nine in the fourth. Her grandson, Dr. Michael Honywood, Dean of Lincoln, in King Charles the Second's time, and whose monument is in the Minster, used to relate, that he was present at a dinner given by her to a family party of two hundred of her descendants[a]. Of her own issue, which consisted of seven sons and nine daughters, Robert, the eldest son, married Dorothy, the daughter of John Crook, LL.D.[b], Anthony, the second, married Mrs. Anne Gybson, Arthur, the third, Elizabeth Spencer; Walter was the fourth, and Isaac the fifth, who was killed at the battle of Newport, June the 20th, 1600; the two other sons died young Of the daughters, Catherine married, first, William Flete; and, secondly, William Headmarsh, or Henmarsh· Priscilla, to Sir Thomas Engeham, or Ingeham, Knight, Mary, to George Morton; Anne, to Sir Charles Hales, Knight, Grace, to Michael Heneage, from whom are descended the Earls of Winchelsea, and Nottingham, Elizabeth, to George Woodward, Susan, to Mr. Beecham, or Rancham, Bennet, to Henry Croke, the second son of Sir John Croke and Elizabeth Unton, and Dorothy, to his brother William Croke[c].

Hakewill, the first writer who gives a printed account of Mrs. Honywood, quotes an Epigram from Theodore Zwinger, which was made upon a noble lady of the Dalburg family of Basil, as applicable to her.

Mater ait natæ, dic natæ, filia, natam
Ut moneat, natæ plangere filiolam.

" The mother said to her daughter, daughter, bid thy daughter tell her " daughter, that her daughter's little daughter is crying[d]."

[a] Letter from Mr Francis Brocklesby, at the end of the sixth book of Leland's Itinerary, by Hearne, p 105

[b] I know not who this was, or whether of our family

[c] Hasted's History of Kent, vol ii p 442 Morant's History of Essex, vol ii. p 168. The names of the husbands are spelt differently in these two books

[d] Hakewill's Apologie of the Power and Providence of God, folio, 1635, p 252, and

Mrs. Honywood was a very good and pious woman, and zealous in performing all the charitable offices of Christianity. The poor, the distressed, and the afflicted, partook of her bounty, and were benefitted by her advice and consolation. In the persecutions, during the reign of Queen Mary, she used to visit the prisons, and administered comfort and relief to the unhappy sufferers. But, like many other good and pious persons, she was afflicted with religious melancholy, and despaired of her own salvation She was frequently visited by some of the most eminent divines, who endeavoured to heal her wounded spirit, by the various arguments of Scripture and reason, unhappily without effect. In a conversation with the celebrated Mr John Fox, the author of the Martyrology, whilst all his advice and consolations were ineffectual, in the agony of her soul, having a Venice glass in her hand, she broke forth into this expression, "I am as surely damned as this glass is broken," which she immediately threw with violence to the ground. The glass however rebounded again, and was taken up whole and entire The event seemed miraculous, yet she took no comfort from it, but continued long after in her former disconsolate condition: until at last, as Dr. Fuller relates it, "God "suddenly shot comfort, like lightning, into her soul, which once entered, "ever remained therein: so that she led the remainder of her life in spi-"ritual gladness" This she told herself to the Reverend father Thomas Morton, Bishop of Durham, from whose mouth Dr. Fuller received the relation[e]: and the glass was long preserved in the family[f].

During the time she continued in this unhappy state of mind, she consulted, amongst others, as a spiritual adviser, Mr. John Bradford, a celebrated divine, and preacher; who was committed to prison soon after Queen Mary's accession, and continued there near two years and an half. Amongst a great number of letters, written during his confinement, and preserved by Bishop Coverdale and Fox, are three to Mrs. Honywood, and one at least to her sister, Mrs. Joyce Hales[g]. The writings of

from him, Dr. Derham, in his Physico Theology, p 178 Edition 1727 Fuller's Worthies, Kent, &c.

[e] Fuller's Worthies, Kent, p 85 [f] Morant's History of Essex, vol ii. p 168, 170

[g] Myles Coverdale's Letters of the Martyrs, p 426 A small black-letter, quarto, published in 1564. Fox's Book of Martyrs, vol. iii f 271, &c Edit 1684 The account

most of the divines of that period are deeply tinctured with the doctrine of abstract faith, predestination, and election In these letters, the consciousness of a well-spent life, the zealous performance of all the duties of religion, and the satisfaction arising from sincere, though imperfect, endeavours to serve God, are not thought of sufficient importance to be introduced as topics of consolation. The sinner is to be recovered from despair by a firm faith, that she is the beloved daughter of God, the citizen of heaven, and the temple of the Holy Ghost; independently of any obedience or merit on her part. All doubts to the contrary are pronounced to be only the suggestions of Satan, and that whilst she has this belief, no sins can be imputed to her. Admitting the soundness of the principle, the letters are written with zeal and fervour, with good sense and eloquence[h].

When the time of Bradford's sufferings approached, and he was to be carried to Smithfield to be burnt, Mrs. Honywood resolved to accompany him. Not deterred by the tumult, and the crowds which assemble upon such occasions, she pressed forward with undaunted courage, and stood as near to him as possible though such was the pressure of the mob, that her shoes were trodden off, and lost. On their arrival at the place, Bradford went boldly up to the stake, and laying down flat on his face on one side of it, as a young man who suffered with him did on the other, they continued in prayer for some little time, till the Sheriff told them to rise. When they were got up, Bradford took up a faggot, and kissed it, as he did the stake. When he pulled off his clothes, he desired they might be given to his servant, "who," he observed, "was poor." After he was chained to the stake, he held up his hands and face to heaven, and said aloud, "O England, England, repent thee of thy sins!" Then, declaring that he forgave, and asking forgiveness of all the world, and requesting the people to pray for him, he turned his head about to the young man who was chained to the same stake behind him, encouraged him, and said, "Be of good comfort, brother, for we shall have a merry supper with the "Lord this night." They both appeared to be void of all fear, and

of Bradford, in Fox, with some of his letters, occupies 68 pages of double columns, closely printed, in folio

[h] See some of these letters in the Appendix, No. XXXII

shewed not the least alteration of countenance. In the midst of his tortures, Bradford embraced the flaming reeds that were near him and the last words which he was heard to say, were, "*Strait is the way, and nar-" row is the gate, that leadeth to salvation, and few there be that find it.*" When the affecting scene was over, after disengaging herself from the crowd, Mrs. Honywood was obliged to walk barefoot, from Smithfield to St. Martin's, before she could purchase a new pair of shoes[i].

She survived till the month of May, in the year 1620, when she died at the great age of ninety-three years.

There is a picture of her at Coleshill in Hertfordshire, the seat of the Lord Viscount Folkestone, son of the Earl of Radnor, who is descended from her, as is likewise his lady, through her mother, Lady Mildmay. She appears to be a handsome hale woman, of about fifty or sixty years of age, with some red in her cheeks, and of a cheerful countenance. Her dress is a close jacket, buttoned, with a sort of loose gown over it, of black silk. She has a small ruff, and a large hood, which falls over her back, and comes over part of her left arm In her left hand is a book, and at one corner of the picture her epitaph. Lady Mildmay has another picture of her, with the Venetian glass in her hand In the family manor house at Marks-Hall, in Essex, in the dining-room, was an original picture of her, in a widow's dress, with a book in her hand. On the right side of her hat was this inscription in golden letters, Ætatis suæ 70 On the other side, An°. Dni 1597[k]. In the library belonging to the Cathedral of Lincoln, which was founded by her grandson, Michael Honywood, D. D. who was Dean there, is his picture painted by Adrian Hanneman[l].

The arms of Honywood are, argent, a chevron between three hawks' heads erased azure.

Those of Atwaters, sable, a fesse wavy, *voided* azure, between three swans, proper[m].

Mrs. Honywood was buried in Lenham Church, near her husband, though a monument was erected to her memory at Marks-Hall, in Essex, by her eldest son, Robert Honywood, with the following inscription

[i] Fox, ibid Fuller s Worthies, Kent, p 85
[k] Morant's Hist of Essex, vol ii p 170
[l] Walpole's Anecdotes, vol ii p 214
[m] Hasted's Kent, vol ii p. 442.

"*Here lieth the body of Mary Waters, the daughter and coheir of* "*Robert Waters, of Lenham, in Kent, Esquire, wife of Robert Hony-* "*wood, of Charing, in Kent, Esquire, her only husband, who had at her* "*decease lawfully descended from her,* 367 *children,* 16 *of her own* "*body,* 114 *grandchildren;* 228 *in the third generation; and* 9 *in the* "*fourth. She lived a most pious life, and in a Christian manner died* "*here at Marks-Hall, in the* 93*d year of her age, and in the* 44*th of* "*her widowhood,* 11*th of May,* 1620[n]."

The inscription on the monument of her grandson, Dr. Honywood, in the Minster at Lincoln, are these.

MICHAEL HONYWOOD, S. T. P. CELEBERRIMÆ ILLIUS MATRONÆ MARIÆ HONYWOOD, ΜΑΚΡΑΙΩΝΟΣ, ΚΑΙ ΠΟΛΥΤΕΚΝΟΥ, E NEPOTIBUS POST NULLUM MEMORANDUS, HIC JUXTA SITUS EST, COLLEGII CHRISTI APUD CANTABRIGIENSES OLIM ALUMNUS ET SOCIUS; PIETATIS, PACIS, LITERARUM, STUDIOSISSIMUS; QUIBUS UT VACARET, PATRIAM, PERDUELLIUM CONJURATIONE PERTURBATAM, FUGIT, XVII POST ANNOS, IN TRANQUILLAM, CAROLO SECUNDO REDUCE, REDIIT; DEINCEPS COLLEGIO HUIC LINCOLNIENSI DECANUS ANNOS XXI PRÆFUIT. VIR PRISCA SIMPLICITATE, MORUM PROBITATE, LIBERALI MAGNIFICENTIA, INSIGNIS; QUA QUIDEM UNICA MONUMENTUM SIBI CUM LITERIS DURATURUM POSUIT; UTPOTE QUI CLAUSTRI HUJUS ECCLESIÆ DILAPSO IN LATERE, EXTRUCTA PRIUS SUMPTIBUS NON EXIGUIS BIBLIOTHECA, EAM POSTEA LIBRIS NEC PAUCIS NEC VULGARIBUS LOCUPLETAVERIT. TANDEM, SPE VITÆ IMMORTALIS, MORTI, HONYVODIOS LENTO PEDE INSEQUENTI, LUBENTUR SE OBTULIT, DIE VII MENSIS SEPTEMBRIS, ANNO ÆTATIS SUÆ 85, SAL. HUMANÆ 1681.

[n] Fuller's Worthies, Kent, p 85 Hakewill's Apology, book iii. ch 5 sec 9 Hearne, in Leland, vol vi. p 4 The words, "*Here lieth the body of,*" are omitted in some of these copies, which are probably the most correct, as she was buried at Lenham, and this of course was only a cenotaph It is omitted on her picture at Coleshill See the Genealogy of Croke, and Honywood, No. 38. from an emblazoned roll, penes me.

Upon a stone on the pavement is an English inscription, which states her descendants the same as on her own monument

William Croke, by his will, made the 17th of January, 1638, to which there is a codicil, dated the 22d of April, 1642, directed his body to be buried in the chancel of the church at Chilton· but there is no monument there to ascertain the time of his death[o]. By his wife, Dorothy Honywood, he had several children, Alexander, Edward, Francis, Elizabeth, and Catherine. Of his son and heir, Alexander, I shall speak presently. Edward was born February the 11th, 1602, and died young. Francis was born, the 6th of September, 1605, married Alicia Castle, and lived at Steeple Aston, near Deddington, in Oxfordshire He was buried there, the 2d of August, 1672, by Daniel Greenwood, the Rector, who published at Oxford, in quarto, in 1680, his sermon, preached upon the occasion, from Isaiah, chap. lvii verses 1st and 2d. "The righteous perish-"eth, and no man layeth it to heart· and merciful men are taken away, "none considering that the righteous is taken away from the evil to come. "He shall enter into peace, they shall rest in their beds, each one walk-"ing in his uprightness[p]." His children were, Dorothy Bell, Sarah Hore, Anne Coxeter, Elizabeth Croke, and Francis[q]. Elizabeth, born June 21st, 1597, married John Keling, Esquire; and Catherine, who was born October the 12th, 1598, was the wife of Richard Davis, otherwise Puleston[r], who had a son named Samuel[s].

Alexander Croke, Esquire, the eldest son of William Croke, and Dorothy Honywood, was born on the 23d of February, 1594. He was a member of the Inner Temple, and married two wives.

His first was Anne, the sole daughter and heir of Richard Brasey, of Thame, in Oxfordshire, by his wife, Mary, the daughter of Richard Danderidge, Esquire, of Berkshire. Richard Brasey was the son of John Brasey, of Northfield, in Worcestershire. She died young, and was

[o] Will, penes me [p] Wood's Fasti Oxon. Part ii col 775 [q] Will of Alexander Croke, who calls them his "nieces" and their receipts for his legacies, penes me [r] From the entries in an old book in MS being Solomon's Proverbs, arranged in methodical order Penes me See Appendix, No XXXIII and the Vellum Pedigree [s] Will of William Croke

buried at Chilton, under a flat, black, marble slab on the pavement of the church.

On a brass fillet round the stone is written,

HERE LYETH ANNE CROKE, WIFE OF ALEXANDER CROKE, ESQUIRE, DAUGHTER AND HEIRE OF RICHARD BRASEY, OF THAME, IN THE COUNTY OF OXNON, GENT. WHO DYED THE 22 DAY OF MARCH, AN. DNI. 1622, AND IN THE 22d YEAR OF HER AGE.

On a brass plate in the middle.

GOD'S LOVE AND FAVOUR IS NOT KNOWN ALWAYS
BY EARTHLY COMFORTS, NOR BY LENGTH OF DAYS,
FOR OFTEN TIMES WE SEE WHOM HE LOVES BEST
HE SOONEST TAKES UNTO HIS PLACE OF REST.
LONG LIFE ON EARTH DOTH BUT PROLONG OUR PAIN,
IN HAPPY DEATH THERE IS THE GREATEST GAIN.

She had only one son to survive her, Richard, who was born the 12th of October, 1619.

The arms of Brasey are, sable, a bend between two dexter arms, couped at the shoulder, clothed in chain mail argent[t].

His second wife, whom he married in 1624, was SARAH BEKE, the daughter of Richard Beke, Esquire, of Haddenham, in the county of Buckingham, and Colubery Lovelace[u]. They appear to have lived first at Dinton till his father's death, as their three first children, George, William, and Colubery are registered there, in 1625, 1627, 1631. This marriage formed another affinity with the families of Bulstrode and Whitelocke; besides a nearer connexion with those of Lovelace, Beke, and Mayne, of which I shall proceed to give some account[x].

COLUBERY LOVELACE was the daughter of Richard Lovelace, Esquire, and sister to Sir Richard Lovelace, who was created Lord Lovelace, Baron of Hurley, in the third year of Charles the First. John Lovelace, who died in 1558, possessed of the manor of Hurley, was grandfather to the first Lord Lovelace, and, according to Lysons[y], was Knighted

[t] Vellum Genealogy. Visitation of Oxfordshire, Coll. Gonvil et Caius, Cantab.

[u] Marriage Settlement, penes me.

[x] For the Bulstrodes, Whitelockes, Maynes, and Bekes, see their Genealogy, No. 34.

[y] Mag. Brit vol. i. p. 299

in the wars, went on an expedition with Sir Francis Drake, and built the mansion-house with the money he gained in that adventure. Lord Lovelace married, to his first wife, Catherine, daughter of George Hill, and widow of William Hyde, Esquire; by whom he had no issue. His second wife was Margaret, daughter and heir of William Dodsworth, citizen of London, by whom he had two sons, John and Francis; and two daughters, Elizabeth, who married Henry, son and heir of Sir Henry Martin, Knight, and Martha, who wedded Sir George Stonehouse, Baronet.

His son John, the second Lord Lovelace, married the Lady Anne, daughter of Thomas Lord Wentworth, and Earl of Cleveland; and dying in 1670, left issue, John, his only surviving son, and three daughters, Anne, who died unmarried, Margaret, married to Sir William Noel, of Hinkley Malory, in the county of Leicester, Baronet; and Dorothy, to Henry, son and heir of Sir James Drax, Knight.

John, the third Lord, was an early friend to the Revolution, but as he was going to join the Prince of Orange with a considerable force, was made prisoner. On the accession, however, of the Prince to the throne, this nobleman was made Captain of the Band of Pensioners. He lived in a most prodigal and splendid style, which involved him in so much difficulty, that a great part of his estates were sold, under a decree in Chancery, to pay his debts. He married Margery, one of the daughters and coheirs of Sir Edmund Pye, of Bradenham, in Buckinghamshire, Baronet; by whom he had a son, John, that died an infant, and three daughters, Anne, Martha, and Catherine, whereof the first and last died before their father without children and his Lordship dying without issue male, the barony of Wentworth descended to his only surviving daughter Martha, and the title of Lovelace to John Lovelace, the son of William, the son of Francis, the second son of Richard, the first Lord Lovelace. His mother was Mary, daughter of William King, of Iver, Bucks. John, the fourth Lord Lovelace, died in his Government of New York, on the 6th May, 1709. He married Charlotte, the daughter of Sir John Clayton, Knight, by whom he had three sons, John, Wentworth, and Nevil: Wentworth died a month before his father.

John, the fifth Lord, survived his father about a fortnight, when his brother Nevil became his heir, and the sixth and last Lord Lovelace, and

No. 39.

GENEALOGY OF LOVELACE.

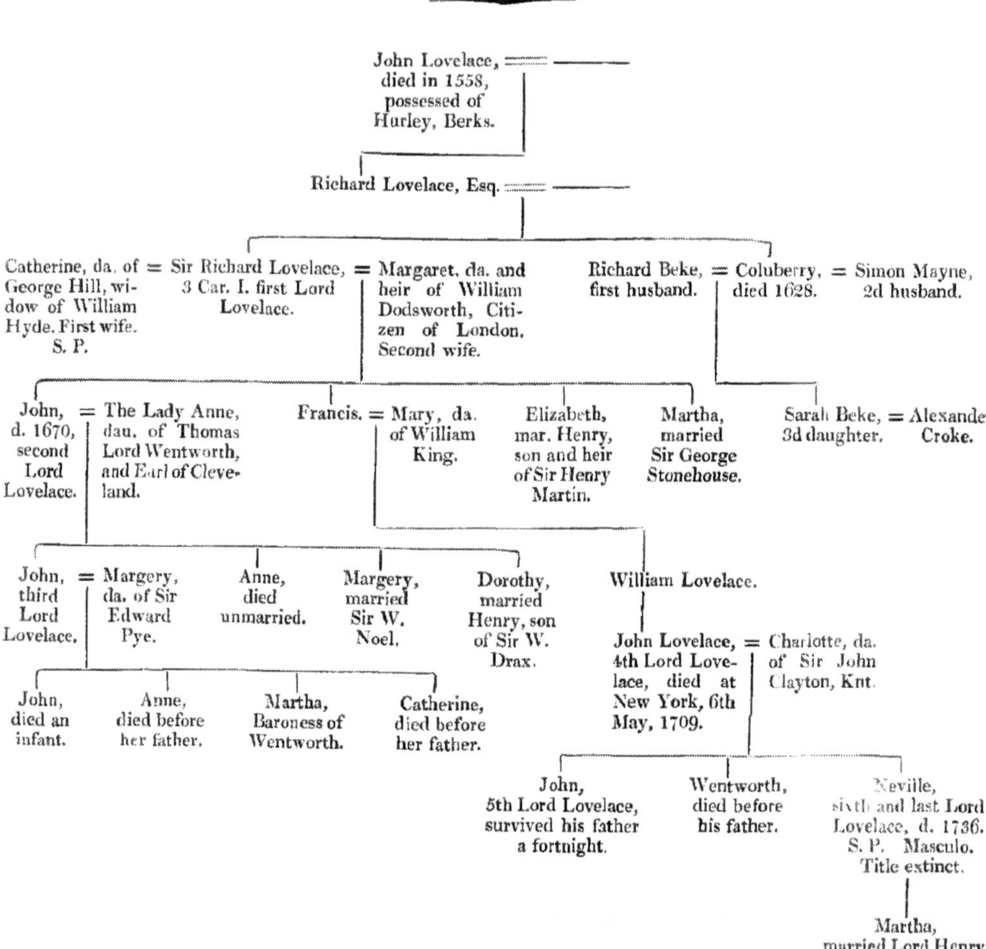
John Lovelace, died in 1558, possessed of Hurley, Berks.
Richard Lovelace, Esq.
Catherine, da. of George Hill, widow of William Hyde. First wife. S. P.
Sir Richard Lovelace, 3 Car. I. first Lord Lovelace.
Margaret, da. and heir of William Dodsworth, Citizen of London. Second wife.
Richard Beke, first husband.
Coluberry, died 1628.
Simon Mayne, 2d husband.
John, d. 1670, second Lord Lovelace.
The Lady Anne, dau. of Thomas Lord Wentworth, and Earl of Cleveland.
Francis.
Mary, da. of William King.
Elizabeth, mar. Henry, son and heir of Sir Henry Martin.
Martha, married Sir George Stonehouse.
Sarah Beke, 3d daughter.
Alexander Croke.
John, third Lord Lovelace.
Margery, da. of Sir Edward Pye.
Anne, died unmarried.
Margery, married Sir W. Noel.
Dorothy, married Henry, son of Sir W. Drax.
William Lovelace.
John Lovelace, 4th Lord Lovelace, died at New York, 6th May, 1709.
Charlotte, da. of Sir John Clayton, Knt.
John, died an infant.
Anne, died before her father.
Martha, Baroness of Wentworth.
Catherine, died before her father.
John, 5th Lord Lovelace, survived his father a fortnight.
Wentworth, died before his father.
Neville, sixth and last Lord Lovelace, d. 1736. S. P. Masculo. Title extinct.
Martha, married Lord Henry Beauclerk, d. March 3d, 1788, aged 79 years. Buried at Stanmore.

dying in 1736, the title became extinct. His daughter Martha married Lord Henry Beauclerk, died March 3d, 1788, aged seventy-nine years, and is buried in Stanmore Church, Middlesex.

The arms of Lovelace were gules, on a chief, indented, sable, three martlets argent[z].

Colubery Lovelace had two husbands. The first was RICHARD BEKE, ESQUIRE, of Haddenham, the son of Richard Beke, Esquire, of White-Knights, in Berkshire, Equerry to Queen Elizabeth, and Elizabeth, aunt of Sir Thomas Read, of Boston (or Barton) in Berkshire; which Elizabeth died in 1606[a]. Queen Elizabeth, in her twelfth year, granted to Richard Beeke, Gentleman, one of the Esquires of her stables, the site of the mansion house in Haddenham, late purchased of the Lord North, and a water-mill, for forty years, rendering £80, for the mansion, and £6, for the mill[b].

By Richard Beke Colubery had several sons and daughters, Henry, who married Frances Rilliard, and had a son Richard, who married a daughter of Sir Thomas Lee; Margaret, who married Colonel Lilburne, Marmaduke, whose wife was Elizabeth Slater, of Haddenham; William; James; Elizabeth, married to Thomas Dover; Anne, married to William Gape; and Sarah, the third daughter, who was the wife of Alexander Croke. Richard Beke died in the year 1605.

The second husband of Colubery Lovelace was SIMON MAYNE, ESQUIRE, of Dinton, in Buckinghamshire. She had two children by him; a son named Simon Mayne; and a daughter called Colubery Mayne, who married Thomas Bulstrode, Esquire, the grandson of Edward Bulstrode and Cecily Croke. Simon Mayne died on the 13th day of July, 1617, when his widow erected a monument to his memory, against the wall in Dinton church, with the following inscription.

[z] This account of the Lovelace family is from Banks's Extinct Peerage. See Genealogy, No. 39.

[a] Elizabeth Beke, in her will dated 18th March, 1605, appointed her son, Richard Beke, her Executor. On the 16th of June, Colubery Beke, his widow, took out letters of administration *de bonis non*. The inventory of his goods at Haddenham and Binfield, taken after his death, is dated 20th May, 1607, penes me.

[b] Pat Roll. in Brown Willis's MSS vol. 40 fol. 80.

HERE LIETH THE BODY OF SIMON MAYNE, LATE OF DINTON, ESQUIRE, WHO HAD TO WIFE COLUBERY LOVELACE, DAUGHTER TO RICARD LOVELACE, OF HURLEY, IN THE COUNTY OF BERKS, ESQUIRE, BY WHOM HE HAD ISSUE, ONE SON AND ONE DAUGHTER, SIMON AND COLUBERY. HE DIED 13 JULY, THE 40th YEAR OF HIS AGE, ANNO DOMINI 1617. IN REMEMBRANCE OF WHOM, COLUBERY HIS WIFE, AS A TOKEN OF HER NEVER ENDING LOVE, HATH CAUSED THIS MONUMENT TO BE ERECTED.

MAIENI PIETAS, PROBITAS, SAPIENTIA, CANDOR,
MENS SUBMISSA, FIDES, SPES, AMOR, INTEGRITAS,
NUNC DESIDERIUM FACIUNT, IMITABILE VITÆ
EXEMPLAR MODO QUÆ PROPOSUERE BONÆ.
OMNIBUS ERGO MAGIS GEMMIS, TITULIS, MONUMENTIS,
SIC DECORATAM ANIMAM NUMINIS AULA CAPIT.

NERE TO THIS PLACE A MIRROR LIES
OF PATIENCE AND HUMILITIE
DEVOTION WAS HIS EXERCISE,
WHICH LED HIM TO ETERNITIE.
HIS SOULE IN BLISS, HIS CORPSE IN CLAY,
SHALL MEET AGAIN, AND LIVE FOR AYE.

His wife, Colubery Mayne, died in 1628 She made her will on the 18th day of July in that year, in which she directed her body to be buried in the parish church of Donington als Dinton, near the place where the body of her late husband, Simon Mayne, lay buried, and that her executors should provide one or two decent grave-stones, sufficient for them both, and her said late husband, herself, and their two children to be pictured thereon, and cause the same to be laid orderly over the place where her husband lay buried The will, which is long, contains such bequests as a rich widow might be expected to make to her children, relations, friends, and servants, according to the respective degrees of her affection for them[c]. In pursuance of the directions in her will, a large flat stone was laid over the relicts of herself and her husband, near the entrance into the chancel in Dinton church ; with the effigies of herself, her

[c] Will penes me

husband, and her two children, engraved on brass plates, with the following simple inscription, in the black letter.

Simon Mayne, Esquire, and Coluberry, left issue, Simon and Coluberry. He died 13 July, 1617. she 10th Jan. 1628.

The coat of arms of Mayne is under it. Ermine, on a bend, three dexter hands couped at the wrist

Her son, Simon Mayne, was a minor at his mother's death, and by her will, she bequeathed the wardship of him, which she had by a grant from the King, to her son-in-law, Alexander Croke, and Sarah his wife, with the benefit of all his lands, and the use of all her goods and chattels in Dinton, Winchendon, and Cudington, till her son attained the age of twenty-one years Upon condition that, during the minority, Alexander Croke should keep and maintain him, with meat, drink, lodging, apparel, and other things needful, at school, the University, or the Inns of Court, with all necessary expences befitting his estate and calling, and that with all loving and respective usage. And she gave to her son, when he should accomplish his full age, the wardship and benefit of his marriage[d].

Under the friendly tutelage of his brother-in-law, it must be supposed that his education corresponded with the wishes and directions of his discreet mother. Influenced probably by the gentlemen of Buckinghamshire, and his neighbour Ingoldsby, as he grew to manhood, he ranged himself on the side of the patriots, and was a Member of the Long Parliament. In 1654, we find him in the commission for the county of Buckingham, under the ordinance for "ejecting scandalous, ignorant, and insufficient "schoolmasters." And he was one of the Commissioners for settling the militia in the same county in 1659[e].

Upon the erection of the High Court of Justice for trying King Charles the First, he was appointed one of the Judges, attended most of the days of the trial, and finally affixed his name and seal to the warrant for the execution[f].

After the Restoration, upon the King's proclamation for those who had given judgment against Charles to appear, he surrendered himself. As one of the Judges, he was excepted by name out of the Act of Indemnity[g].

[d] Will ut supra [e] The printed ordinances. [f] Nalson's Trial of King Charles
[g] 12 Car. II cap 11.

When he was brought to trial with the other regicides, in his defence he said, that "he had pleaded not guilty, not as denying the fact, but because "his conscience told him that he had no malice or ill intention to his "Majesty." He acknowledged the fact of his sitting in the High Court of Justice, and lay at his Majesty's feet for mercy, alledging "that he was "an ignorant, weak man in the law." He admitted his hand and seal to the warrant, but asserted that "he knew not of the King's bringing "up, and never was at any committee" He stated, "that the importu-"nity by which he signed it was known to many there. He was un-"willing to it, and was told, What fear was there, when forty were there "before, and twenty were of the Quorum? He was thereupon drawn in "to set his hand to it. He never plotted, or contrived the business. "There was a gentleman that plucked him down by the coat if he offered "to speak in the House, and told him he should be sequestered as a delin-"quent, and said, Will you rather lose your estate than take away the King's "life[h]?" Mayne was found guilty, and condemned Six only of the King's Judges were executed. The rest, including Mayne, were reprieved, and he continued in prison till his death, which took place in 1661. He was buried at Dinton.

This family became possessed of the manor of Dinton about 1606. Upon the attainder of Simon Mayne it was forfeited to the Crown, but was restored again to the family, and was sold in 1727, by Simon Mayne, grandson of the regicide, to John Vanhattem, Esquire. It is now possessed by the reverend William Goodall, who married the natural daughter and residuary legatee of Sir John Vanhattem, son to the first purchaser[i].

It may not be improper to mention here a man, who was clerk to Simon Mayne, I suppose in his capacity as a Justice of the Peace, and who was a singular character. His name was John Bigg, and he was born in 1629. He had been originally possessed of tolerable wealth, was looked upon as a pretty good scholar, and of no contemptible parts. Upon the Restoration, in despair for the final ruin of the good old cause, he grew melancholy, betook himself to a recluse life, and lived in a cave under ground at

[h] Trial of the 29 Regicides, page 308 Ed 1679

[i] Lysons's Magna Britannia, Dinton, Bucks, vol i part 3 page 550 Dinton register Information from Mr Goodall, &c.

Dinton. His clothes were composed of innumerable patches, chiefly of leather, as were his shoes. He lived entirely upon charity, but never asked for any thing except leather, which he would immediately nail to his clothes. Three bottles were suspended from his girdles, one for strong beer, another for small beer, and a third for milk, which were given and brought to him, as was his other sustenance. He died in 1696. There are two pictures of him, a painting in oil of small size, in the possession of Sir Scrope Bernard Morland, Baronet, of Winchendon in Buckinghamshire, which has been etched by Richardson; and a drawing, belonging to Mr. Goodall of Dinton; they were all taken from the sign of an ale-house, called the Hermit. Two of his shoes are still preserved, of a large size, and made up of pieces of leather nailed on, one is in the Ashmolean Museum at Oxford, the other in the collection of Sir John Vanhattem, who some years ago had his cave dug up, in hopes of finding something curious, but nothing was discovered[k].

To return to Alexander Croke. His second wife, Sarah Beke, whose connexions we have stated, died in 1667. On a flat black marble at Chilton is this inscription over her.

HERE LIETH THE BODY OF SARAH CROKE, SECOND WIFE OF ALEXANDER CROKE, OF STUDLEY, IN THE COUNTY OF OXFORD, ESQUIRE, AND DAUGHTER OF RICHARD BEKE, OF HADDENHAM, IN THE COUNTY OF BUCKS, ESQUIRE. SHE DIED IN THE 67th YEAR OF HER AGE, AND IN THE YEAR OF OUR LORD 1667.

The arms are, Croke, with an annulet, impaled with two bars, indented. On a chief three annulets[l].

Alexander Croke died in 1673, the following inscription is on the black marble slab which covers his remains.

HERE LIETH THE BODY OF ALEXANDER CROKE, ESQUIRE, SOMETIME OF CHILTON, AFTERWARDS OF STUDLEY, IN THE COUNTY OF

k Letter from T. Hearne to Browne Willis, in Letters by eminent persons in the Bodleian Library, and Ashmolean Museum, vol. i. page 247 Inscription under Richardson's Etching, and other information Amongst the servants of Colubery Mayne, Simon's mother, appears one John Bigg As this legacy was given in 1628, and the Hermit was not born till 1629, this could not be the same person, but perhaps was his father.

l This is different from the coat of arms in the vellum Genealogy

OXFORD, WHERE HE DIED, IN THE 78th YEAR OF HIS AGE, AND IN THE YEARE OF OUR LORD 1673, BEING SON OF WILLIAM CROKE, ESQUIRE, AND GRANDSON OF SIR JOHN CROKE, BOTH OF CHILTON.

Arms, Croke, quarterly, with an annulet.

His funeral sermon was preached by the Reverend Daniel Greenwood, the Rector of Steeple Aston, in Oxfordshire, and which was published at Oxford in 1680. The text was from the second Epistle to the Corinthians, the sixth chapter, and the seventh and eighth verses. "By the "word of truth, by the power of God, by the armour of righteousness on "the right hand and on the left, by honour and dishonour, by evil report "and good report: as deceivers, and yet true." The uncle of Mr. Greenwood, Doctor Daniel Greenwood, was made Principal of Brazen-nose by the Parliamentary Committee, and being removed upon the Restoration, he and his wife retired to Studley, where they lived till her death, when the Doctor went to live with his nephew at Steeple Aston[m].

Alexander Croke had a numerous family. By his first wife, Anne Brasey, he was the father of Richard Croke, who was born October the 12th, 1619, and died before him, of whom hereafter: and of John, born July the 10th, 1622, and who died the same year. By his second wife, Sarah Beke, he had George, who was born August 29, 1625, and died in 1627; William, born February the 26th, 1626, of whom likewise more will be said; Simon, born July the 16th, 1629, and died in 1649; Colubery, born September the 11th, 1631, and died August the 20th, 1652; Elizabeth, born March the 26th, 1634, and died in 1641; Thomas, born November the 5th, 1636, and who died the same year; and, lastly, Sarah Croke, born May the 9th, 1640[n]. The last, who died in 1691, married Edmund West, Esquire, Serjeant at Law, of Masworth, who left an only daughter named Sarah[o].

The descendants of Alexander Croke formed two separate families, deduced from his sons Richard, and William: between whom, by settle-

[m] Wood's Fasti, Oxon. part ii. col. 771, 775.

[n] MS. entries. Appendix, No. XXXIII.

[o] Did she afterwards marry John Poynter, Esquire, of Kellshall in Hertfordshire? as William Croke in his will in 1702, the elder brother of the Reverend Alexander Croke, leaves a ring to his cousin Sarah Poynter the elder, and another to his cousin Harvey. Did another sister marry a Harvey?

ments, and his will, he divided his estate at Studley. The mansion house, with the lands in Oxfordshire, and a part of those in Buckinghamshire, he gave to John, the son of his eldest son, Richard, who died before him The remaining part he settled upon his second son, William We have already given an account of a conversation between him and his uncle, Sir George Croke, respecting the mode of disposing of his property: which however did not take effect exactly in the manner then proposed. I shall treat *first* of Richard and his descendants[p] and *next* of William[q]

[p] In the tenth Chapter

[q] In the eleventh Chapter

CHAPTER X.

The eldest branch of the descendants of Alexander Croke

THE eldest son of Alexander Croke by Anne Brasey, his first wife, was RICHARD CROKE. His wife's name was Anne, he lived at Lewknor in Oxfordshire, was born on the 12th of October, 1619, and died, before his father, March the 9th, 1663, according to the modern mode of computation. By his will, which is dated the 1st of March, 1663, and was proved on the 5th of May following, he directed that his body should be buried at Chilton, but there is no memorial of him there. The executors were his father, his brother William, his honoured brother-in-law, Sir John Fettiplace, Baronet, Edmund Fettiplace, Esquire, and his son John[a]

He had a large family, eight sons, and seven daughters, who are all mentioned in his will; John, Richard, Ferdinando, Alexander, Edward, George, Charles, and Thomas Anne, born in 1641, Mary, Elizabeth Sarah, Frances, Colubery, and Arabella Mrs. Croke was left a widow with fifteen children, who all standing in a row in mourning to see the King, Charles the Second, go by in his way to Oxford, the road from London to Oxford being near Lewknor, they engaged his Majesty's attention, and occasioned him to enquire what family they were[b] She was living in 1674, when her children Sarah, Frances, Colubery, George Charles, and Thomas, were under age[c].

His eldest son and heir was JOHN CROKE, Esquire, who appears to have been usually called Captain Croke, from having served his country in the Trained Bands, the Militia of former times He was married, on

[a] Was his wife, Anne, sister to Sir John Fettiplace, or does he call him brother-in-law because his brother William married Sir John's sister? The former I think is the most probable The latter seems very far fetched Will, penes me

[b] From the information of Mrs Hicks, an old woman who had lived in the family

[c] A receipt of that date penes me

No. 40.

GENEALOGY OF NORRIS, AND BERTIE, EARL OF ABINGDON

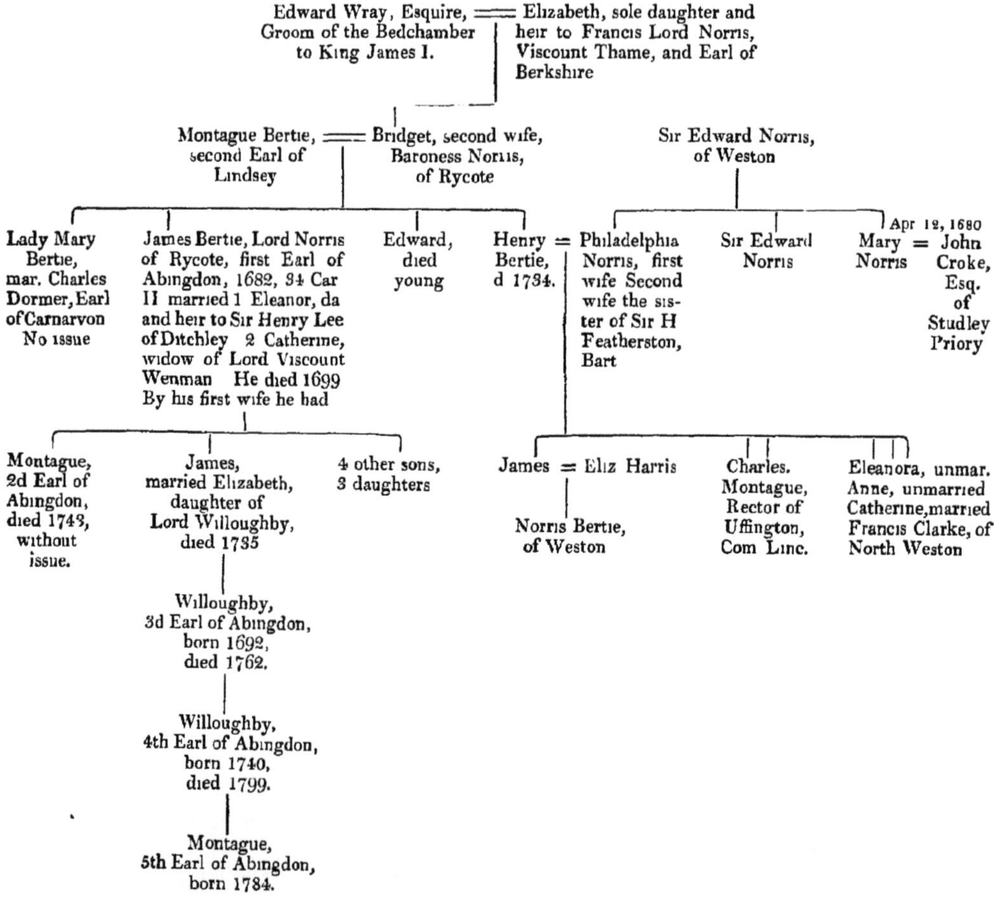

the 12th of April, 1680, to Mary Norris, sister to Sir Edward Norris, of Weston on the Green[d], whose other sister, Philadelphia, married the Honourable Henry Bertie, the first Earl of Abingdon's brother, whose sister, Lady Mary Bertie, was the wife of Charles Dormer, Earl of Carnarvon[e]. Hearne walked to Studley in 1716, and has left an account of his visit. He says, that Mrs. Croke was an handsome woman, which appears likewise by her picture in my possession: that she used to be much at the Earl of Abingdon's, both at Rycote and Witham; and that it was at the Earl's house that Captain Croke courted her[f].

John Croke's brother Edward was a singular character. He was in the army, in the regiment of the Blues, and served abroad, where he had his leg shot off Upon his return, not having realized much property in the profession of war, and having a high spirit, he procured from his brother an appointment in the alms-house at Studley, founded by Sir George Croke Here he lived, and having thus secured an independence which gratified his honourable feelings, he frequently visited at his brother's house, where his company was always acceptable, as he was a facetious companion, and abounded in anecdote, and other convivial qualities. He had entertained a notion that he should live to the age of old Parr, and used to rise very early every morning, and go to a certain spring in the neighbourhood to drink, and wash his hands and face[g]. With respect to the usual allowances of clothes, fuel, and pay, which were given by the founder, he was, of course, upon the same footing with the other alms-people, but it appears by the old accounts, that better linen was supplied to him. That of the others was *Lockram*, at thirteen pence the ell, in 1698; but for Mr. Edward Croke, six ells and an half of *Dowlace* were purchased, at fourteen pence halfpenny the ell, to made him two shirts: the reason stated is that the *Lockram* was too narrow. He was likewise appointed to the office of reading prayers in the alms-house, for which twenty shillings a year is allowed[h] I have his picture in the dress of the alms-people

The manner of the death of her youngest son, Edward, was very afflicting

[d] Albury parish register. [e] Collins's Peerage, vol III p 510 [f] Hearne's account of his walk to Studley, 31 March, 1716, MSS Journal Bodleian Library Appendix, No XXXIV [g] It was at the Warren. From old Mrs Hicks, supra [h] Old accounts, penes me

to Mrs Croke. After having given him a proper correction for some bad words, she left him shut up in a closet, and went to make a visit to her sister-in-law, Lady Carnavon. In the mean while he was taken ill, and, notwithstanding every possible assistance, he died before her return. From this unfortunate event, and, according to Hearne's account, from the supposed unfaithfulness of her husband, she became melancholy, and was principally confined to her chamber for several years before her death[i].

John Croke died about 1714[k] His children, by Mary Norris, were four sons, and a daughter named Richard, John, James, Edward, and Charlotte. Richard was a Student of Christ Church, in Oxford, died young, and is buried in the chapel at Studley. I have his picture painted after his death.

Here lieth the body of Richard, eldest son of John Croke, Esquire, and Mary his wife He was born the 14th of August, 1683 *died May 28th,* 1698

Their son Edward, before mentioned, is buried there likewise, with the following inscription.

Here lieth the body of Edward, the son of John Croke, Esquire, and Mary his wife He died Oct. 24, 1694 *aged* 2 *years and* 11 *months*

John Croke, the eldest surviving son, was deformed, had an impediment in his speech, and was weak in his intellects, so as to be incapable of managing his affairs and therefore gave up his estate at Studley, to his brother James, for an annuity of one hundred pounds a year.

James Croke, the second son, was High Sheriff for Oxfordshire, in 1726, and died in the same year, unmarried[l]. I have his picture. Upon the death of James Croke, the Studley estate reverted to his brother John, who, unwilling to have the trouble of managing it, gave it to his sister Charlotte.

This was Charlotte Croke, who was born in 1587, and succeeded to the mansion at Studley, upon the death of her brothers, John and James. She married William Ledwell, Esq. and died May the 5th, 1763.

[i] Mrs. Hicks [k] Hearne's account [l] Hearne's Diary, vol. 101.

They had an only daughter, who died before them, at the age of seventeen, the 16th of June, 1748. Her husband survived her till the year 1766 She gave the mansion house, at Studley, with the rest of the estate, to her cousin, Alexander Croke, Esquire; and thus the two parts of that estate, which had been divided by the former Alexander Croke, were again united in the person of his descendant.

She was buried in the chapel at Studley, with an handsome monument to her memory, with the following inscription.

" *This stone is erected to the memory of Mrs. Charlotte Ledwell, of* " *Studley, wife of William Ledwell, Esq and youngest daughter of John* " *Crooke, Esq. and Mary his wife. She was in faith and practice a* " *true Christian. After a long and painful illness, which she bore with* " *saint-like fortitude and resignation, she died on the 5th day of May,* " 1763, *aged* 76.

" *If here thy Tears, O Reader, fall,*
" *While Memory to thy Thought*
" *Shall Ledwell's various Worth recall,*
" *By me this Rule be taught;*
" *Like her, Thou Pilgrim of a day,*
" *Thy Task of Life attend,*
" *Then may'st thou find to Heav'n the Way,*
" *And Glory in thy end* "

Arms, Ermine, two flanches, lozengy, or and, azure, impaled with Croke.

The monument of her daughter is similar to Mrs. Ledwell's, and has this inscription.

" *Beneath this Stone lyeth the Body of Mary Ledwell, only Daughter* " *of William Ledwell, Esq. and Charlotte his wife, of this Place. A* " *young Lady blessed with all the excellent Qualifications of Mind and* " *Body, which might make her Agreeable to her Friends, or Happy in* " *herself. Tho' young in years, yet was she aged in virtue, who having* " *spun out her short thread of Life, yet lived long enough to finish a com-* " *pleat course of Piety and Goodness*

" *Stop. Courteous Reader, but one moment here,*
" *And, if thou canst, refrain the generous tear!*

" But if the bloom of Piety and Youth,
" If perfect Goodness, Constancy, and Truth;
" If modest Virtue join'd to modest Sense,
" If Honour, Honesty, and Innocence,
" If such like Virtues could thy soul have moved,
" Thou must this blooming Virgin have approved
" All weeping ask why this Sun rose so bright
" To set so soon and hide its grateful light
" Why in the morn it stopt its chearing ray,
" And left us mortals in the dawn of day
" But weep no more at this her early fate,
" As she is fixed in that eternal state,
" Where Bliss for ever bears an ample sway,
" Where Mirth shall never cease, nor joy decay,
" For see! the rising Fair forsakes her tomb
" And soars triumphant to her native home
" Go then, blest Maid! enjoy what God has given,
" And with the Saints unite a Saint in Heaven.

" She died the 16th day of June, 1748, in the 17th year of her age "

Arms, a lozenge, quarterly, first and fourth, Ledwell, second and third, Croke.

CHAPTER XI.

The youngest branch of the descendants of Alexander Croke.

WE proceed next to WILLIAM CROKE, the eldest son of Alexander Croke, by his second wife, Sarah Beke. We have seen that his father settled upon him the principal part of the Studley estate, in Buckinghamshire. He was born on the 26th of February, in 1627, and married Susan, the daughter of Edward Fettiplace, Esq of Swinbrooke, in the county of Oxford. Through this lady, we claim another descent from Beatrice, the natural daughter of John, the first King of Portugal, and consequently a relationship to the House of Braganza, the reigning family of that country[a]

The ancestor of the Fettiplace family came in with William the Conqueror, and held a high office under him In 1661, John Fettiplace was created a Baronet. The whole of the male line of the Fettiplaces failing in 1746, the estate fell to Thomas Bushell, Esquire, son of Robert Bushell, of Cleve Pryor, in Worcestershire, Esquire, who married Diana, daughter of the first Baronet, and who assumed the name of Fettiplace, by Act of Parliament[b]. This race I believe is likewise extinct[c].

William Croke died in 1702, and was buried at Chilton, where, upon a flat stone in the chancel, is this inscription to his memory.

" *Here lyeth the body of William Croke, Esquire, late of Chilton, in*
" *the county of Bucks, son of Alexander Croke, Esquire, by his second*
" *wife, who died October the 6th*, 1702, *in the 77th year of his age. He*
" *married Susan the daughter of Edward Fettiplace, Esquire, of*
" *Swinbrook, in the county of Oxford, by whom he had* 6 *sons, and* 5
" *daughters.*"

[a] See the Genealogy of Unton and Fettiplace, Book IV Chap 3 and No 24.
[b] 20 Geo II ch 30 [c] Collins s Baronetage

The monument of Susan Croke is adjoining, which states the same facts, and that she died the 17th of May, 1712, in the 86th year of her age.

The arms are, Croke with an annulet, impaling gules, two chevrons, argent, for Fettiplace

Their children were, Sarah, born the 15th of November, 1653, and died the 6th of April, in 1727, unmarried, in the 74th year of her age, as is stated upon her monument at Chilton William, born July the 25th, 1655, and died the 19th of January, 1705, without issue. He was educated at Magdalen Hall[d], and is buried at Chilton The Reverend Alexander Croke, of whom more hereafter, was born July the 23d, 1657. Susanna, born the 5th of September, 1660, died September the 16th, 1662. John, born the 4th of March, 1661, died the 22d of December, 1663. Edward, born May the 15th, 1663, living in 1695 Jane, born the 15th of May, 1665, living in 1695. George, born the 2d of February, 1668, and died the 1st of July, 1669 Elizabeth, born January the 26th, 1670, she married George Wren, son of Thomas Wren, Rector of Kelshal, in Hertfordshire, by whom she had an only daughter. He died February the 22d, 1709, aged 28, and was buried at Kelshal[e]. George, born the 22d of May, 1672[f].

In his will, dated the 10th of May, 1695, after settling his property upon his own family, he leaves rings and other small memorials to Sir Thomas Lee, Baronet, his nephew, Samuel Poynter, and his two sisters, Richard Ingoldsby, Esquire, and Simon Mayne. And he constitutes his wife Susan, John Poynter, Esquire, of Kelshal, in Hertfordshire, Richard Beke, Esquire, and Thomas Dunster, Doctor in Divinity, his executors. His sons William, Alexander, and Edward, and his three daughters, Sarah, Jane, and Elizabeth, were then living[g]

The Reverend ALEXANDER CROKE was the second son of William Croke, and Susan Fettiplace, and was born in 1657. Having originally been a younger son, he was educated in the Church as his profession: he

[d] His name written in books, 1674 and 1678, Wm Croke, Aulæ Magd

[e] Salmon's Hertfordshire, p 350

[f] The names and dates are taken from the entries in an old book, and I believe were written in it by William Croke. See Appendix, No XXXIII.

[g] Will, penes me

was admitted a Scholar of Wadham College, in Oxford, on the 29th of September, 1676 took his degree of Master of Arts in 1681 · and was elected Fellow of that Society on the 4th of July, 1682[h].

During his continuance there, he seems to have been intimate with Creech, one of the principal poets of that time. Creech, in his translation of Theocritus, has dedicated the twentieth Idyllium to him, under the name of "his good-humoured friend, Mr. Alexander Croke, of Wadham "College." The subject is the cruelty of "a City Maid"

By his relation, Sir Thomas Lee, he was presented to the Rectory of Hartwell, near Aylesbury, and I have some of his sermons there preached They are in the full manner of Barrow, and are creditable to his talents as a preacher, and a conscientious parish minister. Upon the death of his elder brother William in 1705, he became the representative of his family, and succeeded to that part of the Studley estate which had been settled upon it.

He married Jane, the third daughter of Anthony Eyans, Esquire, of Begbrook, in Oxfordshire[i], by whom he had two sons and three daughters. By his epitaph in Chilton church, it appears that he died on the 27th of November, 1726, in the 69th year of his age.

The arms on his monument are, Croke, with a crescent, impaled with, a fesse, charged with three balls, in chief a greyhound, currant.

The children were, Sarah, born in 1703, and died of the small pox the 24th of April, 1728, in the 25th year of her age, she was buried at Chilton, and her monument was erected by her lamenting mother. Mater mœrens posuit. Alexander, his son and heir. William Croke, of Aylesbury[k]. Jane, married to William Wood, Esquire, son of Thomas Wood, Doctor of Laws, who wrote the Institutes. Another daughter, whose name is not known.

Alexander Croke, Esquire, the eldest son of the Rector of Hartwell, and Jane Eyans, was born on the 24th of February, in 1704. He received the earliest part of his education at the public school at

[h] The books at Wadham College

[i] I have her picture, painted by Mortimer, father of the celebrated artist She holds a rose It is a poor performance

[k] In a copy of Croke's Reports is written, "Wm Croke de Aylesbury, 1750, e dono "Sam Croke de Crooke Com. Lanc Armigeri" I know not who the latter was

Thame, which was formerly of great repute[l]: and afterwards he was entered as a Gentleman Commoner of Wadham College at Oxford. When he was twenty-two years of age, he married an heiress, and the ceremony was performed at Hartwell, on the 12th of July, 1726. This was Miss Elizabeth Barker, who having been baptized on the 24th of October, in 1708, was in her eighteenth year, and was the only daughter of Richard Barker, Esquire, of Great Horwood, in Buckinghamshire, by his wife, Abigail Busby, who was likewise an heiress. She was handsome and accomplished; having received her education at Cavalier's school, in Queen's Square, then the most fashionable establishment for forming young ladies. When I knew her, in her old age, she preserved the remains of her former beauty, and she had the correct and elegant manners of the females of the last age. By this marriage he acquired the estates at Marsh Gibbon, which had descended from the Busbys, and that of Batchford in Gloucestershire from the Barkers. After their marriage, till the death of her brother William Busby, they lived at Dinton in Buckinghamshire, when they removed to Marsh Gibbon[m].

As this lady was descended from the two families of Barker and Busby, it may be proper to give some account of them. The family of the BARKERS had been settled for many years at Great Horwood. Through the line of Fiennes, Lord Say and Sele, they claimed kindred with William of Wykeham, by the benefit of this pedigree, which was thus transmitted to the Croke family, many of them had obtained admission into the opulent foundations of Winchester and New College[n]. Of these, *William Barker*, born in 1604, was Fellow of New College, was created Doctor in Divinity, in 1661, for his laudable sermons preached before the King and Parliament at Oxford, during the Rebellion. He was Rector of Hardwick, in Buckinghamshire, and Prebendary of Canterbury, and died 26 March, 1669. In his epitaph in Hardwick church, it is said, that "he was always "noted for his orthodox sermons, his innocent wit, and his candid "manners[o]."

[l] Warton's Life of Sir Thomas Pope, page 365.

[m] For the account of Marsh Gibbon, see the Digression at the end of the lives of Alexander Croke and Elizabeth Barker.

[n] Collins's Peerage, vol. i. page 337. See Genealogy, No. 42. from a MS. Genealogy made in 1572, and continued to the present time.

[o] Wood's Fast. Oxon. ii. col. 822.

H. S E.

DEPOSITUM GULIELMI BARKER, RECTORIS DE HARDWYCKE, CANONICI CANTUARIENSIS DIGNISSIMI, QUONDAM NOVI COLL. IN OXON. SOCII, ET DOCTORIS IN ALTIORI THEOLOGIÆ SPÆRA MERITO COLLOCATI, QUAM FREQUENTIBUS ORTHODOXIS CONCIONIBUS, SALIBUS INNOCUIS MORUMQUE CANDORE ORNAVIT. IMITENTUR POSTERI. NATUS A°. DOM CIƆIƆCIIII. DENATUS MART. XXVI. CIƆIƆCLXIX.

Hugh Barker took his degree of Doctor of Laws, and followed with success the profession of an Advocate in the Civil Law He was admitted into the society of Doctor's Commons the 9th of June, 1607, was Chancellor of the diocese of Oxford, and for his learning and integrity was promoted to the highest station in that profession, the Deanery of the Arches[p]. He died in the year 1632, and was buried in New College chapel, under an handsome monument, erected to his memory by his widow, who was Mary, the daughter of Alderman Pyott. He is represented in his doctorial robes under an arch, in marble. It was the work of Nicholas Stone, a celebrated statuary, who had fifty pounds for executing it[q]

H. S. E.

Hugo Barker L L Romanarum studio, scientiâ, professione, doctoratu, insignis. Qui multos annos juri cognoscendo, interpretando, dicundo, impendit, eo successu ut ejus neque consultores prudentiam, neque clientes fidem, neque integritatem adversarii, desiderarent. In quo, præsidium sibi positum sensit Ecclesia, quo res suas, ritusque tueretur, Clerus, quo dignitatem assereret suam, populus quod insimularet non invenit. Quem hisce virtutibus gestus Dioces. Oxon Cancellariatus reverend. apud London Curiæ de Arcubus Decanum fecit, et celeberrimi ibidem Juris consultorum Collegii Presidem. Cui hoc quod vides, lector, monumenti heic inter sacra familiaria condito, sicut ipse præceperat, Wickami olim è societate et sanguine, dolentibus bonis omnibus, Maria conjunx piissima mærens posuit, Anno Domini MDCXXXII.

[p] Wood's Hist et Antiq Univ. Oxon. lib ii Fast Oxon Coote's Catalogue of English Civilians, page 69. Epitaph Genealogy, Harl MSS. No 1193 page 34 b

[q] Walpole's Anecdotes of Painting in England, vol ii page 48 Ed 12mo.

The coat of arms on the monument is Barker, impaled with a lion passant on a fesse, and in chief three other charges.

In the same chapel is another inscription.

H. S. E.

Hugo Barker filius natu maximus Hugonis Barker de Horwood Magna in Com. Bucks Arm. natus 7° *die Jan.* 1684, *obiit* 22°. *die Dec* 1690. *Richardus Barker Armig. et nuper hujus Coll. superioris ordinis commensalis in fratris sui memoriam P.*[r]

Johanna, the sister of Richard Barker, married the Reverend *Thomas Wood, Doctor of Laws*, and Rector of Hardwick in Buckinghamshire, who wrote the two Institutes of the Civil, and the English, Law He was first a Barrister of Gray's Inn, and afterwards Commissary and Official of the Archdeaconry of Bucks He was a man of talents and industry, and had the merit of being the first person who reduced the immense chaos of the laws of his country into a clear and regular system, upon which succeeding times have not been able to improve. To him Blackstone is entirely indebted for his method, arrangement, and the principal substance of his Commentaries. He has only clothed Wood's solid materials in more extended and elegant language, and, by the addition of historical deductions, has formed a composition, if not more valuable to a lawyer, yet better calculated for general reading. In this work Doctor Wood derived great assistance from his knowledge of the civil law which is not only in itself extremely beautiful as a body of laws, founded in justice and good sense, well arranged, and couched in the most perspicuous and expressive language, but it had the good fortune to meet with commentators who were polite scholars, and elegant writers, whilst the English law, notwithstanding its superior excellence, as the code of a free nation, as yet continued to be a rude and undigested mass of legal learning. Doctor Wood died July the 12th, 1722, aged sixty-one[s]. He was related to Anthony à Wood, but I

[r] Wood's Hist Univ Oxon. by Gutch, page 223 I imagine this Richard Barker must have been the husband of Abigail Busby, who had a younger brother named Hugh, probably born after the death of the boy here buried, and of the same name

[s] See a letter from him to Dr Charlett, dated June 2, 1717, complaining of his corpulency, in Letters from the Bodleian Library, vol. ii p 32 There is an original portrait of him in the Warden of New College's Lodgings

Robert Barker, Esq. of Culworth, Northamptonshire, second son. = Mary Danvers, from whom the Barkers and Crokes are Founder's kin at Winchester. See Geneal. No. 42.

er of
New-
sister
ott.

Robert Barker, third son, died July 6, 1636, aged 70. = Marie, daughter of Wm. Smith, LL.D. of Brickhill, Bucks. died 1653, aged 75.

Thomas Barker, first son.

Maria Jones, first wife. = Hugh Barker, M.D. of Newbury, second son, died 1687. = Joanna, daughter of —— Goddard, of Woodhey, Hants, second wife, died 1667.

William Barker, D. Rector of Hardwic first son, born 16 died unmarried 16

er of
ood,
of
wood.

~~Martha~~ Margaret married
1. ~~[illegible]~~ Castillion, of [illegible] Berks. afterwards Vicar of Louth
2. Charles Craycraft. of Louth, co Lincoln

Martha m^d John Gerard of London

Martha Gerard only child m^d Thos. Marsh

Martha Marsh only child m^d P. Thos Adams Esqr of Bushey [illegible] Hants

Hester, daugh. of —— Heysham, married 1697, second wife, survived him. = Hugh Barker, Esq. of Great Horwood, died 1704. = Elizabeth, da Richard Whi of Tidderley, first wife, die

Jane Elizabeth.

Abigail Busby, first wife, See Genealogy, No. 43. = Richard Barker, Esq. of Great Horwood, Will dated 1718, and died 1719. = Anne Peak, Esq. of Bedford, survived hir died 1753.

Alexander Croke, Esquire, of Marsh Gibbon, married 1726, died 1757. See Genealogy, No. 44. = Elizabeth Barker.

Abigail, Esther, Richard, died young.

Hugh
left h
enseir

The coat of arms on the monument is Barker, impaled with a lion passant on a fesse, and in chief three other charges

In the same chapel is another inscription.

H. S. E.

Hugo Barker filius natu maximus Hugonis Barker de Horwood Magna in Com. Bucks. Arm. natus 7°. *die Jan.* 1684, *obiit* 22°. *die Dec.* 1690. *Richardus Barker Armig. et nuper hujus Coll. superioris ordinis commensalis in fratris sui memoriam P.*[r]

Johanna, the sister of Richard Barker, married the Reverend *Thomas Wood, Doctor of Laws*, and Rector of Hardwick in Buckinghamshire, who wrote the two Institutes of the Civil, and the English, Law He was first a Barrister of Gray's Inn, and afterwards Commissary and Official of the Archdeaconry of Bucks. He was a man of talents and industry, and had the merit of being the first person who reduced the immense chaos of the laws of his country into a clear and regular system, upon which succeeding times have not been able to improve. To him Blackstone is entirely indebted for his method, arrangement, and the principal substance of his Commentaries He has only clothed Wood's solid materials in more extended and elegant language, and, by the addition of historical deductions, has formed a composition, if not more valuable to a lawyer, yet better calculated for general reading In this work Doctor Wood derived great assistance from his knowledge of the civil law: which is not only in itself extremely beautiful as a body of laws, founded in justice and good sense, well arranged, and couched in the most perspicuous and expressive language, but it had the good fortune to meet with commentators who were polite scholars, and elegant writers; whilst the English law, notwithstanding its superior excellence, as the code of a free nation, as yet continued to be a rude and undigested mass of legal learning. Doctor Wood died July the 12th, 1722, aged sixty-one[s] He was related to Anthony à Wood, but I

[r] Wood's Hist Univ Oxon by Gutch, page 223 I imagine this Richard Barker must have been the husband of Abigail Busby, who had a younger brother named Hugh, probably born after the death of the boy here buried, and of the same name

[s] See a letter from him to Dr Charlett, dated June 2, 1717, complaining of his corpulency, in Letters from the Bodleian Library, vol. ii. p. 32. There is an original portrait of him in the Warden of New College's Lodgings.

No. 41.

THE GENEALOGY OF BARKER.

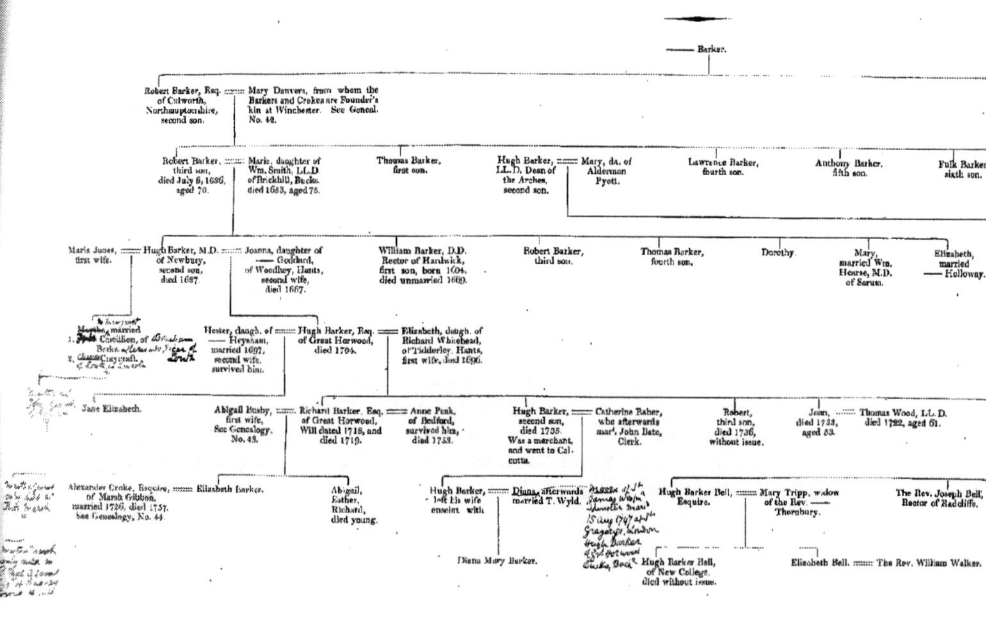

GENEALOGY FROM WILLIAM OF WICKHAM, TO THE BARKER AND CROKE FAMILIES.

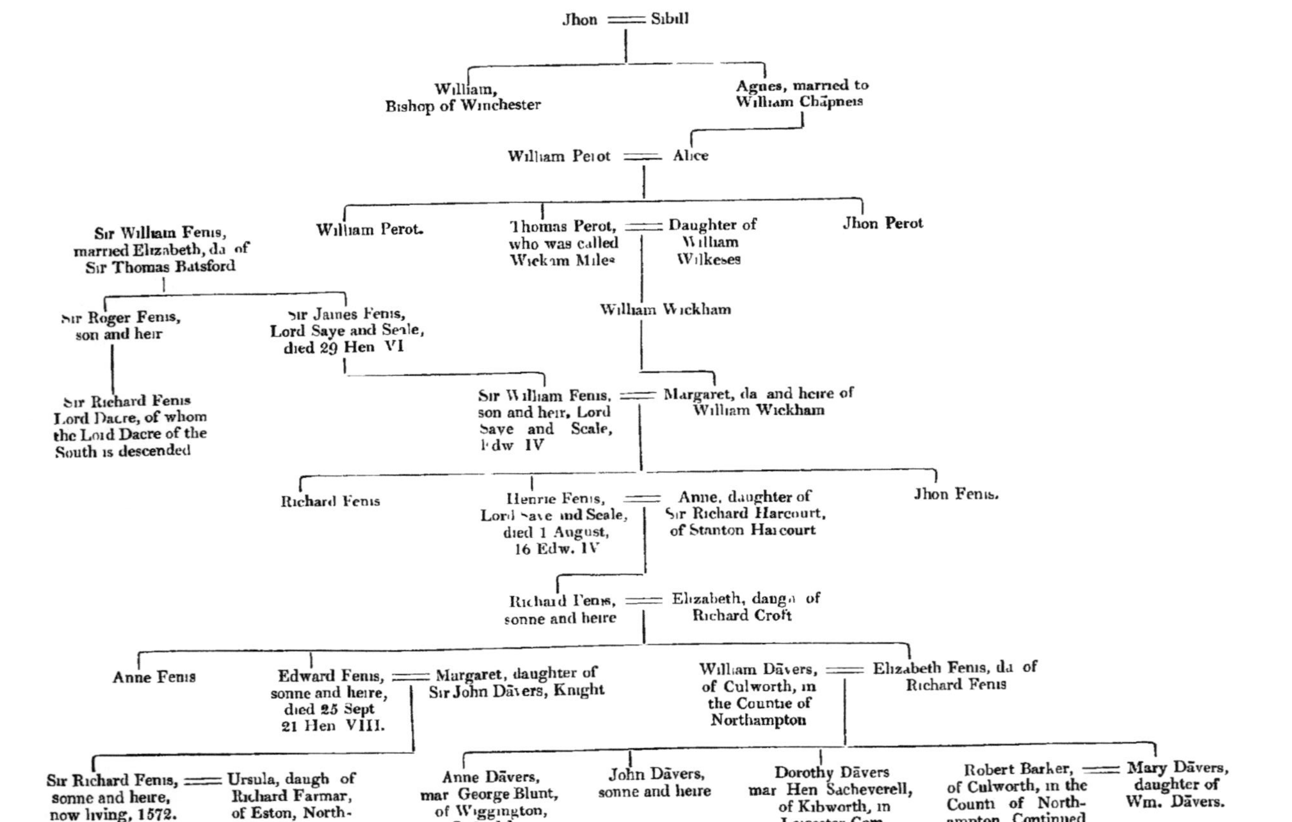

From a Vellum Pedigree, in the family, which agrees with a Pedigree in the Harleian MSS **No.** 1102, *which is a Visitation of Buckinghamshire, by Philpot and Ryley,* in 1634

have not been able to trace out the exact consanguinity. Johanna died in 1733, aged 53 years, Their son, William Wood, married Jane, the sister of Alexander Croke, of Marsh Gibbon. Besides the two Institutes, Dr. Wood wrote an anonymous pamphlet, intitled, "An Appendix to the "Life of Bishop Seth Ward." This was a severe censure upon the pleasantries of Dr. Walter Pope in his Life of Bp Ward, and for the liberties he had taken with his cousin Anthony à Wood[t] For any farther particulars of the Barker family, see the annexed genealogy[u].

The earliest account we have of the BUSBY family extends only to JOHN BUSBY of East Claydon in Buckinghamshire In deeds and old pedigrees he is styled Yeoman, and Goodman John Busby, and a rich shepherd[x]. How he acquired the very considerable property which he possessed is not known. He purchased the estate at Marsh Gibbon of Richard Abraham, Sir Edward and Sir Henry Cary, in 1610, and that at Addington, in 1625, of Sir John Curzon of Waterperry[y] He died the 11th of June, 1635, and was buried in the church at Addington.

These estates descended to his son, ROBERT BUSBY, ESQUIRE, who was a Barrister, and a Bencher of Gray's Inn; who had two wives, Elizabeth Kendricke, whom he married in 1629, and, secondly, Abigail, the daughter of Sir John Gore, of Gilston in Hertfordshire: and, dying on the 15th of September, 1652, in the fifty-second year of his age, was likewise there buried[z]. He left three sons by his second wife, John, Robert, and William, and as many daughters, Hester, Elizabeth, and Abigail.

SIR JOHN, the eldest son, who succeeded to the estate at Addington, was knighted June 25, 1661, by King Charles the Second, out of respect to the memory of his father-in-law, Sir William Mainwaring, who was slain in the King's service in the civil wars in defending Chester[a]. His *first wife*, Judith, was the daughter of Sir William Mainwaring by his

[t] Nichols's Literary Anecdotes, vol i. p. 50 n [u] I have a grant of arms from Sir Edward Bysse, Clarencieux king of arms, to Anthony à Wood, of Merton College, Oxford, son of Thomas à Wood, of the same University, his heirs and those of his father, or, a wolf passant, sable, armed and langued, gules, a chief of the second. A crest, on a helmet a wolf's head erased sable, collared and issuing out of a crown mural, or Dated the 1st of May, 1661 Doctor Wood bore the same arms Genealogy, No. 41. [x] Browne Willis's MSS vol. 21. folio 32. [y] Browne Willis's Collections for Bucks, p 113 [z] Monument at Addington [a] Kennet's Chronicle, p 482

wife Hester, who afterwards married Sir Henry Blount, Knight, of Tittenbanger in Hertfordshire, and by that her second husband she was mother to Sir Thomas Pope Blount, Baronet, Charles Blount, and four other sons, and a daughter, Frances, married to Sir Thomas Tyrrell, Baronet. Judith died the 28th of December, 1661, in the nineteenth year of her age, and is buried at Ridge in Hertfordshire[b]. She left two children, but the son died young, and the daughter, Hester, married the Honourable Thomas Egerton, of Tatton Park in Cheshire, and died in 1724[c].

Sir John Busby's second wife, to whom he was married the 3d of November, 1662, was Mary Dormer, daughter of John Dormer, Esquire, of Lee Grange in Buckinghamshire, who died in 1714, in the seventy-first year of her age. She had five daughters, and nine sons, and was buried at Addington. Most of his children died before him[d].

Sir John Busby himself died the 7th of January, 1700, aged sixty-five. On his monument he is styled, "learned, Deputy Lieutenant, and Colonel "of the Buckinghamshire Militia."

His son and heir was THOMAS BUSBY, Doctor of Laws, who was instituted to the living of Addington on his father's presentation, in 1693, and died in 1725, leaving two daughters, by his wife, Anne, daughter of John Limbry, of Hoddington, Esquire.

Abigail, daughter of Sir John Busby, by his second wife, married the Reverend Harrington Bagshaw, who was father to the Reverend Thomas Bagshaw, since Rector of Addington.

Of the two daughters of Doctor Busby, *Jane* died single in 1780, and *Anne*, the eldest, married Sir Charles Kemeys Tynte, Baronet, of Halsewell in Somersetshire. She died without issue, in 1798, and left the estate at Addington, away from her own relations, to a number of noble persons in succession.

The second son of Robert Busby, and Abigail Gore, was named after his father, was a woollen draper in Saint Andrew's, Holborn, and, in 1663, married Grace, the daughter of Sir Henry Cary of Devonshire, by whom he had one son, Robert, and six daughters. After his death she married —— Sydenham

[b] Chauncy's Hertfordshire, p 503 [c] Collins's Peerage, vol ii tit Bridgewater, and Sharpe's Registrum Roffense, under Penshurst Monument at Addington [d] Monument there

Of the daughters of Robert Busby and Abigail Gore, Hester married Thomas Saunders of Haddenham in Buckinghamshire, in 1655, by whom she had issue, Elizabeth, born in 1638, and died unmarried in 1661, and Abigail, who was born October 14, 1647, and married, first, Edward Shiers, Esquire, of the Inner Temple, and, secondly, Samuel Tryst, Esquire, whom she survived, and died in 1707, in the sixtieth year of her age.

The third son was WILLIAM BUSBY, ESQUIRE, who was also a Barrister of Gray's Inn, and resided at Marsh Gibbon. His wife was Elizabeth Metcalfe of London, a widow, whom he married in 1680. His will is dated in 1704, about which time he died, and his widow survived till 1733 They had three children, John, William, and Abigail. I have his portrait, and that of his wife.

JOHN BUSBY, born in 1681, was a man of philosophical pursuits, and a Fellow of the Royal Society. He obtained a patent from King Charles the Second for a new invented method of drying malt by hot air[e], as the Earl of Berkshire had a similar patent from Charles the First, for a new kiln for the same purpose[f] It appears that at last he studied physic, and perhaps took his degree in medicine, as I find him styled Doctor Croke, and he had many books in that science, and furnaces for chemical experiments. He died without issue about 1727. I have his portrait.

WILLIAM BUSBY, ESQUIRE, the second son, born in 1685, was a Barrister of Gray's Inn, and lived at Marsh Gibbon. He married, in 1725, his cousin, Mary Busby of Addington. He died the 4th of August, 1733, and his widow survived him. His picture is extant. Having no issue, his sister ABIGAIL inherited his property at Marsh Gibbon[g]. She was born in 1683, and in 1709 became the wife of RICHARD BARKER.

[e] See his printed proposals, Appendix, No XXXV [f] Whitelocke's Memorials, p. 24 a

[g] Wood, in his Diary, vol 142 p 26, 1734, says, Dr *Thomas* Busby, a civilian, formerly of University College, died lately at Marsh His books, which are valuable, are to be sold This must be William Busby There is a tradition that Doctor Richard Busby, the celebrated Head-Master of Westminster School, was of this family Gentleman s Magazine for January, 1795, page 15, where are many particulars relating to the Busby family Genealogy of Busby, Browne Willis's MSS vol 19, and his History of the Hundred of Buckingham See Genealogy of Busby, No. 43

ESQUIRE, of Great Horwood. Besides Abigail, Hester, and Richard, who died infants, they had an only daughter, ELIZABETH BARKER, married to Alexander Croke, Esquire Abigail died on the 18th of August, 1712, of the small pox, which succeeded a miscarriage, in the twenty-ninth year of her age, and was buried at Marsh Gibbon, where there is a neat monument to her memory Her husband afterwards married Anne Peck of Bedford, who survived him.

The inscription upon Abigail Barker's monument is as follows

M. S.

Abig Barker, Rich. Barker de Horwood Magna in com Bucks armig. conjugis dilectissimæ, necnon Gul Busby in eodem com. armig et Elizabethæ uxoris filiæ unicæ charissimæ Quæ puerperio (abortu scilicet et variolis simul infirmata) vita spoliata est, Aug. 18. Anno Domini 1712, ætatis suæ 29.

H. C. M. Posuit.

A coat of arms, Barker impaled with Busby.

Alexander Croke lived at Marsh Gibbon, kept a pack of hounds, and acted as a Justice of the Peace for Buckinghamshire. He died the 15th of June, 1757, and was buried at Chilton[h]

Elizabeth, his wife, survived him. She continued to live at Marsh Gibbon till after the marriage of her youngest daughter, Richarda, to Dr. Wetherell, when she removed to Oxford. She lived till the 17th of October, 1786, when she died of the small pox, and was buried in Saint Peter's church in that city, being in the seventy-eighth year of her age[i].

The arms of Busby are, or, three darts, reversed, in pale, sable. On a chief of the second, three mullets pierced of the first Crest on a wreath, a stag's head erased, transfixed with a dart

Of Barker, argent, three bears' heads, erased, gules, muzzled, or. In chief three ogresses.

Alexander Croke, of Marsh Gibbon, and Elizabeth Barker, had seven children: Richard, born the 20th of June, 1727, and died young, Alex-

[h] His Epitaph

[i] On her monument she is stated as having been aged eighty-five years, but this is a mistake, as she was born in 1708

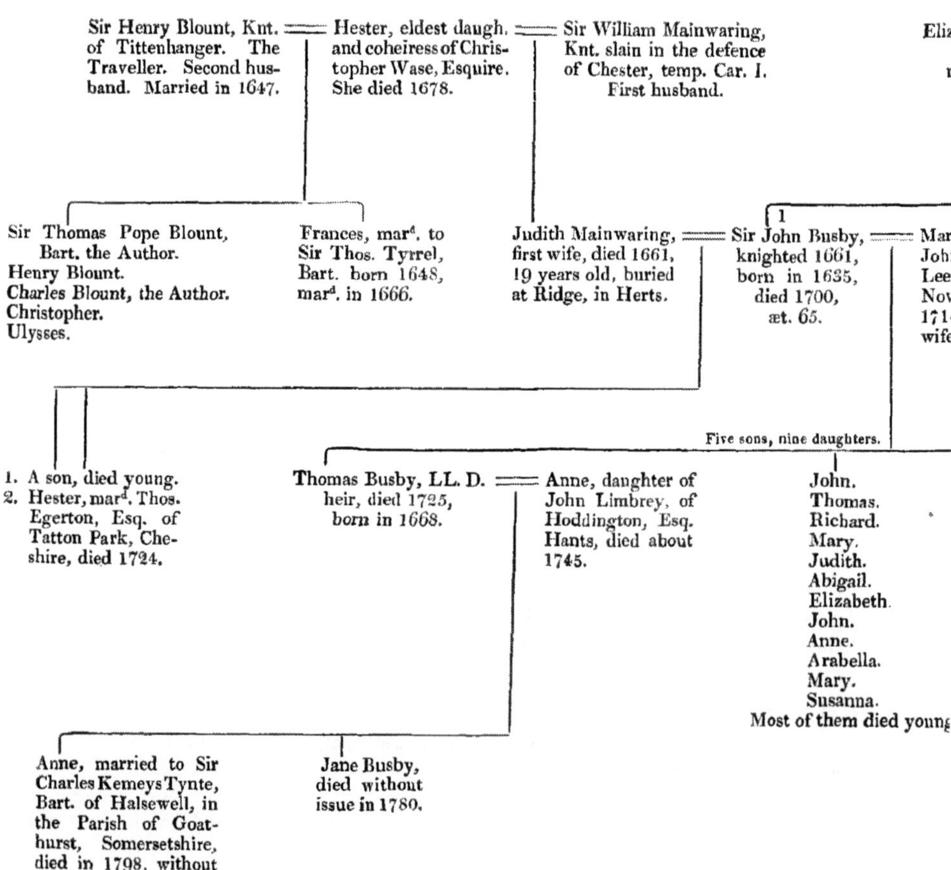

Sir Henry Blount, Knt. of Tittenhanger. The Traveller. Second husband. Married in 1647.
Hester, eldest daugh. and coheiress of Christopher Wase, Esquire. She died 1678.
Sir William Mainwaring, Knt. slain in the defence of Chester, temp. Car. I. First husband.
Eliz
Sir Thomas Pope Blount, Bart. the Author.
Henry Blount.
Charles Blount, the Author.
Christopher.
Ulysses.
Frances, mar^d. to Sir Thos. Tyrrel, Bart. born 1648, mar^d. in 1666.
Judith Mainwaring, first wife, died 1661, 19 years old, buried at Ridge, in Herts.
1
Sir John Busby, knighted 1661, born in 1635, died 1700, æt. 65.
Mar
Joh
Lee
Nov
171
wife
Five sons, nine daughters.
1. A son, died young.
2. Hester, mar^d. Thos. Egerton, Esq. of Tatton Park, Cheshire, died 1724.
Thomas Busby, LL. D. heir, died 1725, born in 1668.
Anne, daughter of John Limbrey, of Hoddington, Esq. Hants, died about 1745.
John.
Thomas.
Richard.
Mary.
Judith.
Abigail.
Elizabeth.
John.
Anne.
Arabella.
Mary.
Susanna.
Most of them died young
Anne, married to Sir Charles Kemeys Tynte, Bart. of Halsewell, in the Parish of Goathurst, Somersetshire, died in 1798, without issue.
Jane Busby, died without issue in 1780.

ESQUIRE, of Great Horwood. Besides Abigail, Hester, and Richard, who died infants, they had an only daughter, ELIZABETH BARKER, married to Alexander Croke, Esquire. Abigail died on the 18th of August, 1712, of the small pox, which succeeded a miscarriage, in the twenty-ninth year of her age, and was buried at Marsh Gibbon, where there is a neat monument to her memory. Her husband afterwards married Anne Peck of Bedford, who survived him.

The inscription upon Abigail Barker's monument is as follows

M. S

Abig. Barker, Rich. Barker de Horwood Magna in com. Bucks. armig. conjugis dilectissimæ, necnon Gul Busby in eodem com. armig et Elizabethæ uxoris filiæ unicæ charissimæ. Quæ puerperio (abortu scilicet et variolis simul infirmata) vita spoliata est, Aug. 18. Anno Domini 1712, ætatis suæ 29

H. C. M. Posuit.

A coat of arms, Barker impaled with Busby.

Alexander Croke lived at Marsh Gibbon, kept a pack of hounds, and acted as a Justice of the Peace for Buckinghamshire. He died the 15th of June, 1757, and was buried at Chilton[h].

Elizabeth, his wife, survived him. She continued to live at Marsh Gibbon till after the marriage of her youngest daughter, Richarda, to Dr. Wetherell, when she removed to Oxford. She lived till the 17th of October, 1786, when she died of the small pox, and was buried in Saint Peter's church in that city, being in the seventy-eighth year of her age[i]

The arms of Busby are, or, three darts, reversed, in pale, sable. On a chief of the second, three mullets pierced of the first. Crest on a wreath, a stag's head erased, transfixed with a dart.

Of Barker, argent, three bears' heads, erased, gules, muzzled, or. In chief three ogresses.

Alexander Croke, of Marsh Gibbon, and Elizabeth Barker, had seven children: Richard, born the 20th of June, 1727, and died young, Alex-

[h] His Epitaph

[i] On her monument she is stated as having been aged eighty-five years, but this is a mistake, as she was born in 1708

No 43

THE GENEALOGY OF BUSBY

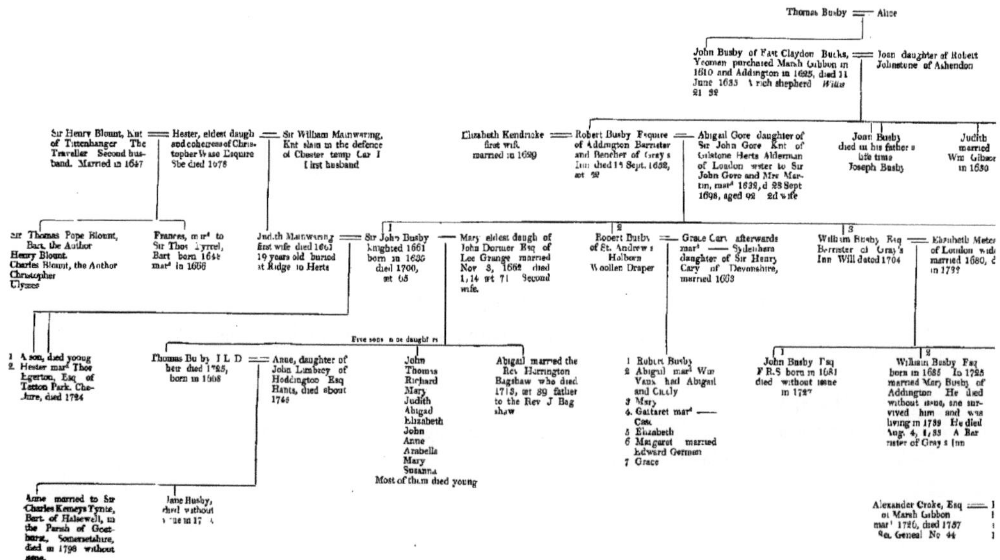

ander, born at Dinton, the 27th of November, 1728: Elizabeth, born at Dinton, the 27th of January, 1730, and died unmarried the 20th of February, 1799, aged seventy years, and was buried at Saint Peter's church in Oxford. Anne, born at Dinton the 29th of March, 1731, and died the 10th of February, 1759 Abigail, born at Marsh Gibbon the 13th of July, 1735, and died the 27th of December, 1821, Jane, born the 7th of June, 1738, and died young; Richarda, born the 28th of October, 1745, married the Reverend Nathan Wetherell, and died the 13th of November, 1812[k].

[k] From the entries in their mother's prayer book Richarda was probably so christened in memory of her grand-father, Richard Barker, but the name occurs elsewhere, there was a Richarda, Marchioness of Saluzzo, who married Nicholas the Third, Marquis of Ferrara

DIGRESSION THE SECOND.

The History of Marsh-Gibbon, from Brown Willis[a]

MERSHE or Marsh Gibwen, derives its name from its situation in a marshy place The adjunct name of Gibwen being from an owner or proprietor of lands here, or the principal lessee tenant under the capital lords.

In the time of the Norman invasion it was surveyed in Domesday Book, thus

Terra comitis Moritonensis, in Lamua Hundred.

In Mersa tenent Monachi de Grestein xi hidas de comite Terra est xiii carucatarum In Dominio iv hidæ. Et ibi sunt iii carucatæ Ibi xvii villani, cum iii Bordariis, habentibus x carucatas Ibi viii Servi. In totis valenciis valet et valuit semper viii libras.

Hoc Manerium tenuit Ulfus filius Bergerete, et vendere potuit.

Et unus homo Bondi stalre habuit ibi dimidium hidæ, et vendere potuit

The monks of Grestein hold eleven hides in Merse of the Earl of Moreton. The arable is thirteen carucates There are in Demesne four hides, and there are three carucates. There are seventeen villains, and three cottagers holding ten carucates. There are seven servants. In the whole it is worth and was always valued at 8l.

Ulf, son of Bergerete, held this manor, and could sell it.

And a certain man, a groom of Bondi, held here half a hide, and could sell it

Terra Will Filii Ansculfi

In Merse tenet Ailric de Wilhelmo iv hidas pro i Manerio Terra est v carucatarum. In Dominio ii et quinque villani, cum iii bordariis habentibus iii carucatas. Ibi iii servi. Pratum v caru-

Ailric holds of William Fitz-Ausoult four hides in Merse for one manor The arable is five carucates, two are in Demesne, and there are five villains, with three cottagers, having three caru-

[a] In his History of the Hundred of Buckingham 4to

catarum, silva xxx porcorum. Valet et valuit semper lxx solidos; istemet tenuit tempore Regis Edwardi, sed modo tenet ad Firmam de Wilhelmo, graviter et miserabiliter.

cates There are three servants; meadow for five carucates; and mast for thirty hogs. It is and was always worth seventy shillings He himself held it, (viz. Ailric) in King Edward's time, but now holds it in farm of William heavily and miserably loaded

This Earl of Moreton, whose name was Robert, being brother by the mother's side to William the Conqueror, he made him Earl of Cornwall, anno 1068, in the second year of his reign, and gave him no less than 29 manors in this county of Buckingham, as we are told in Dugdale's Baronage, vol. i. whereof this of Mersh being one, he bestowed it on the Abbey of Grestein, in Normandy, of his father's foundation, and so it continued part of the Demesnes of that monastery, together with the advowson of the church, till both were procured, about the year 1365, by the De la Pole's, in which family they continued till the year 1441[b], when the manor being separated from the advowson, was by Will. de La Pole, Earl of Suffolk, and Alice his wife, given to Ewelme Hospital Co Oxon. (of their foundation,) by letters patent of King Hen. VI. In which hospital it remained under certain demises till 1605, 3 Jac. I. when that King endowing the Professor of Physick in the University of Oxford, with the Mastership of Ewelme Hospital, and annexing it thereto, this manor thereby became vested in the possession of that Professor: and he is, by virtue of the tenure of that office, Lord of the principal manor of this place, and so remains, anno 1735, in conjunction with the rest of the members of this Hospital, viz. the Reader, and thirteen poor men, who are all united in a corporate body. and act accordingly in that capacity, by granting leases, &c as other possessors of manors do.

As to the other manor of Fitz-Ausculfs (described also in Domesday Book) it seems very soon to have come to Walter Giffard, Earl of Buckingham, for he held it about anno 1112, 12 Hen I. who, having in the year 1162, 8 Hen. II[c]. founded an Abbey, called Nutley, or Notley, within his park of Crendon, he gave thereto the tythes of Mershe; but he

[b] Pat 20 Hen VI. p 2 m 19. [c] See Parochial Antiq. p 118, 147, 211

dying, anno 1164, 10 Hen II without issue, his lands were divided among his heirs; and this his manor of Mershe came to his next kinsman, Richard Strongbow, Earl of Strigoul, whose daughter and heir Isabel, marrying William Marshall, Earl of Pembroke, he in her right became possessed thereof, and gave, anno 1190, 1 Ric. I a very great fine to the King, for livery of Earl of Giffard's lands, among which is recounted this manor; which on the death of his successor, William Marshall, came to his brother Richard Marshall, but he seems to have made little account thereof, for Warin Basset[d], a younger son of Alan Basset, Baron of Wycombe, as a relation and heir of the Marshall's, laid claim to it, and disputed the right of patronage with the Monks of Grestein: but they making it appear to the Bishop of Lincoln, that they stood seized of this advowson by the gift of the Marshall's, his plea was set aside but the issue male of Marshall failing in this reign, their lands became divided among several proprietors, among whom were the Damory's, who claimed Demesnes here temp. Edw. I. And anno 1317, 11 Edw. II. Richard Damory, Knight[e], obtained a grant of free warren at Mershe, and also at Bix Gibwen, which last manor descended to him from the heiress of Gibwen, from whom, as I presume, he inherited lands here; for the Gibwens were possessors of considerable estates in this county, Geffry de Gibwen being as it seems in King John's time, about 1210, Lord of Great Linford in which year he gave lands at Willen to Snelshall[f] Priory, and in King John's and the beginning of Hen the Third's time, he, the said Jeffry Gibbewin occurs one of the King's Justices[g] I also find that Roger de Somery, anno 1291 19 Ed I. descended from the heirs of Fitz-Ausculf, held lands here at Mershe. But the chief and principal heir of the Fitz-Ausculfs seems to have been the Beauchamps, for anno 1260, 44 Hen III there was a tryal at the assizes, held in the ancient county town of Buckingham, for lands at Mershe[h], which were held by William Beauchamp, senior, by knights' service And his heir, Guy Beauchamp, Earl of Warwick, anno 1312, 6 Edw II. is returned to be seized of the manor of Mershe; which the Montacutes had also a title to. For, anno 1315, 8 and 9 Edw. II. the King confirmed to the Abbey of Grestein, the do-

[d] Parochial Antiq p 207. [e] Ibid p 375 [f] Ex Registro Snelshall [g] Madox's Excheq [h] Parochial Antiq p 255

nation and concession which John de Montacute (of the family of Montacute, who were afterwards Earls of Salisbury) made of the manor of Mershe, with its appurtenances, and of the advowson of the church of the said manor, and also the grant of one hide[i] of land in the said village, given to that convent, by Baldwin, son to Thomas de Haldeham, and Isabell Montacute· after which I find no other claimants to this manor.

However, after the dissolution of foreign monasteries, their lands coming to the crown, I presume their possessions in this parish, as well as what belonged here to the Montacutes, being likewise so escheated, remained parcel of the royal property, till the reign of Edw. IV when that King, by letters patent, anno Reg. 22, 1482, gave this second manor, then known by the name of Westbury, or the Bury Manor, to the Company of the Cooks, in London, which he had, anno Regni 12, 1472, incorporated For so it appeared at a tryal at law, anno 1578, 20 of Elizabeth, at the assizes holden for this County of Buckingham, at Aylesbury[k], wherein the aforesaid grant is set forth, and the title of the conveyance of this manor, by the Master and Warden of the said Company of Cooks which Company, by deeds, dated Nov. 30, 1530, anno 31 Hen. VIII. sold their right and interest therein to Robert Dormer, Esq. who, next year, 1531. suffered a fine and recovery thereof, and after five years possession, anno 1536, reconveyed all his title and interest therein to William Howell, who, dying seized thereof, Nov. 30th, 1557, was succeeded therein by John Howell, his eldest son and heir, on whose death without issue, anno 18 Eliz. 1576[l], the Cooks' Company laying claim to the premises, were at the aforesaid tryal at law, anno 1578, cast, and a verdict obtained against them, and the premises adjudged to the purchaser, William Howell's heir, who was one Henry Howell, as may be seen in Plowden's Commentary, wherein the case is set forth at length. And in this family of the Howells this manor[m] continued for upwards of an hundred years; and they held courts for the same; till Edward Howell, by lease and release, dated June the 14th and 15th, anno 1639, 15 Char. I conveyed his property herein to Richard Francis[n], whose descendant, Thomas Francis, dying 1698, his widow, Anna Maria Francis, by deed of lease and release, dated April

[i] Parochial Antiq p. 370 [k] Vide Plowden's Commentary, fol 551. [l] Ibid viz. Plowden [m] Ex evidentiis hujus Manerii. [n] Ex evidentiis hujus Manerii

9th and 10th, 1701, conveyed it in fee to John Townsend and his heirs, and in this family it still remains, anno 1735 And as lord of the manor of Westbury, or the Bury Manor, they claim suit and service over nine yard and three quarters of land in this parish, as does Ewelme Hospital over forty-nine yard land and three quarters The whole extent of the parish being computed to contain fifty-eight yard land and a half, or about two thousand eight hundred acres.

The advowson of this church, after having passed from the convent of Giestein to the De la Poles, escheating to the Crown, anno 1475, after the death of Alice De la Pole, Duchess of Suffolk, has belonged to the royal patronage ever since, except temp. Hen. VIII. when Charles Brandon, Duke of Suffolk, held it, as may be seen in the Account of the Institution to the Rectory.

TO proceed with the children of Alexander Croke and Elizabeth Barker. Their youngest daughter, Richarda, married the REVEREND NATHAN WETHERELL, who was born on the 14th of June, 1726, the son of Cornelius Wetherell, of the city of Durham styled in the Oxford Matricula, Gentleman In his native city he probably received his school education, and he was entered a Commoner of Lincoln College, on the 20th of April, 1744[a]. He was elected a Fellow of University College, on the foundation of William, Bishop of Durham, upon the 24th of January, 1750; and was admitted to his degree of Master of Arts on the same day[b].

During the time that he continued Fellow, it does not appear that he was one of the College Tutors with Best and Coulson: in the register only one person is entered, as being under his tuition. After he was in Orders, he served the church of Marsh-Gibbon in Buckinghamshire, about fourteen miles from Oxford, as Curate to Doctor Schutz Having been early impressed with proper notions of religion, he performed the important duties of a parish Minister with exemplary zeal and piety Here he formed an acquaintance with Miss Richarda Croke, the youngest daughter of Alexander Croke, Esquire, whom he afterwards married.

At University College, several men, who became eminent in different pursuits, were his contemporaries and intimate friends. Of these the principal were, Charles Jenkinson, afterwards Lord Hawkesbury, and Earl of Liverpool[c]: George Horne, President of Magdalene College, Dean of Canterbury, and finally Bishop of Norwich[d]. William Jones of Nayland[e]: Peter Waldo, a man of fortune, who, like Nelson, was a sincere Christian, and bore testimony to the truth of the doctrines which he professed by some excellent and pious writings[f]. Sir Robert Chambers, elected Fellow of University from Lincoln College in 1762,

[a] His subscription in the University Register is, Termino Paschatis, Ap. 20, 1744 Nathan Wetherell è Coll Linc Generosi filius.

[b] From the Registers of the University, and of University College [c] Entered a Commoner of University College, March 13, 1745 [d] Elected Scholar, March 15, 1745. [e] Entered July 9, 1745. [f] Entered April 2, 1748.

afterwards successor to Sir William Blackstone as Vinerian Professor, and a Judge of the Supreme Court at Calcutta George Croft, a man of talents and learning, who filled an useful situation in the north of England for the education of youth[g] Sir William Jones, the celebrated orientalist, elected Fellow in 1764· Doctor John Shaw[h]: and finally, the two illustrious brothers, Sir William Scot, now Lord Stowell, who was elected Fellow the 14th of December, 1764, and John, Lord Eldon, the Lord Chancellor of England[i]. Such a cluster of brilliant talents it would be difficult to find in one society, and within so short a period. To these may be added, of other Colleges, Doctor Hodges, who became Provost of Oriel; Doctor Patten, of Corpus Christi; George Berkeley; Samuel Glasse; and Doctor Nowell, Principal of Saint Mary Hall, who preached a sermon before the House of Commons on the 30th of January, 1772, for which he received the thanks of the House, which were ordered afterwards to be expunged, on account of its high tory principles.

In union with some of these excellent divines, it is no reflection upon the memory of Doctor Wetherell, that he warmly espoused the opinions of John Hutchinson. The doctrines of the Hutchinsonians were strictly conformable to those of the Church of England, and were liable rather to the imputation of an excess of orthodoxy, than of any tincture of methodism, or any other species of Sectarian error. No great prejudice can well be entertained against principles which could produce the elegant and pious Commentary upon the Psalms, and the masterly treatises of Jones, yet it must be admitted, that their interpretations of Scripture were sometimes fanciful, and that many of their tenets, though founded in truth, were carried too far. These doctrines occasioned much controversy at that time, but as they are now almost forgotten, it may not be improper to state them shortly; as they are displayed by the learned Rector of Nayland, one of their ablest advocates[k]

[g] Entered as a Servitor, Oct 23, 1762 [h] Entered May 14, 1764, at fourteen years of age [i] He entered May 15, 1766 All from the College Register

[k] John Hutchinson was born in Yorkshire in 1674, and died in 1737 He was Steward to the Duke of Somerset, and derived most of his peculiar doctrines from the study of Hebrew. See Floyd's Biography, vol iii the Lives of Bishop Horne, and Jones of Nayland, and their works. Duncan Forbes on Hutchinsonianism, and the several pamphlets which appeared in the controversy.

1. The followers of Mr. Hutchinson give to God the pre-eminence in every thing.

2. They hold that only one way of salvation has been revealed to man from the beginning of the world: videlicet, the way of faith in God, redemption by Jesus Christ, and a detachment from the world: and that this way is revealed in *both Testaments*

3. That in both Testaments, divine things are explained and confirmed to the understandings of men, by allusions to the natural creation.

4. They are confirmed Trinitarians, and are kept such by the Hutchinsonian philosophy, of *fire*, *light*, and *air*, the three agents of nature, on which all natural life and motion depend, and in Scripture signify the three supreme powers of the Godhead, in the administration of the spiritual world.

5. On the authority of the Scriptures, they entertain so low an opinion of human nature, under the consequences of the fall, that they derive every thing in religion from revelation or tradition; and that natural religion is deism in disguise, the religion of Satan.

6 The Hutchinsonians are attentive to the types and figures of the Scriptures.

7. In natural philosophy, they are *sure* Sir Isaac Newton's method of proving a vacuum is not agreeable to nature. They hold it more agreeable to nature to suppose a circulating fluid, and that attraction is no physical principle.

8. In natural history, they maintain, that the present condition of the earth bears evident marks of an universal flood.

9. That what commonly passes under the name of *learning*, is a knowledge of heathen books, and should be admitted with great precaution.

10. Of the Jews, they think that they are the inveterate enemies of Christianity: never to be trusted as our associates in Hebrew or divinity; and as dangerous apostates from *true Judaism.*

11. They are of opinion that the *Hebrew* is the primæval, and original language; that its structure shews it to be divine, and that a comparison with other languages shews it priority.

12 That the *Cherubim* were mystical figures of great antiquity, and great signification symbolical of the Divine Presence: and that all *animal-worship* amongst the heathens was derived from them.

Such were the doctrines of these learned men, and, since many of them rested upon the etymologies and grounds of the Hebrew language, it formed a considerable feature in their studies. For a whole winter, Wetherell, Horne, Jones, and Martin, employed themselves in examining and settling all the roots of that language, and in collecting materials for a new Lexicon The fruits of a faithful and laborious scrutiny were communicated to Mr. Parkhurst, who used them in his Lexicon[l].

Although a truly humble and devout spirit pervades all the works of Sir Isaac Newton, they conceived a strong prejudice against his philosophy, which they thought was not altogether consistent with the Scriptures, and the account of the creation given by Moses; and that it might be employed as an engine against Christianity A subscription of three hundred pounds a year for three years was entered into by the friends of Jones, to supply him with an apparatus for trying experiments, to confute the false, and to establish the true, philosophy, of which, fifty pounds were supplied by Wetherell. The result of these experiments was several treatises, written by Jones; but how far he succeeded in his ultimate object, I am not enough acquainted with the subject to decide[m].

Three sermons, preached at Saint Mary's in 1756, by Patten, Wetherell, and Horne, replete with the Hutchinsonian doctrines, gave occasion to some replies, and were followed by an angry controversy, now deservedly gone into oblivion[n].

On the 28th of August, 1764, he was elected Master of University College, upon which occasion he took his degree of Bachelor in Divinity on the 22d, and that of Doctor on the 27th of the November following. Soon after his appointment he married Miss Richarda Croke, on the 22d of April, 1765[o].

In the years 1768, 1769, 1770, 1771, he filled the office of Vice-Chancellor: during all which time the Earl of Litchfield was Chancellor, and so continued till the 17th of September, 1772. Frederic Lord North was elected to succeed him on the 3d of October, 1772: Doctor Fothergill, Provost of Queen's College, being then Vice-Chancellor[p].

During his Vice-Chancellorship, a proposal was brought forward to

[l] Life of Jones, page 42. [m] Lives of Jones and Horne. [n] Ibid [o] Registers of the College, and of Marsh Gibbon [p] University Register

make some changes in the academical habits. It can scarcely be conceived how much the University was agitated, and divided into parties, by this apparently uninteresting question. The Convocation House was frequently a scene of violence and confusion. The clamours after some time subsided; the alterations, which were reasonable and proper, were at length adopted; and Doctor Wetherell gained great credit from all sides for his prudent conduct during this storm, for impartiality and good temper, and his exertions to promote reconciliation and tranquillity.

Principally through the interest of his friend Charles Jenkinson, Doctor Wetherell received the appointment of Dean of the Cathedral of Hereford, in the room of Doctor Francis Webber, Rector of Exeter; in which he was installed the 9th of November, 1771; as he was in the Prebend of Norton Canons, on the 22d of September, 1775, and in the Prebend of Cublington, the 4th of September, 1777, both in that Cathedral He was likewise installed Prebendary of Westminster on the 5th of May, 1775, in the place of Doctor James Cornwallis, made Dean of Canterbury[q]. It has been said that he twice refused the Deanery of Canterbury, and once an Irish Bishopric The latter may be easily accounted for, but there seems no reason for his refusal of the other preferment.

Amongst the friends of the Dean may be enumerated Doctor Johnson, whom he usually visited in London, and who often dined with him when at Oxford. His name appears occasionally in the various memoirs of the celebrated moralist. There is a letter from Johnson addressed to him on the 12th of March, 1776, respecting the books printed at the Oxford press, recommending a larger profit to be allowed to the booksellers, and giving a detail of the progress of a book from the printer to the reader[r]. In the same year, Johnson went to Oxford with Boswell, and called upon the Dean In the course of their conversation, Wetherell said, "I would "have given an hundred guineas if he would have written a preface to his "Political Tracts, by way of a discourse on the British Constitution." Boswell seconded him, and "thought there was a claim upon him for it." Johnson was displeased with the dialogue, and burst out, "Why should "I be always writing[s]?" Doctor Johnson presented him with a copy of those Tracts.

[q] The Registers at Hereford and Westminster [r] Boswell's Life of Johnson, vol ii p 443 [s] Ibid p 461

Once when he was dining at University College, Johnson was rather out of spirits. At dinner, to shew his attention to the lady of the house, he asked her "how many children she had?" Mrs Wetherell told him the number, and added, "that if all the Doctor's learning was divided "amongst them, she should desire no better provision for them" Johnson was highly pleased with this flattery, and was in high good humour the rest of the evening.

When Charles Jenkinson offered himself to represent the University in Parliament, Wetherell and Horne supported him, but he was not elected, and his friends incurred great abuse for what was called departing from the old interest[t]. In 1780, Mr., afterwards Sir William, Jones, upon the resignation of Sir Roger Newdigate, was proposed as a candidate to succeed him in the representation. Finding no probability of success, he signified his intention of declining to give his friends any farther trouble; and, amongst others, by a letter addressed to Doctor Wetherell, on the 2d of September, 1780, in which he complains of uncandid usage even from his own college. In fact Jones had discovered principles of a republican tendency, which were not in harmony with those of the University, and his Ode to Liberty had given considerable offence[u].

However studious in his youth, as he advanced in life, Doctor Wetherell seems to have relaxed from his literary pursuits. None of his writings were ever published, not even a sermon: nor was he considered as a profound scholar, or an eloquent preacher, but he possessed a talent, which, "though no science, is fairly worth the seven"—the knowledge of mankind: and he obtained preferment, and riches, beyond what his original views in life seemed to promise. Besides his wife's fortune, and his regular income, which was now considerable, some large fines occasionally fell to him in his ecclesiastical benefices: and he was appointed residuary legatee by Mrs. Croke, his wife's mother, by her sister, Miss Elizabeth Croke, who died unmarried at an advanced age; and by an old gentleman of the name of Wood, a relation to his wife, who was the son of Doctor Wood, the Rector of Hardwick, in Buckinghamshire, and had acquired a moderate fortune in trade.

The property thus industriously acquired was not suffered to remain

[t] Life of Horne [u] Lord Teignmouth's Life of Sir William Jones, p 228 Ed 1807

idle; it was employed in a profitable speculation. A canal was projected by his friend Sir Roger Newdigate, formerly of University College, to convey the coals from his pits near Coventry, to Oxford. It was, I believe, the first which was made in England, except the Manchester canal; and was considered as a bold undertaking. Doctor Wetherell was a principal promoter of it, and adventured deeply The American war intervened, and the times became bad, the affairs of the canal were in a ruinous state, neither principal or interest were forthcoming, and the original shares of a hundred pounds sank to fifty. Doctor Wetherell, being so materially involved in the concern, had no chance of safety but by supporting its credit, and he purchased many shares at that depreciated value. At the peace, things took a new turn, the profits increased, and an unlooked for event happened, which raised them beyond the most ardent expectations of the proprietors. By an union with the Grand Junction Canal, the Coventry Canal became part of the great line of communication between an extensive manufacturing district, and the metropolis. The dividends were raised to thirty-three pounds upon every hundred pounds share, and each share now sells for seven hundred pounds. By this fortunate occurrence, the Dean's property was multiplied in a prodigious degree, and may fairly be estimated at near one hundred and seventy thousand pounds.

The Dean, though short in stature, was of a strong, sanguine constitution; and, except occasional head-aches, to which he was much subject, enjoyed uninterrupted good health: which was preserved by his habits of temperance, and daily exercise; and he retained all his faculties in a good old age. Something of a paralysis, but of which the effects were not very visible, seems to have constituted his last illness, he laid down as to sleep, and, without any emotion, breathed his last, in his eighty-second year, on the 29th of December, 1807. He was a man of a good understanding. and of a sincere piety strict and conscientious in the performance of the duties of his station, as a clergyman, and as Master of the college, over which he presided for forty-three years. never neglecting to attend the public service of the church, or omitting domestic prayers in his own family. He constantly retained the primitive practice of fasting on Fridays, and during Lent; and was an exact observer of the sabbath. In the intercourse of life, he was an affectionate husband, an indulgent parent, and a considerate master; charitable to the poor, and kind and friendly to all. Possessed of these amiable qualities, with good temper and cheerfulness, his society was always pleasant and agreeable.

He was buried under a neat monument in the chapel of University College, with the following inscription.

H. S. E.
Nathan Wetherell, S. T P.
Herefordiæ Decanus,
Ecclesiæ Westmonast. Præbendarius,
Necnon hujusce Collegii
Per annos plus quam XLIII.
Magister vigilantissimus.
Vir quidem vere venerabilis,
Benevolentia æque ac pietate
Si quis alius
insignis.
Idemque
ob ingenii lenitatem,
et morum suavitatem
nemini non charus.
Natus XIV. Jun. 1726, obiit 29 Dec. 1807.
Anno ætatis suæ LXXXII.
Marito
Tam de se
Quam de XII liberis superstitibus
Optime merito
Ricarda Alex. Croke Arm. filia
Monumentum hoc
P C.

The coat of arms of Wetherell is, argent, two lions, passant, guardant sable. On a chief indented, of the second, three cups with covers, or Crest, a demy lion rampant, sable, bearing in his paws a covered cup or

Mrs Wetherell survived him near five years, and dying on the 13th of November, 1812, aged sixty-nine years, was buried at Cowley They left twelve children. 1 Nathan Croke Wetherell, who was a Barrister. 2. Robert, first, Fellow of New College, and afterwards Prebendary of Hereford, Rector of Newnton Longville in Buckinghamshire, and Vicar of Stanford in Berkshire. He married Anne Meriwether. 3. Charles, a Barrister, King's Counsel, and Member of Parliament, first for Shaftesbury, and now for the city of Oxford. 4. Margaret, married to the Reverend George Shepherd, Doctor in Divinity, Rector of Saint Bartholomew's near the Bank, in London, and Preacher at Gray's Inn. 5. Richarda, married to Colonel Love Parry Jones, and has one daughter. 6. Richard, Rector of Nutgrove, and Vicar of Westbury, both in Gloucestershire. In 1796, he married Caroline, only daughter of Thomas May, Esquire, of Pashley in the parish of Tisehurst in Sussex, upon whose death he succeeded to the estate there. He has a large family 7. Henry, Rector of Thruxton, and Kingston, and Vicar of Kentchurch, all in Herefordshire. 8. Sarah, married in 1800 to the Reverend Thomas Lane Freer, Rector of Handsworth, in Staffordshire, and Vicar of Wasperton, in Warwickshire. The Freers are an old family, of which was the Mrs Lane, who rode before King Charles the Second, in aiding his escape. They have three children, John Lane Freer, Richard Lane Freer, and Mary Lane Freer. 9. Charlotte, married, in 1804, to Richard Spooner, Esquire, son of Isaac Spooner, Esquire, of Elmdon in Warwickshire. They have several children. 10. Mary, married, in 1801, to the Reverend John Clutton, Doctor in Divinity, Canon of Hereford, Rector of Kinnersley, in Herefordshire, and Vicar of Lidney, in Gloucestershire. 11. Elizabeth, married, in 1811, to the Reverend Edward Rowden, Master of Arts, formerly Fellow of New College, and now Vicar of Highworth in Wiltshire. They have several children. 12. James, Fellow of New College, now Prebendary of Hereford, Vicar of Lyonshall in Herefordshire, and perpetual Curate of Upton Saint Leonard's, near Gloucester. His lady was Lucy Huntingford, niece to Doctor Huntingford, the Bishop of Hereford.

My father, ALEXANDER CROKE, the eldest surviving son of Alexander Croke, of Marsh Gibbon, and Elizabeth Barker, was born at Dinton, on the 27th of November, 1728. He was educated, first, at New College School, at Oxford, and afterwards at Thame School, which was then a public seminary of some celebrity: and where he had for his contemporaries, the Lord Cobham, afterwards Earl Temple, and the sons of many other persons of consequence in the neighbouring counties. As his father, by his hounds and other gaieties, had at least not increased his property, he prudently determined to bring up his son to a lucrative profession. He was accordingly bred to the law, and commenced the practice of it at Aylesbury, in Buckinghamshire, where he resided many years.

On the 23d of March, 1754, he married Anne, the daughter of the Reverend Robert Armistead, Master of Arts, Rector of Ellesborough, in Buckinghamshire. The ceremony was performed at St. Gregory's church, in London, by the Reverend Mr. Reyner, and James Revett, Esquire, of Chequers, which is in the parish of Ellesborough, gave her away. Her mother's maiden name was Mary Dobson, and she was related to the families of Citizen, Tourle, and Clutton, in Sussex. Mr. Armistead died in 1745. A memorandum which is in Hammond's Paraphrase on the New Testament, is a proof of the care which he took of his daughter's religious welfare. "April 19th, 1741, I give this book to my daughter, Ann Armi-"stead, and desire her never to part with it. Robert Armistead." He gave her likewise Barrow's Sermons, which I have, in which is written, "Given "to my daughter, June, 1742." Upon the second of October, after the marriage, she came to live at Aylesbury.

We have before seen in what manner the first Alexander Croke divided the Studley estate between his two sons; and that Charlotte Croke, the last surviving heir of the eldest son, married William Ledwell, Esquire. Under the power which she had reserved to herself upon her marriage, having no child living, she settled that part of the estate upon her husband for his life, with remainder to my father. Mrs. Ledwell died on the 5th of May, 1763, and Mr. Ledwell on the 28th of May, 1766, when my father came into the possession of the mansion, and the Oxfordshire part; and thus the whole of the Studley estate became again united.

My mother died on the 8th of March, 1768, of a long and painful disorder, and was buried at Ellesborough on the 14th. She was a religious, amiable, active, and sensible woman. I was too young to be able to form a correct opinion of her merits; but I recollect a conversation between her and the apothecary, who was a Presbyterian, about predestination, in which she asserted, what probably she felt, the freedom of her own will. A child of ten years of age could not be supposed to comprehend much of arguments upon a subject, which has puzzled men of higher intellects, but it made an impression upon me, which may have inclined me, during the rest of my life, to a stronger tendency towards the Arminian, than the Calvinistic, side of that abstruse question.

We left Aylesbury on the 18th of May, 1771, and came to reside entirely at Studley. The next year, on the 11th of February, 1772, my father married a second lady, Sarah, the daughter of the Reverend Thomas Evans, Master of Arts, and Vicar of Sandridge, near St Alban's, to which he was presented by Sarah, Duchess Dowager of Marlborough, the 24th of April, 1744, and he died in 1774. She was a most excellent woman, and proved perfectly a second mother to me and my sister; and we lived in the most intimate friendship with her till her death, many years after Her niece married Colonel Harness, who died, as well as his eldest son, in the East Indies, and left a widow, and two amiable daughters.

My father was a man of the strictest honour and integrity, and of a sound understanding and judgment, without affecting any of those shewy pretensions to talents, which are so apt to impose upon the world Indeed for coxcombs and pretenders of every kind, he always entertained great contempt, and usually treated them with a peculiar kind of humour. The latter part of his time was imbittered by disease and weakness. The healing springs of Bristol afforded him no relief, and he died of a consumption, soon after his return from that place, at his own house at Studley, on the 30th of November, 1777, at the early period of forty-nine years, and he was buried at Chilton.

Mrs. Croke survived him till the 20th of April, 1806 Her death afforded a singular instance of the frailty of human life. As she was sitting by the fire, in moving her chair, she fell, broke her leg, and, after lying for six months in misery, was tranferred to a happier state.

The children by the first marriage, for there were none by the second, were, Jenny Sarah Elizabeth Croke, born the 25th of January, 1755. Alexander Croke, born Feb 29th, 1756, and died the 16th of August, 1756. Anne, born the 17th of June, 1757, and died March the 19th, 1758. Alexander, born July 22d, 1758. William le Blount, born March the 18th, 1760, and died the 5th of June, 1761, having been choked by a crumb of new bread. Of all these, one daughter, Jenny Sarah Elizabeth, and myself, were the only children who survived their infancy.

JENNY SARAH ELIZABETH CROKE, the only surviving daughter, received her education at a school at Eton. When she was grown up, she usually passed her winters with the Lady Elizabeth Lee, the daughter of the Earl of Harcourt, and the wife of our cousin Sir William Lee, at Hartwell. With Lady Elizabeth she sometimes visited at Nuneham, and was introduced to the elegant and literary society, which often assembled there, Horace Walpole, Mason, Jerningham, and the Fauqueres.

On the 15th of April, 1777, she married John Parker, Esquire, of Storth Hall, in Yorkshire, and an eminent Solicitor in London, which proved an unfortunate connexion. On his estate in Yorkshire was a fine trout stream, the delight of his early years. From the great centre of mercantile adventure at Manchester, ramifications extended into all the neighbouring counties, and a cotton-mill was erected upon this rivulet. The profits were known to be considerable, the concern was to be sold, and the demon of avarice prompted Mr. Parker to become the purchaser, in conjunction with another gentleman. The emoluments of this manufactory induced him to launch out still farther Large sums were expended upon a very extensive establishment at Exeter. wealth was rolling in in a full tide, but great fluctuations took place in the cotton markets· Mr. Parker was unskilled in the nature and tricks of commerce, he became the dupe of some artful villains, and, in a short time, was totally ruined After their misfortunes, they retired to Beckley. Mr. Parker died on the 26th of March, 1805, in the 56th year of his age, and his widow on the 23d of July, 1814, aged 59 years which was to me the irreparable loss of the most affectionate of sisters, and the best of women!

You may wish perhaps, my children, to be informed of some particulars relating to your father, of events which happened before you were born, or when you were too young to understand them, and our descendants may have some little curiosity to know something of the person who collected these memoirs. For your gratification, and perhaps instruction, I am willing to encounter the imputation of egotism, in giving you some account of my own life.

I was then the only surviving son of Alexander Croke, and Anne Armistead, and I was born on the twenty-second day of July, 1758, at a quarter after seven o'clock, on a Saturday morning, at Aylesbury, and was baptized on the 12th of August. At the age of nine years I was afflicted with a complaint upon my lungs, which continued a long time, and was nearly fatal. It left behind it a sense of weakness, dejection, and oppression, which I never entirely overcame. When I was about ten years of age, my mother died, but I was too young to feel her loss very sensibly.

After having been at two or three rudimental schools, I was finally placed for education under the care of the Reverend Thomas Shaw, Vicar of Bierton, near Aylesbury, in the year 1767, with whom I continued till my removal to the University. Mr. Shaw was the father of two sons, who afterwards distinguished themselves in the paths of science and literature. The eldest, the Reverend John Shaw, Doctor in Divinity, is Fellow of Magdalen College, and published an edition of Apollonius Rhodius's Argonauts, with learned notes. The work was abused, with all the vulgarity of German critics, by the celebrated Brunck, but it was generally considered as the work of an elegant, if not of a laborious, scholar, and the preface was allowed to be a good specimen of classical Latinity. Against the supercilious censures of Brunck, we may produce in its favour the judgment of a British critic, not inferior in any respect to the German, and certainly as little disposed to flatter, Gilbert Wakefield, who recommended it to Charles Fox, as the best edition of that pleasing poet, in the correspondence which passed between them, after that eminent statesman had retired from public life, and had returned to his early and favourite studies of Grecian literature[q].

The younger son, Doctor George Shaw, was educated as a physician. He was a member of Magdalen Hall, in Oxford, afterwards he studied physic, and the sciences connected with it, at Edinburgh, and in London, and took the degree of Doctor in Medicine; although he never attended to the practice of his profession. His studies were devoted to the pleasing pursuits of natural history, and he became one of the first zoologists and botanists in Europe. Soon after his father's death, he obtained a situation of all others best adapted to his habits, that of one of the Librarians of the British Museum. His works are well known. His British Zoology may be considered as the standard work upon that subject, and of his Na-

[q] Letters between Fox and Wakefield.

turalist's Miscellany, it was said by Doctor Parr, "that he wrote the best "Latin of any man since the time of Erasmus." He had likewise a turn for poetry, and wrote several short pieces of great merit. Both the sons were remarkable instances of early genius, and were entered at the University at fourteen years of age. George, at twelve, could repeat the whole of Horace by heart. The abilities of his sons, of whom the eldest, before his removal to the Charter House, and the youngest, entirely, had been educated by their father, had induced some of his friends to persuade Mr. Shaw to undertake the education of their children, and the number was gradually increased to thirty.

In this amiable and superior society I continued for eight years, during the latter part of the time rather as one of the family, than as a pupil. The dispositions of the mind are as communicable as the affections of the body. Besides the usual routine of Greek and Latin, I was very naturally attracted by the fascinating pursuits of my friend Doctor George Shaw, with whom I passed many delightful hours in experiments of philosophy and chemistry, and in wandering, with perfect freedom, and in a sort of intellectual luxury, through the various paths of science and literature, at a time of life when every acquisition in knowledge produces a charming sensation. The years which I passed at Bierton, I always looked back to as some of the happiest of my life, and I there acquired a general love for science, which has been a never-failing source of amusement, during the whole of my life.

At a proper time, I was entered a Gentleman-Commoner of Oriel College, and went to reside, in February, 1776, under the tuition of Mr. Flemming, who was a tutor of the old school, and much attached to the scholastic logic. This science, since the time of Locke, had for a while lost its credit at the Universities. Aristotle has since been reinstated in his didactic chair. From this study I thought I derived considerable benefit in my future pursuits. After this gentleman had taken a college living, I was pupil to the worthy and excellent Doctor Eveleigh, afterwards Provost of the college. In those days, books were not much in fashion amongst the young men, and I was led by example, more than from inclination, to pass a dissipated, rather than an industrious, life. Something I read, but it was chiefly at home in the vacations, and, upon the whole, I never recalled to my mind my five years residence at Oxford with much pleasure or satisfaction Were the time to come over again, I would have spent it very differently.

In 1777 my father died, and I was left to be my own master. Soon after I came of age, I wished to improve my estate, by the drainage and inclosure of the large common of Otmoor. I took a great deal of pains, and was at a considerable expence about it, and I communicated the result of my enquiries to the other proprietors, in a small pamphlet. In a business which was for the benefit of all persons concerned, and in which I had no separate interest, I might have expected to obtain some credit, and thanks, for my public spirit On the contrary, I was assailed on all sides, and was treated as a common enemy. This patriotic attempt ended in a paper war with the Earl of Abingdon, who had originally suggested the inclosure to me, and five law-suits, by which, as I gained nothing, I was not much benefitted by decisions in my favour with costs. The drainage and inclosure were afterwards accomplished by some other persons, at above four times the expence for which it might have been done at the time, and in the manner, in which it had originally been proposed.

I continued at the University till 1780, when I quitted Oxford, and resided in chambers, first, in Lincoln's Inn, afterwards in other chambers in the Temple, and finally in Harcourt's Buildings. In 1786 I was called to the bar, as a member of the Inner Temple. But although I had studied the theory of the law, I never engaged in the practice of it, or attended much in Westminster Hall. I returned many briefs which were sent me by the kindness of my friends. Having a competence, which though small, as I was then saddled with a mother's and a grandmother's jointures, was sufficient for the wants of a young man without ambition, or extravagance, I was not pressed by necessity to make any exertions. In truth, my habitual bashfulness, the effect probably of the illness before mentioned, disqualified me in a great measure for the bar, which requires a greater degree of confidence and self-possession than I ever was master of, and, which may perhaps be looked upon as a folly of no small magnitude, I had strangely conceived a great contempt for every thing which seemed mercenary, and was connected with a pecuniary remuneration. Yet I was not altogether idle: I employed my time in reading the best writers in different branches of literature, and, besides the Greek and Latin classics, I obtained some insight into the French, Italian, Spanish, and German languages, with a little Hebrew, and still less of Arabic, which I learned of professor Carlyle, partly with a view of visiting the regions of the East, and partly for the purpose of writing the history of the Crusades, neither of which intentions I executed

In the year 1794, being weary of an idle life, and seeing the necessity of a profession, I determined to become an Advocate in the Civil and Ecclesiastical Courts, in Doctor's Commons; and with that view re-entered at Oriel College, and began attending the proper courts In this design, I met with very flattering encouragement from Sir William Scott, with whom I was previously acquainted from his connexion with University College.

On the eleventh of August, 1796, I married, from the purest and most elevated motive to that important connexion, an honourable and disinterested love. It was the most prudent and fortunate act of my whole life, and the principal source of all my future happiness. I found my mind exalted and refined by an attachment to the virtues of an amiable female, every pleasure seemed doubled by communication, and every misfortune was alleviated by the soothings of affection.

In 1797, I took the degree of Doctor of Laws, and in Michaelmas term was admitted into the society of Advocates, in Doctor's Commons A severe illness the next year had nearly put an end to all farther views. The usual year of silence, imposed upon Advocates on their admission, expired upon the third of November, 1798. The Civil Law Bar was at that time richly furnished. It could boast of the elegant learning, the various talents, and the playful imagination of Scott the plain capacity for business of Nicholl the cool argumentative powers of Arnold the masterly acquaintance with the law and practice of the Courts of Swabey · and the comprehensive mind, and the overbearing, but sometimes obscure, eloquence of Lawrence, the friend of Burke The junior Advocates, who came into the profession about the same time with myself, were likewise in every way highly respectable. In the time of war, the Court of Admiralty affords a plentiful harvest, and I was admitted to a share of the business, and the emoluments, fully adequate to my expectations.

Having taken some notes of an important case relating to the marriage of illegitimate minors, I was solicited to publish them. I prefixed an introductory essay upon the laws of illegitimacy in general; which was designed as a specimen of the manner in which I conceived law should be studied as a liberal science, by first ascertaining the general principles upon which it is founded in nature and reason, and then examining the manner in which they have been carried into effect, in the institutions of different nations[r]. This was one of many researches of the same kind which I had pursued in a course of study, recommended to me by a great master of the science.

The credit which I gained by this essay soon found me another employment. Mr. Schlegel, a Danish Professor, had published a scurrilous book against the conduct of Great Britain towards neutral nations, and the proceedings in the Courts of Admiralty[s]. I was requested by some persons high in government to answer it. My reply was published early in 1801[t], and I received the most flattering testimonies of their approbation from Lord Teignmouth, Lord Loughborough, Sir William Grant, Lord Sidmouth, Lord Grenville, and other great and eminent persons—the latter honoured me with some observations upon it, but the greatest, because the most discriminating applause, was bestowed upon me in the Anti-jacobin Review for September, 1801, at that time conducted by Mr. Canning and other men of talents in the confidence of government. I had planned, and in part executed, a more general inquiry into the rights and duties of belligerent and neutral nations, which seemed little understood, and

[r] A Report of the Case of Horner against Liddiard, upon the Question of what consent is necessary to the marriage of Illegitimate Minors, determined on the 24th of May, 1799, in the Consistorial Court of London. By Sir William Scott. With an Introductory Essay upon the Theory and History of Laws relating to Illegitimate Children, by Alexander Croke, LL.D. London, 1800. Butterworth.

[s] It was intitled, Sur la visite des Vaisseaux Neutres sous Convoi, ou Examen impartial du jugement prononcè par le Tribunal de l'Amirautè Angloise, le 11 Juin, 1799, dans l'affaire du Convoi Swèdois. Par J. F. W. Schlegel, Docteur et Professeur en Droit à l'Universitè de Copenhague, Assesseur Extraordinaire de la Haute Cour de Justice, membre de plusieurs societés savantes. Copenhague, 1800, and translated into English, Debrett, London, 1801.

[t] Intitled, Remarks on Mr. Schlegel's Work upon the Visitation of Neutral Vessels under Convoy. By Alexander Croke, LL.D. London. White, 1801.

were greatly and designedly misrepresented by the enemies, secret and avowed, of Great Britain. My subsequent appointment, but more particularly the able manner in which almost every question, which could occur, had been discussed, and set to rest, in the luminous sentences of Sir William Scott, prevented my completion of the work.

In the same year, I received an offer of being appointed a Judge of one of the Vice-Admiralty Courts in America. Complaints of unjust decisions, delays, and exorbitant fees, had been made against those courts, both by British subjects and foreigners, which had at length attracted the attention of the government. It was thought proper, by lessening the number, by extending the jurisdiction, and by increasing the salaries of the Judges, to give them greater dignity, and to induce English advocates to accept of those offices. An Act of Parliament was passed for that purpose in July, 1801[u]. In August, in the same year, I had the honour of being offered, without solicitation, the first appointment upon this new establishment, with the choice of my station either at Jamaica, Martinique, or at Halifax in Nova Scotia. My salary was to be fixed at two thousand pounds a year, besides fees, and it was agreed that upon my return, after a residence of six years, I should receive an annuity of half that sum. The new jurisdiction of each of these courts extended to every part of his Majesty's dominions on the other side of the Atlantic, as well on the continent of America, as in the islands: from Canada to the Gulf of Mexico, and including the West Indies.

This offer was considered with all the deliberation which was due to its importance to my future welfare. On the one side, present profit, the chance of future advancement to the higher honours, and greater emoluments in my profession, at home, and the unpleasantness of a banishment from England. In the other scale, the uncertainty of business, the caprice of clients, the chances of ill-health, the labour and confinement of the bar, the probability of a peace, the certainty and independence of a fixed salary, and of a provision for life, the credit and dignity of the judicial office: all these and other circumstances were duly weighed in the balance of prudence, by myself and my friends. After some hesitation, I resolved to

[u] 41 Geo. III. chap. 96. See the Preface to Stewart's Reports.

accept of the appointment, and, in selecting my situation, I preferred the severe, but healthy climate of Nova Scotia, to all the luxuries and all the dangers of the West Indies.

Upon obtaining this appointment, I had the honour of being introduced to his Royal Highness the Duke of Kent, who had resided many years in Nova Scotia, and was very partial to that country. Nothing could equal his Royal Highness's condescension and kindness to me With that minuteness of attention which so much distinguished the good old King, he enquired into all the particulars of my intended voyage, and the establishment I proposed to take with me. He recommended one of his own servants, who had been with him in that country, as likely to be useful to us from his local knowledge. He took great pains to procure a cook for us, in which however he did not succeed, and we had several notes from him upon the subject. I was indebted likewise to him for several letters of introduction to the Governor, and other persons at Halifax.

The warrant from the Lords of the Admiralty to the Judge of the Admiralty to make out my patent issued on the 13th of August, 1801. On the 10th of September, I went on board the Jason, a merchant ship, under convoy of the Alcmene frigate, at Portsmouth, with my wife, my son Alexander, then a little boy in petticoats, and my daughter Adelaide, a child in arms. After a tedious voyage of nine weeks, we arrived in Halifax harbour on the 11th of November. We were received with great honour and civility. In a few days after our arrival, a vessel came to announce that preliminaries of peace had been signed on the 1st of October, between the King and the French Republic, which were afterwards completed by the definitive treaty of Amiens. This reduced the business of the Prize Court almost to nothing, and my only judicial occupation was the trial of revenue and navigation causes, which were very few, till the declaration of hostilities against France, on the 10th of May, 1803, and the declaration of war by the United States, on the 18th of June, 1812, supplied me with ample materials for employment.

By the King's mandamus, I was appointed a member of his Council for the province, with rank immediately after the Chief Justice, who is President of the Council. Soon after my arrival in Nova Scotia, the King's charter for founding an University at Windsor came over, and I was appointed one of the Governors. They were directed to make a body of statutes, and the Bishop of Nova Scotia, the Chief Justice, and myself, were named as a Committee to prepare them. The statutes were drawn up entirely by myself, and were adopted, without alteration, by a majority of the Governors amongst whom great dissentions prevailed, and continued long, to the great prejudice of the new institution. These contests were originally occasioned by some statutes which had been drawn up by the Bishop, in which he had contrived to give himself, as Visitor, more power than the other Governors thought justifiable, or indeed consistent with his visitorial duties, and which they therefore refused to adopt.

During my residence of fourteen years, I found my situation, and the country, extremely pleasant. The climate was healthy, and not disagreeably severe, and I had employment just sufficient to occupy, without fatiguing, the mind. Part of the time we resided in the town of Halifax but chiefly at a house, which I purchased, about a mile off to which we gave the name of *Studley Minor*. The situation was beautiful, and commanded views of the harbour, the town of Halifax, the country round it, and the fine water of the north-west arm, with its accompanying banks of native forest. This grand scenery was seen to advantage in a rude walk, through my own wood; and a retired spot, where I erected a little edifice, and named it the *Temple of Peace*, was a delightful retreat for meditation or converse. The following inscription was placed in it.

ΑΣΥΧΙΑΙ.

I

Ye who, all-weary, guide your wandering feet
  'Midst life's rough crags, which piercing thorns intwine,
Awhile beneath this lowly roof retreat,
  Sacred to Peace, a pure though rustic shrine.
Fly hence, swoln Pomp, to every vice allied,
  Inconstancy, to nuptial vows untrue,
Comus, with frantic Riot by your side,
  And mad Ambition's ever-restless crew,
Hence! for in vain ye deem no mortal sees
Your inly-sickening hearts, unfit for scenes like these.

II.

These myrtled knolls demand far other guests
  And where the darkening woods unbounded spread
O'er Earth's primæval rocks their gorgeous vests,
  By human hand untamed, save where its head
Yon massy tower lifts o'er the western main,
  And looks to Britain, there let Innocence,
With sweet Simplicity, enchanters twain!
  On every flower, and shrub, that joys the sense,
Unfading charms, celestial grace bestow,
Such as their votaries feel, and only they can know

The society of Halifax was varied and agreeable, and it had acquired a superior tone from the long residence of the Duke of Kent. It consisted of the principal officers of Government, and of the army and navy, with some of the inhabitants. During the time we were there, the Governors' families were, Sir John and Lady Wentworth, Sir George and Lady Prevost, Sir John and Lady Coape Sherbrooke. The Admirals' families were, Sir Andrew and Lady Mitchell, Admiral and Lady Emily Berkeley, sister to the Duke of Richmond, Sir John and Lady Borlase Warren. The Commandants of the garrison were, the Generals Bowyer, Gardiner, the personal friend of Stanislaus, King of Poland, Hunter, Darrack, and Sir Thomas Saumarez all of whom except the two first had wives and families. The Commissioners of the Dock Yard were, the Captains Inglefield and Wodehouse. These, with Dr. Inglis, the Bishop, Chief Justice Blowers, the worthy Dr. Stanser, the Rector of Saint Paul's, and since Bishop, some other divines, lawyers, physicians, merchants, and occasional visitors, such as Lord Selkirk, and Mr. Ambassador Foster, contributed to compose a society sufficiently numerous and respectable for all purposes of comfort or pleasure. We had subscription balls, and a neat theatre, where plays were performed by the gentlemen of the garrison. An annual visit to Windsor, forty-five miles from Halifax, with the other Governors of the College, when an examination of the students took place, and other little excursions, varied the uniformity of the scene. Some amusement I occasionally found in writing little pieces of poetry, which pleased my friends, though they may not immortalize my name*. The fineness of the scenery induced me to attempt landscape painting, and if not the works of a Claude or a Poussin, my pictures gave some idea of a country little known at home, and after our return, served to recall to our remembrance the places where we had spent so many years.

On the 6th of December, 1808, the Governor, Sir George Prevost, sailed upon an expedition against the island of Martinique, which had been surrendered to France by the treaty of Amiens. I was specially appointed by His Majesty, as well as by the Governor's general commission, to administer the affairs of the province in his absence, under the title of President and Commander in Chief.

At Sir George Prevost's departure, the Legislature was sitting, and my appointment had been formally announced to them in his farewell speech. Upon entering upon my office, I repaired to the Council Chamber, and took the oaths. The members of the House of Assembly were summoned to attend there, and I addressed them in the following words:

"*Mr* PRESIDENT, *and Gentlemen of his Majesty's Council,*

"*Mr* SPEAKER, *and Gentlemen of the House of Assembly,*

"His Majesty having signified his pleasure, that, during the absence of his Excellency Sir George Prevost, on a military service, the government of this province should devolve upon me, I have called you together to communicate to you such his Majesty's instructions, and my acceptance of the important trust.

"Anxious as I must feel, to perform the duties of this administration to his Majesty's satisfaction, and to the benefit of the province, it cannot but afford me a subject of great consolation, that this event has taken place at a period, when my imperfect abilities may be assisted by the united wisdom of the two great legislative Councils, at this time assembled. Though, in the execution of this office, I may, perhaps, receive some aid from the habitual attention to the transactions of nations, and to the British laws and constitution, to which my professional studies have been necessarily directed, and though I may have acquired some little

* A few of them are printed in the Appendix, No XXXVI.

knowledge and experience in the concerns of this country, during a considerable residence here; yet I shall ever consider, that the surest grounds of information, and the safest rules for my governance, are to be derived from your advice and suggestions In what must depend upon my own efforts, I shall endeavour, with the most heartfelt zeal, and unremitting application, to promote the honour of his Majesty's Government, and the safety, prosperity, and happiness, of the province, in a systematic combination with the good of the whole united British empire; with which the best interests of every particular part are equally and inseparably connected.

" The flattering picture of political affairs in general, and the encouraging statement of the increased revenues, agriculture, fisheries, and commerce of this province, which were laid before you by his Excellency at the commencement of the session, and the proper objects which were then pointed out to your attention, to give permanency to those improvements, render it unnecessary for me to say any thing upon those topics

" The present aspect of the subsisting hostilities, and of our various national relations, and the probability that the government of the United States will be ultimately actuated by enlightened views for the welfare of their country, under the favour of Providence, and through his Majesty's energetic and successful exertions, seem to promise a continuance of the tranquillity which we have hitherto enjoyed, and which affords so blessed a contrast to the calamities inflicted by the Almighty upon so large a portion of the world. Should any unforeseen events, however, require the employment of a military force, our confidence in the regular troops supplied by his Majesty's paternal care for our defence, is greatly increased by the return of that able and experienced commander, Major General Hunter; and the high state of the discipline of the militia, arising from the late regulations, seconded by the spirit and ardour of individuals, affords a substantial pledge, that the province will likewise find an adequate protection in its own resources, and that its inhabitants are well qualified to display the noble union of the characters of the citizen and the soldier

" In the mean time, I must offer up my wishes and prayers for the success of the expedition, and that our worthy Governor may speedily return, crowned with fresh laurels, in addition to those he has already so honourably acquired; when I may resign with satisfaction the administration of the province into the hands of those, who are so much more capable of conducting it."

This speech was answered by loyal and complimentary Addresses from the Council, and the House of Assembly, but this friendship was not of long continuance. The House of Assembly, presuming upon the weakness of a temporary administration of the government, thought it a favourable time to promote their own views. They had two standing rules of policy, the one was to exhaust the treasury, and, by that means, to make the government dependent upon them for the necessary supplies, and the other was to vote as much money as possible for roads, of which the members, or their friends, being commissioners, or contractors, or otherwise interested, the emoluments came directly, or indirectly, into their own pockets Both these objects they now endeavoured to obtain by larger grants of money, for different services, and particularly for roads, than had ever been made, and far beyond all probability of a revenue adequate to supplying them They had assumed likewise a power of naming a new colonial agent, and commissioners to correspond with him, without an act of the legislature, or the consent of the Governor

In consequence of these encroachments upon the executive power, and this wasteful expenditure of the public money, when the Appropriation Bill was brought up into the Council Chamber by the Speaker and the House of Assembly, and offered to me for my approbation, according to the forms of the British Parliament, which are punctiliously observed in the colonial legislatures, I refused my assent to it. This occasioned much indignation The House of Assembly debated with great heat for two days upon it, with their doors closed. Violent resolutions were passed, and at length a Committee waited upon me, to inform me, "that they had no "further business before them," the usual form observed before a Session was closed. Upon which, I went down to the Council, and prorogued the legislature with the following speech.

"*Mr* PRESIDENT, *and Gentlemen of his Majesty's Council,*
"*Mr.* SPEAKER, *and Gentlemen of the Assembly,*

"The Assembly having informed me by their Committee, that they have no business whatever before them, at the end of a Session which has been protracted to a longer duration than the subjects proposed to be considered might have seemed to require, it remains only for me to dismiss you from the fatigues of public exertion, to the more tranquil happiness of your domestic relations. In your private stations you will, no doubt, continue to exercise the same zeal for the prosperity of the country, which has influenced your conduct in your collective capacity, by the encouragement of industry, and the promotion of peace, and a due submission to the laws

" The inactivity of the season of the year, and the interruption of intercourse during the winter months, have precluded the information of any material change in public affairs, since I last had the honour of addressing you. The situation of Spain, though not yet arrived at its crisis, from the invincible ardor of patriotism, which animates the whole of that interesting country, continues to hold out a promise of relief to the subjugated nations of Europe, and to augur, though remotely, the happy return of peace, which has been so long banished from the world, but the unhappy state of a neighbouring country, distracted by party violence, and occasionally instigated by the suggestions of passion, rather than by the sound dictates of reason, and of a beneficial policy, suggests the precaution of providing against the most unfavourable alternatives, and amongst other means, more particularly by a diligent and spirited execution of the laws for exercising and disciplining the militia.

" *Gentlemen of the Assembly;*

" I have to acknowledge, with the sincerest thanks, the liberal and ample supplies which you have granted to his Majesty, for the exigencies of his government The continuance and amendment of those revenue laws, where utility has been demonstrated by experience, require little observation, but I must congratulate you, with the warmest sentiments of approbation, upon the honourable manner in which you have fulfilled your engagement to his Majesty, by your provision towards defraying the expences of providing arms for the militia, by a tax extremely unexceptionable.

" *Gentlemen of his Majesty's Council, and of the Assembly,*

" It is matter of deep concern to me, that I have been under the necessity of refusing my assent to a Bill, which had received your joint approbation. Disposed as I am to consult the wishes of such respectable bodies of men, and inclined as I should feel even to sacrifice my own opinions to yours, upon affairs of lesser consequence, I should be guilty of a breach of the important trust which has been confided in me by his Majesty, if I should give my assent to laws, which I conceived to be highly exceptionable, in relation either to his Majesty's rights, or to the welfare of the province.

"I have already communicated my reasons for this dissent, and shall again proceed to state them to you One of my objections to this Bill is from the large amount of the sums appropriated by it, in conjunction with the Bounty Bills, far beyond the expenditure of any former years, without any peculiar emergencies to require, or any probability of a material increase of revenue to justify, the extension. The appropriation for expenditures to take place within the year exceeds so far every calculation of revenue expected to be received within that period, and the payment of considerable sums will therefore be so much protracted, that it has been thought necessary to introduce into the Bill a clause for the payment of interest upon the warrants after they become due. By these great appropriations, the expences of this year would exhaust not only the unpaid duties of the last, but the greater part of the funds necessary for the supply of the ensuing year, even under the supposition that the present taxes will be continued. The consequence of this absorption of the past, and anticipation of the future, revenue, will be an exhausted state of the treasury, not only during the present, but likewise during the succeeding year, and what every man who wished well to the country would strongly deprecate, the new measure of the commencement of a debt upon interest If such a profuse lavishment of the revenue, which within the ordinary restrictions is amply sufficient for every useful purpose, consistent with the actual state of the country, would be scarcely adviseable in any common situation of affairs, how much more improvident must it be considered, when a few weeks may render it necessary to place the province in a state of defence, at which important conjuncture, by the operation of this Bill, not a shilling would be found in the public chest to pay and furnish the militia, to defray the expence of any military preparations, or for other necessary service of Government.

"The next objection to the Appropriation Bill is founded upon a clause, which enacts, that it shall be lawful for the Lieutenant Governor, or the Commander in Chief, to draw out of the treasury of the province, by warrant, in favour of the Commissioners appointed to correspond with the Agent of the province, any sum or sums of money, not exceeding two hundred guineas, to be remitted by them to the special Agent of the province, to enable him to defray any expences which may be incurred, for promoting the general interests of the commerce and fisheries of the province.

"For the object there stated, that of promoting the commerce and fisheries of the province, I can assure you with the greatest sincerity, that I possess as much zeal and earnestness as their warmest advocate, and I am truly sorry that the clause introduced into the Bill for that purpose is such as cannot receive my approbation. That any agents of the province, distinct from the two general accredited agents, have been constituted by a lawful authority, I am perfectly uninformed. Of the existence of the Commissioners there mentioned, by whom, by what authority, or for what purpose, they have been appointed, I am equally ignorant. It is impossible therefore for me to recognize persons under either of those descriptions. If, as I have been given to understand, for no communication upon the subject has been made to me from either branch of the legislature, the Council and the Assembly have concurred in appointing a special agent, and have each nominated Commissioners, for the purpose of corresponding with him; to say no more of it, it is a measure novel and unprecedented, and I think that the circumstance would require me, particularly during a temporary exercise of the Government, to employ a considerable degree of caution and deliberation, before I could be induced to give a consent to such material innovations upon the usual mode of transacting colonial affairs. But my objection is not founded merely upon the novelty of the proceeding. For the Council and the Assembly to appoint persons, and to invest them with authority to act, when their own power and existence is suspended or determined, without any Bill or Law for that purpose, without the knowledge, consent, or concurrence of the executive branch of the Government, does appear to me to be an unusual and unwarrantable assumption of power, and a dangerous encroachment upon the prerogative of the Crown.

"Unpleasant as it is to be driven to the exercise of this right of dissenting from Acts which have been agreed to by his Majesty's Council and the Assembly, and approving as I do of the greater part of the provisions of this Bill, it is much to be lamented that it should have passed both branches of the legislature with such exceptionable matter, as to occasion its final rejection. I trust, however, that the province will suffer no injury from the loss of this Bill, and that the revenue will be applied by Government in a manner more œconomical, but equally conducive to the prosperity of the country; but whatever may be the consequences, in the part which I have acted, I have done what I conceive to be my duty, and I shall resign the government at the appointed time, with the consolation of reflecting, that my short administration will not have been marked with the imputation of having opened a road for intrenchments upon the Constitution, of having left the province destitute of the means of defence in the hour of danger, or of having entailed upon it an empty treasury and an incipient debt.

Council Chamber,
Jan. 26, 1809

ALEX. CROKE."

Whilst I was President, I corresponded officially with the first Lord of the Treasury, and the Secretaries of State, Lord Castlereagh, Lord Liverpool, Lord Bathurst, and Lord Hobart, concerning the affairs of the province, and the politics and proceedings of the United States, which were then verging towards hostilities; and likewise with the British Ambassadors in that country, Mr. Erskine, and Mr. Foster. I held regular levées, the returns of every public department were made to me, and I commanded a body of ten thousand militia men.

Sir George Prevost arrived from the conquest of Martinique on the 15th of April, 1809, and resumed the government. He soon convened the legislature, and, as he loved popularity, he gave his consent to a new Appropriation Bill, which contained almost all the improvident grants which I had objected to, except that for the payment of the colonial agent. The consequences which were foreseen succeeded. The treasury was soon completely emptied, the public officers were unpaid, a considerable debt was incurred, the financial affairs of the province were greatly embarrassed, when the United States declared war there was no money to pay the militia, and it became necessary to have recourse to a paper currency to supply the wants of the Government.

At the end of that year, I had an unpleasant altercation with Sir George Prevost respecting a trial for piracy, which I refused to attend, amongst other reasons, because I had doubts as to the validity of the commission, under which the court for the trial of pirates was constituted. Sir George wrote home upon the subject to the Earl of Liverpool, with copies of the correspondence which had passed between us The whole was by him transmitted to the King's Advocate, and the Attorney and Solicitor General, for their opinion upon the points in question. They decided against me, and advised, that it should be signified to me, his Majesty's Government expected that I should attend those trials on future occasions. In giving this opinion, the great law officers had entirely overlooked an Act of Parliament, passed but a few years before, in which new regulations were enacted respecting the trials of pirates in the colonies, and by which *all the existing commissions for them were annulled and declared void*[y], and new ones directed to be issued. No new commission had been granted for the province of Nova Scotia; but these men were tried, and one of them condemned and executed, under the old one, thus revoked. In consequence of my subsequent application, stating these facts, a new commission was issued in 1813.

In the year 1810, I went over to England for a few months, with my son George. We sailed from Halifax on the 14th of January, and landed at Portsmouth, after a very stormy voyage, on the 10th of February Sir John and Lady Wentworth came over in the same convoy. I was happy to see my friends, and was received by them with a flattering cordiality. I placed my son George at Mr Richards's at Winchester.

Nothing worth mentioning occurred during my stay in England, unless it were the civilities which I experienced from his Royal Highness the Duke of Kent. Any little circumstances which display the private manners, and domestic life, of persons in such exalted stations, are interesting, and I shall therefore relate exactly what passed in my intercourse with him. Upon my arrival, of course I paid my respects to his Royal Highness, and received an invitation to breakfast, at Castle Hill Lodge. The time fixed was ten o'clock, and I was punctual to the appointment. After passing through the usual guards of porters, and servants in spendid

[y] Statute 46 Geo III 1806

liveries, I was ushered into the Breakfast Room; his Royal Highness soon made his appearance, and received me with great condescension and kindness. The breakfast things were of elegant sêve china, with a silver urn; he made the tea himself, and no servant waited. I was pressed to take some chocolate, which was brought in by his valet, who he informed me always made it, thought no one equal to himself in that employment, and would be much mortified if I refused It was certainly very good, and was flavoured with cinnamon. The Duke's manner was gracious, and one felt perfectly at ease with him. He talked much, and of a variety of subjects, amongst which Halifax and Nova Scotia formed a principal part. He entered a great deal into his own affairs, and complained of ill usage from the public, and more particularly from his own family, and he stated many circumstances of a very private and confidential nature, which I shall not relate. He said that he had been accused of cowardice in not venturing his person amongst the mutineers at Gibraltar, but that he had actually gone down to them, when they appeared to be in such a state of intoxication and madness, that the officers who accompanied him absolutely forced him away, as no good could possibly be done with men in such a situation, and so utterly incapable of hearing reason. After breakfast we got up, and walked about the room. He shewed me the pictures in that and other apartments. There was a full length of Louis the Eighteenth, painted, as he informed me, by a lady. A drawing of the Princess Amelia, which he particularly pointed out to me. There was a painting of himself by Lawrence, just finished. I observed that it was the best likeness of him which I had seen, upon which he told me that he was having it engraved, and would send me a print from it. His Royal Highness never forgot his promises, and after my return to Halifax, I received the print handsomely framed, with a polite note. He wished me much to go to Windsor to pay my respects to the King, but I was so near my departure, that I did not go. After a moderate stay, his Royal Highness made us a bow, which was the signal for our departure, and we accordingly took leave; when he made an apology for having only asked me to breakfast, as at that time he dined early, and drove out Madame de Saint Laurent every evening, and therefore gave no dinner parties.

The history of an invitation to dinner will afford a striking example of his Royal Highness's punctuality and attention. This invitation was sent to me to Osborn's Hotel, where I had been staying, but as I had left London, it lay there for many weeks unattended to, till enquiries having been made after it by his Royal Highness, it was at last returned to him by the penny post. After my return, upon receiving again his note of invitation, he transmitted it to Halifax, with an explanation of the circumstances, and expressing great indignation that it should have been *opened*, " which," he said, " had never happened to him before ; " as when letters bear the name of *Peers*. or Public Functionaries in the " corner, and they are returned, from being unable to find out the person to " whom they are directed, they are uniformly sent back unopened." He accompanied it with his " best regards," and sent it " that I might be " satisfied of his intentions towards me, although most unluckily they failed " in reaching me."

He always expressed the greatest kindness, and the most favourable opinion of me Soon after the commencement of the American war, having occasion to write to him upon another subject, I freely gave him my sentiments upon the real nature of the war, the temper of the United States, and the situation of our own colonies ; I took the liberty of suggesting that it was not by concessions, but by rapid and vigorous measures, that the war ought to be carried on. In his answer of the 28th of October, 1812, he assured me, that he " was particularly grateful for my communi- " cation, and not a little flattered that the opinions therein expressed were " so congenial with his own—but I fear," he added, " it would be very " difficult to make our friends here see matters in the light that you and I " do Still I do not despair of it, and it shall not be my fault if I do not " turn your most judicious observations to public advantage." In another letter he concluded by saying, that " whenever I returned to England, he " hoped that I should not forget that I should always be a welcome visitor " at Kensington." Some other complimentary letters I had the honour of receiving from him, which I could not copy without too many blushes.

On my return to Nova Scotia, I went on board the packet at Falmouth the 19th of September, and arrived safe the 29th of October.

On the 25th of August, 1811, Sir George Prevost sailed for Quebec, having been appointed Governor General of North America, when the administration of the government of Nova Scotia again devolved upon me during the Interregnum. Sir John Coape Sherbrooke, the new Governor, arrived on the 16th of October following.

In the year 1813, the sectaries in England, ever upon the watch to undermine the Church, introduced into the province of Nova Scotia their two favourite engines, the Lancastrian school, and the Bible Society. The person employed for this purpose had been pay-master of one of the regiments, and not originally of so sanctified a character, before he had undergone a conversion in Portugal. The real nature of these societies was not then so well understood as afterwards, and they met with great success. The Governor, Sir John Coape Sherbrooke, even the Bishop, and the principal persons in the province, at first supported them, and Mr Bromley came over under the express patronage of the Duke of Kent, who had great influence in the country. I saw immediately the tendency of these institutions, and determined to oppose them. I published a letter in the Halifax paper upon the subject, which is printed in the Appendix[z]. This gave occasion to a very long controversy in the public papers, in which above eighty pieces appeared on different sides, of which twenty were written by me. The eyes of the members of the Established Church began to be opened, the Society for the Promotion of Christian Knowledge at length superseded the Bible Society, and the national schools those of Mr Lancaster.

The Duke of Kent, who had become a warm patron of all those sectarian societies, supported his missionary with all his authority and influence. A letter was shewn about, in which his Royal Highness had done me the honour to censure me in strong language for opposing these plans. Upon which I transmitted to him the two first printed papers, in which I had publicly stated the reasons of my conduct, and I added some complaints of his asperity towards me. He returned an answer, dated on the 7th of April, 1814, through a third person, by whom I had made the communication, in which he said, "I am led to express my regret that one who is "so justly esteemed for his great professional talents, and many private "virtues, should upon the important subject of religion exhibit a temper "and dispositions, in my opinion very far from corresponding with the

[z] No XXXVII

"mild and liberal doctrines which it teaches. All the censure I can have "presumed to pass upon the conduct of the worthy Judge as an opponent "of the British system, in my correspondence with Mr. Bromley, must I "think have been confined to the expression of my mortification, that an "individual so well capable from education, talents, and station in society, "to become a friend to the poor and illiterate of *all classes and denominations*, should from *narrow-minded prejudices* so much circumscribe the "sphere of his usefulness, by imbibing false alarms for the safety of the "Church In short, the Judge's sentiments upon religious toleration and "general education are so totally different from mine, that however I may "admire the principle of conscientious rectitude, under which he no "doubt acts, I must lament, that it strikes so deep at the root of that true "benevolence which would encourage universal improvement in the mind, "morals, and character of all around him. I can only state how much I "lament, that any original subscribers to the British system of education "in America should have withdrawn their support, as I must believe the "circumstance to have arisen more from the *particular influence of prejudiced minds*, than as the result of a candid enquiry into the merits and "principles of the institution."

In 1814, Mr Stewart, the Solicitor General of Nova Scotia, published, in an handsome volume, Reports of the principal cases decided by me in the Court of Vice-Admiralty, at Halifax, from the commencement of the war in 1802, to the end of the year 1813[1]. They have the merit at least of correctness, as they were taken entirely from my own notes: many of them had been previously printed at the particular request of the counsel, or parties interested These Reports render it unnecessary for me to say any thing of the nature of the business in which I was chiefly employed during my residence in Nova Scotia. I trust they bear internal evidence of the care and industry with which I conscientiously endeavoured to execute

[1] **Reports of Cases, argued and determined in the Court of Vice-Admiralty, at Halifax, in Nova Scotia, from the commencement of the war, in 1802, to the end of the year 1813, in the time of Alexander Croke, LL D., Judge of that Court: by James Stewart, Esq a member of His Majesty's Council, and Solicitor General for the Province of Nova Scotia. Res Judicata pro veritate accipitur Dig London: printed for J. Butterworth and Son, Fleet Street, 1814.**

the duties of my important office, in which I had the arduous task of sitting as umpire between my own countrymen, and the subjects of other nations, as well neutrals, as enemies; of inforcing the maritime rights, and of maintaining the high character of Great Britain for impartial justice to all the world.

The war being apparently ended, by the success of the allies, the banishment of Buonaparte to Elba, and the peace with the United States, there was little employment for a Judge of the Admiralty in Nova Scotia, and I obtained permission from Government to return to England. In the mean time intelligence arrived that Buonaparte was again seated upon the throne of France, and that fresh hostilities had commenced with that country. Nevertheless, I pursued my original intention, and went on board the packet on the 7th of July, 1815, with my whole family. When we arrived near the English coast, a vessel of war of suspicious appearance came in sight, and bore down upon us. As she did not answer any of our signals, it was concluded that she was a French cruizer, our decks were cleared, and every preparation was made for an engagement. There was no possibility of our making any effectual resistance, as she was greatly superior in size and guns to our vessel, and there seemed every probability, that, after a battle, in which we *Civilians* might lose our lives or our limbs, but could acquire no honour, we might look forward to a long captivity in France. At the critical moment, when she came just within gun shot, to our infinite satisfaction, she hoisted British colours, and sent a boat on board us, with an officer, who informed us of the battle of Waterloo, which was just over, that it was not known what had become of Buonaparte, but that it was suspected that he was endeavouring to make his escape to America; and the vessel was the Pelorus, which was cruizing to intercept him. Never was there a greater change from sorrow to joy, and we sat down to our breakfast with unspeakable comfort On the 29th of July, after a favourable voyage of three weeks, we arrived at Falmouth, where we heard that Buonaparte was in safe custody at Plymouth. On Saturday, the 5th of August, after a pleasant journey from Falmouth, through Exeter, Glastonbury, Wells, Bath, and Oxford, we arrived at Studley Priory about four o'clock, where we found our two sons, Alexander and George, and my whole family dined together with an heartfelt satisfaction, which those only can appreciate who have experienced long absences, from their mother country, and painful separations from their dearest connexions.

On the 23d of December, 1815, I tendered my resignation to the Lords of the Admiralty, which was accepted on the 26th. His Majesty's government granted me the annuity of one thousand pounds a year, which had been agreed upon, and was authorized by the Act of Parliament for constituting the Courts of Vice-Admiralty, and I received the King's Letters Patent for it, under the Great Seal, bearing date the 14th of March, 1816. And on the 5th of July in the same year, the Prince Regent bestowed upon me the honour of Knighthood.

I was apprehensive that the Duke of Kent was not well pleased with the decided part which I had taken against his *protegè*, Mr. Bromley, and the Lancastrian and Bible Societies; but I was assured, by gentlemen who had the honour of being in his confidence, that I had no reason to be alarmed, for that his Royal Highness was a man of the *most perfect liberality, and never thought the worse of any person for differing from him in opinion.* Upon these assurances I waited upon him, when I was received with a marked coldness, and an intimation was given me by one of his confidants, that I might spare myself the trouble of farther visits, as I should not be again admitted to the Royal presence. I then discovered that the *liberality* of the *liberales* extends only to those of their own sentiments, and that the *saints* can *persecute*, as far as they have the power. Thus ended the only Royal friendship with which I have had the happiness of being honoured[b]!

Returned thus to my own country, with a competent income, free from the slavery of business, and master of my own time, I might have expected to pass some years of the autumn, or winter, of life, with comfort and tranquillity, in the bosom of my family, the performance of my duty, the improvement of my mind in piety and knowledge, and the innocent pursuits and pleasures of a rational being. But how uncertain is human happiness! After some previous symptoms, I was taken suddenly ill with

[b] Since I wrote the above, his Royal Highness is gone to appear before the sovereign judge of princes, as well as of common men, and who knows the secrets of all hearts. From him he will receive the reward of his works done upon earth, according to their real motives, and principles Peace be to his manes!

giddiness and sickness, in the Bodleian Library, where I was making researches for these collections, on the 29th of July, 1819. This attack proved the prelude to a most calamitous illness, upon the 17th of September, an oppression of the brain, which produced the effects of a lethargy. For many days I lay totally senseless, at other times I was delirious, and I had no recollection afterwards of what had passed for nearly a fortnight. On the 24th of September, I seemed convulsed, my pulse began to fail, I was thought to be in great and imminent danger, and my life was totally despaired of. By the assistance of the physicians of Oxford, the Doctors Wall, Bourne, and Kidd, and the application of powerful remedies, I was relieved from this situation, so distressing to my beloved wife, and my other friends, and I was gradually restored to health, and strength. My recovery was thought by the physicians to have been almost miraculous, to me it appeared altogether so. I hope I am sufficiently thankful to my heavenly Father for this his great mercy in delivering me from the snares of death which encompassed me, and that I shall ever consider this new portion of worldly existence as graciously bestowed upon me, to enable me to work out my salvation, and to be the better prepared for that state of eternal happiness, which God has promised to those who faithfully serve him. The remainder of my life, whether short or long, does not seem likely to be marked by any great variety of events, and little more will remain to be added to this account than the day of my departure.

Providence has blessed me and my dear wife Alice with eleven children, named, Alexander, Adelaide, George, Jane Sarah Elizabeth, Wentworth, Anne Philippa, Charlotte, John, Frances Mary Territt, Le Blount, and another Alexander. Of all these, the eldest Alexander alone is no more.

The fondness of a parent may be excused for calling to mind, and committing to paper, the few and uniform events of the life of a beloved son, who was taken away at the immature age of one and twenty. And yet, if I am not deceived by paternal affection, I cannot but think that this simple narrative will be interesting, and that the example of so excellent a young man will be useful, even to those who were not personally acquainted with his merits.

Alexander Croke was born in Gloucester Street, Queen's Square, on

On the 16th July at All Saints Church, Paddington, JOHN CROKE, Esq., of Corton House, Radnorshire, sole survivor of the issue of the late Sir Alexander Croke, of Studley Priory, Oxfordshire, [illegible] daughter of the [illegible] of [illegible], county Leitrim, and widow of JAMES [illegible] CROKE, Commander R.N. [illegible]

Monday the twenty-third day of April, 1798, at twenty minutes after seven o'clock in the morning. He was baptized at Queen Square Chapel, now St. George the Martyr's Church, by the Reverend George Huddesford, the author of Salmagundi, and other poetical pieces. Mr. and Mrs. Parker and myself were the sponsors. He was a very delicate child, and often unwell: when he was about two months old he was given over. At about three months, the 18th of July, he was placed with Mrs. Moore, a healthy young woman at Walworth, and his health was much improved. He was a very pretty child, and ladies often stopped his nurse to enquire to whom he belonged, observing that he must be a lady's child, and not her's. On the 29th of April, 1799, he was inoculated with the small pox, vaccination not being then known, and on the 26th of March, 1800, we took him home to our hired house at Walworth. In the beginning of May, 1801, he was ill of a fever, and was attended by Dr. Latham.

The same year, he accompanied us to Nova Scotia. We embarked at Portsmouth on the tenth of September, 1801, and arrived at Halifax on the eleventh of November, he being then above three years and a half old. He was much admired as a fine lively child, with uncommon sense for his years. He shewed, even then, a remarkably correct *tact*, and a sensibility to the peculiar character and situation of those with whom he conversed: his conversation to one person being very different from what it was to another, and suitable to their particular case.

He continued with us in Nova Scotia till 1806, when he came to England, under the care of Captain Sir Robert Laurie, Baronet, on board the Milan. This had been a French frigate, called La Ville de Milan, having been built by that city, carrying 46 guns, but intended for a seventy-four, and which had been brought to, and engaged in a most severe and gallant action, by Sir Robert, in the Cleopatra, of thirty-two guns only, the French ship being double her force in size, compliment of men, and weight of metal. The Ville de Milan would have been taken but for an unlucky accident, by which the Cleopatra was rendered immoveable and in consequence was compelled to surrender. Both vessels were reduced to perfect wrecks, and were taken possession of by Captain Talbot, who came up soon after the action in the Leander, without a gun being fired. After they were taken, the Milan was given to Sir Robert, as a just reward for his gallantry. Alexander went with great alacrity, and confessed, when he was older, that his reason for wishing to go to England was, "that he thought he should have no more lessons to learn" By such trifling, and often unobserved motives, are the wishes and actions of children, and their determination to this or that mode of life or profession, frequently directed! They sailed on the 6th of February, at 10 o'clock, and arrived at Portsmouth. During the voyage, he gained the favour of Sir Robert Laurie, and every person on board, by his spirit and resolution, good-humour, and liveliness. "I assure you," said Sir Robert, in a letter which I received from him at Spithead, "it was with much regret, myself "and officers parted with him. A better disposed, or more charming boy "could not be. Alexander has many friends in the Milan, and will never "want them wherever he goes."

He was now nearly eight years of age, and had been entirely educated by his mother, except a little Latin which I had taught him and few boys of his standing were ever better instructed. Upon his arrival in England, he was placed under the care of the Rev Charles Richards, at Hyde Abbey School, at Winchester, preparatory to his going to a public school. His conduct here, as Mr Richards informed me, "was distinguished by "diligence, good temper, and regularity: in his education he shewed a "fine capacity, and was making all the improvement which could be de-"sired." Soon after he came from Halifax he was nearly choked by a plum stone.

I came to England for a few months in 1810, brought his brother George with me, and placed him at Mr Richards's; but during my stay here, Alexander was removed to Harrow. Doctor Butler was the Head Master, and he was boarded in the house of the Reverend Mark Drury.

During our absence in Nova Scotia, he passed his holidays with my sister, Mrs. Parker, at Beckley, who had all the affection and attention of a parent for him. Besides his aunt, he met with great kindness from many other friends, with whom he sometimes passed part of his time. During the holidays, he used to ride to Oxford three times a week, to be instructed in Greek and Latin, by the Rev. Mr Firth, of Corpus Christi College; which he continued whilst he was at Harrow.

In the Christmas holidays of 1811, and afterwards, he attended the Abbè Bertin, at Oxford, to learn French. The Abbè had left France in the Revolution, and resided 25 years at that University, teaching French, and was a man of learning and respectability. The gentlemen of the University treated him with great attention, and he was particularly intimate with the Bishops of Oxford, Randolph, and Jackson, with whom he spent much time at Cuddesden. Alexander was a great favourite with the Abbè, and Bishop Jackson having once seen him on horseback, sent a message by Bertin, that "he should be happy to see him, and would "shew him his palace." In the Christmas holidays of 1812, the Abbè invited him to call upon him at Cuddesden, where he was upon a visit, to be introduced to the Bishop, but on the day he went there, the Bishop happened not to be at home. On his return, the Bishop sent him another message, that "he should be happy to see him without waiting for a re-"gular introduction," yet he never repeated his visit Upon the restoration of the monarchy, the Abbè returned to France, and at his departure gave Alexander, as a token of his friendship, Vertot's Revolutions Romaines, and the works of Monsieur Coffin, Rector of the University of Paris, in Latin prose and verse, with assurances that he wished he could have seen him come to the University, that he should be happy to see him at Abbeville, and hoped he would remember that "there was once a "Frenchman who had a great regard for him." Such was the general esteem he met with.

On the 23d of July, 1814, he suffered a great loss in the death of Mrs Parker. With every proper feeling upon this occasion he shewed good sense and steadiness, far above his years, which were only sixteen. He informed us of the melancholy event by a letter, in which he says, "I "received a letter from you, containing your praise and approbation of my "compositions, which had made me as happy as possible.—George's re-"covery, the prospect of seeing you all soon, and the more immediate "expectation of these holidays, had all conduced to perfect my felicity, "but it was ordained to be otherwise. How shocking is the task which "devolves upon me, of informing you, for I must no longer hesitate, of "the death of our most dear, and ever to be lamented, aunt, which took "place on Saturday, at about ten minutes before one o'clock, at Studley. "Never was any thing more awful or sudden" He then describes her catching a cold, which ended in an inflammation on her lungs, and their sending for Doctor Bourne. Alexander was at Harrow, but was sent for. To his great agony, she was dead before his arrival "Thus," he proceeds,

" my dear father, distressing as it has been to me, I have related to you " these sad particulars, which I leave to you to break to my dear mother. " You will be equally shocked, but I hope my mother will not be too " much afflicted, at the idea of our being left alone, and will have confidence " in our friends Thus it has pleased the Almighty to deprive us of her, " who has been to us as a parent, the loss is irreparable till your return, " but still I do not repine, I grieve The Lord gave, and the Lord hath " taken away, blessed be the name of the Lord. Even in this affliction " there are blessings. How thankful am I that this did not take place " before; every thing conduces to shew how kind have been the dispens- " ations of Providence, dear George's recovery, the prospect of your " return, &c. must have all rendered her happy, had she any idea of her " death. O could she but have lived to see you again! The greatest " portion of our happiness will be taken away, and I fear we must meet " under affliction. Upon thinking of the pleasures of these holidays, some- " thing used lately to whisper to me, that they would be debarred, and thus " it has pleased God to do it. But enough of these melancholy effusions. " Whatever you may intend to do, with respect to your return, I hope " you will have sufficient dependence on my prudence. I have consulted " my friends in every measure." He then mentions the civilities he had received, and the invitations which had been given to him and his brother George, "but," he observes, " all our visits may be a diversion of our at- " tention, but they cannot be a pleasure. How I dread sending this " letter to you I am alarmed for the affliction of my dear mother · but " I hope the Almighty will enable her to bear it. I am comforted by " knowing, that my poor aunt received a letter from me, and one from " you, a day or two before her death." In another letter he says, " Cala- " mitous as this may be at present, I hope the Almighty will alleviate our " afflictions. I trust that she is now a saint in heaven, free from all her " anxieties and labours."

In a subsequent letter, he gives an account of the kindness of his friends upon this melancholy occasion, for which he says he shall ever be thankful and he adds, " this last sad event has doubled my wishes and anxiety " about your return; I trust the Almighty will grant you all a safe one, " and although perhaps it may not take place just yet, I trust you will " consider us here under sufficient human protection, (and, I trust, under "the protection of God;) and again I will repeat, I hope you have suffi-"cient confidence in me. Shocking is the doubt to me, whether you are "still happy, or now afflicted. (As he did not know whether we had "received his former letter, giving an account of my sister's death.) I hope "my poor mother's health may not be injured by the shock. Sometimes "I think Providence will manage every thing for us all, and that we shall "not suffer any thing material by my dear aunt's death, and therefore "snatched her from her innumerable troubles and anxieties, of which none "but ourselves can have any idea This now reminds me of what she has "told me, that *no one knows what poor aunt has gone through.*

"*Durum, sed levius fit patientiâ*
"*Quicquid corrigere est nefas.*

"It makes me very melancholy to think that I am about to leave this "house (Beckley,) where I have spent so many happy days, and that I "may perhaps never enter it again. Adieu." In after times, and particularly in his last sickness, he frequently recollected with a melancholy pleasure the happy days which he had spent with his aunt, in his early youth. He often stood for some time on a spot, from whence he could see the church, and repeated, "Ah! poor Beckley!" evidently much affected.

In another letter, after he had been informed of our intention of returning to England, he says, "I have had great pleasure and amusement "these holidays, but I look forward to real happiness after my leaving "Harrow. The Almighty has taken away one, but *He* will restore to me "two parents, I trust. What happy preparations would my poor dear "aunt have made for you all! What a recompence would she have "thought it for all her anxieties!"

During his continuance at Harrow, he was remarkable for propriety of conduct, and shewed considerable abilities. Though the letters which are usually written by school-masters are frequently matters of course, yet I believe that those which were written by his preceptors, both at Winchester and Harrow, were sincere, and dictated by a genuine regard for him, founded upon real merit. In a letter of the 28th of November, 1814, brought to me by Sir James Cockburn, the Governor of Bermuda, Mark Drury says, "It affords me real pleasure and satisfaction "to inform you, that your son has conducted himself with the greatest "propriety, ever since you confided him to my care and attention. "His improvement fully corresponds with my expectations, and his "rank amongst his associates as a scholar is a most agreeable recompence "for his assiduity and talents. When you come to England, you will, I "trust, acknowledge that I do not draw a flattering, but a true, picture of "my young friend. His general behaviour to Mrs. Drury and myself is "most exemplary, and has created in our minds a most sincere interest "in his happiness. My friend, Sir James Cockburn, was desired by me "to state to you, as accurately as possible, my sentiments of your son's "qualities and progress. Sir James is a sensible man, and well ac-"quainted with human nature. I conceive therefore you would derive "singular pleasure and comfort from the representation of a gentleman, "who has frequently conversed with me on the subject of my letter, and "who has also been able to form an opinion of your son's attainments, by "the different interviews which occurred, when Sir James resided in our "parish. On a late melancholy occasion, (the death of my sister, Mrs. "Parker,) your son behaved with uncommon sensibility and propriety. "He consulted my advice, though it was unnecessary; indeed we live "together as much like two friends as you can conjecture. If our friend "had not offered his hospitable mansion at that time, under my roof your "son would have met with a comfortable reception. Indeed he will "always be considered in my family as a connexion of real value." In another letter, upon the occasion of his death, he confirms these sentiments "The sad event afflicted me and Mrs. Drury most severely "The dear good fellow always behaved to us as an affectionate son. He "never required reproof. It would be fortunate if all young men were "equally correct in mind and conduct. He must be happy."

The account thus given by Mr. Drury was fully confirmed by Sir James Cockburn, who spoke of him in the most flattering terms, and informed me that he was considered as the best scholar, and, to use the words of Doctor Butler, as the "crack boy," of the school. His verses were frequently "read up" by the master, which was the custom of Harrow, when they were particularly good, and he obtained a great many prize books for his poetical exercises. He had quite a little library of them, including handsome editions of Lucretius, Aristotle's Poetics, Longinus,

Cicero de Oratore, De Finibus, and his Tusculan Disputations, Oudendorp's Cæsar's Commentaries, Thucydides, Pindar, and Lucan

As he was then fit for the University, he quitted Harrow upon the 26th of July, 1815. His farewell verses were said to have been one of the best compositions which had ever been made upon a similar occasion.

Farewell Verses at leaving Harrow.

Βαινομεν αχνυμενοι, θαλερον κατα δακρυ χεοντες.

At length, five years elapsed, with painful heart,
I bid adieu to Harrow, and depart.
Must I then go, and ev'ry tempest brave,
Launch into life, and seek the troubled wave?
And will not Time restrain his swift career,
That pleas'd awhile I yet may tarry here,
A parting look at Lyon's structure cast,
And waken sweet remembrance of the past?
Then stop, my muse; and, ere I take my way,
Crown this last labour, and inspire the lay.
Seats of my youth! Alas, a busy train
Of joys, now fled, excites my mournful strain;
In contemplation starts the silent tear,
Recalling to my view each happy year;
My heart recoils whilst of those days I tell,
And on those hours, as if now present, dwell.
While blushing Spring still linger'd o'er the plain,
And Summer swift advanced his ardent train,
How oft have I through yon lone church-yard stray'd,
Where Lanfranc's steeple measures out its shade;
And, pausing, view'd beneath the village scene,
The sports loud echoing of the joyous green;
Or gaz'd where Windsor's turrets meet the eye,
Bright with the sun, when first he mounts on high;
Or where Augusta's clouded temples rise,
And smoky volumes mingle with the skies.
Sweet was the time, when 'neath the oak's broad shade,
I oft reclining sought th' Aonian maid,
Sang Britain's triumphs o'er her conquer'd foes,
Gallia's fell tyrant and her num'rous woes;
Or Nature's myst'ries when I dar'd t' explore,
Or trace the fables told in days of yore.

How fresh, how happy shone the coming day,
When all, in pleasure, cheerfulness, and play,
Enjoy'd their pastime, and from study free,
Renewed their sports, and gave their hearts to glee
These were thy joys, delightful Ida, these
Beguil'd the hours, and taught e'en toil to please
Oh! that, his course thus pleasantly begun,
Man e'er should cease in happiness to run!
All sport, unweeting, but grim Death stands near,
And fate relentless marks its victims here
Long will these pleasures of our early days
Entitle Harrow to my ardent praise,
And all these blithesome scenes of play and mirth
Endear its name, and well enhance its worth.
Yet these are transient—but that nobler toil,
Those youthful studies by the midnight oil,
Which first my mind exalted, and at length
By hope encouraged, gave it early strength,
Have left a treasure, that will ever last,
And time, swift gliding, ne'er its fruits shall blast
Where'er I go, this benefits me still,
And must with gratitude my bosom fill.
Farewell, my Teachers; first indeed to you
My warmest thanks and all my praise are due
Your cares I hope to cherish while I live,
And feel the precepts ye were wont to give.
Accept this humble tribute of my Muse
Nor what the glowing heart inspires, refuse.
If ever Virtue's riches should be mine,
In Wisdom's honours if I e'er should shine,
To you, kind Guardians, I shall owe my fame,
And bless th' instructions, whence that learning came[d]

ALEXANDER CROKE.

Read over by Dr. Butler in the school, July 24, 1815

The four lines in Italics seem to have been too truly prophetic of his own future fortunes, and on that account are tinged with a deep melancholy pathos which all must feel.

[d] For a specimen of his Latin verses, see Appendix, No XXXVII b

To the great joy of our two sons, after a favourable voyage of three weeks, we landed at Falmouth from Nova Scotia, on the 29th of July, 1815. I wrote to inform them of our arrival, and desired them to repair immediately to Studley to meet us. We reached that place about four o'clock, on the 5th of August, where we found Alexander and George ready to receive us, and, for the first time, our whole family dined together, to our unspeakable joy and happiness; though the death of my poor sister was a great drawback upon our pleasure.

Alexander having left Harrow continued with us the whole summer. He had been entered as a Commoner at Oriel College, the 9th of December, 1814, and he went now to reside, on the 21st of October, 1815. My old friend Doctor Eveleigh, the Provost, died the very day he entered, and Doctor Copleston had succeeded him. Messieurs Davison, Whately, James, and Keble, were successively his tutors, and the college was in the highest repute for discipline, learning, and abilities. For an account of his conduct here, I shall introduce a letter from Mr. Davison.

To Sir Alexander Croke.

Dear Sir,

The conduct of your son, during the time that he has been with us, has been such as to receive the strongest approbation of his college. He has been most consistent in regularity of manners and habits, and seems to have laid on him the foundation that will make him a valuable character in life. With a strong sense of duty and principle, he has an ingenuous modesty of disposition, which renders him a pupil whom it is a most agreeable office to instruct or direct. We have hitherto found him studious and attentive, with a real desire for his own improvement, without which there can be no success, and in his classical reading he has made a considerable progress.

I remain, Dear Sir,

Your faithful humble servant,

Oxford, July 2, 1816. JOHN DAVISON.

With regard to his studies, whilst at Oxford, he was most attached to the classics, and took little pleasure in mathematics. For Latin verse he always retained the fondness which is generally acquired at public schools.

Although not required at the University, he sometimes made a copy of verses instead of a theme; as once when the thesis given was, *Our native soil*, he translated the 137th psalm into lyrics, which was much approved of by his tutor, and was thought very applicable to the subject. In 1816, he wrote for the Chancellor's prize, upon the subject of *The Druids*, but did not obtain it, though he found the practice and exertion employed in the composition of service to him.

Upon his first entering at Oxford, I thought it necessary to guard against the ill consequences which might arise from his conceiving that he was a young man of fortune. I told him therefore, candidly, that although I had a tolerable estate, yet that as I could not make one of my sons rich and leave the rest in poverty, I must provide for all my children, and therefore that he had to expect but a moderate income from me. It would be necessary therefore for him to follow some profession, not for the name only, but as a means of gaining an honourable livelihood. I left the choice to himself, gave him time to consider of it, and stated the nature of the different professions, and the prospects which they afforded him. Upon his return home at Christmas, he told me that he wished to study the law, and to be called to the bar, a determination of which I approved, as I thought that it was best suited to his situation in life, and that his application and talents would afford a reasonable probability of success. Accordingly, on the 27th of April, 1816, he was entered of the Inner Temple, my own Inn of Court, and that of our great ancestor Sir George Croke. On the 28th of October he passed his first examination for his degree by Messrs. Cotton and Keble with credit, in Herodotus, three books of Euclid, the Eclogues and Georgics of Virgil.

But all these fair hopes were early destroyed, and, in fact, terminated with his departure from Harrow. From that period, his health began to decay, and he continued declining during the whole of his continuance at Oxford. From being strong, hearty, and lively, as he described the state of his health in a letter to me, he grew pale and thin by degrees, his strength was reduced, his nerves, sight, and memory, and his faculties, in general, grew weak. In June, 1816, by riding fast after dinner, he hurt his stomach, from which he never recovered. By this weakness, indigestions, and irregularity in the viscera, and the uneasiness which they occasioned, he was prevented from entering into the ordinary pleasures of life, and was unable to apply himself with any degree of vigour to his studies; at some times he was totally incapable of reading at all, and even was deprived of the use of his voice. Although therefore his strong sense of duty impelled him to exert himself, he was not able to do more than what was absolutely necessary for his lectures and terminal examinations, and even this degree of application he was at last obliged to give over. Except occasionally some lyrics, and the poem on the Druids, he seems to have done nothing in reading, or writing, beyond the mere routine of the college, and he very early abandoned all idea of taking a degree in the higher classes; which, as well as his obtaining some of the prizes of the University, his masters at Harrow had confidently expected from him.

And indeed, the last term he was at Oxford, he was most unwillingly compelled to appear very deficient at the collections, or examinations which are held in the college, before the vacations, having been able to make little use of his time, and, as he expressed it, "to make less return "for the attention of his teachers." For this apparent negligence, of which his instructors were not made acquainted with the reason, he incurred, for the first time, what appeared to be their just displeasure, and received a reprimand from the Provost. Reproaches, to which he was entirely unaccustomed, I believe dwelt much upon his mind, and he wrote a letter, on the 2d of July, 1818, to the Provost, to communicate to him the cause of his seeming negligence, in which he explained fully the state of his health, and that "the frequent returns of pain, inconveniences, and morti-"fications that he experienced, had prevented him from any serious "exercises of mind or body, for hours together, so that he was not at all "times able to read over his lectures, and made it impracticable for him "to enter into that active intercourse with others, and even with his "friends and school-fellows in the University, which is peculiar to young "men." It had however been admitted to him, at the time of his reprimand, that he had been regular in his attendance at chapel, upon which he observes, in the true spirit of a religious mind, that "this had been a "service of perfect freedom, and although he had been sometimes obliged "to absent himself, and it had often been painful to him to appear in the "evening, yet he was happy that it had been always in his power to be "in chapel before the service was begun."

To this letter the Provost returned a very kind and friendly answer

Oriel College, July 9, 1818

My dear Sir,

I have just read with great concern the statement you have sent me of your impaired health. I was not aware that you suffered to the extent you speak of, nor indeed that you suffered from general indisposition at all. I am too sensible of the distress caused by indigestion, not to sympathize most sincerely with a fellow sufferer. If any thing of this kind had been suspected by us last term, you cannot suppose we should have expressed the displeasure we did. I wish you had at the time stated this plainly and distinctly. No one accuses you of idleness, or want of excellent principles, and a good heart It only appeared to us that there was a constitutional languor, which called for some stimulus. You have now explained the case in such a way, as to secure you from every thing like reprimand in future, and I am sure all those under whose care and authority you are placed will act towards you with the greatest tenderness

In expressing my sincere wishes for the re-establishment of your health, I must also repeat the high opinion I have always entertained of your character, and remain, my dear Sir,

With great regard,

Yours very sincerely,

E. COPLESTON.

Yet although his prospects of worldly happiness and honours were so soon clouded, and ultimately destroyed, Providence had other, and better, things in store for him From his childhood, he had always been a good and prudent young man, with a proper sense of his duties, and his later valetudinarian state of health contributed to preserve him from many of the temptations of youth, and awakened him to a still more serious consideration of divine things. He then thought that the accident of his having been nearly choked with a plum stone "was a merciful dispensa-"tion of Providence, ordained for his correction." The very day on which he hurt his stomach, June 4th, 1816, and which was the beginning of that specific complaint which ended in his dissolution, he began to read two chapters every day in the Bible, in Mant's edition, with the notes, commencing with Genesis, and the Acts of the Apostles; a practice which had been suggested to him by Mr. Rolleston, of University College, in a sermon at St. Mary's. He considered this as another great mercy, and observed upon it, "that it would seem as if his heavenly Father had "given him his word to teach him how to amend his life, at the same "time that he laid these calamities upon him." His continual illness, his sense of God's goodness, the study of the Bible, together with the serious considerations which entered into his mind when he began to receive the Sacrament, assisted by the Divine grace, had produced a religious state of soul, as perfect in every Christian virtue as perhaps human nature will admit of, and gradually prepared him for the kingdom of heaven, a blessing infinitely more valuable than all the wealth and greatness which the world could have bestowed.

From June 1816, when he met with the accident before mentioned, to the same month in 1818, he continued to be an invalid, but without much alteration for the worse, and his stomach was not so far deprived of its powers as to prevent him from eating moderately. But having hurt it again three or four times in the term preceding the long vacation in that year, by having been compelled to walk too soon after dinner, about Oxford, with friends and visitors, a circumstance which always very much disordered him, and the weather having been uncommonly hot at that time, he was rendered extremely weak, and his complaint was greatly increased. From that period his digestion was so impaired, that he was never able to take more than one third of his usual quantity of food; indeed if he eat more than about three table spoonfuls at once, his stomach was overloaded, and he was uneasy for three or four hours afterwards. Nor could he drink till about an hour after his meal, and that by sipping leisurely, without bringing on an indigestion. It seemed upon the whole, that it was the quantity of food, whether solid or liquid, rather than the quality, which disagreed with him. To use his own words, "it was no "more possible for him to go regularly through a dinner from soup to de- "sert, eating or drinking just as it happens, than it would be to empty a "tureen filled with meat, vegetables, and soup, into a tea-pot" It was another inconvenience to him, that he could not venture to eat soon after exercise, and was obliged to sit completely still for an hour or two after meals, and that he could not move from place to place, or use the smallest exercise, during that time, without bringing on an indigestion

From an amiable disposition, and a wish not to give uneasiness to his friends, he had concealed his real state of health, and we had no idea that he was seriously ill, till about the 20th of September, in 1818, when he explained his situation to me fully, in a letter, from which I have given most of the above account. Till then we had attributed his abstemiousness and singularity more to whim, and a fantastic system of physic, and valetudinarianism, which people often adopt, than to any real disorder, and we were therefore endeavouring to laugh him out of it His good humour readily excused our joking, and his good sense induced him to adhere to a plan which was necessary to his comfort. The opinions of the medical men, who had been consulted, contributed still more to deceive us. Upon his first accident, Mr. Grosvenor, and Mr. Tuckwell, two eminent surgeons at Oxford, were applied to, and on the 30th of March, 1818, I took him to Doctor Latham. They were unanimously of opinion that his complaints proceeded merely from weakness, occasioned by his growing, and his youth, and prescribed steel, and such medicines, with every flattering assurance of a speedy recovery.

After his letter had made me acquainted with the full extent of his disorder, I sent him to London, on the 20th of October, 1818, for the best medical advice He consulted Carlisle, who was equally positive that it was merely a case of weakness, without any local injury having been received in the stomach, and recommended the same class of medicines, and diet, which he had before taken He stayed three weeks in London, and shocked us inexpressibly, by the dreadful change which had taken place in that short period. Upon his return, on the 7th of November, he was reduced to a mere skeleton, his eyes were sunk in his head, and his voice was altered, and hollow. As Mr. Carlisle had spoken with confidence of the probability of his recovery, we still entertained hopes from the effects of his medicines. No benefit was received; he gradually grew weaker, and could scarcely bear any food at all. Doctor Bourne was sent for, and at his first visit despaired of a recovery. His brother George was expected home in a few days from Harrow. He said he wished only to live to see him. He arrived on Wednesday the 9th of December, but on that day Alexander felt himself so weak, that he went to bed at four o'clock. On the 10th, he came down to breakfast, and stayed up till about four. The next day, Friday the 11th, he got up for a short time, but he fainted away, and when he recovered, he told his nurse that he thought he was dying.

The next day, Saturday the 12th, he was unable to get up I thought it proper to have some discourse with him respecting his situation. About eleven o'clock in the morning, I went into his room, and finding him easy, and composed, I entered into conversation with him, to prepare him for receiving the sacrament, Mr. Jenkins being expected to come that morning to administer it.

I began by observing, that in his afflictions, and during his long and painful disorder, he had had the greatest consolation which could be enjoyed, in the consciousness that he had led a good and religious life, and that for a year or two past, his time had been almost entirely spent in the duties of holy reading and devotion.

He assented to my observation, and said, "I am perfectly easy and "happy in that respect I have always endeavoured to follow the example of my Saviour, and, like him, I have always been meek, and serving, "in the world[e]. I have never been a man of the world. If it should "please God to take me, I have no doubt of my salvation."

Finding him in this excellent state of mind, I sent for his mother, as I knew it would give her the greatest happiness Upon her arrival, he repeated nearly the same things, and added, "It has been my practice for "more than two years to read two chapters every day in the Bible, with "the notes, and I think that it has given me a better idea of the Christian "religion than reading long treatises would do From this practice, I "may say that I out-shone all the other young men at college at the divinity lectures My reading the Bible prepared my mind to perform my "duty properly at church. I wish you all, particularly my brothers and "sisters, to do the same. I leave my Bible with notes to you, my father, "as a legacy. But you are learned, and do not want it, but it will do "for them all to read; and I wish that the Prayer Book with notes, now

[e] See Luke xxii. 26, 27.

"about to be published as a companion to the Bible, may be procured, "and read also.

"I thank God, and I think it a great blessing, that I was born of a "good family, and of virtuous parents, who have set me a proper ex- "ample, and have instructed me in the way I should go. It is impossible "to know what God Almighty, with whom a thousand years are but as "one day, and one day as a thousand years, has ordained in respect to our "family, but I trust that they will all do well, and that not one of them "will fall into condemnation. My father, you may think it childish, but "it always strikes me, that boys do things without considering or under- "standing them, or without thinking what connexion they may have with "their future life George's carpentering for instance. Our Saviour when "a boy, was probably brought up to that trade. George was intended "for the church, but that is now altered.

"I wish to receive the Sacrament, and if I look at my pocket-book, I "can tell how often I have had that honour." (Upon looking into his pocket-book, after he was no more, it appeared that he had regularly set down every time of receiving it, and that the last was on Whit-sunday, the 10th of May, opposite to which he had written, "10th, Received the "Sacrament the 15th time.")

I asked him if I should read to him, or say any prayers He thanked me, and hastily and earnestly mentioned the fifty-third chapter of Isaiah. but said that we should have prayers by and by, and as I was afraid of fatiguing him, I did not read to him, and he did not mention it again

He then said, "I do not know what I have done to be cut off so early "in my youth. If I recover, I have laid down a plan for my future life. "I may recover, as I do not think my vital powers are affected, but I "have no objection to be carried by angels into Abraham's bosom. My "sufferings have been great, but they are nothing in comparison to what "some experience, who have no hopes of eternal life How horrid, how "dreadful, must be the prospect of those, who know from their wicked "lives that they must be lost everlastingly. I have not been like the fool- "ish virgins, who, when the Lord came, applied to the other virgins for "oil for their lamps. I have endeavoured to keep my lamp trimmed, and "I am not now to seek."

This is all I was able to recollect of his discourse at this time, perhaps not entirely in the order in which he delivered it, but perfectly correct as to the substance, and mostly as to the words. He afterwards talked of indifferent subjects, with his mind perfectly easy, and unembarrassed

Soon after this conversation, Mr. Jenkins came, and administered the Sacrament. Lady Croke, my daughter Adelaide, Mrs. Marshall, our housekeeper, Mrs. Jones, one of his nurses, and myself, received it with him. He seemed very devout, and made the responses firm and loud, lying in bed. The remainder of the day, and during the whole of Sunday, he was very weak, occasionally in great pain, but seemed to suffer most from restlessness, often requiring to be turned in his bed, which was attended with great trouble and pain from his soreness within side. On Sunday morning he wished us to go to chapel to pray for him, and, at night, his brothers and sisters, with his mother and myself, took leave of him, about eleven o'clock, and all kissed him He was then perfectly sensible, but restless, and as no particular change had taken place, it appeared to us that he might have continued in the same state for some time, but about one o'clock, he seemed to be a little light-headed, wished, with some impatience, to get up, and to go down stairs; and complained of their wanting him to go to Beckley, which he said would kill him. They endeavoured to quiet him by telling him that every body was gone to bed, but he observed, that if his father was there he would dress him in a minute, and would not let them serve him so cruelly. Upon this I was called up, and found him calm and composed, but unable to speak articulately. He wanted something which we could not understand, and to every thing of his usual wants which we mentioned, he shook his head He then lay perfectly quiet, muttered to himself for a little while in a faint murmur, his lips just moving, and in a short time ceased to breathe, without any struggle, groan, or emotion, at twenty minutes past one o'clock on Monday morning, the 14th of December, 1818.

During his illness, he sometimes seemed to consider himself as near his end; as when he told the boy who attended him, that he should have all the money which would be found in his purse; but more generally he used to say that he thought his vital powers were not affected. Such is the self-deception, and the unwillingness to die, which is peculiar to human nature, even in the best of men! Or rather, such was God's special mercy to him, that although he had a sufficient sense of his danger to prepare for that awful event, yet he was relieved from the most alarming apprehensions of approaching death, which is naturally painful to all How wonderful must have been his surprise, and how exquisite must have been his sensations, when he awoke from death, which he knew not that he had passed through, and found himself so unexpectedly in the regions of the blessed, and was received and congratulated by his Saviour, the holy angels, and the souls of good men made perfect, amongst whom, we humbly trust, were some of his dearest friends and relations!

In his last illness, besides the Bible with notes, he read daily in the Prayer Book. Nelson's Festivals, and Taylor's Holy Living, were two other books which he used, and he observed, that "in time he should come "to Taylor's Holy Dying." He read, morning and evening, two prayers which I had drawn up for his brother George, and which he kept in a drawer in his dressing table, with a quire of whitybrown paper to kneel on. He observed once to Mrs. Marshall, who assisted him in going to bed, that "he had been used to say his prayers to her when he was a "child."

On a paper, in his pocket book, are two lists of certain Psalms, over which he had written, "Best." The first list consists of the 72d, 19th, 24th, 63d, 85th, 65th, 96th, 98th, 99th, 23d, 80th, 81st, 22d, 29th, and the 45th. The second list contains the 18th, 34th, 90th, 91st, 42d, 43d, 50th, 68th, 77th, 78th, 84th, 103d, 104th, and 107th, and he refers to notes 71 and 75, upon Psalm the 119th, and note 11 upon the 51st Psalm.

Of these two lists it may be observed, that the *first* consists of psalms of the sublimest character, and those which are most prophetic of Christ, and his kingdom. But the *second* list is composed of Psalms adapted to individuals, and contain complaints of the shortness of life, of afflictions, and disquietude of soul, of hope in God, trust in his deliverance, thanks for mercies received, and descriptions of the blessedness of God's service. These were probably the Psalms which he felt to be most in harmony with his own state of mind in his illness. But the notes, to which he last refers, may be considered as exhibiting the exact picture of his own soul, in the very last stage of life. "It is good for me that I have been afflicted, "that I might learn thy statutes. There is a class of most important "duties, which can only be practised in affliction; namely, patience and "composure under distress, pain, and affliction a stedfast keeping up of "our confidence in God, and our dependence upon His final goodness, "even at a time when every thing present is discouraging and adverse, "and, what is no less difficult to retain, a cordial desire for the happiness "and comfort of others, even then, when we are deprived of our own. "The possession of this temper is almost the perfection of our nature. "But it is then only possessed when put to the trial tried at all it could "not have been in a life made up only of pleasure and gratification. It is "in the chambers of sickness, under the strokes of affliction, amidst the "pinchings of want, the groans of pain, the pressures of infirmity; in "grief, in misfortune; through gloom and horror, that it will be seen, "whether we hold fast our hope, our confidence, our trust in God; "whether this hope and confidence be able to produce in us resignation, "acquiescence, and submission[f]." "From whatever quarter afflictions come "upon us, they are the judgments of God, without whose providence nothing befalls us His judgments are always right, or just, duly proportioned to the disease and strength of the patient, in sending them "God is faithful and true to his word, wherein He hath never promised "the crown without the cross, but hath, on the contrary, assured us, that "one will be necessary, in order to our obtaining the other, and that they "who are beloved by him shall not sin with impunity, nor go astray without a call to return[g]." "The soul that is truly penitent dreads nothing "but the thought of being rejected from the presence, and deserted by the "Spirit, of God. This is the most deplorable effect of sin, but it is one "that in general, perhaps, is the least considered and regarded of all "others[h]." To the searching trial of severe and long-continued afflic-

[f] Note 71, to the 119th Psalm, in Doyly and Mant's Bible, from Paley, on verse the 71st, It is good for me that I have been afflicted, &c.

[g] Note 75, on the verse, I know, O Lord, that thy judgments are right, and that thou in faithfulness hast afflicted me. From Bp Horne.

[h] Note to Ps. li v. 11. Cast me not away from thy presence, and take not thy Holy Spirit from me From Bp Horne

tions, it was the will of the Judge of all mankind to expose his virtues, and he passed through them triumphantly. In pain, and distress, he performed in the highest degree the appropriate duties of patience, and composure; of resignation and submission to God's will; of a full confidence in him, and a sincere anxiety for the happiness of others. This temper, justly styled by Doctor Paley, *the perfection of our nature*, he fully possessed, and as he bore his cross meekly, so he has no doubt received the crown of immortal glory!

Such was the truly religious life and character, and such the happy death, of this excellent young man. In this account of him, I have described his feelings and state of mind, and the history of his sickness, in his own words, and I have chiefly taken the particulars of his outward conduct from the disinterested testimony of others. A few more circumstances remain to be added, to complete the account. He was a handsome, well-formed young man, of a manly, and not of an effeminate appearance, and without the smallest alloy of vanity, self-conceit, or affectation. In his countenance there was a mixture of good sense, and mildness, which was uncommonly interesting, and which prepossessed even strangers in his favour There was something peculiarly elegant in his manner, his attitudes, his motions, and his manner of speaking, which I could not but observe even in his last conversations with Doctor Bourne. When he was well, he was very active, and was always cheerful, even in his last illness, as far as pain and weakness would permit it. To his aunt, his father and mother, and his instructors, he was dutiful and affectionate; for his brothers and sisters he had the kindness, care, and consideration, rather of a parent than of a brother, and paid the greatest attention to their welfare, and the propriety of their conduct. To the servants, and every body about him, he was mild and compassionate, and often took opportunities of instructing them, and giving them good advice. His piety was quiet, without parade, cant, or moroseness, and he contented himself with doing his own duty, without censuring others By his equals, and his young friends, he was universally beloved, and was respected and esteemed for his goodness, even by those who could not follow his example He had the very unusual, and almost singular, talent in a young man, of being able to advise, and even to reprove, his acquaintance and friends of his own age, not only without offending their self-love, or provoking their ridicule, but so as

Sir Alexander Croke – D.C.L.
and

even to increase their esteem for him · and they admitted the justness of his opinion, though they could not always follow it. As a proof of this I shall introduce part of a letter, written by a fellow collegian to his brother George after his decease

" Thank you, my dear Croke, for the early information you gave me of " our mutual loss. I hope you will not think it impertinent in me, now " that time, I trust, has worn off the first sting of grief, to testify to you " the high regard, which from the time that I had more opportunity of " knowing him, I have always entertained for your dear brother. He was " indeed a friend to me, not merely an acquaintance, with whom I could " pass an evening to enjoy his conversation, and admire an apt quotation, " or a witty turn he often shewed himself qualified for this, yet many do " this, some perhaps better than he But a real friend is not often to be " found. I mean one, who dares reprove. This your brother would " do, and in so mild and friendly a way, that though just, and sometimes " severe, his remark, the manner in which it was conveyed, has afforded " an additional tie to his friendship."

He was buried in the church at Beckley, on the 21st of December; his sisters Adelaide, and Jane Sarah Elizabeth, his brothers George, and Wentworth, and myself, attended the funeral; Mr. George Cooke performed the service, his Tutor, Mr James, and Mr Henry Bishop, both of Oriel, Mr. Grantham, junior, Mr. Loveday, and Mr Davie vicar of Waterperry, Fellows of Magdalen College, and our minister, Mr Jenkins, all clergymen, held up the pall.

I shall now conclude this melancholy history with the wish of one of his friends,

MAY OUR LAST END BE LIKE HIS!

END OF VOL I

Sir Alexander Croke died 27 Dec 1842 at Studley Priory, co Oxford – in his 85th Year. He published an Essay on the Origin & Progress of Rhyming Latin verse at Oxford 1828 – Regimen Sanitatis Salerni – in 1831 –
A long memoir of him is in the Gent Mag for March 1843 – Vol 19 p. 315

Milton Keynes UK
Ingram Content Group UK Ltd.
UKHW020625071223
433866UK00005B/89

9 781015 945296